IISS

Strategic Survey
2008
The Annual Review
of World Affairs

published by

Routledge
Taylor & Francis Group

for

The International Institute for Strategic Studies
Arundel House | 13–15 Arundel Street | Temple Place | London | WC2R 3DX | UK

The International Institute for Strategic Studies

Arundel House | 13–15 Arundel Street | Temple Place | London | WC2R 3DX | UK

Strategic Survey 2008

First published September 2008 by **Routledge**
4 Park Square, Milton Park, Abingdon, Oxon, OX14 4RN

for **The International Institute for Strategic Studies**
Arundel House, 13–15 Arundel Street, Temple Place, London, WC2R 3DX, UK

Simultaneously published in the USA and Canada by **Routledge**
270 Madison Ave., New York, NY 10016

Routledge is an imprint of Taylor & Francis, an Informa business

© 2008 The International Institute for Strategic Studies

DIRECTOR-GENERAL AND CHIEF EXECUTIVE Dr John Chipman
EDITOR Alexander Nicoll

ASSISTANT EDITOR Dr Jeffrey Mazo
CONTRIBUTING EDITOR Jonathan Stevenson
MAP EDITOR Jessica Delaney
EDITORIAL Dr Ayse Abdullah, Katharine Fletcher, Sarah Johnstone, Carolyn West
DESIGN/PRODUCTION John Buck
ADDITIONAL MAP RESEARCH James Howarth, Catherine Micklethwaite
CARTOGRAPHY Steven Bernard

COVER IMAGES PA
PRINTED AND BOUND IN GREAT BRITAIN BY Bell & Bain Ltd, Thornliebank, Glasgow

This publication has been prepared by the Director-General of the Institute and his Staff, who accept full responsibility for its contents, which describe and analyse events up to 30 June 2008. These do not, and indeed cannot, represent a consensus of views among the worldwide membership of the Institute as a whole.

British Library Cataloguing in Publication Data
A catalogue record for this book is available from the British Library

Library of Congress Cataloguing in Publication Data

ISBN 978-1-85743-468-2
ISSN 0459-7230

Contents

Strategic Geography (after p. 184)

Index of Regional Maps

Index of Maps

June 2007

29 **United Kingdom:** Two unexploded car bombs are found in central London, two days after Gordon Brown succeeds Tony Blair as prime minister. On 30 June, a car is driven into the terminal at Glasgow airport. A group of foreign-born doctors is arrested.

July 2007

3 **Japan:** Defence Minister Fumio Kyuma resigns after saying the atomic bombs dropped on Japan in 1945 were inevitable.

4 **Palestine:** BBC journalist Alan Johnston is released after 114 days in captivity in Gaza.

7 **Iraq:** Truck bomb in northern town of Amirli kills more than 150 people.

10 **Pakistan:** Troops storm Red Mosque in Islamabad, where militants had been under siege for a week. More than 100 people are killed.

11 **United Kingdom:** Four men are convicted of failed bombings in London on 21 July 2005 and sentenced to life imprisonment.

14 **Russia:** President Vladimir Putin signs presidential decree suspending Russia's participation in the Conventional Forces in Europe Treaty.

16 **Bangladesh:** Former Prime Minister Sheikh Hasina arrested and charged with corruption.

16 **North Korea:** UN inspectors confirm Yongbyon nuclear reactor has been shut down.

16 **United Kingdom:** Four Russian diplomats are expelled over Russia's refusal to extradite suspect in the 2006 London murder of former agent Alexander Litvinenko. Russia later expels four UK diplomats.

20   **Pakistan:** Supreme Court reinstates Chief Justice Iftikhar Chaudhry, four months after his suspension by President Pervez Musharraf, which had prompted nationwide protests.

20   **Serbia:** Plan for independence of Kosovo taken off UN Security Council agenda in the face of Russian opposition.

20   **United States:** US launches diplomatic offensive in Middle East region, increasing military aid to Israel and Egypt, stepping up arms sales to Saudi Arabia and other Gulf states, in effort to isolate Iran, bolster Iraq and boost chances of Middle East peace.

22   **Turkey:** Ruling AK Party wins general election with 47% of nationwide vote.

24   **Iran/US:** Iranian and American ambassadors to Iraq hold second round of talks on Iraq in Baghdad.

24   **Libya:** Five Bulgarian nurses and a Palestinian doctor are released after eight years in captivity in Libya. They had been condemned to death on charges, which they denied, of deliberately infecting Libyan children with HIV-infected blood.

27   **India/US:** Governments agree terms of civil nuclear cooperation deal, sparking a political storm in India.

29   **Japan:** Ruling Liberal Democratic Party loses control of upper house in election. Prime Minister Shinzo Abe says he will not resign.

31   **Sudan:** UN Security Council agrees to send force of 20,000 military and 6,000 police personnel to Darfur in combined UN–African Union peacekeeping mission.

August 2007

13   **United States:** Karl Rove, key adviser to President George W. Bush, resigns, followed on 18 August by Tony Snow, White House spokesman, and on 27 August by Alberto Gonzales, attorney general.

14   **Iraq:** More than 500 people killed by four bombs in two villages of Yazidis, Kurdish religious minority, in northern Iraq.

16   **United States:** José Padilla,US citizen arrested in 2002 and held in military custody for three years, convicted in civilian court of plotting to kill people overseas and supporting terrorism.

19   **Thailand:** New constitution approved in referendum, with 57.8% of those voting – turnout was 57.6% – supporting it, clearing the way for elections to be held.

23   **Pakistan:** Supreme Court rules that Nawaz Sharif, former prime minister, has the right to return from exile.

26   **India:** Two bomb explosions kill 42 people in Hyderabad amusement park and restaurant.

27   **Japan:** Prime Minister Shinzo Abe shuffles cabinet in bid to regain support.

28   **Turkey:** Abdullah Gül, foreign minister in previous AK Party government, elected president, the first with an Islamist background.

29   **Iraq:** Moqtada al-Sadr, radical Shia cleric, announces suspension of activities by Mahdi Army for six months, following fighting between rival Shia groups in Karbala.

September 2007

2   **Lebanon:** Lebanese army takes control of Palestinian refugee camp, ending three-month stand-off with Islamic militants in which more than 400 people died.

3   **Bangladesh:** Khaleda Zia, former prime minister, arrested on corruption charges.

3   **Iraq:** British troops complete withdrawal from Basra city, with 5,000 remaining based at airport.

4   **Pakistan:** Two bombs kill 25 people, including intelligence personnel, in Rawalpindi.

5   **Germany:** Three men arrested on suspicion of planning attacks on Frankfurt airport and American facilities in Germany.

6   **Algeria:** Bomb attack kills 20 people in town of Batna. On 8 September, truck bomb kills 37 people, mostly coast guard officers, in town of Dellys. Responsibility is claimed by al-Qaeda in the Maghreb.

6   **Australia:** China and Australia jointly announce that they will hold an annual security dialogue, and agree A$35bn deal on supply of liquefied natural gas to China.

6   **Syria:** Israeli jets launch air strikes in Syria, which protests to the United Nations. According to some intelligence reports, the attack was on a partly constructed nuclear reactor.

10   **Iraq:** General David Petraeus, US commander in Iraq, tells Congress that US forces in Iraq could be reduced by 30,000 by July 2008, and that most US military objectives in Iraq were being met. On 13 September, Bush confirms the troop reduction and says 5,700 will be home by Christmas.

10   **Pakistan:** Former Prime Minister Nawaz Sharif returns to Islamabad from exile in London but is arrested on corruption charges and immediately deported to Saudi Arabia.

12   **Japan:** Prime Minister Shinzo Abe resigns. On 25 September, Yasuo Fukuda succeeds him following parliamentary vote.

12   **Russia:** Prime Minister Mikhail Fradkov resigns and is replaced by Viktor Zubkov, chairman of the Federal Financial Monitoring Service.

16   **Iraq:** The killing in Baghdad of 17 Iraqis by personnel of Blackwater, US private security company on contract to the US State Department, triggers Iraqi protests and investigations in Washington.

17   **Sierra Leone:** Ernest Bai Koroma, opposition leader, becomes president after defeating Vice President Solomon Berewa in run-off election.

22   **Myanmar:** As protests led by monks against military regime escalate, Aung San Suu Kyi, opposition leader under house arrest, is allowed to greet monks

outside her house. On 26 September, military rulers begin violent crackdown on protests, resulting in the deaths of 13 people – though unofficial estimates are higher – and arrests of hundreds of monks. UN envoy Ibrahim Gambari meets Aung San Suu Kyi on 30 September and Senior-General Than Shwe, the military leader, on 2 October. On 11 October, UN Security Council passes resolution condemning violence, calling for dialogue with Aung San Suu Kyi and release of all detainees.

25 **Chad:** UN Security Council approves peacekeeping force for Chad and Central African Republic to protect refugees from Darfur. Force to be made up of 3,000 EU troops and 300 UN police.

October 2007

6 **Pakistan:** President Pervez Musharraf wins re-election by electoral college, but awaits Supreme Court ruling on his eligibility to stand.

8 **Iraq:** UK announces it will reduce troops in Iraq from 5,500 to 2,500 by spring 2008. However, in March 2008 the drawdown is paused at 4,000.

18 **Pakistan:** Former Prime Minister Benazir Bhutto returns from exile. Bomb attack on her motorcade in Karachi kills 140 people.

18 **Turkey:** Parliament authorises government to order raids into Iraq in pursuit of PKK Kurdish rebels; US urges Ankara not to take military action as violence between the two sides continues.

20 **Iran:** Ali Larijani, chief negotiator on nuclear programme, resigns and is replaced by Saeed Jalili, a deputy foreign minister. In May 2008, Larijani is elected speaker of parliament.

21 **Poland:** Opposition Civic Platform party wins general election, ousting Law and Justice party. On 9 November, Donald Tusk becomes prime minister, replacing Jaroslaw Kaczynski.

22 **China:** Four new members, including Shanghai party chief Xi Jinping, are appointed to the nine-member Standing Committee of the Chinese Community Party's Politburo

25 **Iran:** US tightens sanctions, targeting the financing of the Iranian Revolutionary Guard Corps as well as the defence ministry and three banks.

28 **Argentina:** Cristina Fernández de Kirchner wins election and succeeds her husband, Nestor Kirchner, as president.

31 **Japan:** Government orders end to naval refuelling mission for coalition warships in Indian Ocean after six years, because parliament fails to agree on continuing it.

31 **Spain:** National Court convicts three men of murder in the 2004 Madrid train bombings in which 191 people died. Three alleged masterminds are acquitted. Eighteen people are convicted of lesser offences. Seven leading suspects had blown themselves up when police tried to arrest them.

November 2007

2 **Sri Lanka:** Tamil Tigers' political chief, S.P. Thamilselvan, killed in bombing raid.

3 **Pakistan:** President Pervez Musharraf declares emergency rule, replaces Chief Justice Iftikhar Chaudhry, and suspends the constitution. Hundreds of opposition activists are arrested. Lawyers who take part in widespread protests are beaten up.

7 **Georgia:** President Mikheil Saakashvili declares temporary state of emergency after police break up demonstration outside parliament. Independent television station is stopped from broadcasting. He blames Russia for unrest. On 8 November, he calls early presidential elections in January 2008.

14 **France:** Nine-day wave of strikes and protests hits France – particularly public transport – over President Nicolas Sarkozy's plans to reform public-sector pensions.

20 **United States:** *New York Times* reports that US Defense Secretary Robert Gates halted the reduction of US bases in Europe, freezing the number of troops at 43,000. The number had been set to drop to 24,000 by end-2008 from 62,000 in 2005.

22 **Colombia:** President Alvaro Uribe ends mediation effort by Venezuelan President Hugo Chávez to arrange exchange of hostages held by the FARC guerrilla group.

24 **Australia:** Kevin Rudd becomes prime minister as his Labor Party defeats John Howard's Liberal–National coalition government in elections.

25 **Pakistan:** Nawaz Sharif returns to Pakistan following intervention by Saudi Arabia, where he was in exile.

27 **Israel/Palestine:** Israeli and Palestinian leaders, meeting with President Bush and other leaders at Annapolis, Maryland, agree to engage in negotiations with a view to reaching an agreement by end-2008.

29 **Pakistan:** Pervez Musharraf is sworn in as civilian president after resigning as army chief

December 2007

2 **Russia:** United Russia Party of President Vladimir Putin wins 64% of vote in parliamentary elections. Western governments question the fairness of the polls.

2 **Venezuela:** President Hugo Chávez loses referendum vote on constitutional changes that would have enabled him to be president indefinitely

3 **Iran:** US publishes National Intelligence Estimate saying that Iran terminated its nuclear-weapons programme in 2003, though it continued other nuclear activities. President Mahmoud Ahmadinejad claims a 'great victory'.

10 **Russia:** President Vladimir Putin endorses the candidacy of Dmitry Medvedev, first deputy prime minister and Gazprom chairman, to succeed him in elections due in March 2008. Medvedev says Putin should then become prime minister.

11 **Algeria:** Two car bombs in Algiers kill more than 30 people including 17 UN employees. An al-Qaeda affiliate claims responsibility.

12 **Bosnia:** Dragomir Milosevic, former Bosnian Serb general, sentenced to 33 years in prison by UN war-crimes tribunal over siege of Sarajevo in 1994–95.

13 **Portugal:** EU leaders sign reform treaty, including many elements of proposed 'constitution' rejected by French and Dutch voters in 2005.

15 **Indonesia:** UN members, at climate-change conference in Bali, agree to launch two-year negotiating process on set of emissions targets to replace Kyoto Protocol.

18 **United States:** US says it has met 2004 target of halving nuclear-weapons stockpile five years early, and plans further 15% reduction.

19 **South Korea:** Lee Myung-bak, candidate of the conservative Grand National Party, easily wins presidential election, defeating the ruling liberal United New Democratic Party. In February 2008, he is cleared to take office after a special prosecutor finds that he was not involved in a stock-market share-rigging scandal.

27 **Kenya:** Presidential elections result in victory being declared for incumbent President Mwai Kibaki, but violence, protests and looting break out after the opposition candidate, Raila Odinga, rejects the result and claims the count was rigged. Foreign monitors express concern about the vote count. By early January, some 600 people are reported to have been killed and some 250,000 displaced. US Africa envoy Jendayi Frazer holds meetings with the two leaders.

27 **Pakistan:** Benazir Bhutto is assassinated in a suicide-bomb attack at an election rally in Rawalpindi. It is unclear whether she was shot before the bomb was detonated. Her 19-year-old son Bilawal, a student in the UK, is appointed to lead the party and her husband, Asif Ali Zardari, will run it. Elections are delayed from 8 January to 18 February.

January 2008

5 **Georgia:** Mikheil Saakashvili is re-elected president with 52% of the popular vote.

15 **Afghanistan:** US announces plan to send 3,200 marines to Afghanistan.

15 **France:** United Arab Emirates and France sign agreement under which a French naval base will be established in Abu Dhabi.

16 **Sri Lanka:** Government formally withdraws from six-year-old ceasefire with Tamil Tigers.

23 **DR Congo:** Government and rebel leaders including General Laurent Nkunda sign peace deal intended to end conflict in Kivu region of eastern Congo.

23 **Palestine:** Tens of thousands of Palestinians from Gaza, frustrated at Israeli blockade, flood over border into Egypt to buy supplies, after Hamas blows a hole in the border fence. The breach lasts for 12 days.

23 **United States:** José Padilla, US citizen held since 2002 as an 'enemy combatant', sentenced to 17 years in prison for conspiracy to murder and kidnap and support terrorists.

24 **Japan:** Refuelling of coalition warships in Indian Ocean resumes after Prime Minister Yasuo Fukuda forces through legislation.

27 **Afghanistan:** Paddy Ashdown, British former UN supremo in Bosnia, withdraws from consideration as UN 'super-envoy' to Afghanistan after President Hamid Karzai makes clear he does not favour the appointment. On 6 March, UN Secretary-General Ban Ki Moon appoints Norwegian diplomat Kai Eide to the role.

February 2008

2 **Chad:** Rebels launch assault on N'Djamena, the capital. In the ensuing fighting, government forces with French help beat back the attack. On 14 February, President Idriss Déby declares 15-day state of emergency in attempt to restore order after the coup attempt, in which more than 100 people died.

6 **Thailand:** Democratically elected coalition government, including many allies of former Prime Minister Thaksin Shinawatra who was ousted in a 2006 military coup, is sworn in following elections. On 28 February, Thaksin returns from exile to face corruption charges.

9 **Turkey:** Parliament approves constitutional amendments relaxing ban on women wearing headscarves in universities.

11 **Timor Leste:** President José Ramos-Horta is shot and severely wounded in an assassination attempt and is flown to Australia, where he recovers. Prime Minister Xanana Gusmão is also targeted but is unhurt. Rebel leader Alfredo Reinado is killed in the attack on the president. State of emergency is declared and Australia sends additional troops.

17 **Afghanistan:** More than 100 killed in suicide-bomb attack on crowd watching dogfight near Kandahar.

17 **Kosovo:** Kosovo declares independence from Serbia, which declares the move illegal. It is recognised by the United States and some European countries, but not by many other countries.

18 **Pakistan:** The parties of former Prime Ministers Nawaz Sharif and the late Benazir Bhutto win the largest number of seats in the parliamentary election, in a significant setback to President Pervez Musharraf. The parties agree to form a coalition government. On 24 March, Yusuf Raza Gillani of the Pakistan People's Party is elected prime minister. He immediately frees all the judges under arrest, including former Chief Justice Iftikhar Chaudhry. However, political dispute continues over judges' reinstatement.

19 **Cuba:** Fidel Castro steps down as Cuba's leader after 49 years in power. His brother Raúl Castro is appointed president.

21 **United States:** US Navy ship fires missile to destroy damaged US satellite over Pacific Ocean.

28 **Kenya:** President Mwai Kibaki and opposition leader Raila Odinga sign power-sharing deal following mediation by Kofi Annan, former UN secretary-general. Odinga is nominated to newly created post of prime minister.

March 2008

1   **Israel/Palestine:** More than 100 people killed as Israeli forces attack Gaza in retaliation for rocket attacks.

2   **Russia:** Dmitry Medvedev elected president with 70% of votes.

3   **Iran:** UN Security Council passes third resolution imposing sanctions on Iran over its nuclear programme.

3   **Ukraine:** Russia's Gazprom reduces gas supplies to Ukraine over payment dispute which is resolved on 5 March, when supplies are restored.

8   **Malaysia:** Ruling National Front coalition suffers large fall in parliamentary majority in elections, and loses control of four state assemblies. Its worst result since independence in 1957 foreshadows a period of turbulence in Malaysian politics.

8   **Serbia:** Prime Minister Vojislav Kostunica resigns over disagreements on relations with the European Union following Kosovo's declaration of independence. Elections called for 11 May.

10   **China:** Authorities in Lhasa, capital of Tibet, arrest monks protesting against Chinese rule. As protests grow in the following days, shops and cars are set on fire and tear gas is used to disperse crowds. Dalai Lama, Tibet's exiled spiritual leader, urges end to violence and calls on Beijing to begin discussions with Tibetans. Beijing reports ten deaths in riots on 14 March, which bring Chinese crackdown. Other estimates are higher. Protests spread to other provinces. From 30 March onwards, protests greet the Olympic torch as it is carried through world capitals ahead of the August 2008 Beijing Olympic Games, prompting many cities to shorten its route. Beijing blames the Dalai Lama for the protests in Tibet. But on 24 April, state media report that Chinese officials will meet his representatives.

11   **United States:** The Federal Reserve and central banks in Europe take coordinated action to inject money into the international financial system in an effort to ease the funding difficulties suffered by banks as a result of the eight-month-old credit crunch. On 16 March, the Fed orchestrates the emergency sale of Bear Stearns, a US investment bank, to J.P. Morgan. The sale price is a fraction of the former share price, and the Fed provides financial backing for the transaction. The Fed cuts US interest rates seven times between September 2007 and May 2008.

22   **Taiwan:** Ma Ying-jeou of the Kuomintang party wins presidential election with 58% of the vote, defeating Frank Hsieh, candidate of the ruling Democratic Progressive Party.

25   **Iraq:** Government forces launch an assault on militia groups in Basra, triggering heavy fighting with the Mahdi Army headed by Shia cleric Moqtada al-Sadr. US and Iraqi troops also attack Mahdi Army positions in the Sadr City area of Baghdad, and fighting spreads to other cities. Militiamen put up fierce resistance, and ignore the demands of Prime Minister Nuri al-Maliki to lay down their arms. President George W. Bush praises Maliki's offensive, and the US military provides support. However, Maliki orders an end to the Basra

operation after a week, with no clear accommodation or outcome. Several hundred people are killed in the fighting.

29 **Zimbabwe:** Following parliamentary and presidential elections, the electoral commission's slowness in releasing results leads to accusations of rigging. Nevertheless, results announced on 3 April show that the Movement for Democratic Change opposition party, led by Morgan Tsvangirai, won 99 seats in parliament, defeating President Robert Mugabe's ruling Zanu-PF party which won 97. Results of the presidential election released on 2 May give Tsvangirai 47.9% and Mugabe 43.2%. However, under electoral rules, if no candidate wins 50%, a run-off should be held. During the period before the delayed results, the government is accused of launching a campaign of violence and intimidation against opposition supporters across the country, and tens of thousands of people are reported to have fled their homes. A run-off election is set for 27 June.

April 2008

3 **Afghanistan:** France commits to send 700 more troops to Afghanistan, Georgia 500 and Poland 400 with eight helicopters.

3 **Romania:** NATO leaders, meeting in Bucharest, agree to admit Albania and Croatia to the Alliance, and that Macedonia will be admitted once it has resolved a dispute with Greece over the country's name. Leaders refuse to grant Membership Action Plan status to Ukraine and Georgia, in spite of US demands to do so.

6 **Russia/US:** Presidents Vladimir Putin and George W. Bush issue a declaration agreeing on a 'Strategic Framework' at a meeting in Sochi. They agree to develop new arrangements following expiration of the START treaty in 2009, and to engage in a dialogue on missile threats. While noting Russia's objection to US plans to site missile-defence equipment in Poland and the Czech Republic, the declaration says that Moscow 'appreciates the measures that the US has proposed and declares that if agreed and implemented such measures will be important and useful in assuaging Russian concerns'.

6 **Sri Lanka:** Tamil Tiger suicide-bomb attack kills Highways Minister Jeyaraj Fernandopulle and 13 others.

10 **Nepal:** Elections are held for a new assembly that will write a new constitution. Results, published two weeks later, show that former rebel Maoists won 220 out of 601 seats. The Nepali Congress Party came second with 110 seats. Assembly votes to abolish the monarchy and on 11 June King Gyanendra steps down and leaves the royal palace, as efforts to form a government continue.

10 **United Kingdom:** High Court rules that the UK government acted illegally in 2006 when it halted a corruption inquiry into a deal between Saudi Arabia and arms manufacturer BAE Systems. Judges say it surrendered to blatant Saudi threats.

15 **Italy:** Silvio Berlusconi's centre-right coalition wins control of both houses of parliament. On 8 May he becomes prime minister for the third time.

20   **Paraguay:** Fernando Lugo, a former Catholic bishop, wins presidential election, ousting the Colorado Party after 61 years in power.

24   **Syria:** US releases intelligence data indicating that Israel's September 2007 air-strike was on a partly constructed nuclear reactor being built by Syria with North Korean assistance. The facility was destroyed.

May 2008

1   **Somalia:** US missile strike kills Aden Hashi Ayro, military commander of Islamist insurgent group al-Shabaab, in town of Dusamareb.

2   **Myanmar:** Cyclone Nargis hits southern areas of Myanmar, killing 78,000 people and leaving 56,000 missing, and affecting 2m people, according to official figures. The ruling military junta is widely criticised over its efforts to help the affected areas, and for its refusal to allow foreign aid to flow freely, even after a visit by UN Secretary-General Ban Ki Moon. US, French and British naval ships off the coast are not allowed to unload aid materials or use much-needed helicopters.

6   **Lebanon:** Government order to close down Hizbullah's telecommunications network sparks protests and riots. Hizbullah gunmen set up roadblocks and take over most of western Beirut. Some 65 people are killed in street violence. A ceasefire deal, mediated by the Arab League, is reached after government drops the measures to which Hizbullah had objected. On 21 May, the factions reach an agreement at talks in Qatar, under which a new national unity government is to be formed under Prime Minister Fouad Siniora, and General Michel Suleiman becomes president.

8   **Russia:** Dmitry Medvedev takes office as president and appoints his predecessor, Vladimir Putin, as prime minister. Putin heads the United Russia Party.

12   **China:** Earthquake in Sichuan province kills some 70,000 people and leaves nearly 5m homeless. Government mounts massive rescue and reconstruction effort.

13   **India:** Eight bombs kill 63 people in Jaipur, western India.

13   **South Africa:** Anti-immigrant violence breaks out in poor townships and spreads, resulting in some 50 deaths and causing thousands to flee over the following two weeks.

21   **Israel/Syria:** Tel Aviv and Damascus announce that talks have been taking place on a comprehensive peace agreement through Turkish mediation.

21   **Spain:** Javier López Peña, leader of Basque separatist group ETA, is arrested in France.

25   **Colombia:** Rebel group FARC says its top commander, Manuel Marulanda, died of a heart attack in March. Two other commanders were recently killed and a female leader surrendered.

June 2008

5 **United States:** US Air Force chief and Air Force secretary forced to resign following inquiry into mishandling of nuclear weapons and components.

6 **Israel:** Shaul Mofaz, transport minister and a deputy prime minister, says Israel will attack Iran if it continues to develop nuclear weapons.

7 **United States:** Hillary Clinton concedes defeat to Barack Obama, leaving him to fight as the Democratic Party's candidate for the presidency against Republican John McCain.

11 **Pakistan:** Islamabad protests after US air-strike kills 11 Pakistani soldiers near the Afghan border.

12 **China:** Taiwan and China agree to host representative offices and to begin regular direct flights.

12 **Ireland:** Voters reject the EU's Lisbon Treaty in a referendum. The treaty, intended to streamline the workings of the EU, cannot be put into effect until all 27 members ratify it. European leaders say ratification process should continue.

12 **United States:** Supreme Court rules that detainees at Guantanamo Bay have the right to challenge their detention in American courts.

13 **Afghanistan:** Raid on prison in Kandahar frees 350 Taliban prisoners. NATO and Afghan forces launch offensive against Taliban fighters in outskirts of Kandahar.

19 **Israel/Palestine:** Ceasefire between Israel and Hamas begins in Gaza.

19 **Nigeria:** Militants attack Shell's Bonga oil platform, 120km off the coast of the Niger Delta, temporarily stopping production.

22 **Saudi Arabia:** Saudi Arabia agrees at an emergency summit of consumers and producers called because of surging oil prices to increase production by 200,000 barrels per day to 9.7m.

22 **Zimbabwe:** Morgan Tsvangirai, opposition MDC leader, pulls out of 27 June presidential run-off election following extensive violence against supporters. He takes refuge temporarily in Dutch Embassy. The UN Security Council condemns the violence and says the elections could not be free and fair. On 29 June, Robert Mugabe is sworn in as president.

23 **Iran:** EU joins US in freezing assets of Iran's Bank Melli as part of pressure to halt enrichment of uranium.

24 **Germany:** Government says 1,000 more troops will be made available to be sent to Afghanistan, potentially raising German total to 4,500.

27 **North Korea:** Cooling tower at Yongbyon reactor is destroyed to show government's commitment to ending nuclear programme. It also hands over requested details of nuclear programme. In return, Washington promises to lift some economic sanctions and to begin process of removing North Korea from US list of state sponsors of terror.

1 **Perspectives**

For the world's larger powers, this was a year taken up by domestic and economic concerns while they awaited the beginning of a new period in international affairs. This new start would come once the next American administration had established itself in Washington. That great-power relations would go, in effect, on hold was inevitable given that the 'lame-duck' status of the administration of President George W. Bush was more than usually pronounced. The United States was widely thought to have suffered a substantial loss of authority and credibility across the world since the 2003 invasion of Iraq. Its ability to influence international affairs had been weakened to an extraordinary degree. But other governments were conscious that the United States still remained the world's most powerful country, and an essential pillar of international security. Therefore, it was natural that they should watch the US election campaign with close interest and await the arrival of a new administration in January 2009.

While they did so, the leaders of major powers were mostly preoccupied by domestic developments. China's determination that the 2008 Olympic Games should go smoothly was underlined by its testy response to modest international protests about its rule of Tibet. Russia's leadership entered an unusual and uncertain phase as Vladimir Putin handed the presidency to Dmitry Medvedev, but instead became prime minister. India's coalition government struggled to survive arguments about a civil nuclear accord with the United States, though it eventually won a vote of confidence in parliament. In Europe, the future of closer integration within the European Union was again thrown into doubt by Irish voters' rejection of the Lisbon Treaty. President Nicolas Sarkozy gave France a much higher profile internationally and pressed an ambitious reform agenda at home, though so far without major tangible results.

The attention of governments around the world was increasingly focused on a nexus of pressing economic problems: the triple shock in the markets for credit, oil and food. There was a severe loss of confidence in the international banking system triggered by excessive lending to finance property purchases, which resulted in some of the world's largest banks being forced to seek infusions of new capital. Meanwhile, oil prices soared to record levels, and food prices were also under strong upward pressure. All these phenomena derived from a strong period of worldwide economic growth, and all threatened to slow the pace of growth significantly. At mid 2008, the signs were that economic performance was proving quite resilient, and that the world would not be tipped into a widespread and deep recession. However, the full impact was yet to be seen.

Among the issues that regularly provide the stuff of discussions about international security, Iran's nuclear programme remained an extremely pressing problem. The United States and the largest European countries sought to exert maximum pressure on Tehran to stop enriching uranium. But, in perhaps the most surprising development of the year to mid 2008, America's intelligence agencies released a National Intelligence Estimate in November 2007 in which they judged that Iran had halted a nuclear-weapons programme in 2003 in response to international scrutiny and pressure. The immediate effect of this declaration was to halt speculation that Bush might attempt a military strike on Iranian nuclear facilities before leaving office – even though this possibility could still not completely be ruled out. The broader effect was to undermine international efforts to keep up the pressure on Tehran to stop its nuclear work.

Some comfort was to be found, at least for the time being, in an improvement of conditions in Iraq, where politically motivated violence declined markedly following the American troop 'surge' and tactical changes that began in early 2007. In another positive development, North Korea began to take steps towards dismantling and disclosure of its nuclear programme. On 27 June 2008 the cooling tower of its Yongbyon nuclear reactor was destroyed as a show of Pyongyang's will to carry out a series of steps agreed with Washington following a reversal of America's hard-line refusal to negotiate. North Korea also provided documents about its programme. The United States in return moved to lift some sanctions and to remove North Korea from the list of 'state sponsors of terrorism'. While there was still a long way to go before North Korea could be deemed disarmed, and while it had failed to follow through on previous agreements, this seemed to be progress achieved by negotiation.

In both the Iraqi and North Korean cases, progress was made following changes to the Bush administration's approach – though right-wing former officials accused it of capitulating to Pyongyang. More broadly, efforts to repair the damage done to America's international relations in the earlier Bush years were being made by experienced hands who had been brought in to smooth the Bush administration's late days – in particular the defence secretary, Robert Gates.

However, there were worrisome events in a number of troubled countries. In nuclear-armed Pakistan, a multi-faceted political drama was being played out, punctuated by acts of violence that killed many people, including former Prime Minister Benazir Bhutto. While there were no major successful terrorist attacks on industrialised countries, plots continued to be uncovered, and evidence given in trials of terrorist suspects revealed links to masterminds and training camps in Pakistan. Conflict worsened in Afghanistan and Sri Lanka and continued in Somalia and Sudan, while there seemed little prospect of a resolution of the Israel–Palestine issue in spite of Washington's efforts to engineer an accord. Myanmar's military regime quelled protests by Buddhist monks, and later further angered foreign governments as it prevented an adequate flow of international aid to victims of a cyclone that devastated its coastal region. One long-running conflict appeared, however, to be moving towards a conclusion: in Colombia, a number of leaders of the FARC rebel group were killed or captured and the organisation was tricked into releasing its highest-profile hostage, the former presidential candidate Ingrid Betancourt.

In Africa, political violence erupted following elections in previously harmonious Kenya, while in Zimbabwe Robert Mugabe lost all claims to legitimacy as he used violence and intimidation to avoid being toppled in the second round of a presidential election after coming second in the first round. These developments emphasised the chronic fragility of the world's poorest continent, as foreign powers competed for its natural resources while many African countries lacked adequate governance, and many conflicts and ethnic rivalries persisted. The unwillingness of African leaders to condemn Mugabe was especially discouraging.

Fallout from the Bush presidency

The next president of the United States will inherit leadership of a country whose international standing is widely perceived to have diminished over the last eight years. He will be acutely conscious of global perceptions of the deleterious results of Bush's main decisions, even though policy shifts have begun to produce partial remedies. He will, however, have an enormous opportunity to remedy the situation: damage to American prestige, while it may take some time to repair, does not have to be lasting.

Of course, the new president may not agree with this judgement of what has happened under Bush. *Strategic Survey* is obliged to make an assessment each year that is inevitably open to reassessment in light of later events or new analysis. For example, it may in future be judged that, if there was a reduction of American authority, this was part of an inexorable secular re-ordering of power in a globalised world. Or later events may tend to justify Bush's essential judgement in 2001 that the Western world must engage in a long-term war against Islamist extremism that trumped other strategic concerns – and may therefore support a more favourable view of his main actions. However, while the threat from Islamist terrorism was self-evident, the judgement that tackling it should subordinate all other strategic interests met only faint echoes outside the United States. Indeed, there is a strong view that the actions of the United States solidified and increased the threat that it was facing.

Still, that the possibility of future reassessment needed to be borne in mind was suggested when, on 15 June 2008, Bush was a guest for dinner at 10 Downing Street, the official home of British prime ministers. Gordon Brown, the current resident, invited a group of British historians to meet him, reflecting the two leaders' shared enthusiasm for the study of history. Some of the guests were avowed fans of Bush, while others had been vitriolic critics. However, the fact that the conversation was reportedly about previous centuries, and not about the twenty-first, should perhaps serve as a caution about the inherent danger of attempts to give considered judgement on the correctness and effectiveness of the key strategic decision of the century so far. That decision was taken by Bush in response to the 11 September 2001 terrorist attacks on the United States, when he declared a 'global war on terror' – a decision amplified by his later characterisation of Iraq, Iran and North Korea as forming an 'axis of evil'.

Nationwide grief and anger provoked by the 11 September attacks on America, in which some 3,000 people died, provided an understandable background: a leader faced with such a shock to the nation must be seen to undertake determined action that has a credible chance of preventing a recurrence. Yet Bush's reaction seemed even at the time to be misguided in its characterisation of the problem and in the course being set to deal with it. The free rein that was then given to the neo-conservative view that the whole Middle East/Gulf region could and should be permanently changed by American action, with or without the support of allies, seemed a further misjudgement. The detention without trial of terrorist suspects at Guantanamo Bay, abuses of prisoners in Iraq and elsewhere, and the repeated killing of civilians by the US military, then seemed to expose an America that, in its reaction to the 11 September atrocity, had suffered an erosion in the values that had been its own best advertisement. Later, as American troops struggled to quell growing insurgencies in chaotic Iraq and Afghanistan, as the wave of post-11 September sympathy for the United States was replaced by widespread distaste for its actions and mistrust of its words, and as many key allies kept their distance from Washington, Bush appeared to have allowed a huge tactical setback – the 11 September attacks – to trigger a possible longer-term decline. The military might of the United States was seen to be not so mighty after all, and America's voice might no longer be heard.

The declaration of a 'war on terror' was the step from which these consequences followed. It conflated a number of separate threats and attempted to shape them into a single overriding one in a way that subordinated America's other strategic interests. The 'war on terror', because of its unclear nature – if it really was a war, who and where was the enemy and how would it be won? – was open to manipulation both in the United States and elsewhere. For example, it was not difficult for Islamist groups to paint it as a war against Muslims, especially as that was in fact how many Americans interpreted it. As events unfolded, it therefore acted as an inspiration to extremism. In Washington, it was also not difficult for neo-conservatives to persuade a president who had declared 'war' that rogue states which were trying to obtain weapons of mass destruction were all part of the same problem – and also formed part of a status quo that the United States could no longer tolerate. The countries were, after all, on the US government's list of 'state sponsors of terrorism'.

Bush's decision to make an attack on Iraq part of the 'war on terror' had damaging consequences. It cast the problem to be dealt with as a rogue regime with weapons that could fall into the hands of terrorists. The regime and its supposed weapons were therefore the target of the narrowly defined military campaign plan closely overseen by Donald Rumsfeld, the defence secretary. The instigators of the invasion deliberately did not involve themselves in the ground realities of Iraq: they believed they could surgically lance the problem, and withdraw. Therefore, they did not plan for the realities, and they were not concerned as the post-Saddam Hussein looting began in Baghdad. 'Stuff happens', said Rumsfeld. The American forces in Iraq in April 2003 therefore had no mission. They did not seek to impose security on government-less Iraq by, for example, securing arms depots, and in any case they did not have the numbers to do so because of the limited nature of the invasion plan. Because the administration had imposed its own conceptual framework on Iraq, as a country desperate for liberation from its oppressor, it failed to anticipate the political and insurgent forces that would emerge following the disappearance of Saddam Hussein's dictatorship – and therefore it rapidly lost control of the country, which had in effect become a failed state overnight. Only when Rumsfeld was replaced, three and a half years after the invasion, was Bush persuaded to adopt a policy that could address the true ground realities, and the situation in Iraq began to improve.

The 'axis of evil' was a further example of Bush's imposition of an American conceptual paradigm that failed to reflect real-life politics and American strategic interests. It placed Iraq and Iran in the same bracket as weapons proliferators with rogue regimes that fostered terrorism, but ignored the fact that the two countries were deadly enemies. Thus, by destroying the Iraqi part of the 'axis', and getting bogged down in internecine conflict in Iraq, and putting in government in Baghdad political parties that had strong links with Tehran, Bush handed an extraordinary strategic win to Iran, which gloried in its much-advanced status as a regional leader and was able to pursue its nuclear ambitions with relative freedom from fear of American military intervention.

Meanwhile, Osama bin Laden and Ayman al-Zawahiri, the al-Qaeda leaders, remained at large nearly seven years after the 11 September attacks. Some al-Qaeda leaders had been killed or captured in various countries. In Iraq, where al-Qaeda had blossomed following the American-led invasion, Sunni communities had turned against it and were increasingly rejecting the involvement of jihadists in their affairs. However, al-Qaeda and related groups around the world continued to recruit new adherents and to plot acts of terrorism.

Following these failures, the loss of traction in international affairs that the United States has suffered during this period is evident. For example, even though Bush was able to assemble a meeting on Middle East peace at Annapolis, Maryland in November 2007, and to obtain commitments to reaching agreement on a two-state solution by December 2008, there seemed little prospect that this could be achieved. The many visits and exhortations of US Secretary of State Condoleezza Rice appeared to have little effect on the protagonists, each of which was in any case so divided internally as to preclude success – barring a miracle breakthrough in the final months of 2008.

A further example was to be found in Afghanistan, where deep differences of approach emerged within the NATO forces, damaging the unity of the international community's efforts to bring security and construct a durable nation. At heart, these differences stemmed from a rejection by some alliance members of the American forces' 'kinetic' approach, which they believed to be counter-productive. America was unable to impose its will on allies, making only partial progress in its efforts to persuade them to contribute more troops and equipment and to alter their rules of engagement so as to play a bigger role in combat against Taliban insurgents. These problems became serious with the proliferation of national 'caveats' on the way forces could be used. Maintaining the fiction of Alliance solidarity within the practice of serial exceptionalism became an impossible task. Also within NATO, allies flatly refused America's demands that Georgia and Ukraine be advanced towards membership of the Alliance. Meanwhile, the process of hedging against an American decline that had been in evidence around the world for some time continued to be seen. In the Gulf, Arab countries have sought to expand their global contacts on both economic and security fronts, in effect hedging their bets for the future in spite of their continuing close links with the United States. For example, the United Arab Emirates and France agreed in 2008 on the establishment of a French military base in Abu Dhabi. Asian countries have also for some years been developing new security structures that, as in the case of the East Asia Summit, did not include the United States, even though Washington retains a pivotal security role in the Asia-Pacific region. In Latin America, the United States has lost influence as its general foreign-policy approaches too easily coincided with Latin American caricatures of the meddling 'gringo'.

To many people, the poverty of the Bush administration's vision of international affairs was indicated by the progress that seemed to be made when its approach was altered – for example, regarding Iraq and North Korea. Meanwhile, the path towards a rehabilitation of American relations with allies was already being trodden following the departure of Rumsfeld and the arrival of seasoned officials without an ideological agenda. In particular, Gates, a former head of the Central Intelligence Agency, proved an effective and statesman-like defence secretary. His style of polite candour did not shrink from firmly advancing the administration's views, for example on Iran or on the need for allies to play a stronger role in Afghanistan. But he also repeatedly laid stress on the longer-term perspective, and the permanent mutual interest of America and its allies and friends in ensuring international peace and security. He also appointed new leaders of the armed forces and emphasised their responsibility to focus urgently on capabilities needed for modern operations.

The consequences of Bush's key strategic decisions and of his past unilateralism will be evident to his successor, and will present both opportunities and challenges. The democratic candidate, Senator Barack Obama – who would be America's first black president – opposed the Iraq War from the first, was committed to a 'careful' withdrawal from Iraq and has advocated direct talks with problem countries such as Iran. While his views exposed him to right-wing criticism, there were also conservative elements to his foreign-policy outlook. Senator John McCain, his Republican opponent, was relying on his own military career, his political experience and the image of his party as being tougher on security issues. At 72, he would be the oldest man to assume the presidency. He has retained the language of the 'war on terror', saying that radical Islamic extremism was 'the transcendent challenge of the twenty-first century'. Obama's view was that terrorism was not the only threat facing the United States.

The triple shock

While the next US president will inherit a demanding international security agenda, his first concern – and that of other world leaders – is likely to be for the state of the economy and financial markets. The past year has seen an extraordinary convulsion in the Western world, with a sudden drying up of credit occurring at the same time as a surge of inflationary pressure, leaving central banks torn between lowering interest rates in order to ease credit and bolster economic growth, and raising them in order to restrain inflation. Rising prices were seen especially in fuel and food. Both the credit squeeze and the inflationary pressures were the consequence of a long period of global economic growth which had steadily boosted demand for goods while inflation had remained under control and finance had been easily available. The 'triple shock' in the markets for credit, fuel and food ended these benign conditions, and caused a slowdown in economic growth, especially in the industrialised West. However, the full extent of global economic effects remained to be seen at mid 2008.

The financial crisis blew up in August 2007 as problems emerged in the market for securitised mortgages – home loans that had been sold by the lenders to financial institutions, which in turn packaged them into complex financial instruments. Amidst an economic and property boom in the United States, many home loans had been made to 'subprime' customers, with a poor credit rating and a low ability to service their debt. As US house prices began to fall, their ability to repay their loans weakened, and the rate of defaults grew. This called into question the valuation of the securitised pools of mortgages, which had become far removed from the original lender. The inability of fund managers to value investment funds that held these instruments set in motion a chain reaction in which many financial institutions with large holdings of mortgage-backed securities were forced to write down their value and take losses on them. At the same time, they became wary of lending to each other because they were unsure of each others' solvency. The interbank lending market, the very foundation of the international financial system, dried up. Central banks were forced to step in to lend money to banks in order to maintain the system's liquidity. Among the high-profile casualties of this turbulence were Bear Stearns, the US investment bank which was absorbed in a state of collapse by the larger JPMorgan Chase with the help of the US Federal Reserve, the central bank; and Northern Rock, the fifth-largest UK bank, which had relied on borrowing from the short-term money markets to fund its home-loan portfolio, and was taken into state ownership. Some of the world's biggest banks, including Citigroup and Merrill Lynch of the United States and UBS of Switzerland, had to arrange large injections of new capital after writing down the value of their assets, and other banks also raised new capital. In July 2008, the US Treasury was forced to step in to support the mortgage companies Fannie Mae and Freddie Mac, which either own or guarantee half of all US mortgages. This indicated that the crisis had not yet run its course.

One consequence of the crisis was that government-backed investment funds, particularly in Asia and the Gulf, acquired significant equity stakes in a number of large Western banks by helping to shore up their capital. The emergence of these large 'sovereign-wealth funds', mostly swelled by receipts from sales of oil, gas and other commodities, seemed likely to pose a range of strategic questions in the future.

The so-called 'subprime mortgage' crisis was a classic example of a financial crash in which a 'bubble' in asset prices leads to investors taking on excessive exposure – often in new, inadequately regulated instruments – without fully understanding the risks involved. The other two aspects of the triple shock, the surges in oil and food prices, were equally classic: rising demand encountered supply constraints.

The rise of oil prices fed into concerns expressed by many governments about longer-term security of energy supplies, and thus attracted attention for reasons beyond the considerably increased fuel costs being borne by consumers and, in countries which subsidise energy prices, taxpayers. Crude oil prices, at about \$140 a barrel at mid 2008, were some four and a half times their levels four years previously, and more than 85% higher than a year ago. The fall in the dollar's value on currency markets contributed to this rise. In inflation-adjusted terms, crude-oil prices were about 35% above the high reached in 1979 following the 1970s oil-price boom. The rapid rise of recent years reflected increased demand, particularly from China and other developing countries with strong economic growth rates. Demand rose to the point at which existing supply capacity was almost all being utilised, with the effect that even small additional supply constraints, such as temporary interruptions or slowing of the flow from any particular producer, had a large impact on market prices. While the world has very large unexploited oil reserves, most producing countries have not reacted quickly to invest in new supply capacity. According to a recent study by the International Monetary Fund (IMF), 'the supply response to robust demand growth and high prices has been sluggish, and there is now widespread consensus that the production and distribution capacity will be slow to build up, reflecting soaring investment costs [and] technological, geological and policy constraints'. The 2008 annual report of the Bank for International Settlements (BIS) said the costs of increasing capacity had risen sharply: 'For the four largest private sector oil companies outside OPEC, the cost of developing new oil reserves rose by between 45 and 70% over the period 2003–6'. While slower economic growth may inhibit demand, the IMF noted that oil-futures-market prices reflected an expectation that 'only high prices will induce the capacity expansion needed for continued robust oil demand growth'. Thus, the market expectation was that oil prices would remain at much higher levels than those seen in recent years.

The factors driving food prices were much the same as those for oil: strong economic growth, particularly in developing countries, was boosting demand. Rising incomes have boosted demand for cereals and for meat, which in turn requires more grain consumption as feed for livestock. The BIS also noted that 'subsidies for biofuel production have increased the demand for maize and soybeans, which has in turn raised the prices of other food crops by diverting production away from them'. According to the IMF, production of ethanol accounted for about three-quarters of the increase in global maize production in 2006–07. Again, rising demand for food has run into limitations on supply. Production of major food crops has not matched the increases in demand, and stocks have fallen to low levels. As in the oil market, prices have been boosted by disruptions to supply such as those caused by poor weather conditions. Oil price rises have increased production and transport costs. In addition, countries that have previously been large food exporters have acted to restrict exports as they have sought to limit the impact of global price rises on their own populations. In markets for food commodities, however, it is possible that supply constraints may be overcome more quickly than in the energy markets through investment in new capacity.

Taken together, the combination of financial distress and commodity-price inflation left the prospects for the world economy extremely uncertain at mid 2008. While a continued slowing of global growth seemed almost inevitable, the more precise effects and the degree of the economic impact were impossible to predict. This left policymakers across the world not only confronting a global situation fraught with risk, but also having to take difficult economic decisions under extreme political pressure, given the sensitivity of all electorates to the costs of fuel, food, homes and borrowing.

Developments in the 'arc of crisis'

A defence and security White Paper published by the French government in June 2008 identified an 'arc of crisis' as the first of four critical zones of the world in which European interests were especially at risk. While there had been earlier attempts to define such arcs, the one traced by France ranged from the Atlantic coast of northwest Africa though the Middle East and Gulf region to Afghanistan and Pakistan. Although it acknowledged that the countries involved in no way constituted a homogeneous whole, the White Paper said that radical Islam, sectarian tensions and fragile regimes 'constitute an explosive mixture'. It noted the presence of terrorist networks, nuclear-weapon and ballistic-missile programmes, and the risk that sectarian divisions seen in Iraq could spread more widely. The White Paper said European countries were bound to have to engage more in the entire arc in the future to prevent and manage crises.

While the delineation of such a zone is open to debate, it does provide a useful framework to consider the events of the year to mid 2008. Events along the 'arc' were mostly negative and had a number of common elements.

Beginning at the eastern end in nuclear-armed Pakistan, the rise of militant Islamist groups came into sharp focus in July 2007 when security forces laid siege to and eventually stormed the Red Mosque in the heart of Islamabad, the capital, which had been taken over by radicals conducting a campaign against the government. More than 100 people were killed. Militant groups were becoming increasingly active in the ungoverned tribal areas of Pakistan, where Osama bin Laden was still presumed to be hiding. From these areas, close to the border with Afghanistan, the groups fuelled the Taliban insurgency across the border, which Taliban fighters were freely able to cross. They were also believed to be responsible for a series of bomb attacks within Pakistan, including two attempts – the second of which succeeded – on the life of Benazir Bhutto, the former prime minister. These attacks, in which hundreds died, underlined the threat posed by violent extremism to Pakistan and the intersection of its problems with those of the wider world.

However, the Pakistani establishment was meanwhile engaged in its own internal existential battle. In mid 2007, US-backed President Pervez Musharraf faced a lawyers' revolt after he suspended the chief justice, whom he had to reinstate following a Supreme Court ruling. Under pressure from all sides, Musharraf desperately sought to remain in office. To be sworn in as president for a new term, he would have to step down as head of the army. His method was to win the presidential election while still the army chief, then declare a state of emergency and sack the Supreme Court, replacing it with judges who would formally approve his election as president. This being done, he took off his army uniform and was sworn in as a civilian president the next day. Elections for a new parliament were then to be held. He had made a deal with Bhutto under which she would return from exile and contest parliamentary elections without facing long-standing corruption charges. Her long-time rival Nawaz Sharif, the former prime minister ousted by Musharraf in a military coup, was not part of the deal, but Musharraf was later persuaded by Saudi Arabia to let him return from exile as well. The elections, which were delayed by Bhutto's assassination, were won by her party, but to form a government it had to enter a coalition with Sharif's party. By mid 2008, the durability of these new political arrangements was still unclear, with a weakened president, a deeply divided coalition government, a defiant judiciary, and an army adversely affected by an unsuccessful six-year front-line campaign against militant Islamist groups in the tribal areas bordering Afghanistan.

The prospects for future stability were no more comforting across the Durand Line in Afghanistan, where the efforts of international and Afghan forces to put down the Taliban insurgency continued to be unavailing in spite of some tactical successes. The insurgency spread to new areas and increasingly adopted tactics such as suicide bombings and improvised explosive devices, copying methods used in Iraq. The international community made little headway towards a much-needed common and comprehensive approach to tackling Afghanistan's problems. Instead, it remained divided by arguments about the military commitments and tactics that were needed. President Hamid Karzai faced re-election in 2009, but his authority had been undermined by pervasive government corruption and the failure to spur economic development.

In Iran too, President Mahmoud Ahmadinejad faces elections in 2009. He has come under severe pressure because of poor management of the economy, but on foreign policy he has been supported by Supreme Leader Ayatollah

Sayyid Ali Khamenei. Given the intricate machinations that ensured conservatives would do well in the 2008 parliamentary elections (although not hard-line supporters of Ahmadinejad), the likely outcome of the presidential vote is hard to predict. A December 2007 declaration by American intelligence agencies that Iran had ceased a nuclear-weapons programme in 2003 was a major boon to Ahmadinejad in his domestic political struggles. In contravention of four United Nations Security Council resolutions, Iran pressed ahead with its enrichment programme, which is believed by many experts to have no ultimate purpose other than the development of a nuclear-weapons option. On the diplomatic front a familiar pattern was repeating itself, as the UN agreed to tighten sanctions, while Europe put new proposals to Tehran with American support, and Iran delayed its response. At the heart of this impasse was Iran's refusal to suspend uranium enrichment. Meanwhile, verbal sparring and sabre rattling continued between Iran and Israel, and in July 2008 Iran very publicly tested missiles, including one that could reach Israel. While top American military officers made clear their belief that military action against Iran would be unwise, the situation remained vulnerable to sudden escalation in spite of the US intelligence agencies' verdict, which had been thought to rule out an American attack during the Bush administration. The American presidential election will have a crucial bearing on the Iranian confrontation, with Obama advocating direct talks and McCain sticking to a harder line. However, there had already been signs of a partial change of tack by the United States, which joined EU-led 'pre-negotiations' with Iran in Geneva on 19 July 2008 and was considering posting diplomats to Tehran for the first time since the seizure of the American Embassy in 1979.

American tactics were altered far more substantially in Iraq. The troop 'surge' of early 2007 was accompanied by the establishment of outposts intended to increase security within residential areas of Baghdad. Although Iraq's capital remained a violent and dangerous city, over the year to mid 2008 it began to move towards sustainable security, with organised politically motivated violence declining markedly. Moreover, Sunni communities moved to reject the jihadist extremists who, since the American invasion, had taken root among them. This new 'awakening' dealt a heavy blow to the insurgency, although bomb attacks causing large casualties still occurred. Meanwhile, the Iraqi government, whose writ had previously not extended beyond the secure 'Green Zone' of Baghdad, began to assert itself. There were signs that Iraq was regaining the workings of a state, all of which had collapsed following the American-led invasion. The operations of two groups that had been the main drivers of rampant civil strife, al-Qaeda in Mesopotamia and the Shia militia Jaish al-Mahdi controlled by Moqtada al-Sadr, have been largely constrained. The US–Iraqi military campaign against al-Qaeda broke its organisational capacity and radically reduced its geographic areas of operation. Key Jaish al-Mahdi strongholds were taken by the Iraqi Army.

However, the progress towards stability, both political and military, that had occurred since the surge remained vulnerable to unresolved political divisions. The responsibility to move towards a longer-term reconciliation of these divisions rested firmly with the Iraqi elite as American influence on Iraqi politics declined. While this was not unwelcome in Washington, future developments will again depend to a large extent on the approach to be adopted by the incoming US administration, with Obama planning a large drawdown of American forces and McCain more willing to maintain commitments for as long as he feels necessary.

For Iraq's Gulf Arab neighbours, events in Iraq and Iran continued to be worrisome. In particular, Saudi Arabia felt a strong risk from jihadists returning from Iraq. Arab states viewed with equal apprehension Iran's nuclear ambitions and the possibility of a military conflict because of them. The Iranian influence on Shia-dominated Iraq seemed set to be a long-term concern for them, as was the lack of progress towards a two-state solution to the Israel–Palestine dispute. The prospects for Middle East peace did not seem to be advanced in spite of an American push to force an agreement by the end of Bush's term. Internal divisions and weak leadership on both the Israeli and Palestinian sides appeared to preclude any possibility of a lasting accord being reached. Lebanon's vulnerability to political turbulence was underlined by an eruption of violence in May 2008, which left lingering concerns about the potential for radicalisation of its Sunni community. A more positive development was the commencement of peace talks between Israel and Syria with Turkish mediation, although this was balanced by evidence released by the United States indicating that a Syrian facility destroyed by an Israeli air raid in 2007 was a nuclear reactor that was under construction with assistance from North Korea.

Moving further westwards along the French-defined 'arc', conflict continued in Somalia between Islamist militias and Ethiopian-backed government troops, and the country continued to lack a functioning government. The long-running conflict in western Sudan continued, and in July 2008 the chief prosecutor of the International Criminal Court, in a contentious move, sought a warrant to arrest Sudanese president Omar al-Bashir on charges of genocide. Further west in the Maghreb, authoritarian regimes were facing an increasing threat from al-Qaeda-linked Islamist organisations, which carried out a growing number of bomb attacks.

Across this sweep of countries, there were few encouraging developments over the past year in disputes and problems of long standing. Islamist radicalisation, or the risk of it, was an element common to many of the countries. The gains made in Iraq against al-Qaeda in Mesopotamia were a welcome exception to the pattern. Also positive were counter-radicalisation efforts such as a programme to rehabilitate jihadists in Saudi Arabia, and the gains made by Indonesia and the Philippines in combating jihadist groups.

Non-traditional views of security

Over recent years, new views have begun to permeate international thinking about what constitutes a security issue, and about new approaches to solving issues that were previously viewed mainly from a military perspective. This reflects recognition that the regional or local conflicts that have proliferated since the end of the Cold War may be prevented and ended more effectively if the full range of causes and contributing factors is taken into account. It reflects lessons learned from progress made in some troubled regions, such as the Balkans, and from the intractability of other conflicts, such as in Afghanistan, the Middle East and Africa. More broadly, governments have been increasingly open to suggestions that issues such as climate change and commodity-price rises may have a security aspect.

This more wide-ranging assessment of security was reflected in the declaration of the 2008 NATO Summit in Bucharest, which laid stress on a 'comprehensive approach'. Leaders were heavily influenced by the difficulties of quelling the Taliban insurgency in Afghanistan and of securing a stable future for the country. Modern security challenges 'cannot be successfully met by NATO acting alone', they acknowledged. 'Meeting them can best be achieved through a broad partnership with the wider international community, as part of a truly comprehensive approach, based on a shared sense of openness and cooperation as well as determination on all sides.' This would bring together civilian and military efforts, and would require cooperation with non-governmental organisations and local bodies. The leaders said: 'It is essential for all major international actors to act in a coordinated way, and to apply a wide spectrum of civil and military instruments in a concerted effort that takes into account their respective strengths and mandates.' They endorsed an action plan that covered areas such as planning and conduct of operations, training and education, and enhanced cooperation with other actors – for example, the African Union and the European Union. Some of these – and particularly the EU – may in fact be better fitted than NATO to combine civil and military instruments and thus to contribute to a comprehensive approach.

While still to be put into practice, the leaders' commitment seemed potentially to be an important step towards the unified international approach that had been desperately needed in Afghanistan. It was linked to shifts already being made in the approaches to defence and security of NATO member countries, many of which have steadily reduced their perceptions of direct threats to their territorial sovereignty but have detected growing indirect threats, such as from regional or even distant conflicts, terrorism and weapons proliferation. For example, the French White Paper of June 2008 explicitly linked external and domestic security, and the capabilities that were required to ensure both. In the United States, there has also been a growing realisation that purely military prosecution of the 'war on terror' would not bring lasting solutions. While far from fully formed, such thinking was seen in the troop surge tactics in Iraq and in the reconstruction funds administered by American commanders in areas of Afghanistan. It remains to be seen whether full-blooded social engineering and nation building can be sustained over the time horizons suggested.

The serious challenges posed by ethnic and sectarian conflicts, as well as by nuclear proliferation, are not ones that can be fully dealt with by Western governments alone. Recruiting the active involvement of leading powers from other regions in combating such threats will require a level of comfort with policy approaches in Washington that, for the past seven years, has not been present. Building a new level of confidence – and thus restoring some of the bulwarks of international security – will be a pressing task for the next president of the United States.

2 Strategic Policy Issues

The intelligence services of the world's largest nations had not fully digested the implications of the end of the Cold War when the impact of international terrorism became horrifyingly clear on 11 September 2001. It was already obvious that new organisational structures would be necessary to replace those that had been focused on the Soviet bloc. The attacks on New York and Washington, in which 3,000 people died when hijacked aircraft were flown into the World Trade Center and the Pentagon, added extreme urgency to demands for intelligence reform. Then, in 2003, a US-led coalition invaded Iraq, partly because American and British intelligence analysis had indicated a threat from that country's weapons of mass destruction programmes. While the existence of such programmes had been well established by past United Nations inspections, the invading forces found neither weapons nor evidence of their recent existence. Reforms of intelligence services have since been drawn up and put into effect. Those of the United States are examined in the first essay below. This is followed by an essay on reforms in the United Kingdom.

A third strategic policy essay in this chapter considers the responses of countries bordering the Arctic Ocean to post-Cold War developments such as melting icecaps and competition for energy resources.

Reshaping Intelligence: America's Reforms

For the United States, the terrorist attacks of 11 September reflected failure on many fronts. Among these, it seemed clear that there had been a massive intelligence failure. The intelligence community had not connected the available information – for instance, about men from the Middle East who were learning to fly in American flight schools, but who showed no interest in take-offs and landings. There were organisational failings, too: agencies had withheld information from each other, for instance that two of the would-be hijackers had been tracked into the United States by summer 2001.

In the eyes of many, these intelligence errors were compounded when the George W. Bush administration's assertions that Iraq possessed weapons of mass destruction (WMD) proved to be false. American agencies could argue that they were not alone, since even the intelligence services of countries opposed to the war believed evidence of programmes would be found – but it was still a failure. Secretary of State Colin Powell's speech to the United Nations Security Council on 5 February 2003, which drew heavily on intelligence purporting to prove the existence of Iraq's WMDs, proved a lasting embarrassment. Powell, following close consultation with CIA Director George Tenet, reported, for example, that Baghdad possessed mobile biological-weapons production facilities on trucks and rail cars. Iraq's descent into a quagmire of violence and civil war put greater focus on how the United States had been led to attack and occupy the country.

Some immediate steps were taken in response to the 11 September attacks. For example, the Department of Homeland Security (DHS) was created in 2002, bringing together some 20 federal agencies and creating an Office of Intelligence and Analysis. The subsequent intelligence-reform process, however, was driven largely by official investigations into the 11 September attacks and Iraq. In 2002, Bush established a bipartisan committee, the National Commission on Terrorist Attacks upon the United States, to look at all aspects of the attacks. Its findings, widely praised for clear reporting and writing, were published in 2004 as *The 9/11 Commission Report*. The commission made several proposals regarding intelligence, and reform began in earnest with the passing of the Terrorism Prevention and Intelligence Reform Act of 2004. Also in 2004, following the Iraq invasion, Bush set up a bipartisan committee with a specific remit to consider intelligence capabilities. Its findings were published in 2005 as the *Final Report of the Commission on the Intelligence Capabilities of the United States Regarding Weapons of Mass Destruction*. The WMD Commission extended the agenda of intelligence reform.

Outlines of reform
Both commissions made clear that they saw an enormous challenge that would be the work of years, not months.

While the 9/11 Commission made specific recommendations, the broadest and most far-reaching was its proposal to foster coordination among the many agencies by emulating the military in separating the 'organise, train, and equip' function from the deployment of intelligence personnel. Under this concept, the existing agencies – such as the CIA, the FBI, the Defense Intelligence Agency

(DIA) and the National Security Agency (NSA) – would, like the military services, be responsible for building the intelligence forces, but those forces would be deployed by new 'national intelligence centers', which would be shaped by issue or function, rather than by organisation or the source from which data was collected.

The centres would be thus be the intelligence community's equivalent of the military's unified commands. In Iraq, for instance, Central Command (CENTCOM), the regional command for the Middle East, managed the war, but the troops were provided by the military services, which executed operations under CENTCOM's direction. By analogy, a National Counterterrorism Center would be established as the 'unified command' in the 'war on terror', carrying out intelligence analysis and planning operations; the CIA and other agencies would provide the analysts and other personnel and would conduct required operations such as intelligence gathering.

The 9/11 Commission also saw a need not only to create the technical infrastructure through which intelligence could be shared, but also to rethink the web of 'need to know' and other security requirements that tended to frustrate effective sharing of information. Its main specific recommendations, which were followed up in the 2004 Act, were the following: create a national intelligence director, and make the CIA director separate from the national intelligence director; establish a national counter-terrorism centre and national intelligence centres.

Create a national intelligence director

The commission argued that the absence of an individual with overall responsibility for coordinating the nation's intelligence capabilities contributed to the failures that permitted the 11 September attacks. These had, in fact, been more of coordination at the working level than of broad strategic direction, and the mere fact of the attacks was enough to spur marked improvement in day-to-day coordination, along with a change in mission at the FBI. Nevertheless, the need for better strategic management of the intelligence community was seen to be pressing. In the WMD Commission's words, the community was 'fragmented, loosely managed, and poorly coordinated'.

The logic was to give a new national intelligence director powers that the existing position of director of central intelligence (DCI) lacked: authority over budgets for the intelligence agencies other than the CIA, over hiring and firing senior leaders, and over setting standards for intelligence personnel and infrastructure. Since 1946, the head of the CIA had also been the DCI, responsible for coordinating the activities of all intelligence bodies. Under the proposal, the position of DCI would be replaced by a director of national intelligence (DNI) separate from the CIA director.

This was hardly a new idea; rather, it was a hardy perennial. In one assessment conducted by RAND of 31 studies of or proposals for reforming intelligence between 1948 and 2002, the top three recurring themes were expanding the DCI's authority; creating a director of national intelligence; and giving the DCI more tools to manage the community. Nor was the proposition that DCIs had previously lacked the authority now proposed for the DNI quite so clear-cut. Veterans observed that the earlier DCIs could have had sufficient authority had the president so desired, and given appropriate orders to the secretary of defense. In the Carter administration, when intelligence budgets were falling, DCI Stansfield Turner exercised considerable control over the entire intelligence budget, and built a serious programme-analysis staff to aid him. Nevertheless, the 2004 Act, in establishing the DNI position, explicitly granted the holder more authority than had been available to the DCI.

The law gave the DNI authority to appoint the director of the CIA, subject to Senate confirmation. For all other intelligence-agency heads, save one, the DNI was given a veto through the requirement that the director concur in the appointment made by the cabinet secretary (Defense, State, Treasury, and so on) for whom the intelligence agency worked. The exception was the directorship of the DIA, where the law stated only that the DNI had to be consulted.

There were inevitable arguments between and among agencies and in Congress about the precise authority to be given to the DNI. Constraints were imposed. The sticking point in the congressional negotiations was the exact power of the DNI over intelligence operations located in the Department of Defense, especially the big technical collectors of data – the National Security Agency (NSA), the National Geospatial Intelligence Agency (NGA) and the National Reconnaissance Office (NRO). These agencies account for the vast bulk of the national intelligence budget, and no secretary of defense had been eager to cede authority over them to the DCI. Donald Rumsfeld, the secretary of defense at the time of the act, was similarly reluctant to surrender authority to the new DNI. In eleventh-hour negotiations, Congress also trimmed the proposed powers of the DNI to reallocate money and people – for example, to move more than a hundred people to any particular new joint intelligence centre.

The importance of these constraints was not clear, and the DNI's authorities continued to be at issue during the rewriting of the main order covering intelligence, Executive Order 12333, during 2007 and 2008. The term of the first DNI, John Negroponte, who served from 2005 to 2007, provided little indication of whether the limitations were substantial, or whether he was disinclined to try to stretch them. In principle, he had considerable programmatic authority: the director develops the National Intelligence Program (NIP) – that is, the broad budgets for all 16 national intelligence agencies – and determines broad personnel policy covering civilians in all the agencies. In that sense, the DNI's authority over the nation's intelligence budget is roughly comparable to that of the secretary of defense over total defense spending.

The challenge for the DNI, however, is not simply a matter of the position's formal authority. As the capabilities of collection systems such as imaging and eavesdropping satellites have improved, they have become increasingly important to warfighters for tactical purposes, and the distinction between strategic and tactical intelligence has become blurred. The overlap increases competition for resources: the same satellite system can locate insurgent combat units in Iraq for warfighters and help keep tabs on suspicious nuclear facilities in Iran for the benefit of policymakers.

The intelligence community and the Pentagon thus increasingly share assets, and competition over whose needs are more important has intensified. It is hard to short-change warfighters in that competition, but support for them risks being open-ended – more is always better – with expensive duplication. In the short run, striking the balance depends on relations between the DNI and the secretary of defense. In the longer run, something like the Key West accords of 1947, which hammered out the authorities of the new secretary of defense and the service chiefs, may be required.

Make the CIA director separate from the national intelligence director

A key element in the creation of a DNI was to separate the person in charge of the intelligence community from what had been the DCI's principal asset: the foreign espionage and analysis capabilities of the CIA. This arrangement was potentially to the disadvantage of both the DNI and the CIA director.

In the past, no DCI had wanted to surrender direct management of the CIA, fearing that the loss of 'troops' would mean a loss of power. The 9/11 Commission, while it recognised this risk, argued that clandestine operations were tactical and required close attention. In addition, if the DNI ran the CIA as the DCI had done in the past, he would be an advocate for CIA budgets while at the same time the manager of overall intelligence funding – a conflict of interest. The commission noted that the law charges the CIA with *foreign* intelligence, while a critical task for the DNI is to coordinate intelligence across the foreign–domestic divide.

The commission also argued that a DNI who continued to run the CIA would have an overwhelming workload, even worse than that of the DCI:

The DCI now has at least three jobs. He is expected to run a particular agency, the CIA. He is expected to manage the loose confederation of agencies that is the intelligence community. He is expected to be the analyst in chief for the government, sifting evidence and directly briefing the President as his principal intelligence adviser.

The commission hoped a national intelligence director would be able to exercise the third responsibility while spending most of his time on the second role. In practice, DCIs had tended to focus on the CIA, running the agency that was theirs to command; running operations abroad was interesting and politically delicate, with constant tactical management required.

The CIA director was meanwhile left with a primary responsibility to build a better espionage capacity for the nation. The task included, in the 9/11 Commission's words,

> transforming the clandestine service by building its human intelligence capabilities; developing a stronger language program, with high standards and sufficient financial incentives; renewing emphasis on recruiting diversity among operations officers so they can blend more easily in foreign cities; ensuring a seamless relationship between human source collection and signals collection at the operational level; and stressing a better balance between unilateral and liaison operations.

The CIA director at the time, Porter Goss, who was appointed in 2004 and resigned in 2006, made this almost his exclusive priority. However, he was notably unsuccessful. The Goss era was characterised by weak and uncertain leadership and divisive office politics. Goss, previously a member of Congress, brought his Congressional staff with him, leading to the departure of many of CIA's most experienced operational managers (including Stephen Kappes, who later returned as deputy to Goss's successor, Michael Hayden).

The Bush administration also made the CIA director the national manager of human intelligence, with a deputy charged with the wider responsibility of overseeing human intelligence across the community. This initiative holds promise of better coordinating CIA and Pentagon HUMINT operations, all the more so as Secretary of Defense Robert Gates moved to rein in some of the more controversial Pentagon intelligence activities, such as the sending of small teams, called military liaison elements, into countries – including friendly ones – at times without the knowledge of the American ambassador. However, managing HUMINT across the government will remain difficult. On the foreign side, political reporting by foreign service officers is a major source of 'intelligence', but those officers do not regard themselves as intelligence collectors.

Creation of the DNI position has not solved all problems. The DNI still has to balance two jobs. Negroponte took over management and delivery of the crown jewel of analysis, the President's Daily Brief (PDB), which had been the CIA's product. However, Negroponte's relatively brief tenure mostly involved building the DNI bureaucracy, and reinforced the argument of sceptics that the position would simply add one more layer of organisational clutter. Negroponte, a career diplomat whose most recent appointments had been as Ambassador to the United Nations and to Iraq, had the air of a man who had taken the job out of duty rather than real interest or commitment. After less than two years, he accepted the position of deputy secretary of state. It could be argued that his willingness to trade the DNI post for the deputy position did not reflect well on the reshaping of intelligence and the post itself. His successor, Michael McConnell, a career military intelligence officer and former NSA director, sought to pick up the pace of reform with a 500-day plan that emphasised 'jointness' among intelligence agencies. As an example of the institutional challenges he faced, McConnell's moves to streamline training provoked resistance from agencies to the DNI even having a role in evaluating their programmes, much less consolidating them. After three years, there is not much evidence that the DNI has had a significant impact on major intelligence programmes.

The 9/11 Commission had recommended that the CIA cede responsibility for directing and executing paramilitary operations to the military. Like its other major recommendations, this had a long history. The arguments for giving control to the military have been, historically, the ones the commission cited: the requisite capabilities are military, the task has not been a continuous priority for the CIA, and it makes no sense for the nation to build two parallel capacities. The counter-argument is that the military is less agile and discreet, and cannot act covertly – a concern that may have diminished as the special forces have developed a wide variety of units and types of operations. The commission found that the Afghanistan precedent of joint CIA–military teams was a good one. It suggested that CIA capabilities and people should be integrated into military-directed teams, giving both the CIA and military's special-operations forces a role. The 2004 bill was silent on this issue. Both organisations remain in the paramilitary operations business.

Establish a National Counterterrorism Center

While intelligence agencies gather and analyse information about many fields affecting national security, the impact of the 11 September attacks placed particular urgency on countering terrorism. The 9/11 Commission proposed the creation of a National Counterterrorism Center (NCTC) that would be responsible, like a unified command within the military, for bringing together information and planning. The centre would task intelligence collection requirements both inside and outside the United States, and would 'perform joint operational planning, assigning lead responsibilities to existing agencies and letting them direct the actual execution of the plans'. The centre would thus be responsible for both joint intelligence and joint operational planning. The model is explicitly that of military joint staffs, and the centre would play the roles of both J-2 (intelligence) and J-3 (operational planning).

A Terrorist Threat Integration Center (TTIC) had already been created in 2003 to 'connect the dots' of intelligence, both foreign and domestic, that could provide warning of terrorist threats to the homeland. Under the commission's proposal and the 2004 Act, this became the NCTC. The centre was left to work out exactly what the planning task, labelled 'strategic operational planning', would entail and how it would work.

For intelligence analysis, the NCTC, like the TTIC, was to absorb analytic talent residing in the CIA's Counterterrorist Center (CTC), the FBI's Counterterrorism Division (CTD) and in the Defense Intelligence Agency's Joint Task Force Counterterrorism (JTFCT). In effect, the NCTC became the 'campus' for a confederation, bringing together several hundred officials from the CTC and the CTD, plus smaller numbers from other agencies, at its headquarters at Liberty Crossing near Tyson's Corner, Virginia, not far from the CIA's Langley headquarters.

On the strategic operational planning side, however, the NCTC drew on a limited inheritance. The CIA's Counterterrorist Center, for instance, was located with the CIA's clandestine operators, the Directorate of Operations, and was more engaged in providing operational support to intelligence operations abroad than it was in pure analysis. The NCTC, however, was set up neither to execute operations – those would be left to the agencies – nor to make policy, which would be left to the president and the National Security Council. It was to assign responsibilities for operations to lead agencies but not to direct the execution of those operations. On the positive side, the conception of the NCTC is rooted in the understanding that the counter-terrorism mission is intelligence-rich and thus that planning needs to be intelligence-driven. It brought the interagency process under one roof, with a permanent set of agency representatives – at about the one-star level – housed at the NCTC. However, it was not clear what was meant by 'strategic operational planning', and to what extent the NCTC could influence the planning of the major agencies, especially the military.

Establish National Intelligence Centers

The NCTC represented the first attempt to structure the entire US intelligence system in a new way. Under the Cold War approach, US intelligence collection was organised around sources – signals, espionage and imagery – while analysis was organised by agency. This configuration had logic when the intelligence community had one overarching target, the Soviet Union. There were relatively few consumers of intelligence material. Pride of place was given to secret sources which an agency 'owned'. In effect, the collectors were asked: what can you contribute to understanding the puzzle of the Soviet Union?

In the modern era the situation has changed fundamentally. Rather than a single threat, there is a multiplicity of dangers to which intelligence agencies must be alert and about which they need to gather information. Rather than relying only on secret sources, an intelligence agency must process a mass of information from many sources, many of which are public, such as the Internet. The wide variety of threats that could affect national security means that many government agencies, rather than just a few, may need to be supplied with intelligence material. Urgent action may be necessary to head off threats.

Under the 9/11 Commission proposal, new centres would bring together analysts, information collectors and operations specialists around problems or issues, rather than being structured to reflect collection sources or existing agencies. Issue-oriented centres had in fact existed in the intelligence community since the mid 1980s. Although they had reported to the DCI, they were in practice dominated by the CIA. This proposal moved them to remit of the DNI and, in principle, made them more central as focal points for intelligence and operations. The 2004 bill licensed their creation but had little to say about specific centres other than the NCTC. Neither Negroponte nor his successor McConnell pushed the concept forward.

There are several concerns about organisation by centres. First, establishing new centres implies that they should be staffed by experts from other agencies. But there is little tradition of intelligence officers moving between organisations, and little incentive for them to do so – despite tentative efforts by the DNI to require of intelligence officers something like the 'joint' appointments that are a prerequisite for senior leadership in the military. Secondly, the technical difficulties of creating new amalgamated structures were made obvious at the NCTC, where analysts' computers continued to be accompanied by a half dozen 'pizza boxes', each housing a hard drive for a different agency information source that had to be integrated by the analysts. Thirdly, the big analytic agencies such as the CIA, FBI and DIA resist thinking of themselves as force providers; they regard themselves as the doers. Well before 2004, agencies expressed concern about 'centeritis', the rise of specialised or issue-oriented bodies, like the CTC or the Counter-Narcotics Center. Agency staff tend to think of personnel assigned to those centres as lost to the real work, which continued to happen back home at their agency. Changing that view to regard the real work as done by the centres, with the agencies in a supporting role, would entail a sea change in organisational culture. Fourthly, there is concern that the centres would be very much inclined to focus on current intelligence, and would tend to produce worst-case analyses. This would be a serious problem. Unified commands in the military do tend to have short time horizons and to worry about worst cases, for understandable reasons: if war broke out today, they would have to fight it. In a similar way, the centres would be the first ones blamed if crises developed without warning, and their plans would be the first ones exposed if remedies failed. So the bias toward current intelligence and dramatic over-warning that now afflict all of US intelligence – a theme that runs through the WMD Commission report – could get worse.

If issue-oriented centres assume a central role in the US intelligence community, the overall system should also allow for countervailing pressures. For example, the existing National Intelligence Council – a kind of strategic think tank formerly part of the CIA and now under the DNI – would lean against the wind and offer protection from the urgency of the immediate. In response to a WMD Commission recommendation, the NIC created a long-range analysis unit. The CIA previously had a Strategic Assessments Group to perform a similar long-range role, but its fate is cautionary: it was disbanded in 2006 on the grounds it had not 'produced' enough.

Issue-based centres other than the NCTC might serve as focuses for the intelligence community. Acting on a WMD Commission recommendation, the Bush administration created a National Counter Proliferation Center, structurally very different from the NCTC. The proliferation centre was conceived as small and focused on overseeing collection and analysis. Planning and operations was left to wider inter-agency groupings. There is also a National Counterintelligence Executive (NCIX), which builds on an earlier organisation, and is less a centre in the 9/11 Commission's sense than a focal point for the specialised task of counter-intelligence.

There are risks in organising intelligence by problem, rather than by agency or information source, beyond preoccupation with the immediate. Focusing on non-state threats risks underappreciating developments in states. The more centres are embodied in bricks and mortar, rather than being 'virtual' organisations, the more they risk outliving their usefulness if national priorities and threat perceptions change. Moreover, the more specific the definition of the problems, the more likely it is that intelligence will be blind-sided in the future by something for which there was no structure to collate information and plan action.

Domestic intelligence: a new approach for the FBI

The 11 September attacks prompted immediate calls for a new domestic intelligence service, separate from the FBI. Senator Bob Graham (D-FL) argued it was time to look seriously at an alternative to the FBI approach and do what many other nations had done: put domestic intelligence in a non-law-enforcement agency. The 9/11 Commission pointed to the limitations imposed by the FBI's culture of case-based law enforcement, saying that FBI agents were trained to build cases, and thus developed information in support of their own cases rather than as part of a broader more strategic intelligence effort. One example was the case of Zacarias Moussaoui, the so-called 'twentieth hijacker', now serving a life sentence for conspiracy to murder. When agents from the local FBI field office looked in August 2001 at the flying lessons he had been taking at a Norman,

Oklahoma school, they did so in ignorance of the fact that the same field office had been interested in the same flight school two years earlier because a man thought to be Osama bin Laden's pilot had trained there. However, both commissions decided, and Congress agreed, that the arguments for creating a separate domestic intelligence service were not persuasive and that the FBI should be given time and encouragement to build its own intelligence capacity.

FBI director Robert S. Mueller, who had been in the post for one week on 11 September 2001, was keenly aware of the pressure to cede domestic intelligence to a new agency. He moved quickly to reorient the bureau toward prevention and intelligence, sending a reorganisation plan to Congress in November 2001. He centralised management of the bureau's counter-terrorism programme. Arthur Cummings, special agent in charge for counterterrorism at the Washington Field Office, explained the rationale: 'There is no such thing as a local terrorism problem. Something might happen locally, but within two seconds, you discover national and international connections.' Today, the FBI website says that the bureau's top priority is to 'protect the United States from terrorist attack'.

The FBI's budget more than doubled between 2001 and 2008, from $3.1 billion to $6.4bn. It increased the number of joint terrorism task forces (JTTFs), which bring together FBI agents, state and local law enforcement officials, and representatives from other federal agencies to investigate terrorism cases, from 34 to 101. Yet the JTTFs remained primarily in the business of investigation, especially because Mueller promised after 11 September that no tip would go unpursued. The JTTFs sought to avoid conflict in investigations by assigning them to particular federal, state or local agencies and then insuring that they did not cross in harmful ways.

In May 2003, Mueller took a further step by creating a more independent Office of Intelligence, recruiting Maureen Baginski from the National Security Agency (NSA) to head it, and naming her executive assistant director of intelligence (she has since left the post). Her mandate was to create state-of-the-art processes and standards for intelligence gathering throughout the bureau; to spot and rank gaps in intelligence; and to evaluate field-office performance in closing those gaps. Field Intelligence Groups (FIGs) in each field office would analyse and disseminate intelligence, and would serve as central points of contact both among field offices and between them and headquarters personnel with regard to intelligence issues. The WMD Commission worried, however, that intelligence still lacked clout: 'The Directorate of Intelligence may "task" the field offices to collect against certain requirements … [but] its "taskings" are really "askings".' In early 2005, only 38 of the bureau's 1,720 intelligence analysts worked within the Directorate of Intelligence itself.

The bureau quickly embraced the recommendation of the WMD Commission. The next stage of reorganisation, in 2005, put the beefed-up Office of Intelligence back together with counter-intelligence and counter-terrorism in the National Security Branch (NSB), with the intention of creating an intelligence branch with a relationship to the DNI similar to those of NSA and NGA – not managed day-to-day by the DNI but looking to that office for budget and broad guidance. In effect, the FBI had created a service within a service, though without a formal personnel track. Later, the bureau did create an intelligence career track (one of five) for special agents as part of its general effort to upgrade the status of intelligence within the organisation.

Terrorism is a matter for both intelligence and law enforcement, and the wall that used to separate the two, within the FBI as well as between and among agencies, has been all but erased. Officials seeking intelligence can share information with colleagues who are investigating a criminal case. However, another major terrorist attack on the United States would certainly raise the question again of whether a new domestic intelligence agency was required.

The challenges ahead

An important challenge for the DNI is to break down stovepipes in data collection and to consider how best the government should obtain the information it needs. Collection systems consume the bulk of the intelligence community's budgets but, as the WMD Commission said, 'the intelligence failure in Iraq did not begin with faulty analysis. It began with a sweeping collection failure.'

The sheer volume of the take from collection, even from secret sources, let alone public sources, threatens to overwhelm processing capacity. One problem has been that collection produces too much data and too little information. According to the WMD Commission, in the case of Iraq, both imagery and signals intelligence 'produced precious little intelligence for the analysts to analyse'. This is partly because traditional methods are now of less value. US techniques for collecting data, especially through satellite imagery, have become well understood by targets. Meanwhile, tried-and-tested Cold War espionage practices will not work against terrorist targets; al-Qaeda operatives do not, for example, frequent embassy cocktail parties.

There is a need to be less passive in data collection and quicker to innovate. For signals intelligence, this means getting closer to targets; for example, pinpointing particular mobile phones or computers before their signals disappear into the enormous volume of international communication. In the field of imagery, it means using smaller platforms, both satellites and unmanned aerial vehicles, more stealth technology for all platforms, and more of the spectrum, going beyond infrared to 'hyperspectral' imagery. For espionage, it means drawing on the ethnic diversity of the United States (and other countries) in recruiting spymasters and having agents operating outside the official cover of American embassies abroad.

The WMD Commission, like other such panels, called for improvement in America's espionage, or human intelligence. However, while the demand was understandable, expectations on this front should not be high. American experience with officers working under non-official cover is viewed as mixed at best. Such agents are seen as expensive to deploy and sustain, costly for the limited information they can provide, and requiring both substantial risks and dealings with unsavoury people. That such practices do not come easily to the American system means that the United States will likely continue to depend on friendly countries and associates with access and methods unavailable to its own agents.

Even if human intelligence continues to be a shortfall, the US intelligence community does have access to a vast array of information. For example, terrorists – like everybody else – leave a trail through travel, telephone calls, Internet use, purchases and so on. In tandem with the development of information technologies, the technical capabilities of the intelligence agencies to generate information, such as imagery from spy satellites, have mushroomed. Each new generation of collection systems dramatically increases the intelligence take, especially in imagery. However, the capacity to process and analyse the data has fallen far behind. For example, the NSA is capable of collecting the equivalent of the contents of the US Library of Congress every six hours.

With such a huge amount of data available, the big collectors of signals and imagery intelligence, NSA and NGA, will be tempted to solve their processing problem by turning a fire hose of data on intelligence analysts. Should there be another intelligence failure, an agency could say that it had at least passed on the data. A better balance is thus needed between investments in the emerging new-generation collection systems and enhanced forms of analytical capability. The DNI, as he seeks to reduce stovepiping in collection agencies, should have a role in developing more analytic capacity and making trade-offs.

The WMD Commission suggested that the DNI create an 'integrated collection enterprise' for the intelligence community, coordinating the entire cycle from planning new systems, to developing strategies for deploying systems against priority targets, to processing and exploiting the information produced. Steps towards this included the establishment of the centres for counter-terrorism and counter-proliferation, and the appointment of issue managers for North Korea, Iran and Venezuela/Cuba, intended to focus on particular intelligence problems, especially in collection. In addition, a National Intelligence Coordination Center (NIC-C) has been set up, though it is still a work in progress. The Integrated Concepts Development Office (ICDO) also has a remit to push innovation with regard to particular intelligence challenges, especially in collection.

Performance in the area of intelligence analysis has been heavily criticised. There was strategic analysis aplenty on al-Qaeda before 11 September: for example, there was an item in the president's Daily Brief in August 2001 entitled

'Bin Laden determined to strike in US'. Yet for the new Bush administration, committed to other priorities, the warning was general, not specific. There was no tactical warning of particular attacks that might have led to action. The WMD Commission said of intelligence before the Iraq War that the 'failure was in large part the result of analytical shortcomings; intelligence analysts were too wedded to their assumptions about Saddam [Hussein]'s intentions'. The Senate Select Committee on Intelligence was equally scathing about the October 2002 National Intelligence Estimate on Iraq, concluding that 'most of the major key judgments ... either overstated, or were not supported by, the underlying intelligence reporting. A series of failures, particularly in analytic tradecraft, led to the mischaracterisation of the intelligence.'

There are no easy solutions for improving analysis. Higher quality cannot be produced by legislation, reorganisation or exhortation. The shortcomings of US intelligence analysis run deep in organisational culture. The major agency, the CIA's Directorate of Intelligence, was and still is hierarchical, dominated by generalist analysts and quite risk averse. Before 11 September, most agencies used computers primarily to sort messages; they have been slow to move into network analysis, data mining and the like. Nor did they make much use of formal methods like the Delphi interactive forecasting technique or other ways of aggregating subjective judgements. Current and future threats to the United States, such as terrorism, are global and changeable, blurring distinctions between and among crime, terrorism and war. Analysts may have to think more like detectives, trying to see patterns amidst incomplete information. The DNI and the CIA director will need to oversee experiments and pilot projects, many of which may involve quite dramatic departures from current practice. Finally, the asymmetric nature of modern threats means it is important to understand the interplay between the United States and its adversaries – that is, understanding what the 'blue' side is doing as well as the 'red'. But that runs directly against a powerful norm in US foreign intelligence: 'Thou shalt not assess America or Americans'.

There is also an enormous challenge of pooling information. The heart of the issue is existing practice in which each intelligence agency controls the information it produces, making it hard to share with other US intelligence agencies, let alone get information to state and local authorities. Some 700,000 law-enforcement officers in 18,000 government jurisdictions, as well as private-sector managers of critical infrastructure, are involved daily in combating terrorism, but security procedures are designed to limit information to those with a 'need to know'. The fundamental challenge is to reshape how the US government thinks of information, and how it should be produced, used and controlled. For example, simply to speak of 'information sharing' implies that agencies 'own' their information and that it is theirs to share as they see fit. It also implies that the sharing is in one direction, from the collecting agencies to bodies that use the information. But in dealing with modern threats, consumers of information are also producers; for example, a local police force acting on information may also be a provider of information.

The JTTFs established by the FBI are a step towards better cooperation. So too is a newer and promising DHS initiative, 'fusion centres'. These are intended to complement the JTTFs, which work on cases once identified. Fusion centres are meant to assemble strategic intelligence at the regional level. They too seek to bring together federal, state and local officials, and to involve the private sector. The responsibility of the centres is to fuse foreign intelligence with domestic information to facilitate improved policymaking on issues of counter-terrorism, crime and emergency response. This is challenging, and fusion centres are experiencing adjustment difficulties, including poor or absent communication between centres. Not all fusion centres have state-wide intelligence systems. They also do not all have access to law-enforcement data or private-sector information. The lack of interoperability of different agencies' systems, widely criticised directly after 11 September, still exists. Because of the huge number of systems and the resulting duplication, reviewing incoming information is extremely time consuming. The goal is not just a two-way street for data, it is to jointly produce useful information across the far-flung American federal system. Effective sharing of information will not be a panacea, but would be an important step forward.

The next director of intelligence will inherit a structure that is very much a work in progress. From the beginning, the task of reshaping American intelligence was partly a matter of organisation – but only partly. How business is done within the stovepipes – for instance, in fostering innovation in intelligence analysis – is as important a finding ways to make trade-offs across them. Even on an issue like training, the DNI's efforts to increase interoperability are meeting push-back from the agencies that resist diluting their 'brands'. The next DNI will have an opportunity, but the window is closing. Those observers who worried from the beginning that the new structure would just add one more layer of officialdom may have been correct.

Intelligence Reform in the UK

Intelligence reform in the UK since the start of the new millennium has been driven by two main factors: the realisation that pre-war intelligence on Iraq's WMD holdings had proven incorrect; and the need to respond to the threat posed by Islamist extremist terrorism. The first attracted much public attention but resulted in few substantive changes to the structure of the UK intelligence community. The second has had more impact, but there has not been a net fundamental shift in the way the UK intelligence community functions.

Since the end of the Second World War, the UK's intelligence capabilities, though in no way comparable to those of the United States, have nonetheless been more substantial than those of most medium-ranking powers. The UK's permanent seat on the UN Security Council, its front-line position during the Cold War and a long-running process of decolonisation ensured that intelligence played an important role in policy formulation. Apart from its own intelligence resources, the UK also benefited significantly from its membership of the 'Five-Eyes' intelligence alliance comprising Australia, Canada, New Zealand, the UK and the United States, and from the UK–USA agreement which allowed for an unprecedented level of cooperation and information-sharing in the arena of signals intelligence (SIGINT).

Many UK government departments and agencies have intelligence-gathering functions, but formally speaking, the intelligence community comprises the Security Service, also known as MI5, which is responsible for monitoring threats within the UK; the Secret Intelligence Service (SIS), also known as MI6, which collects intelligence overseas predominantly by means of human intelligence (HUMINT); and Government Communications Headquarters (GCHQ), which is responsible for SIGINT collection. These organisations are collectively referred to as 'the agencies'. The Defence Intelligence Service (DIS), tasked to meet the intelligence needs of the Ministry of Defence, is predominantly an analytical service but also engages in collection by technical means, including imagery (IMINT) and electronic signals intelligence (ELINT). It is not formally included within the agencies but collaborates increasingly closely with them.

At the heart of the UK intelligence community is the Joint Intelligence Committee (JIC), created in 1936. It is made up of the agencies, the DIS and the main government departments that are intelligence 'customers', and is situated in the Cabinet Office, which works for the prime minister and co-ordinates government departments. The JIC has 24 members, and representatives from other departments can be invited to attend when relevant issues are under discussion. The JIC's functions are to collect, prioritise and disseminate the intelligence requirements of customer departments and to monitor the degree to which these have been met; it does not exercise line-management responsibility over the agencies. However, a senior Cabinet Office official – whose title over recent years changed from intelligence co-ordinator to security and intelligence co-ordinator, then to permanent secretary, security, intelligence and resilience – is responsible for monitoring the agencies' management practices and use of resources, and negotiating these resources with the Treasury as accounting officer for the Single Intelligence Account (SIA) from which the agencies are funded. (From 2004 to 2007, the posts of JIC chairman and accounting officer for the SIA were combined, but have subsequently separated with the permanent secretary holding the overall budget, and a separate JIC chairman appointed.) Political oversight of the agencies is the responsibility of the home secretary in respect of the Security Service and the foreign secretary in respect of SIS and GCHQ.

One of the JIC's key functions is to produce intelligence assessments that represent an official British government view of a particular issue or situation. This is in contrast to the US system where policymakers draw on a range of competing assessments from different parts of the intelligence machinery. JIC assessments can reflect dissenting or competing views, though in practice this happens rarely. They are compiled by the JIC's own Assessments Staff, which is made up of some 30 analysts seconded from a range of government departments for fixed terms typically of three years. Staff from the MoD and Foreign Office tend to predominate. When the Assessments Staff was established in 1968, the intention was to create a permanent cadre of career analysts, but this proved impossible given the difficulties of creating a career structure in what was then a highly compartmented community with limited possibilities for staff inter-change. JIC assessments are compiled from all available sources of information, including open source and secret intelligence. All relevant agency reports are channelled to the Assessments Staff, but the agencies also disseminate single-source reports directly to customer departments. There is no formal requirement for intelligence to be assessed by the JIC before action is taken on it; that is a matter of judgement for policymakers.

The configuration and size of the UK intelligence community remained rela-tively static throughout the Cold War. However, following the collapse of the Soviet Union, the UK government began to question the resources being devoted to intel-ligence. Within the Treasury, the department driving the process, there was an apparent ideological reluctance to invest in capacity: all resource expenditure had to be justified in terms of demonstrable outcomes. The Security Service, engaged in a long-running campaign against Irish republicanism, was largely unaffected. However, SIS suffered a 25% reduction in numbers during the 1990s. During this period, it had to adapt to a new range of transnational threats including Islamist extremist terrorism, serious and organised crime and WMD proliferation. At the same time, SIS was having to adapt to being placed on a statutory footing under the Intelligence Service Act of 1994 – prior to that the British government had never formally acknowledged SIS's existence – and becoming subject to parliamentary oversight, as well as dealing with enhanced legal compliance arising out of legisla-tion such as the Regulation of Investigatory Powers Act (RIPA).

The Iraq War

The pressure on resources affected intelligence analysis of Iraq's WMD pro-grammes. For much of the 1990s the intelligence community depended for its knowledge of these programmes on United Nations weapons inspectors, who secured wide-ranging access in Iraq and uncovered substantial weapons pro-grammes that contravened UN Security Council resolutions. GCHQ, and to a lesser extent SIS, provided intelligence support to the inspectors. But SIS, realis-ing that it would never be able independently to replicate the levels of access enjoyed by the UN, concentrated its resources on WMD programmes in other countries, for example Iran's clandestine nuclear-enrichment programme, the activities of the A.Q. Khan network, and Libya's activities. The relative lack of focus on Iraq was to have important consequences once it became clear that President George W. Bush's administration had taken the decision to overthrow the regime of Saddam Hussein.

In the run-up to the US-led invasion of Iraq in 2003, the government of then Prime Minister Tony Blair was committed to supporting American action against Saddam. Seeking to build popular support for the case for war, the government published a dossier based on intelligence assessments prepared by the JIC on the threat posed by Iraq's WMD programmes. At the time of publication, the dossier, entitled *Iraq's Weapons of Mass Destruction: The Assessment of the British Government*, was not viewed by experts as especially controversial; indeed it attracted some criticism for its apparent lack of substantive new information. However, it made headlines because of its claim that the Iraqi military was able to deploy chemi-cal and biological weapons within 45 minutes of a decision to do so. It was this 45-minute claim that was to reverberate afterwards, as Blair was accused of delib-erately exaggerating the threat that Saddam posed. The controversy turned into a political crisis when a BBC radio programme reported in May 2003 that the document had been transformed 'to make it sexier' on the orders of the prime minister's office, with the 45-minute claim being inserted just before publication even though intelligence agencies were uncertain of its accuracy. The BBC report cited an unnamed source, whom it described as 'one of the senior officials in charge of drawing up the dossier'. The official in question was soon unmasked as Dr David Kelly, an MoD scientist and a WMD expert, who committed suicide two days after testifying before a Parliamentary investigating committee.

Following these events, and as it became clear that Iraq possessed no WMD, several inquiries were held to consider the conduct of the government and its engagement with the intelligence community in making the case for war. The first of these, an investigation by Lord (Brian) Hutton, a senior judge, into the cir-cumstances surrounding Kelly's death, touched only tangentially on intelligence issues. Hutton focused on the inclusion in the dossier of the 45-minute claim, but his report dismissed the allegation that the government had 'sexed up' the dossier in order to make the case for war more compelling. The chairman and director-general of the BBC resigned. This was followed by a House of Commons Foreign Affairs Committee report on 'The Decision to go to War in Iraq', and an investigation by the Intelligence and Security Committee on 'Iraqi Weapons of Mass Destruction – Intelligence and Assessments'. Neither report made any specific recommendation in relation to the future organisation or conduct of the UK's intelligence services. Initially the British government had been reluctant to countenance any investigation into the intelligence community, fearing that to do so would constitute a costly distraction from the conduct of current intelligence operations. But in February 2004, in response to growing political pressure, Blair appointed a committee of senior figures headed by Lord (Robin) Butler, a former top civil servant, with the following terms of reference:

> To investigate the intelligence coverage available in respect of WMD pro-
> grammes in countries of concern and on the global trade in WMD, taking into
> account what is now known about these programmes; as part of this work, to
> investigate the accuracy of intelligence on Iraqi WMD up to March 2003, and
> to examine any discrepancies between the intelligence gathered, evaluated and
> used by the government before the conflict, and between that intelligence and
> what has been discovered by the Iraq survey group since the end of the conflict;
> and to make representations to the Prime Minister for the future on the gather-
> ing, evaluation and use of intelligence on WMD, in the light of the difficulties of
> operating in countries of concern.

Butler's terms of reference were deliberately narrow in scope. In contrast to the United States, there was no sense that the UK's intelligence collection, assessment and dissemination machinery was fundamentally broken, nor was there any particular desire to make the intelligence community a scapegoat for political decisions in which intelligence had ultimately played an ancillary role. The Butler Report, published in July 2004 and entitled *Review of Intelligence on Weapons of Mass Destruction*, sought to set matters in context by pointing to four recent cases relating to WMD in which the intelligence picture had been shown to be correct. These were the exposure and dismantling of the A.Q. Khan network; the decision by Libya to renounce their WMD programmes; the Iranian nuclear programme; and North Korea's proliferation activity. Butler emphasised the difficulty of collecting intelligence in an area where secrets were so closely guarded, and the problems inherent in making sense of detailed technical information which could often appear ambiguous.

It was, however, clear that in respect of Iraq, things had gone wrong. The failure to locate WMD in Iraq made some of the pre-war intelligence seem discredited. Butler identified a number of areas for attention within the collection agencies (particularly SIS), within the assessment processes, and with the public presentation of the intelligence case. The review's recommendations, all of which were accepted without qualification, fell well short of a demand for radical reform.

In respect of SIS, the key issue was the validation of sources. Butler made the point that SIS intelligence coverage of Iraq had come from sources in the regime rather than émigrés or dissidents, thereby reducing the risk that the resultant reporting was deliberately biased or misleading. But of the five main sources on which SIS had relied, only one had had direct access to intelligence on WMD, with the others deriving their information from sub-sources. This was an entirely legitimate approach, but one which imposed a substantial obligation to test the bona fides of the sub-sources. Following the Iraq invasion, the intelligence from one source was 'withdrawn', meaning that the service no longer had confidence in the validity of the material. That from two others was placed in doubt. This pointed to a lack of rigour in applying validation standards which, when properly deployed, had served the intelligence community well.

Butler focused on changes in SIS procedures which might have contributed to this lack of rigour. Traditionally, SIS case officers (that is, those who ran agents and produced reports) had been under separate line management from the officers who issued the reports and who were responsible for quality control. But in the decade following the end of the Cold War, this system had been replaced by a culture of integrated teams in which case officers and reports officers sat together under the same line management. The change was partly a function of manpower constraints. But it was also dictated by a desire to engender a service culture in which officers took responsibility for 'end-to-end' intelligence production and to develop the nimbler operational response that was needed to deal with a new generation of transnational targets. The new arrangement did, however, carry the risk of a reduction in the status of the reports officers who, with some exceptions, tended to be junior and inexperienced – and hence less able to resist pressure to issue reporting of questionable authority.

To address this issue, SIS appointed a senior officer answerable to the director for operations and intelligence to assume line-management responsibility for all reports officers and to implement a programme of professionalisation and quality control. A policy decision was taken to develop a separate career stream for reports officers within SIS as part of a wider restructuring and to give it equal status with the operational stream, whose members had traditionally been seen as SIS aristocracy. These changes coincided with a move to open recruitment – already well established in the Security Service and GCHQ – to replace the traditional 'tap on the shoulder'. This was driven by a desire to grow faster and to enhance diversity among SIS recruits.

It is as yet too early to judge whether these changes have produced any significant improvements. However, they need to be seen in the context of Butler's recommendations regarding the UK's wider analytical community, in particular the JIC Assessments Staff and DIS. In respect of the former, the recommendation was that the security and intelligence co-ordinator review the size of the Assessments Staff and in particular consider whether they have available the volume and range of resources to ask the questions which need to be asked in fully assessing intelligence reports and in thinking radically ... This review should include considering whether there should be a specialism of analysis with a career structure and room for advancement, allowing the Assessments Staff to include some career members.

This recommendation went to the heart of the Iraqi WMD issue. The problem was not so much one of intelligence analysis as of the inability of the UK's analytical community to put themselves into the minds of those whose behaviour they were analysing. In his book *Know Your Enemy* examining the JIC's performance between the Second World War and 1968, former JIC Chairman Percy Cradock highlighted this as a persistent shortcoming in the committee's otherwise creditable performance. In the same vein, no effort was made by the JIC or policymakers to think radically about the pre-invasion failure of the UN inspectors to find militarily significant quantities of WMD. At no point did anyone consider the possibility that, to contradict former US Defense Secretary Donald Rumsfeld, absence of evidence might in fact indicate evidence of absence.

Following Butler's recommendation, some progress has been made towards establishing a UK analytical community. A head of profession has been appointed in the Cabinet Office to recommend on professional training, standards and career structure. However, the position commands no resources, has no line-management responsibilities and can only advise and seek to exercise influence. An additional move has been to organise courses in intelligence analysis at King's College, London, to provide consistent methodology and standards. In spite of these steps, there is so far little evidence within the Assessments Staff of a permanent cadre of analysts becoming established. For this to be a realistic prospect there needs to develop within the wider UK analytical community a culture of secondments and cross-posting, since no single part of this community is big enough to sustain a separate career structure for analysts. The disposition to do this appears to exist, but it is likely to require significant and sustained senior management focus to bring it about.

That Butler should make recommendations regarding the JIC itself was to be expected in view of the controversy surrounding the Iraq dossier. He highlighted the JIC's failure to consider the wider political and social content of Iraq's WMD programmes: intelligence on WMD had been a Category One requirement, whereas intelligence on Iraq's politics had been only Category Three. Understanding Iraqi politics better might have caused analysts to ask more searching questions about why Saddam behaved as he did, and to take into account his concerns about Iran and internal dissent. It might have resulted in a better appreciation of how brittle the regime was and provided a more sober appreciation of how hard it would be to replace. Most importantly, excessive focus on the technical aspects of WMD without understanding the political context of WMD programmes risked arriving at judgements disproportionately based on a worst-case interpretation of the science.

Butler also criticised the failure in some JIC assessments to highlight the limitations and uncertainties regarding some of the intelligence. This had led to 'more weight being placed on the intelligence than it could bear'. His recommendation that such language should be incorporated in JIC assessments has been put into effect. The recommendation that attracted the most public interest concerned the position of JIC chairman, and in particular its independence. The review said that 'we see a strong case for the post of Chairman of the JIC being held by someone with experience of dealing with ministers in a very senior role and who is demonstrably beyond influence and thus probably in his final post'. The current and former JIC chairmen, respectively Alex Allan and Richard Mottram, have both broadly met this criterion. However, it may prove difficult to sustain this approach over the long term: the events of 2002–03 militate against the post being held by a professional intelligence officer and it may be difficult to attract senior civil servants with policy backgrounds meeting Butler's description.

A related issue on which Butler touched was the need for better communications within the analytical community. This referred specifically to the community of experts on proliferation issues, and spoke of the need to create a 'virtual network' of experts within government 'who would know each other and consult easily'. In the medium term, a possible solution that addresses this specific issue as well as the wider issue of connectivity within the totality of the UK's analytical community is SCOPE, the UK government's high-classification IT system for disseminating intelligence. Now in the process of being introduced, SCOPE represents a step forward in terms of being a 'pull' rather than a 'push' delivery system – that is, the intelligence is posted on the network and those who are entitled to and need to see it can access it and mine it. It also offers interactive communication, and hence may be able to deliver the outcome envisaged by Butler. But SCOPE has, in common with many government IT projects, been the subject of substantial delays and it is unclear whether all the intended functionality in the system will be available. Sharing of intelligence, though inherently desirable, can never be total and will always be subject to some restrictions depending on the nature of the source. While collecting intelligence is of no value unless that intelligence can be used, there will always be trade-offs between the desire or need to take action and the need to preserve sources which may not easily be replaceable.

Regarding the DIS, Butler criticised the fact that its experts had not been allowed to see one key piece of SIS intelligence which had been inserted into the government's dossier. He asked whether 'steps were needed to integrate the work of the DIS more closely with the work of the intelligence community' and expressed support for ongoing efforts to ensure that the DIS served wider national priorities as well as defence priorities, and that it had the resources it needed to service these priorities. He also recommended that DIS staff, as well as the JIC Assessments Staff, should have access to the intelligence community's staff counsellor to provide them with a confidential mechanism for expressing ethical or other concerns. Following progress in these areas, there is satisfaction within the intelligence community about the levels of cooperation that now exist with the DIS. However, a recent MoD capabilities review appeared to have determined that DIS analysts were part of the administrative 'tail' rather than the operational 'teeth', as a result of which the chief of defence intelligence has been required to reduce their numbers by 20%. It is hard to reconcile this decision with the spirit of Butler's recommendations.

Impact of the counter-terrorism agenda

Looking beyond the Butler review, wider developments within the UK intelligence community have been driven by the counter-terrorism agenda and the related requirement for SIS and GCHQ to provide intelligence support for UK military expeditionary deployments. The first major innovation within the UK intelligence community was the creation in 2004 of the Joint Terrorism Assessment Centre (JTAC). The centre, located in the Security Service headquarters in London, was originally designed to act as a clearing house for the large quantities of terrorism-threat intelligence which would have overwhelmed the capabilities of any single agency, and which in any case needed to be considered in a wider context. It comprises representatives of some 16 departments, each of whom has access to the network of their parent department. In addition to managing threat intelligence, JTAC undertakes studies of specific aspects of transnational terrorist threats and analyses of longer-term trends, as well as engaging with the British and international academic communities. JTAC has undoubtedly been a success and has been much visited by delegations from other countries, some of which have established similar organisations. The degree of inter-agency collaboration and trust involved in establishing JTAC has been remarkable, and few countries have found this easy to emulate. But JTAC may find it challenging in the longer term to attract high-quality talent and to build up a longer-term corpus of expertise and tribal memory.

The counter-terrorism agenda has had a substantial impact on the Security Service. The dimension of the threat to the United Kingdom from the 'enemy within' became clear as a result of the 2005 London bombings. On 7 July 2005, three morning rush-hour underground trains and a bus were attacked by suicide bombers, resulting in 52 deaths. Two weeks later, an almost identical attack failed when the bombs failed to detonate. Subsequently, a large number of groups and individuals, many of Pakistani origin, have been arrested on suspicion of terrorist activities. As a result of an investigation code-named *Crevice*, five men were jailed in 2007 for conspiring to set off fertiliser bombs in the UK, and in the *Rhyme* investigation six men were convicted of conspiring to bomb targets in Britain and the United States. In 2008, eight men arrested in 2006 went on trial accused of conspiring to blow up transatlantic airliners with liquid explosives. Following these and other events, the government moved to double the size of the service, from 2000 to 4000, by 2011.

The extent of the focus on terrorism is underlined by the fact that the Security Service has stopped all non-terrorism activity with the exception of a residual effort on counter-espionage, counter-proliferation and Northern Ireland. While this is an understandable response to the particular nature of the threat in the UK, it must be seen as a high-risk approach as it devotes either few or no resources to a range of other security threats. How long this will prove sustainable remains to be seen.

In a further move, having previously relied on police Special Branches for coverage outside London, the Security Service has opened eight regional offices working with newly formed police regional counter-terrorism and intelligence units. SIS and GCHQ are represented in the regional offices, a degree of cooperation which appears to counter suggestions that the UK should establish a separate counter-terrorism service.

SIS, though also heavily focused on the counter-terrorism agenda, has meanwhile sought to maintain coverage of a wider array of issues and threats and to ensure a good geographical spread. It has, however, significantly reduced its involvement in work on serious organised crime, transferring much of this to a newly created Serious Organised Crime Agency, though retaining some involvement in counter-narcotics work. A major new element of SIS work, as for GCHQ, has been the development of intelligence support for UK forces deployed overseas, particularly in Afghanistan and Iraq. This activity, performed in conjunction with the UK military's own field HUMINT teams, has imposed strains on a service that remains smaller than at the height of the Cold War. But it has produced a new generation of campaign-hardened officers with strong language abilities, constituting a valuable resource base for the future. Meanwhile, the growth of the service is to be accelerated following the allotment of a higher budget in 2008. For the future, SIS faces a major challenge in sustaining levels of covert intelligence collection in a world of far greater openness and accessibility of personal data. Doing this may entail significant additional costs.

For its part, GCHQ has for some time been grappling with two issues. First, it has needed to move away from the secretive and compartmentalised culture of the Cold War towards a more open and customer-focused approach. Secondly, it faces challenges posed by the explosion of global connectivity and in particular the Internet. The first issue significantly influenced the design of GCHQ's new headquarters, in Cheltenham in the west of England. Popularly known as the 'doughnut', the building has open-plan offices and multiple public areas intended to facilitate communication and consultation. Though cultural change on this scale invariably takes time, the early signs are that the new approach has had some results, especially in terms of a readiness to engage more actively with outsiders. The second challenge is a long-term one: the proliferation of new communications systems will make it increasingly hard for GCHQ to offer assurance about the breadth of its coverage and will inevitably impose the need to set priorities.

Possible future steps

The British intelligence community has thus undergone a degree of change, though this falls well short of a radical transformation. Whether this is sufficient to meet the intelligence challenges of the twenty-first century has yet to be seen. In terms of collection capability, the UK is arguably not badly placed. Its collection agencies are now better resourced, and have developed a culture of increasing collaboration and interoperability. The government's previous inclination to reduce intelligence resources has given way to recognition of a world of uncertainty and multiple threats. This was in evidence in the publication in 2008 of a new National Security Strategy.

However, more could be done to professionalise some aspects of the UK's intelligence performance. First, a unified intelligence academy could be established to provide a basic training course for all new entrants to the intelligence community before they pursued their specialisations. This would also serve as a staff college for members of the intelligence community about to assume senior management positions. It could actively promote and facilitate interchange within the intelligence community, and act as custodian of best practice and standard-setting.

Secondly, the performance of the UK intelligence community could be enhanced by creation of an analytical community with a developed career structure and sense of identity, enabled and empowered to challenge conventional wisdom. As illustrated earlier, some components of such a community are in place, but it could be argued that insufficient drive, focus and resources have been devoted to bringing it into being. In this context, there is a case for re-examining the working of the JIC and considering whether its operation is adequate to cope with an environment in which multiple threats present themselves simultaneously.

Finally, further work could be done to educate the British public on what intelligence can and cannot be expected to achieve. In the very strident and political debate about the intelligence on Iraq, there was a tendency to present the available information in terms of absolutes, neglecting the delicate and qualified judgements that intelligence analysts are require to make and to present to their political masters. The government, by presenting intelligence data in a public document with the intent of supporting its political case, was partly responsible. But to prevent similar problems in the future, it seems clear that still greater openness will be required of intelligence agencies so that their work is better understood – and trusted – by politicians and the public alike. In this context, a current proposal to make the Intelligence and Security Committee, until now a cross-party panel drawn from both houses of parliament and reporting directly to the prime minister, into a full parliamentary select committee, could be a positive move. No government, and no intelligence agency, will want to allow the chaotic exposure in 2003 of intelligence practices, and of the interplay between agencies and government, to be replicated in the future.

Towards a Wider High North? Strategic Issues in a Changing Arctic

For more than 15 years after the end of the Cold War, interest in strategic developments in the Arctic steadily faded. In recent years, however, the region has gradually come back into focus. The issue of climate change now joins a complex mix of national interests affecting a number of countries: these include energy and mineral resources, fishing, new shipping lanes and technological developments. The region is still subject to territorial disputes, and governments must also take into account the voice of indigenous populations. Recent developments are altering the military-strategic picture and the results are difficult to predict.

For centuries the Arctic (here geographically defined as the region north of the Arctic Circle at 66°66'N) has been of strategic interest to the states around the Arctic Ocean basin, as well as other countries. National policies in the region were influenced by commercial interests and were supported by scientific and military resources. The remoteness, extreme climate and generally difficult conditions also shaped the strategic pattern and contributed to its unique circumstances. With the onset of the Cold War, the region's military-political standing took on new importance. Intercontinental ballistic missiles turned the Arctic into a focus for the two superpowers. Ballistic-missile submarines (SSBNs) hid under the Arctic ice cap to ensure the invulnerability of nuclear second-strike capability. Surveillance systems were developed and deployed by both sides, and over the decades these became very elaborate. Meanwhile, the United States, the Soviet Union and other countries continued with scientific exploration, fishing, whaling and mining, and later with oil and gas exploration.

The 'New Cold War' of the 1980s saw a renewed interest in what had become known as 'the High North'. Moscow had, since the 1960s, aimed to build up naval power. A coastal navy with an essentially defensive posture was no longer enough; a blue-water fleet as well as a nuclear second-strike capability was now the goal. Naval bases for Soviet strategic SSBNs and for the fulfilment of Soviet aspirations in the Atlantic were sited on the Kola Peninsula, where the only available year-round ice-free ports were to be found. In response, the United States and its allies developed strategies designed to thwart Soviet aspirations to enter the North Atlantic, to protect the sea routes between Europe and America and to counter the Soviet nuclear threat. The logic of the Cold War dictated that this part of the Arctic – the northernmost part of the Scandinavian peninsula and the sea to the north of it – became highly militarised, and tensions at times ran high.

With the end of the Cold War, strategic interest in the Arctic gradually waned. Surveillance systems largely remained operative and in place and nuclear submarine patrols continued, but at a much lower level. In some respects the Cold War never completely ended in this part of the world. Now, however, several factors influencing the Arctic are changing. This essay considers some of the issues.

Principal regional issues
Climate change and new shipping routes
Although prognoses of global warming involve a large degree of uncertainty, the best available scientific data, summarised by the Intergovernmental Panel on Climate Change (IPCC), the UN's climate body, is at its highest degree of certainty when describing climatological developments in the Arctic. Global warming is already having far-reaching effects; recent observations point to rapid shrinking of the polar ice sheet and melting of permafrost – soil which had been permanently below freezing point.

Both will affect the Arctic profoundly. The shrinking of the ice sheet will cause it to disappear completely in some areas that previously were permanently iced over. The effects on wildlife and fisheries aside, this will create new circumstances for exploitation of energy resources, as well as for shipping and naval operations. Much of the infrastructure of the Arctic region was constructed on the presumption that the ground would remain frozen year-round. Thawing of the permafrost would mean that it would need to be reinforced or even rebuilt. Housing, airports, roads, electricity grids, pipelines, mines and pumping stations for oil and natural gas would all be affected. The cost is hard to calculate, but would be substantial. In addition, the permafrost traps vast volumes of frozen methane, a greenhouse gas which, if released into the atmosphere, contributes to global warming.

If current trends continue, three new sea lanes of communication (SLOCs) will open. The Northeast Passage (running from the Barents Sea via the Kola

Peninsula along the north coast of Russia, into the Bering Sea and out into the Pacific), has until recently been inaccessible to shipping for most of the year. It seems likely that it will, within five to ten years, be open to traffic for most of the northern summer, and parts of it for longer periods. The Northwest Passage (from the west coast of Greenland and west through the Canadian northern archipelago and north of Alaska to the Bering Sea and the Pacific) will, if current climatological predictions prove correct, be open to shipping within 10–15 years. A North Polar Route, passing over the geographical North Pole, could be open for year-round traffic in 30–40 years. The main advantages of this route will be that it is shorter than the other two and will run across the open sea. Shipping could use these routes even sooner, given a thin summer ice sheet, using convoys led by ice-breakers. (See map on page II of Strategic Geography section).

The opening of one or more of these SLOCs would have regional and global effects. A Northeast Passage from Europe to Asia would be substantially shorter than the shortest routes currently available, halving, for example, the distance from Hamburg to Yokohama. It would avoid traditional chokepoints such as the Suez Canal, the Malacca Strait and the Panama Canal, and could be used to circumvent problems such as congestion, piracy and open conflict. New shipping lanes connecting Asia with Europe and America would have an impact on global trading patterns, and new transit and terminal ports would require large investments by governments and shipping companies.

Management of the new SLOCs will be an issue for states with territories in the Arctic as well as for other countries and business interests. In 1996 Canada, Denmark, Finland, Iceland, Norway, Russia, Sweden and the United States established the Arctic Council as a high-level forum to promote cooperation, coordination and interaction.

One further effect could be that the heightened role of Arctic territories would lead to aspirations for greater autonomy or independence among indigenous populations, since increased shipping activities would offer them the opportunity for a more stable economic base.

Energy potential

The Arctic is widely believed to hold vast undiscovered energy and mineral resources, although their precise extent is difficult to quantify – different models used to calculate energy resources provide different estimates and surveys of the region are incomplete or lacking. According to the US Geological Survey, up to 25% of the world's undiscovered oil and gas resources are to be found in the Arctic, including up to 110 billion barrels of oil to the east of Greenland. In the Norwegian exclusive economic zone, proven reserves are around 370 million barrels of oil and 800bn cubic metres of natural gas. About three-quarters of these are to the north of Norway in the Norwegian Sea rather than the Barents Sea, and their ownership is thus not in dispute. Some Russian researchers claim that commercially available resources in the Russian Arctic amount to 11bn barrels of oil and 15 trillion cubic metres of gas, while others estimate as little as 700m barrels of oil and 5tr cubic metres of gas. Whether these resources can be exploited on commercially viable terms depends on technology, climate and market prices. The Arctic is also believed to contain reserves of valuable minerals and raw materials such as coal, nickel, copper, tungsten, lead, zinc, gold, silver, diamonds, manganese, chrome and titanium.

With its long Arctic coastline, Russia has a great deal at stake; the region's resource potential has always been part of Moscow's strategic thinking. For example, initial appraisal work has already taken place in the vast *Shtokman* field in the Barents Sea which, if fully developed, would be the largest offshore gas field in the world – it is estimated to contain 3.8tr cubic metres of gas and 37m tonnes of gas condensate. Gazprom, the state-controlled gas company, has signed an agreement with Total of France and StatoilHydro of Norway on developing the field. However, while Russian energy companies declare the Arctic to be a priority, in practice they are encountering difficulties in exploiting known reserves, due partly to the government's nationalistic investment and ownership policy. Exploration of new fields is thus slow and Russia may currently lack the capacity to extract unexploited reserves. Moscow's policy priority for the time being may therefore be to ensure that no other country can take control of these resources.

Canada has the longest Arctic shoreline of any nation, and the potential for energy exploitation largely motivates its Arctic policy. Extraction is currently small scale, at only about 0.7bn cubic metres of gas per year, partly due to lack of proper infrastructure, and also because most of the potential resources are hidden under the ice. Canadian offshore oil extraction is at about 100m barrels a year.

The Arctic has not been a high priority for the United States and it will probably fall to the next administration to develop US policy further. American energy extraction in the Arctic is relatively modest: about 0.86m barrels per day (b/d) of oil in Alaska, for example.

For the United States and Canada, energy production is unlikely to lead to a significant increase in energy transport in the Arctic, even in the longer term. Most oil and gas is transported by pipeline, but an increase in transport of liquefied natural gas (LNG) from Canada is a possibility. For Russia, on the other hand, transport of energy through the Arctic will be important in the short term. Sea transport will be primary, since the road network in the region is poorly developed. Oil transport from the Barents Sea region is estimated to increase by 50% by 2020. The Northeast Passage offers Moscow an opportunity to exert influence; Russia could act unilaterally to regulate transport close to shore to further its own interests. With the opening of other ice-free SLOCs through the Arctic the influence provided by control of the Northeast Passage may wane over time.

Territorial disputes

Access to potential resources and shipping routes is complicated by several long-standing territorial disputes. Some have remained unsettled or unmitigated for strategic reasons – it has simply not been in the interests of the parties to settle their differences – while others have been impossible to resolve due to the extreme conditions (thick ice makes surveying islands and the seabed difficult or impossible). Some of the more important disputes include:

- In the Barents Sea, Norway and Russia are at odds over whether their border should be drawn from the land border due north towards the North Pole (the Russian position) or be drawn as an extension of the land border (the Norwegian position). Agreement was recently reached over a small part of the area close to land.
- The United States and Canada dispute whether the Canadian northern archipelago is to be treated as Canadian territorial waters or as part of its exclusive economic zone. The right to innocent passage of ships without prior notice is at the core of Washington's claim. The incomplete mapping of the seabed makes a definite resolution difficult and the United States has not signed the 1982 United Nations Convention on the Law of the Sea (UNCLOS), which complicates the matter further. During the Cold War both parties were content to let the dispute remain unresolved, with US warships operating freely near or even in Canadian waters. Now, however, as part of a more robust Arctic policy, Canada wishes to reach a settlement.
- There are differences of interpretation over the multilateral 1920 Svalbard Treaty, under which Norway has limited sovereignty over the Svalbard archipelago, north of the Arctic Circle. Economic activity is allowed there by all states party to the treaty, and the islands – of which the largest is Spitsbergen – are permanently de-militarised and neutral. However, the development of international law has led to differing interpretations of the treaty. Norway claims that it applies only to the land territory and four nautical miles out to sea, and that the maritime area between four and 200nm is part of Norway's exclusive economic zone. Norway has received no open support for its claim. The issue is complicated and has a long history, and large interests are at stake, given the potential oil and gas resources.

Arctic governments are already taking action so as not to lose influence and control over natural resources, and to avoid being usurped by other states. For example, in summer 2007, a Russian expedition in mini-submarines placed a titanium flag on the seabed at the North Pole to strengthen Moscow's claim to the Arctic waters – and specifically that the undersea Lomonosov ridge was a continuation of the continental shelf north of Siberia. Immediately afterwards, Denmark sent an expedition north of Greenland with a leased Swedish ice-breaker to conduct oceanographic surveys (ironically, a Russian nuclear-powered icebreaker was also leased to support the expedition). The purpose of the expedition was to seek evidence to support Denmark's claims to the Lomonosov ridge. The Norwegian and German foreign ministers then met on Spitsbergen and announced joint plans to exploit energy reserves and to study the effects of global warming on the North Pole.

The scramble by Arctic nations to explore and map the seabed is in support of their respective sovereignty claims to the UN's Commission on the Limits of the Continental Shelf. The delineation of the continental shelf needs to be mapped in order to support claims under the provisions of UNCLOS. Every coastal state has the right to a 200 nautical miles exclusive economic zone (EEZ) from its baseline. Beyond that limit, the coastal state has to support its claim based on geological criteria and present data to the commission for review. However, the territorial disputes are unlikely to be resolved quickly. While they continue, they could contribute to increased military tension, but it is unlikely that they will lead to open conflict. As long as UNCLOS remains as a reasonably effective framework, the process will in all likelihood remain mostly orderly.

Arctic states and their policies

The Arctic states – those with territories in the Arctic or with claims to it – are all in the process of adopting or updating their Arctic policies in light of the new possibilities created by global warming. The process is dynamic and interactive; smaller states on the whole have to take into account the actions and policies of the larger ones, and shape their policies accordingly.

Norway

Norway's interests in the Arctic include substantial energy resources. Its priorities, expressed in official documents, are to develop neighbourly relations with Russia; to take full responsibility for combating illegal fishing and to provide good stewardship of fisheries resources; to extract the energy resources of the Barents Sea; to improve living conditions for all inhabitants of the north; and to take all actions in the Arctic in light of environmental and climate-related factors. Norway's focus is mainly limited to the region nearest to it; the Arctic as a whole is not discussed other than to state that climate change, energy resources under the seabed and new SLOCs will mean challenges to Norwegian interests. Oslo recognises that this might entail friction with other states in the region.

A northwards shift in the focus of Norwegian security policy is under way. After the Cold War, international crisis-management and peace-support operations had become the main focus for the armed forces, but this is now being balanced by renewed efforts in the northern region, where Norway sees a requirement for crisis-management capabilities, including surveillance assets, training, cooperation and decision-making functions. Several of these requirements have already been addressed, and the most recent defence budget included a slight increase in defence funding and provision for relocation of some bases to the northern region. The chief of the Norwegian Defence Staff, General Sverre Diesen, has said that if Norway wants to exert any influence in NATO operations in the north, it has to be able to provide relevant components for such operations, even though the risk of conflict is deemed low. In all likelihood Norwegian defence posture in the north will be augmented and NATO exercises are likely to increase in coming years.

Relations with Russia are an important concern. The increased importance Russia is placing on its base complex on the Kola Peninsula is expected to lead to a larger military presence in the region, which in turn is likely to generate more interest from NATO countries, particularly the United States. Among other maritime security concerns is the need to protect and enforce Norway's rights in its waters, including those affected by the dispute over the Svalbard Treaty. Meanwhile, the growth of maritime transport already seen in this part of the Arctic, which is expected to continue, increases the burden of protection, for instance against sabotage.

Denmark

Denmark is responsible for defence and security of the vast territory of Greenland, even though Greenland's 57,000 inhabitants (84% native Greenlanders) have had home rule (*Grønlands Hjemmestyre*) since 1979. Although Denmark's defence stance has changed considerably since the Cold War, switching away from national defence and towards capabilities for international operations such as those in Iraq and Afghanistan, the security of Greenland will continue to demand resources for the protection of its sovereignty. Security is maintained through a permanent presence of patrol and oceanographic ships. A few bases are permanently manned, and some air-patrol and air-transport assets are also deployed. The long-range dog-sledge *Sirius* patrol keeps a regular watch on the frozen territory. In addition, under a 1951 treaty between Denmark and the United States, Washington has rights to use the territory of Greenland in defence of the American continent. The base at Thule (Pituffik) is important as part of the US missile-early-warning system and for communication with satellites in polar orbit, and is being upgraded to play a part in the new US missile-defence system.

The possibility of large undiscovered oil, gas and mineral resources has led Denmark to conduct extensive oceanographic surveys to establish the extent of the continental shelf north of Greenland. As other Arctic states are also in the process of making similar and potentially overlapping claims, there was some haste to its 2007 expedition to map the Lomonosov ridge. There are also several territorial disputes in Greenland's neighbourhood: with Canada over Hans Island, which lies in the strait between Greenland and Canada's Ellesmere Island; with Norway over the newly discovered Tobias Island/Tuppiap Qeqertaa (only discovered, under the permanent sea ice, in 1993); and in all likelihood over not yet formulated claims on parts of the Arctic Ocean by Russia and Canada.

Greenland's status as a part of Denmark is the subject of domestic debate. While public opinion in Greenland supports a long-term goal of full independence, it had been thought that the economic and physical resources of the island would not be sufficient. However, the prospect of income from energy, minerals and shipping has rekindled the independence debate. All Danish parties represented in parliament agree that if Denmark is no longer welcome on Greenland, it will leave, but in that case, Denmark would no longer wish to pay for Greenland's defence and security. Those who favour independence claim that new financial resources derived from future incomes from shipping, oil and gas would enable Greenland to pay for the security of its territory by agreement with some outside power. This is in fact the situation today, but it is paid for by the government in Copenhagen. A change in Greenland's status, usually discussed in terms of a ten- to 20-year time scale, might therefore happen considerably faster. Whether a fully independent Greenland would seek a closer relationship with the United States, lean toward Canada or wish to maintain a link to Denmark, other Nordic nations or the EU remains an open question.

Iceland

Iceland has had to reconsider its security and defence policy, especially in light of the withdrawal of US forces from the naval air station at Keflavik in 2006. Although the US decision offended Iceland, the US–Icelandic Defence Treaty of 1951 nevertheless remained in force. A short time after the American withdrawal from Keflavik, Russian long-range strategic bomber patrols resumed in the region, followed by naval activity. With Iceland's membership of NATO seen as a cornerstone of its security, NATO has offered limited airspace surveillance until 2011, to which France, the United States, Spain, Denmark and Norway will contribute. Iceland's security predicament also led to formal security dialogues with the United Kingdom, Canada and Germany. A memorandum of understanding was also signed with Norway in May 2007. Iceland has not responded to a Russian offer of security talks.

Parallels with the Cold War should not be exaggerated. There have been no Russian incursions into Icelandic airspace or territorial waters. Reykjavik's concerns are more about maritime security, energy and natural resources. However, the strategic importance of Iceland will be re-emphasised by the growth in shipping of cargo, oil and gas transport in and around Icelandic waters. Whatever lies behind the change in Russian operational patterns, it is causing uncertainty and highlighting the possibility of military posturing amidst the scramble for Arctic energy resources. Iceland will be torn between the benefits that oil and gas transport and new shipping lanes could bring and the risk of negative effects on its security. Risk management will therefore be an important element of domestic debate on security issues.

Canada

Canada's assertion of sovereignty over territories in the Arctic has been an important new element of its national security policy. In announcing a Canada First defence strategy in May 2008, Prime Minister Stephen Harper said that in former years 'we did almost nothing to assert our sovereignty in our North, in our Arctic'. Unveiling plans for a significant renewal of Canadian defence equipment, he said the strategy would 'improve surveillance of our land and coastal borders'. The government's major annual policy statement, the 'Speech from the Throne', had asserted in October 2007 that 'the Arctic is an essential part of Canada's history ... but the North needs new attention. New opportunities are emerging across the Arctic, and new challenges from other shores. Our government will bring forward an integrated northern strategy focused on strengthening Canada's sovereignty, protecting our environmental heritage, promoting economic and social development, and improving and devolving governance, so that northerners have greater control over their destinies.' The speech announced plans to build an Arctic research station, focusing on environmental science and resource development. It also said that 'as part of asserting sovereignty in the Arctic, our government will complete comprehensive mapping of Canada's Arctic seabed'. In addition, Canada's Far North and the Northwest Passage would be guarded by new Arctic patrol ships and expanded aerial surveillance. Harper also announced plans to expand the size and capabilities of the Canadian Rangers, a local volunteer paramilitary group recruited from the indigenous Inuit population. An Arctic training centre would be established for the Canadian armed forces, providing specialised training in cold-weather military operations, search-and-research techniques and 'sovereignty enforcement'. In addition, a new naval station with a deep-water docking and refuelling facility is to be built at Nanisivik, strategically located on the Northwest Passage, and is intended to provide a home for the new offshore patrol ships.

In fact, Canada had been moving to assert its rights in the Arctic region for some years. In 2005 then Minister of Defence Bill Graham flew by helicopter to Hans Island. Canadian military personnel had landed on the football-field-sized island the previous week and planted the Canadian flag. Sovereignty over the island had been disputed since the international maritime border was drawn in 1973, and there had been several visits, and flag-plantings, since then, most recently by Danish sailors in 2003. Graham's visit, however, stirred up the dispute, and led to new negotiations between Denmark and Canada. It also caused domestic political problems when Canadian maps were updated in 2007, based on new satellite imagery, to show the island falling athwart the agreed international maritime boundary, rather than to the western, Canadian side. During the Cold War it had suited both Ottawa and Washington to leave the issue of transit rights in the Northwest Passage unresolved, but in recent years Canada has sought to give the passage the status of Canadian territorial waters, while the United States wants the passage to have the status of an international strait, which grants the right to innocent passage for ships and submarines.

Russia

The Soviet Union claimed territory between the border with Norway and the Bering Strait all the way to the North Pole, with the exception of Spitsbergen, where it was party to the 1920 Svalbard Treaty. A number of Arctic expeditions were undertaken in the 1930s to support these claims. The claims were never accepted by the other Arctic states, and they were finally dropped when Russia ratified UNCLOS in 1997. In 2001, Russia claimed the undersea Lomonosov and Mendeleev ridges all the way to the North Pole as part of the Siberian continental shelf, in accordance with the provisions of the treaty. The claim was rejected as insufficiently founded and Russia intensified its surveying efforts. In 2003 Russia re-established a polar research station, and the head of the Federal Security Service (FSB) flew to the North Pole the following year to plant a Russian flag on the ice. This was followed in 2007 by the expedition with ice-breakers along the Lomonosov ridge and the planting of the flag on the seabed using mini-submarines, accompanied by statements that Russia could now include the ridge in its exclusive economic zone. Some Russian politicians did acknowledge that this would have to be discussed with other nations and within the UN system. Russia's claims were rejected by the other Arctic states. Long experience of exploration in the Arctic means that Russia has a more developed infrastructure than the United States or Canada and a larger population in the region than the other Arctic states. For these reasons, Russia claims to have a better right to the region. Russia accepts the Svalbard Treaty and is the only one to operate, under the terms of the treaty, a coal-mine – albeit a loss-making one – on Spitsbergen.

Russian Arctic policy over the past decade has been driven by the prospect of resource-driven economic growth, and by the state's centralisation of economic power. Military and civilian interests have become more closely coordinated, and there has been an increase in military funding. Russia's *Maritime Strategy for 2001–20* emphasises the importance of free access for Russian naval forces to the Atlantic, the Northern Fleet's important role in the defence of Russia, and the significance of the Northeast Passage for economic development. It also mentions exploration, extraction of natural resources, defence of Russian interests in the Arctic and limiting the presence of foreign navies. The Russian navy recognises that the growing national income from export of oil and gas can lead to higher budgets, while the oil industry, in turn, is taking military interests into account by limiting its operations in the Murmansk area. New oil-transit terminals have instead been built further east in the White Sea.

Russia increasingly emphasises the threat from NATO in the Arctic and the role of the military in defence of Russian interests there. Russian military officers speak of infiltration from Norway and other NATO members through military exercises, and of a militarisation of the Arctic designed to put pressure on Russia. They claim NATO is striving for control of global SLOCs. Proposals for nature reserves and limitations on economic activities in the Arctic by environmental groups are seen as attempts to weaken Russia. Another concern is that the Western powers could try to establish an 'operational control line', beyond which Russian naval forces would be unable to operate, with naval and air forces between the North Cape and Spitsbergen to contain Russian shipping.

To counter these perceived threats Russian rhetoric emphasises the need to use military means. Sea lanes and oil platforms must be protected and the projected increase in shipping and other economic activity will demand more naval resources. The base complex on the Kola Peninsula – Russia's only year-round ice-free ports in the Arctic at present – is seen as critical for its submarine-based nuclear deterrent. Some Russian military analysts see the Arctic as compensation for the losses suffered with the collapse of the Soviet Union; it could make possible stable development as a great power and provide Russia with a comparative advantage. The FSB has formed a new Arctic directorate and established border-control stations along the Northeast Passage. Test-firing of strategic missiles has been intensified and naval-aviation exercises have resumed from Russia's only aircraft carrier, the *Admiral Kuznetzov*. When patrols with strategic bombers were resumed in 2007, Arctic bases in Tiksi, Vorkuta and Anadyr were reactivated. The same year an ambitious military procurement programme stretching to 2015 was promulgated; one of its objectives is to make the Russian navy the second most powerful in the world by 2027. Two new carrier groups will be built, one for the Far East and one for the Arctic, beginning construction in 2015.

United States

Policy statements on Arctic issues by high US officials are few and often general in character; the United States uses the Arctic Council as the main multilateral forum for discussion of Arctic issues. However, America's hitherto low profile in the Arctic is likely to change. In May 2007 President Bush asked the US Senate to ratify UNCLOS, arguing that it would strengthen America's ability to pursue its interests, not only in the Arctic but worldwide. The Foreign Affairs Committee sent the matter to the floor of the Senate at the end of October. All US governmental agencies, and a majority in the Senate, favour ratification, but a number of conservative Republican senators are opposed. Treaties require a two-thirds majority for ratification. Should UNCLOS be ratified the United States would be able to claim exclusive economic zones and it would be easier to come to agreement with Canada over rights to passage through Canadian waters.

The Arctic will likely increase in importance for the United States as an arena for military operations and exercises. The US Navy and Coast Guard will want to increase their knowledge and experience of Arctic conditions. Currently, the Coast Guard operates three ice-breakers, launched in the late 1970s, and this fleet needs replacement or refurbishment. There may be a need for more ice-breakers, given projected increases in shipping around Greenland and north of Alaska. The region is also becoming more important for gathering intelligence on Russian operational capabilities, with fixed sensors, active and passive sonar and radar installations, submarines, reconnaissance aircraft and ships all playing their part. As far as is known, the fixed underwater sensors placed during the Cold War to help protect vital transatlantic SLOCs against submarine attack were never completely abandoned. The region also remains important for defence of the territorial integrity of America and its allies, but the United States no longer has a permanent combat-aircraft presence in Iceland and there is significantly less prepositioning of equipment in Norway than in the past.

Some of the earlier dynamic and logic of the Cold War may return, but would involve parties beyond just the United States and Russia. In coming years US missile defence will become operational and will further increase the importance of the Arctic in times of crisis as a defensive zone against intercontinental missiles. No new sites for permanent ground-based interceptors seem likely in the short term, but increased deployment of *Aegis*-equipped ships in the Bering Sea, the Norwegian Sea or the North Atlantic is a possibility. Since the different components of missile defence need to be developed, tested and exercised, an increased naval presence in the Arctic seems likely, but would not mean many new land-based installations or ground forces.

Military-strategic consequences

In the next two decades access to energy and other raw materials, transport and distribution routes and the strategic nuclear balance will continue to guide policies and actions of states with interests in the Arctic. Larger countries will set the framework within which smaller Arctic states will form their security policies. For the latter, international treaties and conventions will be central pillars.

The prognosis for continued melting and retreat of the ice, coupled with continued high energy prices, may contribute to increased interest in a military presence to signal long-term intent and to monitor the activities of others. This does not exclude the risk of small-scale crises and incidents, which in turn could affect political climate negatively and complicate cooperation on resource extraction and fisheries. Patrols could be undertaken by coast-guard rather than naval units, since coast-guard units are often seen as less contentious. More military units with capabilities for Arctic service are likely to be established, especially in states which have few at present, such as the United States.

The Arctic will remain important, and perhaps even increase in importance, on the nuclear-strategic level, due to technological advances in early-warning systems and missile defence and the increasing role of Russia's Northern Fleet for Moscow's nuclear forces. SSBNs based on the Kola Peninsula constitute Russia's nuclear second-strike capability. After the Cold War, Russian SSBN patrols in the North Atlantic and Arctic Ocean dwindled considerably, to the occasional patrol or even to zero. Russia has given modernisation of nuclear systems high priority. The Arctic similarly remains important as a patrol area for US, British and French SSBNs and SSNs as well as for submarine-based reconnaissance. The Western powers kept such patrols going after the Cold War, but at a lower level. Even if gradual reduction of the Arctic sea ice reduces the opportunities for covert SSBN patrols below the ice, the Arctic's importance for the strategic nuclear balance will remain. Apart from its role as a launch zone for submarine-launched ICBMs, the Arctic would also be an important approach route for US strategic bombers and land-based ICBMs with potential targets in Asia, as it would also be for Russian or Chinese land-based strategic missiles aimed at North America. If new or emerging nuclear states in Asia were able to develop long-range missiles to target the United States, the missile trajectories would also cross the Arctic.

Russia expressly sees the Arctic as an area for expansion and economic exploration. The United States has, so far, paid little attention to the Arctic apart from its military-strategic role. However, it is unlikely that Washington would be willing to allow Russia to acquire a dominant role in the region.

Conclusion

It seems likely that the Arctic – as a result of improved access and technological development – will be characterised by both increased economic and military activity. Projections of climate change, as much as the change itself, will act as a driver for developments in national policy. The risk of 'missing the bus' will galvanise governments into action and others will follow.

However, analysis and prediction of how the Arctic will develop is complicated. There are a number of outstanding questions, the answers to which will determine how the Arctic will look in ten to 20 years. Will it be an arena for geopolitical power games? To what extent will military means be used in support of perceived interests? To what extent will the major Arctic states dominate the region's agenda? How will the smaller Arctic states develop their policies and assert their sovereignty? What will be the role of external actors with perceived interests in the Arctic?

One way to approach these questions is to look at two scenarios from either end of the spectrum of potential developments. In the best-case scenario – 'Arctic Bliss' – cooperative trends prevail and conventions and treaties are developed to regulate the Arctic. The territorial issues are managed within the UN framework, and more and more states accept UNCLOS as the main framework for arbitration. Shipping is regulated: Arctic standards are established, reducing the risk and impact of marine accidents and environmental disasters. SLOCs are carefully surveyed and managed responsibly, and infrastructure is developed. Realisation among most Arctic states that energy and mineral resources have to be extracted responsibly to the benefit of all contributes to openness for investment, further reducing the risk of friction and conflict. The military-strategic situation involves a low-key nuclear presence, but few new conventional military capabilities are developed for the Arctic. International debate over an Arctic Treaty along the lines of the 1961 Antarctic Treaty leads to a comprehensive agreement.

At the other end of the spectrum looms an 'Arctic Great Game' scenario. Here, territorial disputes remain mostly unresolved and continue to handicap development. Narrowly defined national interests take precedence. Extensive energy exploration and fishing, as well as unsafe shipping, generate friction. There are frequent incidents and occasional crises. The sensitive natural environment suffers extensive damage. More and more military resources are required to protect national interests, and further friction is generated. The nuclear dimension, which involves substantial screening forces, also contributes to a larger military presence.

It seems reasonable to expect that the outcome will fall somewhere between these extremes. The strategic debate on the Arctic during the latter part of the Cold War was almost exclusively focused on the military-strategic situation in the Barents Sea and Northern Scandinavia, termed by then Norwegian Minister of Defence Johan Jörgen Holst 'the High North'. Today the phrase 'Wider High North' would encompass all the factors that have until recently remained frozen or dormant. It could offer a useful context in which the whole range of problems could be discussed. With some problems being solved or mitigated, others remaining unresolved and generating difficulties, the outlook is that, even if the melting of the ice is not manageable, the new strategic situation of the Arctic will be.

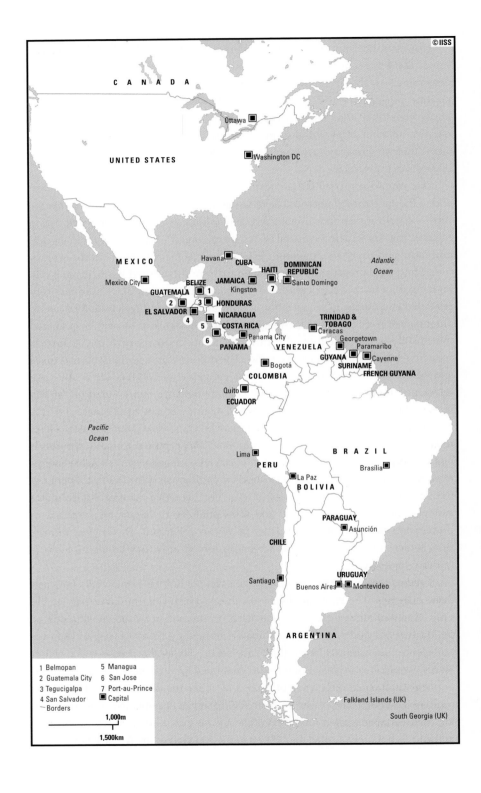

© IISS

C A N A D A

Ottawa

UNITED STATES

Washington DC

MEXICO

Havana   CUBA
Mexico City   HAITI   DOMINICAN
                    BELIZE   JAMAICA   REPUBLIC
              GUATEMALA   1   Santo Domingo
          2   3   Kingston   7
  EL SALVADOR   HONDURAS
          4
          5   NICARAGUA
              COSTA RICA   TRINIDAD &
          6   TOBAGO
          PANAMA   Panama City   Caracas
                    VENEZUELA   Georgetown
                                          Paramaribo
                         GUYANA   Cayenne
                    Bogotá   SURINAME
                    COLOMBIA   FRENCH GUYANA

          Quito
              ECUADOR

Atlantic
Ocean

Pacific
Ocean

                              B R A Z I L
          Lima   Brasília
          PERU
              La Paz
          B O L I V I A

                    PARAGUAY
                         Asunción

          CHILE

                    URUGUAY
          Santiago   Buenos Aires   Montevideo

A R G E N T I N A

Falkland Islands (UK)

South Georgia (UK)

1 Belmopan   5 Managua
2 Guatemala City 6 San Jose
3 Tegucigalpa   7 Port-au-Prince
4 San Salvador   ■ Capital
~ Borders

1,000m

1,500km

3 **The Americas**

The United States: An Extraordinary Election Campaign

On the second of May 2008 Mildred Loving, a 68-year-old black woman, died of pneumonia in Central Point, Virginia. In the same town 50 years earlier, she had been asleep in bed with her new husband, a white man, when sheriff's deputies broke into their house and arrested them both. The Lovings had been legally married in adjacent Washington DC, but this did not spare them several nights in jail and a plea-bargained felony conviction for violating the state's Racial Integrity Act that resulted in suspended one-year jail sentences and a 25-year banishment from the state of Virginia. The sentencing judge, Leon Bazile, explained that the Virginia law, enacted in 1662, was in service of God's purpose when He placed the races on separate continents to prevent their mixing. The Lovings paid court fees and left the state to set up house in Washington. But they grew homesick for family, friends and the easy rolling hills of rural Virginia, and in 1963, with the civil-rights movement gaining momentum, Mildred Loving wrote a letter about her plight to US Attorney General Robert F. Kennedy. Kennedy replied that she should contact the American Civil Liberties Union. ACLU lawyers took the Lovings's case through Virginia's courts and up to the US Supreme Court, which, in 1967, reversed their conviction and effectively overturned the United States' remaining anti-miscegenation laws.

The *Washington Post* and *New York Times* published obituaries for Mildred Loving a few days after her death, on Tuesday 6 May. Neither paper remarked on the overlapping significance of that Tuesday: to do so might not have been appropriate to an obituary, but in any event, as the papers went to press, no one knew that the day would end with the decisive victory of Senator Barack Obama in his long and drawn-out contest for the Democratic Party's nomination as candidate for president of the United States. His big win over Senator Hillary Clinton in that day's North Carolina primary, and her meagre win in Indiana, extinguished any residual chance that Clinton might overcome Obama's lead in delegates to the Democratic nominating convention.

Barack Obama is the fruit of 'miscegenation' – between a black Kenyan father and a white Kansan mother. He was born in 1961 in Hawaii, a newly admitted American state which, by nature of its location and heterogeneous population, was relatively tolerant on racial matters, and did not, in any event, have a law that stigmatised his very existence. But growing up a black boy in America in the 1960s meant becoming politically conscious in an era of civil-rights struggle: the struggle was glorious and inspiring and, in many respects, triumphant, but it could not in a decade erase the humiliations and oppression inflicted daily on the descendants of slaves. For most of that decade the Lovings were still banned as a couple from crossing south over any of the Potomac River bridges that a President Obama could reach in a 20-minute walk from the White House. If, in the last year of the 1960s, eight-year-old Barack himself had been driven through Virginia or any southern state in a car with his white mother, he almost certainly would have encountered hostility and abuse. Obama grew into adolescence and manhood during the 1970s, a decade in which the desolation of riot-torn cities, the growing drug scourge, fears of urban crime and the unsettled nature of race relations – all in the context of economic and foreign-policy crisis – helped to feed a conservative political backlash among whites. Meanwhile, Obama was moving into the social circles of black college students who felt the anger, the disappointed expectations and the confusion of an African-American middle class that was trying to find its place in the racially polarised, crisis-torn and palpably violent America.

Obama's election in 1990 as the *Harvard Law Review*'s first black president led to a contract for his first book, *Dreams From My Father*, in which he set down his struggles with selfhood and racial identity in these years. He seems to have worked hard to embrace his black identity for the purpose of transcending it. In his electrifying speech to the 2004 Democratic convention in Boston, which nominated John Kerry for president, Obama spoke eloquently of the falsity of imagining that America was so utterly divided between conservatives and liberals, whites and blacks, or the religious and the secular. Since then, he has continued to articulate a distinctive and upbeat brand of American national-ism. It has been reported that he thinks of himself as a liberal version of Ronald Reagan, insofar as Reagan reached beyond traditional conservatives to assemble a game-changing coalition that famously included so-called 'Reagan Democrats'. Obama's supporters claim that he can similarly defy the categories of recent American polarisation.

The post-racial image that is part of this political strategy is necessary politically and valuable in its own right. But it should not be allowed to obscure the magnitude of what happened in American politics in 2008. That one of the two major political parties nominated a black man to be president testifies to the impressive journey that America has navigated in the 47 years since he was born. The nomination and very plausible election of Obama to the presidency does not mean that America has eradicated racial injustice or antagonism. It does mean, however, that the United States has undergone a deep and historically rapid transformation.

Amazing campaign

Obama was not the only phenomenon of this American election year. Had he lost, Hillary Clinton would have been the first woman to win the Democratic nomination for president. Moreover, in terms of sheer improbability, the resurrection of Republican Senator John McCain after political near-death was almost as remarkable. McCain had to draw the political equivalent of an inside straight against odds set by a record and a philosophy significantly out of step with the conservative base of his party. He voted against President George W. Bush's tax cuts: the reason he gives now is Reaganite, that there were no corresponding spending cuts; but the reason he gave at the time was liberal populist, that it offended his conscience to give big tax breaks to the very wealthy. His campaign-finance reforms were particularly hated because they threatened the fundraising prowess of conservative and anti-abortion groups. He stood against the anti-immigrant fever that swept the Republican Right in the years 2006–08. He stood with Democrats to oppose any equivocation on the definition and prohibition of torture. And he has co-sponsored legislation for a 'cap-and-trade system' to impose significant limits on American carbon emissions.

During the primary campaign McCain tacked well to the right on most of these matters. Even so, as far as Democrats are concerned, McCain was probably the most formidable candidate that Republicans could have chosen. He staked a claim to more moderate, 'national-greatness' conservatism, with strains of Teddy Roosevelt progressivism. He had a small chance, therefore, with help from unaccustomed good news in Iraq, to restate and rehabilitate some elements of the Bush administration's otherwise discredited foreign policies.

The political climate was forbidding for any Republican, however. The party was led, at least nominally, by a uniquely unpopular second-term president. Not counting the impeached Richard Nixon, there have been three other two-term presidents in the post-Second World War era – Dwight D. Eisenhower, Reagan and Bill Clinton. Only Reagan was followed by a president from his own party. Yet, in stark contrast to Bush, each had public approval ratings well over 50% as the voters chose their replacements. Having lost their majority in both the

Senate and House of Representative in 2006 mid-term elections, the Republicans now confronted an array of candidates for their nomination who, each in his different way, posed a challenge to the reigning conservative consensus. Early front-runner Rudolph Giuliani, the former mayor of New York City, was a social liberal on such matters as civil rights for homosexuals and abortion; he planned to compensate among the religious and rural Right with his promise to keep America on the offensive in the 'war on terror'. Former Massachusetts Governor Mitt Romney also had a moderate-to-liberal record when he presided over that liberal state; in the campaign he risked the label of 'flip-flopper' for veering sharply to the right, but his bigger vulnerability may have been that he was a devout Mormon in a party whose evangelical base considers Mormonism to be a non-Christian cult. Former Kentucky Senator Fred Thompson, a character actor in Hollywood and a star of the popular TV legal drama 'Law and Order', was once considered the conservatives' saviour, but after his late entry into the race he ran a lacklustre campaign and faded quickly from serious contention. The one second-tier candidate who proved able to break away from the pack was former Arkansas Governor Mike Huckabee. He was an ordained minister, an evangelical Christian who set himself apart from much of the Christian Right by insisting he was a 'conservative ... just not angry about it'. His engaging sense of humour and comfort with cultural cross-currents – he played, for example, in a rock band – were among the assets that propelled him to victory in the first contest, the Iowa caucus on 3 January, where he beat Romney, the early favourite. But Huckabee, too, was out of step with much of Republican orthodoxy, emphasising issues of socio-economic equity above the shibboleth of tax cuts.

The absence of a conventionally conservative candidate, together with the pessimism and anger engendered by the immigration issue and the performance of the Bush presidency, gave a highly uncertain configuration to the Republican race. Well into autumn 2007, Republican leaders feared a long fight for the party nomination, with no candidate winning decisively and several competitors remaining contenders, perhaps as far as the nominating convention in September 2008. This fear was compounded by expectations that Democratic front-runner Hillary Clinton would wrap up her contest early, and focus fire on the Republicans while they bled in a protracted civil war.

What happened was precisely the opposite. Giuliani's early front-runner status was the consequence of his high name recognition and prestige associated with his leadership of New York City in the immediate aftermath of 11 September 2001. Once conservative voters learned of his positions on such issues as abortion rights – not to mention his own volatile marital history – he started to sink in the polls. Huckabee won Iowa, creating something of a sensation by defeating the financially well-endowed Romney who had spent many months canvassing the state. But it was McCain who, having fallen into financial straits and campaign disarray, hung on stubbornly and by late 2007 started rising again in the polls. McCain established his surprising comeback with victory in New Hampshire's primary a few days after Iowa, triumphing again in the state where he had almost knocked George W. Bush out of the race eight years earlier. He went on a week later to win North Carolina, the state where he'd met his demise in 2000 in a bitterly fought contest against Bush. McCain had therefore fulfilled what had become almost an iron law of Republican politics – that the eventual nominee must win two of the first three contests in Iowa, New Hampshire and North Carolina. Giuliani was effectively knocked out of the race by a poor showing in Florida, where he had staked the success of his entire campaign; Romney won Michigan, Nevada, Wyoming, Maine, Massachusetts, Montana, Utah, Minnesota, Colorado, North Dakota and Alaska, but never managed to convince the bulk of evangelical conservatives, on whom he'd been banking, why they should choose him over Huckabee. McCain effectively clinched the nomination by winning nine of 21 contests on so-called 'Super Tuesday' on 5 February – which constituted, in effect, a national primary. Nine days later Romney dropped out and endorsed McCain. Huckabee, drawing the continued support of disaffected conservatives, surprisingly bested the presumed nominee in 2 more states, but he dropped out on 4 March when it became clear that McCain would beat him in Texas.

It was, instead, the Democratic nominating contest that ended up seeming endless. A strong field of candidates included former New Mexico Governor and UN Ambassador Bill Richardson, Delaware Senator Joseph Biden and Connecticut Senator Christopher Dodd. The three clear front-runners, however, were Clinton, Obama and John Edwards, a former North Carolina senator who had run for the nomination four years earlier and ended up as Senator John Kerry's vice-presidential running mate in the general election campaign. Edwards, an accomplished former trial lawyer, was a passionate and eloquent populist. Although never quite able to achieve traction against the two 'glamour' candidates, Obama and Clinton, Edwards did have the effect of pushing the centre of the candidates' debate perceptibly to the left on such issues as universal health insurance.

Until December, Clinton held on to a double-digit lead over Obama. Political experts generally emphasised that national polling at this stage had little predictive value regarding the state-by-state battle (Giuliani was, at this point, also still ahead), but it was remarkable that Clinton was also ahead among black voters, who remembered fondly the presidency of her husband, Bill Clinton, and who also apparently doubted that a black man could be considered a viable contender. Clinton and her campaign team worked hard to convey an aura of inevitability, and an image and a record of steely competence. 'She simply does not make mistakes' became common refrain among political cognoscenti, and this perception appeared to have affected the calculations of Democratic primary voters who –

still embittered by the Bush–Gore election dispute in 2000 and angry at the Bush administration – were concerned above all about which Democratic standard-bearer could fight back and win against the 'Republican attack machine'. The Democratic argument about 'electability' was thereby transformed – Clinton, notwithstanding the national hate campaign conducted against her in the 1990s, and worries even among supporters about high negative ratings in public-opinion surveys, was deemed by many to be the most likely winner.

Early assessments of Obama's candidacy were meanwhile affected by his uneven campaign performance. He had the capacity to inspire crowds, and there were early suggestions that his mixed race, personal history and eloquence could help improve the catastrophically low opinion of the United States around the world. Comparisons were made to the intelligence and charisma of the slain John F. Kennedy or his brother Robert, also assassinated, or even Obama's fellow Illinois politician Abraham Lincoln – whose presidency was the culmination of a comparably limited political career. Yet a politically less auspicious comparison also presented itself: that of Adlai Stevenson, another Illinois intellectual, who was the darling of 1950s Democratic liberalism, but who led his party through a decade of defeats against Eisenhower. The fear of some Obama enthusiasts was that their candidate might fit the archetype of Stevenson or the 1968 contender Eugene McCarthy – beloved by highly educated and often affluent liberals, but perhaps too coolly cerebral to thrive in mass politics.

That worry never went away entirely, but it was largely forgotten on the evening of 3 January 2008, when Obama pulled off a stunning victory in Iowa. Winning a close race in a nearly all-white state dominated by rural voters opened up vistas of possibilities. The moderately conservative *New York Times* columnist David Brooks captured the mood well when he wrote that night:

This is a huge moment. It's one of those times when a movement that seemed ethereal and idealistic became a reality and took on political substance ... Whatever their political affiliations, Americans are going to feel good about the Obama victory, which is a story of youth, possibility and unity through diversity – the primordial themes of the American experience. And Americans are not going to want to see this stopped. When an African-American man is leading a juggernaut to the White House, do you want to be the one to stand up and say No?

Five days later, on the back of polls predicting a second straight Obama victory, New Hampshire voters stood up and said 'no'. Clinton's narrow victory over Obama established her reputation for grit and perseverance – in the same state where her husband in 1992 was able to call himself the 'comeback kid'. And it set the pattern for five months of sometimes bitter see-sawing between the two contenders. Obama won South Carolina, with its large, and now energised, black population, by a huge 2–1 margin. On Super Tuesday Clinton won most of the big populous states, including New York and California; but Obama won many of the smaller ones: the net result was an effective tie. Through the rest of February, Obama racked up easy victories in such states as Maryland, Virginia and Wisconsin. (Obama won all 11 primaries and caucuses held between Super Tuesday and 4 March, while raising $1 million per day in campaign contributions.) By this time he had, crucially, opened up a consistent lead of about 100 so-called 'pledged' delegates to the nominating convention. This was in large measure the fruit of what had been revealed to be his campaign's superior organisational skills. The Clinton team, expecting the race to be won through psychological momentum after a string of wins up to Super Tuesday, had neglected to adequately organise for, or in some cases even understand, the rules in states that held caucuses rather than primaries. In Texas, for example, delegates were allocated in both a primary election and a parallel caucus; Clinton won the primary but came out of the state with fewer delegates because of the Obama campaign's caucus performance.

Though Obama's delegate lead was relatively small, the mathematics started looking forbidding for Clinton. Democratic primaries awarded delegates in proportion to vote share, unlike the winner-take-all contests on the Republican side, so even double-digit victories could only produce small net gains in delegate totals. Clinton's only real hope was to convince enough of the so-called 'superdelegates' – some 800 party leaders and elected officials who are automatically entitled to cast a vote at the convention – that Obama would be a losing candidate in the general election. To turn that hope into a strategy, however, was inevitably a fraught enterprise because the most salient reason that he might be unelectable was his race. Obama supporters had already been angered when Bill Clinton, commenting on his wife's loss in South Carolina, noted that black civil-rights activist Jesse Jackson had also won the state when he ran for president in 1984 and 1988. A Clinton campaign surrogate, ex-New York Senator Geraldine Ferraro, who had made history of her own in 1984 as the first female vice-presidential nominee of a major party, raised a furore by telling a newspaper reporter in March, 'if Obama was a white man, he would not be in this position'. Such comments had to be disavowed, to varying degrees, by the Clinton campaign. But the most explosive interjection of race into the campaign came in the form of a gift, of sorts, to the Clinton campaign from the retired minister of the Chicago church that Obama had attended for over 20 years. YouTube videos from the Reverend Jeremiah Wright's sermons, long available, started being played and replayed with feverish intensity on network and cable news television. In these sermons Wright could be seen crying 'God damn America', suggesting that the 11 September attacks constituted 'chickens coming home to roost' for America's misdeeds in the world, and endorsing a conspiracy theory, which has amazing currency among American blacks, holding that HIV/AIDS was manufactured by US government scientists to kill African Americans. Obama had been close to Wright; the title of his second book, *The Audacity of Hope*, was taken from a Wright sermon. It wouldn't be enough to say, although true, that Wright was a complicated figure, a US Navy and Marine veteran who served during the Vietnam War; that his church was welcoming to whites and tolerant of homosexuals; and that the prophetic tradition of African-American churches could be jarring when heard or witnessed out of context. Strikingly, one person who did say as much was the Republican candidate and former preacher Huckabee, who observed vis-à-vis Wright: 'I grew up in a very seg-regated south. And I think that you have to cut some slack ... to people who grew up being called names, being told "you have to sit in the balcony when you go to the movie. You have to go to the back door to go into the restaurant. And you can't sit out there with everyone else. There's a separate waiting room in the doctor's office. Here's where you sit on the bus..." And you know what? Sometimes people do have a chip on their shoulder and resentment. And you have to just say, I probably would too.'

But the circulation of Wright's sermons opened a potentially huge trap for Obama, a chasm of white anxiety and anger about corresponding anger and resentment on the part of blacks, and a bundle of doubts about whether black America considered itself truly American. This was the handle that right-wing media figures latched onto – by alleging inadequate patriotism they had the bonus of maintaining plausible deniability while reminding white voters of their disquiet about certain elements of black culture. The patriotism allegation carried nativist and religious subcurrents: for months chain e-mails had circulated the false allegation that Obama was a secret Muslim (hard to deny too vigorously without implying that there was something wrong with being a Muslim). Obama added to his own troubles with an ill-advised comment at a private fundraising event in San Francisco, where he suggested in rather too intellectual a mode tht the Democrats' difficulties with rural voters stemmed from an economic back-sliding and bitterness that made them 'cling' to a culture of guns, religion or suspicion of immigrants.

Obama had sought to present himself as 'post-racial', but in the storm of these controversies he had no choice but to address himself directly to the issues raised by his skin colour. He did so in an eloquent and thoughtful speech, which he wrote himself and delivered in sober circumstances in Philadelphia. He con-demned Wright's incendiary statements, but added: 'I can no more disown him than I can disown the black community. I can no more disown him than I can my white grandmother – a woman who helped raise me, a woman who sacrificed again and again for me, a woman who loves me as much as she loves anything in this world, but a woman who once confessed her fear of black men who passed by her on the street, and who on more than one occasion has uttered racial or ethnic stereotypes that made me cringe'. Crucially, Obama discussed African Americans' continuing disadvantages and resentments along with the fact that most 'working- and middle-class white Americans don't feel that they have been particularly privileged by their race. Their experience is the immigrant experience – as far as they're concerned, no one's handed them anything, they've built it from scratch' – but are sometimes made to feel that they must pay in perpetuity for the injustices of slavery and segregation. Obama cited a line from William Faulkner, who knew as much as any writer about the inseparable stories of white and black America, and who wrote, 'the past isn't dead and buried. In fact, it isn't even past'.

This speech may well go down in history as a major document in the history of American race relations. But it was not enough to overcome Obama's structural disadvantage against Clinton in large, ethnically diverse states such as Ohio and Pennsylvania, both of which she won handily. The Clinton team used these victories to press their case to superdelegates that Obama could not win over the white working-class voters that a Democrat would need to win the White House. Actually, a more precise examination of the counties where Clinton won big against Obama revealed a more specific problem – Obama had failed to persuade voters in Appalachia, the mountainous region that extends south along the western parts of New York, Pennsylvania, eastern and southern Ohio, eastern Kentucky and Tennessee, all of West Virginia, and into northern regions of Georgia, Alabama and Mississippi. These were some of the poorest counties in the country, populated by struggling white descendants of Scots-Irish settlers, who for centuries have maintained a distinct culture and world-view. Clinton trounced Obama in West Virginia's and Kentucky's May primaries, where some voters were not shy about expressing frankly racist opinions to journalists. Obama also fared poorly against Clinton among Catholic voters. What started to become clear was that the ups and downs of the Democratic primary campaign were influenced less by momentum and events and more by the demographic contours of the primary calendar. Clinton enjoyed a rebound late in that schedule not because she raised new doubts about Obama, but because Pennsylvania, West Virginia and Kentucky – states where she enjoyed this demographic advantage – had scheduled their primaries for late in the season. Clinton herself did appear to undergo an impressive transformation: from the establishment claimant of 'inevitability', to a tough and tireless tribune for working-class women. With Obama still ahead in pledged delegates, however, it was never plausible that superdelegates would stand up and say 'no' to their party's first African-American nominee. On 3 June, the date of the last primary, Obama declared victory. A few days later Clinton conceded.

The choice

For the general election in November 2008, American voters faced a choice of two attractive and very different candidates. McCain would be, at 72, the oldest president ever inaugurated for a first term and, with a body suffering considerable stiffness and pain, was not a particularly vigorous septuagenarian. The reason for this condition, however, was inspiring: the skeleton of the Vietnam War Navy pilot was fractured in many places when his plane was shot down in a bombing run; confined and tortured for years in a North Vietnamese prison, he was offered early release as the son of a prominent admiral, but he refused to accept any favours over his imprisoned comrades. McCain had established a reputation for wit and irreverence as well as a record of seeking bipartisan coalitions and friendship in the Senate. Obama, too, promised to move beyond the polarisation of the 16 years under Presidents Bush and Clinton. So the election seemed to offer a clear way forward out of the American public's deep disillusion with the Bush administration.

But whatever the promise for the future, Americans remained mired in present anxieties, with eight out of ten surveyed voters telling pollsters that they thought the country was moving in the wrong direction. Economic worries were paramount. Job growth throughout the Bush administration had been slow, and the cyclical recession that the US economy appeared to enter on the eve of the election was compounded by financial crisis. After the contraction of the great information-technology bubble of the 1990s, the US economy had been revived and expanded by a second speculative bubble in housing prices. In 2007, that bubble, too, dramatically burst. Falling house prices revealed the fragility of a financial system that had been greatly leveraged through the creation of complex securities that packaged together disparate assets including an unknown quantity of so-called 'subprime' mortgages ('subprime' refers to the borrower's creditworthiness). No one could quite figure out what share of financial institutions' balance sheets were subprime, but the answer mattered a lot more if house prices were falling rather than rising. By August 2007, problems were emerging in financial markets.

Mortgage defaults increased and financial institutions starting looking at one another warily – the extent of risk was unknowable. The crisis spread well beyond the housing and credit sector. Economic growth slowed down in the last quarter of 2007 and first quarter of 2008. As asset-backed securities suffered defaults, banks stopped lending to each other. On 22 January a massive Wall Street sell-off moved the Federal Reserve to announce an 0.75-percentage-point cut in interest rates, to 3.5%, the largest single cut in more than 20 years. Major American and foreign banks were forced into large write downs of the value of their assets, and had to turn to the capital markets for new funding to shore up their equity capital and avoid bankruptcy.

In March the Federal Reserve organised a JPMorgan Chase buyout of the investment bank Bear Stearns at a fraction of the $170 at which the shares had been trading the previous year. Two of Bear Stearns's hedge funds had collapsed and clients had withdrawn $17 billion in two days. To avert a panic and shore up liquidity, the Federal Reserve reduced its base rate again, to 2.25%. But interbank lending remained tight. More reasons for wariness would be revealed in July: Fannie Mae and Freddie Mac, the two government-sponsored mortgage giants, had lost at least $11bn in the crisis, and the Treasury was forced into announcing emergency support measures.

By summer 2008, US unemployment had risen to 5.5%, gasoline prices hit $4.11 per gallon, and house prices had fallen faster than in any year since the Great Depression. The downside for the US and world economies was somewhat mitigated by strong growth in the world's emerging economies. The full financial and economic effects of the credit crisis were yet to be seen. Economic distress was likely to sour the American discourse on interaction with the rest of the world. Three big campaign topics were trade, immigration and energy policy (with all of its implications for the environment).

While it was always possible that improved economic conditions would change the national mood regarding trade, there were also signs that the high-water mark of American free-trade ideology had been reached. In 2007, only 59% of surveyed Americans thought that international trade was benefiting the country, down from 78% in 2002. In the early primaries, the populist calls for a more defensive US trade posture were led by Edwards on the left and Huckabee on the right. As the primary calendar brought them to the large industrial states, Ohio and then Pennsylvania, Obama and Clinton vied to outbid each other in promising that their administrations would see the renegotiation of the North American Free Trade Agreement (NAFTA), which Clinton's husband had touted as one of his key economic achievements. Obama also promised, during the Iowa caucus campaign, to fight a new trade pact with South Korea, and proposed a 'Patriot Employers Act' to reward companies that do not outsource their labour. It is hard to know how much of this anti-trade talk in 2008 might translate into policy in 2009. One member of Obama's economic-policy group got into trouble by telling Canadian diplomats not to worry too much about the Democrats' rhetoric. McCain has remained firmly attached to free-trade policies, and travelled during the campaign to Canada and Latin America to highlight them. But, as the huge and still impoverished labour supplies of China, India and other emerging markets are increasingly tapped into the global economy, it would be foolish to imagine that the pain thereby inflicted on much of the US middle classes can safely be ignored.

The public reaction to a second great manifestation of open economies – the international movement of labour – has been even more emotional. Republican politics at the grassroots level were seized by virulent agitation against illegal immigration. One single-issue candidate for the White House, Congressman Tom Tancredo, set the tone, but he was joined by others such as Romney and Giuliani. McCain was the only major Republican candidate who refused to join the anti-immigrant cause; given that all the Democrats were working hard to court Hispanic voters, this would seem to augur well for a calm approach to the issue. However, a Bush-backed immigration bill, which would have given a path to citizenship for some 12m illegals already in the country, was brought down by Republican opposition in Congress. McCain, although he had backed the bill, was not willing on the campaign trail to promise he would bring it back unless the Right had been appeased with sharper enforcement. Even a President Obama would likely have some difficulty getting the bill through Congress unless his election were accompanied by a Democratic landslide in House and Senate seats.

Probably the most fundamental economic problem confronting the United States, like the rest of the world, was the combined crisis of soaring global oil prices and potential climate catastrophe. It was possible that the coincidence between expensive oil and growing environmental consciousness would prove fortuitous. Certainly in the year leading up to summer 2008, the US debate on climate change seemed transformed. McCain and all of the Democratic candidates had promised to push through Congress a 'cap-and-trade' scheme for reducing carbon emissions. In October former Vice President Al Gore, together with the UN's Intergovernmental Panel on Climate Change, were awarded the Nobel Peace Prize for their work in sounding the global-warming alarm.

One might have thought this to be a good time to explain to Americans that high oil prices, however painful, were a requirement for shifting away from a carbon-intensive economy, and would have to be made permanent through government policy. However, there is probably no good time to tell Americans that $4-per-gallon gasoline needs to be permanent. During the spring primaries, McCain and Clinton both proposed gas-tax 'holidays' to ease the summer burden on motorists. Obama, sensibly, decried the proposal as a gimmick. He showed less political courage, however, in backing subsidies for maize-based ethanol; this time it was McCain who had the courage and common sense to oppose. Evidence was growing that maize ethanol was not a very efficient way to produce fuel, and therefore not genuinely carbon light; the industry, moreover, was adding to the spike in global food prices; and the package of support for maize ethanol included egregious tariffs against Brazilian cane-sugar ethanol, which is carbon efficient and is not, so far at least, taking land away from food production.

By summer it was clear that there would be no serious action on either energy or climate in the last months of the Bush administration. The administration's only proposals on energy were federal help to the same nonsensical biofuel, and proposals to allow oil exploration and drilling in Alaskan wilderness reserves and off America's coasts. On climate, the cap-and-trade bill introduced by Senators Joseph Lieberman and John Warner in October had failed by June.

America to the left?

A major change in government energy and carbon policies will be tough to bring about. There was some evidence, though, that Americans were at least taking the climate problem more seriously: from 2003 to 2007, the percentage of surveyed citizens who said they worried 'a great deal' about global warming rose from 28% to 41%. This was not the only area where the American political terrain appeared to be sloping left, in favour of the Democrats. They favoured Obama's plan to raise the top income-tax rate from 35% to 39.6%, and to raise capital gains taxes from 15% to 25%; they were left cold by McCain's counter-bid to make the Bush tax cuts permanent. And they were increasingly Democratic in their thinking about the fact that America remains the only advanced industrial country without a universal guarantee of health insurance. Democratic efforts to redress this anomaly go back to the Harry S. Truman administration – that is, roughly to the same time that Britain introduced its National Health Service. But the opposition from conservatives, private insurance companies and, until recently, doctors' associations, was always decisive.

The most recent effort had been, of course, early in President Bill Clinton's first term, in the form of a proposal prepared by a task force under the direction of Hillary Clinton. It went down to spectacular defeat amidst the same cries of 'socialised medicine' that had been hurled against Truman's proposals.

In 2007 and 2008, all the major Democratic candidates proposed ambitious plans for universal insurance. Obama's was perhaps less ambitious than the others, insofar as he considered it politically inopportune to mandate Americans to buy the insurance that he proposed the federal government subsidise. The Democrats hoped they had learned necessary political-strategic lessons from the Clinton-era debacle. They were also heartened by a growing change in doctors' views of the matter, and they reasonably hoped to have considerably increased majorities in the 2009 Congress. Even if Obama's polling lead over McCain was thin, the Republican Party had become toxic in many voters' estimations, and in the Senate, more Republican than Democratic-held seats were up for election. Moreover, the Congressional Democrats were proving more adept at wielding even their current small majorities. One incident, highly dramatic if slightly obscure in its policy details, illustrated this. The last surviving Kennedy brother, 77-year-old Senator Edward Kennedy, was a long-time champion of universal care. In the late spring he had to absent himself from the Senate for surgery to remove a brain tumour, and for follow-on chemotherapy. But on 9 July he was flown covertly, against his doctors' advice, from Boston to Washington to cast a decisive vote on a bill to move funds back into doctors' Medicare payments, and away from federally subsidised private accounts that had been instituted under Bush. The Senate chamber erupted into riotous cheering when he arrived to cast a vote that took Republicans by surprise, and gave them no time to plot a counter-strategy. Democrats viewed their victory, in Paul Krugman's words, as a first successful blow 'in the fight against creeping privatization'.

Foreign policy

With domestic issues favouring the Democrats, the McCain campaign counted on being able to exploit the Republicans' traditional advantage on national-security issues. The line of attack was familiar. In May 2008, in a speech before the Knesset to celebrate Israel's 60th anniversary, Bush attacked those who 'seem to believe that we should negotiate with the terrorists and radicals, as if some ingenious argument will persuade them they have been wrong all along'. Bush continued:

> We have heard this foolish delusion before. As Nazi tanks crossed into Poland in 1939, an American senator declared: 'Lord, if I could only have talked to Hitler, all this might have been avoided.' We have an obligation to call this what it is – the false comfort of appeasement, which has been repeatedly discredited by history.

Democratic supporters of Obama reacted with anger; Republican candidate McCain supported the president, and the White House claimed to be puzzled that Obama's campaign would assume that the president was talking about him. This was a clever denial, intended to be unconvincing. Very early in the presidential race, at a YouTube debate on 23 July 2007, Obama had been asked whether he would be ready to meet, 'without precondition ... with the leaders of Iran, Syria, Venezuela, Cuba and North Korea'. Obama had replied that he would indeed be ready. This was widely assumed to be a gaffe; the Clinton campaign immediately pounced, calling Obama's statement 'irresponsible and frankly naive'. Obama's aides asked him if he wanted to retract, or at least clarify, his remarks. Yet while it is pretty clear that the campaign had not intended to stake out new ground, once in possession Obama decided to hold onto it. Throughout the campaign they carried talking points arguing that, throughout the Cold War, presidents as diverse as Kennedy, Nixon and Reagan had seen the value in direct talks with enemies far more dangerous than those listed above, that it was absurd to view 'talk' as some kind of 'reward', and that the conventional wisdom that equated negotiation with appeasement had led, in Obama foreign-policy adviser Samantha Power's words, into Iraq, 'the worst strategic blunder in the history of U.S. foreign policy'.

More broadly, the Obama foreign-policy posture was a distinctively conservative one. In contrast to the Bush administration's signature promotion of democracy in the Middle East and elsewhere as a US national-security imperative, Obama stressed the universal importance of human 'dignity', telling an interviewer that only when basic material 'aspirations are met' would space 'open up ... for the kind of democratic regimes we want'. He downplayed the 'war on terrorism', telling another interviewer that 'problems of terrorism and groups that are resisting modernity ... is one of the severe threats that we face. I don't think it's the only threat that we face.' He expressed admiration for the statecraft of former President George H.W. Bush, and the ostentatious realism of such Bush advisers as General Brent Scowcroft. One area where the Obama vision was less conservative was in a commitment to confront genocide – this reflected the views of Power, a key adviser whose intellectual development focused on genocide in the Balkans and Rwanda. In general, however, and even though his team was imbued with the moderate hawkishness of most Democratic foreign-policy elites, the Obama world view reflected an appreciation of the dangers of over-reaching idealism.

Obama had opposed the Iraq War when he was still an Illinois state senator; this was an early and perhaps decisive advantage in the Democratic primary race over Clinton, who had voted in favour of the 2002 Senate resolution that Bush had claimed as authority to invade. Obama insisted that he was no pacifist; he opposed 'dumb wars' rather than war in general. He had also opposed the 'surge' of US troop levels that Bush ordered in early 2007, and its apparent success in quelling Iraq's violence posed for Obama something of a quandary. He continued to maintain that he would set a withdrawal schedule to remove the bulk of US combat troops from Iraq within 16 months of taking office. He and his campaign got into trouble whenever they tried to hint at flexibility and nuance in their approach: Power herself had to leave the campaign not long after she told a British television interviewer, '[the senator] will, of course, not rely on some plan that he's crafted as a presidential candidate or a US Senator ... What he's actually said, after meeting with the generals and meeting with intelligence professionals, is that you – at best case scenario – will be able to withdraw one to two combat brigades each month' (although the proximate cause for her resignation was her description of Hillary Clinton as 'a monster' to another British interviewer). In June, Obama himself said in a press conference that his plans would be 'refined' on the basis of advice from generals and facts on the ground; this set off a storm of speculation about his 'flip-flopping', so that a few hours later he called another press conference to insist that the 16-month schedule still held. He almost always added a variation on the line, 'what I do believe is we've got to be as careful getting out as we were careless getting in'. But he left no doubt that he intended to withdraw as soon as was prudently feasible, that he would use some of the troops this would free up to focus on greater military effort in Afghanistan, which he considered, along with Pakistan, the more vital source of terrorist threat.

Obama needed to transcend the assumption that the most salient issues of national security can be framed as a question of sufficient toughness, of Churchillian resolve and refusal to appease enemies and aggressors. Such certainty had an able advocate in McCain, who on the campaign trail regularly declaimed that 'the transcendent challenge of the twenty-first century is radical Islamic extremists'. This was moral clarity at the expense of common sense, but it did have political, aesthetic and moral resonance, and it was helped by McCain's steadfast position in favour of the Iraq War and the surge. There was reason to believe that the 'Anbar Awakening' involving local accommodations with Sunni tribes would undermine Iraqi state-building in the long run, and there were largely coincident factors for greater calm including a tactical truce from Moqtada al-Sadr's Mahdi Army. Still, McCain's argument was compelling because it was straightforward: he supported the surge when almost everyone else was looking for an exit; the killing had unquestionably diminished; his opponents were ready for surrender while he was set on victory.

The sources of McCain's foreign-policy positions are eclectic and, arguably, not altogether coherent. He was a conservative opponent of Reagan-administration military deployments to Beirut, of the Bush/Clinton mission to Somalia, and to early arguments for US intervention in Bosnia. By the time of the Kosovo War, however, he joined neo-conservatives in backing Clinton's interventionism. He stood with neo-conservatives outside the Bush administration in backing the invasion of Iraq and criticising the paucity of troops and mismanaged occupation. His campaign advisers included unrepentant neo-conservatives and traditional Republican realists, and his speeches reflected this tension: he proposed, for example, the radical step of expelling Russia from the Group of Eight industrialised nations (G8); yet he emphasised in another speech the importance of resuming serious strategic arms-control negotiations with Moscow. It would require McCain's election as president for the world to find out whether this neoconservative–realist tension would result in foreign-policy creativity, or paralysis.

The Bush administration, meanwhile, continued to move towards the realist end of that spectrum. In the confrontation with Iran, its hand was arguably forced by events, including a December 2007 National Intelligence Estimate (NIE) reflecting the consensus of US intelligence agencies that Iran had ceased work on nuclear weaponisation in 2003. This was only an apparent bombshell – actual weapon design and construction is much less difficult or important than Iran's ongoing programme to master uranium-enrichment technology.

Nonetheless, the NIE's release seemed to take the option of US military strikes against Iran's nuclear facilities off the table (although Israel might feel so threatened as to strike itself, or persuade the United States to do so). In July 2008, US Undersecretary of State for Political Affairs William Burns travelled to Geneva to join European and Iranian negotiators; this marked the highest-level official contact between the United States and Iran since the 1979 takeover of the US Embassy in Tehran. This meeting continued a general trend of greater US emphasis on diplomacy. US negotiator Christopher Hill made substantial progress with Pyongyang on implementing the February 2007 'Six-Party' agreement to 'disable' North Korea's nuclear programme in exchange for economic aid and easing of sanctions. Following the violent schism between a Fatah-dominated West Bank and Hamas-ruled Gaza in summer 2007, Bush and Secretary of State Condoleezza Rice pushed for a 'shelf peace treaty' to be signed by the end of their administration, even in full recognition that neither side was in a position yet to implement it. (It did not, however, appear likely that it would even be signed.) Even in Iraq, the administration arguably undermined McCain's hard line by agreeing to a 'time horizon' with Iraqi Prime Minister Nuri al-Maliki for withdrawing US troops. (A few days later Maliki went further and endorsed Obama's timeline.)

Out of the hole?

In late July 2008, Obama left the United States for a trip to Afghanistan, Kuwait, Iraq, Jordan, Israel, Germany, France and Britain. It was a trip that drew intense media interest, and a speech scheduled for Berlin's Tiergarten was expected to draw huge, adoring crowds. The McCain campaign complained, with some reason, that this was an unusual campaign stunt, but their complaints were undercut somewhat by the fact that McCain had been taunting his opponent for months because he had not recently travelled to Iraq. Stunt or not, however, the Obama trip underscored a remarkable new political reality: it was now considered an important qualification for a presidential candidate to be liked in Europe – even in France.

Both McCain and Obama could be expected to improve America's standing in the world. Both men had promised to close the Guantanamo Bay detention facility for terrorist suspects, and to rehabilitate America's reputation for observing the rule of law. They were both evidently sincere, but the task would not be easy. On 12 June the US Supreme Court ruled, on a 5–4 decision, that the constitutional right to habeas corpus extended to the American base on Cuba and to its 'enemy combatants', including non-US citizens. This ruling effectively invalidated administration claims that detention at Guantanamo placed them outside the reach of US law, and the Court also found that the military tribunals set up to review the detainees' combatant status improperly allowed hearsay evidence while denying defendants their proper legal assistance and access to evidence. The ruling was close and contested – dissenting Justice Antonin Scalia wrote that 'it will almost certainly cause more Americans to be killed' – but the Court had been consistent in rolling back the administration's legal theories regarding the 'war on terror'.

Obama, who had taught constitutional law at the University of Chicago, claimed that the suspects could be put on trial, with proper safeguards and modifications, in the traditional court system. McCain, who had suffered torture in Vietnam, argued that the military commissions could be reformed to be fair and workable. Either candidate, upon becoming president, would face a moral and ethical problem. There was no question that swept up among the original detainees in Guantanamo and other facilities were a considerable number of essentially innocent people. Some had already been released, but there were others whom the United States had no idea where to send, since home countries were worried about the security implications of taking them. Many had been abused in the course of 'enhanced interrogation'. A 17 June 2008 Senate Armed Services Committee hearing revealed that interrogation trainers in Guantanamo used a chart that was copied verbatim from a 1957 Air Force study of what happened to US Korean War prisoners in Chinese hands. The techniques that were described included 'sleep deprivation', 'prolonged constraint' and 'exposure'. The only thing that Guantanamo interrogators did not see from this chart was its original title: 'Communist Attempts to Elicit False Confessions From Air Force Prisoners of War'.

Canada's Conservative Foreign Policy

Canadian Prime Minister Stephen Harper has headed a relatively stable minority Conservative government since coming to power in early 2006. Notwithstanding disagreements over the government's handling of such issues as the environment and the conflict in Afghanistan, the official Liberal opposition under Stéphane Dion has so far proven unwilling to initiate a no-confidence vote that could, if successful, trigger a federal election. Neither of the other major political parties, the New Democratic Party (NDP) and the Bloc Québécois (BQ), have sufficient seats in parliament to bring down the government independently and have been limited to verbally criticising current government policies.

Harper emphasised domestic priorities to unseat the governing Liberals in the last federal election, but once in office found himself managing a number of pressing international issues that overshadowed this electoral agenda, such as the mass evacuation of Canadian citizens from Lebanon in 2006 and the ongoing

Canadian military mission in Afghanistan. The current government's term in office will be judged on its handling of foreign affairs and defence. Recognition of this fact can be seen in the Conservative government's 16 October 2007 Speech from the Throne, which devoted an entire section to the need for 'Strengthening Canada's Sovereignty and Place in the World'. As the speech, read by Governor General Michaëlle Jean, noted, 'Rebuilding our capabilities and standing up for our sovereignty have sent a clear message to the world: Canada is back as a credible player on the international stage.'

The current government, expanding upon the promises of its Liberal predecessor, has consecutively increased defence expenditures as part of its 'Canada First' defence strategy. The official 2007/08 defence budget was C$16.9bn, indicating the government is on track to achieve its original promise of allocating C$19bn to defence by 2010. If supplementary funding is included, the original budgetary goal for 2010 will be achieved one year earlier – an estimated total of $19bn has been earmarked for 2008/09, which places Canadian defence expenditures as a percentage of gross domestic product (GDP) on a par with German and Danish spending at 1.3%. The government is on its way to fulfilling the goal, noted in the 2005 Conservative policy declaration, of increasing defence spending as a percentage of GDP to the European average of the North Atlantic Treaty Organisation (NATO).

The Conservatives' 'Canada First' strategy includes an emphasis on both sovereignty protection and expedition-oriented military force. The government has announced major acquisitions of equipment with important dual-use capabilities in support of both aims. In 2006, this included a fleet of strategic and tactical airlifters (with 4 strategic-lift CC-177 *Globemaster* III aircraft expected to be delivered by 2008), medium-to-heavy-lift helicopters, medium transport trucks and three multi-role Joint Supply Ships (JSS). This was followed by the announcement of additional acquisitions, including 100 *Leopard* II main battle tanks; an immediate short-term loan arrangement for 20 additional tanks for current operations in Afghanistan; up to eight Arctic offshore patrol vessels; and the modernisation and life extension of the existing fleet of *Halifax*-class frigates and CP-140 *Aurora* long-range surveillance and reconnaissance aircraft. Many contracts have not been signed and cost overruns may still lead to project cancellations, but it was remarkable that C$30bn in military equipment and upgrades (including in-service support) generated so little controversy or public reaction.

These acquisitions have taken place even though an official 'Canada First' defence-strategy document that would clarify the meaning of this approach and offer long-term strategic guidance to the Canadian military has yet to be released. The Canadian government has instead opted to publicly outline the strategy in recent speeches by Harper and Minister of National Defence

Peter Mackay in May 2008. The speeches emphasised the need for long-term and continued investment in four pillars – people, infrastructure, readiness and equipment – that form the basis for Canada's military capabilities. Critically, the strategy promises eventually to replace a number of ageing platforms with 15 new naval ships, 10–12 maritime patrol aircraft, 65 fighter aircraft and a number of land combat vehicles. Funding for these new acquisitions will be made possible by an automatic 2% annual increase in the defence budget from 2011 to 2028. These commitments will be partially overseen by Lieutenant-General Walter Natynczyk, who was promoted to chief of the Defence Staff in July 2008 as a replacement for the charismatic General Rick Hillier.

Replacements are urgently required for many critical and expensive capability platforms, such as the increasingly obsolescent fleet of fighter aircraft, destroyers and even frigates. Personnel costs are also expected to steadily rise as Ottawa struggles to fulfil its pledge to boost the size of the Canadian military. This was originally expected to reach 75,000 regular members and 35,000 reservists, though the recent speeches have instead reduced this number to 70,000 and 30,000 respectively. As noted in a recent performance report, personnel-retention problems and operational commitments have posed significant obstacles to the planned expansion of the Canadian military. But there are additional doubts whether the Canada First defence strategy's modest promise of automatic defence-budget funding until 2027/28 will be sufficient to cover such a significant recapitalisation programme. The lack of a detailed and long-term planning document for these capital acquisitions, expected to be included in the original Canada First defence-strategy document, has only reinforced concerns over the long-term funding of the Canadian military.

The Canadian combat role within NATO's International Security Assistance Force (ISAF) in Afghanistan, where 87 military personnel and one diplomat have been killed since 2002, remains a controversial and increasingly unpopular mission. Canada's military casualties have declined since 2006, but Taliban insurgents inflicted a greater number of attacks and civilian fatalities in 2007. Canada's operation in Afghanistan is expected to continue to drain scarce defence resources and limit any fundamental rebuilding of the Canadian military. This commitment has cost an estimated C$3.5bn since 2001, and is projected to cost nearly C$1bn per year in future given the current operational tempo and level of military contributions in Kandahar.

The Independent Panel on Canada's Future Role in Afghanistan was created by the prime minister in October 2007 and tasked with providing expert, non-partisan advice on Canada's role in Afghanistan. The Manley Panel, as it has become known, was made up of several influential former ambassadors and bureaucrats and chaired by former Liberal Deputy Prime Minister John Manley. The final report, released in January 2008, recommended a continued commitment in Kandahar after 2009 and an increased emphasis on diplomacy, reconstruction, development and the training the Afghan National Security Forces. Yet this recommendation was contingent on two key factors: the commitment of an additional battle group (roughly 1,000 troops) to Kandahar by NATO or other allies, and the acquisition of medium-helicopter lift capacity and unmanned aerial vehicles (UAVs). The Liberal Party, which played a key role in originally committing Canada's military in 2001 and choosing to transfer this contingent to the turbulent Kandahar region in 2005, gradually accepted the need for a continued – if reduced – Canadian combat role in Afghanistan after the 2009 deadline. The Manley Panel's recommendations were ultimately accepted by both parties, and a compromise motion on Afghanistan – which, subject to the outlined conditions, extends the mission in Kandahar to 2011 – was approved by parliament on 13 March 2008. This outcome is indicative of the government's cautious and conciliatory approach to the Afghanistan issue, which has seen the Conservatives seek to build bi-partisan consensus with the Liberals in order to eliminate the Afghanistan mission as a possible election issue.

Canadian officials were successful in having the Manley Panel's conditions met at the NATO Summit in Bucharest, Romania, in April 2008. France agreed to send a battalion of 700 troops to the eastern region of Afghanistan and the United States confirmed the deployment of a battalion of marines to work with the Canadians in Kandahar. The panel's second condition, on the need for new equipment, was partly fulfilled by Poland's agreement to offer the use of its Mi-17 transport aircraft, with plans for the UAVs to be leased and six additional CH-47-D *Chinook* helicopters purchased from the United States. Yet the summit did not resolve the contentious use of restrictions, or 'caveats', by many NATO members that limit their participation in combat operations.

The Conservatives' 'Canada First' approach includes a nationalistic element of protecting Canadian sovereignty. The government has been vocally opposed to any US border-security measures that could damage trade between the two countries, and in April 2008 blocked a US company's C$1.3bn takeover bid for a Canadian company involved in developing space technology, including the state-of-the-art *Radarsat-2* satellite. Harper has also been active in trying to protect Canadian citizens who have been jailed in such places as China, Bulgaria and Saudi Arabia.

Sovereignty protection also involves the use of the Canadian military to reinforce Ottawa's claims in the disputed Northwest Passage, which will likely become a major shipping route because of climate change, and the northern Arctic region, with its potentially large oil and gas reserves. On both issues, Canada has been challenged by the United States, Norway, Denmark and especially Russia, which sent research submarines to plant its flag close to the North

Pole in August 2007. The planned procurement of up to eight Arctic patrol vessels is meant to reinforce the Canadian presence in the North. In addition to pursuing this capability platform, the government has planned for the establishment of an Arctic Warfare Training Centre and a deep-water port in the Canadian Arctic; an increase in the size and capabilities of the Arctic Rangers (the Inuit and First Nations militia that patrols the Far North); a comprehensive mapping project of Canada's Arctic seabed; and an increase in Canada's surveillance capabilities using existing surveillance aircraft and the space-based Polar Epsilon project, which will use *Radarsat*-2 for the wide-area surveillance of Canada's Arctic and ocean approaches.

While the government has spent a large amount of time dealing with the military commitment to Afghanistan and, to a lesser extent, buttressing Canadian claims to the Arctic, it has also moved to put a 'conservative' stamp on other elements of Canada's international policy. Harper strained diplomatic relations with Beijing after publicly meeting with exiled Tibetan spiritual leader the Dalai Lama in late 2007. Canada pushed for Pakistan's expulsion from the Commonwealth after the country's military government imposed emergency rule in November 2007.

The Conservatives have also been less wedded to multilateral organisations than their Liberal predecessors. Canada took the notable steps of voting against a UN Declaration on the Rights of Indigenous Peoples and not supporting a European Union-led UN initiative to establish a global moratorium on capital punishment. Perhaps more controversially, the government joined with Washington in supporting the Asia-Pacific Partnership on Clean Development and Climate as a more limited alternative to the Kyoto Protocol, and proved to be an increasingly isolated obstructionist at the 2007 Bali conference which aimed to establish a global framework to succeed the Kyoto Protocol. The government also displayed a more cautious attitude towards multilateral non-proliferation activities by refusing to co-sponsor a UN resolution encouraging states to sign and ratify the Comprehensive Nuclear Test-Ban Treaty and abstaining from another resolution that called on nuclear-weapons states to lower the operating status of their nuclear weapons, which was seen as potentially inconsistent with the government's support for NATO's nuclear deterrence policy.

The government also plans to revamp Canada's annual C$4.1bn foreign-aid budget, which has been growing steadily over the last several years with the goal of doubling 2001 spending levels by 2010. The new 'conservative' foreign-aid policy is expected to redirect aid to fewer countries and more carefully target states that prioritise responsible governance and economic policies. Afghanistan will continue to be Canada's largest aid recipient, but the policy will also place a renewed emphasis on the Americas, where the government has shown a strong interest in free-trade agreements and development projects. Canada has also renewed its commitment to doubling aid to sub-Saharan Africa from 2003 levels to C$2.1bn in 2008, and remains the fourth-largest donor to the Darfur mission (C$441m since 2004).

The Conservatives' approach to international affairs has been greeted with enthusiasm from Washington and seems to have contributed to an overall improvement in Canada–US relations, even though Harper has also made an effort to not appear too close to the deeply unpopular Republican US president. However, in early 2008 leaks that appeared to be linked to Ottawa contradicted Democratic presidential candidate Barack Obama's statement that no meeting took place between members of his campaign and Canadian officials on the subject of the North American Free Trade Agreement (NAFTA). 'NAFTA-gate', as this incident became known, embarrassed the potential Democratic presidential nominee and resulted in a rebuke by Obama of the perceived meddling by the Conservative Canadian government – with its close ideological affinity to the US Republican Party – in the Democratic Party's primaries.

The Conservative government's tenure in office coincided with Canada becoming a major secure oil supplier to the United States, largely as a result of the accelerated investment in and development of the Alberta oil sands. Harper has gone so far as to proclaim that Canada is an emerging 'energy superpower'. Yet such a claim seems exaggerated at best. Contrary to the spirit of the government's emphasis on sovereignty, the Alberta oil sands are largely controlled by private, foreign companies that pay relatively small royalties to the Canadian government; in any event, the federal government has very little jurisdiction over the country's oil resources, which under the constitution are controlled by the provinces. While certainly helping to smooth Canada–US relations, Canada's role as a major energy supplier displays little strategic direction and is unlikely to result in significant international influence.

In April 2008 Harper's government had exceeded the term of office of his predecessor Paul Martin's Liberal government, but Canada's opposition parties remain deeply suspicious and critical of the Conservatives' foreign-policy agenda. The NDP and BQ have been stridently opposed to Canada's military commitment to ISAF; the Liberals have begun formulating a foreign policy that, while accepting the current military deployment to Afghanistan, has placed a higher priority on multilateral activism and diplomatic nuance. Meanwhile, the mission in Afghanistan, given that it is widely perceived by Canadians as a largely American military operation, may still become a pivotal election issue before its expected end in 2011. The government has achieved some notable tactical successes on the international stage, but its approach remains fundamentally contested, and Canadian hard-power capabilities remain vulnerable to challenges.

Latin America: Slower Movement to the Left

Latin America's twenty-first-century shift to the left – halting at times and in some places, but nevertheless palpable – was encapsulated in Guatemala. On 14 January 2008, Alvaro Colom was sworn in as Guatemala's first centre-left candidate since Jacobo Arbenz, who was overthrown in a US-backed coup in 1954. Colom, known for his work with the United Nations to repatriate refugees after Guatemala's 36-year civil war ended in 1996, won a second-round victory over Otto Pérez Molina, a former army general in the bloody conflict that left 200,000 dead. Colom's social-development platform and promises of greater inclusion for Guatemala's indigenous population helped him secure the support of the country's poverty-ridden rural areas, while Pérez Molina's vows to fight crime with a *'mano dura'*, or strong hand, won him widespread support in violence-wracked urban and suburban sectors. After a campaign marked by high levels of political violence that killed dozens, Colom garnered 52.8% of the vote in the 4 November 2007 run-off, while Pérez Molina received 47.2%. Colom now faces the monumental tasks of combating drug-fuelled crime, which has claimed the lives of 25,700 people over the last five years, and easing the hardship of the 51% of Guatemala's 13m citizens who remain in poverty.

Comparable challenges face many governments in the region. Each has three basic options: maintain traditional alignment with the United States; turn sharply and antagonistically to the left, following the populist lead of Venezuelan President Hugo Chávez; or strike some balance between the two. While Chávez's approach held sway for several years, the resulting instability and economic dysfunction appear to have induced greater moderation. Across Latin America, his brand of radicalism may be yielding to the more calibrated and accommodating left-of-centre policies of Brazilian President Luiz Inácio 'Lula' da Silva.

Colombia's managed conflict

Spillover from Colombia's 40-year civil war has embroiled its neighbours and prompted international leaders to offer their assistance in forging peace. Conservative President Alvaro Uribe's *Plan Patriota*, the largest military offensive in the history of Colombia's conflict, launched in 2004, took the fight to Colombia's largest illegal armed group, the Revolutionary Armed Forces of Colombia (FARC), forcing them to retreat from the cities to their stronghold in Colombia's southern jungles. Homicides have dropped by 40%, kidnappings by 83% and terrorist attacks by 61%, making Uribe spectacularly popular with the Colombian people. Following a constitutional amendment to allow consecutive presidential terms, he was overwhelmingly re-elected in 2006.

The Colombian government has continued to aggressively pursue FARC in southern Colombia, both through direct military confrontation and by seeking to cut off its narco-trafficking income through the US-funded Plan Colombia, which supports interdiction and crop eradication, mainly by the Colombian military. Operations in southern Colombia have increased tensions with Colombia's neighbours, as FARC has sought refuge across the border in both Venezuela and Ecuador. Additionally, the Ecuadorian government has complained that spraying of drug crops with the herbicide glyphosate along the border has caused health problems among the population. Quito's plans to seek recourse from the International Court of Justice at The Hague, and pressure from the United Nations, compelled Uribe to move away from controversial aerial spraying in favour of strictly manual eradication programmes.

While Colombia's counter-insurgency campaign has reduced FARC's numbers from 18,000 to an estimated 11,000 and cut its drug income by a third, the guerrillas have maintained their operational capacity and, since 2005, have engaged in a brutal counter-offensive, increasing popular support for negotiations. FARC holds some 700 hostages, approximately 40 of whom it considers 'political assets'. Among these political hostages were former presidential candidate Ingrid Betancourt, who holds dual French and Colombian citizenship, and three United States military contractors abducted in 2003. Betancourt, who had been held since 2002, the three Americans and 11 Colombian military and police personnel were rescued, without a shot fired, on 2 July 2008 by Colombian intelligence officers who tricked the rebels into handing them over.

In June 2007, in part at the behest of French President Nicolas Sarkozy, Uribe unilaterally freed FARC Foreign Minister Rodrigo Granda and began the process of releasing over 180 other FARC rebels on condition that the group demobilise. Rather than reciprocate with a hostage release of its own, however, FARC continued to insist that Uribe grant them a demilitarised zone from which to negotiate. Earlier in the decade, however, FARC had used such a zone to expand its operations.

Despite notoriously rocky relations with Venezuelan President Hugo Chávez, who has frequently assailed Colombia for its close relationship with the United States, in August 2007 Uribe accepted Chávez's offer to mediate a hostage exchange with FARC, authorising opposition Senator Piedad Córdoba to assist in the negotiations. But Venezuelan–Colombian relations deteriorated in November, when Uribe dismissed Chávez from his role as mediator for allegedly overstepping his bounds by directly contacting members of the Colombian military. Chávez, with support from Córdoba and the hostages' families, continued in his efforts. On 10 January 2008 FARC released two hostages to representatives of the Venezuelan government in a move rebels said resulted from the efforts of Chávez and Córdoba. The guerrillas released four more hostages on 27 February. To the consternation of the Colombian government, the United States and the European Union, all of which consider FARC a terrorist organisation,

Chávez began campaigning for FARC to be designated a legitimate army, characterising it as 'insurgent forces that have political and Bolivarian goals' worthy of respect. This was clearly an unpopular position. On 4 March 2008, millions of Colombians marched against FARC and rallies were held in solidarity in 131 cities around the world, including Caracas.

On 1 March 2008 a purportedly retaliatory Colombian cross-border raid into Ecuador touched off the region's most serious diplomatic conflict in decades, exacerbated by long-standing tension spilling over from the Colombian conflict and inflamed by Latin America's ideological divides. The raid scored Colombia's most significant victory to date against FARC in killing the guerrillas' second-in-command, Raúl Reyes. This victory, however, came at considerable cost to Colombia's hostage-release efforts and its relations with its neighbours. Reyes had been the guerrillas' point man in hostage negotiations. Although Ecuadorian President Rafael Correa's initial response to the raid was rather muted, when he was informed by Ecuadorian officials that contrary to Colombia's representations it had initiated hostilities, Correa hardened his stance and accused Uribe of either being 'poorly informed' or 'having brazenly lied'. On 2 March, Correa broke off diplomatic ties with Colombia, sending 3,200 troops to the border, and began a six-nation tour to build support for his demand that the Organisation of American States (OAS) condemn Colombia's violation of Ecuadorian sovereignty.

In turn, Chávez, an ally of Correa, ordered ten battalions to the Colombian border, held a minute of silence for Reyes on his weekly radio and television broadcast, and accused Uribe of being a pawn of the 'imperialist' United States, which sought to foment conflict with Venezuela. He warned that a similar incursion into Venezuelan territory, which Uribe has long claimed is a refuge for FARC, would result in war. Uribe ordered Colombian troops to stay away from the border with Venezuela. The conflict appeared to be a 'microphone war', as it was unlikely that Chávez would want to disrupt lucrative Colombian–Venezuelan trade. Relations with Mexico were also strained by Uribe's denunciation of Mexican students killed in the raid, and ties with Costa Rica became tense as evidence of communications between Costa Rican politicians and FARC emerged. Uribe subsequently released information contained in documents from FARC laptops recovered during the raid indicating that the organisation had sent Chávez approximately $150,000 while he was in prison in 1992 after his failed coup attempt, that Chávez had pledged or given $300 million to the organisation, and that Correa had accepted campaign funding from FARC and strengthened ties with the rebels during his presidency. Correa and Chávez denied these allegations, insisting that any ties their governments had maintained with FARC were intended to facilitate a hostage exchange between it and the Colombian government. Uribe nevertheless threatened to file charges against Chávez with the International Criminal Court (ICC) for his support of terrorism.

At the Rio Group Summit on 7 March 2008, Latin American presidents urged the three Andean leaders to normalise their relations. Uribe subsequently pledged not to breach the Ecuadorian border and to drop his legal threats against Chávez. On 18 March, the crisis officially ended when the OAS issued a compromise resolution 'rejecting' but not 'condemning' Colombia's violation of Ecuadorian sovereignty while reiterating the commitment of its member states to work together against insurgents and criminal organisations. But the underlying issues of border spillover and the need for a multilateral counter-insurgency approach remain. In an attempt to jump-start negotiations with FARC, on 27 March the Uribe administration announced that it would release the Colombian government's FARC prisoners if FARC were to free its hostages, including the ailing Ingrid Betancourt. As an inducement, Sarkozy offered refuge in France for the freed rebels. But FARC has repeatedly insisted that the two FARC fighters currently held in prisons in the United States, known as 'Sonia' and 'Simon Trinidad', must be included as part of any hostage-for-prisoner swap. Trinidad was convicted in July 2007 for conspiring to kidnap the three American contractors in 2003, and in January 2008 given the maximum sentence of 60 years for this crime.

The contents of the documents found in Reyes's computers are likely to create further regional tensions. As of May 2008, the Colombian government had disclosed only a small fraction of the 16,000 recovered documents and photos. Leaked files indicated that high-level Venezuelan officials, including the chief of military intelligence and the interior minister, had met with FARC commanders and issued promises to help the guerrillas obtain funds and a variety of weapons. According to the documents, Venezuela offered to help FARC purchase surface-to-air missiles, capable of fending off the air power critical to the gains the Colombian military has made against the organisation in recent years. In addition to acting as a middleman with international arms dealers, the Venezuelan government apparently also offered to help fund arms purchases, allow FARC to use a Venezuelan port to receive weapons, and help the guerrillas travel to the Middle East for missile training. In return, Venezuela purportedly wanted military training in guerrilla tactics in order to resist a putative US invasion. Files also describe a meeting with Chávez in which the Venezuelan president talked of creating safe havens for the guerrillas along the border, and in which Venezuela was apparently interested in forging some sort of a joint security plan with FARC. While the accuracy of the information cannot be wholly verified, and may reflect a degree of wishful thinking or misinformation, Interpol concluded on 15 May 2008, after two months of forensic research, that the recovered files were in fact FARC's and had not been tampered with by the Colombian government. Chávez, however, denounced the investigation as a 'show of clowns' and continued to insist that the laptops were fabricated and planted by the

Colombian government to drum up conflict with Venezuela and encourage US efforts to oust his government.

While Colombia's struggle against FARC has continued, Uribe has made significant strides towards formal peace with the country's second-largest guerrilla group, the National Liberation Army (ELN), having conducted preliminary talks in Havana since December 2005. After the eighth round in August 2007, both sides were optimistic, with ELN head negotiator Pablo Beltrán describing the process as having progressed 'halfway' to a framework for peace talks. Uribe has said his government is willing to consider the ELN a legitimate political party if they agree to a ceasefire, release their hostages and end kidnapping, but questions remain about whether the ELN will be willing to meet government demands to concentrate its forces in a demilitarised zone and hand over membership lists to monitor such an arrangement.

The Colombian government's demobilisation of 30,000 right-wing pro-state paramilitary fighters from the United Self-Defence Forces (AUC) has come under heavy scrutiny. Under the controversial Justice and Peace Law (JPL), promulgated by Uribe, low-level combatants were given amnesty and paramilitary commanders offered reduced sentences and freedom from extradition in return for demobilisation and admission of their crimes. As paramilitary leaders began detailing their crimes over the first half of 2007, the anger and frustration of the Colombian populace swelled. Over 70,000 victims of paramilitary violence have come forward. Many of these victims and their sympathisers consider the terms of the AUC's demobilisation too lenient and are frustrated with the slow pace of investigations. In July 2007, the Colombian Supreme Court ruled that rank-and-file paramilitary fighters were not eligible for pardon, and AUC leaders threatened to end their cooperation. Uribe sought a Congressional remedy to the situation, and the jailed paramilitary leaders are unlikely to forfeit their guarantee against extradition to the United States. Nevertheless, dissatisfaction with the peace process will probably remain high on both sides. While many Colombians sought harsher remedies for AUC impunity, the Colombian government's priority was to keep paramilitary fighters from rearming. Many fighters have regrouped into armed gangs engaged in drug trafficking and other criminal activities. The OAS documented 22 such illegal armed groups, such as the increasingly notorious 'Black Eagles', which posed a new challenge to the Colombian state.

The Uribe administration has also been burdened by the so-called 'para-politics' scandal linking the government's domestic supporters with paramilitary groups. Evidence of government–paramilitary collusion began to surface in 2006 after the seizure of a former AUC commander's laptop, and grew in 2007 as the confessions of paramilitary leaders detailed their government connections. By April 2008, 31 members of Congress were imprisoned and another 31 were under investigation, most from Uribe's governing coalition. Thus, 20% of the country's legislature had been implicated in the scandal, in addition to several high-ranking officials, such as the president's former intelligence chief. On 22 April, the president's cousin and confidant, former Senator Mario Uribe, was arrested for criminal conspiracy after he was denied asylum in Costa Rica. The president subsequently revealed that he was himself under investigation for alleged involvement, along with his brother Santiago, in the 1997 massacre of 15 peasants by the paramilitaries during his tenure as governor of Antioquia. He denounced the allegations, saying they were merely a ploy by his political opponents to tie him personally to the scandal. They countered that he had tried to interfere with the independence of the judiciary. More broadly, however, he has been strongly supportive of the related investigations and prosecutions.

The para-politics scandal appeared to hurt Uribe's political allies in local and regional elections in October 2007. While Uribe's governing coalition won significant victories, including 15 governorships, parties linked to the scandal lost mayoral races in Colombia's major cities. Samuel Moreno of the leftist Democratic Pole won the powerful position of mayor of Bogotá, and smaller leftist parties won mayoral races in both Medellín and Cali. While prospects for opposition parties have certainly strengthened ahead of the 2010 presidential elections, Uribe remained popular among the Colombian people, with approval ratings consistently above 70%. According to an August 2007 poll, over 50% of Colombians wanted the president to seek a third term, which would require another constitutional amendment, on the basis of fears that the country's security successes could evaporate without Uribe's leadership. Although FARC is no longer strong enough to keep people from the polls, 29 candidates were still assassinated in the October 2007 elections, at least half of them by FARC. Uribe said he would consider running in the 2010 elections, but some Colombians fear extending the presidential term limit will threaten long-standing democratic traditions.

Despite Uribe's continued popularity at home, the para-politics scandal has tarnished his personal credibility among many in Washington and provided fodder for those seeking to change US Colombia policy. Former US Vice President Al Gore went so far as to cancel his participation in an environmental conference in April 2007 after hearing that Uribe, whom he accused of having links with par-amilitary death squads, would be present. That same month, US Senator Patrick Leahy (D-VT) suspended 25% of military aid to Colombia based on evidence of military–paramilitary collusion. In June and September 2007, the US House of Representatives and Senate, respectively, passed bills that would reduce aid to Colombia and shift its focus away from military programmes in favour of social and economic development assistance. Citing human-rights abuses and the Colombian military's involvement in the deaths of trade-union leaders, congressional Democrats indefinitely postponed a vote on the US–Colombia free trade agreement (FTA) signed by Uribe and US President George W. Bush.

The Bush administration came to the defence of its ally, pointing out that violence against all sectors of the Colombian populace declined during Uribe's tenure, and by some 50% against union members. Bush attempted to force a vote on the FTA by submitting the agreement to Congress in April 2008 for fast-track approval, meaning that it would have 90 days to approve or reject the bill. A mere two days later, however, the House voted 224–195 to remove the fast-track provisions of the FTA. Bush urged Congress to reconsider, insisting that the trade agreement was vital to supporting the United States' strongest ally in a region in which anti-US populist sentiment was rising. Uribe has not given up hope of reviving the FTA. In a surprise move on 13 May 2008, he announced the extradition of 14 jailed paramilitary leaders, including the notorious Salvatore Mancuso – previously exempt under the terms of their demobilisation agreement – to the United States on drug-trafficking charges. Uribe said the paramilitaries violated this agreement by continuing to conduct criminal operations from behind bars and failing to pay reparations to victims. Colombian human-rights activists have voiced concerns that these leaders will face lesser sentences in the United States. While many in the US Congress applauded the extraditions, prospects for the FTA remain bleak.

The Bush team also argued that continued American military assistance to Colombia was crucial to Colombia's efforts against FARC as well as to success in the wider war on drugs. Sceptics have long cited the failure of the $5bn spent on Plan Colombia to stem the flow of drugs to the United States. The Bush administration contends that the drug war is beginning to show results, citing the rising price and declining purity of cocaine in the United States from January through September 2007. While the nature of US assistance to Colombia may change in coming years, Colombia is certain to continue to receive significant aid and attention from Washington due to its position as a key hemispheric ally.

Venezuela: more bluster, less traction

Hugo Chávez continues to be Latin America's most vocal critic of what he claims are Washington's imperialist, free-market economic models for the region which have failed to curb its persistent poverty and inequality. Venezuela's vast oil reserves have enabled Chávez to finance populist projects across the continent, and allowed him to shore up key regional allies. Yet festering problems of crime, corruption and economic mismanagement at home have fuelled domestic opposition to the Venezuelan president, threatening the future of his radical populist agenda both at home and abroad.

Chávez, a former army colonel whose 1992 coup attempt had failed, was resoundingly elected in 1998 on the strength of promises to use the country's oil wealth to displace the country's oligarchic elite and benefit its poor majority. He then inaugurated his so-called 'Bolivarian Revolution', a nationalist, populist agenda which pledged to replace Venezuela's discredited oil-dependent clientelist institutions with a 'popular democracy' in which the president was directly accountable to the people. Chávez 're-founded' the nation in 1999 with a new constitution, the first in a long series of reforms to consolidate power in the office of the presidency and the person of Chávez. Implementation of Chávez's revolutionary social agenda, however, was stunted by his less-than-revolutionary economic policy: the politicised distribution of oil revenues. Facing low oil prices when he entered office in 1999, Chávez resorted to the very orthodox stabilisation policies he had campaigned against, and as the country's economic crisis deepened the president's approval rating crashed from 70% to 30%. This remaining 30% of support represented Venezuela's poorest of the poor, who continued to be fiercely loyal to Chávez despite their worsening circumstances. These core supporters, in addition to the president's remarkable political resilience and acumen, helped Chávez weather a coup attempt in April 2002, national strikes in 2002–03 and a recall referendum in August 2004.

Chávez turned the opposition's efforts against him into opportunities to consolidate his power, portraying his political opponents as counter-revolutionary elites, while windfall oil revenues in 2004 breathed new life into his Bolivarian Revolution. The failed recall referendum left Chávez's opposition fragmented, allowing the pro-Chavez contingent known as *chavistas* to score major victories in local and regional elections in October 2004. Over the course of 2005, allies of the president took control of the Supreme Court, National Electoral Council (CNE), ombudsman, attorney general and comptroller general, and in December an opposition boycott allowed them to consolidate their power by sweeping the elections for the National Assembly. Chávez scored his largest victory to date in the December 2006 presidential elections, in which he was re-elected with 62% of the vote. In January 2007 the National Assembly granted Chávez the power to govern by decree for 18 months and largely circumvent the democratic process.

With a renewed mandate and control over all three branches of government, Chávez vowed to consolidate his Bolivarian Revolution by implementing 'twenty-first century socialism' throughout Venezuela. Over the course of 2007, however, Chávez's attempts to extend his political control fragmented his support base and fuelled the rise of a stronger, more broadly based opposition wary of Chávez's authoritarian proclivities. Attempts to force his loose coalition of parties into a single entity, the United Socialist Party of Venezuela (PSUV), led to discord within Chávez's movement as several parties, such as Podemos, refused to relinquish their independence. In a December 2007 referendum Chávez sought to reform the constitution so as to declare Venezuela a socialist state, allow for indefinite presidential re-election, and extend presidential power over the Central Bank, universities and local governments. The president's ex-wife not only criticised Chávez's attempts to hold onto power through the referendum, but proposed Venezuela amend its constitution to reduce Chávez's term from six to four years. Retired General Raúl Baduel, whom Chávez replaced as defence minister in July 2007, also campaigned for a 'no' vote in the referendum. Chávez's May 2007 refusal to renew the license of opposition television station RCTV gave the opposition a cause around which to rally in protest and helped stimulate the rise of a vibrant student movement, which lent credibility to the opposition. Further attempts to polarise Venezuelans, such as calling his opponents 'traitors' and warning that a vote against him amounted to a vote for Bush, created a tense and combative environment but failed to mobilise the president's supporters. The referendum was narrowly defeated, by 51% of the vote, with voter turnout a low 56%.

Chávez's oil-funded social programmes improved health care, reduced illiteracy and unemployment, and helped poverty rates decline from 43% in 1999 to 28%, yet many problems remained. Despite oil prices of over $100 a barrel, Venezuelans were plagued by spiralling crime, shortages of basic goods, and the continent's highest rate of inflation (22.5% in 2007). In addition, allegations of corruption in government bureaucracies and the state-run oil company PDVSA left many Venezuelans feeling that the country's oil wealth was once again being siphoned off by those at the top of the political hierarchy to the detriment of ordinary citizens. Thus, disillusionment spread among the poor, upon whose unwavering support Chávez was once able to depend.

Chávez's swift acceptance of the referendum results, however, helped revive his democratic credentials, as regional leaders praised his concession. He initially vowed to press on with his socialist agenda, which he could have attempted to push through piecemeal given his powers of decree and extensive control over Venezuela's National Assembly. Yet the president soon adopted a more conciliatory approach, saying he would slow down his revolutionary efforts and concentrate on alleviating the day-to-day problems plaguing his fellow citizens. Reaching out to the opposition, Chávez pardoned many accused of participating in the 2002 coup attempt. And in his January 2008 cabinet reshuffle, Chávez replaced his radical vice-president, dispatching him to launch the president's new political party, the PSUV. Chávez also replaced his financial and planning ministers, issued a new currency, and eased price controls in hopes of addressing some of Venezuela's economic problems. Chávez declared that 2008 would be a year for 'revision, rectification and relaunching'.

Emboldened opposition parties in January 2008 agreed to band together to launch joint candidates ahead of the November local and regional elections. In order to retain their broad-based support, however, the opposition will have to articulate an affirmative alternative to, rather than a mere rejection of, Chávez.

To counter such a prospect, Chávez reached out to the disaffected members of his movement, floating the idea of reviving the Patriotic Pole, the coalition that brought him to power in 1998. Chávez also declared that he had not relinquished plans to amend the constitution in order to run in the 2012 presidential elections.

On the international front, Hugo Chávez's manoeuvres have been vigorous, involving governments or sub-national groups throughout the continent. They have also been complex, usually serving the dual purpose of extending and consolidating his network of allies abroad while drumming up domestic support against an 'external enemy'. Chávez has cast his regional aspirations in terms of counterbalancing American imperialism in Latin America, and his incendiary anti-US rhetoric has sought to divide the region between *chavistas* and *imperialistas*. Chávez has been friendly to governments hostile to the United States, such as Cuba, Iran, Syria and Libya, while using benefits from oil revenues to entice other leftist governments into uniting with him and his allies. US–Venezuela relations chilled after the 2002 coup attempt, when the Bush administration failed to denounce the coup leaders, and continued US support for Venezuelan opposition groups fuelled Chávez's accusations that Washington sought to topple his government to take control of Venezuela's vast oil reserves. Chávez has frequently warned that the United States was planning to invade or destabilise Venezuela, often with the supposed help of Colombian military or paramilitary groups, especially when he faced heightened domestic discontent.

He has also used the threat of invasion by the United States to justify his country's soaring arms purchases from Russia, worth over $3.5bn, including fighter aircraft, helicopters, and 100,000 Kalashnikov assault rifles. Venezuela has also made plans to build a Kalashnikov munitions factory in addition to buying Russian submarines and sniper rifles. These dealings have to some extent destabilised the region by emboldening Chávez. In March 2008 Chávez intervened in the bilateral confrontation between Colombia and Ecuador over Colombia's raid on FARC in Ecuadorian territory, probably gave safe haven to FARC in Venezuelan territory, and demanded FARC be taken off international terrorist lists. Revelations, leaked from the Interpol-certified documents uncovered in the raid, that high-level Venezuelan officials agreed to provide funds to FARC as well as help them secure weapons in return for guerrilla training to help Venezuelan troops resist a US invasion, led some in Washington to call for Venezuela to be added to the US State Department's list of state sponsors of terrorism. The charges were dismissed as fraudulent by Chávez. The Bush administration appeared unlikely to acquiesce to these demands, however, as the resulting sanctions would disrupt the flow of the 1.58bn barrels of oil per day from Venezuela to the United States, which accounts for 10–12% of US oil imports. A May 2008 Senate Foreign Relations Committee study also warned that sanctions could strengthen Chávez's hand by stoking anti-US sentiments in both Venezuela and the region as a whole. Meanwhile, Chávez's support for FARC may isolate him somewhat in the international arena, given that other governments failed to follow Venezuela's lead in considering FARC legitimate belligerents.

Compounding regional frictions, Venezuela has become a conduit for Colombian cocaine. Due to hostile relations with Washington, Chávez suspended US drug surveillance flights in 1999, and in August 2005 ended formal cooperation with the US Drug Enforcement Agency on the pretext that its counter-narcotics taskforce was a front for espionage operations. Drug seizures have since fallen, while illegal flights to Haiti and the Dominican Republic have risen. Meanwhile, as Colombia and Mexico have beefed up counter-narcotics operations, Venezuela has become an increasingly attractive alternative for drug traffickers. According to US officials, narcotics traffic through Venezuela rose 40% over 2007 and roughly a third of Colombian cocaine now transits the country en route to the United States and Europe. Many Venezuelans living along the border with Colombia complained of increased drug-related corruption and violence, and drug-fuelled gangs appeared to be on the rise in Caracas. Chávez, however, rejected criticism by the United States on the drug issue and insisted that Venezuela remained vigilant in rooting out drug trafficking.

Chávez has sought to counter Washington's influence in Latin America by forging alternatives to US-backed institutions and alliances. Venezuelan aid to allied leftist governments in Bolivia, Ecuador, Nicaragua and Argentina helped those countries reduce their reliance on the International Monetary Fund (IMF) and the World Bank, allowing them to follow more populist development policies, in support of which Chávez and his regional allies launched the Bank of the South in December 2007. Additionally, Chávez dampened US plans to forge a Free Trade Agreement of the Americas by forming the Bolivarian Alternative for the Americas (ALBA), which sought to foster regional economic and energy integration while focusing on socio-economic development for the poor. ALBA, however, became increasingly politicised and inflammatory, as Chávez called for the organisation to create a military alliance against the United States and urged its members to pull their foreign reserves from US banks.

The Venezuelan leader also curried favour amongst Latin American nations by providing access to Venezuela's immense oil resources. The Petrocaribe alliance offers preferential oil agreements to 15 countries in Central America and the Caribbean, which currently owe $1.2bn to Venezuela; this figure is expected to grow to $4.5bn by 2010. Similarly, Chávez created Petrosur and Petroandina, and is seeking to unite these various regional energy integration agreements into an overarching Petroamericas initiative. Chávez also built or pledged to build jointly owned oil refineries in Cuba, Jamaica, the Dominican Republic, Ecuador,

Nicaragua and Brazil. These projects helped cement Chávez's regional alliances in addition to reducing Venezuelan dependence on United States refineries and markets. To extend his regional clout, Chávez provided Cuba with nearly 100,000 barrels of oil per day, and cast himself as the natural heir to Fidel Castro as leader of the Latin American left. In December 2007 Chávez also relaunched an oil refinery that had been left idle since the collapse of the Soviet Union. In return for his assistance, Castro helped Chávez implement his social agenda by providing him with the assistance of thousands of Cuban doctors. According to Havana, the two countries have signed deals worth $7bn. Chávez continued to maintain a close relationship with Castro, who stepped down as Cuba's leader in February 2008, while also stressing that Cuba and Venezuela will continue their close alliance.

Chávez's oil-funded diplomacy has not been well received by a number of regional governments. In Peru, Chávez's support for radical populist candidate Ollanta Humala in the 2006 elections led to icy relations with the victorious Alan García. The proliferation in Peru of Venezuelan-funded 'casas de ALBA' (or 'ALBA houses') – which provide social services to impoverished locals and serve as propaganda centres for *chavismo* while condemning 'yanqui imperialism' – caused García to denounce Chávez's continued interference. In El Salvador, Venezuela has angered the right-wing government and its US allies by sending the president's cousin and head of PDVSA's Caribbean operations, Asdrubal Chávez, to meet with municipal governments run by the leftist Farabundi Marti National Liberation Front (FMLN) party. The Salvadoran and US governments fear Chávez will use his oil wealth to back an FMLN presidential candidate in the 2009 elections as he did for the Sandinistas in Nicaragua by providing discounted oil to Sandinista-controlled municipalities. Chávez has also been accused of covertly and illegally financing the presidential campaign of Cristina Fernández de Kirchner in Argentina.

More broadly, Chávez's polarising rhetoric has alienated many, sometimes subverting his international agenda. In June 2007, he accused Brazilian senators of 'parroting' the United States after they criticised his closure of RCTV, fuelling opposition to Venezuela's entry into Mercosur among Brazil's legislature. The following November he sparked a highly publicised argument with Spanish diplomats at the Iberoamerican Summit, prompting Spanish King Juan Carlos to tell Chávez to 'shut up', and sowing discord at a meeting expressly devoted to 'social cohesion'. Even among his close allies, such as Ecuador and Bolivia, many Latin Americans are wary of their governments becoming too beholden to the domineering Venezuelan president.

Ultimately, the viability of Hugo Chávez's campaign to extend and consolidate his regional influence will turn on how well he is able to grapple with the problems of Venezuela's economy. The revenues upon which his oil diplomacy, as well as his domestic social agenda, depend may be in jeopardy if operations at PDVSA continue to decline. The state-run oil company's output has declined by 20% since 2002–03, when Chávez laid off thousands of competent but politically disloyal workers after national strikes. Furthermore, the funds for investment PDVSA requires to extract oil from new fields in the Orinoco region have been diverted into Chávez's domestic social agenda. Additionally, his direct control over PDVSA has generated fears of nationalisation among foreign investors. In June 2007, Exxon Mobil and Conoco Phillips pulled out of their investments in the Orinoco when Chávez forced foreign oil companies to give majority stakes to the Venezuelan government. In fact, Chávez's economic policies are damaging the Venezuelan economy beyond just the oil sector. Overall foreign investment has also declined, registering a net outflow of $543m in 2006, as Chávez took steps to nationalise the telecommunications and electricity sectors and threatened to take over other businesses and banking institutions. Lack of investment, an overvalued currency, and price controls have led to shortages of basic goods. The government's robust spending of oil revenues has increased inflation, which is hardest on the poor. Unless the Venezuelan government takes serious steps to rectify these economic problems, Chávez will face increasing domestic discontent, damaging the prospects for his 'Bolivarian Revolution' at home and abroad.

Ecuador's quest for political stability

Ecuadorian President Rafael Correa was elected in November 2006 on promises to seize greater control over the country's finances, wrest power from Ecuador's corrupt and exclusionary political elite, and funnel the nation's oil wealth into social programmes. In the absence of adequate democratic channels for popular discontent, over the past decade Ecuador's underprivileged majority has frequently taken to the streets in mass protests, toppling three presidents in nine years. Most recently, Lucio Gutiérrez was ousted from the presidency in April 2005 after he instituted the very orthodox economic policies he had campaigned against. Correa is the country's eighth president in the past 11 years, and he hopes to be the first in this succession to survive a full term.

Declaring the end of Ecuador's 'long dark night of neo-liberalism', Correa has sought independence from the international financial institutions and foreign companies he blames for Ecuador's inequality. In April 2007, Correa ejected World Bank officials from the country, and the following July ordered IMF representatives to clear out of their offices in the Central Bank. While Correa has frequently threatened to default on Ecuadorian debt, he has thus far been pragmatically consistent in debt repayment. And although many Ecuadorians have clamoured for Correa to seize control of the country's oil and mining operations, he has avoided outright nationalisations for fear of lawsuits costing Ecuador billions of dollars. Correa has, however, sought to extend Ecuadorian control over these sectors via other means. In October 2007, the president implemented by decree a tax hike on the oil windfall profits of foreign companies, raising the rate from 50% to 99%. He subsequently used oil companies' reluctance to pay the astronomical tax as leverage to get them to renegotiate their contracts with the Ecuadorian government, turning participation contracts into service agreements giving Ecuador greater control. In January 2008, Correa cancelled 587 mining concessions on the grounds that the foreign companies had failed to pay environmental-protection fees. Additionally, he floated the idea of having international institutions pay Ecuador $350m in grants and debt reductions to refrain from Amazonian oil drilling, an action the Ecuadorian president argued was in the best interests of the global community.

Appealing to Ecuadorians' rejection of US-backed economic policies, Rafael Correa has, to a certain extent, modelled himself after Chávez and embraced his 'twenty-first century socialism'. Correa has openly criticised Bush, denounced prospects for a free-trade agreement with the United States, and repeatedly insisted that Ecuador will not renew the US lease on Manta air-force base, which expires in 2009. Yet Correa has refrained from completely alienating the United States, lobbying for extension of the Andean Trade Preference and Drug Eradication Act (ATPDEA), voicing his continued support for cooperation with the US military, and seeking to maintain Ecuador's independence from Venezuela in many respects. Correa has not joined ALBA, declined Chávez's offer to purchase Ecuadorian bonds (as he had done in Argentina), and rejected the notion of joining Venezuela in a strategic alliance against the United States. At the same time, Ecuador has become increasingly dependent on Venezuela with respect to its oil sector. While Ecuador is South America's fifth-largest oil producer and an exporter of crude, its oil production has been declining over the past few years, and reversing this trend is the centrepiece of Correa's plan to boost economic growth. Ecuador's single-largest import item is refined fuel. Venezuela has replaced the United States as Ecuador's primary supplier of such fuel. Additionally, Chávez inaugurated the first of two oil rigs, sold to Ecuador at a discount, in February 2008 and Venezuela committed to building a $5.5bn oil refinery in Ecuador.

Colombia's March 2008 bombing of the FARC camp in Ecuadorian territory, and Correa and Chávez's united opposition to it, exacerbated protracted tensions between Ecuador and Colombia over their shared border. Ecuadorians have long been wary of being dragged into the Colombian conflict, and Correa has requested international monitoring of the border. Colombia and Ecuador fundamentally differ in their approaches to security and drug trafficking. Correa launched Plan Ecuador in April 2007, which he proclaimed would contrast with the US-backed Plan Colombia by prioritising conflict resolution over military action. Correa has also suggested reducing sentences for low-level drug traffickers. Although the Ecuadorian military has repeatedly clashed with FARC and reportedly destroyed 71 FARC camps in 2006–07, Ecuador has long refused to consider FARC a terrorist group. Neither, however, does Ecuador consider FARC a legitimate insurgent group, citing its lack of compliance with the Geneva Convention. Correa has appeared keen on reducing the guerrillas' influence in his country, and in December 2007 launched a probe into FARC's Ecuadorian operations, suspecting a correlation between FARC incursions and sabotage of infrastructure. Correa has also tried to diminish the influence of the narco-traffickers and illegal armed groups by reinvigorating economic and infrastructure projects in border towns. Ecuador objects to Colombia's aerial spraying of drug crops along the border as dangerous to people as well as the environment and as driving the economically taxing flow of Colombian refugees – up to 250,000 so far, according to the UN.

Correa's primary focus has been reform at home, where he is attempting to 're-establish' the Ecuadorian government with a new constitution. Correa repeatedly clashed with Ecuador's opposition-dominated Congress, which he advocated disbanding and replacing with a Constituent Assembly charged with drafting the new constitution, and subsequently holding new elections. While his detractors accused him of having authoritarian tendencies along the lines of Chávez, Correa insisted he was legitimated by the 'will of the people'. The president's position was reinforced by an April 2007 referendum in which 82% voted in favour of a Constituent Assembly. Elections for the assembly were held on 30 September 2007, and Correa's National Alliance (AP) won 80 of the 130 seats. Aligning themselves with eight deputies from smaller parties, the AP secured the two-thirds majority needed to approve elements of a new constitution. On 29 November, to Correa's delight, the Constituent Assembly voted 110 to 20 to suspend the highly unpopular Ecuadorian Congress and assume that body's legislative duties.

Disbanding Congress, however, has caused the Constituent Assembly to become bogged down in day-to-day legislative affairs, such as increasing taxes on the wealthy, and political manoeuvring, such as the January ousting of opposition leader and former congress head Alvaro Noboa, whom Correa defeated in the 2006 presidential elections. Thus, although the Constituent Assembly was supposed to have finished drafting the new constitution by May 2008, it only began to work on the preamble in February. Additionally, the Correa administration accused members of the Constituent Assembly from Lucio Gutiérrez's Patriotic Society Party (PSP) of attempting to bribe AP members to vote against the new constitution. Scandals also damaged the credibility of the Correa government. Finance Minister Ricardo Patiño was censured in 2007 for attempting to manipulate the bond market. Correa's combative stance in defence of Patiño caused his popularity to decline from 76% in April 2007 to 56% by August, where it hovered. The approval ratings of the Constituent Assembly have also been on the decline, dropping from 62% in November 2007 to 38% in February 2008. The primary reason for this drop, according to polls, was the assembly's slow progress in drafting a new constitution. In any event, progress is likely to be slow and divisive. In February 2008, hundreds of citizens from the business-oriented region of Guayaquil, whose mayor Jaime Nebot has emerged as one of Correa's strongest opponents, delivered a declaration of their demands for the constitution, including greater regional autonomy.

The most serious threat to Correa's agenda, however, comes from the destabilising potential of mass mobilisations by Correa's supporters who are frustrated with the slow pace of change and disillusioned by the government's inability to address their immediate needs. In November 2007, Ecuadorians in the Amazonian province of Orellana took to the streets to protest Correa's failure to fulfil promises of increased infrastructure investment. The protesters' tactics quickly escalated from road blockades to seizure of oil installations and bombing of bridges. State-run Petroecuador's oil production dropped by 20% in the following weeks, threatening Ecuador's ability to meet its contractual obligations. Correa declared a state of emergency and sent in the military to quell the protests. The mayor and 22 others were arrested on charges of sedition. Correa also sacked his interior minister and the head of Petroecuador, placing the oil company under the command of Ecuador's navy. The Orellana episode touched off a row between Correa and the Constituent Assembly when AP deputies sought to free the 23 people arrested. Correa threatened to resign, and the Constituent Assembly quickly backed off, but perceptions that Correa governs in an authoritarian manner and ultimately seeks to extend his power through the Constituent Assembly and the new constitution hardened.

Ecuador remains in desperate need of democratic institutions through which its citizens can channel their discontent and seek redress for their grievances. It is unclear whether the Constituent Assembly will be able to build such institutions through a new constitution, which would be Ecuador's twentieth since independence in 1830. The current constitution is only ten years old and, despite language about founding a 'pluricultural' and 'multiethnic' society to incorporate long-excluded sectors, it has failed to bring stability.

Bolivia's fragile federalism

Much like his counterparts in Venezuela and Ecuador, Bolivian President Evo Morales has launched a 'peaceful revolution' that centres on resource nationalisation and 'refounding' the country. An indigenous leader of Bolivia's prominent coca growers' union, Morales appealed to various factions within the country's powerful social protest movement and was instrumental in the massive popular mobilisations that, in June 2005, toppled the country's second president in 20 months. In the ensuing December 2005 presidential elections, Morales's radical populist platform won him 54% of the vote, giving him the strongest mandate of any president since Bolivia's return to democracy in the 1980s. Morales is Bolivia's first indigenous president, and his indigenist agenda has reinvigorated struggles for native sovereignty throughout the region. Rather than being imposed from above, like Chávez's Bolivarian Revolution, Bolivian indigenism has emerged from the masses of the country's long-excluded indigenous majority and takes its cues from grassroots leaders. Morales thus gains legitimacy from his indigenous ties, but also remains beholden to a powerful movement he does not directly control.

Despite having South America's second-largest natural gas reserves, Bolivia remains its poorest nation, with 67% living in poverty and 37% in extreme poverty. There is anger among Bolivia's indigenous peoples over hundreds of years of foreign exploitation of their natural resources. In 2006, Morales deployed troops to the country's gas fields, declaring they would be nationalised, thus forcing foreign companies to renegotiate contracts to give Bolivia a majority stake in all projects. He went on to place operations under the control of the state-run company Yacimientos Petrolíferos Fiscales Bolivianos (YPFB). The move was highly popular among Bolivians, and Morales claims that government control over the economy has risen from 6% when he took office to 20% today. Bolivia's income from gas and oil skyrocketed from $188m in 2001 to $2bn in 2007, when the government budget ran a surplus for the first time in 40 years. With these funds, Morales has invested in popular social programmes, though many of his constituents feel he has not redistributed this wealth to a great enough extent.

The nationalisations, however, made foreign companies wary of investment. The Brazilian state-owned company Petrobras, for example, suspended its Bolivian investments until December 2007. Under-investment and mismanagement also kept YPFB from being able to meet its export obligations to its neighbours, and it may be forced to renegotiate its Argentine contract. Morales hoped to remedy this through what he hailed as an 'all-time record' of investment commitments worth $1.5bn from Brazil, Iran and Venezuela in 2008. Unless Bolivia is able to boost its natural-gas production it will be unable to take full advantage of rising regional gas demands, and Morales will thus miss an important opportunity to garner the resources necessary for his social revolution.

Morales is also struggling to provide what he believes will be a more equitable distribution of resources and political power within Bolivia and seeking to enshrine these principles in a new constitution. Progress on this front has been halting, as Morales has met strong opposition from the wealthier and more mixed-race eastern states of Santa Cruz, Tarija, Pando and Beni. These states form a crescent-shaped region known as the Media Luna, and they have been striving for greater local autonomy, particularly as to land and resource distribution. Bolivia's Constituent Assembly was elected in July 2006 and given a year to draft a new constitution, but in that time it failed to approve a single statute. When the Assembly extended its deadline until 14 December, several indigenous organisations mounted protests, maintaining that the president should have ensured the passage of a new constitution by the deadline and complaining that the Constituent Assembly was not representing their interests. The assembly's slow progress was due, in large part, to opposition efforts to bog down the proceedings by pressing the divisive issue of whether Bolivia's capital should be moved from La Paz to Sucre. Opposition supporters favoured the move while Morales' backers opposed it. Protests prompted the Constituent Assembly to exclude the issue altogether and call a recess.

Failing to reach an accord, on 24 November 2007 delegates from the president's Movement Towards Socialism (MAS) party reconvened the assembly in a military installation and pushed through a draft constitution, despite an opposition boycott. Violent clashes outside the meeting left three dead and 130 injured. The new draft was approved by 136 of the 138 delegates present, well below the necessary two-thirds threshold of the 255-member assembly, yet the Morales government declared that measures needed to be approved by only two-thirds of those present. In the face of another boycott, the Constituent Assembly ratified the new constitution on 9 December with 164 votes. On 28 February 2008, Morales's supporters blocked opposition lawmakers from entering the congressional session, which approved a national referendum on the constitution. The referendum, as well as a vote on whether landholdings should be capped at 5,000 or 10,000 hectares under the new regime, was slated to be held in mid 2008. The opposition, however, refused to accept the new constitution, denouncing the undemocratic manner in which it was approved and threatening to boycott the national referendum. Lacking recourse to the Constitutional Court because all but one justice has resigned or been forced out, the opposition appealed for mediation. This effort, however, was dealt a blow in January 2008 when OAS Secretary General José Miguel Insulza declared that text of the new constitution adhered to democratic principles.

The decision by MAS to muscle through the new constitution fuelled autonomy demands. On 15 December 2007, the governors of the Media Luna region unilaterally declared autonomy and vowed to hold local referendums to ratify their decisions. The first was held in Santa Cruz on 4 May 2008 amidst clashes between pro- and anti-autonomy factions in which dozens were injured and one person killed. Morales denounced the referendum as illegal and his supporters boycotted the vote, leading to a landslide victory for pro-autonomy measures. At the heart of the debate over regional autonomy lies the issue of gas revenues. The gas-rich eastern provinces wish to maintain more control over gas royalties while communities in Bolivia's largely indigenous western highlands want these revenues redistributed. The new constitution would also provide greater political power for the country's 36 indigenous groups, allowing them to control their communities' distribution of land and resources as well as dispensation of justice. On the national level, the constitution would give the federal government greater control over the economy, restrict private landholdings, popularly elect judges, and allow the president to be elected to a second consecutive term. Morales has reached out to his opposition to a certain extent, offering to explore ways in which their demands for regional autonomy would be compatible with the framework of the new constitution. Yet as long as Morales continues to force through reforms that impinge upon the wealth of the Media Luna, such compromise is likely to remain out of reach.

The inability of elected politicians to stop Morales from forcing through reforms unfavourable to the opposition has increasingly led many anti-government protesters to resort to violent tactics, including arson and bombings against pro-government politicians and trade unions. No real threat of a secessionist armed struggle has arisen, but Morales put the military on alert in December 2007, warning that he would deploy troops against 'criminal' autonomists. The president has been cautious about actually engaging the military in violent clashes with protesters – for example, he ordered the army to relinquish control of an airport in Santa Cruz in the face of mounting protests – in hopes of avoiding the fate of Bolivia's last elected president, Gonzalo Sánchez de Lozada, who was toppled following deadly clashes between protesters and the military.

Hugo Chávez has aggravated the Bolivian opposition by vowing to intervene should the 'oligarchy' or its US sympathisers attempt to oust or assassinate the Bolivian president. Chávez and Morales have become staunch allies, joining forces on the Bank of the South, ALBA and a joint oil company, among other ventures. Morales also established diplomatic relations with Iran, which has promised $1bn in investment over the next five years. Bolivia has become heavily dependent on Venezuelan aid, which rivals the United States' contribution of over $120m, and which is used to bankroll Morales's populist initiatives. Chávez has also been instrumental in helping Morales implement his policy of 'zero cocaine but not zero coca'. Venezuela funded the first of two plants to 'industrialise' coca, with the intent of making products such as tea and herbal medicines. Morales, furthermore, has pledged to spend $300,000 to develop legal markets for coca, but this will remain a contentious proposal given that the UN refuses to change its stance on the illegality of coca consumption in any form. Morales's coca policy, which includes expanding Bolivia's legal growing area from 12,000 to 20,000 hectares, has strained relations with the United States. The Bolivian government has put an end to the US-backed forced eradication policies that led to deadly encounters between the government and Morales's coca-growing base of support. Yet Morales insists Bolivia has been vigilant in its efforts to crack down on cocaine trafficking, seizing 431 tonnes of the drug and arresting 4,178 suspected traffickers in 2007.

The United States, for its part, has attempted to maintain working relations with the Morales administration both to further its counter-narcotics aims and to counter Chávez's influence. In September 2007, Washington once again certified Bolivian cooperation on the drug front, enabling the disbursement of $34m in aid. US–Bolivian relations, however, have remained rocky and Morales has repeatedly charged that the United States is attempting to destabilise his government. In January 2008, Morales accused Washington of supporting 'irregular' police intelligence operations in Bolivia, and the ensuing diplomatic row was made worse the following month when a US Embassy official was accused of asking a Fulbright scholar and Peace Corps volunteers to spy on Cubans and Venezuelans in Bolivia. The official was charged with espionage and banished from the country. While US Ambassador Philip Goldberg attempted to repair relations, acknowledging the 'inappropriate' nature of the official's behaviour, Morales accused Goldberg himself of directing a conspiracy against his administration and the new constitution, and threatened to evict both Goldberg and the US Agency for International Development, which he says supports the opposition. The primary threat to the stability of the government, however, is not 'outside agitators' but rather the danger Morales faces from mass protests levied by the far left and far right in Bolivia. He has the difficult task of attempting to bring the opposition back to the bargaining table and into the political process while balancing the demands of his constituents, who are discontented with the slow pace of reform. Having served two years at the helm, Morales has outlasted each of Bolivia's last three leaders, but he is not yet safe from the threat of being toppled by the mass mobilisations he once led.

Peru's extroverted economy

A major earthquake in August 2007 and the extradition of notorious ex-president Alberto Fuijmori from Chile in September did not seem to distract Peru from its steady economic expansion. President Alan García Pérez of the centre-left Partido Aprista Peruano (APRA) began his five-year term in July 2006, his second run after a disastrous tenure from 1985–90. García faces the delicate challenge of proving the effectiveness of his pro-market policies to an electorate that nearly brought to power the leftist, Venezuela-backed Ollanta Humala. With APRA occupying only 36 of the 120 seats in Congress, which was also elected to a five-year term in 2006, García confronted considerable obstacles to passing legislation without building consensus within the fractured party system. As García continued to avoid the short-term, populist fixes that plagued his first term, the Peruvian government found it more difficult to convince the 40% of its population in poverty that it was doing enough to help them. Impoverished indigenous groups, alienated from the central government, shut down roads and cities with heated street protests. García's five-year term is likely to be a balancing act between Peru's macroeconomic successes and its frustrated internal unrest.

Peru is currently proving its economic mettle. The government's 2008 budget still estimates GDP growth at 6.2%, down from 7.2% in 2007 mainly due to the recent earthquake. Peru's inflation rate is the lowest in Latin America, at about 2.3%. Credit-rating agencies have awarded Peru investment-grade status, possibly in response to García's pledge to cut Peru's foreign-debt level to 10% of GDP. Peru owes much of its economic growth in the past two years to the boom in export-commodity prices, especially minerals. Exports were expected to increase by more than 10% in 2007, reaching $26.2bn. The García administration has been promoting the $1bn modernisation of a state-run oil refinery and construction of an export terminal for the Camisea liquefied-natural-gas project. The project is estimated to increase Peru's GDP by 0.5% annually beginning in 2010. In hopes of becoming a net hydrocarbon exporter, Peru has also opened up around 540,000 square kilometres for exploration, yielding discoveries by foreign firms such as Argentina's Plupetrol and France's Perenco. Peru's state oil and gas investment agency, Perupetro, expects between $800m and $1bn in oil and gas investment in 2008.

Mining continues to account for half of all exports and more than 34% of foreign investment, including noteworthy contracts from the United States and China. Copper prices and production continue to increase with growing demand from Asian markets. Increased exploration and development of natural resources, however, has met staunch resistance among indigenous and environmental groups. In its excitement for exploration, the government reneged on plans for protected areas along the coast and in the rainforests of the Amazon. Moreover, some development contracts have encroached upon reserves for indigenous groups, sparking deadly protests between local activists and police. Similarly, the mining industry has met strong resistance from farmers over water rights and from indigenous communities protesting the mines' harmful effects on the environment.

One of Peru's most significant economic successes to date was the passage of a free trade agreement with the United States. Signed in April 2006 under then-president Alejandro Toledo, the Peru Trade Promotion Agreement (PTPA) allows Peruvian goods permanent duty-free access to US markets and opens up Peru's market to most US industrial and agricultural exports. The agreement will significantly expand the market for Peruvian agricultural goods. Although the agreement divided Democrats in the US Congress, who insisted on adding components protecting labour rights and the environment, Congress finally approved the measure in November 2007, a year and a half after it was signed. Detractors in Peru argued that it would only benefit Peru's wealthier coastal residents and that US imports could cripple local industry, leading small farmers to turn to illicit crop production and coca cultivation. Yet the agreement broadly aims to protect United States security interests in Latin America, building a closer economic alliance with Peru to counter the influence of anti-American leaders like Chávez and aiding the war on drugs by opening new markets for legal crops as alternatives to coca leaves. Peru produces about a third of the coca crop globally, second only to Colombia. Previous efforts along these lines have been frustrated, however. The United States' 1991 Andean Trade Preference and Drug Eradication Act (ATPDEA) granted duty-free access to many agricultural exports in Andean countries with an eye towards encouraging farmers to develop crops such as artichokes, coffee and hearts of palm. Aerial herbicide spraying has had little effect on coca production, often simply causing a shift in cultivation to other regions. Despite these measures, coca-leaf production grew approximately 8% from 2005 to 2006, and 92% of this coca is channelled into drug production.

The García administration's National Strategy 2007–11 focused, through the National Commission for Development and Life without Drugs (DEVIDA), on alternative development and the prevention of illicit drug consumption, cultivation and trafficking. However, in response to increased violence, García has taken a hard-line approach to coca production, ordering drastic eradication responses such as bombing cocaine production sites within Peru. In turn, violent groups hired by farmers to protect trafficking routes increased attacks on police, judges and attorneys, killing five police officers in autumn 2007. The groups were likely remnants of the Maoist Shining Path guerrilla movement, which was still mobilised in small numbers in the Apurímac and Ene River Valleys.

García also worked hard to improve relations and expand free trade with members of the Asia-Pacific Economic Cooperation Forum (APEC): Peru will host the annual APEC conference in 2008, recently signed an agreement with Singapore, and is pursuing trade agreements with Australia, Korea, Canada, Mexico and China. García has welcomed Chinese investment in mining, manufacturing, and ports, and has negotiated several preliminary agreements with Chinese President Hu Jintao on the path to a free trade agreement. García was quick to defend China's controversial Taiwan and Tibet policies in the months leading up to the 2008 Beijing Olympics. He also hoped to support China in its negotiations for the de-nuclearisation of North Korea. China is Peru's second biggest trading partner, eclipsed only by the United States.

Despite macroeconomic successes, the Peruvian government laboured to convince the public that it was adequately addressing poverty. In 2006, García promised an 'investment shock' of over $1bn in public investment in one year. García's platform included the transfer of $3.5bn from the federal government to local departments to finance projects in agriculture, infrastructure, healthcare and education. The programmes, however, have achieved little so far. Most progress was made in the coastal areas and in Lima, while rural communities saw little development. Although the overall poverty rate in Peru fell by more than 4% in 2006, the rural provinces of Apurímac and Ayacucho reported a 10% increase, according to a poll by Ipsos Apoyo. In response, peasants turned to leftist alternatives, including those touted by Chávez. García, not surprisingly, opposes Chávez's Bolivarian Revolution and during the 2006 elections condemned the populist president as a 'midget dictator with a big wallet'. Despite the central government's decidedly anti-socialist agenda, Chávez enjoys substantial support among rural and indigenous populations in Peru. Since his establishment of ALBA, pro-Chávez solidarity groups and 'ALBA houses' have proliferated in rural Peru. The governor of Peru's Puno province, near the border with Bolivia, has voiced strong support for Chávez and has threatened to secede from the national government.

Peru's government encountered an unexpected challenge on 15 August 2007 when a magnitude 8.0 earthquake killed over 500 people and injured thousands of others. The quake hit off the coast of Pisco, a port city about 200km south of Lima, and also shook the agricultural centres of Ica, Chincha and Paracas. More than 80,000 Peruvians were displaced, about half of whom lacked title to their homes and possessions, complicating the process of reclaiming lost territory and property. The Peruvian government established a $95m fund to finance reconstruction efforts and received aid from several countries, including the United States and Venezuela. The quake critically damaged the Pan-American Highway, Peru's main transportation artery, which hindered the transport of the region's booming agro-exports. The García administration estimated that the earthquake could reduce economic growth by about 0.5%, with economic losses predicted to reach between $10bn and $20bn. García was criticised for not taking more immediate action, but studies have shown an increase in his approval ratings since the earthquake.

Another test of Peru's democratic institutions came in September 2007 with the extradition of Alberto Fujimori to Peru by a Chilean tribunal. Fujimori faced seven charges of corruption and human-rights violations committed during his ten-year presidency between 1990 and 2000, and a 30-year sentence. Though he was largely credited with curbing rampant inflation and defeating two leftist insurgencies, the Shining Path and the Tupac Amáru Revolutionary Movement, nearly 70,000 Peruvians were killed by guerrillas and soldiers during the counter-insurgency campaign. The corruption charges included bribes to lawmakers and journalists, illegal wire-tapping and the transfer of $15m in state funds to Vladimir Montesinos, the former intelligence chief who is currently serving a 20-year jail sentence. Human-rights charges included Fujimori's complicity in the activities of the Colina Group, a military intelligence squad believed to have executed 25 civilians in 1991 and 1992. Fujimori contends that he was unaware of the group's existence. In a smaller case completed in December 2007, he was sentenced to six years for ordering an illegal search of the apartment of Montesinos's wife in 2000. Despite Fujimori's crimes, he retains a substantial political following. His daughter Keiko Fujimori won a seat in the Peruvian Congress in 2006, receiving three times more votes than any other candidate and emerging as a considerable political force. She is likely to run for president in 2011 on liberal macroeconomic policies and redistributive social programmes with the support of a brand-new political party, Fuerza 2011, uniting *fujimoristas*.

Brazil's successful third way

Brazilian President Luiz Inácio 'Lula' da Silva has been forging a highly effective leftist alternative to the radical populist policies being implemented in many parts of Latin America. Brazil's first working-class president, Lula has been resiliently popular because of the success of his economic policies, which have combined fiscal austerity with targeted social programmes. Under Lula the Brazilian economy has grown steadily, if slowly, with GDP increasing 5.3% in 2007, and the central bank has been fiercely committed to keeping inflation low. Unemployment has decreased while real wages and consumption have risen. Meanwhile, Lula has cut extreme poverty in half through his Bolsa Familia programme, a conditional cash-transfer arrangement which has benefited 11m families. Based on these successes, Lula has become the most popular president in Brazilian history. As of February 2008, a month into his second term, the president's approval rating was 66.8%, its highest level in five years.

Notwithstanding sound economic policies, in 2006 Brazil suffered its worst corruption scandal in a dozen years, leading to the indictment of 40 government officials, including the president's former chief of staff. Various corruption scandals continued to plague the Lula administration, toppling several cabinet members and forcing government ally Renan Calheiros to resign as president of the Senate. Additionally, the administration's credibility was dealt an extreme blow when mismanagement of the country's aviation system, overseen by the Ministry of Defence, led in July 2007 to the worst airline crash in Brazil's history. The credibility of Lula's Workers' Party (PT) has suffered, placing it in a weak position ahead of the October 2008 municipal elections and raising concerns about the 2010 presidential elections. Lacking a clear successor to the popular president, some in the PT have begun to favour amending the constitution to allow Lula to run for a third consecutive term. Lula, however, has rejected the idea, saying that it would be 'playing with democracy'.

Support for the PT could further erode if it is unable to get the president's legislative agenda through Congress. Shifting alliances with the Brazilian Democratic Movement Party (PMDB), upon which the PT depends to secure a majority vote, have made congressional relations difficult and halting. Over 140 accords signed between Brazil and foreign governments, dating back as far as 1994, await legislative approval. In December 2007, the PT failed to secure the votes necessary to approve renewal of a tax bill the government needed to fund $22.5bn of its 2008 budget. While Lula attempted to hike taxes by decree, the opposition challenged this move in the courts. Thus, the president may have difficulty financing the expansion of his Bolsa Familia programme as well as his Accelerated Growth Program (PAC) designed to stimulate Brazil's sluggish growth by spending approximately $252bn on transportation, energy and infra-structure development.

Lula and his party also lost the backing of some of the more radical elements of their constituency, who felt the president's social programmes did not go far enough in addressing Brazil's extreme inequality. In April 2007 the Landless Workers Movement (MST) launched protests in 15 of the country's 27 states and led land occupations in ten others. The MST accused Lula of inflating land-redistribution statistics and appeasing wealthy farmers by distributing only pub-licly held lands. Furthermore, the MST contended that the government's ethanol policy was fuelling agribusiness by encouraging the development of sugar plan-tations, particularly as US investors were buying large tracts and thus pushing up land prices. Indicative of the growing chasm between the MST and the PT, in June 2007 the MST refrained from inviting Lula to speak at their national assembly as they had in the past. Yet while the MST has vowed increased land occupations, their support appeared to be eroding somewhat as the government successfully redistributed more and more land. Fifty MST protesters were met by 400 counter-protesters in the town of Taió in February 2008, marking the first time the MST was directly confronted by opposing demonstrations. Lula, more-over, has been affirmatively attempting to neutralise their accusations. In January and February 2008 alone, he made plans to expropriate 255,000 hectares of land, exceeding the total for all of 2007. The president also announced a follow-on programme to his popular Bolsa Familia, designed to target rural poverty by assisting 38m families by 2010.

Lula has also begun to tackle drug-fuelled crime in Brazil's urban areas. According to the United Nations, 80 tonnes of cocaine enters Brazil each year, and domestic consumption of the drug rose 30% in 2007. Brazil now consumes 15% of the world's cocaine. Lula sent 1,350 soldiers into Rio's *favelas* in June 2007, seeking to wrest power from the drug traffickers that had taken effective control of these slum areas. Two months later he launched a comprehensive $3.3bn national-security plan aimed at restoring order to Brazil's cities in an effort to stem the violence that claims the lives of over 40,000 Brazilians a year.

On the international front, many Brazilians have been frustrated that Hugo Chávez's aggressive oil-funded diplomacy and radical populist rhetoric have eclipsed what they feel is their country's natural leadership role as South America's largest country and economy. Relations between Brazil and Venezuela became particularly strained after Chávez supported Evo Morales's decision to nationalise Bolivian gas fields, in which Brazil had invested heavily and upon which Brazil depends for 50% of its gas. Relations soured further in May 2007 when Chávez harshly rebuked Brazilian senators after they denounced his decision to close the opposition television station RCTV, prompting the senators to stall ratification of Venezuela's entry into Mercosur and leading Chávez to threaten withdrawal from the agreement. But Lula has sought to curtail Venezuelan influence through engagement rather than antagonism, repeatedly voicing support for Venezuela's entrance into Mercosur, and for further economic and energy integration between the two countries. Lula has also endorsed Chávez's democratic credentials, defending Chávez's democratic record at the November 2007 Iberoamerican Summit.

Nevertheless, Brazil's increased spending on arms was most likely due to Venezuela's recent military purchases. Brazilian military commanders insisted that their operational capacity has suffered from lack of investment in new weaponry and technology, compromising the country's 'power of persuasion' and ability to defend its borders. Lula thus announced a 2008 defence budget increasing military spending by over 50%, approaching $5bn. In February 2008, Brazil signed a strategic alliance with France, providing for the purchase of French arms and the transfer of technology so that Brazil can one day manufacture its own weapons. While the likelihood of direct military conflict remains low, increased Brazilian arms spending has stoked fears of a regional arms race.

Lula's main weapon for offsetting Chávez's regional influence, however, has not been military but energy policy. While Chávez has secured allies with preferential oil deals, Lula has countered with ethanol diplomacy. In August 2007, Lula and Chávez simultaneously campaigned for energy accords in the region, with Chávez courting South American allies while Lula travelled to Mexico and Central America to sign agreements furthering biofuel development. Brazil's ethanol production has also strengthened its relationship with the United States. The Bush administration sees ethanol production both as a way to decrease US dependence on foreign oil and to counterbalance Chávez's oil-driven influence, particularly in Central America and the Caribbean. Lula has also made trips to Europe and Africa to encourage ethanol investments. Prospects for Brazil's future energy policy were enormously boosted in November 2007 when Lula announced the discovery of massive oil reserves off the coast of Rio de Janeiro, which may allow Brazil to become a major oil exporter in the next five to ten years. In marked contrast to Chávez, who seeks to keep oil prices above $100 a barrel, Lula announced Brazil's intention eventually to join OPEC to fight for low oil prices on behalf of poverty-stricken, energy-deprived nations. Via ethanol and oil policy and its pragmatic approach to leadership in foreign affairs, Brazil is likely to garner growing regional influence in coming years.

Argentina's uneasy populist experiment

Argentine First Lady Cristina Fernández de Kirchner, a lawyer and senator, was elected president on 28 October 2007, in large measure due to her husband Nestor Kirchner's considerable success in guiding the Argentine economy out of crisis after its 2001 collapse. During his presidency, the country's economy grew by over 8% each year, fuelled by strong exports and high levels of government spending. Since 2002 unemployment has dropped from 21% to 10%, and poverty has decreased from over 50% to 27%, making Kirchner remarkably popular among Argentina's poor. Kirchner, furthermore, pre-paid Argentina's debt to the IMF, freeing the country from the financial institution that many Argentines blamed for their economic hardship.

Kirchner's populist economic policies, however, have created imbalances in the country's economy. Inflation has been steadily rising, hitting the poor who comprise Kirchner's key support base hardest, but also eating away at the incomes of the middle class. Support for the Kirchner administration eroded somewhat as the government was accused of tampering with inflation statistics, declaring inflation was only 8–10% while independent economists estimated it as twice as high. Purchasing power significantly decreased, and citizens frustrated with the government's refusal to acknowledge it held periodic protests outside the National Statistics Institute (Indec). Argentina also faced a looming energy crisis partly due to a price freeze that has increased energy demand while restricting investment in the sector. Argentines pay only 60% as much for energy as their neighbours. Bolivia's inability to meet its export contract with Argentina worsened the situation, and Argentina has faced shortages in the colder months, leading to blackouts and factory lay-offs.

Mounting economic problems and spiralling crime eroded Kirchner's support among the middle class, and in mid 2007 his allies lost several key municipal elections. Buenos Aires, for instance, elected its first centre-right mayor. Kirchner also faced disillusionment within his base, which triggered massive strikes in 2007. Protesting teachers in his home state of Santa Cruz forced out their governor, a Kirchner ally, and threw eggs at the visiting minister of social development, Kirchner's sister. The opposition accused the president of ruling in an authoritarian manner, noting that he had passed more decrees than Congress had passed laws. The administration also suffered from a series of scandals in 2007, tarnishing the image of rectitude Kirchner had worked hard to project in contrast with the corrupt administration of Carlos Menem in the 1990s.

Nevertheless, Kirchner remained relatively popular, with approval ratings over 50%, and polls indicated that he could have won the October presidential elections. On 2 July 2007, however, he announced that he would step aside for his wife to run. At the time, Fernández was polling about ten percentage points behind her husband, but observers speculated the couple had made the decision for her to run so as to alternate presidential terms and circumvent Argentina's limit of two consecutive four-year terms. Kirchner will be eligible for re-election in 2011. Fernández sought to strike a balance between continuing her husband's popular economic policies and making the changes Argentines felt were still necessary, using the slogan 'change is just beginning' and focusing her campaign on building her international credentials. Many Argentines, particularly among the middle and upper classes, felt their country needed to distance themselves from the firebrand Chávez and strengthen relations with the United States and Europe. Kirchner had forged strong relations with Chávez, as Venezuela bought some $5bn of Argentine bonds, which Argentina could not sell on the international bond market after its 2002 default. Venezuela's economic assistance helped Kirchner pay off the country's IMF debt. Venezuela has also sold fuel to Argentina under preferential terms. Unsurprisingly, Kirchner had a somewhat antagonistic relationship with the United States. In March 2007, Kirchner allowed Chávez to hold a counter-rally during President Bush's visit to Uruguay. When US officials criticised the move, Kirchner accused the United States of having 'forgotten about Argentina' when the country needed financial help. Many Argentines, however, hoped that the more conciliatory Fernández could repair relations with the United States as well as international lenders and investors. To strengthen her international credentials, Kirchner sent his wife on a series of state visits. Additionally, the president helped shore up her support among the poor with a pre-election spending spree of $4.44bn in September 2007.

Fernández's opposition remained fragmented, failing to effectively capitalise on the discontent of many Argentines over crime, corruption and inflation. Ahead of the October elections, 62% of voters believed corruption was on the rise, 76% that insecurity was growing, and 80% that inflation was increasing. Fernández's main competitors were former Economy Minister Roberto Lavagna, whose campaign slogan was 'stop inflation, vote Lavagna', and Congresswoman Elisa Carrió, who campaigned against corruption. While these candidates attempted to target the areas in which the Kirchner administration, and thus the Fernández campaign, was weak, the opposition failed to band together to mount a concerted campaign or provide an appealing alternative. Fernández won an impressive first-round victory, garnering 45% of the vote in a field of 14 candidates and becoming the first woman to be elected president of Argentina. Kirchner, meanwhile, angled for the presidency of his Justicialista Party (PJ).

Fernández was sworn in on 10 December 2007, and less than a week after she took office hopes for better relations with Washington were dashed. US prosecutors indicted four Venezuelans and one Uruguayan, charging them with being undisclosed agents of a foreign government operating in the United States. The defendants were linked to a cover-up of an alleged attempt by the Chávez government to funnel nearly $800,000 to Fernández's campaign in a suitcase belonging to a Venezuelan intercepted in Argentina. The allegations drove Argentina closer to Venezuela, as Fernández and Chávez vehemently denounced the incident as a US fabrication. Fernández restricted her contact with the US ambassador to Argentina. In March 2008, US Secretary of State Condoleezza Rice, in turn, refrained from visiting Argentina on her Southern Cone diplomatic trip. While many Argentines had hoped Fernández would improve relations with European investors, the country's new economy minister quickly announced he would not renegotiate the $26bn of debt owed to international investors who had refused Argentina's 2005 debt restructuring. Additionally, the minister indicated that renegotiating the $7bn owed the Paris Club was not an 'urgent' priority. Argentina is thus likely to continue to be heavily dependent on Venezuelan bond purchases as well as short on overall foreign investment.

Fernández also declined to end her husband's policy of promulgating unrealistically favourable inflation figures. In January 2008, the Argentine government announced inflation had only been 8.5% in 2007, prompting further protests outside the Indec offices. While Fernández suggested changing the methodology used to calculate inflation, as of May 2008 it had not been done, and the IMF has threatened to lodge a formal complaint against Indec. In an attempt to mitigate the country's economic problems, on 11 March 2008 Fernández increased agricultural-export taxes, sparking weeks of strikes and protests by farmers. Fernández refused to lift the taxes, saying that they were needed to facilitate redistribution from wealthy farmers to Argentina's poor. Yet the poor she purported to be benefiting could end up suffering from food shortages. Fernández also raised export taxes on the energy sector in hopes of curbing the country's looming energy crisis, and signed energy accords with Venezuela to protect the country in the event of shortfalls from Bolivia.

Ultimately, Fernández faces difficult policy choices. To stem mounting inflation and energy crises, she will need to cut government spending and lift price controls, yet these are the very policies that made her husband so popular and helped her win the presidency. Fernández's underprivileged support base would undoubtedly be unhappy with such changes in the short term. If she continues down the populist road, however, the poor will suffer, as rising inflation and energy shortages are hardest to bear for the most vulnerable sectors of the populace.

Mexico: Calderón's statesmanship
Since taking office in late 2006, centre-right president Felipe Calderón has become widely popular, enjoying an approval rating of 66%. This is a credit to Calderón's

political skill, given that he was elected by a margin of less than 1% in the bitterly divisive presidential elections of July 2006. The president's popularity has been buoyed by the strength of the Mexican economy. While overall growth has been sluggish, in 2007 Mexicans benefited from significant increases in job creation and foreign investment, and for the first time Mexico's inflation rate was lower than that of the United States. Though Calderón has generally advocated conservative economic policies, he has also eased the financial burdens of Mexico's poor with, for example, price freezes on tortillas and fuel. Calderón's popularity was also attributable to his remarkable ability to bridge the country's political divides. Calderón's opponent in the 2006 elections, Andrés Manuel López Obrador, has been a polarising influence, continuing in his refusal to concede defeat and attempting to undermine the Calderón administration by launching a nominal shadow government. Yet the president has reached out to his opposition, promoting 'national reconciliation'. Calderón's predecessor, Vicente Fox, failed to meet high expectations in large part because he was unable to get Congress to approve his legislative agenda. In contrast, Calderón has managed to induce Congress to pass long-overdue pension, tax and judicial reforms by forging alliances with opposition parties.

Calderón's energy-reform proposal met less success. Mexico's state-run oil company, Pemex, has faced steadily declining output and is in desperate need of investment to fund oil exploration if the country is to remain a net oil exporter in coming years. Mexico is currently the world's sixth-largest oil producer, and Pemex revenues finance 40% of the government's budget. In order to secure the funds Pemex requires, Calderón suggested opening the company up to private investment, currently prohibited by the constitution. Many Mexicans vehemently opposed the idea and consider keeping Pemex out of foreign hands an issue of national pride and sovereignty. Capitalising on this sentiment, López Obrador re-emerged on the national scene, leading thousands in protest against the private investment plan. His Democratic Revolution Party (PRD), however, has limited traction due to its own internal squabbles. López Obrador's refusal to acknowledge the legitimacy of the Calderón government has threatened to split the PRD between members who wish to work with the government and those who seek to stand in radical opposition. These tensions came to a head when the March 2008 elections for party leadership degenerated into mutual accusations of election fraud by López Obrador ally Alejandro Encinas and his more moderate competitor, Jesus Ortega.

In addition to facing the relatively loyal opposition of the more radical elements of the PRD, the Calderón administration has also suffered from militant attacks by the leftist People's Revolutionary Army (ERP). The ERP engaged in a series of bombings of Pemex oil pipelines in July and September 2007. The guerrillas vowed to continue their attacks until the government released three

ERP activists the group contended were detained by the Fox administration for involvement in violent protests in Oaxaca in 2006. The Mexican government, however, insisted the activists were not in their custody. The bombings, meanwhile, not only disrupted Pemex's already low production, but also undermined the security efforts at the heart of Calderón's domestic policy.

Soon after taking office in December 2006, Calderón launched the largest counter-narcotics offensive in Mexican history, deploying 30,000 troops to combat the drug-related violence that claims the lives of over 2,000 Mexicans per year. Mexican drug gangs began to increase in prominence after the Colombian Cali and Medellín cartels were dismantled in the 1990s. (In 2000, just two-thirds of the cocaine in US markets travelled through Mexico, compared with 90% today.) Calderón's offensive scored enormous successes over the course of 2007, leading to the arrests of over 20,000 people involved with drug trafficking or organised crime, including several top members of drug gangs and their paramilitary armies. In October 2007, Mexico made the largest cocaine seizure in history. A total of 45 tonnes were confiscated in 2007. US officials credited the effort for sparking price hikes in US cocaine markets. The Calderón administration also sought to purge Mexico of corrupt law enforcement elements, and in June 2007 the president removed all 284 federal police chiefs to investigate their ties to drug gangs. Successes in disrupting the operations of these drug gangs, however, led to a spike in violence as groups competed for access to remaining trafficking routes. Additionally, the narco-traffickers engaged in brutal reprisals, leaving beheaded bodies in public spaces and assassinating high-level officials, including National Police Chief Edgar Eusebio Millán Gómez in May 2008.

Calderón's counter-drug initiative led Mexico and the United States to forge closer ties in the realm of security. In March 2007, Calderón and Bush established the Mérida Initiative, in which they agreed to increase US–Mexican security cooperation in the spirit of taking 'shared responsibility' for combating Mexico's drug scourge. Bush officially launched the initiative in October 2007, announcing his intention to provide Mexico with $1.4bn over three years for counter-narcotics training and weaponry. Bush requested an initial disbursement of $500m in counter-narcotics aid for 2008, a dramatic increase from the $47m per year allocated for Mexico in 2007.

Despite strengthening ties with the United States in the counter-drug arena, Calderón maintained his independence from the US government in other respects. In June 2007, for instance, Calderón did not hesitate to rebuke US legislators for their failure to pass immigration reform. The Mexican president characterised it as a 'grave error' and warned it would be detrimental to border security insofar as, lacking legal avenues for migration, Mexicans would be encouraged to cross into the United States illegally. Nor has Calderón's close relationship with Washington kept him from forging closer ties to radical leftist governments in the region. The president restored diplomatic relations with Cuba and Venezuela, and in January 2008 he restructured Cuba's $400m debt to Mexico. Calderón's talent for bridging ideological divides may help him exert a unifying and moderating influence in regional politics as he has done at home.

Nicaragua: Ortega's calculated inconsistency

When the former revolutionary Daniel Ortega became president of Nicaragua in January 2007, he did so with only a 38% popular mandate. By the hundredth day of his administration, 50.4% of the population saw 'no hope' for Ortega's government, and 65.4% either did not support him at all or supported him with hesitation. The lack of confidence in the president's leadership came, in part, from his association with the Sandinista National Liberation Front (FSLN)'s Marxist government of the 1980s, which once held up to Nicaragua the promise of economic development through a vehemently anti-US socialist system, but which left power in 1990 with pocketfuls of national wealth and state assets. It also came from a general scepticism toward the Nicaraguan central government, which has been unable, at least since the country's liberalisation in 1990, to address the country's intense poverty, lack of resources and sluggish economic growth. In the year and a half after his inauguration, Ortega walked a fine line between populist development politics and a strategy of large-scale international investment and diplomacy, while his sometimes scorching anti-American rhetoric seemed to be polarising an already divided support base.

Domestically, Ortega struggled to boost his opinion ratings, most notably through populist reforms. On 30 November 2007, he promulgated a national network of Citizen Power Councils. As decentralised barrio-based organisations, they were intended to encourage participatory democracy and build consensus among civil society, NGOs and national and local government. Ortega's hope was that they would serve as an arm of the executive branch, helping to coordinate administrative efforts. The councils have been highly controversial: the Supreme Court called them 'illegal, illegitimate, and non-existent', and numerous detractors suggested that Ortega created them to build support for questionable administrative decisions, including the appointment of his wife, Rosario Murillo, as executive spokesperson and chief of staff. There was also fear that Ortega would use the councils to maintain effective personal or FSLN power when his term expired. Whatever his intentions, the councils were distinctly populist, along the lines of Hugo Chávez's Local Public Planning Councils. Less controversially, Ortega undertook to build new hospitals, to develop infrastructure in Managua, and to initiate a 'Zero Hunger Program' that aimed to raise 75,000 families out of poverty in five years. Thus far, however, his policies do not seem to have had the desired impact. In October 2007, his popular support was down to 28% and in March 2008 it had dwindled to 21%.

In his year and a half in office, Ortega has pursued what has been labelled an 'indiscriminate' foreign-policy agenda. On one hand, he aligned himself closely with Cuba and Venezuela. In a speech on 26 September 2007, he expressed solidarity with the Castro regime in the face of the United States' long-term embargo, lambasting 'global imperialist capitalism' and criticising Bush as the steward of the 'most impressive tyranny of humanity'. He also supported Chávez's attempt at constitutional reforms in 2007. In turn, Venezuela agreed to give Nicaragua $600m in development assistance and to forgive $31.8m in Nicaraguan debt. Moreover, as part of ALBA, Venezuela pledged $250m to Nicaragua for a new oil refinery, which will process 150,000 barrels of Venezuelan oil daily, in addition to a petroleum plant and affordable housing. In 2007, Venezuelan oil sales under ALBA totalled 2m barrels, at $135m. On the other hand, Ortega agreed to renew an IMF lending programme and to uphold CAFTA-DR in the face of stiff criticism from opponents in the National Assembly. He also welcomed Brazilian and other Latin American investors in the construction, banking, textile and energy sectors. These attitudes were consistent with Foreign Minister Samuel Santos López's insistence that Nicaragua does not want to pick one economic or political model and denigrate all others. The goal for the administration is to maintain 'relationships of sincere friendship with the USA' and throughout the Americas.

The Nicaraguan government showed surprising commitment to the US-led drug war in 2007 and 2008. In *Operation Gladiator*, Nicaraguan authorities confiscated 2,000kg of cocaine from a transport boat off the Pacific coast. In 2007, authorities seized 23 tonnes of cocaine, 82kg of heroin and $6m in cash. They arrested nearly 2,000 people connected with international drug rings, including 115 foreign nationals, and dismantled 14 drug-smuggling groups. Among Nicaraguans, there has been unexpected popular support for anti-drug policies; polls and surveys conducted in March 2008 indicated that 54.6% believed that police anti-drug efforts had had positive effects. In December 2007, however, Ortega lectured Colombian President Alvaro Uribe on conflict resolution, saying it was time to 'put an end to the fight in the only country remaining in Latin America with a conflict'. Then, in March, when the Colombian military began raids into Ecuador to hunt members of FARC, Ortega severed diplomatic relations with Colombia, calling the foray an act of 'political terrorism'.

Beyond the Western Hemisphere, Nicaragua cultivated several eyebrow-raising diplomatic ties. In June 2007 Ortega spoke of an 'undefeatable' unity between Iran and Nicaragua, based on common ideals of 'independence, peace and justice'. In autumn, Iran opened a diplomatic mission in Managua, naming Ismael Pour as chief of mission. At the end of 2007, Ortega waived visa regulations for Iranian and Syrian diplomats and foreign service officers. In the past year, Nicaragua and Iran have further collaborated on trade deals, exchanging agricultural exports for oil and alternative-energy resources. Iran also agreed to fund a $350m seaport, five dairy processors, four hydroelectric plants, and 10,000 low-income homes in Nicaragua. Ortega and North Korean President Kim Jong Il also restored relations in the past year. Ortega lauded Kim's 'military-first' policy as a symbol of the country's indefatigable independence and as a statement of national sovereignty in the face of international pressure against his government. The two states concluded limited free-trade agreements, and North Korea named an ambassador to Nicaragua.

These budding relationships were evidence of Nicaragua's increasing alignment with extra-hemispheric strategic interests, and they set many observers in Washington on edge. Given Washington's anti-terrorism commitment, Ortega's invitation to Iranian President Mahmoud Ahmadinejad was, for many US policymakers, a step in the wrong direction. Nicaraguans also had reservations. The Nicaraguan newspaper *La Prensa* noted that Ortega's courting the 'bellicose axis' of Venezuela, Iran and North Korea had aggravated tensions with Colombia, Costa Rica, Honduras and Mexico. In an apparent departure from his anti-establishment 'strongman' stance and a June 2007 denunciation of the UN as having 'run its course', Ortega made a bid for a Nicaraguan to assume the 2009 UN General Assembly presidency. In March, Nicaragua won the support of the Latin American and Caribbean Group, and in June it won the UN post. Ortega named Rev. Miguel D'Escoto Brockmann, a former foreign minister, to take the position. The United States, though it energetically and successfully precluded Venezuela from winning a UN Security Council seat in 2006, did little to resist less-powerful Nicaragua's move for the less-powerful General Assembly post.

Overall, Ortega seemed to be navigating the range of Western Hemisphere ideological currents quite deftly. Foreign Minister López noted that Nicaragua wanted to keep good relations with both Venezuela and the United States as 'a very practical, realist and objective matter; it is not something of an ideological nature'. Given Ortega's small popular mandate, it is indeed in his country's best interest to position his government favourably with both countries. But to do this, as many of Ortega's opponents in the Nicaraguan National Assembly have pointed out, the president would do well to quiet his anti-American and anti-capitalist rhetoric. As of mid 2008, the prudent course appeared to be to encourage the steady flow of US and European aid and investment.

Cuba's unconvincing regime change

The end of Fidel Castro's half-century rule in Cuba came on 19 February 2008. Following intestinal surgery in 2006, Fidel had placed his brother Raúl in temporary control of the government, in what was the first major interruption in Fidel's administration since his revolutionary movement came to power in 1959. Having been re-elected to the National Assembly in January 2008, Fidel wrote in his resignation letter: 'I will not aspire to or accept the post of President of the Council of State and Commander-in-chief'. This time, it seems, Fidel has stepped down for good.

In the five years following the Soviet collapse, the Cuban economy contracted by 35%. In response, Fidel Castro and a team of reform-minded economists led by Finance Minister Carlos Lage instituted a gradualist programme of economic revision. This 'Special Period' opened up the island to foreign tourists and investors, and licensed farmers and entrepreneurs to create their own markets. It also permitted exchange in US dollars, which freed up currency markets and encouraged remittances from Cuban expatriates. At the turn of the twenty-first century, once the economy had begun to stabilise and grow, Fidel terminated the 'Special Period' and started a counter-reform to shore up the socialist state. In 2002 Fidel pushed through a constitutional amendment, backed by a dubious popular referendum, declaring the socialist system 'irrevocable' in Cuba. The government immediately began cracking down on dissenters, arresting 75 opponents and handing them long prison sentences.

Castro followed this move with a financial austerity programme that consolidated the Central Bank and pared down the Ministry of Finance. In July 2003, the government outlawed the US dollar, substituting the Cuban convertible peso. A brief financial downturn following this reform lowered confidence in the government's ability to handle fiscal policy; it also demonstrated to US policymakers that, whatever the 1990s may have suggested, Fidel Castro had no intention of loosening his grip. These apprehensions were confirmed when, in 2004, the Castro administration forced foreign-owned industries to form joint ventures with the Cuban government or risk expulsion. A similar piece of legislation the following year revoked entrepreneurial licenses from several thousand domestic business owners, eliminating half the country's private sector. Leading up to Fidel's retirement, the Cuban government instituted a sweeping programme intended to stimulate the country's weak economy and to increase the power of the socialist state. This, and amplified anti-US rhetoric, suggested that the Cuban government was tightening its grip as Castro prepared to leave the political stage.

It remains to be seen whether this reassertion of socialism will persist in the post-Fidel era. Five days after Fidel's resignation, the National Assembly selected the younger Castro as interim president and defence minister for 50 years – to fill the power vacuum. Many international observers had expected Lage to win the nomination and held out hopes that his appointment would facilitate speedier economic reforms. In the event, the decision to elevate Raúl, which sidestepped many of the assembly's qualified and reform-minded younger candidates, indicated that the old guard of party 'historicos' was still largely in control of the Cuban state.

With Raúl in power, continuity can be expected for at least three to five years. While Raúl is not the charismatic and radical revolutionary that his 'irreplaceable' brother was, neither is he the great liberaliser – the 'Gorbachev of Cuba' – that democratic states, in particular the United States, would have hoped for. Since taking office, he has pushed through several limited economic reforms, streamlining the planning bureau to make it more efficient and revising the federal wage system to raise the standard of living for Cuban workers. In March 2008, he authorised farmers to purchase seeds and fertiliser and to lease uncultivated land from the state to boost the current-account balance, which remains in steep deficit due to estimated annual food imports of $2bn. The younger Castro has also agreed to renew licences for small businesses, but the legislature has made the licensing process far too complex for most applicants to navigate. The 100,000–150,000 private business licenses granted between mid 2007 and mid 2008 covered less than 3% of Cuba's workforce. Raúl proposed legislation granting Cubans permission to travel freely, to rent their homes, to buy and sell titled property, and to purchase automobiles without special government authorisation. In addition, he allowed computers (though not Internet service), mobile telephones and media players to be purchased privately. But genuine structural liberalisation remained far off. The new president stated in his inaugural address that any major policy shifts would 'preserve the role of the state and the predominance of socialist property'. With Raúl Castro in power – and his brother still alive – change will indeed come gradually.

The younger Castro continued building relations with the Latin American left – in particular, Nicaragua, Bolivia, Ecuador and Venezuela. In 2007, Chávez sent Cuba 92,000 barrels of oil daily, in addition to $1.5bn in development assistance. Trade with Venezuela, moreover, helped to boost GDP growth in Cuba, which crested above 10% in 2005 and remained around 6.5% in 2008. Under Venezuela's ALBA programme, the younger Castro and Chávez agreed to a barter deal, whereby Cuba will pay for Venezuelan oil and industrial exports with medical services, bananas and sugar. Since Raúl took office, he has also strengthened ties with President Calderón of Mexico. In March, Mexican Foreign Secretary Patricia Espinosa met Cuban Foreign Minister Felipe Pérez Roque. They agreed to normalise relations, strained since then President Vicente Fox temporarily closed the Mexican mission in Havana in 2004 over disputes relating to Cuba's human-rights practices. Mexico also agreed to restructure $400m of Cuba's debt. Outside the hemisphere, Raúl has been deepening ties with China, which maintained its position as Cuba's second-largest trading partner in 2007. He also began talks with the United Arab Emirates, whose state-owned Dubai Ports World is slated to make a $250m overhaul of Cuba's port at Mariel.

Despite Cuba's recent transition, the United States has remained inflexible in its policy, showing no signs of removing the 40-year-old trade embargo against the island. In fact, the most recent shift in US policy was towards greater severity, as Bush instituted measures to 'hasten the end of Cuba's dictatorship' in 2004. These included tightening economic sanctions, stiffer travel restrictions, and limitations on remittances sent to Cuba. The United States also dedicated $59m to bolster democracy-building programmes and civil-society organisations in Cuba. To make bilateral matters even testier, Venezuela and Cuba demanded that Luis Posada Carriles – a former CIA operative convicted of immigration fraud in the United States, allegedly connected to an anti-Castro terrorism campaign, including an assassination plot against Fidel Castro, and released in 2007 from prison – be extradited. But US courts have stalled, straining already tense relations. Moreover, for many Latin Americans, the United States' hesitancy called into question its multilateral commitment to combating terrorism in the Western Hemisphere.

On the day of Raúl Castro's inauguration, US Secretary of State Condoleezza Rice urged the Cuban state to use this opportunity to begin a peaceful transition by 'releasing all political prisoners, respecting human rights and creating a clear pathway towards free and fair elections'. Until that happened, the Bush administration would almost certainly maintain the embargo, lest it 'send a poor message about US toleration both of Cuba's patterns of unsavoury behaviour and its totalitarian system'. Although Washington is indeed interested in building democratic institutions on the island, it will probably refrain from attempting to impose liberal reforms directly. The future of US policy toward Cuba depends in large part upon the upcoming US presidential elections. The Republican candidate John McCain said that he would not extend aid or drop the embargo unless Cuba made a dramatic shift. Democratic candidate Barack Obama suggested lifting travel bans, offering incentives for the Cuban government to democratise, and engaging Cuban leaders without preconditions.

Reacting to pressure from European leaders to begin a democratic shift, Raúl Castro agreed to sign covenants under the UN Universal Declaration of Human Rights in February 2008. Whether or not he follows through with the commitments stipulated in the agreements will largely determine whether Cuba can expect substantive change from their new president. The early signals were unclear at best. On 15 February 2008, Raúl freed four long-serving political prisoners. Yet a week later Cuban courts dealt another prison sentence to a dissenter cited for 'dangerousness'. Human-rights observers estimated that there were 200 or more political prisoners in Cuba's penitentiary system. Cuba's January 2008 parliamentary elections were no less discouraging. In a typical Cuban fait accompli, 614 candidates contested – and, of course, won – 614 National Assembly seats. Yet the 95% voter turnout suggested that the Cuban people, if not their government, were more than ready for a *Cuba libre.*

Turbulence in Haiti

The past year was one of mixed blessings for the Western Hemisphere's poorest and politically weakest state. Haitian President Rene Préval made significant progress in forming a coalition in the central government and stabilising a state that has been persistently dysfunctional. However, the island was rocked by the growing global food crisis, and showed signs of potential breakdown. Although the Brazilian-led UN Stabilisation Mission (MINUSTAH) made headway in curtailing the brutal gang-related violence in the cities, the mission does not seem close to withdrawal. Head of Mission Edmond Mulet said that Haiti needed an effective police force of at least 22,000 members before the UN can leave; its strength is currently 8,000.

In February 2006, in a controversial election overseen by UN peacekeepers, Préval was chosen as Haiti's first president since the bloody coup that overthrew Jean Bertrand Aristide in 2004. In April 2006, legitimate parliamentary elections ushered in a new central government. Préval laboured to build political consensus between his own party, the Front for Hope, and five other major parties. During 2007 the government cracked down on corruption, sacking a number of state officials. Most notably, on 6 June 2007, a Haitian court indicted Franck Ciné, chief executive officer of HaiTel, Haiti's leading telecommunication's company, and three key stockholders in Société Caribéenne de Banque, for fraud and expropriation of funds during the bank's collapse. The main challenge, however, remained security. Beginning in February 2007, the 9,000-strong MINUSTAH force, in coordination with the Haitian National Police (PNC), undertook an offensive against criminal gangs around Haiti's major cities, focusing on Cité Soleil, a notorious slum north of Port-au-Prince. In addition to killing many of the cities' top gang leaders in heavy fire-fights during neighbourhood raids, the force arrested more than 700 gang members. Aside from a spate of extra-judicial lynchings in July 2007, Haiti's cities remained relatively stable after the end of the push, as kidnappings and targeted attacks on UN troops declined. But many prisons were filled beyond capacity, and at least two threatened to collapse completely. Should that occur, MINUSTAH and the PNC would likely lose what little ground they have gained, as gang leaders and other criminals flood back into circulation. Neither the UN nor the Haitian government has adequately dealt with the poverty and lawlessness underpinning the criminality of Haiti's marginal communities.

Haiti has also been particularly hard-hit by the emerging global food crisis. Food prices rose 40% in 12 months, against a core inflation rate of 8.5%. Some 78% of the population is classified as extremely poor – that is, living on less than $2 per day – and those people have had to limit their diets to scarce cereals and, disturbingly, cakes of mud, oil and sugar. Some Haitian farmers had to sell off property and assets to feed their families, and many consumed their seed stores, which will likely lead to a more difficult recovery next year. Estimates place unemployment at 50–70%, although the country's extensive informal sector complicates these figures. The food crisis also stimulated a wave of emigration: the US Coast Guard apprehended 972 unauthorised Haitian migrants between October 2007 and April 2008, up from 376 in the same period in 2006.

The food crisis sparked riots in several Haitian cities in March and April 2008. As of May 2008, 20 Haitians and one Nigerian UN peacekeeper had been killed, and a mob of several thousand people smashed the front gate of the Presidential Palace in Port-au-Prince before they were dispersed by UN troops firing tear gas and rubber bullets. Looting and riots kept food supplies from getting off the docks in port cities, and in one instance, a group plundered a UN warehouse holding emergency hurricane food stores. Préval urged the country to avoid violence and authorised food subsidies that would cut the cost of rice by 15%. He also encouraged US and European leaders to change their biofuel policies, arguing that increased demand for corn used for ethanol production had driven up prices. The UN pledged to distribute 8,000 tonnes of food in Haiti through the World Food Programme and UNICEF. In April, MINUSTAH began allocating 14 tonnes of grain in Port-au-Prince. The OAS also agreed to supply 400 tonnes of rice, and the World Bank made a grant to reduce the burden of increasing food prices.

Whether Préval's government can withstand the pressures of the hunger crisis, political incapacity and insecurity is debatable. There was talk among Haitian citizens of 'rising up' to change the situation. Aristide, having taken leave of the island in 2004, seemed to be looking for an opportunity to return as pressure against the Préval administration rose. On 12 April, 16 of the 27 senators in the Haitian National Assembly voted to dismiss Prime Minister Jacques Edouard Alexis, demanding that Préval replace him with someone 'competent'. Such disruptions underscored the fragility of Préval's coalition. If present conditions persist, Haiti may face a return to the political turbulence from which it has suffered relentlessly in previous years.

A new beginning?

The preoccupations of the Bush administration in other parts of the world and consequent inattention to Latin America (save for counter-narcotics), US policies perceived as aggressive and reckless (exemplified by the Iraq War), and Chávez's anti-American oil diplomacy and contagious populism have unquestionably caused a pronounced diminution of the United States' once-dominant influence in Latin America. But there remain strong and important American partners, such as Colombia, Peru and Chile, whose President Michelle Bachelet rejected Chávez's offer of subsidised gasoline for Santiago's hobbled public transportation system in November 2007. Moreover, even leaders sharing Chávez's leftist populist bent have begun to apprehend the risks to political stability and economic integrity of fully adopting his policies. Chávez himself has lost both political traction in Venezuela due to the under-performance of his economic measures, and some persuasive power in the region. For these reasons, Lula's third way, which involves affirmatively maintaining an independent foreign policy rather than overtly spurning Washington, appears to be emerging as the more attractive political model for Latin American governments. Should it take firmer hold, the region on the whole would be expected to merely maintain or only slowly increase the distance from the United States it has established over the last several years. But Bush will be gone in January 2009. Depending on who is elected as the next US president in November 2008, that prognosis could change.

Thus, while an era of US hegemony in Latin America appears to have ended, any new American administration would be expected to make a serious effort to recoup American leverage. Both Republicans and Democrats recognise that China is interested in making geopolitical inroads into Latin America, and that further erosion of American influence could make that easier. Should McCain prevail, continued strong support for the 'war' on drugs, reluctance to alter Cuba policy and stasis on immigration policy would be likely, with a push for liberalised trade – for example, the US–Colombia FTA – the probable avenue of major policy revision. Should Obama triumph, policy on Cuba and counter-narcotics could see significant revision via, respectively, more energised efforts to integrate illegal workers, more 'carrots' to Havana to induce reform, and greater interest in demand-side measures. Although congressional Democrats have blocked the US–Colombia FTA over human rights and domestic economic concerns, those could ease sufficiently after the election to permit its passage.

More broadly, Obama would be expected to work hard to rehabilitate America's tarnished image abroad, with greater multilateralism and respect for international law and consensus, while McCain would be expected to make earnest, if less intense and resolute, attempts to do so. Whoever wins, Washington's concern for and attention to the region seems bound to increase. To a greater or lesser degree, US policy is likely to reinforce the constraints on anti-American populism reflected in an evolving regional preference for Lula's pragmatism over Chávez's antagonism.

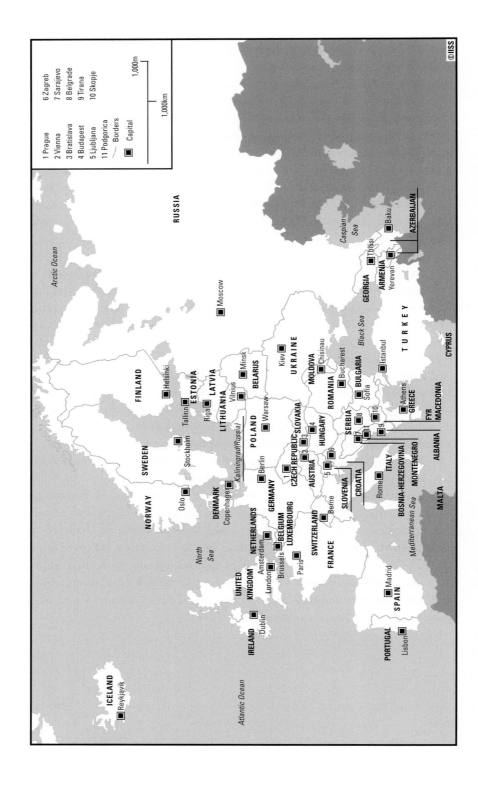

4 Europe

European countries were largely preoccupied by economic and domestic issues in the year to mid 2008. All were affected by the difficulties in international credit markets that originated in the United States. In France, President Nicolas Sarkozy made little headway in his ambitious programme to reform the economy, and the public was transfixed for some time by his private life. In Germany, Chancellor Angela Merkel consolidated her position at the head of the 'grand coalition', but in the United Kingdom, Prime Minister Gordon Brown's control over the government and the ruling Labour Party seemed to be weakening only a year after he took over from Tony Blair. In Italy, media baron Silvio Berlusconi became prime minister for the third time, while in Poland a period in which twin brothers were president and prime minister ended when the centre-right Civic Platform party defeated Jaroslaw Kaczynski's conservative Law and Justice party, and Donald Tusk became prime minister.

Efforts by European leaders to settle outstanding issues over the pace of European integration came to a shuddering halt in June 2008 when voters in Ireland rejected the European Union's Lisbon Treaty. Ireland was the only country to put to a popular vote the decision on whether to ratify the treaty, which would streamline the workings of the EU to reflect the substantial expansion of its membership. It was signed by EU heads of government in December 2007 but required ratification by all 27 members to be put into effect. An earlier version, styled as an EU constitution, had been resoundingly rejected by French and Dutch voters in 2005, forcing a moratorium on EU reform that leaders had hoped to end with the Lisbon Treaty. While some larger countries wished Dublin to organise a second referendum that, they hoped, would have a different result, a more likely outcome seemed to be a further period of impasse. Repeated rejection by voters of reforms that leaders saw as both necessary and innocuous seemed to indicate a lack of connection between electorates and the EU. This may signal an end for the foreseeable future to the long trend towards ever-closer EU integration. The de facto outcome may be a period in which smaller groups of European countries take steps towards closer interaction in areas in which they are comfortable to do so – such as with the euro, which 15 EU members now use as their currency.

One area in which there seemed some prospect of revitalising European efforts was defence and security. Sarkozy indicated that he would like France to return to the integrated military structure of NATO, which it had left in 1966. In tandem with this, he wanted the EU to step up its defence capabilities, with more ambitious goals for intervention capacity and enhanced instruments to plan and operate missions. While the United States indicated its support, it was not clear what momentum France would be able to muster among its European partners during its period of rotating presidency of the EU in the second half of 2008.

France: Frustrated Hopes for Radical Change

To say that Nicolas Sarkozy had a tumultuous first year in office would be an understatement. The judgement of the French press as 2008 approached its mid-point was almost universally negative: too much smoke and mirrors, too little focus, too many broken promises, too many half measures and too few decisive breakthroughs. France, in short, had experienced none of the fundamental change – the Sarkozian buzzword was *rupture* – so boldly heralded during the election campaign in 2007.

Never in the history of the Fifth Republic had a recently elected president enjoyed such instant high approval ratings (69% in summer 2007) or suffered such a rapid fall in them (36% in May 2008). There was virtually no prospect of the full employment and 3% growth rates predicted by the candidate. The country still suffered from low economic growth (1.7% was forecast for 2008), an inflexible labour market and an unsustainable level of national debt (rising in 2007 to €1.2 trillion, or 64.2% of GDP). At a press conference on 8 January 2008, the president bluntly announced that 'the state coffers are empty'. In the municipal and regional elections in March 2008, his right-wing coalition lost control of a large majority of French cities and *départements.*

Some of the disapproval derived from Sarkozy's high-profile private life, his lightning divorce from his wife Cecilia and rapid marriage to the singer Carla Bruni. French citizens love to read celebrity gossip, but they prefer their president to embody the gravitas that had characterised Sarkozy's predecessors. Discontent also sprang from general disillusionment with a president elected with huge political capital, who had given the appearance of unlimited energy, focus and determination, but who had delivered so little of substance and had alienated people from many walks of life, not to mention increasing numbers of his own political associates. Strikes, protests and demonstrations had brought onto the streets, from late summer 2007 onwards, transport workers, students, health practitioners, scientific researchers, fisherman and truckers. Although the president proved unyielding on pension reform and the short-circuiting of the 35-hour work week, few groups of voters felt that he had satisfactorily delivered on his promises for domestic reform.

The one area where opinion about Sarkozy's progress was more nuanced was foreign and security policy. The main initiatives he had promised during the 2007 election concerned Europe, the Mediterranean, Africa, the Middle East and defence policy. The thrust of much analysis and commentary in these policy areas was not so much that nothing of substance had happened, but that the president had embarked on what was often presented as a perilous new course involving *rupture* from the basic tenets of Gaullism. This view was somewhat paradoxically showcased on 8 April 2008 when the National Assembly debated a motion of censure against the government over its policy with regard to both NATO and Afghanistan. The charge was that Sarkozy, by preparing for France to return to the integrated command structure of NATO, and by sending additional French troops to Afghanistan, had simply aligned French policy with that of Washington. The irony came from the fact that the charge of breaking with Gaullism was formulated by the Socialist opposition, while the ostensible heirs to Gaullism in the ruling UMP party appeared to offer solid backing to the president. Only one right-wing deputy, the maverick Nicolas Dupont-Aignan, voted with the Socialists. The motion was massively defeated. The Socialists had gambled on unleashing a wave of discontent within the ranks of the Gaullists, but UMP deputies were canny enough not to fall into the trap.

Defence and security initiatives

Sarkozy's first year on the diplomatic and security front will be judged mainly on three major interlocking initiatives of which the results have yet to be seen: a White Paper on defence and security policy published in June 2008, an attempt to relaunch the EU's European Security and Defence Policy (ESDP), and the plan to return to the integrated command structure of NATO (which in itself signified a strong desire for much-improved relations with the United States).

Reintegration with NATO

The president's reputation as a 'friend of America' was well established before his election. Several high-profile visits to the United States, including a summer 2007 holiday in New England and a speech to the US Congress in November

2007, left no doubt that he intended to re-cement France's ties to its 'oldest ally'. The high point of this new approach came with his decision, first hinted at in August 2007, to bring France back into NATO's integrated command structure, from which President Charles de Gaulle had removed it in 1966 following repeated protests against American domination of the Alliance. Both François Mitterrand and Jacques Chirac had attempted to renegotiate a new, closer, relationship between France and NATO. Neither overture had worked out, although France did rejoin the NATO Military Committee in 1994.

Sarkozy's NATO plan has been the subject of much comment. Was it true, as some journalists claimed, that the president had 'confessed' to being emotionally inspired by a 1960s Michel Sardou song, 'Les Ricains' (the Yanks), which was composed as a protest against de Gaulle's decision to break with NATO, and whose key line was '*Si les Ricains n'étaient pas là, vous seriez tous en Germanie*' (if the Yanks hadn't arrived, you'd all be Germans)? Or was his rapprochement with Washington the result of a strategic calculation that the United States, whatever the mistakes of the George W. Bush administration, was now a beleaguered Goliath in a turbulent world, desperately in need of support and understanding from its closest friends? Some combination of these explanations is probable. At mid 2008, it remained unclear whether Sarkozy would succeed where his predecessors had failed, and what difference the change would make both to France's role within NATO and to internal Alliance debates over the future.

While much commentary on Sarkozy's first year stressed his Atlanticism and detected a genuine *rupture* with the Gaullist heritage, the true picture was more nuanced. First, France had in fact been heavily involved with NATO since the end of the Cold War. It had deployed as many troops on NATO missions as other leading Alliance members, and had commanded both KFOR in Kosovo and ISAF in Afghanistan. Since 2004 its presence at the two main NATO commands in Mons, Belgium and Norfolk, Virginia had risen to over a hundred officers. Since France's presence in the Alliance's decision-making structures has not been commensurate with its significant contribution to NATO's military activities, it has been suffering from a self-imposed shackle. Ending this isolation is manifestly perceived in Paris as being in France's best interest. A further argument is that the widespread view of France as being sceptical of NATO as a US-dominated organisation has led to newer NATO and EU members, many of which are close to Washington, taking a jaundiced view of the EU's role in defence activities, and seeing ESDP as a French 'alternative' to NATO. In addition, partly as a result of self-marginalisation, France has in effect been reduced to playing an obstructionist role in NATO, applying the brakes to initiatives such as enlargement and a new strategic concept. A return to the NATO command structure could dispel all these problems.

Sarkozy announced on 17 June 2008 that France would return to the integrated command structure in time for NATO's 60th anniversary summit in April

2009. While there has been much speculation about the terms that France would exact, it is even possible that the move is viewed in Paris as being so much in French interests that it could in effect be unconditional. However, Sarkozy set two objectives which France would wish to pursue as corollaries to its return. The first is that appropriate command posts are made available to French officers to reflect the new status. This will undoubtedly be one consequence of a sweeping restructuring process that NATO is likely to undergo over the next few years. The second is that ESDP should be given a new boost under the French presidency of the EU in the second half of 2008, and that Washington should finally give ESDP its unequivocal blessing. Even if these goals are achieved, however, it is unlikely that France's heightened participation in NATO will bring fundamental changes to the nature of the Alliance, and Paris' fundamental approach, based on the triptych *'ami, allié, mais non-aligné'* (friend, ally, but non-aligned), is unlikely to change.

Sarkozy moved to meet American concerns about NATO's mission in Afghanistan. At the April 2008 NATO summit he said France would send 700 more troops, bringing the total to around 3,000. While the new contingents will not be sent to Helmand province, where NATO wanted more combat troops, they will be assigned to the eastern provinces where US forces are battling al-Qaeda. This will allow some American troops to be redeployed to Helmand, and will demonstrate France's willingness to join the United States in fighting global terror networks and to help tip the balance of the struggle in Afghanistan.

Defence and security priorities adjusted

France's capacity to intervene in theatres such as Afghanistan was a key theme of a long-awaited White Paper on defence published in mid June 2008. The document set five main thrusts to French defence and security policy over the next 15 years: knowledge-based security and intelligence; deterrence; intervention; prevention; and protection. Its principal ambitions were threefold. The first was to recalibrate French conventional forces in such a way as to make them more usable within a European and alliance framework, framed not by the Cold War but by the realities of the twenty-first century: globalisation and strategic uncertainty. The second was to lay the groundwork for an ever-increasing cooperation between the instruments of both external and internal security – particularly with respect to counter-terrorism. The third was to show a lead in fleshing out the contours of a future, genuinely European, grand strategy.

The traditional trumpeting of France's nuclear capacity has, under Sarkozy, undergone important shifts. Speaking at the launch of France's fourth strategic nuclear submarine, *Le Terrible*, in March 2008, the president made explicit reference to the deterrent value of the NATO Alliance, and also stated that France's nuclear deterrent benefited its EU partners in that any potentially hostile state contemplating an attack on any EU member state would have to weigh the fact that it was tightly integrated to France, with its nuclear capacity. In addition, Sarkozy indicated an apparent willingness to contemplate missile defences as a complement to deterrence. Finally, an announcement that the airborne component of the French nuclear deterrent (*Mirage* 2000 and *Rafale*) was being cut by 30% presaged an eventual alignment with the United Kingdom's maintenance of a nuclear deterrent carried only in submarines. These significant adjustments suggested that France was beginning to rethink some of the fundamentals of its sacrosanct national deterrence posture.

In the White Paper, the army turned out to be the sacrificial lamb in a policy review which began as a root-and-branch probe into all aspects of defence but ended up as a classic cost-cutting exercise. Defence spending will be held at around 2% of gross domestic product. The overall force levels in the army will be cut from a present level of 154,000 to 131,000. The ambition will be to be able to deploy 30,000 troops on overseas missions, with a reserve force of 10,000 assigned to internal-security missions. The air force sees its fighter aircraft fleet reduced from 330 to 300 and transport aircraft cut from 100 to 70. The navy will see its frigate fleet reduced from 25 to 18, with continuing uncertainty over the hypothetical second aircraft carrier. 54,000 jobs will be cut in support or administrative services and the budget ratio reversed from 60% personnel/40% equipment to 40/60%. Equipment spending will rise from €15.5bn to €18bn per year from 2009 to 2020. Military space spending will double from its 2008 level of €380m.

European defence

As France took the rotating presidency of the EU for the second half of 2008, Sarkozy was widely expected to propose a revitalisation of the organisation's defence role. Addressing parliamentarians on 9 January 2008, he vowed to fight for a common defence policy, asking 'how can we think that Europe, one of the richest regions in the world, can live without defending itself?' Implicitly, this constituted yet another subtle shift in France's defence discourse, which hitherto had explicitly recognised that collective defence was the core function of NATO – though the EU's Lisbon Treaty also envisages collective action by the EU if a member is attacked.

One element of the French proposals was likely to be development of an EU operational planning headquarters in Brussels. With the EU currently able to use NATO assets under the 'Berlin Plus' arrangements, this was likely to be opposed by those countries, including Britain, which fear that NATO's competence to deal with crises will be eroded and that money will be wasted on duplication and the building of new bureaucracies. However, Paris seemed determined to push ahead with the proposal. During his presidential campaign, Sarkozy also touted the notion of an ESDP *directoire* involving France, the UK, Germany, Italy, Spain and Poland. Leaked proposals later spoke of a 'mutualisation' of forces between these countries, each contributing 10,000 men to a 60,000-strong strategic force, which would act as a 'pioneer group' under the terms of the Lisbon Treaty's 'permanent structured cooperation'.

Heightened cooperation between France and the United Kingdom, the two countries that jointly launched the EU into the defence arena in 1998, was also viewed in Paris as desirable. Sarkozy paid a state visit to London in March 2008, but plans that emerged from talks with Gordon Brown, the British prime minister, fell short of being visionary. At the macro level, they claimed to 'share a common analysis of the organisation of the 21st century international order' and boasted plans for international development and the resolution of international crises. At the European level, it appeared that the main motivation for cooperation was financial rather than political or strategic. With both countries suffering from cost overruns in their procurement programmes, pooling of resources could reduce the degree to which programmes will have to be curtailed. In addition to cooperation on aircraft carriers already under way, they discussed sharing in-service support for A400-M transport aircraft, addressing critical shortfalls in helicopter provision, setting up a joint defence research and development (R&D) fund of €100 million a year, and cooperation on missile projects. But this did not come close to representing a strategic breakthrough on the lines of the St Malo agreement of 1998.

On defence spending, French proposals were likely to be largely hortatory. The proposed spending benchmark for the 'Big 6' was 2% of GDP, the same as the target level for NATO members. But of the top six EU members, only France and the UK currently exceed this level: exhortation alone was unlikely to close the gap. Particular emphasis was likely to be placed on R&D: it was widely repeated in French defence circles that whereas the US spent €67 billion annually on R&D, the EU figure was around €9bn. While the growing demands of international crises and the rising costs of defence equipment might indicate higher spending was necessary, the immediate solution seemed to lie rather in closer coordination of defence assets between European nations: rationalisation, integration, sharing and pooling. Sarkozy called for European countries to stop wasteful duplication and pool orders for equipment, while also abandoning the *juste retour* principle under which each nation's industry was allotted work on a programme based on the size of that nation's order. This would permit more effective procurement and rationalisation of Europe's defence industries. But by mid 2008, his calls had not gone beyond rhetoric.

Activist diplomacy

On other foreign-policy issues, Sarkozy appeared at least to dabble with *rupture*. His electoral campaign had stressed humanitarian intervention, and this initially assumed unfamiliar and original forms. His personal intervention in July 2007 (through the intermediary of his then-wife Cecilia) to release five Bulgarian nurses and a Palestinian doctor who had been held in a Libyan jail since 1999 and sentenced to death for allegedly infecting Libyan children with HIV, initially brought him enthusiastic plaudits. In December, however, it became clear that the price exacted by Libyan leader Muammar Gadhafi was a week's state visit to France, during which the volatile ex-sponsor of terrorism took a large step towards international rehabilitation at the cost of daily embarrassment for his host. Foreign Minister Bernard Kouchner and Rama Yade, secretary of state for human rights, refused to meet Gadhafi, and Yade publicly denounced him even while he was pitching his Bedouin tent in the gardens of the Hôtel Marigny: 'Colonel Gadhafi must understand that our country is not a doormat on which a leader, terrorist or not, can come to wipe the blood of his crimes off his feet', she declared. Sarkozy nevertheless managed to clinch several trade deals with Libya, including the supply of two missile systems worth $411m and a nuclear-powered seawater-desalination plant.

The president's energetic attempts to bring about the release of the Franco-Colombian political hostage Ingrid Betancourt were less successful, even though they appeared to confirm that he was prepared to put his own reputation on the line in the cause of justice. Betancourt, a former Colombian presidential candidate with joint Colombian and French nationality, had been held, along with some 50 other hostages, for six years by the FARC rebel group in the jungles of Colombia. In short order, Sarkozy publicly intervened with Colombian President Alvaro Uribe and Venezuelan President Hugo Chávez to mediate with the FARC, which both the United States and the EU consider to be a terrorist organisation. He said he would be prepared to go into rebel-held areas of the jungle to negotiate personally for Betancourt's release. In January, former vice-presidential candidate Clara Rojas and congresswoman Consuelo González were released, largely through Chávez's efforts, but not Betancourt. Sarkozy's dramatic interventions therefore came to nought, while demonstrating again his impulsive and spontaneous dimension. However, on 2 July 2008 Betancourt, along with three US Defense Department employees and 11 Colombian police and military personnel, was rescued by Colombian forces in a bloodless operation.

Meanwhile, the president gave full rein to Kouchner to exemplify the government's new approach to humanitarian intervention by orchestrating a succession of initiatives with regard to the crisis in the Darfur region of Sudan. Within two weeks of joining the government, Kouchner proposed the establishment of 'humanitarian corridors' from Chad to allow the provision of international relief supplies to the people of Darfur. The scheme, which might have involved up to 25,000 EU, UN and African Union (AU) forces, was rapidly shot down as impractical both by the Chad government and by the international community. Undeterred, Kouchner then proposed an EU force to protect the refugee camps in Chad, which were by summer 2007 teeming with some 450,000 refugees from Darfur and neighbouring Central African Republic (CAR) as well as internally displaced persons from Chad. After months of intra-EU wrangling over troop levels, military equipment, leadership and objectives, the EU mission EUFOR Chad/CAR was launched in March 2008. Although the mission is commanded by an Irish general, France has contributed 65% of the troops, while separately maintaining a garrison in Chad to support the government. The UN-mandated EU operation, geared to protecting refugees, aid workers and UN personnel, is due to last one year and to be succeeded by a more substantial UN force. It purports to be strictly neutral in the ongoing struggle for political dominance in Central Africa among authoritarian governments, rebels and militias, focusing single-mindedly on its humanitarian task. The mission looks set to become the most sensitive and complex of all the EU's overseas operations. The environment in which it is operating is volatile and evolving rapidly, with tens of thousands of armed rebels, militias and bandits inhabiting the same space. Above all, the mission's declared neutrality cannot avoid the central problem in Chad and the CAR, where corrupt, unpopular and highly vulnerable governments are attempting to hide behind the EU's presence to avoid fundamental change. The significant point, however, was that Sarkozy had consciously 'Europeanised' the security framework in a former French colony.

More generally, Sarkozy indicated that the phenomenon of 'Francafrique', under which his predecessors, using networks of personal influence and patronage, had essentially run large tracts of Africa from inside the Elysée Palace, was a thing of the past. He got off to a bad start by selecting former French colonies Senegal and Gabon for his first trip to the continent in July 2007, and by making a highly insensitive (many said racist) speech at the University of Dakar which criticised the 'African peasant' for his inability to break with 'a way of life driven by the seasons' and which patronisingly enjoined his astonished hosts 'not to be ashamed of the values of African civilisation'. But he soon began to promote a view of Africa geared not to perpetuating colonial ties but to regional stabilisation, the development of normal market transactions and the control of immigration flows – in short, as an integral part of French foreign policy. In a widely praised visit to South Africa in March 2008, he declared that France's long-standing defence agreements with several former colonies would be revised to reflect the genuine needs of Africa as a whole, and that France no longer intended to play a policing role in the continent. By prioritising the role of the UN, the AU and the EU in Africa, he intended to help the continent adjust to globalisation. He outlined new aid packages amounting to €2.5bn designed to help 2,000 African companies create 300,000 jobs.

Sarkozy's major concern was immigration: 65% of the 200,000 annual immigrants to France are African and the majority of the 500,000 illegal immigrants entering the EU each year come from Africa. This, he noted, was a problem France and Europe shared with South Africa and might hope to solve through a cooperative approach. The 'anti-foreigner' riots in South Africa in May 2008 seemed to confirm his analysis. Sarkozy's major initiative in this area is an immigration bill which was adopted by the French parliament in October 2007, instituting language exams and DNA testing for prospective immigrants, making family regrouping more difficult by ensuring that visa seekers could not enter the country through the use of fraudulent papers. The new French approach to Africa is pragmatic, intended to offer solutions to the continent's many problems.

One of the most controversial proposals made by candidate Sarkozy was for the creation of a 'Mediterranean Union'. This was the brainchild of Sarkozy's special adviser, Henri Guaino, who was charged by the president with promoting it. The original aim was to create, between the countries on the shores of the Mediterranean, a separate regional regime on the model of the EU. Sarkozy presented this scheme in big-picture terms as the ultimate solution to the clash of civilisations, allowing the world 'to overcome hatred and to make way for the dream of peace and civilisation', including between Israel and Palestine. He also presented it as 'the pivot of a grand alliance between Europe and Africa ... the counterweight to Asia and America'. In October 2007, in a grandiose speech in Tangiers, he invited all Mediterranean leaders to a summit in Paris on 13–14 July 2008, at which the project was to be officially launched. Emphasising above all economic development, he described his project as 'the greatest co-development laboratory in the world'. It was to cover investment and trade, migration, energy, security and counter-terrorism.

From the outset, the idea ran into serious opposition. German leaders were irritated at the explicit exclusion from the scheme of Germany and other non-Mediterranean-shore EU members, who were nevertheless invited, as mere 'observers', to assist in its realisation. In December German Chancellor Angela Merkel became overtly critical, accusing Sarkozy of risking a major split within the EU. Slovenia, assuming the presidency of the EU in January 2008, lambasted the project as unnecessarily undermining both the existing Barcelona Process (the Euro-Mediterranean Partnership scheme, launched in 1995) and the EU Neighbourhood Policy.

At a summit meeting with Merkel on 3 March 2008, realising that his project had helped produce a crisis in Franco-German relations, Sarkozy began to backpedal. He accepted a German proposal that the Union be open to all EU member states and that it be explicitly considered as a fresh start to the stalled Barcelona Process. This was a major climbdown since Sarkozy had initially proposed his project because, in his view, the Barcelona Process had failed. In addition, Sarkozy was prevailed upon to drop some of his more ambitious institutional proposals, such as a Mediterranean Investment Bank and a number of specialised agencies. Merkel's compromise proposal was then endorsed, after lengthy and sometimes heated debate, by the EU at a meeting of heads of state and government on 13–14 March 2008. Support for the idea was stronger on the south side of the Mediterranean, particularly in Morocco, Tunisia and Israel, although Gadhafi, in his inimitable way, roundly condemned the scheme as 'humiliating' to the African and Arab side. Turkey, moreover, was deeply concerned that the union might emerge as an alternative to its long-desired membership of the EU. This fear was laid to rest in mid March when Sarkozy explicitly accepted that the project would in no way affect Turkey's negotiating situation with regard to EU accession. Under these circumstances, the EU member states were all relatively content to relaunch the Barcelona Process, recognising that it had indeed stalled and that, given the strategic importance of relations between the two shores of the Mediterranean, the Sarkozy project may well serve to set it back in motion on a more constructive track. All eyes were on Paris on the eve of Bastille Day 2008, when the heads of state and government of 43 states – only Libya's Muammar Gadhafi failed to attend – assembled at the Elysée to take the project to its next stage. What seemed clear, however, is that, given the parlous state of French finances, the Mediterranean Union scheme, like its Barcelona predecessor, will be essentially funded via the European Commission. Thus, the episode to date was a case of a near-*rupture* being co-opted by France's EU partners and transmogrified into business (almost) as usual.

As for Sarkozy's policy regarding the Middle East and Gulf, Kouchner's highly symbolic visit to Iraq in mid August 2007 – the first by any major French official since the US-led 2003 invasion in which France refused to take part – was widely interpreted as both a statement of France's intention to help out if and where possible, and more generally as yet another sign of fence-mending with Washington. Meanwhile, France's tough approach towards Iran's nuclear programme was maintained. Kouchner stated that war with Iran could not be ruled out: 'We will negotiate until the end. And at the same time we must prepare ourselves ... for the worst ... The worst is war.' However, Sarkozy, visiting New York in late September 2007, insisted that his foreign minister had been speaking metaphorically, implying that 'the worst' – war – was as unacceptable as an Iranian nuclear weapon, and that therefore alternative solutions between these two extremes had to be found. In particular, Sarkozy said severe sanctions – if necessary applied outside a UN mandate – would help unblock the situation. Yet neither in Iraq nor in Iran did France's revised perspective make any real difference to the situation on the ground.

Nor did it in Lebanon, despite energetic efforts by Kouchner. The foreign minister visited Lebanon no fewer than six times between May and December 2007 and Sarkozy received Lebanese Prime Minister Fouad Siniora in Paris in June 2007 and February 2008. In July 2007, Kouchner organised an informal intra-Lebanese meeting at the Château de la Celle Saint-Cloud, aimed at re-establishing a constructive dialogue between the different political blocs partici-pating in the national dialogue. French diplomatic efforts were aimed first and foremost at breaking the internal political impasse which had prevented Lebanon from selecting a president since Emile Lahoud finished his second term in October 2007. However, in May 2008, when Hizbullah, responding to a government attempt to control its communications networks, temporarily took over West Beirut in what was widely perceived as an attempted coup, it was not France – the former colonial power – but the secretary-general of the Arab League and the emir and foreign minister of Qatar who, during five days of intense negotiations in Doha, produced the solution endorsed by all Lebanese parties to elect Michel Suleiman as president and to form a national unity government. France was left with the somewhat uncomfortable role, given the energy it had expended, of applauding from the sidelines. The role of Qatar in the resolution of the Lebanon crisis came as no surprise in Paris, where the Sarkozy administration had already decided to reorient the thrust of France's Middle East policy towards the Gulf. A decision to establish a French military base in Abu Dhabi – the first overseas base outside France's traditional colonial sphere – was an important indicator of the shift.

On the Israel–Palestine issue, France seemed uncharacteristically downbeat. The political class waited eagerly to see when and how Sarkozy's reputation as a firm friend of Israel would manifest itself in terms of *rupture* with the alleged pro-Arab policy of his predecessor Chirac. In the event, no such shift was per-ceptible. Indeed, when Israeli Foreign Minister Shimon Peres visited Paris in March 2008 for a five-day state visit, Sarkozy said baldly that the Jewish state must halt its 'colonisation' on the West Bank as an indispensable step towards peace. Continued settlements, the Quai d'Orsay added, threatened the creation of a viable Palestinian state. In May, Kouchner announced that France had been engaged in 'contacts' with Hamas. This announcement came only days after Bush, on his own visit to Israel, had denounced as 'appeasers' those prepared to 'talk to terrorists and radicals'. France's pronouncements on Israel–Palestine did not fit the image of a country which had broken with Gaullism in order to embrace Atlanticism. Sarkozy's own first visit to Israel came in late June 2008.

Energy not yet matched by effect

Sarkozy's first year has been marked by an extraordinary profusion of initiatives and developments, many of them accompanied by intense media fanfare. He has suffered a loss of popularity, due partly to his private life, but has time to regain it. On the domestic front, he has faced down massive protests from all those who feared losing out through his liberal reforms, but the reforms themselves, given the parlous state of the French economy, ultimately failed to set the country off on a new and firmer footing. He has revamped France's defence and security policy in a manner that creates a strong relationship between external and internal capabilities and refocuses the scope for French military intervention away from Africa and on the 'arc of crisis' stretching from the Maghreb to Pakistan. In foreign policy, he has begun to forge a new, more positive relationship with the United States, though the full outcome must await the arrival of a new American president and agreement on France's return to the command structure of NATO. Similarly, Sarkozy's desire to give new impetus to the defence role of the EU has yet to bear fruit, with no sign of a groundbreaking agreement with the United Kingdom. Elsewhere on the diplomatic front, only the move away from the ex-colonial approach to Africa can be seen as a radical departure, though Sarkozy and Kouchner have been far more activist in their efforts, for example, in Colombia and Lebanon. Sarkozy's ambitious goal of a Mediterranean Union was rapidly watered down in the face of strong European opposition. In short, the story was one of massive energy but limited impact – so far.

Germany: Constraints on Action Debated

The centre-right Christian Democratic Union/Christian Socialist Union (CDU/CSU) grouping led by Chancellor Angela Merkel enjoyed increasing support over the year to mid 2008, while the Social Democratic Party (SPD) was pushed more and more into the role of the junior partner in the grand coalition as its showing in opinion polls slumped. Several poll results released in early June 2008 put the SPD at between 20% and 25% nationwide compared to the 34.2% it received in the 2005 federal elections. By comparison, the CDU/CSU polled at 34–36%, unchanged from its result of 35.2% in the last elections. With unemployment continuing to decline to 3.28m in May 2008, a drop of some 530,000 in a year-on-year comparison, and economic growth surprisingly robust in 2007 and early 2008, Merkel and her party received most of the credit for Germany's strong performance, even though the basis for it was in part laid by welfare reforms introduced by the previous SPD-led government. The SPD came under pressure from the pacifist Left Party, established in June 2007 through the merger of the PDS and the WASG. The PDS had been formed in 1990 out of the former governing party in East Germany, the SED, whereas the WASG was founded in January 2005 by left-wing activists disappointed with the then SPD-led federal government. As the Left Party began to make inroads among former SPD voters (polling at 14–15% in June 2008 compared to a result of 8.7% in the 2005 elections), there were attempts to strengthen the SPD's profile and emphasise its differences from the CDU/CSU in, among others, the field of foreign and security policy. The SPD struggled to unite two powerful internal factions, the modernist and reform-oriented part and the traditional left wing, a struggle complicated by weak leadership. The SPD is on its third chairman since then Chancellor Gerhard Schröder stepped down from the chairmanship in early 2004.

Germany's troop deployment in Afghanistan continued to arouse vigorous political debate. Meanwhile, the discovery of a major jihadist terrorist plot led to a rethinking of the degree of Germany's vulnerability to international terrorism. The need for a substantive debate on German security-policy priorities appeared to be growing, although it is unlikely to occur before the next national elections scheduled for autumn 2009. The government continued to resist growing international pressure to increase its commitment to NATO operations in Afghanistan – although it later said it would make more troops available – and to remove restrictions on the activities of its deployed troops. Senior German politicians believed domestic political opposition to such changes was prohibitive.

Afghanistan: a delicate balancing act

In September 2007, the government approved a new Afghanistan policy, jointly drawn up by all the ministries involved, which declared the stabilisation and consolidation of Afghanistan to be in Germany's direct and vital interest. The concept was based on two principles: 'no security without reconstruction and development' and 'no reconstruction and development without security'. The government pledged that it would maintain its military contribution until Afghan security forces had the capacity to provide security in support of a government backed by a majority of Afghans. The policy also made clear that Germany would continue to focus its efforts on the north of the country. Funding for civilian assistance was raised from €20m to €100m in 2007 and €125m in 2008. Shortly afterwards, the parliamentary mandates allowing for the deployment of German troops to the NATO International Security Assistance Force (ISAF) and the US-led *Operation Enduring Freedom* were extended with a clear majority in the Bundestag.

The run-up to these parliamentary votes saw an intense political debate. It became clear that the SPD was vulnerable to political pressure from the left, with the Left Party calling for withdrawal of German troops from Afghanistan. The September 2007 party congress of the Green Party, which had been part of the centre-left coalition government which first sent German troops into Afghanistan, was dominated by activists who exposed a deep rift in the party by demanding that its members of parliament vote 'no' on both the ISAF and *Operation Enduring Freedom* extensions. While the CDU/CSU and opposition Free Democrats (FDP) expressed their support for both missions, individual parliamentarians dissented from the party line.

The domestic debate was fuelled by diverse and sometimes outright conflicting results from opinion polls. For example, one poll from August 2007 indicated that more than 60% of Germans favoured withdrawal from Afghanistan, while another one from September/October of the same year showed some 60% support for German participation in ISAF in general. The latter asked for support for the 'peace mission of the United Nations in Afghanistan (ISAF)' whereas the former used the terminology 'NATO operation in Afghanistan', which might explain some of the variation. More detailed analysis based on separate polling data revealed that only about half the people polled said they were familiar with the main facts of the Afghanistan deployment, more people opposed the use of *Tornado* reconnaissance aircraft in Afghanistan than supported it, and an absolute majority were against German participation in combat operations. Aware of the domestic constraints, Franz Josef Jung, defence minister from the CDU party, argued that Afghanistan needed 'security and reconstruction and development: that is the wider concept. That's why I think these calls for simply more and more military involvement are misguided.'

Against this background, a letter sent to Jung by US Secretary of Defense Robert Gates in January 2008 caused uproar in Germany. Gates asked for an additional 3,200 German troops, more helicopters and the lifting of restrictions, or 'caveats', so that German troops could join other coalition forces in combat operations across Afghanistan. At the annual Munich Security Conference in February, Gates said that 'some partners should not have the luxury to focus on stabilisation and reconstruction missions while thereby forcing other partners to carry an unproportionately high share of the fighting and dying'. He warned of a two-tier NATO and said this would 'effectively destroy the Alliance'.

Although Gates said he had sent similar letters to other Allied governments, his words hit a raw nerve. Jung stood firm, arguing that 'it would be a big mistake to neglect [Afghanistan's] North, which is half the size of Germany, to withdraw troops from there or to rotate them through different regions'. He said the mandate already allowed for support of Allied troops by German soldiers *in extremis* throughout Afghanistan – though the circumstances in which this could occur remained unclear. At the same Munich conference, Foreign Minister Frank-Walter Steinmeier (SPD), asking allies to acknowledge the development of German troop deployments, said: 'I don't see the [wisdom] of jeopardizing the good work we are doing in the north by spreading the Bundeswehr forces thinner to cover all Afghanistan'. Meanwhile, member of parliament and CDU/CSU foreign-policy spokesman Eckart von Klaeden commented that 'the tone and content of [Gates'] letter are completely inappropriate', and the parliamentary leader of the Green Party, Fritz Kuhn, maintained that 'we have to fulfil our tasks in the north, that is no walk in the park'. By the time of the NATO Bucharest Summit in early April 2008, the row had calmed down, with US President George W. Bush saying in a German media interview: 'I do not want to demand from other countries what they cannot do politically'. Asked whether he would press in Bucharest for German deployments to the south of Afghanistan, he responded 'no, that will not happen'.

In addition to the use of *Tornados* in the south and the *in extremis* condition, Germany was taking other small steps in the direction demanded by Washington and other Allies. From July 2008 on, it was due to provide a 250-strong rapid-reaction force in northern Afghanistan, previously contributed by Norway. It also deployed additional personnel to Kunduz to beef up force protection in response to an increase in rocket attacks on the German camp. With the German ISAF deployment hitting the mandated ceiling of 3,500 personnel, there were indications that the next extension, due in October 2008, might see a lifting of the ceiling to 4,500. However, it seemed extremely unlikely that significant changes to the German position beyond raising the ceiling could occur before the parliamentary election scheduled for autumn 2009. Given the timing of the elections, there was a risk that parliamentary extension of the Afghanistan mandates could become a campaign issue.

Terrorism: Germany as target

The government scored a major counter-terrorism success when a jihadist plot was thwarted in September 2007. *Operation Alberich*, begun in October 2006 after US intelligence agencies intercepted emails between Germany and Pakistan, led to the arrest of two German converts to Islam, Fritz Gelowitz, 28, and Daniel Martin Schneider, 22, and a Turkish national, Adem Yilmaz, 29, on 4 September 2007. The operation involved some 300 personnel, including a joint German–US task force in Berlin. The three individuals were caught in the act of mixing chemicals to make explosives at a holiday home they had rented in the Sauerland region of western Germany. At the time of the arrest, all the material necessary for making bombs, including detonators and hydrogen peroxide, had been gathered. German law-enforcement personnel bugged the rented apartment and car of the suspects and overheard conversations that indicated a plan for three car bombs. The possible targets included Frankfurt international airport, US military installations at Ramstein, US military barracks in Hanau and nightclubs frequented by US personnel. However, in July 2007 police had replaced the 12 barrels of hydrogen peroxide acquired by the group with a lower concentration to eliminate its potential for bomb-making. Investigators waited as long as possible before arresting the suspects in order to accumulate evidence; the assumed intended date of attack was in mid September 2007. The cell was found to be linked to the Islamic Jihad Union (IJU) of Pakistan, a spin-off of the Islamic Movement of Uzbekistan. The fact that the IJU, of which the declared goal was to internationalise jihad, had successfully recruited German nationals and a Turkish national (Turks make up by far the majority of Germany's Muslims) raised considerable concern among German counter-terrorism experts. While it remained unclear whether the incident was an isolated affair, it raised questions about Germany's threat assessment. The issue of Germany as a target of jihadist terrorism had first gained prominence in the public at large with the attempted bombings of two commuter trains on 31 July 2006. In that instance the bombs failed to go off due to deficient bomb-making skills on the part of the terrorists.

In early 2008 additional worrying signals appeared. Germany's domestic intelligence agency pointed to an increasing number of websites calling for an attack on German soil, some of them in German and others in Arabic with German subtitles. A link to the presence of German troops of Afghanistan was assumed. At the same time, there was evidence that the number of German nationals travelling to Pakistan was increasing. In March 2007 Pakistan's Inter-Services Intelligence agency detained two German nationals who were thought to have visited training camps. A 500-page study entitled 'Muslims in Germany' conducted by researchers at the University of Hamburg and supported and published by the German Ministry of the Interior in 2007 suggested that 6% of the approximately 3.5m Muslims living in Germany showed acceptance of 'massive forms of political/religious motivated violence'. Earlier estimates had put this number at 1%. While this latest result was slightly biased because the data included only urban Muslim populations in Germany and overrepresented young Muslims, and might tend to overestimate the acceptance of violence, it was founded on a composite index of eight items related to religiously motivated violence. The authors of the survey-based study estimated that some 10–12% of Muslims in Germany could potentially be radicalised, and put the proportion of Muslims in Germany who subscribed to a fundamentalist interpretation of Islam at 40%. While it was unclear whether the findings were due to a change in methodology, they nonetheless added to the perception that Germany might increasingly find itself a direct target of jihadist terrorism.

The national security debate

As the debates on Afghanistan and terrorism continued, a position paper on national-security policy was presented by the CDU/CSU parliamentary group in May 2008. It argued that Germany could only meet current security challenges in cooperation with other countries and by pursuing a comprehensive security policy that aimed to prevent risks from turning into conflicts. Key goals, it said, should be to fight terrorism, prevent proliferation and promote disarmament, secure access to resources, address the effects of climate change, and mitigate and resolve conflicts. The CDU/CSU parliamentarians made four recommendations for security policy. First, networked homeland security had to be improved, with the armed forces to be involved in dealing with major natural disasters, terrorist attacks or accidents, and European cooperation had to be strengthened. Secondly, civil–military coordination across different government areas should be strengthened to improve international crisis management and prevention. Thirdly, a national security council should be set up to improve analysis and coordinate crisis response. Finally, the government and private sector should improve partnership on technology development. The recommendations ran into opposition, partly because of a turf battle between the SPD, which currently holds the Foreign Ministry – which could lose influence if a national security council is created – and the CDU/CSU, which holds the ministries of Interior and Defence as well as the Chancellery.

Critics pointed out that the position paper did not provide additional guidance on the use of the armed forces for international missions. CDU/CSU politicians had argued that Bundeswehr personnel taking part in EU or NATO missions, in particular in rapid-reaction formations such as EU battlegroups or the NATO Response Force, should be exempted from the general legislation governing their deployment. Instead, legislation allowing for a simplified and faster procedure should be introduced to cover rapid-reaction scenarios. These arguments, however, were severely undermined by a 7 May 2008 ruling of the constitutional court, Germany's highest court, that the deployment of German AWACS personnel to fly reconnaissance missions over Turkey during the 2003 invasion of Iraq had been unconstitutional because it was not put to a parliamentary vote. The SPD–Green coalition government had argued these missions were routine NATO obligations and thus did not require a vote. The constitutional court rejected this logic, saying that a parliamentary vote was necessary for all missions that might result in combat. The judges took the view that all missions in which German personnel were armed and allowed to use force fell into this category.

The CDU/CSU parliamentarians deliberately styled their position paper as an attempt to trigger a substantive and widespread domestic debate. However, like a 2006 government White Paper on security policy, it failed to shift the ground significantly because of the sensitivities in political culture, party politics, and events such as the constitutional court ruling. It is unlikely that the CDU/CSU draft will be tabled for consideration before the 2009 elections. Meanwhile, external pressure on Germany to adapt its security-policy orientation is likely to remain as strong as the domestic constraints that limit the freedom of action of policymakers.

United Kingdom: Brown's Travails

When Gordon Brown arrived at his Downing Street office in London for the first time as prime minister on 27 June 2007, he wasted no time in seeking to distinguish himself from Tony Blair, his predecessor. In a 352-word statement, he used the word 'change' eight times and said he would lead a 'new government with new priorities'. The son of a Scottish Presbyterian minister, he quoted his school motto: 'I will try my utmost'.

Blair's decision to step down after ten years in office had opened the way for Brown, his long-time rival, to win the Labour Party leadership, and hence the premiership. Brown's desperate desire to succeed Blair had been obvious in the long-drawn-out internecine conflict that had dogged Blair's tenure. Finally, with the comfort of a healthy majority in Parliament and three years before he was required to call a general election, Brown appeared in a strong position to impose his own vision.

A year later, however, his government was floundering. The Labour Party was growing impatient with Brown's failure to fashion an electorally appealing purpose, and was struggling to cope with his awkward leadership style. David Cameron, the Conservative opposition leader, launched stinging verbal attacks that Brown could counter only with dogged recitations of the (Blair) government's achievements. The malaise was felt throughout the country: in local council elections on 1 May, Labour's share of the vote was the lowest for 40 years. The maverick Labour mayor of London, Ken Livingstone, was ousted by an almost equally maverick Conservative, Boris Johnson.

Brown's expression of his government's goals was rooted in the policies that he had pursued during ten years as Blair's finance minister. Labour had come to power in 1997 partly because of widespread dissatisfaction with the performance of public services, particularly in health and education. The key to Blair's and Brown's success was initially to put the government's finances on a sound footing and to adopt a pro-business approach that did not seek to reverse the market-oriented, anti-socialist reforms carried out by Margaret Thatcher in the 1980s. To give greater assurance that inflation would be kept under control, Brown made the Bank of England, the country's central bank, free to set interest rates independently of the government. Having thus established trust in the government's 'prudence', Blair and Brown then poured money into state-provided health care and schools. As prime minister, Brown has repeatedly expressed his passionate belief in giving opportunities to all parts of society, and in particular to the children of poor families – the government claims to have brought 600,000 children out of poverty since 1997, and aims to eradicate child poverty by 2020. Job creation and improved public services were Brown's constant themes. His upbringing instilled a faith in hard work and duty. In his view, the government has a duty to help the unemployed, but the unemployed have a duty in return to train for and find work. New forms of training so as to optimise opportunities represented a shift of resources from welfare to education, with the aim of making Britain a successful participant in a globalised economy, rather than a victim of it.

While Brown believes deeply in these goals, Blair also shared them. Brown has seemed unable to fashion and articulate a platform for his government that goes beyond them. Blair, by contrast, had been a bold player on the international stage, finding common cause with the United States as a matter of explicit strategy, deploying British troops abroad on many occasions, and putting himself in the forefront of international initiatives on Africa and climate change. But his decision to take part in the 2003 invasion of Iraq damaged him irremediably, particularly as it was founded on what proved to be an overstated case regarding Baghdad's weapons programmes. Brown's view of the Iraq venture was closely held: he had publicly expressed his support, though in the fewest possible words. In devising an approach distinct from that of his predecessor, he had conflicting impulses: to exit from Blair's most unpopular venture, but at the same time to maintain a close relationship with the United States – just not one that, in the words of one of his ministers, was 'joined at the hip'.

Here lay the essence of Brown's problem: on Iraq and on most other controversial issues during his first year in office, he seemed unable to resolve his own internal conflicts and strike a path forward. He avoided decisions and, when forced to decide, produced solutions that were neither one thing nor the other. He repeatedly fell between two stools, thereby nullifying any political advantage that might be gained on a particular issue, and ceding the ground to the opposition. He was lampooned for having agitated obsessively for a decade to become prime minister, only to have little idea of what he wished to do once in power.

Foreign and defence policy: 'hard-headed internationalism'
Brown inherited a British military presence in Iraq and Afghanistan, and a terrorism threat underscored by the July 2005 London bombings and the subsequent discovery of several unsuccessful plots. The broad lines of his approach were evident from the first as he announced a plan to publish a national security strategy and reconfigured Cabinet sub-committees to create a National Security Committee. The government would in future announce 'a single security budget', he said. Observers of the armed forces found plenty to confirm their long-held suspicion that Brown had no empathy with the military. His decision to 'double-hat' the defence minister, Des Browne, by giving him additional ministerial responsibility for Scotland, seemed calculated to offend the defence community.

Of all foreign-policy issues, the military presence in Iraq was inevitably the most pressing for Brown, as it represented what many voters saw as the Blair government's most glaring failure. It was not long before David Miliband, the foreign minister, was seeking to create a distinctly British case for keeping a military presence in Iraq – and thus for reducing it. Decisions about troop deployments in Iraq, he said, must reflect circumstances in the southern province of Basra, for which Britain had responsibility, rather than those in Baghdad, where the Americans were in charge. The two situations, he said, were 'very very different'. By October, all British troops had withdrawn from Basra city to the airport, and Brown announced that their number would be cut from 5,500 to 2,500 by spring 2008. They were now in an 'overwatch' role, concentrating on training of Iraqi soldiers. There were suggestions – vigorously denied by the British military – that the UK presence in the south had proved a failure. When the Iraqi government launched attacks on militants in Basra in March 2008, American forces moved to support them, but British troops hardly became involved. Brown was prepared to ignore American distaste for the reduced UK role. His solution, however, pleased nobody: by mid 2008, Britain had not yet withdrawn from Iraq as many voters wanted; but its troops were unable to influence events in Iraq and seemed to have no clear reason for remaining – a situation that was unsatisfactory for UK forces, for the Iraqi government and for Washington.

In November, Brown sought to enunciate his foreign policy. In a speech, he said the United States remained Britain's strongest ally: 'I have no truck with anti-Americanism in Britain or elsewhere in Europe'. More broadly, he described his approach as 'hard-headed internationalism'. The second element of this phrase was easier to understand than the first. He was internationalist, he said, in the sense that 'global challenges need global solutions and nations must cooperate across borders – often with hard-headed intervention – to give expression to our shared interests and shared values'. He was hard-headed 'because we will not shirk from the difficult long term decisions and because only through reform of our international rules and institutions will we achieve concrete, on-the-ground results'. While the speech provided little further clue as to the implications of this approach for policy, the National Security Strategy, published in March 2008, offered some elucidation: 'We will be hard-headed about the risks, our aims, and our capabilities. We will adopt a rigorous approach to assessing the threats and risks to our security, and the options for tackling them. That means being clear and realistic about our aims, and about the capabilities we and others have to achieve them.' The document went on to say: 'In an increasingly interdependent world, we cannot opt out of overseas engagement. But overseas especially we need to be realistic, and set realistic expectations, about what we can achieve.'

The repeated use of 'realistic' seemed to shed light on what Brown had meant by 'hard-headed'. It suggested an intention to be more cautious about undertaking military ventures and to lower expectations of what they might achieve. This seemed a deliberate – albeit not very transparent – move to eschew what might have been seen as the more starry-eyed ambitions of Blair to 'make a difference' in the world through British military action. Complementing this picture, Brown's major new suggestion, floated to European leaders and at the UN, was to develop new civilian capabilities to help rebuild damaged countries. In his November speech, he said: 'I propose that, in future, Security Council peacekeeping resolutions ... should make stabilisation, reconstruction and development an equal priority; that the international community should be ready to act with a standby civilian force including police and judiciary who can be deployed to rebuild civic societies'.

In spite of this more reserved stance, Brown's government has continued to demonstrate full commitment to the NATO operation in Afghanistan, where 7,800 British troops are deployed. By July 2008, UK forces had suffered 83 combat deaths, as well as 14 deaths in a military aircraft crash, since military operations began there in 2001. More than half these deaths had occurred since the start of 2007. British participation was maintained in spite of tensions with the government of President Hamid Karzai, who objected to secret discussions with Taliban militants and blocked the appointment of Paddy Ashdown, the British former UN supremo in Bosnia, to a similar coordinating role in Kabul. While Brown called for other NATO European countries to share the combat burden in southern Afghanistan being shouldered largely by Britain, Canada and the Netherlands, the mission continued to have popular support within the UK, helped by press coverage of the deployment of Prince Harry, a soldier grandson of Queen Elizabeth II.

The long commitments in Iraq, Afghanistan and elsewhere have put a heavy strain on the armed forces, which number just 180,000 active service personnel, excluding reserves. Although the defence budget, at some £30bn, is the world's second largest in hard-currency terms and is supplemented by additional funding for operations, it is seen by defence analysts as inadequate to support the tempo and nature of British military activity, which regularly involves combat. Difficulties in funding an ambitious equipment-procurement programme became particularly evident over the past year. Following the sudden departure of the government minister responsible for defence procurement, who was widely admired but opted to pursue a passion for motor racing, policy entered a state of drift. Brown was apparently unable to decide whether to cancel some equipment programmes to narrow a funding gap, and the likely result was that all would be further delayed. The frustration felt in the defence community boiled over in November when five former chiefs of defence staff, as well as other senior figures, fiercely criticised the level of defence funding, and Brown personally, in a debate in the House of Lords. Decrying the government's claims to have increased the defence budget, a former admiral accused it of using 'smoke and mirrors' to disguise cuts and said that at the defence ministry there was 'blood on the floor as the defence programme is slashed to meet the desperate funding situation'. Brown responded that he 'wanted to see the armed forces properly equipped with the resources they need'.

Another important area of foreign policy, Europe, provided an example of the prime minister falling between two courses of action. He indicated that he wanted to be in the forefront of creating new ideas for the European Union. In his November foreign-policy speech, he said: 'I want to play my part in helping the European Union move away from its past preoccupation with inward-looking institutional reform and I will work with others to propose a comprehensive agenda for a Global Europe – a Europe that is outward looking, open, internationalist, able to effectively respond both through internal reform and external action to the economic, security and environmental imperatives of globalisation'. Brown played a full part in the negotiations that led to the EU's Lisbon Treaty, which replaced the attempt to agree an EU constitution that had failed in 2005. He resisted feverish calls from opposition parties for a UK referendum to be held. However, when the moment came in December for Europe's leaders to gather to sign the treaty, he contrived to be absent. Instead, he went to Lisbon later on the same day and signed the treaty by himself. Thus, he opened himself to criticism from pro-Europeans and sceptics alike.

The continuing threat of terrorism

The new government did not have to wait long to face a full-scale terrorism alert. Less than 48 hours after Brown took office, two cars containing petrol, gas cylinders and nails were found abandoned in central London, one of them outside a crowded nightclub. They did not explode. A day later, a car also packed with gas canisters was driven into the main entrance of Glasgow Airport in Scotland and caught fire. Again, there was no explosion. One of the two men in the car later died of his injuries. Police investigations resulted in the arrest of several foreign-born doctors.

While this was the most dramatic such event of the year to mid 2008, there was a constant stream of arrests, trials and convictions related to terrorism offences. One group, linked to the men jailed for the unsuccessful London bombings of 21 July 2005, was convicted of attending and operating terrorist training camps in the UK. Another group was jailed after discovery of a plot to kidnap and kill a British Muslim soldier. A female shop assistant at Heathrow airport was convicted of owning terrorist manuals, and was also shown to have communicated regarding airport security with a man separately convicted of preparing to commit terrorism overseas – her conviction was later overturned on appeal. Among trials still under way were those of eight men accused of plotting to blow up transatlantic airliners with liquid bombs, and of three men who, according to prosecutors, were linked to the 7 July 2005 London bombers.

The extent of the Islamist extremism problem in Britain was indicated in a rare speech in November 2007 by Jonathan Evans, director general of the Security Service, also known as MI5. Some 2,000 people, he said, had been identified as posing a threat, and 'we suspect that there are as many again that we don't yet know of'. The rising number was partly due to better coverage by intelligence agencies, but also to a steady flow of extremist recruits. Terrorist attacks were not random acts by disparate, fragmented groups, but were part of a deliberate campaign by al-Qaeda. Young people and children were particular targets for radicalisation. 'I do not think that this problem has yet reached its peak', he said.

The National Security Strategy sought to quantify the threat of terrorism. Placing it first in the list of 'threats and risks', it said that the UK 'faces a serious and sustained threat from violent extremists, claiming to act in the name of Islam'. Networks and individuals aspired to cause mass casualties, to mount suicide attacks, to use chemical, biological and radiological weapons, to target critical national infrastructure, and to use new methods including electronic attack. The document, however, added a qualification:

> While terrorism represents a threat to all our communities, and an attack on our values and our way of life, it does not at present amount to a strategic threat. But it is qualitatively and quantitatively more serious than the terrorist threats we have faced in the past, and it is likely to persist for many years.

This qualification seemed important: while not belittling the dangers, it moved British policy further along a separate track from that of the Bush administration's 'global war on terror'. It was sharply different, for example, from the campaign rhetoric of John McCain, the Republican presidential candidate, who refers to what he calls 'radical Islamic terrorism' as the 'transcendent challenge of our time'.

Brown took a number of steps to strengthen British defences against terrorism. Among these were improvements to border security and the addition of further resources and technical capabilities to the intelligence services. These were welcomed, but Brown again put at risk the political capital that might be derived. His government stuck doggedly to a proposal to extend the period that terrorist suspects could be held without charge from 28 to 42 days, by far the longest in Europe. This was roundly criticised by civil-liberties advocates and many Labour MPs, and seemed even to have little support among the police, intelligence or judicial experts.

Political and financial turbulence

By mid 2008, it was clear that Brown faced political difficulties. He did not need to call an election for two more years, but would be expected to do so by mid 2009 if he followed the practice of his predecessor. Opinion polls, while not a reliable guide when taken mid term, indicated that Labour would lose its parliamentary majority. Among the ranks of Labour MPs, many of whom would lose their seats in such a circumstance, there began to be rumblings about the leadership, although no real alternatives to Brown had yet emerged. In an attempt to freshen his government and Labour's image, he had promoted a bevy of younger politicians to ministerial office. But after 11 years in power, the ruling party's parliamentary benches contained plenty of disaffected members who had lost ministerial jobs or had been repeatedly passed over for them.

Brown had damaged his prospects in his handling of several issues. First, he flirted with the idea of seeking an electoral mandate of his own in an autumn 2007 election – a bold but risky option. He allowed close political associates to fuel a brief frenzy of media speculation, prompting David Cameron to challenge the prime minister to call an election even though the Conservative leader perhaps privately wished for more time to prepare. Brown's eventual decision not to call one then appeared weak, even though it was clearly the prudent course.

Secondly, the government's uncertain handling of problems in the banking system undermined Brown's reputation for competent handling of financial matters. As the effects of the US subprime mortgage crisis spread around the world, Northern Rock, a mortgage lender based in northeast England, found itself in September 2007 unable to obtain funding in the money markets to support its loan portfolio. The government authorised the Bank of England to provide emergency finance. But customers with savings in the bank, concerned about the safety of their deposits, rushed to withdraw them, forming long queues outside branches. Britain thus experienced its first run on a bank since that on Overend, Gurney & Co. in 1866. Within three days Alistair Darling, the finance minister, was forced to guarantee all deposits in Northern Rock. This allayed the panic. But by offering unlimited loans to preserve the bank's liquidity, and by guaranteeing all its deposits, the government had in effect taken control of it. It was evident that the authorities needed to engineer a rapid fire sale within the private sector – as the US Federal Reserve later organised for Bear Stearns, another institution bankrupted by the mortgage crisis – or nationalise Northern Rock. But it was not until February, five months after the emergency began, that Darling announced the lender's nationalisation.

The third misstep was the most surprising. As finance minister, Brown had introduced in 1999 a starting rate of income tax of 10% to help low-income households. In 2007, in his last budget before becoming prime minister, he announced its removal, making the starting rate 20%. Brown argued that the 10% rate had been 'transitional', and that benefits to low-income families were provided instead by a higher tax threshold and a range of tax credits, especially for pensioners and families with children. But when the change took effect in April 2008, it became clear that working people on low incomes without children would have higher tax bills. This caused a rebellion among Labour MPs, who felt betrayed. Brown at first doggedly rejected the criticism, but as the revolt continued, he was forced to make a humiliating apology and to promise to compensate fully all those who had been disadvantaged.

These events left Brown, and Britain, facing an uncertain future. The strong, competitive economy remained attractive both to investors and migrant workers, and London was enhancing its status as a global financial hub. But after a decade of prosperity under Labour rule, the economy had, as in other countries, entered a fragile period in which rising fuel and food prices were boosting inflation even as economic activity was slowing as a result of the reduced availability of credit following the mortgage crisis. The outcome could not be predicted, but posed evident risks to the government. Brown's first-year stumbles made him vulnerable to economic and financial developments, to unpredictable events in general, and to machinations within his own party. Having struggled so long to reach the pinnacle, he seemed unlikely to relinquish it voluntarily. It still appeared open to him to consolidate his position if he could show more positive and deft leadership. But it was not clear whether he had the capability to do so.

Developments in European Defence

NATO's mission in Afghanistan remained the top defence and security priority for European countries, almost of all of which had troops deployed there. The EU, meanwhile, continued to move into more demanding areas of both civilian and military crisis management. Moves towards new defence arrangements in Europe were put into doubt by Irish voters' rejection of the Lisbon Treaty, but the EU and NATO edged towards possible improved cooperation, even though obstacles remained. The United States signed an agreement with the Czech Republic, and continued to negotiate with Poland, on installing elements of its ballistic-missile-defence architecture in those countries, but Russia continued vigorously to oppose these plans.

NATO: Afghanistan and the Bucharest Summit

A series of divisive issues confronted NATO as it approached its 60th anniversary in 2009. The absence of clear strategic success in Afghanistan threatened to put at risk the long-term sustainability of its mission there, and there was a growing need for allies to step up their efforts to define a common understanding of their objectives.

As the insurgency in Afghanistan worsened (see pp. 296–305), NATO appeared to have increasing problems in forging a common vision of its mission, with each of the main contributing countries to the International Security Assistance Force (ISAF) seeming to develop its own operational approach. Disputes over risk sharing and the caveats placed by some governments on the activities of their forces continued to simmer. At the Alliance's Bucharest Summit in April 2008, NATO leaders sought to counter worries about the mission's cohesiveness by issuing a declaration entitled 'ISAF's Strategic Vision', which formulated four guiding principles for NATO activities in Afghanistan. First, it was underlined that NATO was committed for the long term and that this was a commitment shared among the Allies. Secondly, NATO would work to enhance Afghan leadership so that Afghan security forces and institutions could eventually ensure the rule of law. This included training and equipment support for the Afghan National Army, which is set to reach some 80,000 personnel by 2010. This principle also involved a progressive transfer of responsibility away from ISAF towards Afghan forces. Thirdly, NATO stressed the need for a comprehensive approach and enhanced civilian–military coordination. The nexus between development and security was highlighted as the main reason to improve unity of effort. Fourthly, NATO leaders pointed to the need to engage Afghanistan's neighbours, in particular Pakistan, to help combat violent extremism and narcotics trafficking.

In the months preceding the summit, tensions over burden-sharing were running high. US Secretary of Defense Robert Gates wrote to his European counterparts asking them to make more troops and equipment available. The Canadian government let it be known that it would withdraw from the Afghanistan mission unless Allies sent at least an additional 1,000 soldiers in support of the operation. France announced that it would send an extra battalion (some 800 troops), Poland pledged an additional 400, the Czech Republic some 120 special-forces personnel, and small increases were also pledged by Romania and Portugal, as well as by soon-to-be-member Croatia. Non-NATO member Georgia also announced an extra 500 troops. Later, Germany said it would make available an additional 1,000 troops from autumn 2008 on. It was also reported that some 18 additional helicopters were made available by Allies for operations in Afghanistan. NATO was able to secure increased commitments, but without resolving the longer-term debate over force generation.

There was disagreement among the Allies on whether Georgia and Ukraine should be admitted to NATO's Membership Action Plan (MAP), a key step on the road to membership. Washington put strong pressure on NATO members to admit both countries, but several, including France and Germany, opposed extending MAP status to these aspirants for a variety of reasons, including territorial disputes in Georgia, an uncertain political situation in Ukraine, and (less openly) because of vocal Russian opposition. Unable to bridge the divide, NATO did not grant MAP status to either country. A compromise was reached in which the summit declaration stated: 'NATO welcomes Ukraine's and Georgia's Euro-Atlantic aspirations for membership in NATO. We agreed today that these countries will become members of NATO.' This phrasing was reportedly inserted into the declaration directly by the leaders after protracted negotiations. However, the two countries still awaited MAP status.

Albania and Croatia were invited to join NATO, and signed the accession protocols on 9 July. Macedonia, which like Albania and Croatia had MAP status and was a candidate for membership, was told it would need to resolve a dispute about its name with Greece before it could be invited to join.

Missile defence

NATO acknowledged at Bucharest that the planned Europe-based US missile-defence assets would significantly contribute to the protection of European allies from long-range ballistic missiles. The Alliance set out to define ways in which these assets could be linked to NATO's own efforts in this area by its next summit, in 2009. Among existing activities of NATO members in this area are the Active Layered Theatre Ballistic Missile Defence Programme (ALTBMD), preliminary work to support potential decisions on a missile-defence system to protect NATO territory and population centres, and cooperation on theatre missile defence with Russia. ALTBMD, to which NATO members have allocated some €700m, is scheduled to reach initial operating capability by 2010, with full operating capability planned for 2015. It is designed primarily to protect deployed NATO forces against ballistic missiles, but could also be used as part of a territorial missile-defence system. It could thus function as a bolt-on to the US system, providing complete coverage of NATO territory.

US plans for Europe-based assets include an interceptor site of up to ten silo-based long-range interceptor missiles to be deployed between 2011 and 2013, and a mid-course tracking radar, currently being used at a US test range in the Pacific, that would be relocated to Europe in 2011. The United States, seeking to counter the perceived threat from Iran's missiles and nuclear programme, wants to site the interceptors in Poland and the mid-course radar in the Czech Republic. In July 2008, following lengthy negotiations, the US and Czech governments signed an agreement, though this had still to be approved by the Czech parliament.

Negotiations with Poland continued. In February 2008, Polish Foreign Minister Radek Sikorski announced the outlines of a basic agreement under which the United States would bolster Polish air defences and contribute to the cost of transforming Poland's armed forces in exchange for Poland hosting the interceptors. Defence Minister Bogdan Klich said the government wanted the Americans 'to seriously involve themselves in the modernization of our armed forces'. These demands were a hardening of the position of the previous government, to reflect the perception that the interceptor missiles would make Poland a target and that it was owed something for supporting the United States in Iraq and Afghanistan.

The US proposals were unpopular in the two countries and were strongly opposed by Russia, which was concerned that its nuclear deterrent would be undermined. Russian President Dmitry Medvedev said the US plans were 'a threat to Russian interests'. Presidents George W. Bush and Vladimir Putin, at their last meeting before Medvedev succeeded Putin as president, issued a joint statement that 'the Russian side has made clear that it does not agree with the decision to establish sites in Poland and the Czech Republic and reiterated its proposed alternative. Yet, it appreciates the measures that the US has proposed and declared that if agreed and implemented such measures will be important and useful in assuaging Russian concerns.' Moscow's response to the signing of the Czech agreement, however, was to threaten to react through 'military-technical methods'.

EU missions expand further

As of June 2008, the EU was conducting 12 crisis-management missions, ten of which were civilian. It launched new missions in Chad–Central African Republic (CAR), Kosovo and Guinea-Bissau. Meanwhile, a police mission to Afghanistan reached operational capability and a civilian–military action in support of the AU mission in Sudan was terminated as planned at the end of 2007, when the AU's mission was handed over to a hybrid AU–UN operation.

The EU, however, was facing persistent weaknesses in both civilian and military capabilities for crisis-management operations. Its potential as a truly integrated provider of crisis-management tools had not yet been realised, a situation that might become increasingly difficult to maintain as the Union takes on more demanding challenges. Better NATO–EU cooperation in international crisis management, however, seemed to be within reach with changes in political assessments in Paris and Washington.

The most ambitious EU military mission to date, a UN-mandated bridging operation in Chad and CAR, was launched on 28 January 2008. The operation, EUFOR Chad/CAR, was scheduled to last for 12 months before being replaced by a follow-on UN force. Deployments began in February 2008, and initial operating capability was reached on 15 March. The force, set to reach a strength of some 3,700, numbered 2,760 by May, with the largest contingents coming from France (1,548), Ireland (379), Sweden (211), Austria (150) and Belgium (150). The operation's commander was Lieutenant-General Patrick Nash of Ireland and the force commander was Brigadier-General Jean-Philippe Ganascia of France. EUFOR deployed with a rear force headquarters at N'Djamena, a force headquarters at Abeche and three battalions in the eastern Chad areas of Iriba, Forchana and Goz Beida. It also deployed a detachment to Birao in CAR. Key objectives were to protect civilians, especially refugees and displaced persons, to facilitate the delivery of humanitarian aid, to assist with the free movement of aid personnel, and to contribute to the protection of UN personnel and facilities. One problem was obtaining sufficient transport helicopters able to operate in the harsh environment.

As Kosovo declared independence in February 2008, the EU formally launched a Rule of Law mission in Kosovo (EULEX Kosovo), intended to support the building of a legal system. It was intended to have a staff of 1,900 police officers, judges, prosecutors and customs officials. Priority areas were the protection of minority communities, corruption and fighting organised crime. EULEX was the first EU mission with limited executive powers in the field of investigating and prosecuting serious and sensitive crime, and was also the first EU crisis-management mission to which the United States would contribute personnel. The failure of Kosovo to win widespread international recognition complicated the mission, since the UN mission in Kosovo (UNMIK) continued to have authority. EULEX was subject to delays because of its unclear legal status and difficulties in staffing and equipping the mission. It was questionable, for example, whether it would be able to take over equipment and files from UNMIK.

Launched in June 2007, the EU's police mission in Afghanistan (EUPOL Afghanistan) was some 230 strong and comprised police and law-enforcement and justice experts, deployed at central, regional and provincial levels. The three-year mission, headed by Brigadier-General Jürgen Scholz, was intended to assist the Afghan government with the creation of civilian policing arrangements. This was the first time the EU had sent civilian personnel into an active conflict zone.

The EU also launched a small security-sector-reform mission to Guinea-Bissau (EU SSR Guinea-Bissau), comprising 15 military and civilian advisers, on 12 February 2008 at the invitation of the government.

In light of the persistent demand for civilian crisis management, the EU created a new chain of command for civilian operations in June 2007. The Civilian Planning and Conduct Capability, comprising an operations unit and a mission-support unit, was a civilian equivalent of the EU military staff. A civilian operations commander, Klees Klompenhouwer, was given strategic command and control of all civilian missions.

The EU's Lisbon Treaty: security and defence implications

The Lisbon Treaty was agreed by EU heads of government in December 2007 and was submitted to member countries for ratification. Of the 27 EU members – all of whom had to ratify the treaty for it to take effect – only one, Ireland, held a referendum. In June 2008, Irish voters threw its fate into doubt by rejecting it. The treaty contained many of the reform measures that had originally been included in an EU 'constitution' rejected by voters in France and the Netherlands in 2005. The challenge facing Europe after the Irish vote was to avoid a further period of introspection (such as occurred after the 2005 votes) when expectations of a stronger EU role regarding international peace and stability were growing. The treaty included an array of measures intended to make the EU more coherent and efficient in this field.

Several clauses would affect future arrangements in the areas of foreign affairs and security. The office of the high representative for the Common Foreign and Security Policy, the post currently held by Javier Solana, would be transformed into the high representative of the Union for foreign affairs and security policy (Articles 18 and 27), and the holder of that future post (often described as an 'EU foreign minister') would also be a vice-president of the European Commission, absorbing the current position of commissioner for external relations. This arrangement could improve coordination between the European Council and the Commission, but also implied a tension in that the future high representative would have to balance the demands of two institutions. A further complication would be that the high representative's responsibilities are not clearly delineated from those of the new permanent president of the Union, another post that would be created under the treaty. Both posts were likely to be largely driven by the personalities of their incumbents. The Lisbon Treaty also envisaged the creation of an EU External Action Service (EAS), comprising officials from both EU institutions and EU member states, designed to strengthen the high representative.

Further significant aspects of the treaty were a solidarity clause (Article 222) and a mutual-assistance clause (Article 42.7), which stirred debate because its wording was such that some observers argued it amounted to a mutual-defence clause. This was a three-way compromise among those member states which desired an EU mutual-defence commitment, those which sought to safeguard their non-aligned status, and those which saw mutual defence as the remit of NATO. The assistance clause called on EU member states to aid each other in case of 'armed aggression' on a member's territory and to do so with 'all means in their power', although military means are not explicitly mentioned. But it said its provisions should not prejudice the defence policy of member states without alliance commitments and that NATO would remain the 'foundation of collective defence' of EU members that are also members of the Alliance. A significant difference between the treaty's mutual-assistance clause and the mutual-defence clause of NATO is that military means are explicitly included in the latter. The solidarity clause would commit EU member states to support each other in the event of terrorist attacks and natural or man-made disasters. While the clause refers to military assets, it is up to member states to decide what kind of assistance they would provide. The wording of the solidarity clause mirrors the EU's Declaration on Terrorism adopted in March 2004. Its importance lies in the ability to employ military resources within the EU for the purpose of consequence management in cases of terrorism or disaster.

The treaty redefined the Petersberg tasks, which set the framework for the operations the EU could undertake. It listed these as 'joint disarmament operations, humanitarian and rescue tasks, military advice and assistance tasks, conflict prevention and peace-keeping tasks, tasks of combat forces in crisis management, including peace-making and post-conflict stabilisation'. It said that 'all these tasks may contribute to the fight against terrorism, including by supporting third countries in combating terrorism in their territories'.

A final treaty innovation in the defence arena that caused much debate was the set of provisions regarding permanent structured cooperation (Article 42.6 and Protocol on Permanent Structured Cooperation), which would allow those member states 'whose military capabilities fulfil higher criteria and which have made more binding commitments to one another in this area with a view to the most demanding operations' to set up a leadership group seeking closer cooperation but within the overall framework of the EU. Permanent structured cooperation would be set up by groups of countries after consultations with the high representative, by qualified majority voting. The treaty would maintain the unanimity requirement for the launch of ESDP missions or activities under the revised Petersberg tasks. The criteria for membership of such groups are controversial and remain undefined. One school of thought argues that the criteria should be demanding, to facilitate creation of new capabilities among committed states, while another believes that permanent structured cooperation should be as inclusive as possible to prevent decoupling of an avant-garde group from the rest of the EU member states.

With the EU's plans thrown into question, cooperation between the EU and NATO continued to be blocked by political obstacles. However, there were signs of shifts in long-held positions. US Ambassador to NATO Victoria Nuland, for example, made it clear that the United States would like to see a strong and capable Europe that continued to build civilian and military capability through both the EU's defence arms and NATO. This was the most positive American endorsement yet of the EU's role in the realm of security and defence. A further sign that cooperation could improve came from France's interest in rejoining NATO's integrated military structure. The debate about whether the EU and NATO were competing or complementary seemed to be losing definition. The biggest stumbling block remained Turkey's unwillingness to discuss substantive questions in meetings between the organisations so long as EU member Cyprus was involved. This impasse remained unresolved.

The Balkans: Kosovo Breaks Away

The most important event in the western Balkans in the year to mid 2008 was Kosovo's declaration of independence from Serbia on 17 February. The ramifications of this decision will play out for years to come. One of its first consequences was the downfall of the Serbian government. However, dire predictions of extensive violence and of a mass exodus of Serbs from Kosovo did not come true.

Albania and Croatia were invited to join NATO at the Alliance's April summit in Bucharest. However, Macedonia's bid to join was blocked by Greece because of a dispute over the country's name. In Bosnia, 18 months of political gridlock were ended by a breakthrough agreement among leaders on police reform in October 2007. This allowed their country to sign a Stabilisation and Association Agreement (SAA) with the European Union on 16 June 2008, the first substantial step on the road to EU membership.

Albania was rocked politically in the aftermath of a massive explosion at a factory in Gerdec near Tirana on 15 March 2008 which left 26 dead. Workers had been dismantling old ammunition so that brass casings could be recycled for scrap and the gunpowder reused. There were also allegations that corruption had allowed old, poor-quality ammunition to be exported to the Afghan security services.

Kosovo: declaration's confusing outcome

Kosovo's declaration of independence was intended to be the last chapter in the dismantling of the former Yugoslavia, but it merely ended one chapter and opened another. Four months on, Kosovo had been recognised by only 43 countries, including the United States and 20 out of 27 EU members. Russia, Greece, Spain, the vast majority of Muslim countries, Brazil, China and India all spurned it.

Five of the six former Yugoslav republics, Serbia, Bosnia-Herzegovina, Macedonia, Croatia and Slovenia, achieved independence in the early 1990s, and the sixth, Montenegro, became independent of Serbia in 2006. As a province of Serbia, however, Kosovo did not have the same *de jure* right to self-determination as the republics, or indeed, according to Serbia, any right at all. About 90% of Kosovo's 2m people are ethnic Albanians, and the region was plagued by guerrilla war and ethnic cleansing from 1996–99. Following the NATO bombing campaign against Serbia in 1999, NATO peacekeeping troops moved into Kosovo and administration of the territory was taken over by the United Nations Interim Administration Mission in Kosovo (UNMIK), which operated under the aegis of UN Security Council Resolution 1244. It later devolved much power to Kosovo's elected institutions.

After riots in Kosovo in March 2004 the UN set in train a process aimed at finding a durable settlement. In February 2006, Martti Ahtisaari, the former Finnish president, was asked to oversee talks between Kosovo's Albanians and Serbia. The parties were willing to compromise on almost all issues other than the question of whether Kosovo would be an independent state. Unable to break the deadlock, Ahtisaari presented a plan to the UN in March 2007, envisaging independence for Kosovo but with a high level of autonomy for its Serbian areas and provisions for special protection of Serbian churches, monasteries and other important monuments. Serbian areas would be allowed to keep special links with Serbia. The plan, which was predicated on a new UN

Security Resolution to replace 1244, foresaw the phasing out of UNMIK over 120 days. NATO troops would stay and a new body, the International Civilian Office (ICO), would be set up along the lines of the Office of the High Representative in Bosnia. Its head, the international civilian representative, would be given extensive powers to intervene in running Kosovo, if necessary. In parallel with the ICO, Ahtisaari planned an EU-led police and justice mission which would help mentor Kosovo's police, intervene in police matters if necessary, and provide international judges in special cases. The mission, EULEX, would provide policemen, including Americans operating under an EU flag, and would comprise some 1,900 personnel.

When planning for these arrangements began, the extent to which a resurgent Russia intended to flex its muscles was still unclear. Kosovo provided Moscow an ideal opportunity. In summer 2007 Russian diplomats thwarted all attempts to pass a new Security Council resolution, arguing that the Ahtisaari plan was a plan for independence and that, since Kosovo was technically part of Serbia, its people did not possess the right to self-determination. Russia's approach partly reflected a concern about the precedent that Kosovo's independence would set. Following the failure of attempts to pass a new resolution, the UN asked a troika of diplomats from the United States, Russia and the EU to make a last-ditch attempt to bridge the gap between the Serbs and the Kosovo Albanians. This, too, failed but the EU used the time to build a consensus on the deployment of EULEX and the ICO, which was to be headed by Pieter Feith, a Dutch diplomat.

Kosovo was prevailed upon to put off a declaration of independence until after presidential elections in Serbia scheduled for 20 January, with a run-off between the top two candidates on 3 February, so as not to tip the balance in favour of the hard-line nationalist candidate. With the elections over, on 16 February 2008 the Council of the European Union formally launched EULEX and appointed Feith as the EU special representative to Kosovo, 'double-hatting' him with the ICO, which was also formally constituted by a group of willing states. The next day Kosovo declared independence amidst scenes of celebrations among ethnic Albanians. Reaction soon set in. On 19 February a mob burned down the two customs posts between Serbian-inhabited northern Kosovo and Serbia, an action warmly applauded by Slobodan Samardzic, Serbia's minister for Kosovo, who said it 'might not be pleasant but it is legitimate'. On 21 February, following a rally of some 200,000 people in Belgrade, the US Embassy was set on fire and others were attacked while a mob went on a looting spree through the centre of the city.

Since 1999 Serbian areas of Kosovo had been only nominally under the control of the UN and Kosovar authorities. This was especially true for the north of Kosovo, where just under half of Kosovo's 100,000–130,000 Serbs live (the remainder are in enclaves scattered throughout the rest of the territory).

Kosovo's Serbs have always been extremely hostile to the idea of independence. On Belgrade's instructions, they had boycotted Kosovo's general and local elections in November 2007, but they still worked in the main Kosovo-wide institutions such as the police, customs and prison services. For the most part Serbian policemen patrolled Serbian areas, especially in the north. As soon as independence was declared this began to break down. Most Serbs employed in the Kosovo Police Service in Serbian enclaves were instructed to leave their jobs. Those in the north continued to work, but were now to be paid directly from Belgrade. Vojislav Kostunica, Serbia's prime minister, declared Kosovo a 'phony' state and said the EULEX deployment would be illegal. The Serbian authorities then went through the largely ritual gesture of annulling the declaration and bringing criminal charges against Kosovo's president, prime minister and parliamentary speaker for an 'unlawful attempt to bring about the secession of a part of Serbia's territory'.

Kostunica then made his intentions clear, saying 'Serbia intends to rule parts of Kosovo where loyal citizens still look to Belgrade for government'. As Serbian ministers toured Serbian areas of Kosovo at will, Samardzic defined the plan as 'functional separation' between Serbs and Albanians – in other words consolidating the de facto partition of the territory. On 18 March the UN hit back, seizing a court in the northern, Serbian part of the divided city of Mitrovica occupied by former employees. In the ensuing melee one Ukrainian peacekeeper was killed and there were many injuries on all sides.

The parties looked to UN Secretary-General Ban Ki Moon for a ruling on how to proceed in the absence of a new UN resolution. On 12 June he wrote to Serbia's President Boris Tadic and Kosovo's President Fatmir Sejdiu. To the latter he wrote that independence had 'operational implications' for UNMIK, 'which require it adjust to developments and to changes on the ground'. To Tadic he said that there would now be 'temporary arrangements that would apply for a limited duration and without prejudice to the status of Kosovo'. The secretary-general's letters did not mention the ICO. To Sejdiu he said he foresaw an 'enhanced' role for the EU in Kosovo, but to Tadic he said only that he would discuss this with Javier Solana, the EU's foreign-policy chief. He was, however, clear that in Serbian areas Serbian police would continue to report to the UN.

These letters created confusion as Kosovo's post-independence constitution came into effect on 15 June. The constitution gave no role to UNMIK, but set out arrangements for the roles of EULEX and the ICO as prescribed in the Ahtisaari plan, leaving many issues unresolved. Full deployment of EULEX was postponed until an unknown date (October 2008 was mentioned as a target) for both political and logistical reasons. The role of the ICO, which had already been established, was unclear if UNMIK continued to exist. It was suggested that EULEX could be brought under the umbrella of UNMIK, but exactly how was unclear. Although

Feith said the ICO and EULEX would operate over the whole of Kosovo's territory, it was clear that this would not happen: staff from both organisations were told they would be unwelcome in Serbian areas. Serbs who wanted to work with them or rent offices to them were threatened. It appeared that the UN would continue to operate in Serbian areas and the ICO and EULEX in Albanian ones.

On 11 May Serbs in Kosovo voted in local elections (as well as in Serbia's general election). As these were Serbian and not Kosovar elections, the UN and ICO said they would not work with the new local authorities in Serbian areas. On 28 June the situation became even more complex with the formation of a Serbian assembly for Kosovo comprising those elected in the Serbian municipal polls on 11 May, further consolidating the partition of Kosovo.

Kosovar Albanians reacted extraordinarily calmly to these developments. There was no Serbian exodus from Kosovo, and Serbia did not mount a much-feared economic blockade of the territory or cut off water and electricity supplies. Roads to and from Serbia remained open. UN police returned to the two burned border posts in the north, though customs officers did not and smuggling became a problem. Serbia said it would not accept Kosovo's presence at international meetings if it was represented as the Republic of Kosovo but would continue to accept the old formula of 'Kosovo/UNMIK'. Belgrade's attempts to stem the tide of further recognition of an independent Kosovo were generally successful.

Serbia: differing reactions

The key issue for the main political parties in Serbia was not so much the question of Kosovar independence itself – they all opposed it – but rather how to react to its declaration, and in particular how to approach countries that recognised it. Kostunica favoured a hard line, arguing that Serbia should abandon or put aside its desire to join the EU if (as they did) most EU states recognised Kosovo. Tadic took a different view, arguing that, whatever happened over Kosovo, Serbia must not abandon the path towards EU membership; not only was this was the best way to secure the future prosperity of its citizens, but Serbia would be in a weaker position to continue the argument over Kosovo if it were isolated.

Following the January 2007 elections Tadic's party, despite winning more seats, had settled into an uneasy coalition with Kostunica, having ceded him the position of premier to secure his support. Relations between the two men turned acrimonious, and it often appeared that the president's party was taking orders from its junior coalition partner. Relations deteriorated further during the presidential elections, in which Kostunica refused to back Tadic. In the first round on 20 January 2008 the winner was Tomislav Nikolic, leader of the hard-line nationalist Serbian Radical Party. The party's founder, Vojislav Seselj, is on trial at the UN war-crimes tribunal at The Hague. In the second round Tadic, who ran on a strongly pro-EU ticket, won with 51.6% of the vote.

Kosovo's declaration two weeks later made it impossible for the government to continue, and parliamentary elections were called for 11 May. Early opinion polls foreshadowed a government made up of the Radicals, Kostunica's party and the small Socialist Party of Serbia (SPS), which under Slobodan Milosevic had led Serbia into the disastrous wars of the 1990s. However, voters appeared to be strongly influenced by developments just before the elections.

Serbia had already completed the work to sign an SAA with the EU – an important step on the path towards membership. However, the signing had been blocked by Belgium and the Netherlands, which argued that Serbia should not be rewarded when it had been deemed not to be cooperating fully with the UN war-crimes tribunal. Carl Bildt, the Swedish foreign minister, and others persuaded them to let Serbia sign, arguing that Belgrade would slip back into isolation if Tadic's party did not win the general election, with negative consequences for the whole of the western Balkans. Serbia signed the SAA on 29 April, and talks opened on reforms to allow Serbs to travel to most EU countries without visas. In another important development, Italian car maker Fiat announced an investment of some €700m in Zastava, its Serbian counterpart, with the prospect of thousands of jobs.

Tadic's party did far better at the polls than expected, taking some 39% of the vote. After weeks of negotiations the SPS and the coalition around Tadic's party signed an agreement on 4 July, stating their intention to form a government.

Bosnia: continued political wrangles

The political roller coaster endured by Bosnians in the year to mid 2008 resulted in extension of the mandate of the high representative and at times aroused fears that the country could sink back into conflict.

The legacy of the Dayton peace agreement which ended the Bosnian war in 1995 was a complex state with two 'entities', one for Serbs (the Republika Srpska) and one for Bosniaks (Muslims) and Croats. A weak central government was overseen by the UN high representative, who had considerable powers. However, the country's progress had been such that it was planned, in 2007, to abolish the Office of the High Representative and to reduce the number of EU and EU-led troops from 6,000 to 2,500 by the end of the year. In the event, a deteriorating political climate and fears about the repercussions of Kosovo's declaration of independence led to the high representative's mandate being pro-longed, although the troop reduction took place as planned.

Several things contributed to the poor political atmosphere. In 2006, modest proposals to reform the constitution failed to secure parliamentary support, causing political stalemate. Elections brought a sweeping victory for Milorad Dodik in the Republika Srpska and the return to centre stage on the Bosniak side of Haris Silajdzic, a hardliner and former premier. Silajdzic demanded the abolition of the Republika Srpska, which threatened to hold a referendum on independence. Police reform was a major bone of contention. Changes demanded by the EU would have deprived the Republika Srpska of its own force. Dodik, who had initially argued that his people would rather keep their own police than join the EU, conceded the change provided that the name of the police of the Republika Srpska could be retained. This was rejected by Silajdzic, who argued that the name was associated with genocide.

In October 2007 Miroslav Lajcak, the high representative, sought to end a long period of wrangling by imposing various political changes and implicitly threatening Dodik, whom he had the power to remove. Bosnia's politicians then struck a deal on police reform which was far less extensive than the EU had originally sought, and in effect put off key decisions. This allowed an SAA to be initialled with the EU on 4 December. Although Dodik had demanded a referendum on independence for Republika Srpska if Kosovo was recognised as an independent state, his rhetoric became more muted after Kosovo's declaration. The implication was that Dodik was primarily interested in preserving the powers given to him under the Dayton agreement. On 22 April 2008 a law on police reform was finally passed, enabling Bosnia to sign an SAA on 16 June, becoming the last western Balkan country to do so. This was regarded as a major step forward, and the abolition as early as mid 2008 of the Office of the High Representative was put back on the agenda. As the high representative and the EU special representative in Bosnia are 'double hatted', the intention is that there should be a seamless transition from the legal power of the former to the influence of the latter, with the EU representative able to cajole where necessary to ensure that the SAA's provisions are carried out.

Macedonia: name dispute blocks NATO membership

Macedonia suffered a major political setback when Greece succeeded at NATO's April 2008 summit in Bucharest in blocking an invitation to Skopje to join the Alliance. At issue was the dispute over the name of the republic, which has dogged it since independence in 1991. Greece called it 'the Former Yugoslav Republic of Macedonia', and sought to impose the use of this name by others. Macedonia rejected Greece's claim that it had territorial pretensions to the Greek part of historic Macedonia. Greece conceded that the republic could include 'Macedonia' in its name but wanted a qualifier such as 'New' or 'Upper' added. Skopje rejected this solution. Greece, further upset by Macedonia's decision to name Skopje's airport after Alexander the Great, is also blocking the opening of Macedonia's discussions on EU membership.

Following the setback in Bucharest, Macedonian Prime Minister Nikola Gruevski called an early election. Macedonia had suffered from political instability throughout 2007 after Gruevski's party, which had won elections in 2006, decided to take as a coalition partner the smaller of the two main ethnic Albanian parties. This led to a four-month boycott of parliament by the larger Albanian party, physical fights between members of the two parties and even scuffles between members in parliament. About one-quarter of Macedonia's people are ethnic Albanians. As elsewhere in the Balkans, power confers considerable political and economic patronage. Elections in Macedonia are conducted on a strictly ethnic basis. On the Macedonian side, Gruevski's party did well in the 1 June election, but on the Albanian side the polls were marred by violence and intimidation. One man died in a shoot-out with police. In areas where there had been trouble, elections were rerun on 15 June. After the election there was speculation as to whether Gruevski, once he had formed a new government, would feel strong enough to strike a deal with Greece – although Macedonians also wondered whether Greece really wanted one.

Turkey: Government Stumbles after Win

Even by Turkey's roller-coaster standards, rarely has a political party witnessed such a dramatic change in its fortunes as that experienced by the ruling Justice and Development Party (AKP) over the past year.

In the general election of 22 July 2007, the AKP was easily returned to power, winning nearly half the popular vote. The party saw the victory as a public endorsement of its record in office. Since coming to power in 2002, it had overseen the longest period of domestic political stability and sustained economic growth in living memory, and had opened formal accession negotiations for membership of the European Union. Few AKP members had any hesitation in predicting even greater success during the party's second term.

But by mid 2008, Turkey was facing a crisis. The AKP appeared paralysed, uncertain how to respond to a case filed in the Constitutional Court to close the party down. Turkey's EU accession process was stalled. Economic growth was beginning to slow, with inflation and unemployment on the rise. Most worrying of all was the deepening polarisation of Turkish society over an issue which has overshadowed political life since the republic was founded in 1923: the role of religion in public life.

The AKP's triumph
The year to mid 2008 began with the AKP weathering a political storm and being returned to office with a resounding electoral victory. The party had appeared to offer something new when elected in 2002 following a recession and a series of corrupt and incompetent coalition governments, but it also had to overcome reservations about its Islamist origins.

Most of the decision-making core of the party had previously served in hard-line Islamist parties which had been closed down by the Constitutional Court for allegedly attempting to undermine the principle of secularism enshrined in the Turkish constitution. Few of the leaders had held high-level positions in these parties; those who had, such as Tayyip Erdogan, who served as mayor of Istanbul from 1994 to 1998, insisted that they had abandoned the radicalism of their youth. They described themselves as 'conservatives' or 'Muslim democrats', who were committed not only to secularism and pluralistic parliamentary democracy but also to Turkish accession to the EU. Hard-line secularists remained unconvinced and suspected that, despite protestations to the contrary, AKP leaders still harboured a long-term Islamist agenda.

In fact, the truth lay somewhere in between. Although it did not appear to desire an Islamic state based on sharia law, the AKP did want a more Islamic society – from its perspective, it wanted to ease the constraints imposed by the traditional interpretation of secularism in Turkey on the Islamic character of Turkish society. In practical terms, this meant changes such as lifting restrictions on religious education and abolishing the ban on women who wore headscarves attending university.

The AKP's initial accession to power was sweeping: in the 2002 election, none of the parties which had won seats in the previous election managed to cross the 10% threshold necessary for representation in parliament. The AKP won 34.3% of the popular vote, giving it 363 seats in the 550-member assembly, ahead of the nationalist Republican People's Party (CHP), which took 19.4% and 178 seats. The remaining nine seats were won by independents. Erdogan, as prime minister, focused on nurturing the economy's recovery from the 2001 recession and passing sufficient democratic reforms to enable the opening of accession negotiations with the EU. Although it had, from time to time, attempted to relax the headscarf ban and encourage religious education, on each occasion the government rapidly backed down in the face of opposition from the staunchly secularist military and from President Ahmet Necdet Sezer, who was able to use his veto to block both legislation and the appointment of several hundred AKP supporters to the higher echelons of the bureaucracy. But this was a confrontation postponed, not resolved. The AKP's supporters and its hard-line secularist opponents were counting the days until Sezer completed his seven-year term in office in May 2007. Under Turkish law, the president is elected by parliament. Given its large majority, the AKP could appoint its own candidate and thus remove the possibility of its laws and bureaucratic appointments being vulnerable to presidential veto.

With a general election due by November 2007, Erdogan initially favoured avoiding confrontation with the secular establishment by putting forward a weak, compromise candidate. But AKP conservatives threatened a revolt unless he nominated someone of stature from within the party, such as Foreign Minister Abdullah Gul, whose wife wore the headscarf. For most hard-line Turkish secularists, the presence of a headscarfed first lady in the presidential palace was in itself a violation of secularism. On 27 April 2007, only days before parliament was expected to elect Gul as president, General Yasar Buyukanit, the chief of the Turkish General Staff (TGS) posted a statement on the TGS website implicitly threatening to topple the government if it pushed ahead with Gul's nomination. The possibility of a coup was averted when, on 1 May 2007, the Constitutional Court – on dubious legal grounds – announced that a quorum of two-thirds of MPs had to be present in parliament for a presidential election to be valid. As a result, all the CHP had to do to prevent Gul's appointment as president was to boycott parliament. The AKP responded by calling an early general election for 22 July 2007.

Since formally opening EU accession negotiations in 2005, the AKP had appeared to lose direction. The EU had become increasingly frustrated by Turkey's failure to pass more democratic reforms or to open its ports and airports to ships and aircraft from the Republic of Cyprus – something Ankara had explicitly promised to do in return for the opening of accession negotiations. In December 2006, the EU suspended negotiations on eight of the 35 chapters of the accession process. By spring 2007, there were signs that the economic boom of the government's first years in office was beginning to lose momentum. The government was also under intense domestic pressure over its failure to curb the death toll in the long-running insurgency of the Kurdistan Workers' Party (PKK).

Pressure from the military, however, was a gift to the AKP. Reinvigorated, the party was able to portray itself as the victim of an undemocratic intervention in the political process and to promise a continuation of the relative stability and prosperity of its first term. The election campaigns of its two main rivals, the CHP and the ultranationalist Nationalist Action Party (MHP), were considerably more vituperative. The CHP lambasted the AKP for its alleged radical Islamist agenda, while the MHP harangued it for its failure to suppress the PKK. MHP Chairman Devlet Bahceli appeared at election rallies with a rope with which he promised to hang imprisoned PKK founder Abdullah Ocalan. Both opposition parties appeared to offer conflict rather than conciliation, gloom rather than hope. Neither had formulated a convincing strategy to handle the impending economic slowdown.

In previous attempts to use its still-considerable public prestige to influence civilian governments, the military had reinforced its public statements with a behind-the-scenes campaign, including discreet meetings with politicians and bureaucrats and briefings to trusted journalists, to undermine the government's credibility. However, the statement posted by Buyukanit on the TGS website did not appear to be part of a well-planned strategy. Its rough grammar suggested that it had been written in haste as an emotional reaction to the prospect of Gul becoming president. Throughout the election campaign, the TGS made no public or private attempts to influence the outcome. Buyukanit seemed to have believed that the website warning would in itself be sufficient to erode support for the AKP. This was a miscalculation.

In the election, the AKP took a much-increased 46.6% of the vote and 341 seats in parliament. The CHP finished second with 20.1% and 112 seats, ahead of the MHP with 14.3 % and 71 seats. The remaining 26 seats were won by independents, 20 of them members of the pro-Kurdish Democratic Society Party (DTP) who had run as independents in order to avoid the 10% threshold applied to political parties. Despite the scale of its election victory, the AKP still did not control two-thirds of the seats in parliament, enabling the opposition to block any government candidate for the presidency by boycotting the vote. However, on 25 July 2007, Bahceli unexpectedly declared that the MHP would participate in the presidential elections regardless of whom the AKP put forward as a candidate. The announcement handed the presidency to Gul, who was formally sworn in on 28 August 2007. Stunned by the electorate's refusal to heed its warning, and unwilling to topple a government so soon after it had won nearly half of the popular vote, the military remained silent.

Moves to relax headscarf ban

Upon re-election, the AKP at first sought to calm the waters following the recent political storm. On election night, Erdogan delivered one of the most conciliatory speeches of his career to exuberant supporters outside the party's headquarters in Ankara. He promised that the government would consult a broad cross section of society before making major decisions and would strive to represent not only those who had elected it but also those who had voted for other parties. However, with Gul installed as president and the military seemingly neutralised, the AKP apparently felt less of a need to consult or compromise.

In September, the party's deputy chairman, Dengir Mir Mehmet Firat, announced the completion of the initial draft of what he described as a new 'civilian constitution prepared by the people', but refused to reveal its contents. Two weeks later, he announced that the text had been finished and submitted to Erdogan. Such secrecy fuelled secularist fears that the government was finally going to implement an Islamist agenda, beginning by lifting the headscarf ban in universities.

The AKP was aware that further electoral success was dependent on lifting the ban. Around 65% of Turkish women, and an estimated 90% of adult female AKP voters, cover their heads. The ban meant they were, in effect, prevented from receiving a university education. Nor could the AKP continue to justify its failure to lift the ban by citing possible opposition from the presidency or the military. The assumption among both AKP supporters and opponents was that the party would attempt to lift the ban in the new constitution. In late November 2007, Erdogan announced that the draft text would be published by the middle of the following month. But the deadline passed without the document being made public.

The first sign that an attempt to lift the headscarf ban was imminent came on 10 December 2007, when Gul appointed Yusuf Ziya Ozcan, a relatively unknown sociology professor, as head of the Higher Education Council, which oversees university education. Traditionally, the council has been headed by one of the rectors of Turkey's 115 universities. Ozcan, whose main previous administrative experience had been as head of a university department, was close to the AKP leadership and a fierce opponent of the headscarf ban. As rumours that the AKP was planning to abolish the ban intensified, protests were led by the judiciary, another bastion of Turkey's secular establishment. In January, Public Prosecutor Abdurrahman Yalcinkaya threatened the AKP with judicial sanctions after Erdogan publicly called for a lifting of the ban on the headscarf even if it symbolised a desire for the creation of an Islamic state. The Council of State, Turkey's highest administrative court, issued a warning that any attempt to abolish the ban would be a violation of the principle of secularism enshrined in the constitution.

Erdogan, however, was undeterred. Under Turkish law, constitutional amendments require the support of at least two-thirds of parliament. In January, Erdogan was approached by the MHP – which also included a large number of headscarfed women among its supporters – with a proposal to lift the ban by amending the constitution. He immediately cancelled a planned trip to the annual meeting of the World Economic Forum in Davos, Switzerland, and remained in Ankara to draft the constitutional changes. On 9 February 2008 the constitution was amended to prevent anyone being denied access to education except for a reason openly stated in law. In fact, it was debatable whether the amendment lifted the headscarf ban as, in 1989, the Constitutional Court had ruled that women covering their heads in universities were violating secularism.

On 23 February, the amendment was published in the Official Gazette. Ozcan immediately issued a directive instructing all universities to start admitting students wearing headscarves with immediate effect. Most university rectors were committed secularists and refused to implement the directive. The CHP immediately applied to the Constitutional Court for the annulment of the amendment.

Ozcan's directive had been issued in the middle of the academic year, when women in the new student intake had long since decided either to attend classes with their heads uncovered or forgo a university education. As a result, the directive had a greater political than practical impact. For many secularists, it was proof of the AKP's determination to lift the headscarf ban whatever the cost. On 16 March 2008, Yalcinkaya responded by formally applying to the Constitutional Court to have the AKP closed down on the grounds that it had become a centre for anti-secular activities. In a 162-page indictment, Yalcinkaya also called for 71 AKP members, including Erdogan and 37 other members of parliament, to be banned from belonging to a political party.

The indictment took the party by surprise. Most members had assumed that, despite his earlier warning, Yalcinkaya would not dare try to outlaw a party which had so recently received such a convincing public mandate. The result was confusion. Some members advocated introducing legal amendments to make it more difficult to close down political parties, and meanwhile to court the EU's support by implementing democratic reforms. Others argued that changing the law just to protect the AKP would be unprincipled, particularly as the government had done nothing when Yalcinkaya had filed a separate case in November 2007 for closure of the Kurdish DTP on the grounds that it had become a centre for separatist activities. The government, while expressing opposition to party closures, made no attempt to pass laws that would have made them more difficult. Privately, some AKP officials argued that closure of the DTP would work to the party's advantage. In local elections due in March 2009, Erdogan was known to be targeting major gains in the DTP's heartland in the predominantly Kurdish southeast of Turkey.

On 5 June, the Constitutional Court upheld the CHP's appeal and annulled the constitutional amendments, ruling that allowing headscarfed girls to study at university would be a violation of secularism. Given the AKP's role in passing the amendments, the court appeared to have implicitly endorsed Yalcinkaya's indictment of the party, making it almost certain that it would eventually rule in his favour.

The PKK, the United States and Iraq

The past year saw an increase in the number of clashes between Turkish security forces and the PKK. Since returning to violence in June 2004 after a five-year ceasefire, the PKK has pursued a two-front strategy, combining a rural insurgency in southeast Turkey with an urban bombing campaign in the west. Both elements are part of a war of psychological attrition aimed at pressuring the Turkish authorities into making concessions on Kurdish cultural rights or agreeing to enter into direct negotiations with the organisation.

Most PKK operations in southeast Turkey had been carried out by small units of six to eight militants, who staged ambushes, laid mines or launched hit-and-run attacks on soft targets. However, in September 2007, shortly before the first winter snows put an end to the campaigning season, the PKK began to launch larger-scale attacks, sometimes comprising up to 200 militants, on Turkish army units. The same tactic had been employed in the early 1990s but had been quickly abandoned when the heavy casualties that it inflicted were more than offset by heavy losses suffered when the military called in air support. On this occasion, the PKK appeared to have been looking for a propaganda victory, seeking to inflict losses before withdrawing to wait out the winter in what it assumed was the immunity of its camps in northern Iraq. Some 40 Turkish soldiers were killed in PKK attacks in less than a month.

Under intense public pressure, on 17 October the Turkish parliament authorised the government to launch a military operation into northern Iraq. The Turkish Army began a military build-up on Turkey's border with Iraq. This put the United States in a difficult position; Turkey's recent relations with the United States had been awkward, dominated by the repercussions of the US-led invasion of Iraq in 2003, when Ankara refused to allow the country to be a platform for the invading forces. Facing insurgency and civil war in other parts of Iraq, Washington refused to allow Turkey to move against PKK training camps and forward bases in the mountains of northern Iraq, fearing this could destabilise Iraq's most peaceful region. This refusal to allow cross-border operations had provided the PKK with a psychological and propaganda gift. To both its supporters and enemies, it frequently appeared as if Washington was sympathetic to the organisation, despite repeated US denials. On 5 November, however, Washington lifted its opposition to a Turkish incursion, promising to supply actionable intelligence on PKK positions in northern Iraq and agreeing to limited cross-border military operations.

On 16 December, using imagery provided by the United States, Turkey launched the first of a series of bombing raids on PKK positions in northern Iraq. On 21 February 2008, three battalions of Turkish commandos helicoptered into Iraq to stage a ground attack on PKK units wintering in camps close to the Turkish border. By the time the commandos withdrew on 29 February, the Turkish military claimed to have killed 240 PKK militants for the loss of 27 of its own men and to have destroyed a large number of shelters, training facilities and command centres.

Washington's provision of information to the Turkish military both strengthened its relationship with Ankara and exploded the myth of American sympathy for the PKK. With its camps and bases in northern Iraq no longer immune to Turkish attack, the PKK was forced onto the defensive both militarily and psychologically. When the spring thaw melted the snows in the passes in the mountains that straddle the Turkish–Iraqi border, PKK militants once again began to infiltrate into Turkey. However, Turkish air strikes were now disrupting the organisation's command and supply lines and forcing it to devote resources to protecting its assets in northern Iraq rather than supporting the insurgency inside Turkey.

The Turkish incursions also changed the nature of Ankara's relationship with the Iraqi Kurds. Turkey had long feared that the Iraqi Kurds were merely waiting for the opportunity to break away and form an independent state in the north of the country, which Ankara believed would further fuel the separatist aspirations of its own Kurdish minority. The PKK's camps and bases were located in territory under the control of the semi-autonomous Kurdistan Regional Government (KRG). However, Turkey had preferred to engage only with the central Iraqi government in Baghdad in the belief that dealing directly with the KRG would be interpreted as recognition of its political authority in northern Iraq, which could in turn encourage the Iraqi Kurds to push for independence.

Although it regarded the PKK as a rival, the KRG had been reluctant to move against the organisation's camps, most of which were located in almost inaccessible mountains. It lacked the resources to stage a military campaign in difficult terrain, and also hesitated to attempt to eradicate fellow Kurds – particularly at the behest of Turkey, which many Kurds in northern Iraq regard as an oppressive neo-imperial power. The Iraqi Kurds had also been confident that, however much they antagonised Turkey, the United States would protect them from military retribution.

Washington's decision to allow Turkish incursions into northern Iraq shook the confidence not only of the PKK but also of the Iraqi Kurds, who suddenly felt more vulnerable. The rhetoric of the Iraqi Kurds towards Turkey became more cautious and there were signs that the KRG had begun to restrict the movements of PKK militants outside their mountain hideouts. Aware of this impact, Ankara now had the confidence to change its policy. From April 2008, Turkish officials began to engage directly with KRG officials, offering aid and improved economic ties in return for the KRG clamping down on the activities of the PKK in northern Iraq, particularly its ability to move through the lowlands and source supplies from the local population. However, in July 2008 it was still too early to be sure how long the rapprochement would last or whether it would yield significant results.

Towards a tense and uncertain future
The failure of the military's heavy-handed attempts to prevent Gul from becoming president severely damaged its public prestige and its political leverage. The sharp increase in the AKP's electoral support represented a humiliating reverse for an intensely proud institution which saw itself as embodying the essence of the Turkish nation. However, the size of the AKP's vote also allowed the party's confidence to outstrip its judgement, perhaps setting the stage for its own undoing.

Economic factors contributed to the growing malaise. The government deserved some of the credit for the economic boom of its first term in power, during which gross domestic product increased by an average of 6.8% a year. Some of the expansion was attributable to political stability and improved productivity. But it was also fuelled by an increase in foreign investment and sharp growth in borrowing by consumers and companies. Yet with real wages and levels of unemployment having remained stable, there was bound to be a limit to how long domestic demand could sustain such high levels of growth. In addition, since Turkish exports are heavily reliant on imports of raw materials and semi-finished goods, rapid export growth produced large foreign-trade and current-account deficits. Dazzled by its electoral success, the government failed to heed warnings from business, leaving the economy dangerously exposed when the effects of the international credit squeeze were exacerbated by fears of domestic political instability following the attempt to close down the AKP through the legal system. By mid 2008, both inflation and unemployment were beginning to rise and the debate was no longer about when the economy would slow, but how deep and how long the slowdown would be.

There was a growing sense that the government had become overconfident, while lacking a cohesive strategy. The events surrounding the headscarf ban contributed to this impression. These had a particular effect on liberal Turks, many of whom had been prepared to accept the AKP's denials that it had an Islamist agenda and had voted for it as the party which had done most to boost Turkey's chances of EU membership. AKP officials frequently referred to allowing headscarfed women to attend university as a question of human rights. But there was a marked contrast between the effort expended on the headscarf ban and the government's failure to address other restrictions on human rights in Turkey, including discrimination suffered by non-Muslim minorities and the Alevi community. The attempts to lift the headscarf ban undermined the credibility of Erdogan's election-night pledge to reach out to all sections of Turkish society.

The Constitutional Court was expected to deliver a ruling on the closure case against the AKP in late summer 2008. If, as appears likely, the AKP is outlawed, the country will almost certainly head for an early general election in November or December 2008. But there is no guarantee that fresh elections will resolve the tensions in Turkish society. Both the AKP and its secularist opponents now believe they are locked in a trial of strength which only one side can win. An unequivocal victory for either side could severely damage the social fabric of the country. But, for the moment at least, there is no indication that either is prepared to compromise. Turkey faces the prospect of a sustained period of political uncertainty and instability.

Strategic Geography

2008

Legend

———— subject country
international boundaries

———— other international boundaries

················ province or state boundaries

ANBAR province or state

◾ capital cities

● state or province capital cities

● cities/ towns/ villages

GLOBAL ISSUES: Arctic resources and shipping routes

Although estimates as to the extent of the Arctic's natural resources vary significantly, it could be home to up to a quarter of the world's unexplored oil and gas reserves. As new trade routes open up as a result of global warming and the technology required to navigate these polar waters and to exploit the region's reserves advances, there has been a growing clamour among Arctic nations to claim sovereignty over vital strategic territories. For a detailed discussion of the issues at hand, see Arctic essay on p. 58–71.

National interests in the Arctic region

Russia: The planting of the Russian national flag on the seabed below the North Pole in August 2007, while causing alarm within the international community, was a telling reminder of just how seriously Moscow takes the issue of Arctic sovereignty. In December 2001 it submitted a claim to the Continental Shelf Commission that the Lomonosov Ridge was an extension of the Russian continental shelf, therefore entitling it to claim sovereignty over a vast swathe of the Artic region. While Russia's claim was not approved, the commission requested that it conduct further research and provide more data.

Canada: In October 2007 Prime Minister Stephen Harper announced a series of measures aimed at reinforcing the country's sovereignty and interests in the region, such as a new fleet of Arctic patrol ships, a permanent 1,000-strong garrison and training centre, and an extensive oceanographic survey. It is currently in dispute with the US over the extent of its northern archipelago, as well as with Denmark over the sovereignty of Hans Island.

United States: As a non-signatory of UNCLOS, Washington's ability to assert its territorial claims is somewhat limited, but there is growing domestic support for ratification. The ability to exploit the Arctic's natural resources would enable the US to reduce its reliance on energy imports, which would be considered a vital boost to national security.

Norway: The Arctic issue is a key preoccupation of Oslo's foreign and security policy, as well as being a central commercial interest. Norway is engaged in a bilateral dispute with Russia over the drawing of their national borders north of their continental shelves, an area potentially rich in oil and gas, as well as a multilateral dispute with Russia and most other signatory countries over its interpretation of the Svalbard Treaty of 1920. It is also in dispute with Denmark over the sovereignty of Tobias Island.

Denmark: Copenhagen is asserting its rights over the Arctic through the semi-autonomous territory of Greenland. It is in dispute with Norway over the sovereignty of Tobias Island, as well as with Canada over the sovereignty of Hans Island. It conducted a data-gathering expedition north of Greenland in 2007 in support of its potential claim to the Continental Shelf Commission. In May 2008 it called a summit of the five Arctic powers with the aim of averting conflict over the issue and reasserting confidence in the UNCLOS framework.

Legal framework

United Nations Convention on the Law of the Sea (UNCLOS), 1982 – Replacing the 17th-century freedom-of-the seas doctrine under which the seas beyond a narrow strip around a nation's coastline were 'free to all and belonging to none', the convention was the culmination of a process of UN conferences and agreements which had begun in 1956. It was established in order to allocate responsibility for environmental oversight and to protect fish stocks, but also to grant nations sovereignty over the natural resources contained within 200 nautical miles of their continental shelves. National claims to sovereignty beyond this 200-nautical-mile limit must be made to the **Continental Shelf Commission**, as Russia has done, and to which Norway, Denmark and Canada are thought to be preparing claims. Because it has not ratified UNCLOS, the US is unable to submit a claim to the commission.

Northwest Passage – In September 2007 the European Space Agency declared that, as a result of the summer thaw, these waters were fully navigable for the first time. Canada regards the passage as part of its territorial waters, while the US and EU have called for it to be designated an international sound. At 2,105 nautical miles shorter than the current route through the Panama Canal, it could become a vital trade route between Europe and Asia.

Beauf
Sea

CANADA

Hudson
Bay

Thu

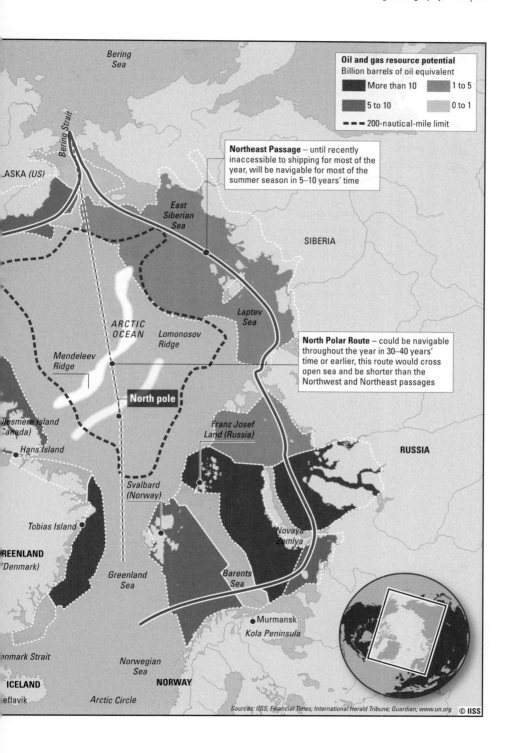

Oil and gas resource potential
Billion barrels of oil equivalent

More than 10
5 to 10
1 to 5
0 to 1
▬ ▬ ▬ 200-nautical-mile limit

Bering
Sea

Bering Strait

ASKA (US)

East
Siberian
Sea

SIBERIA

Northeast Passage – until recently
inaccessible to shipping for most of the
year, will be navigable for most of the
summer season in 5–10 years' time

_Laptev
Sea_

_ARCTIC
OCEAN_

_Lomonosov
Ridge_

North Polar Route – could be navigable
throughout the year in 30–40 years'
time or earlier, this route would cross
open sea and be shorter than the
Northwest and Northeast passages

_Mendeleev
Ridge_

North pole

RUSSIA

_llesmere Island
`anada)_

Hans Island

_Franz Josef
Land (Russia)_

_Svalbard
(Norway)_

Tobias Island

_Novaya
Zemlya_

REENLAND
'Denmark)

_Greenland
Sea_

_Barents
Sea_

● Murmansk
Kola Peninsula

nmark Strait

_Norwegian
Sea_

ICELAND

NORWAY

eflavik

Arctic Circle

Sources: IISS; Financial Times; International Herald Tribune; Guardian; www.un.org   © IISS

GLOBAL ISSUES: Sovereign wealth funds

As the global economy comes to terms with the current credit crunch, much attention has been paid to the activities of sovereign-wealth funds. Their investments in ailing corporations, such as the $6.6bn and $14.5bn received by Merrill Lynch and Citigroup respectively in January 2008, gave them key stakes in the economies of the industrialised world. The funds mostly originate from emerging economies, which are enjoying current-account surpluses based on the profits of their energy and commodity exports combined with record oil prices.

Oil
Commodities
Non-commodity based

US

UNITED STATES

Fund: Alaska Permanent Fund
Estimated assets: $37.8bn

Source of funds:

Year established: 1976

Derived from mineral revenues, its investments include stocks, private equities, real estate and hedge funds

NORWAY

Fund: Government Pension Fund - Global
Estimated assets: $358bn

Source of funds:

Year established: 1976

Investment portfolio includes bonds, equities and derivatives across 42 markets and 31 currencies

NORWAY

US

ALGERIA

Fund: Reserve Fund
Estimated assets: $43bn

Source of funds:

Year established: 2000

ALGERIA

LIBYA

Fund: Reserve Fund
Estimated assets: $100bn

Source of funds:

Year established: 1981

Stakes in Juventus (Italian football club), as well as companies in Middle East, North Africa and Pakistan

Rapid growth of sovereign-wealth funds
Projected ($trillion)

US$11.9 trillion

Sovereign-wealth funds

Official reserves

US$7.9 trillion

Crossover in 2011

2008 2009 2010 2011 2012 2013 2014 2015

SAUDI ARABIA

Fund: Various funds
Estimated assets: $300bn

Source of funds:

Year established: –

Investments focused primarily on US Treasury bonds, although a new fund devoted to foreign investments may be set up

According to Global Insight, an economic-analysis company, these funds 'now represent the most powerful group of global investors'. But while the vital cash injections that they provide, along with their long-term investment outlook, no doubt make them attractive investors, there have been calls to regulate their activities and to encourage greater transparency. In the future, the investments of these funds could be a factor in the global strategic balance. The key funds in the sovereign-wealth market are plotted here.

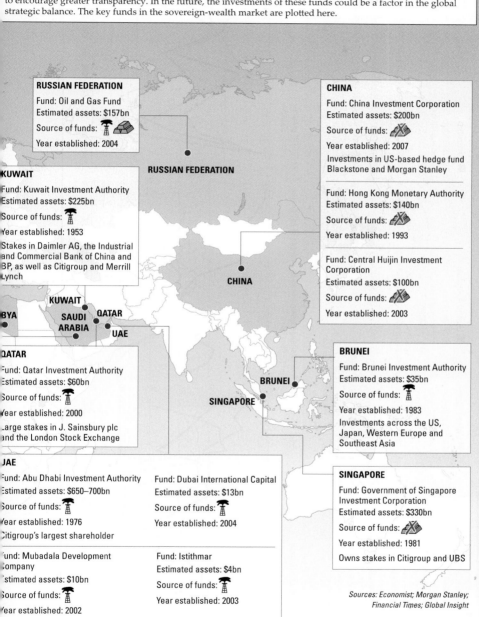

RUSSIAN FEDERATION

Fund: Oil and Gas Fund
Estimated assets: $157bn
Source of funds:
Year established: 2004

KUWAIT

Fund: Kuwait Investment Authority
Estimated assets: $225bn
Source of funds:
Year established: 1953
Stakes in Daimler AG, the Industrial and Commercial Bank of China and BP, as well as Citigroup and Merrill Lynch

QATAR

Fund: Qatar Investment Authority
Estimated assets: $60bn
Source of funds:
Year established: 2000
Large stakes in J. Sainsbury plc and the London Stock Exchange

UAE

Fund: Abu Dhabi Investment Authority
Estimated assets: $650–700bn
Source of funds:
Year established: 1976
Citigroup's largest shareholder

Fund: Mubadala Development Company
Estimated assets: $10bn
Source of funds:
Year established: 2002

Fund: Dubai International Capital
Estimated assets: $13bn
Source of funds:
Year established: 2004

Fund: Istithmar
Estimated assets: $4bn
Source of funds:
Year established: 2003

CHINA

Fund: China Investment Corporation
Estimated assets: $200bn
Source of funds:
Year established: 2007
Investments in US-based hedge fund Blackstone and Morgan Stanley

Fund: Hong Kong Monetary Authority
Estimated assets: $140bn
Source of funds:
Year established: 1993

Fund: Central Huijin Investment Corporation
Estimated assets: $100bn
Source of funds:
Year established: 2003

BRUNEI

Fund: Brunei Investment Authority
Estimated assets: $35bn
Source of funds:
Year established: 1983
Investments across the US, Japan, Western Europe and Southeast Asia

SINGAPORE

Fund: Government of Singapore Investment Corporation
Estimated assets: $330bn
Source of funds:
Year established: 1981
Owns stakes in Citigroup and UBS

Sources: Economist; Morgan Stanley; Financial Times; Global Insight

© IISS

RUSSIAN FEDERATION

CHINA

KUWAIT
QATAR
SAUDI ARABIA
UAE
BYA

BRUNEI

SINGAPORE

GLOBAL ISSUES: Economic slowdown and financial turbulence

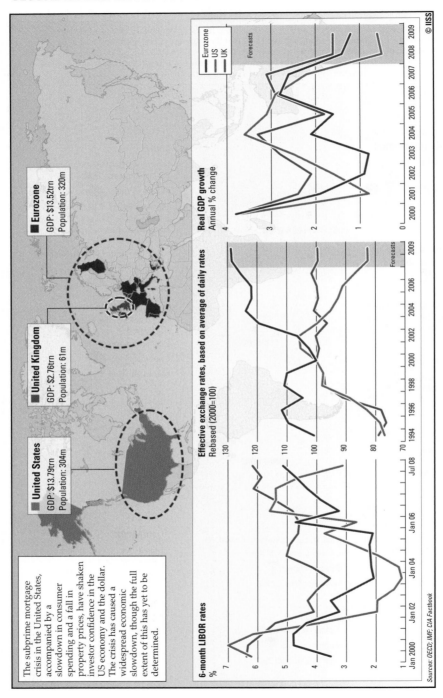

The subprime mortgage crisis in the United States, accompanied by a slowdown in consumer spending and a fall in property prices, have shaken investor confidence in the US economy and the dollar. The crisis has caused a widespread economic slowdown, though the full extent of this has yet to be determined.

United States
GDP: $13.79trn
Population: 304m

United Kingdom
GDP: $2.76trn
Population: 61m

Eurozone
GDP: $13.52trn
Population: 320m

6-month LIBOR rates
%

Effective exchange rates, based on average of daily rates
Rebased (2000=100)

Real GDP growth
Annual % change

Eurozone
US
UK

Forecasts

© IISS

Sources: OECD; IMF; CIA Factbook

AFRICA: Kenya's election crisis

In the wake of presidential and parliamentary elections held in late December 2007, Kenya was shaken by two months of ethnic violence which claimed the lives of 1,200 and displaced up to 300,000. Previously held up as an example of a stable and unified African state while being home to around 40 different ethnic groups, the disputed vote brought simmering ethnic tensions, as well as frustration over corruption among officials, to the surface. Despite the protestations of Raila Odinga of the Orange Democratic Movement (ODM), who believed himself to be the true winner, on 30 December incumbent President Mwai Kibaki, representing the Party of National Unity (PNU) was declared victorious and sworn in hours later. Riots erupted throughout the country as a result, with ethnic Kikuyus, of which Kibaki is one, being targeted in particular. The violence may have cost the economy of Kenya – as the world's biggest exporter of black tea and a popular tourist destination – up to $3.6bn. It is hoped that a power-sharing agreement between the two main parties brokered by former UN Secretary-General Kofi Annan will lead to renewed prosperity and stability in the country.

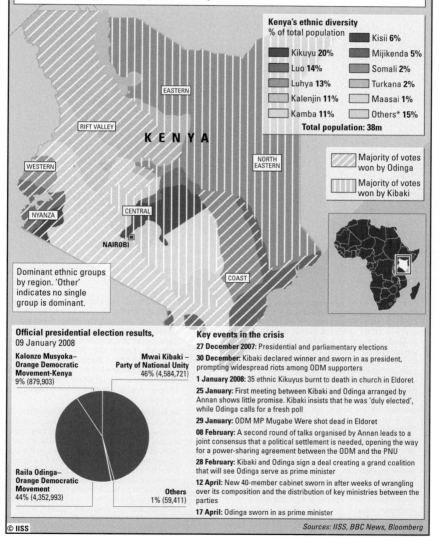

Kenya's ethnic diversity
% of total population

Kikuyu **20%**
Luo **14%**
Luhya **13%**
Kalenjin **11%**
Kamba **11%**
Kisii **6%**
Mijikenda **5%**
Somali **2%**
Turkana **2%**
Maasai **1%**
Others* **15%**

Total population: 38m

Majority of votes won by Odinga

Majority of votes won by Kibaki

Dominant ethnic groups by region. 'Other' indicates no single group is dominant.

Official presidential election results,
09 January 2008

Kalonzo Musyoka–
Orange Democratic
Movement-Kenya
9% (879,903)

Mwai Kibaki –
Party of National Unity
46% (4,584,721)

Raila Odinga–
Orange Democratic
Movement
44% (4,352,993)

Others
1% (59,411)

Key events in the crisis

27 December 2007: Presidential and parliamentary elections

30 December: Kibaki declared winner and sworn in as president, prompting widespread riots among ODM supporters

1 January 2008: 35 ethnic Kikuyus burnt to death in church in Eldoret

25 January: First meeting between Kibaki and Odinga arranged by Annan shows little promise. Kibaki insists that he was 'duly elected', while Odinga calls for a fresh poll

29 January: ODM MP Mugabe Were shot dead in Eldoret

08 February: A second round of talks organised by Annan leads to a joint consensus that a political settlement is needed, opening the way for a power-sharing agreement between the ODM and the PNU

28 February: Kibaki and Odinga sign a deal creating a grand coalition that will see Odinga serve as prime minister

12 April: New 40-member cabinet sworn in after weeks of wrangling over its composition and the distribution of key ministries between the parties

17 April: Odinga sworn in as prime minister

© IISS

Sources: IISS, BBC News, Bloomberg

EUROPE/RUSSIA: Frozen conflicts on Russia's borders

Kosovo's unilateral declaration of independence in February 2008 was firmly opposed by Russia, which fears that the declaration will set a precedent for other break-away states within its sphere of influence.

POLAND

UKRAINE

SLOVAKIA

MOLDOVA **TRANSNISTRIA**

HUNGARY

Chisinau

ROMANIA

TRANSNISTRIA (Moldova)

Capital: Tiraspol

Population: 550–700,000; 32% Moldovan, 29% Ukrainian, 30% Russian

Background
Transnistria claimed independence from Moldova in 1990 after protests against Moldova's own bid for independence from the Soviet Union, which had sparked fears of reunification with Romania. Fighting between Transnistrian and Moldovan forces broke out in 1991 after the former seized control of Moldovan public institutions and lasted until mid 1992, killing hundreds and displacing around 100,000. A Russian-brokered and implemented ceasefire imposed a 10km demilitarised zone on both sides of the Dniestr River. The 14th Russian Army was already in place on the left bank of the Dniestr when violence broke out, and is thought to have aided the secessionists; Russia maintains a troop presence. The territory is unrecognised by the international community

Recent developments
A September 2006 referendum again calling for independence from Moldova was widely endorsed. Reconciliation talks resumed in April 2008 after a seven-year hiatus

Tiraspol

SOUTH OSSETIA (Georgia)

Capital: Tskhinvali

Population: 70–100,000; 66% ethnic Ossetian, 29% ethnic Georgian

Tskhinvali

Background
South Ossetia declared its secession from Georgia in 1990 and its effective secession in 1991. The break-up of the Soviet Union and Georgia's subsequent independence fuelled Ossetian nationalist sentiment and led to violence. Russian peacekeeping troops were deployed to the region in 1992; their continued presence, along with Moscow's good relations with Tskhinvali and offer of Russian passports to South Ossetians, is a source of tension in what are already strained Georgian–Russian relations. The territory is divided from North Ossetia by the Georgian–Russian frontier and is unrecognised by the international community

Recent developments: When President Mikheil Saakashvili took office in 2004 he vowed to protect Georgia's territorial integrity and persuade breakaway states to give up their demands for independence. But in a referendum in November 2006, 95% of South Ossetian voters favoured renewing their claim to independence. Violence continues to flare up sporadically. In April 2008, after Moscow announced its intention to recognise some elements of the Tskhinvali administration as legal entities, the US and EU called on Russia to support Saakashvili's efforts to find a peaceful solution and bring an end to its overt support for the South Ossetian and Abkhazian causes

© IISS

ABKHAZIA (Georgia)

Capital: Sukhumi

Population: 180–200,000;
50% ethnic Abkhaz,
25% ethnic Georgian

Background
Claimed independence from Georgia
in 1994, after two years of violent clashes
with Georgian troops. Up to 2,000 Russian
peacekeepers sent to enforce a ceasefire in 1994 are still
stationed there. In common with South Ossetia, it is
unrecognised by the international community but enjoys good
relations with Moscow: tense Georgian–Russian relations
have been heightened by the presence of Russian troops and
Moscow's offer of passports to Abkhaz residents. Perhaps
more viable as an independent state than South Ossetia as it
has its own coastline, as well as fertile land used for tea,
citrus-fruit and tobacco cultivation

Recent developments
On 21 April 2008, Georgia accused Russia of downing a
Georgian drone over Abkhazia. Moscow denied the charge,
while arguing that Georgian UAV flights over Abkhazia were a
violation of the ceasefire. Russia sent a further 500
peacekeepers, mostly paratroopers, which Tbilisi called 'an
act of aggression'. Although NATO and the EU called for
restraint and the withdrawal of the additional troops, in late
May Moscow sent 400 unarmed 'railway troops' to repair the
destroyed Georgia–Russia railway. Georgia saw the
deployment as a further prelude to large-scale aggression. A
meeting between Medvedev and Saakashvili on 7 June failed
to resolve the crisis.

NAGORNO-KARABAKH (Azerbaijan–Armenia)

Capital: Stepankert

Population: 137,000; nearly 100%
ethnic Armenian

Background
First delineated in the 1920s by the
Soviet Union as the Nagorno-
Karabakh Autonomous Region, this
predominantly Armenian-inhabited area
divides Azerbaijan from its autonomous
territory of Naxcivan to the west.
Violence between Armenians and Azeris
began in 1988 when Nagorno-Karabakh
unsuccessfully petitioned the Soviets for
incorporation into Armenia, which Azerbaijan rejected. Violence
continued beyond the unilateral declaration of independence in
1991, until a Russian-sponsored ceasefire in 1994. It claimed the
lives of 20–30,000 and led to mass population displacements.
The Armenians prevailed and gained control of more Azeri
territory beyond Nagorno-Karabakh's original borders

Recent developments
Violence between Azeri and Armenian troops, such as that in
March 2008, flares up sporadically. Mediation efforts by the
OSCE's Minsk Group have failed to produce a final settlement on
the issue of the disputed territory held by Armenia and there are
still up to one million IDPs. In December 2006, a referendum on
the subject of whether Nagorno-Karabakh should declare itself
a sovereign state was endorsed by 98% of voters, but
Azerbaijan declared the vote illegal. The territory is
unrecognised by the international community, including
Armenia

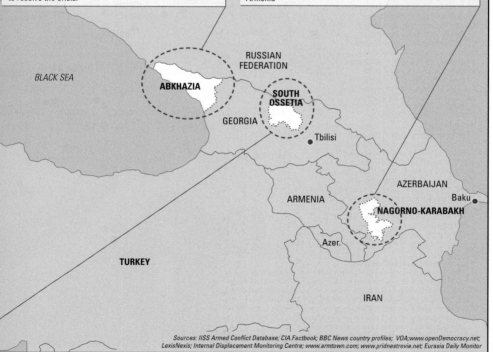

Sources: IISS Armed Conflict Database; CIA Factbook; BBC News country profiles; VOA;www.openDemocracy.net;
LexisNexis; Internal Displacement Monitoring Centre; www.armtown.com; www.pridnestrovie.net; Eurasia Daily Monitor

EUROPE/RUSSIA: Gazprom's grip on Europe

Russian energy giant Gazprom supplies a quarter of Europe's gas, delivering some 150bn m³ in 2007, and is making further strategic investments in the continent's industry. It is involved in gas storage and trading hubs, local delivery, joint-ventures and pipeline projects aimed at securing greater control of delivery to Europe's borders – major examples of which are indicated below. Gazprom's attempts to gain a larger share of pipelines within Europe, however, are meeting some resistance, with talk of an EU curb on ownership of distribution networks by non-EU entities. There are worries that – especially after a cut-off of gas to Ukraine for several days in 2006 – Russia could use energy supplies as a political weapon. The state is the majority Gazprom shareholder, and there is an inevitable blurring of political and commercial interests. President Dimitry Medvedev was company chairman for six years before becoming Russian president. Moscow's strategic priorities are reflected in Gazprom's flagship projects. Already the world's third-largest company by market value, Gazprom looks set to continue its success on the back of rising global fuel prices, renationalisation of private projects and expansion into crude oil, electricity and coal.

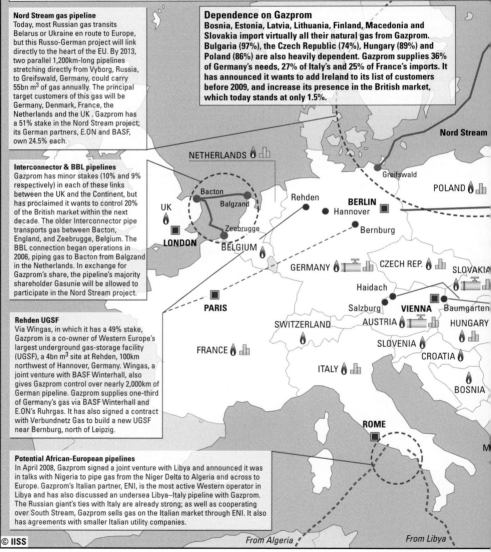

Nord Stream gas pipeline
Today, most Russian gas transits Belarus or Ukraine en route to Europe, but this Russo-German project will link directly to the heart of the EU. By 2013, two parallel 1,200km-long pipelines stretching directly from Vyborg, Russia, to Greifswald, Germany, could carry 55bn m³ of gas annually. The principal target customers of this gas will be Germany, Denmark, France, the Netherlands and the UK . Gazprom has a 51% stake in the Nord Stream project; its German partners, E.ON and BASF, own 24.5% each.

Dependence on Gazprom
Bosnia, Estonia, Latvia, Lithuania, Finland, Macedonia and Slovakia import virtually all their natural gas from Gazprom. Bulgaria (97%), the Czech Republic (74%), Hungary (89%) and Poland (86%) are also heavily dependent. Gazprom supplies 36% of Germany's needs, 27% of Italy's and 25% of France's imports. It has announced it wants to add Ireland to its list of customers before 2009, and increase its presence in the British market, which today stands at only 1.5%.

Interconnector & BBL pipelines
Gazprom has minor stakes (10% and 9% respectively) in each of these links between the UK and the Continent, but has proclaimed it wants to control 20% of the British market within the next decade. The older Interconnector pipe transports gas between Bacton, England, and Zeebrugge, Belgium. The BBL connection began operations in 2006, piping gas to Bacton from Balgzand in the Netherlands. In exchange for Gazprom's share, the pipeline's majority shareholder Gasunie will be allowed to participate in the Nord Stream project.

Rehden UGSF
Via Wingas, in which it has a 49% stake, Gazprom is a co-owner of Western Europe's largest underground gas-storage facility (UGSF), a 4bn m³ site at Rehden, 100km northwest of Hannover, Germany. Wingas, a joint venture with BASF Winterhall, also gives Gazprom control over nearly 2,000km of German pipeline. Gazprom supplies one-third of Germany's gas via BASF Winterhall and E.ON's Ruhrgas. It has also signed a contract with Verbundnetz Gas to build a new UGSF near Bernburg, north of Leipzig.

Potential African-European pipelines
In April 2008, Gazprom signed a joint venture with Libya and announced it was in talks with Nigeria to pipe gas from the Niger Delta to Algeria and across to Europe. Gazprom's Italian partner, ENI, is the most active Western operator in Libya and has also discussed an undersea Libya–Italy pipeline with Gazprom. The Russian giant's ties with Italy are already strong; as well as cooperating over South Stream, Gazprom sells gas on the Italian market through ENI. It also has agreements with smaller Italian utility companies.

Nord Stream

NETHERLANDS

Greifswald

POLAND

Bacton
Rehden
BERLIN
UK
Balgzand
Hannover

Zeebrugge
Bernburg

LONDON
BELGIUM
GERMANY
CZECH REP.
SLOVAKIA

Haidach

PARIS
Salzburg
VIENNA
Baumgarten

SWITZERLAND
AUSTRIA
HUNGARY

SLOVENIA

FRANCE
CROATIA

ITALY
BOSNIA

ROME

From Algeria
From Libya

© IISS

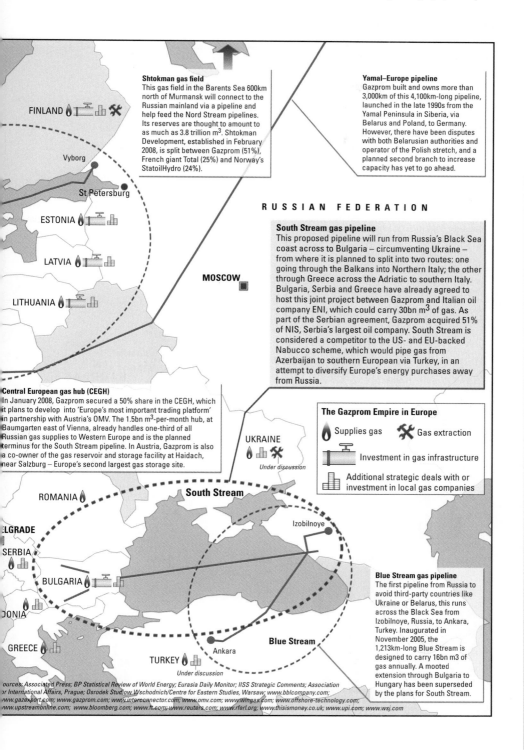

Shtokman gas field
This gas field in the Barents Sea 600km north of Murmansk will connect to the Russian mainland via a pipeline and help feed the Nord Stream pipelines. Its reserves are thought to amount to as much as 3.8 trillion m³. Shtokman Development, established in February 2008, is split between Gazprom (51%), French giant Total (25%) and Norway's StatoilHydro (24%).

Yamal–Europe pipeline
Gazprom built and owns more than 3,000km of this 4,100km-long pipeline, launched in the late 1990s from the Yamal Peninsula in Siberia, via Belarus and Poland, to Germany. However, there have been disputes with both Belarusian authorities and operator of the Polish stretch, and a planned second branch to increase capacity has yet to go ahead.

FINLAND

Vyborg

St Petersburg

ESTONIA

LATVIA

MOSCOW

LITHUANIA

RUSSIAN FEDERATION

South Stream gas pipeline
This proposed pipeline will run from Russia's Black Sea coast across to Bulgaria – circumventing Ukraine – from where it is planned to split into two routes: one going through the Balkans into Northern Italy; the other through Greece across the Adriatic to southern Italy. Bulgaria, Serbia and Greece have already agreed to host this joint project between Gazprom and Italian oil company ENI, which could carry 30bn m³ of gas. As part of the Serbian agreement, Gazprom acquired 51% of NIS, Serbia's largest oil company. South Stream is considered a competitor to the US- and EU-backed Nabucco scheme, which would pipe gas from Azerbaijan to southern European via Turkey, in an attempt to diversify Europe's energy purchases away from Russia.

Central European gas hub (CEGH)
In January 2008, Gazprom secured a 50% share in the CEGH, which it plans to develop into 'Europe's most important trading platform' in partnership with Austria's OMV. The 1.5bn m³-per-month hub, at Baumgarten east of Vienna, already handles one-third of all Russian gas supplies to Western Europe and is the planned terminus for the South Stream pipeline. In Austria, Gazprom is also a co-owner of the gas reservoir and storage facility at Haidach, near Salzburg – Europe's second largest gas storage site.

UKRAINE

Under discussion

The Gazprom Empire in Europe

Supplies gas

Gas extraction

Investment in gas infrastructure

Additional strategic deals with or investment in local gas companies

ROMANIA

South Stream

ELGRADE

SERBIA

Izobilnoye

BULGARIA

JONIA

GREECE

TURKEY

Ankara

Blue Stream

Under discussion

Blue Stream gas pipeline
The first pipeline from Russia to avoid third-party countries like Ukraine or Belarus, this runs across the Black Sea from Izobilnoye, Russia, to Ankara, Turkey. Inaugurated in November 2005, the 1,213km-long Blue Stream is designed to carry 16bn m3 of gas annually. A mooted extension through Bulgaria to Hungary has been superseded by the plans for South Stream.

ources: Associated Press; BP Statistical Review of World Energy; Eurasia Daily Monitor; IISS Strategic Comments; Association or International Affairs, Prague; Osrodek Studiow Wschodnich/Centre for Eastern Studies, Warsaw; www.bblcompany.com; www.gazexport.com; www.gazprom.com; www.interconnector.com; www.omv.com; www.wingas.com; www.offshore-technology.com; www.upstreamonline.com; www.bloomberg.com; www.ft.com; www.reuters.com; www.rferl.org; www.thisismoney.co.uk; www.upi.com; www.wsj.com

MIDDLE EAST/GULF: Progress in Iraq

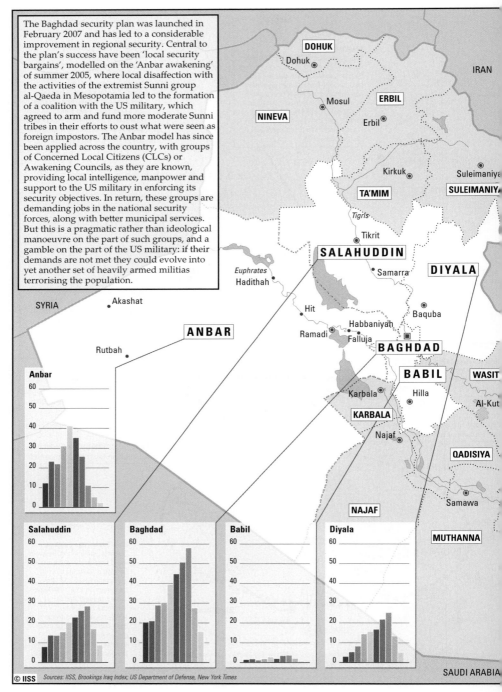

The Baghdad security plan was launched in February 2007 and has led to a considerable improvement in regional security. Central to the plan's success have been 'local security bargains', modelled on the 'Anbar awakening' of summer 2005, where local disaffection with the activities of the extremist Sunni group al-Qaeda in Mesopotamia led to the formation of a coalition with the US military, which agreed to arm and fund more moderate Sunni tribes in their efforts to oust what were seen as foreign impostors. The Anbar model has since been applied across the country, with groups of Concerned Local Citizens (CLCs) or Awakening Councils, as they are known, providing local intelligence, manpower and support to the US military in enforcing its security objectives. In return, these groups are demanding jobs in the national security forces, along with better municipal services. But this is a pragmatic rather than ideological manoeuvre on the part of such groups, and a gamble on the part of the US military: if their demands are not met they could evolve into yet another set of heavily armed militias terrorising the population.

© IISS   Sources: IISS, Brookings Iraq Index; US Department of Defense, New York Times

Integrating the Concerned Local Citizens into a national security force

A key challenge to establishing Iraq's long-term security is the integration of the CLCs into the Iraqi Security Forces, under the direct control of Baghdad. But sectarian politics stand in the way: the Shia-dominated government is reluctant to assimilate these predominantly Sunni organisations into the mainstream police force. A growing number of CLC groups are feeling disenfranchised and threatening to undermine local security frameworks if no commitment to integrating them into a truly national security force can be made.

Overview, as of April 2008

Total officially registered with the US military	**91,641** *
Of which under US military contract (at approx. $300 per month)	**72,000**
Of which serving as volunteers	**19,000**
Of which Shia	**9,500**

*The 25,000 volunteers who formed the 'Anbar awakening' are not included in these figures.

Integration with the Iraqi Security Forces, as of April 2008

Already integrated	**1,738**
Vetted by the Iraqi government and awaiting assignment	**2,000**
In the process of being vetted	**8,000**
Number to be employed by the Baghdad police	**12,000**
Those being transferred to civilian duties	**4,500**
Those to have expressed willingness to join Iraqi Security Forces	**18,000**

Weapons Caches Found by Coalition and Iraqi Forces, 1 January 2004–22 February 2008

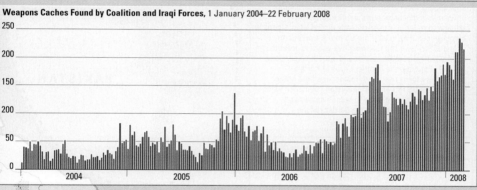

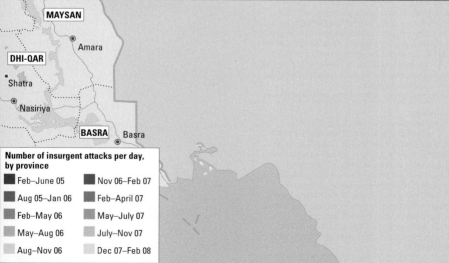

MAYSAN

Amara

DHI-QAR

Shatra

Nasiriya

BASRA Basra

Number of insurgent attacks per day, by province

- Feb–June 05
- Aug 05–Jan 06
- Feb–May 06
- May–Aug 06
- Aug–Nov 06
- Nov 06–Feb 07
- Feb–April 07
- May–July 07
- July–Nov 07
- Dec 07–Feb 08

ASIA-PACIFIC: Pakistan's year of turmoil

The international community will be keeping a close eye on how the new government of Pakistan elected in February 2008 tackles the country's many security problems. Amid signs of a growing movement of both homegrown and imported Islamic extremism taking hold, fears that the country could serve as the next launchpad for a major terrorist attack on the West have been heightened. The stability of this nuclear power has ramifications well beyond its own borders.

Fighting extremism on three fronts

The Federally Administered Tribal Areas (FATA)
A mountainous frontier region with a population of approximately 3.5m where the Pakistani authorities have limited control provides a base for an increasing number of extremist groups who share a broadly Islamist, anti-Western agenda. Establishing more effective governance here is seen as key to the US-led 'war on terror', and the US has been providing the Pakistani security forces with assistance to achieve this goal. There are approximately 120,000 Pakistani troops deployed in the region, working to establish 1,000 checkpoints in an effort to stem the flow of militants and arms across this notoriously porous border. In an attempt to reduce its over-reliance on Pakistani troops to establish security, in 2007 the US made a pledge to spend $750m over the following five years in order to improve infrastructure, health and education services, as well as to train the Frontier Corps, a Pakistani paramilitary force recruited from local ethnic groups. Reports that US forces in Afghanistan have been using Predator unmanned drones to launch missiles at suspected militants across the border remain unconfirmed by either side.

Baluchistan
In common with FATA, Baluchistan has endured a steady flow of both refugees and militants across its rugged territory since the war in Afghanistan began in 2001. The Afghan Taliban's leadership is thought to be based in Quetta, the state capital. While attempting to tackle Islamist extremists in the region, the Pakistani army is also attempting to quell a Baluchi separatist insurgency spearheaded by the Baluchistan Liberation Army, which is seeking autonomy for the ethnic Baluchi people. Its leader, Sardar Akhtar Mengal, was released in May 2008 as part of a pledge by the new BPP-led government to release all political prisoners.

Tehrik-i-Taliban
This indigenous extremist group, led by Baitullah Mehsud, and which has been affiliated to the Afghan Taliban in the past, is thought to be responsible for the assassination of Benazir Bhutto, as well as most other suicide bombings across the country. Despite the reservations of many Western governments, Islamabad is attempting to negotiate a ceasefire which would involve the release of prisoners, compensation for tribespeople affected by violence involving government forces, and guarantees of free movement for Tehrik-i-Taliban members. A key point of contention between the two sides is the presence of the Pakistani army in the FATA.

TURKMENISTAN

Bajaur Agency

Mohmand Agency

Khyber Agency

Peshawar

Kurram Agency   Orakzai Agency

AFGHANISTAN

NORTH WEST FRONTIER PROVINCE

North Waziristan

South Waziristan

PAKISTAN

AFGHANISTAN

Sources: IISS; Time; www.danielpipes.org; Economist; CNN; www.state.gov; Reuters; The Hindu; New York Times

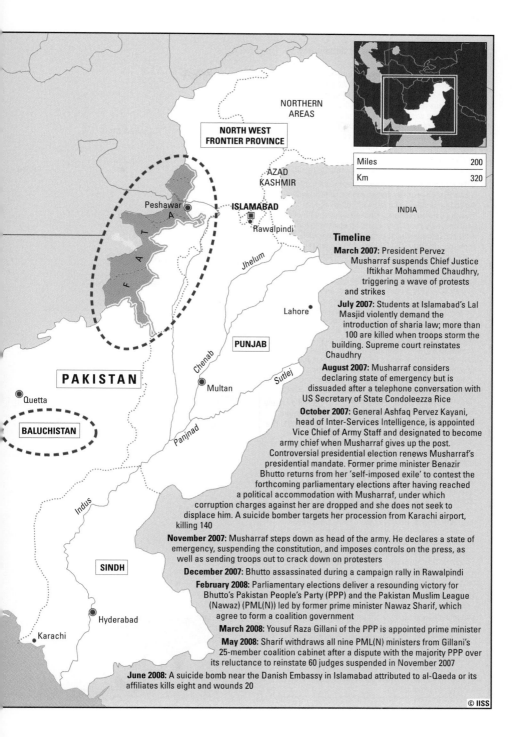

NORTHERN
AREAS

**NORTH WEST
FRONTIER PROVINCE**

AZAD
KASHMIR

Peshawar

ISLAMABAD

Rawalpindi

INDIA

| Miles | 200 |
| Km | 320 |

Lahore

PUNJAB

Jhelum

Chenab

Sutlej

PAKISTAN

Quetta

Multan

Panjnad

BALUCHISTAN

Indus

SINDH

Hyderabad

Karachi

Timeline

March 2007: President Pervez Musharraf suspends Chief Justice Iftikhar Mohammed Chaudhry, triggering a wave of protests and strikes

July 2007: Students at Islamabad's Lal Masjid violently demand the introduction of sharia law; more than 100 are killed when troops storm the building. Supreme court reinstates Chaudhry

August 2007: Musharraf considers declaring state of emergency but is dissuaded after a telephone conversation with US Secretary of State Condoleezza Rice

October 2007: General Ashfaq Pervez Kayani, head of Inter-Services Intelligence, is appointed Vice Chief of Army Staff and designated to become army chief when Musharraf gives up the post. Controversial presidential election renews Musharraf's presidential mandate. Former prime minister Benazir Bhutto returns from her 'self-imposed exile' to contest the forthcoming parliamentary elections after having reached a political accommodation with Musharraf, under which corruption charges against her are dropped and she does not seek to displace him. A suicide bomber targets her procession from Karachi airport, killing 140

November 2007: Musharraf steps down as head of the army. He declares a state of emergency, suspending the constitution, and imposes controls on the press, as well as sending troops out to crack down on protesters

December 2007: Bhutto assassinated during a campaign rally in Rawalpindi

February 2008: Parliamentary elections deliver a resounding victory for Bhutto's Pakistan People's Party (PPP) and the Pakistan Muslim League (Nawaz) (PML(N)) led by former prime minister Nawaz Sharif, which agree to form a coalition government

March 2008: Yousuf Raza Gillani of the PPP is appointed prime minister

May 2008: Sharif withdraws all nine PML(N) ministers from Gillani's 25-member coalition cabinet after a dispute with the majority PPP over its reluctance to reinstate 60 judges suspended in November 2007

June 2008: A suicide bomb near the Danish Embassy in Islamabad attributed to al-Qaeda or its affiliates kills eight and wounds 20

© IISS

ASIA-PACIFIC: Myanmar's trauma

Two decades of frustration for democracy activists

March–September 1988: Disquiet began to grow in September 1987 after General Ne Win chose to withdraw certain bank notes from circulation for superstitious reasons, resulting in many people's savings being wiped out. Millions of pro-democracy demonstrators, led by students, take to the streets. 3,000 killed in subsequent military crackdown.

1990: The National League for Democracy (NLD), led by Aung San Suu Kyi, posts a convincing victory in general elections, but the junta ignores the result.

1993: National Convention launched by the junta, 'a reconciliation process' between the military regime, the NLD and other opposition forces 'aimed at drawing up a new constitution'. Reserving 25% of parliamentary seats for military chiefs, the resultant draft constitution, finally published in April 2008, has been roundly criticised for securing the supremacy of the military even if a civilian government were ever to gain power.

August–September 2007: Protests began on 19 August when 400 people led by pro-democracy activists marched in Yangon. They were motivated by the government's unexpected decision to reduce fuel subsidies dramatically when inflation was already at 40%, effectively doubling petrol and diesel prices. The price of compressed gas used to power buses increased fivefold, leading to overnight price hikes for public-transport fares, while prices for staples such as rice and cooking oil leapt up too. Despite some arrests, protests continued in Yangon and beyond, including at Pakokku near Mandalay, where monks took 13 senior officials and military officers hostage for several hours, in retaliation for their harsh treatment of fellow monks who had joined a demonstration. When a deadline issued by the monks for a government apology expired, the momentum of the protests against the repressive regime and its economic mismanagement grew, with as many as 10,000 monks participating. Unlike the 1988 protests which were led by students, the leading role of the monks, regarded as the country's 'highest moral authority', fuelled hopes that the military regime might finally be forced to relinquish its grip on power. However, the junta's crackdown was comprehensive: around 3,000 monks and activists were arrested, and although the junta admitted to 10 deaths, the true figure may have been closer to 200. International media coverage was severely impeded by a shutdown of Internet and telephone connections.

10 May 2008: Despite international calls for it to be deferred, a referendum on the constitution goes ahead in most of the country, while the vote in delta areas worst hit by Cyclone Nargis is delayed by just 14 days. State media report that the constitution was 'overwhelmingly approved'. Apart from international criticism of the substance of the constitution, there were additional fears that the vote would divert the army's resources from the humanitarian operation at its most critical juncture.

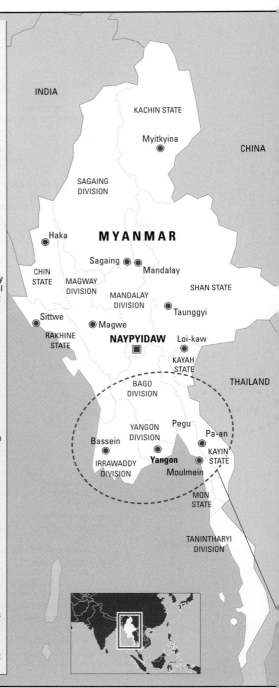

The international community watched in frustration as Myanmar endured a year of political turbulence and natural disaster. The military junta's emphatic response to the September 2007 pro-democracy protests quashed all hope that it might loosen its grip on power, but whether it can ride out the impact of Cyclone Nargis in the same way remains to be seen.

Ethnic-minority groups

Myanmar's population is among the most ethnically diverse in Asia, with its location at a crossroads between India, China and Thailand resulting in over 100 distinct ethnic groups. The annexation of the territory into a province of India by the British in 1886 imposed a single-state structure on this tapestry of separate identities. The country's leadership has been unable to reach a satisfactory accommodation with many groups over issues such as the right to self-determination and disputes over land, resulting in a cycle of ethnic insurgency met with counter-insurgency, resulting in severe human-rights abuses on the part of the authorities and the displacement of hundreds of thousands of people. Ethnic rebel groups stood back from the September 2007 pro-democracy protests.

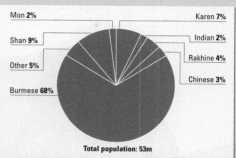

Mon 2%
Karen 7%
Shan 9%
Indian 2%
Other 5%
Rakhine 4%
Chinese 3%
Burmese 68%

Total population: 53m

Cyclone Nargis storm track

Described by UK Prime Minister Gordon Brown as a natural disaster which 'by the actions of a despicable regime ... turned into a ... manmade catastrophe', Cyclone Nargis left 130,000 people dead or missing, and, according to the UN, severely affected 1.6–2.5m people. Two weeks after it struck, around 550,000 were sheltering in temporary settlements in Irrawaddy and Yangon Divisions. The Irrawaddy Delta is the country's key rice-producing region. The military junta failed to take advantage of the 48 hours' notice it had of the cyclone's strength and landfall. Its insistence on coordinating the relief efforts directly prevented international aid and aid workers with considerable experience of disaster relief from getting in, and those who did were often limited to operating in Yangon. The regime did seem more receptive to its immediate neighbours, however, allowing entry to 160 aid workers from countries such as Bangladesh, India, China and Thailand.

Estimated category and wind speed

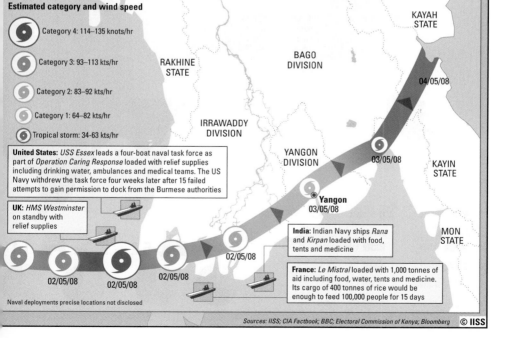

Category 4: 114–135 knots/hr
Category 3: 93–113 kts/hr
Category 2: 83–92 kts/hr
Category 1: 64–82 kts/hr
Tropical storm: 34-63 kts/hr

United States: USS Essex leads a four-boat naval task force as part of Operation Caring Response loaded with relief supplies including drinking water, ambulances and medical teams. The US Navy withdrew the task force four weeks later after 15 failed attempts to gain permission to dock from the Burmese authorities

UK: HMS Westminster on standby with relief supplies

India: Indian Navy ships Rana and Kirpan loaded with food, tents and medicine

France: Le Mistral loaded with 1,000 tonnes of aid including food, water, tents and medicine. Its cargo of 400 tonnes of rice would be enough to feed 100,000 people for 15 days

Naval deployments precise locations not disclosed

Sources: IISS; CIA Factbook; BBC; Electoral Commission of Kenya; Bloomberg © IISS

AMERICAS: The 2008 US presidential election: swing states and battleground

The winner of the US presidential election is decided by the Electoral College. States are allocated Electoral Votes (EVs) according to the number of Senators (2) and Representatives (dependent on population) they send to Congress. The candidate receiving the plurality of votes in a given state receives all its electoral votes (except for Nebraska and New Hampshire, which award votes to the winner of each congressional district as well as to the state-wide winner). 270 EVs are required to win. Election campaigns tend to focus narrowly on a small number of 'swing' states that have large numbers of EVs, are closely competitive, or both. As of 4 July 2008, four months before the November election, the battleground between Republican candidate John McCain and Democratic candidate Barack Obama appeared to be narrowing to a mix of states whose demographics and 2004 results are indicated.

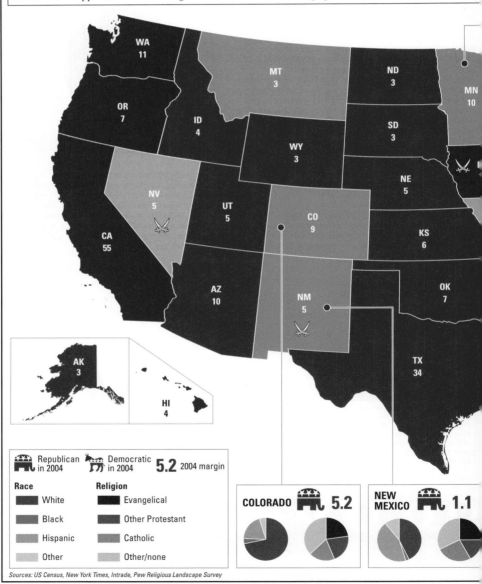

Sources: US Census, New York Times, Intrade, Pew Religious Landscape Survey

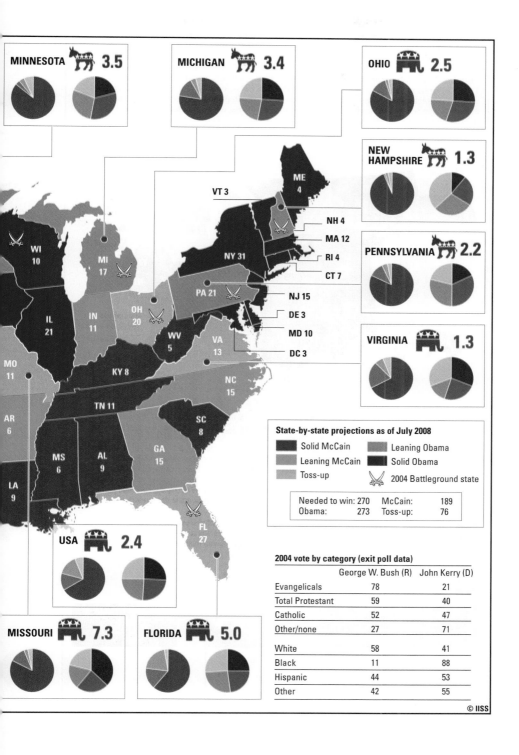

MINNESOTA 3.5

MICHIGAN 3.4

OHIO 2.5

NEW HAMPSHIRE 1.3

PENNSYLVANIA 2.2

VIRGINIA 1.3

USA 2.4

MISSOURI 7.3

FLORIDA 5.0

ME 4
VT 3
NH 4
MA 12
NY 31
RI 4
CT 7
PA 21
NJ 15
DE 3
MD 10
DC 3

WI 10
MI 17
IL 21
IN 11
OH 20
WV 5
VA 13
MO 11
KY 8
NC 15
AR 6
TN 11
SC 8
MS 6
AL 9
GA 15
LA 9
FL 27

State-by-state projections as of July 2008

- Solid McCain
- Leaning McCain
- Toss-up
- Leaning Obama
- Solid Obama
- 2004 Battleground state

| Needed to win: 270 | McCain: | 189 |
| Obama: | 273 | Toss-up: | 76 |

2004 vote by category (exit poll data)

	George W. Bush (R)	John Kerry (D)
Evangelicals	78	21
Total Protestant	59	40
Catholic	52	47
Other/none	27	71
White	58	41
Black	11	88
Hispanic	44	53
Other	42	55

© IISS

AMERICAS: The 2008 US senate election: landscape and prospects

US Senators are elected for fixed six-year terms, staggered so that one-third of the 100 seats are up for election every two years. In the November 2008 election there are 35 seats at stake, two of which are special elections to replace Senators elected in 2006 who have died or retired. In both cases the state governor appointed a temporary replacement, who must now defend the seat. The Democrats have more opportunities for gains, since they only have to defend 12 seats, all of which have incumbents running for re-election, while the Republicans must defend 23 seats, including five where the current Senator is retiring and three which the Republicans won from the Democrats in the 2002 elections, the first elections after the 11 September attacks.

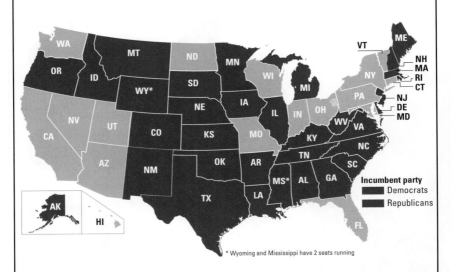

* Wyoming and Mississippi have 2 seats running

Incumbent party
- Democrats
- Republicans

In the 2006 elections the Democrats gained six seats and control of the Senate with a 51–49 majority, including two independents who caucus with them. (In the event of a 50–50 split, the tie is broken by the vice president, in his role as president of the Senate). A partisan majority gives control of committee chairmanships and of the legislative agenda. 60 votes are needed for 'cloture', which cuts off debate and forces a vote, and without which the minority can block legislation or confirmation of presidential appointees through the tactic known as the filibuster. 67 votes are needed to overcome a presidential veto or ratify an international treaty. The Democrats controlled the Senate from 1955–81, after which control changed six times. The Democrats held more than 60 seats in 1959–69 and 1975–79, but only held more than 67 between 1965 and 1967. The Republicans have never held more than 55 seats in the modern era.

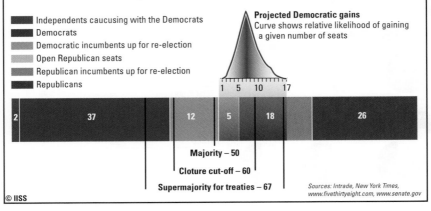

- Independents caucusing with the Democrats
- Democrats
- Democratic incumbents up for re-election
- Open Republican seats
- Republican incumbents up for re-election
- Republicans

Projected Democratic gains
Curve shows relative likelihood of gaining a given number of seats

1 5 10 17

| 2 | 37 | | 12 | 5 | 18 | 26 |

Majority – 50
Cloture cut-off – 60
Supermajority for treaties – 67

Sources: Intrade, New York Times,
www.fivethirtyeight.com, www.senate.gov

© IISS

5 Russia / Eurasia

The past year has tested the resilience of Russia's 'stability' paradigm, established by Vladimir Putin during his eight-year tenure as president. It saw parliamentary and presidential elections, following which Putin handed the presidency to his hand-picked successor Dmitry Medvedev, but remained in government as prime minister. Russia continued to face challenges in its relations with Europe and the United States. During the year to mid 2008, Russia suspended its obligations under the Conventional Forces in Europe (CFE) Treaty and stepped up its opposition to the plans of President George W. Bush to place elements of a US missile-defence system in Poland and the Czech Republic.

Russia continued to project the image of an assertive and confident power. Beneath the surface, however, the fundamentals of its domestic order were in question as its governmental system was fraught with legitimacy problems and insufficient capacity to deliver the reforms necessary to sustain economic growth. The country had rejected democratic accountability and transparency in favour of a state-controlled and elite-based modernisation project. The fundamental political challenge now lay in crafting a new balance of power between Putin, who as prime minister appeared to be determined to retain all the real levers of power, and Medvedev, whose political ambitions remained untested.

It appeared that the government would need to reconcile two opposing economic forces. On one hand there was growing state interference in the economy, evidenced by state corporations assuming control of lucrative enterprises and by the anticipated increase in state funding for major innovation and infrastructure projects. On the other hand, there was a rising, albeit still politically immature, middle class, which had a greater stake in eradicating corruption, establishing

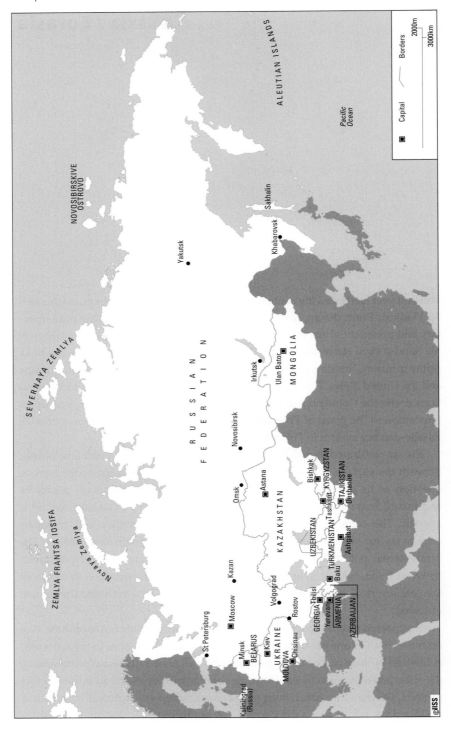

the rule of law and developing modern state institutions. The ability of the state to get the balance between these two forces right will determine whether it can forge longer-term economic and political stability.

In the foreign-policy sphere, Moscow's disappointing implementation of domestic political reforms was a major obstacle to the creation of strategic alliances with Western democracies. Russia lacked the economic and demographic capacity to assert itself as a genuinely equal geopolitical partner for China and India. Its partnerships with neighbours in the Commonwealth of Independent States (CIS) have been propped up by economic growth and rising wealth, but countries in post-Soviet Eurasia have sought to counter Russian pressure by forging stronger relations with other powers in Europe and Asia. Over the past year these trends emerged even among such close Russian allies as Kazakhstan, Tajikistan, Armenia, Uzbekistan and Belarus.

Russia has thus become increasingly inward looking and isolated. It has wasted political capital pursuing bargains with the West on issues such as the CFE, and in some cases has taken risks, as in its relations with Georgia. However, there were signs that Medvedev could adopt a more outward-looking approach and was interested in improved relations with the West, although his limited domestic power-base will constrain his ability to implement a substantially different foreign-policy strategy.

Russia's political transition

The year had been dominated by speculation as to whether Putin – who retained enormous popularity but constitutionally could not stand for a third successive term as president – would change the constitution in order to stay, or would anoint someone as his chosen successor. In the event, the formal transfer of power was a fairly mundane affair. In May 2008 Putin handed the reins of power to Dmitry Medvedev, who had easily won the presidential election, and Medvedev immediately appointed his predecessor as prime minister. It was unclear precisely how the new 'diarchy' would work. It promised to be unpredictable and risky.

Although tensions within the Kremlin over the succession dated back several years, the process really began only months before the elections. Throughout 2007 speculation over the choice of successor surrounded the two deputy prime ministers, Sergei Ivanov and Medvedev. In September 2007, Mikhail Fradkov resigned as prime minister and the Duma confirmed Putin's appointment of the largely unknown Viktor Zubkov as his replacement. Some considered this a sign that Zubkov was a possible candidate for the presidency. Others saw it as a sign of the political downfall of Ivanov, who had been a clear favourite in the eyes of many experts, but whose ambition and independence inspired opposition from powerful Kremlin insiders.

In October 2007, Putin agreed to head the dominant United Russia Party list in the December 2007 Duma elections and hinted that he might become the next prime minister. No Russian president had ever been formally associated with any political party. Elections for the lower house of the Duma on 2 December saw United Russia sweep to victory with 64.3% of the vote. The closest contender was the Communist Party of the Russian Federation, with 11.6%. Only two other parties crossed the 7% threshold needed to gain seats: the far-right Liberal Democrat Party (8.14%) and Fair Russia (7.74%). Both were considered Kremlin allies. Observers from the Organisation for Security and Cooperation in Europe (OSCE)'s Parliamentary Assembly and the Council of Europe's Parliamentary Assembly declared at a news conference that the election 'was not fair and failed to meet many OSCE and Council of Europe commitments and standards for democratic elections'. They accused United Russia of 'abuse of administrative resources' and 'media coverage strongly in favour of the ruling party', and said many election observers had not been granted visas in time.

In mid December, United Russia formally nominated Medvedev as its presidential candidate, ending speculation over Putin's choice of successor. Medvedev announced on Russian state television that he would ask Putin to head the government if he won the election. There were four registered contenders: Andrei Bogdanov (leader of the Democratic Party of Russia), Gennady Zyuganov (leader of the Communist Party), Vladimir Zhirinovsky (leader of the Liberal Democratic Party), and Medvedev. The latter was supported by Putin and five political parties: United Russia, Fair Russia, the Agrarian Party, Civilian Powers and the Russian Ecological Party (the Greens). Several other potential candidates were refused permission to register or were disqualified on dubious grounds. These included the liberals Garry Kasparov and Mikhail Kasyanov (a former prime minister who had become a strong critic of Putin's anti-democratic policies) and the ex-dissident Vladimir Bukovsky. No televised debates between the registered candidates were allowed by the Kremlin and administrative resources were used in many instances to bolster partisan turnout. The elections were held on 2 March 2008. On a turnout of 64%, Medvedev won with 70.28% of the vote; Zyuganov received 17.72%, Zhirinovsky 9.35% and Bogdanov 1.3%. The OSCE boycotted the elections over the severe restrictions placed on them but the Parliamentary Assembly of the Council of Europe's Observer Delegation concluded that no election fraud or major violations had taken place and that the outcome broadly reflected the will of the people, although it did say that not all candidates had received equal media coverage. On 15 April 2008 Putin accepted an offer from United Russia to become its leader and chairman. Medvedev was officially inaugurated as president on 7 May 2008. His first official act was to nominate Putin as his premier.

Most observers believed Putin would remain the real centre of power. Medvedev had no independent power base and owed his election almost entirely to Putin's endorsement and his management of the electoral system. Because the elections had been in effect non-competitive, with no public debates between candidates, and with real opposition candidates barred from running, Medvedev's legitimacy was weak. Should he decide to distance himself from Putin and steer an independent course he would have to establish himself as a real power. It remained uncertain whether his policy agenda was sufficiently different and his capacity for political intrigue sufficiently strong to engineer a real shift of power – although a major crisis could help accelerate such a transition. Meanwhile, Putin's enduring influence did not suggest that the government was ready to implement economic reforms or improve state institutions.

Medvedev's challenges and priorities

Although Putin and Medvedev have worked together for over 17 years, first in St Petersburg and then in the Kremlin, the two men are dissimilar in many ways. A lawyer – only 25 years old when the Soviet Union collapsed – with no links to the KGB or roots in the Soviet Communist Party system, Medvedev is far more integrated into the modern globalised world: he regularly uses the Internet and holds liberal views. He has made it clear that he values freedom, deplores corruption and believes in private-sector initiatives. He may, therefore, seek to supplement Putin's strategy of state-managed modernisation by finding ways to improve conditions for individual entrepreneurs, nascent civil society and the rising middle class, so that they can realise their economic and political potential.

Medvedev, the first post-Soviet Russian leader to come to power with no sense of existential crisis looming over the country, indicated that he intended to undertake technocratic reforms to establish the rule of law and to free entrepreneurs from the tyranny of the bureaucracy. His challenge will be to offer some guarantees that private-sector-led innovation will be encouraged, even though Putin may work further to strengthen state control over the economy. Medvedev proposed a focus on building genuine institutions, improving infrastructure, supporting innovation and attracting investment. During the Putin era, institutions were subject to excessive bureaucracy (now 35% larger than in Soviet times), corruption and undermining of the rule of law. Putin's system also restricted investment and innovation by granting the state more power than it was capable of exercising. For example, the Strategic Industries Law on state corporations, although promulgated under Medvedev, was very much a product of Putin's system. The law authorised the state to limit or prohibit foreign direct investment in 42 sectors of the economy classified as strategic, although many had nothing to do with national security. This was likely to make some of Putin's friends in state corporations very rich, but was unlikely to deliver innovation, modern management and initiative. Speaking at the St Petersburg Economic Forum in June 2008, First Deputy Prime Minister Igor Shuvalov, one of Medvedev's closest allies, warned that too much state influence in the economy was as dangerous as too little.

Medvedev's two most important commitments related to fighting corruption and strengthening the rule of law. These will depend on reducing the power and size of bureaucracy, guaranteeing the independence of the judiciary and enhancing the accountability of corrupt officials at all levels. Medvedev established a commission to develop an anti-corruption programme, and initiated several cases to remove notoriously corrupt judges and to expose governmental interference in court cases and other judicial processes. These measures, while encouraging, did not challenge Putin's inner circle. However, Medvedev has hinted that he might reconsider past and current prosecutions of the management of the oil company Yukos, including its jailed former head Mikhail Khodorkovsky. These had been seen as a fundamental step in Putin's assertion of state control over business.

Another area of concern was freedom of the press. Under Putin the Russian media became subject to almost total state control and extensive censorship. It was used to boost Putin's popularity and often resorted to Soviet-style patriotism and anti-Western propaganda, while limiting access to information on sensitive issues such as Chechnya, corruption and the political opposition. Medvedev vowed to relax control over the media. One of his first major decisions was to block a draft Law on Mass Media, prepared by Putin's allies, which would have granted the state even more power to prosecute journalists and enforce censorship. Although opinion polls have consistently shown that the Russian people are happier and wealthier today than ever before and that a 'colour revolution' is unlikely, the authorities continue to fear 'people power', and carefully control access to information. The experience of former President Mikhail Gorbachev's glasnost policy demonstrated that information revolutions can be powerful drivers for change. It is reasonable to assume that Medvedev will address freedom of the press in earnest only if he believes that it will reinforce his legitimacy rather than further undermine it.

If Medvedev's liberal credentials go beyond rhetoric, his most likely power base will be the rising middle class. In 2001 the Russian middle class comprised approximately 4 million people (or 8m including dependants). By June 2007 it was conservatively estimated at 8–15% of the population, with some estimates as high as 25%, or 35m people. In his inaugural speech, Medvedev stated that he wanted 'as many people as possible to join' the middle class to gain access to quality education and health services. The Kremlin's aim of bringing household incomes in line with the EU average by 2020 also envisages a significant expansion of the middle class. This expansion is likely to significantly affect Russia's economic and political development. In Putin's Russia, however, the middle class, particularly the genuine entrepreneurial part, was excluded from the political process and fell victim to corruption and lack of the rule of law. It is now a constituency that could support Medvedev's aspiration to overcome these problems.

Economic growth and investment

The new Russian diarchy emerged during a period of turbulence in global financial markets. The impact of the turmoil on Russia's economy has, however, so far been limited. At the January 2008 World Economic Forum in Davos, Finance Minister Alexei Kudrin said Russia was a 'haven of stability' for investors in a period of global instability. Gross domestic product grew at a record rate of 8.1% in 2007 – reaching 9.5% in the last quarter – and the budget was again in surplus. Although the Ministry of Economic Development and Trade forecast GDP growth would drop to 7.6% in 2008, foreign investment was expected to rise further to $55–58bn after increasing sharply to $45.1bn in 2007. Rising inflation was one sign that Russia was being affected by international factors. The ministry raised its inflation forecast for 2008 from 8–9.5% to 9–10%, while experts suggested that 15% would be a more accurate estimate. Rising food prices were a major factor.

Russia's stabilisation fund continued to provide a strong underpinning for the economy. Thanks to the high price of oil, the fund grew in 2007 from 2.35 trillion roubles ($89.1bn) to 3.85tr roubles ($157bn). High energy prices and levels of foreign investment have thus shielded the Russian economy from the problems of the financial markets. However, Russia's dependence on commodity exports underscored the vulnerability of its economy.

Meanwhile, Russia's treatment of major foreign investors exposed the weakness of institutions, corruption and the unhealthy relationship between the state and the business community. In mid 2008 a row erupted in the 50:50 joint venture between British Petroleum and TNK, a group of three Russian private investors. It was an open secret that Gazprom had pressured TNK-BP to transfer control of one of its most lucrative gas deposits. The tensions, which resulted in a public row, were interpreted by Putin as a purely private matter – a conflict between shareholders. However, the state's intimidation of the British head of TNK-BP, including lengthy interviews with police and prosecutors, reminded international investors of the ability of Russian businesses to call on state instruments to assist them, for example through environmental regulations (as in the Sakhalin II project) or visa restrictions. Companies such as Gazprom and Rosneft have used these methods to obtain major stakes in lucrative energy projects with little real investment on their part. As long as these practices continue, Russia's ambition to become a global financial centre will have little credibility for the international community.

Military and security policies

Although constitutionally the military and security sectors in Russia are firmly under presidential control, Medvedev neither had personal links to these groups nor relied on them to come to power. However, he began his term by presiding over the first Victory Day military parade in Red Square since the end of the Soviet Union, underlining his responsibilities as commander-in-chief of the armed forces. He later visited a unit of the Strategic Rocket Forces and promised to continue increasing state funding for the military.

Medvedev moved General Yury Baluevsky, the chief of the general staff, to a symbolic role as deputy head of the Security Council, which enjoys no real powers. Baluevsky enjoyed respect among servicemen but came into conflict with Russia's first civilian defence minister, Anatoly Serdyukov, who was appointed by Putin, apparently to clean up corruption at the Ministry of Defence. Although Serdyukov had no experience in defence matters, he had worked with the tax police and was familiar with techniques to expose corruption and fraud. He brought in a team of civilians and engaged in a comprehensive economic audit of the military. He also privatised lucrative Moscow real estate which had been used as a source of shadow income for the military. The government was concerned that the increase in the defence budget from 429bn roubles in 2004 to 956bn roubles in 2008 had resulted in little improvement to conditions for servicemen. A report on conditions in the army, released just days before Baluevsky's dismissal, exposed major problems in accommodation, pensions and abuse of conscripts. The new chief of the general staff, General Nikolai Makarov, is seen as more progressive and politically astute in his approach to defence reform.

Under Putin, a Kremlin faction known as the *siloviki*, economic nationalists with security-service backgrounds, had exerted considerable power. Former KGB officers had come to form the backbone of both the state bureaucracy and state-controlled businesses. By some estimates, over 80% of senior civil servants had security-service backgrounds. Medvedev was offered the opportunity to exercise greater authority, at least symbolically, when two prominent security chiefs were removed from office: Nikolai Patrushev, head of the Federal Security Service (FSB), who was then appointed head of the Security Council; and Viktor Cherkesov, Federal Narcotics Control Service (FSKN) head, who was appointed head of the Federal Agency for the Procurement of Military and Special Equipment. Medvedev also pledged to remove officials from the boards of major state companies, a move that could further weaken the role of the *siloviki*. However, it could take quite some time for Medvedev to weaken their grip.

North Caucasus

Pro-Moscow President Ramzan Kadyrov continued to oversee a major rebuilding programme in Chechnya, which contributed to stabilisation and normalisation in the formerly war-torn republic. Kadyrov demonstrated loyalty to Moscow, delivering over 90% of the vote for Putin's United Russia party in the parliamentary elections and around 90% for Medvedev in the presidential elections. Although several non-governmental organisations (NGOs) alleged procedural irregularities in the elections, these numbers testified to Kadyrov's desire to retain Kremlin support after the transition of power. Moscow continued to channel funds to Chechnya to support reconstruction efforts and maintained an around 80,000-strong military and police presence in the region, but some officials remained concerned over Kadyrov's consolidation of power, which made it difficult for the federal authorities to exercise direct control.

Moscow's strategy to balance Kadyrov's growing power was to support other groups within Chechnya. One of Kadyrov's most prominent opponents was Sulim Yamadaev, commander of the Vostok battalion, a unit of Chechens under the direct authority of the Russian Ministry of Defence. Throughout 2007 and 2008 tensions built between the Kadyrov and Yamadaev factions, each backed by powerful militias that were accused of human-rights violations by local and international NGOs. On 14 April 2008, a road collision near the town of Argun between Kadyrov's motorcade and a Vostok convoy sparked a confrontation. Violence erupted when Kadyrov commanded his militia to detain Vostok battalion members and take control of the city of Gudermes. The Vostok battalion reacted by attacking the barracks of Kadyrov's guards in Gudermes, leading to a fierce gun battle in which nearly 20 people were reportedly killed. Kadyrov called in reinforcements and was only prevented from attacking the Vostok base and the Yamadaev family home in Gudermes by Russian security forces. Following the incident, Kadyrov accused the Vostok battalion of kidnappings, torture and murders. The discovery of the remains of seven people allegedly killed by members of the Vostok battalion prompted Kadyrov, live on Chechen television, to declare the suspension of Sulim Yamadaev as its commander for the duration of the investigation into the deaths. Yamadaev remained in command, however, as the battalion was not under Kadyrov's jurisdiction. The Russian Ministry of Defence later confirmed that it did not plan to disband Vostok or change its command, although its personnel were to be reduced by 30%.

The incident demonstrated the tense relationship between security forces and the fragility of political stability in Chechnya. Kadyrov's grip on power was only partially based on Moscow's support. Increasingly it was underpinned by local militias, operating on the basis of personal loyalty to Kadyrov, his control over financial resources and his efforts to reassert his role as Chechnya's spiritual leader, building on the legacy of his late father Ahmad Kadyrov, former mufti of Chechnya. Ramzan Kadyrov has been overseeing a major Islamic revival in Chechnya; many mosques have been restored or rebuilt and Sufi brotherhoods – traditionally important in Chechnya – granted an increasing role in political and cultural life. Moscow has, thus far, supported Kadyrov's links with the Islamic world at large; it promoted a visit to Grozny by a group of ambassadors from Muslim states. Kadyrov made the hajj to Mecca in 2007 and was warmly received by the Saudi king. Following the visit, Kadyrov sought to require women attending Chechen universities to wear the headscarf. These attempts to politicise Islam and turn it into a vehicle for promoting Kadyrov's personality cult are causing some resistance among a younger generation that is turning towards more conservative Salafist Islam, which has already spread among so-called 'youth jamaats' (local spiritual and community organisations) across the North Caucasian region.

Chechen resistance, increasingly marginalised but nevertheless still active (with several thousand members dispersed in the mountains of Chechnya and some high-profile leaders still active in exile), has been completing its own transition from a nationalist to a global jihadist agenda. In October 2007 an insurgent leader, Dokka Umarov, abolished the cabinet and parliament of the former Chechen Republic of Ichkeria (ChRI) as incompatible with a sharia state, and proclaimed himself emir of a newly established Caucasus Emirate, a territory understood to cover the North Caucasian republics, other Muslim regions in Russia, and possibly Transcaucasia. The move showed the growing influence of fundamentalist Islam on the insurgency and the increasingly regional character of the movement. Umarov's statement included criticism of the West and Israel and support for jihadist fighters in Afghanistan, Iraq and Palestine. Umarov's anti-Western rhetoric created a split with London-based ChRI foreign minister Ahmed Zakayev, who called upon separatist fighters and politicians to distance themselves from Umarov and to pledge allegiance to the Chechen parliament. Chechen field commanders Isa Munayev and Sultan Arsayev publicly sided with Zakayev, although Umarov was backed by militant jamaats in neighbouring republics, increasingly the driving force of the insurgency.

In particular, the militant Sharia jamaat stepped up activities in Ingushetia and ambushed law-enforcement personnel, military convoys and politicians on an almost daily basis. These attacks killed several prominent officials, including the deputy chairman of Ingushetia's Supreme Court, the head of the transport police and the deputy commander of the Ministry of the Interior's Special Task Force Unit. Adding to instability in Ingushetia was growing political tension between the authorities and the parliamentary opposition led by former President Ruslan Aushev. There were repeated calls for the resignation of President Murat Zyazikov, a former FSB colonel. In November 2007 the authorities dispersed a demonstration comprising 700 people gathered to protest unexplained kidnappings, corruption and poor economic conditions. Before the protest Oleg Orlov, head of the Human Rights Centre Memorial, was kidnapped and beaten in an apparent attempt at intimidation. In January 2008 further rallies in the republic's largest city, Nazran, were planned by the opposition. However, a day before the scheduled rally the authorities established 'counter-terrorist zones' in Nazran and the capital Magas, allowing them to detain suspicious individuals, carry out identification checks and restrict public movement. According to the authorities, the measures were adopted in response to intelligence that a major terrorist incident was imminent. The ensuing stand-off led to violent clashes between demonstrators and security forces in Nazran's Accord Square and to the arrest of around 200 protesters. The rally's organising committee blamed the violence on provocations and postponed further demonstrations, creating even more dissatisfaction among the population. In the first six months of 2008, there was a fourfold increase in attacks on police and servicemen in Ingushetia as compared with the same period in 2007.

Instability in Ingushetia, Chechnya and Daghestan, and the rise of radical Islamic groups in the North Caucasus and among migrants from the region to other parts of the Russian Federation, may challenge Russian domestic security in future, although large-scale separatist conflicts are unlikely to emerge. The threat is increasingly dispersed geographically and in terms of agenda, as Islamic underground groups have been radicalised by a mixture of local grievances and global trends. These threats require a combination of responses and will only be exacerbated by the heavy-handed military tactics so often used by Russian security services.

Foreign-policy developments

In 2008 Russia's foreign policy continued to be dominated by traditional concerns such as arms control, regional conflicts and NATO, as well as newer challenges such as energy security and geopolitical concerns over the balance of power in Eurasia.

CFE suspension

In April 2007, Putin threatened to suspend implementation of the 1990 CFE Treaty in response to what Russia viewed as a changed security situation due to US plans to base missile-defence systems in Poland and the Czech Republic. Russia was also aggrieved that NATO members had not ratified treaty revisions agreed in 1999, which addressed Russian concerns. The treaty set strict limits on the number of conventional offensive weapons – tanks, combat aircraft and heavy artillery – that the members of the Warsaw Pact and NATO could deploy between the Atlantic and the Urals. Russia called an extraordinary conference on the CFE in Vienna in June 2007 to demand ratification of the amended treaty.

Its demands were not met, and on 14 July Putin issued a decree suspending observance of treaty obligations, effective 150 days later. A compromise proposed by the United States in autumn 2007 was not accepted and the suspension came into force on 12 December. It did not constitute a full withdrawal from the CFE Treaty, but it did mean that Russia would no longer permit inspections or exchange data on its deployments. As there was no provision for suspension in the CFE, Western signatories declared Russia to be in breach of the treaty when it refused to provide full data on arms stockpiles in December 2007 and allow inspections in the following months.

Moscow provided several explanations for its suspension. Russia was irked by non-ratification of the adapted treaty by NATO member states, and viewed linkage between ratification and Russian withdrawal of troops from Georgia and Moldova as illegitimate. It considered troop withdrawal to be a bilateral issue. Many in Russia were concerned that in the event of a full Russian withdrawal from these states NATO could establish military relations with them, weakening Moscow's strategic influence in regions it views as essential to its security. Moscow also demanded a lowering of NATO ceilings on conventional armaments following the Alliance's enlargement. It argued that Hungary, Poland, the Czech Republic and Slovakia had failed to comply with commitments to adjust their ceilings.

Russia felt threatened by the planned deployment of American forces to Bulgaria and Romania, both of which joined NATO in 2004. The US military planned to use Bulgarian and Romanian airports for training US Army and Air Force personnel, for logistic support for the operation in Iraq and for cooperation with the Bulgarian and Romanian militaries. Russia claimed that these facilities would constitute 'substantial deployments', which fall under the limitations of the adapted CFE. Moreover, Russia feared that US missile-defence facilities in Poland and the Czech Republic would be accompanied by deployments banned by the CFE.

A further Russian concern was that the Baltic states and Slovenia had not signed the CFE treaty; they could therefore legally increase levels of conventional forces and allow emergency deployment of foreign troops and military hardware on their territory. Russia was concerned that the United States or NATO could thus obtain bases or deploy personnel and conventional weapons adjacent to Russian territory. Moscow felt that under such circumstances it would not be able to uphold its CFE treaty commitments to weapons ceilings in northwest Russia, and that the failure of NATO members to ratify the adapted treaty was a deliberate attempt to keep open options with regard to deployment in the Baltic states.

Despite some differences, NATO states have maintained a collective position in negotiations with Russia on CFE issues. Their position has been that they could only ratify the adapted treaty after Russia fulfilled two major commitments it made at the Istanbul Summit in 1999. NATO states acknowledged that Russia had reduced its military hardware levels to treaty limits and that it had closed three of its four military bases in Georgia, but they argued that Russia must still withdraw from the base at Gudauta, in Georgia's breakaway region of Abkhazia, before the United States could ratify the adapted treaty. Russia claimed it had already done so. NATO and the OSCE offered to send a fact-finding mission to Georgia to verify Russia's withdrawal, but Georgia and Russia did not accept. Georgia demanded regular inspections of the base while Russia argued that neither NATO nor the OSCE had a mandate for such inspections, and refused to guarantee the security of such a mission.

The NATO states also demanded that Russian troops withdraw from the Republic of Transdniestr, a separatist region within Moldova with close ties to Moscow. Russia claimed that its troops in Transdniestr were on a peacekeeping mission. NATO states, supported by the EU and the OSCE, wanted this peacekeeping mission to be internationalised, with Russia participating but not in overall command. NATO also argued that Russia needed to remove around 20,000 tonnes of ammunition and 500 Russian servicemen guarding weapons stockpiles in Transdniestr before it could ratify the adapted treaty. NATO members have volunteered financial support to assist with withdrawal from Moldova and Georgia, particularly removal of weapons stockpiles, but Russia has declined these offers.

The United States maintained that 'flank agreements' dealing with areas outside Central Europe could only be dealt with after Russia had withdrawn from Moldova and Georgia. NATO members also stated that renegotiation of flank agreements must take account of Turkish, Norwegian and other European states' worries about Russian troop and weapons concentrations on their borders.

It appeared that no compromise could be reached, although in the long run Russia seemed to have more to lose from the end of the CFE regime than NATO members, which would maintain conventional superiority and would be free to deploy forces in Central Europe if the treaty collapsed. At the NATO–Russia Council meeting in June 2008 the Russian delegation presented compromise proposals.

Missile defence

US plans to install ten interceptor missiles in Poland and a radar system in the Czech Republic provoked an indignant response from Russia, which viewed the bases as a threat to Russian security and as a potential catalyst for an arms race. The United States sought to reassure Russia that the system was intended for use against ballistic missiles from Iran. In June 2007, Putin threatened to target Europe with nuclear or cruise missiles if the US plans were carried out. However, Russia subsequently softened its tone and proposed that, rather than deploying a radar in the Czech Republic, the United States could have access to the Gabala radar site in Azerbaijan, leased by Russia, to monitor missile developments in Iran. Discussions on the proposal took place at the Bush family summer retreat in Kennebunkport, Maine in July 2007. Bush welcomed the offer, but only as an addition to the US plans, rather than as a substitute. US experts later highlighted technical problems with joint use of the Gabala radar. On 11 August 2007, Putin announced that Russia had launched a programme to improve its own strategic defences. A new system, the S-400 *Triomf*, designed to defeat stealth bombers, was put on combat alert at Elektrostal in Moscow oblast. The new *Voronezh-DM* early-warning radar at Lekhtusi, just north of St Petersburg, entered 'experimental combat service' in December 2006, the first stage of a major early-warning programme to be completed in 2015. A similar advanced radar is under construction at Armavir in southern Russia and is expected to enter service by the end of 2008.

US–Russia talks resumed in September 2007 and US experts visited the Gabala site, but no agreement was reached. Putin offered to work with the United States and other European countries on a joint defence system – a proposal first made in 2000. In January 2008 there were reports in the Russian press that the Russian Ministry of Defence planned to change the configuration of troops in Kaliningrad in response to the US plans. Soon after, Putin spoke of a 'new arms race being unleashed in the world'. He reiterated the view that the US bases would threaten Russian security and that Russia would have to re-target its missiles in response. There were further talks in Moscow in March between US and Russian defence and foreign ministers in which the United States offered to allow Russia to monitor the radar remotely and to inspect the interceptor-missile base, but again no agreement was reached. On 6 April, during their final presidential meeting at Sochi, Putin and Bush signed an 11-page Strategic Framework Declaration detailing the spectrum of US–Russian relations. This expressed mutual 'interest' in creating a system for responding to potential missile threats in which Russia, the United States and Europe would participate as equal partners and included provisions for nuclear cooperation between the United States and Russia. The United States, which controls much of the world's nuclear fuel, pledged to help Russia achieve its goal of establishing an international nuclear-fuel-storage facility by importing and storing spent fuel. Although Russia remained opposed to US bases in Poland and the Czech Republic, it conceded that it appreciated US proposals and agreed to intensify dialogue on issues concerning missile-defence cooperation, both bilaterally and multilaterally. 'I do have certain cautious optimism with regard to mutual agreements. I believe that this is possible. But the devil is in the details', Putin said. The US elections and the new Russian administration's review of security policy, including missile-defence plans, could ease US–Russian tensions and provide time for proposals on cooperation to be developed further. However, when the Czech government signed an agreement with Washington in July 2008, which required parliamentary approval, Moscow responded by threatening 'military-technical' measures.

Energy diplomacy

Over the past year, Gazprom continued to extend its tentacles across Europe, striking further deals to expand supplies and invest in the distribution network (see Strategic Geography, pp. X–XI). Russia signed agreements with almost all the states involved in the South Stream natural-gas pipeline project, which would supply gas to southwestern Europe, bypassing Ukraine. The project is seen as a rival to the EU- and US-supported Nabucco pipeline, which would transport gas from the Caspian Sea to Austria via Turkey, Bulgaria, Romania and Hungary, avoiding Russia. South Stream was announced on 23 June 2007 when Russian monopoly Gazprom and the Italian energy company ENI signed a memorandum of understanding (MoU) to build a pipeline from Russia to Italy, with an annual capacity of 30bn cubic metres. The project will include an off-shore section of around 900km under the Black Sea from the Russian Beregvaya compressor station to the Bulgarian coast at Varna. From Bulgaria, there are two possible routes: one north through Romania, Hungary and Austria or Slovenia to northern Italy, and one south through Greece to southern Italy. Gazprom set up a Coordinating Committee for the project on 6 September 2007 and on 22 November Gazprom and ENI signed a supplement to their MoU. On 18 January 2008 the South Stream AG Special Purpose Entity was registered. Analysts predict that the project will cost €10bn.

On 18 January Bulgaria also agreed to join the project and signed a deal giving it a 50% stake in a joint venture that would run the pipeline on Bulgarian territory. On 25 January, Russia and Serbia signed an inter-state agreement on cooperation in gas and oil under which Gazprom bought a controlling inter-est in the state oil company, Naftna Industrija Srbije, and would route a branch of South Stream through Serbia. On the same day Gazprom signed an agree-ment with the Austrian oil and gas corporation OMV giving Gazprom 50% of the Central Europe Gas Hub, a subsidiary of OMV Gas International, although as of June 2008 there was still no inter-state agreement between Russia and Austria. On 28 February, Putin signed a bilateral agreement with Hungarian Prime Minister Ferenc Gyurcsany to set up a joint company to build the pipeline. On 29 April, Greece and Russia agreed on Greece's participation in the project. Tensions between Austria and Gazprom led the company to hold talks with Slovenia in April to discuss involvement in the project, possibly as a warning to Austria that it could be bypassed. Neither country has yet signed on to the project, and the final transit country for the northern branch remains in question. The pipeline is scheduled to be operational by 2013.

The EU's rival Nabucco project was undermined by a lack of alternative suppliers. Azerbaijan is already supplying gas to Europe via the Baku–Tbilisi–Erzurum pipeline, but other sources are more problematic. Iran, which could represent a major alternative, is excluded for political reasons, while Turkmenistan at present sells almost all its gas to or via Russia. Much effort had been made over the past year to promote the construction of the Trans-Caspian gas pipeline from Turkmenistan, a project which had been discussed since the mid 1990s but had failed to make any progress. After the death of Turkmen President Sapurmat Niyazov in 2006, Turkmenistan made some effort to open up and was actively courted by the United States and the EU. Washington sent several high-level delegations to Ashgabat to lobby for the Trans-Caspian pipeline and the EU Troika held a Central Asia ministerial meeting there to signal the importance of the country as a prospective gas supplier for Europe. Active Western engagement improved relations between Turkmenistan and Azerbaijan, which had competing territorial claims over some oil and gas fields in the Caspian Sea. During a historic visit by new Turkmen President Gurbanguly Berdymukhamedov to Baku in May 2008, preliminary agreements were reached to resolve the dispute. However, the major obstacle to the Trans-Caspian pipeline is the unresolved status of the Caspian Sea among the five littoral states (Russia, Kazakhstan, Turkmenistan, Iran and Azerbaijan) and no agreement is expected soon. Turkmenistan signed an agreement with China in July 2007 to speed up the Turkmenistan–China gas pipeline, expected to stretch from Turkmenistan's Bagtyarlyak territory to Xinjiang in China. Construction began in 2007 and the pipeline is expected to be operational by early 2009. The project signals the start of Sino-Russian competition over Central Asian energy resources, as Russia remains dependent on Turkmen gas to meet its domestic and export obligations. Russia has already been forced to significantly raise the price for Turkmen gas under the pressure of competition from China. The lack of clear information about the extent of Turkmenistan's gas deposits leaves Europe the clear underdog in this three-way competition. The government of Turkmenistan is currently conducting an audit of its gas resources, likely to shed some light on whether it could be a significant alternative gas supplier for the EU.

Kosovo and frozen conflicts

Russia vehemently opposed Kosovo's February 2008 declaration of independence from Serbia, arguing that it would not be legal without Serbia's consent. Russia feared that independence for Kosovo would set a precedent for other secessionist movements, and warned that it would consider Kosovo's move when revising its own policy toward Georgia's breakaway regions of Abkhazia and South Ossetia. The Kremlin called Kosovo's declaration illegitimate under international law, and Russian Foreign Minister

Sergei Lavrov warned his US counterpart Condoleezza Rice that it endangered international stability.

The West's refusal to accept a Russian veto regarding Kosovo prompted a response from Moscow, which came, as expected, in the Caucasus. It was not, however, in the form of recognition of Abkhazian and South Ossetian independence from Georgia, but rather in increased links with the territories, including establishing formal relations with the de facto authorities. On 6 March 2008, shortly after Kosovo's declaration of independence from Serbia, Russia announced that it no longer felt bound by the 1996 agreement signed by the Commonwealth of Independent States that imposed economic sanctions on Abkhazia. On 7 March, the parliament of Abkhazia addressed appeals to the Russian Federation Council, the State Duma, and the Secretary-General of the UN to recognise the independence of the Republic of Abkhazia. The Duma passed a resolution calling on the Kremlin to consider 'the expediency of recognizing the independence' of Abkhazia and South Ossetia. The draft resolution also recommended that Russia open missions in Abkhazia and South Ossetia, ease border restrictions and boost economic ties with the breakaway regions. The resolution was not binding but called on the Russian president 'to intensify efforts aimed at the protection of the security of citizens of the Russian Federation, residing on the territories of Abkhazia and South Ossetia' and to consider 'the possibility of the reinforcement of the [Russian] peacekeeping troops in the Georgian–Abkhaz and Georgian–Ossetian conflict zones'. During the NATO Bucharest Summit on 2–4 April, Putin communicated with the leaders of Abkhazia and South Ossetia via letters addressing them as 'president' and promising that Russian support would be 'practical, not declaratory' in nature. On 16 April, Putin signed a decree moving toward the de facto annexation of Abkhazia and South Ossetia. The decree effectively made Abkhazia and South Ossetia autonomous republics of the Russian Federation and opened up direct trade, transportation and political links with the territories. Under the decree, separatist-issued 'passports' and other legal acts will be 'recognized by counterpart state agencies of the Russian Federation.' The United States and the EU urged Russia to repeal the decree.

On 18 April the Abkhaz Ministry of Defence announced it had shot down a Georgian unmanned aerial reconnaissance vehicle (UAV) which had violated Abkhaz airspace. Georgia denied the incident and, on 20 April, Abkhaz president Sergei Bagapsh announced that his forces had shot down another UAV and had found the debris. Georgia accused Abkhazia of provocation, stating that Abkhazia did not have the technical capability to shoot down an unmanned aircraft – only the Russians did. The next day Georgia confirmed the incident, accusing the Russians of shooting down the UAV, and released video footage of the incident as proof. Georgian President Mikheil Saakashvili accused Russia of 'an unprovoked act of aggression against the sovereign territory of Georgia' and called on Russia to reverse Putin's 16 April decision. Moscow denied the claim, and Putin expressed concern to Saakashvili about Georgian military flights over Abkhazia. On 23 April, the Russian Federation Council announced that it had postponed consideration of Abkhazia and South Ossetia's request that Russia recognise their independence. On 25 April, Valeriy Kenyaykin, the Russian Foreign Ministry's special envoy for relations with the CIS countries, told a news conference that if Georgia unleashed a military conflict in Abkhazia or South Ossetia, Russia would use force to defend its countrymen living in those regions.

Over the next few weeks each side accused the other of building up troops in the Abkhaz region. Georgia denied the accusation and Russia claimed it had only introduced 500 additional peacekeepers to bring the level up to 3,000, as stipulated by the 1994 Moscow agreement. On 4 May, the Abkhaz Ministry of Defence announced that two more UAVs had been shot down over Abkhaz territory by Abkhaz air-defence forces. On 8 May it announced that yet another UAV had been shot down and on 12 May it reported destruction of a further two. Georgia denied the incidents, although it later accepted that three of its UAVs had been destroyed. On 16 May, the UN adopted a Tbilisi-backed resolution on the return of refugees to Abkhazia. Russia and Abkhazia criticised the resolution. In late May Russia deployed 400 'railway troops', allegedly to repair the railroad which had connected Georgia and Russia via Abkhazia. Georgia viewed this deployment as an act of aggression on its territory.

As tensions continued to rise, a meeting between Medvedev and Saakashvili in St Petersburg on 7 June yielded no results. Georgia set three conditions for normalising relations: the additional Russian military units should be withdrawn, construction of military infrastructure should cease, and Putin's 16 April decree should be rescinded. However, despite international support, it appeared unlikely that Georgia would get its way. Moscow seemed determined to alter the status quo in Abkhazia to suit its interests.

On 6 July 2008 five mines exploded in the border area between Georgia and Abkhazia. Russia accused Georgia of setting off the mines to stir tension in the region, while Georgia accused Russia of violating agreements by transporting military hardware, including anti-aircraft systems, armoured vehicles and helicopters to Abkhazia – the same weapons Georgia claims are responsible for shooting down their UAVs.

The cycle of escalation demonstrated that Russia and Georgia both had much at stake in Abkhazia. For Saakashvili, who had recently experienced domestic political problems and had failed to make the progress he had wished towards membership of NATO at the Bucharest Summit, it was important to regain control of the breakaway republic, or at least to demonstrate meaningful steps in that direction. For Russia, closer cooperation with the de facto authorities in

Abkhazia was important as it prepared to hold the 2014 Winter Olympic Games in Sochi, fewer than 20km from Abkhazia's hotels and cheap labour.

NATO and the EU expressed concern and called for restraint. In the space of several weeks the French foreign minister, the secretary-general of NATO, the US president and the EU's foreign-policy chief all intervened to facilitate the reduction of tensions and called upon Russia to withdraw its additional forces. In July, German Foreign Minister Frank-Walter Steinmeier, who chairs the Group of Friends of the UN secretary-general for Georgia, unveiled a three-stage peace plan to resolve the Georgia–Abkhazia conflict. The proposals were supported by the international community, including Russia, but rejected by Abkhazia and met with reservations by Georgia. Despite greater Western engagement, it was unlikely that Georgia's calls for the deployment of international peacekeepers under EU or NATO auspices would be met. The challenge was to find a path back to the negotiating table.

Signs of conciliation

In spite of the difficult issues of the CFE, missile defence, Kosovo and Georgia, there were some signs by mid 2008 of a possible thaw in the frosty dealings between Russia and the West. In Bucharest, Putin attended a NATO summit for the first time. While he accused leaders in a closed meeting of not heeding Russia's security concerns, and criticised NATO's promise to eventually make Ukraine and Georgia members as a 'direct threat' to Russian security, his participation revealed a softening of tone. He said Bush was listening to Moscow's criticisms of his missile-defence plans – and the two later issued a joint declaration at their meeting in Sochi.

EU–Russia relations started to show some progress. At an EU–Russia Summit in Khanty-Mansyisk on 26–27 June negotiations began on a new basic treaty between Russia and the EU to replace the ten-year-old Partnership and Co-operation Agreement, although differences over the nature and scope of the treaty made it unlikely that a quick agreement would be reached.

In a speech in Berlin on 5 June, Medvedev announced that Russia 'had come in from the cold' and was actively returning to global politics and the global economy. He stressed that Russia valued a close strategic partnership with Germany and pointedly warned 'of the consequences of marginalising and isolating countries ... and abandoning the creation of general regional collective security systems'. Medvedev said Russia was a European country and 'shared common moral and spiritual heritage' with Europe. He called for a European summit to develop 'a legally binding treaty on European security' that could resolve common arms-control and security concerns. In its conciliatory tone, the speech contrasted markedly with his predecessor's fiery rhetoric in Munich in February 2007 that had raised fears of a new Cold War.

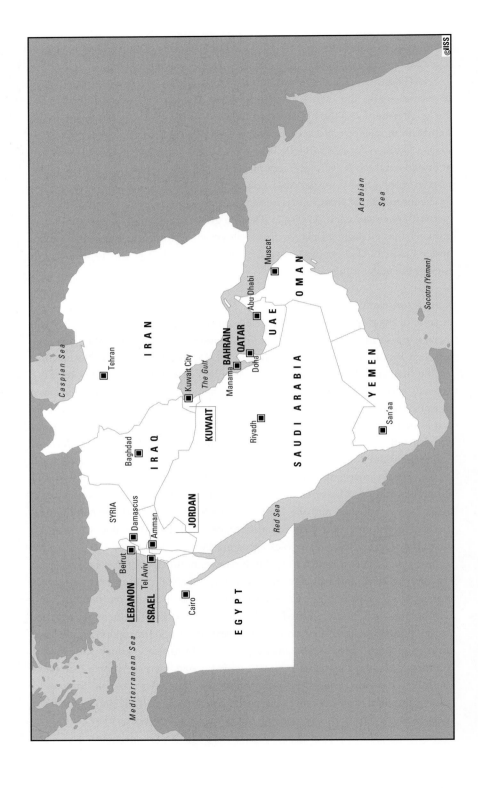

Tension over Iran's nuclear programme remained high during the past year, in spite of a surprise announcement by American intelligence agencies that they believed Tehran had halted its development of nuclear weapons in 2003. Iran pressed ahead with the enrichment of uranium, in defiance of United Nations Security Council resolutions. In neighbouring Iraq, there was a significant fall in politically motivated violence following a change in American military tactics in conjunction with the 2007 troop 'surge' – although Baghdad remained a dangerous place. Five years after the collapse of the organs of government that followed the American-led invasion, there were signs that the workings of the state were resuming. Although the violence of key sectarian groups had been constrained, the United States, as well as Iraq's Arab neighbours, remained concerned about the lack of political reconciliation. In the Middle East, internal divisions and weak leadership on both the Israeli and Palestinian sides appeared to preclude any possibility of a lasting peace accord, in spite of American efforts to force an agreement. Israel did, however, commence talks with Syria.

Iraq: Violence Reduced

Events in Iraq were dominated in the year to mid 2008 by the 'surge', or Baghdad Security Plan, announced at the beginning of 2007 by US President George W. Bush. From February 2007, US troop levels steadily rose from 130,000 to a peak of 175,000 in the middle of November. In military terms the surge undoubtedly worked, creating a pause in Iraq's previously relentless descent into civil war.

However, the plan's main architect, General David Petraeus, head of Multi-National Force in Iraq, always saw the surge as a temporary palliative designed to facilitate a long-term political settlement. The rapid increase in US troops, and their deployment into Baghdad neighbourhoods, was meant to suspend the civil war, creating a 'window of opportunity' for Iraq's politicians to move towards national reconciliation. There was little evidence that this happened. If anything, the year to mid 2008 saw Prime Minister Nuri al-Maliki's government become less representative of Iraq's different factions. That the pause in violence brought about by the surge has not been utilised by Iraq's ruling elite raises questions about the longevity of its effects.

Improved security

There can be little doubt that the surge delivered a large and sustained reduction in violence. In Baghdad itself, the bold use of increased American troops produced a knock-on effect, convincing Iraq's warring factions that the United States was serious about enforcing order. The policy of locating US troops, alongside their Iraqi counterparts, in 68 small forts (Joint Security Stations and Combat Outposts) placed a visible security presence in previously abandoned and strife-torn communities. The security plan saw concrete barriers designed to impede the movement of both death squads and car bombers placed around Baghdad neighbourhoods, or *mahallahs*. Gated communities were set up behind perimeter walls as the US military oversaw the clearance of armed groups from selected areas, conducted a local census and established an identity-card system. Once specific areas had been secured, the barriers built and the security stations staffed, American battalion commanders used their Commander's Emergency Response Programme (CERP) funds to rebuild governmental services in the areas they now controlled. By the middle of 2007, this approach had begun to bear dividends. Although the Joint Security Stations only covered a small number of neighbourhoods, the aggressive deployment of US and Iraqi forces clearly increased security across Baghdad. The rate of sectarian murders fell dramatically. A limited number of displaced Sunnis returned to their former homes, and economic life returned to the shopping and market areas of west Baghdad.

Petraeus was unambiguous in the message he delivered to the US Congress in September 2007: 'the military objectives of the surge, in large measure, are being met'. Violent civilian deaths of all kinds had declined by 45% in Iraq as a whole and by 70% in Baghdad, he said. Within these figures, ethno-sectarian deaths had declined by 55% across the country and by 80% in Baghdad since their peak in December 2006. More detailed US government figures suggested that, across the country as a whole, civilian deaths steadily declined throughout 2007–08. According to figures collated by the Brookings Institution's Iraq Index, 3,500 Iraqi civilians were violently killed in Iraq in January 2007. This figure dropped to 2,700 in February and continued to decline to a low of 550 civilians killed across Iraq in May 2008.

Against this background of military success, Petraeus came under intense American political and military pressure to reduce the number of US troops deployed in Iraq. Senior US military figures, including General George Casey, the army chief of staff, and Admiral William Fallon, then head of the US military's Central Command, which covers the Gulf and Middle East, voiced concern that the extended deployment of such large troop numbers was damaging the military's long-term capacity. In response to this pressure, Petraeus announced in his September testimony that the surge would effectively end in July 2008, with the withdrawal of five brigades, bringing troops back to their pre-surge levels of 130,000. Secretary of Defense Robert Gates had aimed to further reduce troop levels to 100,000 by the end of 2008. However, Petraeus was careful to place numerous caveats on the drawdown, stressing that US troop numbers would ultimately be shaped by events on the ground. This cautious approach was supported by Bush when he publicly committed the government to giving Petraeus 'whatever forces he needed'. By May 2008 the Pentagon had agreed to keep US troop levels at 140,000 until the end of 2009.

Ironically, it was the failure of Casey's own strategy whilst in charge of US forces in Iraq that was cited as a cautionary example. Casey was commander of Multi-National Forces in Iraq from June 2004 until February 2007. During this time he was keen to hand responsibility for security to Iraqi forces as quickly as possible, to meet political pressures from Washington for a rapid reduction in US casualties. This resulted in Iraq's descent into civil war during 2006, when previously pacified areas were once again seized by sectarian militias and insurgents. Petraeus was keen to avoid repeating Casey's mistakes and strove not to see hard-won security advances squandered by speedy troop reductions.

However, in the long term the Iraqi Ministry of Defence (MoD) and its minister, retired Lieutenant-General Abdullah al-Qadir Muhammad Jasim al-Mufraqi, remain at the centre of US transition plans and any future withdrawal strategy. Amidst widespread governmental inefficiency and corruption, the MoD is considered one of the more effective ministries in the government. Because it is sited within the protective enclave of Baghdad's Green Zone, 50 US civilian advisers working in its central building can operate with a heightened degree of security and access. A report to the US Congress in July 2007 asserted that nine out of 13 divisions in the Iraqi army, and 95 out of 101 battalions, were capable of taking a lead role in operations. Of 226,664 soldiers reported to be in the army, congressional estimates assess that 75–80% are Shia, with two of 11 divisions being at least 50% Kurdish. However, the senior ranks of the military are more ethnically and religiously balanced, with three Kurdish divisional commanders, four Shi'ites and four Sunnis.

There was general acceptance that the rebuilding of Iraq's army had been comparatively successful. However, it still suffered from problems with logistics, shortages of qualified leaders, staff retention, militia infiltration in some units, and sectarianism. Overall, it was judged to be years away from functioning effectively without sustained coalition support. There was a major under-manning problem, with most units only able to muster between 60 and 75% of their assigned staff. This was partly due to the policy of allowing soldiers to travel home each month to give wages to their families. There was also an estimated 15–18% annual attrition rate. Both problems were exacerbated by corruption, with muster rolls sometimes padded with non-existent soldiers so that senior officers could skim money off for personal enrichment.

Sectarianism remained a problem in some units, though it was not nearly as pronounced as in the police force or other government ministries. While Shi'ites made up the vast majority of the junior ranks of the army, the senior staff was still dominated by Sunnis and Kurds. This may be because those at the top of the Iraqi army gained their experience either in the Peshmerga (the Kurdish militia) or in Saddam's armed forces, which had an inherent bias towards a Sunni officer corps. Of much greater concern was the overtly sectarian behaviour of some army divisions. The Fifth Division, based in Diyala province northeast of Baghdad, was accused of facilitating arms shipments to Shia militias and of being dominated by both Moqtada al-Sadr's Jaish al-Mahdi (JAM) militia (also known as the Madhi Army) and the Badr Brigade, the military wing of the Islamic Supreme Council for Iraq (ISCI). In July 2007, 30 civilians in Diyala were killed by men wearing army uniforms, and the Fifth Division's Shia commander was replaced at the coalition's behest after repeated complaints that he had been involved in the harassment of Sunni civilians.

In a country deeply enmeshed in violence and long-running sectarian conflict, it is perhaps not surprising that the army was contaminated by religious and ethnic division. The large number of coalition advisers embedded in its ranks and the close interaction between US and Iraqi forces limited the scope for an orchestrated campaign of colonisation by militia groups. However, throughout 2007 there were worrying signs that an extended campaign of politicisation was under way. As part of the campaign to reduce violence, the US military agreed that Maliki could create the Office of the Commander in Chief (OCIC). This was designed to bring greater coherence to the Iraqi armed forces. However, the prime minister used the OCIC to increase his personal control over the Iraqi army. Key prime-ministerial advisers used his authority to move troops, employing mobile telephones to contact officers directly, bypassing the chain of command. The creation of the OCIC undermined the administrative coherence of the MoD and the authority of the defence minister. Analysts judged that this could, if left unchecked, open the Iraqi army to the sustained politicisation that had done so much to undermine the police force. The Iraqi army would then become another sectarian actor, hastening a descent into civil war. Under this scenario, US plans for greater Iraqi control over the military would simply deliver it into the hands of the militias and death squads.

Organisation of violence

One of the great success stories of the surge was the battle against al-Qaeda in Mesopotamia (AQM). The United States estimated that AQM's ability to operate in Baghdad had been drastically reduced, forcing it to regroup in and around Iraq's third city, Mosul, the capital of Nineveh province. The central reason for AQM's troubles was the rejection of the organisation by key sections of Iraq's Sunni community. Throughout 2005 and 2006, AQM had successfully transformed itself from a vehicle for foreign jihadists into a largely indigenous Iraqi organisation. This success, however, may have proved its undoing. By recruiting large numbers of Iraqis into its ranks, AQM brought itself into much closer proximity to the general Sunni population in Baghdad and across the northwest of the country. AQM radicals demanded strict adherence to their austere brand of Islamism, using unrestrained violence to impose their edicts upon society. This ran counter to a more diverse set of approaches to Islam across Sunni Iraq. A ban on smoking was strictly enforced, as were new standards of dress. Local women were forced into arranged marriages with jihadist leaders.

The result was a backlash that led to the creation of the *Sawah*, or 'awakening movement'. In 2006, 12 tribal sheikhs in Anbar province gathered together to form the Anbar Awakening Council, designed to expel AQM from the area. One of the leading figures of the *Sawah*, Sheikh Abdul-Sattar Abu Risha, formed the organisation after AQM had murdered his father and two brothers. Initially, the US military hoped the Anbar awakening would result in irregular Iraqi forces doing much the fighting against al-Qaeda. However, the Anbaris lacked the military organisation and social cohesion necessary to fight against their better-organised and more determined adversaries. Instead, the Anbar awakening was more useful in supplying intelligence and offering local support for US troops. Effective fighting was only possible when closely supported by American soldiers and airpower.

Given the success of the Anbar awakening, Petraeus tried to reproduce it across Iraq. He placed 'local security bargains', deals between neighbourhood militias and the US military, at the centre of consolidating and expanding the security gains made under the surge. Local Sunni allies were sought in the fight against al-Qaeda in Diyala province and in several areas of Baghdad. The approach was later broadened to include support of Shia militias in the south of the country. However, these local security bargains posed a direct threat to the capacity and coherence of the Iraqi state. By funding local quasi-military organisations, the US military may well have been aiding one side of a civil war that was far from over. There was a danger that these newly empowered organisations would contribute to government weakness, further hindering the state's ability to interact with the population. Reflecting recognition of this problem, the creation of local 'neighbourhood watch' organisations was coordinated with a committee for national reconciliation set up by the central government. But given the Iraqi state's incoherence and record of profound sectarianism, there must be grave doubts that the centrifugal dynamics produced by the creation of highly localised security forces could be countered by the Iraqi government at a national level. It was possible that, in nationalising the Anbar model, the US military was simply picking sides in a series of violent local conflicts. This would not result in sustainable security for the Iraqi population but would fuel the dynamics driving the civil war.

An important remaining challenge was integration of the 103,000 armed men involved in 'Concerned Local Citizens' groups (CLCs) – the name given to these quasi-military organisations – into government security services under the direct control of Baghdad. If this did not happen, they seemed likely to degenerate into another group of heavily armed militias terrorising the population. The Shia-dominated government was reluctant to integrate these predominately Sunni organisations into the mainstream police force, which was dominated by militias controlled by national politicians. This led to a number of CLCs voicing frustration and anger with the national politicians and government. In Anbar this resulted in a direct challenge to the provincial governor. In the Baghdad suburb of Ameriya, the local militia commander issued direct threats to Vice-President Tariq al-Hashimi. The situation in Diyala province may be indicative of future problems. Here the Awakening Council became increasingly angry that only 10% of its members had been admitted into the local police force. In protest it threatened not to support the provincial authorities and launched a series of accusations against the local police chief. These disturbances highlighted the danger of encouraging the creation of yet another set of armed groups in Iraq without a clear commitment to integrate them into a truly national security force or rebuild the institutional capacity of the state. The fact that one of the Anbar awakening's key leaders, Sheikh Abdul-Sattar Abu Risha, was murdered by a car bomb in September 2007, just days after meeting Bush, indicated the scale of the security problems still faced by the US military in Anbar, as well as across the whole of Iraq.

In addition to the successes of the surge and the Anbar awakening, another key factor in the steep decline in violence across 2007–08 was al-Sadr's decision to demobilise JAM, which had been one of the main protagonists in the sectarian violence that engulfed Baghdad in 2006. At the beginning of the US troop surge al-Sadr fled to Iran and ordered JAM not to seek direct confrontation with

US forces. However, against a wider background of reduced national violence, intra-Shia tensions increased during summer 2007. The primary cause of the violence within the Shia community was JAM's struggle with its rival militia, the Badr Brigade, for control of southern Iraq. This led to the assassination of two provincial governors: the ISCI governors of the southern provinces of Qadisiya and Muthanna were both killed by car bombs in August 2007. Events reached a peak when JAM and Badr gunmen fought a running battle in the holy city of Karbala during an August religious festival. The death of 52 people outraged Shia public opinion and forced al-Sadr to declare a six-month ceasefire, subsequently extended to a year. Over the 12 months al-Sadr attempted to purge JAM of its more violent, corrupt and sectarian members, setting up a national 'Golden Brigade' to impose discipline and central control. Meanwhile, he tried to re-brand his movement, stressing its political and charitable work, attempting to build its popularity and capacity along the lines of Hizbullah in Lebanon. In conjunction with this attempt to change the image of the movement, al-Sadr himself moved to the Iranian city of Qom to complete his religious studies. If he were to re-emerge from this period of study and isolation as an Ayatollah, a senior religious figure in Shia Islam, his political and moral influence would be greatly enhanced.

The battle between Shia militias in the south of Iraq took place as British influence in the area was deliberately reduced. In February 2007, a month after Bush announced the surge, then British Prime Minister Tony Blair, in preparation for his exit from office, announced to Parliament that the commitment of British troops to Basra would drop from 7,100 to 4,200 by summer. Downing Street briefers went much further, suggesting that this was only the beginning and that British troops would quickly be moved into a single base outside Basra city and from there completely withdraw from the country by the end of 2008. Once Blair left office and Gordon Brown replaced him in June 2008, similar statements were repeatedly made on and off the record by Brown, his senior advisers and high-ranking military figures. The UK military withdrew from the centre of Basra in September 2007, with the remaining forces based at Basra airport where their activities mainly consisted of training Iraqis. British army chiefs were clearly angered by al-Sadr's claim that 'they are retreating because of the resistance they have faced. Without that, they would have stayed for much longer, there is no doubt.' However, senior US officials in Baghdad appeared to agree, stating that 'the Brits have lost Basra'.

From the British withdrawal until March 2008, warring militias and criminal gangs fought among themselves for control of the city and the revenues from the lucrative oil smuggling in the nearby port of Umm Qasr. Eventually this lawlessness forced the Iraqi government to intervene. At the end of March 2008 Maliki moved 30,000 Iraqi troops south to Basra. Although the US military was informed of the operation just before it started, it was not centrally involved. The Iraqi army managed to fight in Basra for two days. However, JAM was entrenched in well-defended positions and put up sustained resistance. Within 48 hours the army ran short of munitions and food. The US military then intervened, deploying its logistical capacity to equip the Iraqi army and sending US special forces and combat advisers to Basra to ensure that the Iraqi military was not defeated. Finally, both US and British air-power and artillery were used against JAM positions. With this added support Iraqi government forces were able to take control of Basra and Umm Qasr, Iraq's only port. JAM retaliated in Baghdad from its stronghold of Sadr city, a 2-million-strong slum in the north of the city, by targeting rockets and mortar fire on the US Embassy in the Green Zone. The Iraqi army sealed off Sadr city and by the end of May negotiated a truce that allowed it to enter the area, arresting over 800 militiamen whilst also seizing heavy weaponry.

If the Iraqi army can retain its hold on both Basra and Sadr city in Baghdad, the military campaigns that began in March 2008 will represent a major victory for Maliki. The re-taking of Basra and the entrance of Iraqi army troops into Sadr city represented a major expansion of governmental power. This, when combined with the successes of the surge, indicated that a coherent Iraqi state might be emerging five years after Saddam Hussein's regime was ousted. However, the sustainability of these advances remained open to question. Petraeus stated repeatedly that the Iraqi conflict must have a political rather than a military solution. The advances made in imposing security on Iraq have not been matched by positive outcomes in the political arena.

Politics: no reconciliation

The momentum delivered by the surge was meant to trigger and ultimately be sustained by the transformation of politics in Iraq. The renewed US commitment to halting Iraq's slide into civil war was specifically designed to create the space for national reconciliation. As violence decreased, Iraq's politicians were meant to negotiate a new national pact designed to end the conflict. During most of 2007, US officials made little attempt to hide their frustration that the American-driven improvements in security had not been matched by improvements in the political situation or state capacity. Against this background, calls for 'national reconciliation' were quietly replaced by lobbying for an improvement in the government's appalling record in delivering services desperately needed by the population. Far from facilitating national reconciliation, the led to a narrowing of the political base of Maliki's government with the loss of key members from both sides of the sectarian divide.

The first political target of the surge was Maliki himself. From his surprise appointment as prime minister in spring 2006, the United States had profound doubts about both his ability and his goals. As prime minister he remained the key vehicle of US influence on Iraqi politics. In spring 2007, both Petraeus and US Ambassador Ryan Crocker made Maliki's continued tenure dependent upon him meeting several demands. The most important change demanded by the United States was that Maliki distance himself from al-Sadr, a politically dangerous course. Maliki had obtained the premiership through the support of al-Sadr's parliamentary bloc, which backed him in order to keep its main rival, ISCI, from taking the job. After losing that battle, ISCI continually plotted for its own candidate, Adel Abdul Mehdi, to replace Maliki. If he were to break his alliance with al-Sadr, Maliki would be left without reliable political support in either the cabinet or the Council of Representatives.

Political tensions within the United Iraqi Alliance, the Shia bloc that won the 2005 elections, first became apparent when Fadillah, a radical Shia party whose main electoral base is in Basra, left the alliance in March 2007 over a row about cabinet posts. Of much greater political importance was al-Sadr's decision in April 2007 to remove his six cabinet ministers from Maliki's government. This created the break from al-Sadr that Crocker sought. Though it made Maliki politically more vulnerable, it improved his relations with Washington. Al-Sadr claimed the removal of his ministers was because the prime minister had refused to set a date for the withdrawal of US troops. Sadrist ministers had used their position to infiltrate militia members into the ministries they controlled. They had also siphoned off government resources for political use. Most damagingly, they had colluded with other Shia ministers to remove public services from Baghdad's Sunni community as part of a wider plan to drive them from the city. The Sadrist ministers' departure from government allowed the prime minister to purge some of the worst sectarian actors from government service, meeting key US demands.

US plans for national reconciliation were seriously set back at the end of July 2007, when the main Sunni political bloc, the Iraqi Accordance Front or Tawafuq, removed its six ministers from the government. The senior Tawafuq politicians and Vice President Tariq al-Hashimi claimed the move was triggered by Maliki's refusal to listen to them. Hashimi demanded much quicker progress on national reconciliation, the release of prisoners and a rewriting of the constitution as the price for their return.

Tensions within the UIA and the departures of both the Sadrists and Tawafuq from the government left Maliki dangerously vulnerable to plots to unseat him. The first attempt came in March 2007, before Tawafuq's withdrawal, when Mehdi struggled to build a majority within the 275-member Iraqi parliament to gain a vote of no confidence against the prime minister. When this failed, former prime minister and non-sectarian centrist Iyad Allawi attempted to build the majority needed. Finally Ibrahim al-Jaafari, another ex-prime minister and former leader of Maliki's own party, Dawa, also unsuccessfully attempted to build the coalition needed to unseat him.

The conspiracies against Maliki failed because two key constituencies could not find a better candidate. The two Kurdish parties, the Kurdistan Democratic Party and the Patriotic Union of Kurdistan, decided that it was better to have a weak prime minister ready to do their bidding than risk replacing Maliki with a stronger candidate. Most importantly, the US Embassy, with all its misgivings about Maliki, could not find a replacement with a realistic chance of gaining a parliamentary majority. Finally, at the beginning of 2008, Maliki's main detractor, the leader of ISCI, Abdul Aziz Hakim, decided that it was better for Maliki to take the blame and unpopularity associated with the job than to replace him with his hapless deputy Mehdi. So Maliki continued to serve as prime minister and strove to build a base to make his position more secure. In effect, he was trying to construct a set of shadow institutions that spread from the prime minister's office across the Iraqi state, tying key civil servants, generals and police officers to him personally. However, the effect was to make Maliki more secure in his position while undermining the coherence and capacity of the state he was trying to control, causing an atmosphere of distrust to spread across the whole government.

The lack of national reconciliation or of a general direction in Iraqi politics was reflected in the difficulties the cabinet and parliament had in passing legislation. In January 2007, the US Congress, increasingly disgruntled about the lack of progress in Iraq, set a series of benchmarks for the government of Iraq to meet. This included the need for parliament to pass a hydrocarbons law to regulate the sharing of revenues and future exploration of oil. Given Iraq's reliance on the export of oil, the hydrocarbons law was one of the most important and controversial issues that the government had to deal with. The problem at the heart of the issue was the extent to which the Kurdistan Regional Government (KRG) could develop its own oil reserves, untroubled by oversight from Baghdad. A compromise in the wording of the law collapsed and in September the KRG passed its own law and began to sign independent development contracts with a number of small international oil companies. The response from Iraqi Minister of Oil Hussein al-Shahristani was swift and uncompromising. He declared the contracts illegal, said that any company dealing with the KRG would be banned from doing business with the national government, and revealed that the Iraqi government had an understanding with neighbouring states that they would not allow the export of Kurdish oil. One positive outcome of the KRG's rush to sign development contracts was to force the Iraqi government to speed up its own negotiations with international oil companies, which then agreed to help reform and develop national oil fields.

The dispute over oil contracts highlighted the profound lack of agreement about the future direction of the Iraqi state. The two Kurdish parties, in alliance with ISCI, wanted as much regional autonomy, short of outright independence, as possible. Maliki, backed by a large majority of Iraqi Arab public opinion, favoured a strong, united Iraqi state based in Baghdad. The fact that the two sides could not reach an accommodation indicated the ruling elite's inability to find a compromise.

Against this background, US policy was increasingly focused on the provincial elections scheduled for 1 October 2008. Washington hoped these would deliver a new generation of indigenous politicians with grassroots appeal, linking the population to their representatives and putting greater pressure on the national government to perform. However, the American fear was that provincial elections would simply empower a larger and bolder group of politicians aligned to al-Sadr, who would demand a quick US withdrawal. US Embassy estimates suggested that al-Sadr's movement might get as much as 60% of the popular vote in the south of Iraq. This would prove problematic, not only for the US government but also for ISCI. If ISCI failed to get a major share of the Shia vote, its claim to be representative of the Shia community would be placed under severe threat. The temptation to use its influence over the state and the security forces to obtain a favourable election result must therefore be high. If the provincial elections were fixed, Sadrists would have little incentive to move away from violence into mainstream politics.

The undoubted success of the surge in reducing sectarian violence in Baghdad has not been matched by a similar breakthrough on the political front. Iraqi politics both in parliament and cabinet are dominated by a group of politicians furthering a highly divisive and sectarian agenda as the best way to guarantee their own influence over national politics. This has created a stagnant parliament unable to pass crucial legislation, as well as high levels of inefficacy and corruption across the whole of the Iraqi state. The Iraqi government is very protective of its own sovereignty. With the current high price of oil, its resources now easily outstrip those that the United States can deploy in Iraq. This means American influence in Baghdad can only continue to decline.

Iran: Continuing Impasse

The drumbeat of confrontation between Iran and the West over Tehran's nuclear ambitions was suddenly interrupted in December 2007, when the United States released an intelligence assessment which determined that Iran's nuclear-weapons programme had been halted in 2003. This was immediately interpreted as meaning that an American military strike on Iranian nuclear facilities would not occur during the presidency of George W. Bush and that the issue was, in effect, being handed to his successor. Pressure on Tehran from Washington and

European capitals was seriously undercut, and Iranian President Mahmoud Ahmadinejad claimed a major victory, which helped him overcome domestic troubles over his failure to deliver on his economic promises.

As the nuclear impasse continued, so did considerable tension over Iran's activities in Iraq. There seemed a real danger that hostility could boil over and degenerate into military conflict as the United States continued to accuse Iran of training Shia militias and supplying devices that were proving lethal against American vehicles. The American and Iranian ambassadors in Baghdad held three rounds of talks about the security situation from May to August 2007, and at times Iran appeared to limit its support for violence in Iraq, but its backing of a wide range of proxies made Tehran's strategic aim difficult to discern. Amidst the tension, one incident in January 2008 almost led to an exchange of fire in the Strait of Hormuz when five Iranian speedboats harassed three US Navy ships and were mistakenly thought to have radioed a bombing threat. In April 2008, a second US aircraft carrier returned to the Persian Gulf and the Pentagon again warned of the 'increasingly hostile role' Iran was playing in Iraq by smuggling weapons that were then used against American troops.

Nuclear programme: diplomatic stalemate, slow technological progress

Throughout the year to mid 2008, Iran continued to work on its nuclear programme in defiance of United Nations Security Council resolutions. But the critical development occurred on 3 December 2007, when the United States declassified the conclusions of a new National Intelligence Estimate (NIE) that Iran had halted its nuclear-weapons work in late 2003 and that such single-purpose activity aimed at developing weapons had not resumed. The NIE, which represented the collective judgement of America's 16 intelligence agencies, contradicted the 2005 NIE assessment that Iran was 'determined to build a nuclear weapon'. The 2007 version reaffirmed that Iran had indeed had a dedicated nuclear-weapons programme until November 2003, including covert uranium-enrichment activity. The report judged that Iran still wanted a weapons capability and was keeping this option open by producing fissile material.

The report profoundly changed the dynamics of the nuclear issue. Notwithstanding the NIE's confirmation of past illicit activity, Ahmadinejad called it a 'declaration of victory'. Israel, France and an unnamed senior UK diplomat were among those who publicly doubted the NIE's conclusion, stated 'with moderate confidence', that work on developing nuclear weapons had not resumed. The United States, Britain, France and Germany insisted there would be no change to their policy of pressure on Tehran to halt enrichment of uranium and related activities. But Russia and China, which just days before had accepted the need for additional Security Council sanctions, now had further reason to delay the UN process.

The motivation and mechanism for releasing the intelligence estimate were, to the outside world, puzzling. The decision appeared to undermine the administration's pursuit of Iran, cast by Bush as a member of the 'axis of evil', as a 'state sponsor of terrorism' and a rogue state intent on developing nuclear weapons and ballistic missiles. It undercut the pressure of America's European allies who, on the nuclear issue, were as hard-line as Washington. In releasing the new assessment, the United States did not appear to be softening its views – indeed, it constantly attacked what it saw as Iran's efforts to stir trouble in Iraq and Lebanon. Robert Gates, US secretary of defense and a former director of the Central Intelligence Agency, speaking at the IISS Manama Dialogue in Bahrain a few days after the NIE release, said: 'The reality is that the timing and the content of the national estimate were determined entirely by the Director of National Intelligence and the policy-making arm of the national government was left to deal with it'. NIEs were independent and had caused confusion about the American agenda many times before. 'The estimate clearly has come at an awkward time. It has annoyed a number of our good friends. It has confused a lot of people around the world in terms of what we are trying to accomplish.'

Those who suspected Iran's nuclear intentions also pointed to its continued development of longer-range ballistic missiles. In September 2007, Iran displayed a new missile, the *Ghadr-1*, at a military parade in Tehran, with a claimed range of 1,800km. Tehran's 26 November announcement of a new 2,000km-range *Ashura* was further evidence of a determination for a strategic reach well beyond its immediate neighbourhood. In February 2008, Iran test-launched a *Kavoshgar-1* rocket that it said was intended to further its nascent space programme, but which is based on the *Shahab-3B* missile and could be put to weapons use. Satellite imagery of the launch site, about 230km southeast of Tehran, showed features that to some analysts were suggestive of North Korean work on the 6,000km-range *Taepo-dong* missile-assembly facility in North Korea.

The NIE helped prolong the diplomatic impasse in which the West called on Iran to halt enrichment of uranium, and Tehran insisted it had the right to develop nuclear capabilities for civil purposes. Without evidence of an active weapons programme, Bush would not have public support for a bombing campaign. And without the backing of a credible military threat, US-led diplomacy had even less chance of persuading Iran to suspend its nuclear programmes.

Regardless of the NIE's conclusions, there was no pause in Iran's efforts to develop nuclear capabilities. Throughout 2007 and the first half of 2008, it continued to expand its enrichment programme in contravention of Security Council resolutions mandating suspension of all enrichment-related activity. Tehran did partly meet the Security Council's demand that it cooperate with the International Atomic Energy Agency (IAEA) to address outstanding questions about its past activity, but it refused the demand to implement the Additional

Protocol on safeguards, even though it had provisionally accepted this before the nuclear confrontation with the West accelerated early in 2006.

Iran also rejected the Security Council's demands that it stop work on building a research reactor at Arak, which would give it an alternative plutonium path to nuclear weapons. As part of its response to the second sanctions resolution of March 2007, it began to refuse required inspection visits to the reactor site. Though it later allowed inspections of Arak, it did not give ground on its refusal to provide design information about new nuclear facilities in advance, as required under an attachment to its safeguards agreement. The IAEA reminded Iran that there was no provision for unilaterally abrogating that condition, and continued to call on Iran to meet its obligation to cooperate with the agency.

In summer 2007, the United States and its European allies sought a third UN sanctions resolution. The second such resolution, UNSCR 1747, had passed relatively quickly on 24 March 2007, only three months after the first sanctions resolution (UNSCR 1737, 23 December 2006). Once Iran failed to meet the 60-day deadline for suspension imposed by the second resolution, the transatlantic allies hoped they could continue to build pressure on Iran. A delay became inevitable, however, when Ali Larijani, Tehran's chief nuclear negotiator, in a 1 June 2007 session with EU foreign-policy chief Javier Solana, appeared to show a readiness for give and take, even though Tehran vetoed the tactical compromises he was ready to make in order to allow negotiations with the P5 plus Germany to begin. In June and July, Larijani held meetings with IAEA Director General Mohamed ElBaradei in which they tentatively agreed to work out an action plan to address outstanding IAEA questions, providing another reason for postponing sanctions. Neither Russia nor China wanted another sanctions resolution tabled as long as Larijani was talking with Solana and working with the IAEA on a timetable.

The timetable was produced in late August in a joint understanding between Iran and the IAEA, whereby Iran agreed to address, in sequence, six sets of outstanding questions about its past nuclear activity, including 'alleged studies' regarding weaponisation. November was set as a target date for closing the issue of past acquisition of first- and second-generation Pakistani centrifuge technology. Closure of other issues would then follow. According to the work plan, no further questions would be left for Iran to answer, and once the work plan had been fully implemented, which ElBaradei said would take three months, IAEA inspections in Iran would return to normal. In Washington, London and Paris, the work plan was seen as another delaying tactic, intended to postpone any further Security Council resolution at least until the end of the year.

Meanwhile, Iran continued to expand its enrichment programme. By September 2007 it had met its interim goal of installing approximately 3,000 centrifuges in the underground fuel-enrichment plant at Natanz. By November, 18 164-centrifuge cascades were operating with uranium hexafluoride, and were producing smallish quantities of low-enriched uranium (LEU). In rushing to meet its 3,000-machine goal, Iran appeared to have violated standard engineering principles under which smaller cascades would be tested for long periods of time. When the IAEA conducted an annual physical inventory in December, it learned that the cascades were operating at only 20% of their design capacity, an indication of technical difficulties. Iran had learned to operate individual centrifuges but apparently had not yet mastered the ability to operate large numbers continuously.

The installed centrifuges were the first module of what is planned to be a 54,000-machine facility. The interim number of 3,000 is significant in proliferation terms because that many centrifuges operating smoothly around the clock could in theory produce 20–25kg of highly enriched uranium (HEU), enough for one implosion-style nuclear weapon, in less than a year. For this reason, international experts had posited late 2009 as the earliest date by which Iran could produce a nuclear weapon. Iran had insisted throughout that it had no intention to produce HEU, only LEU for reactor fuel. If it did attempt to produce HEU at the safeguarded Natanz facility, IAEA inspectors would know immediately. Therefore, if Iran wanted to produce HEU, it would either do so in a clandestine facility or would build up a stockpile of LEU which could later be further enriched to HEU in a few weeks at Natanz if Iran chose to ignore international opinion and withdraw from the Nuclear Non-Proliferation Treaty.

One idea Larijani and his Western counterparts explored was for Iran to agree not to further expand its enrichment work in exchange for the Security Council refraining from imposition of any further sanctions, while diplomats pursued a resumption of formal negotiations. Germany reportedly backed this 'double pause' idea and Britain wavered temporarily, but the United States, France and Britain coalesced around the original position of demanding full suspension of enrichment as a condition for negotiations on a long-term settlement. They argued that a concession that legitimised any level of Iranian enrichment would give it licence to learn how to operate its centrifuges more efficiently. Taking the view that, at this stage of programme development, the number of centrifuges was less important than their performance, they did not want Iran to master the enrichment technology, and thereby be able to replicate cascades in a clandestine facility for HEU production. The stalemate, however, allowed Iran to continue to expand its knowledge base.

In meetings with Iran's leadership during an unprecedented visit to Tehran in October, then Russian President Vladimir Putin apparently again promoted the 'double pause' idea. Larijani told reporters Iran was considering the idea, but Ahmadinejad contradicted him, saying Putin had made no offer. This was the last straw for Larijani, who resigned. Ahmadinejad replaced him with Saeed Jalili, a fellow hardliner. In November talks, Jalili told Solana that nothing proposed in talks to date had any validity, that discussions would have to start afresh, and that Iran would recognise no interlocutor on the nuclear issue other than the IAEA.

One IAEA request Iran did answer was with regard to information about current work on advanced centrifuges. In January 2008, Iran showed the IAEA work on four new centrifuge designs, including test cascades for carbon-fibre-rotor machines it dubbed the IR-2 (second generation Iran centrifuges) and claimed were domestically produced. This could not be verified, and ElBaradei said it would take the Iranians 2–3 years of development before they could reach an industrial-level scale with this new-generation centrifuge.

In February 2008 Washington handed the IAEA additional documents, detailing weaponisation studies, found on a computer hard drive turned over by a defector in 2004, and the IAEA secretariat in turn briefed member states after Iran refused to look at the documents. Iran's answers to other questions from the IAEA work plan were judged either consistent or 'not inconsistent' with the agency's other information. Iran's refusal to answer questions about the weaponisation studies, however, meant that the work plan agreed with the IAEA remained unfinished.

Concerns about the weaponisation studies and the new-generation centrifuges finally provided the basis for a third Security Council sanctions resolution on 3 March 2008. The resolution, which passed 14–0 (Indonesia abstaining) took eight months from the time the first draft was proposed, and only marginally increased pressure on Iran. Resolution 1803 added 13 names to a previous list of 17 Iranian entities subject to an asset freeze and travel ban, and prohibited trade with Iran in certain dual-use materials and technologies. The resolution also authorised the inspection of shipments suspected of containing banned items carried by two airline and shipping companies and called for vigilance in monitoring the activities of certain Iranian financial institutions. Chinese efforts in April to balance the new sanctions with a new incentives package for Iran faltered when the United States and its European allies refused to add to what they believed was the already generous offer still on the table since June 2006. Iran reacted to the latest sanctions with now-typical disdain and chest thumping. On 8 April 2008, designated as National Nuclear Day, Ahmadinejad announced that Iran had started to install another 6,000 centrifuges at Natanz. By July, some 3,700 centrifuges were reportedly in place.

In addition to the UN sanctions, Washington met some success in its efforts to persuade private companies in Europe to curtail transactions with Iranian firms. Deutsche Bank and Commerzbank, the two largest European banks that had continued to do business with Iran, said they too would end their Iran business. Such de facto sanctions drove up costs for Iranian companies. However, a December report by the US Government Accountability Office noted that, since

2003, Iran had signed contracts worth $20 billion with foreign firms to develop its energy resources. It pointed out that Iranian banks subject to sanctions could fund their activities in currencies other than the dollar. Tehran responded to the latest US-led sanctions by shifting business to banks in Asia, Russia and Venezuela, and using go-betweens and front companies in Dubai, Bahrain and elsewhere. The US Treasury in turn moved to impose financial sanctions on Iranian front companies.

In October, the United States further stepped up pressure by targeting the finances of the Quds Force of the Islamic Revolutionary Guard Corps (IRGC) and four state-owned banks, designating them as supporters of terrorism for their activities in Afghanistan, Iraq and the Middle East. The IRGC itself was designated as a proliferator of ballistic missiles. This move marked the first time the United States had tried to punish another country's military and was characterised by US officials as the broadest set of punitive measures imposed on Tehran since the 1979 takeover of the American Embassy. The designations provided the authority to freeze assets, but since no Iranian organisations have assets in the United States, it was more designed to encourage other countries to stop dealing with the named entities or risk being targeted by US sanctions themselves.

With the apparent failure to date of efforts to rein in Iran's nuclear programme, observers in Washington outside the administration increasingly began to look at fallback options. Several academics and former diplomats, including former ambassador to the UN Thomas Pickering, proposed the establishment of an international consortium to produce enriched uranium in Iran, where foreign managers could detect whether Iranian nuclear engineers were engaged in clandestine HEU production. Ahmadinejad, in a speech at the UN, lent support to the idea of an international consortium, although in February he 'withdrew' the proposal, reserving the right to reconsider it if presented with such an offer. Neoconservative columnist Charles Krauthammer called for extended deterrence as the best fallback option: Washington should announce that an Iranian nuclear attack on Israel would be considered an attack on the United States. Employing similar logic and rhetoric, would-be Democratic Party presidential candidate Senator Hillary Clinton said that as president she would obliterate Iran if it launched an atomic attack on Israel. She also said, however, that she would be willing to engage Iran without preconditions. Senator Barack Obama, the eventual Democratic Party nominee, went further by offering personal engagement with Iran. Several prominent Republican statesmen, including former Secretary of State Henry Kissinger, also called for engagement without preconditions. However, Republican Party presidential candidate Senator John McCain offered no change from the Bush administration's position that Iran must first stop enrichment work. He was captured on video singing 'bomb, bomb, bomb bomb Iran' to the tune of the 1960s Beach Boys pop song 'Barbara Ann'.

Ahmadinejad withstands domestic pressures

Foreign affairs have played a greater than usual role over the past year in the struggle for domestic hegemony which has preoccupied the political establishment of the Islamic Republic since its inception in 1979.

Ahmadinejad, who faces presidential elections in 2009, came under persistent attack in large part because of his failure to manage the economy. He was accused of having no economic policy, and of wilfully squandering the opportunities afforded by high oil revenues. His habit of distributing ad hoc cash handouts fuelled inflation. Though Iran was benefiting from the high price of oil, the fall of the dollar diminished Tehran's purchasing power and its international problems hindered trade and investment.

In mid 2007, the government raised petrol prices and introduced rationing to reduce heavy subsidies on imported gasoline (though a major oil producer, Iran lacks refining capacity). The decisions caused unrest, though Iranians quickly adapted by developing a black market. By winter the situation had become critical, as Iranians laboured under the harshest weather in nearly 50 years. With heating oil in short supply, Iran was forced to halt exports to Turkey, while Turkmenistan, a key supplier of natural gas, halted exports in an effort to force Iran to pay it the market price. As the government struggled to reconcile its obligations to both countries, it took intervention by Supreme Leader Ayatollah Sayyid Ali Khamenei to ensure that gas supplies to hard-hit rural areas were restored.

Ahmadinejad's popularity had been slipping since he suffered a reverse in the municipal and council elections in December 2006. However, he received support from Khamenei at every critical juncture. This provided the president with room for manoeuvre, and boosted the already substantial self-confidence of a man with an extraordinary ability to shrug off criticism and indulge in theatrical and nationalistic bombast. While Iran's intellectual and political elite regarded Ahmadinejad's posturing as reckless, ordinary Iranians were intoxicated by Iran's apparent power, evidence for which was seen both in Washington's decision to hold ambassadorial-level discussions in Baghdad over security in Iraq, and Washington's designation of the IRGC as a terrorist organisation. As the March 2008 parliamentary elections approached, Ahmadinejad's opponents calculated that the threat of military confrontation with the United States would encourage Khamenei to distance himself from the president and free up the election process, allowing a coalition of centrists and reformists to win back the parliament. It was widely assumed that the head of the Assembly of Experts, Hashemi Rafsanjani, would use his leverage to persuade the Supreme Leader to relax his control over the forthcoming elections.

In the event, the US NIE was a boon for Ahmadinejad, who viewed it as vindicating his strategy of declaring the nuclear file closed and dealing only with the IAEA. As the threat of conflict receded, Ahmadinejad's political opponents found their strategy in disarray. Far from abandoning his protégé, Khamenei openly endorsed Ahmadinejad's foreign policy and echoed the sentiment that the West had been defeated. Confident that there were no domestic threats to his position, Ahmadinejad moved swiftly to ensure victory in the forthcoming parliamentary elections. The Guardian Council agreed to bar most of the candidates on a list provided by the Ministry of the Interior, a hard-line stronghold. The 1,700 banned candidates included many supporters of political reform. Limited to contesting a small proportion of the 290 seats, reformists cried foul, but their appeal to Khamenei fell on deaf ears. In the most heavily rigged and manipulated election in recent years, the contest amounted to a division of spoils between two hard-line factions – the United Principlist Front, which supported the president, and the Broad Front of Principlists, which included critics of Ahmadinejad. Turnout was reported to be considerably lower than the 65% claimed by the government, and was particularly low in Tehran and other urban areas. The United Principlists won 117 seats, the Broad Principlists 53, independents 69 and reformists 46. Given the fluidity of the factional system, and the ideological proximity of the two major groups, along with the sizeable number of independents, it was unclear how many deputies would support the president. Larijani was overwhelmingly elected the parliamentary speaker, an influential position from which he would exert a restraining influence on Ahmadinejad.

Meanwhile, there was a continued slide in human rights as the government targeted not only perceived 'fifth columnists', but also those it described as general troublemakers and 'thugs'. The campaign against the latter, ostensibly lawless economic racketeers, caused a dramatic rise in public executions. Video clips of executions by hanging were posted widely on the Internet. The government justified its campaign on grounds of social and economic corruption and the need to forcefully establish control. Ayatollah Ahmad Jannati, chairman of the Guardian Council, congratulated the security forces on their work. The public reaction was more mixed, with some arguing that such executions simply dealt with the symptom and not the cause of the moral corruption of society. Others protested against the public nature of the executions. Ayatollah Mahmoud Hashemi Shahrudi, the head of the judiciary, moved to suspend further public executions, although it was unclear whether this decision had been firmly ratified. Similar confusion continued over a Supreme Court ruling in April 2007 overturning the conviction of serial killers in Kerman province. In a judgment which stunned the Iranian legal profession, the court ruled that the killers were justified in seeking to rid society of moral corruption and that the onus lay on the victims to prove their innocence, in which case the perpetrators would be obliged to pay blood money to the victims' families. This ruling was suspended pending a final hearing.

While the crackdown showed the determination of the political establishment to establish moral order and show that it remained in charge, commentators suggested that it revealed a sense of insecurity. This was also indicated by the arrest and imprisonment of several Iranian-American academics accused of fomenting a 'velvet revolution' through the dissemination of divisive ideas. Warnings went out to university students and academics not to participate in foreign conferences, significantly limiting Iran's engagement with the outside world. Ahmadinejad, however, gave a controversial speech at Columbia University in New York, where he was first castigated by the university president, Lee Bollinger, who had been himself attacked for issuing the invitation. Ahmadinejad believed that the Western world laboured under a 'false consciousness' imposed upon them by their governments and that by 'speaking truth to power' he could convince others of the merit of his views. His composure in the face of Bollinger's attack won him plaudits at home. Ahmadinejad's supporters produced a book declaring the president's triumph in the 'metaphysical contest against American academics'.

The pressure on Ahmadinejad arising from an array of political and economic factors seemed unlikely to lessen in the run-up to the 2009 Iranian presidential election. The events of the past year suggested, however, that he could continue to derive political capital from international tensions. While the US NIE of December 2007 at least temporarily removed heat from the confrontation over Iran's nuclear programme, there remained a risk that, as the United States awaited the selection of a new president, these tensions could generate increased military friction.

Middle East: Fading Prospects for Peace

There were few positive developments in Israel, Syria and Lebanon over the course of late 2007 and 2008. Israelis and Palestinians remained at an impasse, as political conditions continued to deteriorate. Lebanon was beset by serious internecine conflict. Syria remained stable, but was revealed to have deepened ties with North Korea with the aim of acquiring nuclear technology. On one salutary note, Syria and Israel began proximity talks towards settling territorial disputes under Turkish auspices.

Hamas's Gaza takeover

On 6 May 2007, the Palestinian Islamist group Hamas rejected a US-sponsored peace plan that had been embraced by its secular Palestinian rival, Fatah, led by Mahmoud Abbas. The plan would have required Hamas to sign up to previously agreed-upon arrangements between the Palestinian Authority (PA) and Israel, which the Hamas leadership, physically split between Gaza and Damascus, was unwilling to do. The defeat of the Israel Defense Forces (IDF) in Lebanon in summer 2006 had strengthened the militant Gaza faction's conviction that Hamas's objectives would be better served by a hard-line stance. The concurrent involvement of the Arab League, which dispatched a delegation to meet Israeli Foreign Minister Tzipi Livni a few days later, on 10 May, raised little hope of a breakthrough. While regional involvement was a constructive diplomatic step from the Arab League's long-term perspective, the organisation's representatives arrived with neither new ideas nor real leverage over the parties, and had a negligible impact.

The situation worsened in mid May. Sporadic clashes between Hamas and Fatah fighters led to power outages and food shortages. The skirmishing stirred hopes on the Israeli side that a civil war – that many thought necessary for the emergence of a Palestinian government capable of negotiating and delivering a reliable peace agreement – would materialise. The model these observers had in mind was the internecine struggle in the late 1940s between Jewish factions in Palestine that resulted in the Labor Zionists' decisive defeat of the Revisionist Zionists and the former group's consolidation of an exclusive hold on power that lasted until 1977. But this scenario badly misread the new correlation of forces within Palestinian society. The election of Hamas in 2005 had shown clearly that the group was a force to be reckoned with and that, under existing conditions, Hamas had more credibility than Fatah, especially in Gaza but also in the West Bank.

To protect his left flank and shore up his flagging authority, Abbas took a more confrontational tone towards Israel. On 6 June, he cancelled one of a series of fortnightly meetings with Israeli Prime Minister Ehud Olmert that had been arranged by US Secretary of State Condoleezza Rice. According to Abbas, Israel had failed to fulfil obligations it incurred in negotiations brokered by the United States, including the unfreezing of Palestinian tax revenues held by Israel and the negotiation and implementation of a ceasefire with Hamas in Gaza. The Israelis blamed Abbas, but were reluctant to release Palestinian tax revenues, mainly because some would inevitably end up in Hamas's coffers. Yet Abbas was scarcely in a position to argue that Hamas's hard line was counterproductive if his own diplomatic efforts yielded no tangible benefits. (Later in the month, Israel agreed to release the Palestinians' money gradually, in an effort to shore up Abbas's authority.)

Abbas's attempt to show backbone did not enhance Fatah's prestige in Gaza. Between 15 and 17 June 2007, Hamas units directly challenged Fatah militia elements in a battle for Gaza City. Fatah, with unintended irony, declared that this battle was the party's 'last stand', but put up little resistance and was quickly routed by better-organised and committed Hamas forces. Within two days, Hamas had asserted unilateral control over Gaza. Subsequently, Hamas showed considerable organisational competence and, despite the miserable conditions prevailing in Gaza, succeeded in exerting a degree of authority that Fatah had never demonstrated. The comprehensiveness of Hamas's control compounded the dilemmas that its seizure of power had posed to Israel and other outside actors. It was becoming increasingly difficult to deny that Hamas was there to stay and enjoyed considerable popular legitimacy despite the fact that its commitment to violence was slowly reducing Gaza to failed-state status.

Furthermore, Hamas's easy victory spurred US fears of an Iranian-backed takeover of vulnerable regional states. Other regional capitals anxious to stave off Iranian penetration – particularly Riyadh – were also worried. Hizbullah's transformation of its ill-judged provocation toward Israel in summer 2006 into a huge propaganda victory, on top of the astonishingly poor Israeli political and military response, had already shifted these fears into high gear. Yet there were no ready options for Washington and its partners. Hamas had given no sign that it was willing to compromise on core issues, while Washington was hemmed in by legal, political and ideological barriers to negotiation. From an Israeli perspective, Hamas's victory provided the opportunity to go after Hamas leaders and fighters without any risk to a peace process revolving around a politically debilitated Abbas. Indeed, Israeli strikes against Hamas could be portrayed as support for Abbas's legitimate rule. The downside to this new dispensation stemmed from the disappearance of Fatah's moderating influence. With Abbas out of the picture, radicalism and, along with it, unfettered Iranian influence and sophisticated weaponry were certain to increase in Gaza.

The combined effect of these developments dictated the next steps. On 17 June, a new Palestinian government headed by Abbas was sworn in on the West Bank, where Hamas influence was kept in check by Israeli security forces and Fatah's militia. The following day, the United States ended the boycott of the PA that had begun when Hamas won the 2006 elections, seeking to strengthen Abbas's hand. Abbas swiftly declared, on 21 June, a policy of 'no negotiation' with Hamas.

In the six weeks following the takeover of the Gaza Strip by Hamas, an estimated 63,000 people lost their jobs because of the collapse of the manufacturing industry when access to raw materials and export markets was cut off. According to *The Economist*, Gaza's population was living on about $1m per day, or 67¢ per person. Olmert, already weakened politically, had made what had come to be perceived by Israeli voters as two related blunders. The first was the unilateral withdrawal of Israel from Gaza, the linchpin of the Kadima Party's policy of disengagement. Rather than purchasing quiet on Israel's southern flank, withdrawal seemed to have laid the foundation for Hamas's resurgence and the constant rocket attacks that were undermining Kadima's political support throughout Israel. The second was Israel's response to Hizbullah's provocation in summer 2006. Against this backdrop, Olmert appeared compelled to up the ante. Starting in June 2007, Gaza's border crossings were closed to all cargo other than humanitarian supplies and selected agricultural shipments. In September, Israel declared Gaza a 'hostile entity' to justify a strong response to Hamas's *Qassam* rocket strikes on population centres in the south.

This process of escalation continued to unfold through the beginning of 2008 and beyond. On 17 January, Israel closed the entry points into Gaza altogether after a spike in the number of rocket launches from the territory. Three days later, Gaza's only power plant, which supplies 30% of Gaza's electricity during the winter, shut down due to lack of fuel shipments, which Israel had suspended. A day later Israel restored permission for the shipment of fuel to the power plant. *Qassam* attacks abated, but only temporarily. The squeeze-Gaza strategy suffered a setback later that month when, in a long-planned manoeuvre, militants broke through the wall on Gaza's southern border with Egypt. Hundreds of thousands of Palestinians crossed into Egypt to replenish their stores, buying fuel, food, spare parts and other supplies. Egyptian President Hosni Mubarak ordered his troops to let them in, saying they were 'starving under siege'. The breaching of the southern barrier was accompanied by a renewal of *Qassam* launches, one of which killed an Israeli civilian in Sderot in late February. In the volatile Israeli political climate, this incident triggered an operation dubbed *Hot Winter* by the IDF, in which a large combined-arms force entered Gaza to neutralise rocket factories and inflict casualties on Hamas forces. The fighting was intense: 110 Palestinians and two Israeli soldiers were killed in five days.

Despite the havoc wreaked by a large-scale IDF incursion and an effective economic blockade, many Palestinians appeared disinclined to blame Hamas for the mayhem. A survey conducted by the Palestinian Center for Policy and Survey Research shortly after *Hot Winter* concluded found that Hamas would win 35% of the vote if elections were held at that time, up four points since December. With a poll rating of 42%, Fatah was still ahead, but its lead over Hamas had been slashed from 18 points to just seven between December and March.

Real crisis, false hope

The persistence of Hamas tenacity and Fatah haplessness presented the Bush administration with an unwelcome corrective to its carrot-and-stick approach to Palestinian politics, intended to delegitimise Hamas and restore the primacy of Fatah. The reverse seemed to be happening. The White House came under increasing pressure from regional allies to renew the formal peace process; they were disinclined to help the United States in Iraq as long as it did little to improve the Palestinians' lot. Saudi King Abdullah bin Abdul Aziz put this sentiment rather tartly, telling the US ambassador that he, the king, 'would not be Bush's Tony Blair'.

Faced with these pressures, Bush announced on 16 July his plan for an autumn 2007 'international meeting' in Annapolis, Maryland that would jump-start a new round of negotiations between Israel and the Palestinians under a diplomatic umbrella provided by as many as 50 participating countries. The meeting eventually took place on 27 November after a series of ominous set-backs, including the defection of a major party, Yisrael Beiteinu, from Olmert's coalition; threats on the part of another party, Shas, to quit if the sovereignty of Jerusalem was placed on the conference agenda; and failure on the part of the principals to agree on what the conference was supposed to accomplish.

Annapolis was an about-face for an administration that had largely ignored the Israeli–Palestinian conflict for seven years and instead devoted the bulk of its regional efforts to Iraq, but now found itself compelled to take a more balanced approach by Arab partners who linked progress in the one to assistance with the other. Initially conceived by the White House as a way to boost Abbas in the wake of Hamas's seizure of Gaza, Annapolis was re-marketed over the course of the summer and autumn as a launching pad for permanent-status negotiations between the Israelis and Palestinians. Given the vast gulf between the positions of the two sides, the civil war raging among Palestinians, and the fading cred-ibility of Israel's government, Bush's insistence that the process initiated by the conference produce a final-status agreement by the end of 2008 gave the looming event a surreal air of improbability. Abbas played along, boldly declaring that the history of Israeli–Palestinian relations would be divided into two distinct historical phases, pre- and post-Annapolis. But there was tremendous scepti-cism on all sides. One Israeli official called it the 'mother of all photo-ops', while a long-time Middle East observer dubbed the summit an example of 'stagecraft' trumping 'statecraft'.

Washington was forced to make several concessions to guarantee the partici-pation of countries such as Syria and Saudi Arabia. Although the White House had initially downplayed expectations that the summit would yield a document, Olmert and Abbas did agree in the end to let Bush read a joint statement of understanding. Both parties agreed to establish a steering committee to 'develop a joint work plan and establish and oversee the work of negotiations teams to address all issues, to be headed by one lead representative from each party', and Olmert and Abbas resolved to hold bi-weekly meetings.

As with any summit, however, what really mattered was what came after-wards. Annapolis had dubious results through mid 2008. The steering committee met as scheduled on 12 December 2007. Olmert and Abbas met in late January, though events in Gaza largely overshadowed the peace talks. In January, Bush travelled to Israel for the first time in his presidency, and made the first visit to the West Bank by a sitting US president. In an interview beforehand with the Israeli daily *Yediot Ahronot*, Bush used some of his toughest language to date on the issue of Israeli settlements, saying he expected the country to keep its promises to dismantle unauthorised outposts built after March 2001: 'The Israeli government has said that they're going to get rid of unauthorized settlements, and that's what we expect, that's what we've been told'. The president also used the occasion to announce subtle but important changes in his position, calling for an end to Israel's 'occupation' and for Palestinian refugees to be financially compensated for the loss of their homes. Although sold as a trip to follow up on progress made at Annapolis, Bush's January visit did little to advance the prospect of Israeli–Palestinian peace. Despite speculation that a three-way meeting might take place, Bush met separately with Olmert and Abbas.

After two days on tour, Annapolis largely receded from the president's agenda. With five additional countries left to visit (Kuwait, Bahrain, the United Arab Emirates, Saudi Arabia and Egypt) in five days, the remainder of his time was occupied with issues such as managing fallout from the war in Iraq, building a coalition against Iran, trying to obtain Saudi support for a boost in oil production, and a host of other bilateral matters. Bush's visit failed to shift regional opinions on Arab–Israeli negotiations. Having exhausted all its energy and influence in getting Arab states to come to Annapolis in November, the administration was unable to secure additional promises of support.

Though it did not receive as much attention as the Annapolis Summit, the December 2007 Palestinian Donor Conference in Paris, which Rice attended, may ultimately prove to be more significant than the Annapolis Summit. At the meeting, donor countries pledged $7bn in aid to support the Palestinian economy and institutional capacity-building, which could transform the lives of the Palestinian people and the prospects for peace in the region.

A brief post-Annapolis calm ended on 4 February 2008 when a suicide bomber struck a commercial centre in the southern Israeli town of Dimona. The strike, which killed one person and injured 11 others, was the first suicide attack in Israel in more than a year. A second bomber failed to detonate his explosive belt and was shot dead by Israeli security forces. Fatah's militant offshoot, the al-Aqsa Martyr Brigade, claimed responsibility. In March, Vice President Dick Cheney undertook a ten-day trip to the region intended to 'reaffirm the president's commitment … toward the two-state solution and efforts to strengthen Palestinian institutions', stopping in Iraq, Oman, Afghanistan, Turkey and Saudi Arabia along the way. After meeting Olmert in Jerusalem, Cheney flew to Ramallah for talks with Abbas and Prime Minister Salam Fayyad. The following month, former US President Jimmy Carter, defying opposition from the Bush administration and Israel, travelled to Syria for talks with President Bashar al-Assad and Hamas leader Khaled Meshal.

May saw Bush's return, this time for Israel's 60th-anniversary celebrations. His speech to the Knesset drew criticism from Palestinians and the broader Arab world, who complained Bush had not done enough to push Israelis on the peace process. He chose not to travel to the West Bank and instead met Abbas at Sharm al-Sheikh, Egypt, at the World Economic Forum. His speech before the forum further raised tensions by criticising the state of human rights and democracy in the Arab world and the absence of women in key positions. His comments also angered Mubarak, his host, who boycotted the speech in response to Bush's own absence during the Egyptian president's opening address. Overall, Bush's peace initiative looked like a half-hearted attempt at eleventh-hour diplomacy, and the peace deal between Israel and the Palestinians propounded by the outgoing president appeared beyond reach before his departure from office.

By June, talks had all but broken down. Olmert and Abbas, who had met only a handful of times since the summit in Annapolis, appeared no closer to agreement on any of the critical issues of refugees, settlements or Jerusalem. By all accounts, their meeting on 2 June in Jerusalem was cool, if not outright antagonistic, with each blaming the other for failing to take the necessary steps to bring about a resolution to the long-standing conflict. Abbas appeared on Palestinian television to announce that he was abandoning his year-old position of refusing to talk to Hamas until it gave up control of the Gaza Strip in favour of direct talks with the group under Arab mediation. This position seemed to stall prospects for a two-state solution indefinitely.

Based on a plan first floated by Yemeni President Ali Abdullah Saleh before the Palestinians in early 2008, the reconciliation proposal under consideration by Hamas and Fatah envisaged a second unity government with the possibility of early elections. March 2008 negotiations in Sanaa had collapsed due to Abbas's insistence that Hamas give up control of the Gaza Strip as a condition for re-establishing dialogue. With Abbas seemingly having dropped this requirement, representatives from both sides met in Dakar, Senegal during the first weekend in June for talks sponsored by Senegalese President Abdoulaye Wade, chairman of the Organisation of the Islamic Conference. A communiqué signed by Hikmat Zeid of Fatah and Emad Khalid Alamy of Hamas was released, praising the talks as having restored 'an atmosphere of trust and mutual respect' between the factions. Hamas leader Ismail Haniyeh, however, cautioned that 'things are still at the beginning and it may take a long time' before the two sides could be reconciled.

Against this bleak diplomatic backdrop, pressure was building for a major confrontation between Israel and Hamas. On 4 June, the barrage of *Qassam* rockets from Gaza into southern Israel claimed its second victim of the year, prompting the Israeli Air Force to step up its air-strikes on the Gaza Strip. One strike led to the death of a Palestinian girl, further inflaming tensions. Egypt responded two days later by deploying hundreds of riot police to the border with Gaza over fears that Gazans would try to storm the Rafah crossing into the Sinai. Israeli officials fanned the flames by openly hinting that a major operation in Gaza could be imminent. Two days later, on 6 June, Olmert announced the government was 'close to a decision' on whether or not to launch a summer military operation in Gaza. On 11 June, the security cabinet voted to pursue an Egyptian-brokered ceasefire with Hamas while leaving open the possibility of a summer military offensive should the negotiations fail. A day later, Hamas fired some 50 *Qassams* at southern Israel, which the IDF construed as a diversionary tactic before a major onslaught on the border fence with Israel. Nevertheless, a Gaza truce went into effect on 19 June. The multi-stage deal would see the IDF slowly lift the siege on Gaza followed by re-opening of the Rafah crossing between Israel and Egypt. The prospect of genuine political progress, however, remained remote.

Debility at the top

Reinforcing this prognosis is the fact that both Olmert and Abbas were acting from positions of weakness. Olmert's term was due to expire in January 2009, and his public-approval rating in mid 2008 was hovering in the mid 30s owing to his missteps in the 2006 summer war with Hizbullah and a corruption scandal involving Morris Talansky, a US businessman. After Olmert narrowly averted an attempt in early June by some Kadima members to hold early leadership primaries, four no-confidence motions were put to the Knesset and a public-opinion poll was released indicating that 61% of Israelis believed the prime minister should step down. Although Olmert managed to survive all the no-confidence motions, a bill sponsored by Likud member Silvan Shalom calling for the dissolution of the Knesset garnered support from 74 members from seven parties, preparing the ground for the government's possible collapse the following week. These developments prompted Olmert abruptly to reverse course, and on 11 June he instructed the party's steering committee to start planning new primaries. On 25 June, he escaped a likely 'yes' vote on a bill that would have dissolved parliament and triggered early elections by agreeing to hold a Kadima leadership vote no later than 25 September. This move, however, cleared the way for his possible removal before the end of 2008.

Among those looking to replace Olmert as leader of Kadima were Transportation Minister Shaul Mofaz, Interior Minister Meir Sheetrit, Public Defense Minister Avi Dichter, and the reported frontrunner, Foreign Minister Tzipi Livni. In the unlikely event that Olmert manages to hold on to his party's leadership, he will still face challenges from Defense Minister Ehud Barak and the Likud's Benjamin Netanyahu, both former prime ministers. Regardless of who is at the helm, and despite early 2008 Israeli opinion polls that showed 64%

of respondents favouring negotiations with Hamas to obtain a ceasefire and prisoner exchange, the hard Israeli line on a Fatah–Hamas reconciliation is likely to remain clear and unchanged. In March 2008, when a deal looked remotely possible, an Israeli official said any such reconciliation would mean an end to peace talks between Israel and Fatah. 'The Fatah leadership has to make a choice … [It] can have a peace process and dialogue with Israel or a coalition with Hamas. But it's clear that you can't have them both.' While Israel participated in separate negotiations with Hamas indirectly through Egyptian mediators from mid 2007, and a ceasefire was reached in June 2008, the truce almost immediately began to fray. The Israeli leadership would be politically hard pressed to engage in all-party talks with a unified Palestinian bloc in the absence of a sustained and durable Hamas ceasefire that seemed unlikely to develop.

The Israelis and Palestinians have both acknowledged that a Palestinian state is unlikely to come into existence this year. In early June, Ahmed Qurei, the chief Palestinian negotiator, told reporters that it would take 'a miracle' to bring about a peace deal with Israel by January 2009, when Bush leaves office. This was not lost on Abbas, who began looking for other lifelines. While representatives of Fatah were meeting in Dakar in early June, Abbas travelled to Saudi Arabia and Egypt to secure Arab support for the Yemeni initiative. Abbas's efforts to bring about 'a national and comprehensive dialogue' between Fatah and Hamas, and his apparent openness to meeting with Meshal, suggested he had concluded that the future lay not in talks with Israel but with Hamas. For the White House, which has sought to isolate Hamas internationally, and an Israeli government that wants the group to renounce violence and recognise the Jewish state, a Fatah–Hamas rapprochement would be unwelcome. The formation of a new unity government could embolden the group's hardliners who, having weathered the storm of the past 12 months, would argue for a continuation of their confrontational approach.

It would therefore present the United States and its Quartet partners with difficult choices. One course would be to encourage Israel to work seriously with Abbas. Israel's early June 2008 decision to transfer frozen tax revenues to the PA, so that it can pay the salaries of Palestinian civil servants, was a step in that direction, but Israel would probably have to take additional, politically wrenching measures to convince Abbas that negotiating with Jerusalem, rather than Hamas, was the best way to preserve his viability. These would include easing of checkpoint restrictions on Palestinians in the West Bank and halting construction of new settlements and expansion of existing ones.

Syria and Israel

The only bright spot on the horizon was the announcement, on 21 May 2008, that Turkey was sponsoring proximity talks between Syria and Israel. Both countries had much to gain from negotiations. Syria was isolated and under increased international pressure, especially due to its dealings with North Korea aimed at acquiring a nuclear capability. These seem to have come to light in early 2007, but the underlying intelligence was undisclosed until well after Israeli aircraft attacked and destroyed the Syrian nuclear facility at Al Kibar in September 2007. Syria and North Korea have long had an arms relationship. Damascus's incentive to acquire nuclear weapons – if that was in fact the purpose of its cooperation with Pyongyang and construction of the installation – would have been raised by its increasing conventional weakness and fear of forceful regime change from the outside. In the immediate aftermath of the US-led invasion of Iraq, the latter concern reverberated strongly in Damascus.

Negotiations with Israel would help alleviate some of Syria's isolation. The main sticking point in the previous round of talks involved the location of the international border with respect to the shoreline of the Sea of Galilee. Since then, the contours of the lake had changed in a way that some observers believed could render the issue moot. Israeli officials, for their part, were looking for help in controlling Hizbullah in Lebanon, which they expected to flow from a peace agreement between Jerusalem and Damascus insofar as Syria, after Iran, remains Hizbullah's strongest ally. Israelis also hoped that a peace agreement would help pry Syria from Iran's influence, isolating the country that had emerged as Israel's main strategic adversary. In mid June 2008, Yoram Turbowicz and Shalom Turgeman, senior advisers to Olmert, travelled to Ankara to prepare an agenda for a possible direct meeting in July. Both sides, however, indicated a head-to-head meeting between Assad and Olmert remained far off. Israeli opposition to returning the Golan Heights to Syria rose significantly after the announcement that negotiations were under way, with a June 2008 joint Hebrew University of Jerusalem and Palestinian Center for Policy and Survey Research survey finding that 67% of Israelis were against returning the Golan, compared to 56% just three months earlier.

In any event, real progress seemed unlikely to occur until 2009 since Assad expects American mediation, which will become politically feasible only once Bush leaves office. At a 14 June news conference with French President Nicolas Sarkozy in Paris, Bush reasserted his inflexible approach to Assad, declaring his message to the Syrians to be 'stop fooling around with the Iranians and stop harbouring terrorists'.

Turbulence to the north

Over the past year, Lebanon experienced considerable turmoil. Fears of renewed civil war returned. The troubles began in early June 2007, when 50 al-Qaeda-inspired militants assaulted a Lebanese army checkpoint adjacent to the Ein al Hilweh Palestinian refugee camp in northern Lebanon. Many of the attackers, variously identified as belonging to Fateh al Islam (Victory of Islam) or Jund al-Shem (Army of the Land of the Semites), were veterans of the jihad in Iraq. Some analysts saw their emergence as blowback from the Iraq War and as evidence of the growing sectarian tensions the war had engendered. The Lebanese government responded harshly. Special-operations forces and armoured units besieged the camps in which the jihadists were entrenched and attacked the camps block by block. Hundreds of civilians perished.

The violence played out against a backdrop of political paralysis in Beirut. The US-supported government of Fouad Siniora and his backers in the March 14th Movement – named for the day in 2005 that a million Lebanese gathered in Beirut to mourn the assassination of Prime Minister Rafik Hariri with suspected Syrian complicity – had been at loggerheads with a Hizbullah-dominated opposition pressing for formal veto power over cabinet decisions. Behind the scenes, Washington and Riyadh were pumping money into the government's coffers and surreptitiously training military special units. These steps were judged necessary to offset Hizbullah's military prowess and the substantial assistance it was getting from Tehran. As the fight against the jihadists in the north was going on, there were glimmers of optimism for the army, which seemed to be performing well. In Washington, the hope was that an army that had dealt so ruthlessly with Palestinians in refugee camps in the north would control Hizbullah in the south with equal zeal. In the long run, this line of thinking went, a truly national army would emerge to ensure the integrity of a constitutional order.

The test of this proposition came sooner rather than later. In May 2007, the Siniora government took several decisions to curb Hizbullah's ambitions. One was to order the dismantling of a secure Hizbullah telephone system the organisation had constructed to block Israel's ability to intercept its communications. As it happened, this autonomous network would also prevent the Lebanese government from listening in on Hizbullah's communications, which made the Siniora government feel all the more vulnerable to a Hizbullah coup. Hizbullah's response was to mobilise its forces and directly challenge the government. Although there was scattered fighting, particularly against Druze militia units, Hizbullah quickly subdued Lebanese army elements in Beirut and established complete control over the city in the space of a day. The Lebanese army proved unwilling to fire on Hizbullah fighters.

With this show of strength, Hizbullah demonstrated that it was the indispensable pivot of Lebanese politics. Following a brief stand-off, the Siniora government and Hizbullah opposition consented to a Qatari-brokered agreement that essentially awarded Hizbullah the veto power it had been seeking and overturned the government decisions that had triggered the showdown. In mid June, Rice made a surprise visit to Beirut to put an American stamp of approval on the new Lebanese government. She said that although Washington would have preferred that Hizbullah not gain greater power at the expense of the US-backed March 14th Movement, the deal was a necessary step for stability.

Strategic disarray

Spring 2008 ended with the failure of a US policy intended to staunch Iranian influence and stymie the growth of Islamist movements in the Levant. Two key US-supported political groups, Fatah and the March 14th Movement, on which Washington had staked its prestige, seemed to be fatally damaged, while Hamas, Hizbullah and their Iranian backer emerged triumphant. Bush's successor will inherit a weaker hand in the Levant than has any previous US president. Given the poor cards the new US president will have been dealt, his most realistic option may be to leverage the one optimistic development of 2007–08 – a nascent Turkish-sponsored negotiation process between Israel and Syria – to reinvigorate conflict resolution in the region with an eye towards establishing true strategic stability. While a 'Syria first' strategy failed President Bill Clinton in 2000, the fact that Syria is now in a more tenuous strategic position than it was then may be grounds for marginally greater hope of success. But that will be rather cold comfort for the incoming US administration.

Saudi Arabia and the Gulf States: Continuity Amidst Instability

The Saudi leadership considers Saudi Arabia a hegemon on the Arabian Peninsula, one of several key players in the wider Middle East and the Muslim world, and a country that is able to balance between the larger global powers because of its oil. Domestically, after a significant period of internal unrest, the Saudi regime appeared firmly in control over the past year. King Abdullah bin Abdul Aziz Al Saud continued to be inclined towards gradual economic and political reform. However, many domestic problems (unemployment and education, for instance) that contributed to earlier unrest remained unresolved. There was also serious concern over the array of destabilising conflicts in the region and, in particular, the number of Saudis actively involved in the Iraqi insurgency, which appeared to be much higher than previously assumed. The return of such jihadis could in future fuel further domestic instability, as those returning from Afghanistan did between 1997 and 2005.

Saudi regional diplomacy

Iraq remains Saudi Arabia's most acute regional concern. The Iranian influence in Iraq and the prospect of a strategic partnership between two Shia-dominated countries worries Riyadh, but the Saudi regime has carefully avoided direct confrontation with Tehran over Iraq. Moreover, the official Saudi position, as expressed during the fourth Iraq Neighbours' Conference in October 2007 in Kuwait and again at the Gulf Co-operation Council (GCC) Summit in Doha, emphasised the unity of Iraq and the importance of a region-wide effort to end the insecurity and instability there. These pleas for unity and cooperation most likely have the dual objective of deflating tensions and of increasing Saudi, and more broadly Sunni Arab, influence in Iraqi politics. A third motivation centres on reducing the radicalising influence that Iraqi unrest has on Saudi jihadists and, in turn, the damage that Riyadh's failure to control them does to its diplomatic standing and credibility, particularly in the United States. While most analysts had taken the view that relatively small numbers of Saudis were involved in the insurgency in Iraq, recent US military reports estimated their numbers as much higher, which could raise doubts in Washington about Riyadh's commitment to stabilising the region. Saudi fighters in Iraq are considered the single largest group of foreign insurgents (about 40%), followed by Libyans and Yemenis.

Though the GCC is a relatively successful sub-regional organisation, its greatest achievements have been in the economic realm. Security matters have proven far more difficult to tackle, mainly because of the size and hegemonic attitudes of Saudi Arabia, the GCC's largest member. There have also been numerous differences on the political level, but these have seldom reached boiling point. For its part, Saudi Arabia has continued efforts to resolve regional conflicts and crises and bring competing parties to the negotiating table in Lebanon and in the Israeli–Arab arena. Iraq remained a less straightforward challenge to Saudi regional diplomacy.

In Lebanon, where Prime Minister Fouad Siniora's embattled government remained in a stand-off with an opposition bloc that included the militant Shia organisation Hizbullah and the followers of Christian General Michel Aoun, Riyadh remained a key supporter of the government. King Abdullah met with Hizbullah representatives in December 2006 and has since carried on efforts to resolve the crisis. These, however, were largely frustrated. Lebanon boycotted the annual Arab League Summit in Damascus on 29–30 March 2008, to which Saudi Arabia and other countries sent representatives. In May, the situation in Beirut and some other parts of Lebanon further deteriorated, leading to instability not seen since the 1975–90 civil war. After several days of violence, Hizbullah seized control of the western part of the capital for several days. In mid May, at the initiative of both Saudi Arabia and Egypt, Arab foreign ministers held an emergency meeting, with Riyadh unimaginatively and timidly sticking to its policy of calling for Lebanese elections in accordance with the country's constitution to end the stand-off among key political factions. Later that month, the emir and prime minister of Qatar mediated talks between Lebanese groups that resulted in an agreement to accept General Michel Suleiman as president.

Saudi Arabia has taken an active diplomatic role in the Israeli–Palestinian conflict, motivated by fears that failure to resolve the conflict would drive Hamas even closer to Iran, but has been frustrated by Iran's ability to influence Hamas through political and financial support. Riyadh brokered the 'Mecca Agreement' for power-sharing between Hamas and Fatah in February 2007. During summer 2007, however, renewed clashes in the occupied territories between Fatah and Hamas culminated in Palestinian Authority President Mahmoud Abbas's dismissal of the national unity government in mid June and Hamas's de facto takeover of Gaza. The Saudi king expressed his disappointment with both sides, though he evinced more sympathy with Hamas than did other Arab players such as Egypt.

In late November, Saudi Arabian Foreign Minister Saud al-Faisal attended the Middle East Peace Conference in Annapolis, Maryland. Saudi officials had been deeply sceptical about the Annapolis initiative, suspecting that it would simply be a photo opportunity. They announced their attendance only after months of haggling with US officials over whether the Saudi peace plan initially mooted in 2002 – involving Israel's withdrawal from land seized during the 1967 war in exchange for full recognition by and normalised diplomatic relations with Arab states as well as the establishment of a Palestinian state – would be discussed. Despite these differences, Washington considered Saudi Arabia's participation in the meeting crucial, and regarded King Abdullah as one of the few leaders in the Muslim world capable of promoting reconciliation between Israel and its Arab neighbours, deemed vital to any comprehensive peace agreement. As many had expected, what little momentum Annapolis may have generated was soon overtaken by unrest on the ground. As of mid 2008, Saudi Arabia appeared disinclined to reopen its mediating efforts.

Relations between Qatar and Saudi Arabia had been bitter since 2002, when the Qatar-based satellite TV station al-Jazeera criticised the Saudi role in the Israeli–Palestinian conflict. Riyadh recalled its ambassador from Doha and boycotted the subsequent GCC Summit in Qatar. In late April 2007, the Qatari emir (accompanied by the chairman of al-Jazeera) met with King Abdullah. After the Qatari government and the station assured the Saudi king that they would stop 'campaigning' against the kingdom, Abdullah agreed to send the Saudi envoy back, to attend the December summit in Doha and to allow an al-Jazeera office in Riyadh. This was a salutary development both for bilateral affairs and for the GCC overall, since other members have often felt compelled to take sides in the rivalry between Qatar and Saudi Arabia. In March 2008 Saudi Crown Prince Sultan spent three days in Doha, symbolising a return to normalcy in Saudi–Qatari relations.

Other divisive issues emerged, however. In February 2008, disputes arose over the accession of Yemen to the GCC. While Saudi Arabia and most other members favoured Yemen's membership, Kuwait expressed reservations. Its official rationale was a disinclination to overstretch the organisation, but there was little doubt that the primary reason was Yemen's support for Iraqi President Saddam Hussein's invasion of Kuwait in 1991. Yemen has since opted to pursue full membership and receives large sums of donor money from GCC states to boost its economy and facilitate its integration into the GCC framework. In March a railway connection was announced between Yemen and the other smaller Gulf states. While analysts believe that Yemen will join the GCC eventually, Kuwait has veto power and may use it.

Major-power relations

Overall, Riyadh's relationship with Washington has weathered the crisis over the 11 September attacks, remaining strong and even being reinforced by arms transfers and military aid. In January 2008, the US State Department officially notified Congress of its intent to sell 900 Joint Direct Attack Munitions kits (JDAMs) to the kingdom. This transaction was part of the American administration's plan to sell at least $20bn of high-tech weaponry to Saudi Arabia and the five other GCC member states. Significantly, the $20bn figure was considered a floor rather than a ceiling, and the ultimate value of the arms sales could be substantially greater. The special Saudi–US relationship was further bolstered when President Bush visited Riyadh in May.

Some have postulated a new regional cold war, pitting the United States and its 'moderate' clients against the Iranian-led 'extremist' camp. While Bush warned, with some hyperbole, that a 'nuclear holocaust' would result if Tehran continued its uranium-enrichment programme, the Saudi government remained worried about Iran's nuclear ambitions, even though Saudi and wider Arab public opinion was largely sympathetic with Iran's assertion of entitlement to a nuclear option. The Saudi government appeared less concerned about a direct nuclear attack from Iran than about the spillover effect of a possible American or Israeli pre-emptive military operation against Iran. Saudi strategists are convinced of Tehran's capacity to launch catastrophic reprisals, primarily on the Arab side of the Gulf and in Iraq, but also in Lebanon and the Palestinian territories. The Saudi elite is thus torn between wanting the United States to do something to stop the Iranian nuclear programme and ensuring that a direct US–Iran military confrontation is avoided. This awkward situation relaxed somewhat after the release of the US National Intelligence Estimate (NIE) on Iran in November 2007, suggesting that Iran had suspended its nuclear-weapons programme in 2003. As a consequence, GCC–Iranian relations began to thaw, and the Gulf monarchies reached out to Tehran with new diplomatic initiatives. Iranian President Mahmoud Ahmadinejad attended the Doha Summit, and weeks later travelled to Saudi Arabia for his hajj pilgrimage at King Abdullah's invitation. In early

May 2008, Tehran announced the signing of a Memorandum of Understanding on security matters with Riyadh, though details have not been released.

Saudi Arabia's continued tightening of relations with Russia exemplifies the kingdom's ability to balance workable relationships with competing global powers. Following up Russian President Vladimir Putin's visit to Riyadh in February 2007, Crown Prince Sultan bin Abdulaziz Al Saud went to Moscow in November of that year. A 'verbal understanding' for the sale of 150 T-90S tanks was reportedly reached, along with an informal agreement whereby Riyadh could purchase up to $4bn worth of arms from Moscow. There were no indications, however, that Riyadh aspired to jettison its special relationship with Washington in favour of an alliance with Moscow. Saudi–Russian relations instead constituted a highly pragmatic partnership driven by a significant, but limited, convergence of interests. For the Saudis, the relationship provided some leverage vis-à-vis Washington and, given the scale of popular domestic anti-American sentiment, yielded political benefits at home.

Similar considerations applied to Riyadh's intensifying relations with Beijing. Saudi Arabia is now China's largest supplier of crude oil, having provided some 528,000 barrels per day in 2007, and has established long-term supply arrangements. China has also become an important market for Saudi Arabia's growing petrochemical industry, and Saudi Arabia has opened part of its domestic oil and gas market to Chinese upstream investments. Equally, if not more, important are Saudi investments in the Chinese downstream sector. Though the scope of Chinese–Saudi security cooperation is hard to gauge, it is generally assumed that China's arms supplies to the kingdom have dwindled over recent years.

Saudi foreign policy vis-à-vis other major powers has been fairly enterprising. In late October 2007, King Abdullah made a four-day, high-profile state visit to the United Kingdom – the first by a Saudi king in 20 years. The trip was marred by mutual recrimination, with the king asserting that the British government had not done all it could to prevent the 7 July 2005 bombings in London, and various British protesters and media outlets making harsh statements about Saudi Arabia's poor human-rights record. Shortly before the London visit, however, Saudi Arabia had signed a deal for the purchase of 72 *Typhoon* fighter jets from Britain (worth £4.43bn), reflecting the strong military and economic ties between the two countries. In early November, King Abdullah became the first Saudi ruler to visit the Vatican, signalling an increased willingness to engage in inter-civilisational and interfaith dialogue.

Domestic affairs: combating radicalism, continued uncertainties

While the Saudi domestic security environment proved relatively stable for most of 2007 and 2008 – the last major terrorist incident was in February 2007, when gunmen killed four French expatriates – there was continued emphasis on counter-terrorism. Threats remained live. In November and December 2007, seven cells that had planned to attack pilgrims, oil installations, security personnel and senior clerics who had condemned terrorist organisations were reportedly captured. In addition, public anti-terrorist campaigning by the official Saudi religious establishment, or ulema, and the government (especially Interior Minister Prince Nayef bin Abdulaziz) continued. On 1 October 2007, the Saudi Grand Mufti issued a fatwa prohibiting Saudi youth from engaging in jihad in Iraq, and in December Prince Nayef strongly condemned mosque preachers who called for jihad and stressed the important role of the ulema and the press in the struggle against the spread of terrorist ideology. In January 2008, a new law was passed authorising prison sentences of up to ten years for anyone convicted of setting up websites in support of terrorism, and up to 5m riyals – more than $1.3m – in fines.

Further evidence of an official commitment to combating radicalism in Saudi Arabia came in March 2008, when a leading newspaper announced government plans to re-train approximately 40,000 clerics through the Ministry of Religious Affairs and the Center for National Dialogue. This report emerged a week after a leading cleric called for the beheading of two liberal Saudi writers. As of spring 2008, the construction of five special detention facilities in Riyadh, Dammam, Jeddah, Qassim and Abha for jihadist sympathisers was under way. These facilities are devoted to rehabilitation and counselling, for which classrooms and lecture halls are included in the design. In addition to the in-prison programme, there will be extended measures to prevent recidivism. These include employment assistance, housing and financial help, and support to families during detention. According to official data, these programmes have a high success rate, but the accuracy of these representations is difficult to verify.

The extent of the rehabilitation programme seems to have anticipated large-scale return of Saudi fighters from Iraq and a pressing need for aggressive intervention in light of the high correlation between the mujahadeen in Afghanistan and the unrest starting with the Khobar Tower attacks in 1997. Nevertheless, the Saudi government remains politically dependent on a religious establishment with a tradition of Wahhabi radicalism and intolerance, and will not act directly against it unless it overtly attempts to undermine the government's authority. Riyadh's opposition to radicalism will continue to be qualified and measured – as with its post-11 September terrorist financing regime, which is fairly strong on monitoring and interdiction but very weak on prosecution.

Sectarianism within the kingdom is an ongoing problem. The Shi'ites in Saudi Arabia have long been victims of systematic discrimination, which has led them to form a political opposition. The tone and content of that opposition, however, has changed since Abdullah acceded to power. Where previous Shia discontent often took the form of direct challenges to the Al Saud, the current version – with the exception of the militant stance of the Saudi Hizbullah, which has limited influence – has been more positive and less confrontational, stressing that the Shi'ites belong to the Saudi Arabian nation and are entitled to equal rights within that framework. Shia leaders are increasingly participating in official political forums, such as the Majlis al-Shura, the municipal councils and the National Dialogue, through which a wide range of religious intellectuals – both Sunni and Shia – are encouraged to make their views heard. Iran's influence among Saudi Shi'ites has not been strong, and has further diminished since the death of Ayatollah Muhammad al-Husayni al-Shirazi in 2001. Most Arab Shi'ites consider Iraqi Ayatollah Ali al-Sistani their spiritual leader, while others may follow Sayyid Muhammad Hussein Fadlallah, also an Iraqi.

The softer line will probably continue, especially given that community leaders have expressed their confidence that cooperation with the Saudi state will better their situation. Shia leaders and the Saudi regime continue to stress the oneness of the nation and regard the Sunni–Shia divide in Saudi Arabia as an internal issue – a position that tamps down the impact on Saudi Arabia of sectarian strife and rhetoric in the wider Middle East. Yet discrimination against Shi'ites continues. Although they make up a majority of the Saudi state oil company ARAMCO's employees, promotion opportunities are still scarce and Shi'ites are largely excluded from the police and the army. In addition, the labelling of Shia Muslims as polytheists or unbelievers by influential clerics continues, though others distance themselves from such portrayals and, most important, they have no official regime support. While sectarian fighting in Iraq to some extent heightens these tensions, only a large-scale return of battle-hardened Sunni fighters from Iraq is likely to disrupt the overall balance that keeps sectarian differences in Saudi Arabia in check.

Considerable hopes for political reform were raised after 2001, and subsequent changes within the kingdom, such as the National Dialogue or the municipal elections in 2005, fulfilled some of them, but developments since then have been disappointing. The municipal councils have largely proven toothless, no changes have been made to the role of the Majlis al-Shura, the two human-rights organisations within the kingdom have largely limited themselves to politically safe issues such as domestic violence, and results of the 'Saudisation' of the workforce and changes in school curriculum have been minimal. Since new elections are to be held in 2009 and the election code of 2005 was formulated only for that particular set of elections, it remains to be seen whether the new code might incorporate further liberalisation – for instance, by changing the proportion of elected and appointed members, which for 2005 was 50% each.

The *mutawwi'in* (the religious police, or officially, the Committee for the Promotion of Virtue and the Prohibition of Vice) is controversial. Reported incidents of its misconduct have increased. They have included two fatal car crashes following chases; the highly publicised case in which 50-year-old Umm Faisal, her 21-year-old daughter and their Indonesian maid were arrested for allegedly inappropriate dress, taken on a harrowing automobile ride, and then abandoned by the roadside; and the fatal beating of a man suspected of having alcohol in his home. Women's rights also remain a controversial issue. While women have been allowed to stay in hotels alone, they still need written permission of their male guardians to travel unless they are over 45. The king has rhetorically endorsed lifting the ban on women driving, but only 'when the country is ready for it'.

The oil boom and the Saudi economy

The rise of global oil prices has swelled current-account surpluses of Saudi Arabia and smaller Gulf monarchies. Saudi Arabia remains the world's largest oil producer and the only one with sufficient surplus capacity to influence global supply and thus pricing as a 'swing producer'. For this reason, Bush visited the kingdom twice in 2008 to ask the Saudis to increase production, only to be disappointed, though the government later agreed to raise it by 200,000 barrels a day. During 2007 the Saudi Arabian Monetary Agency increased its foreign assets by $80bn. In contrast with the boom periods of the 1970s and early 1980s, economic reforms, improvements of the private-sector business environment and large-scale infrastructural and industrial development have prevented excessive capital flight. Nevertheless, the turbulence in financial markets has had several countervailing effects on the Saudi economy. First, as the riyal is firmly connected to the dollar, the latter's position has had a direct negative impact on Saudi domestic liquidity and especially non-dollar imports. Secondly, oil prices have been more volatile. Finally, the rise in global food prices has pushed up inflation, which is forecast at 8% for 2008.

Government spending has risen roughly 15% annually in recent years. While the largest outlays continue to be for security, medical care, education and infrastructure, there is a budget surplus even at the most conservatively estimated oil-price levels. Consequent extra spending can thus be directed towards salaries, subsidies and other benefits, limiting the impact of higher inflation. Although privatisation, diversification and foreign investment have progressed in recent years, in part due to Saudi Arabia's December 2005 accession to the World Trade Organisation, unemployment has stayed high even though the Saudisation of the workforce has been a standing policy goal. Saudis still primarily occupy jobs in the subsidised, semi-governmental sector, while private-sector employers have continued to resist employing them on the grounds that they are more expensive and less productive than foreign labourers. Almost 75% of Saudi citizens are under 30, and youth unemployment is near 30%, which makes that sector vulnerable to political dissent, radicalisation and ultimately terrorist impulses. Only serious educational and social reforms are likely to remedy this persistent problem.

The Gulf states: slow liberalisation

Like Saudi Arabia, Kuwait, Bahrain, Qatar and to a lesser extent the United Arab Emirates and Oman are moving fitfully towards political and economic liberalisation. Kuwait witnessed a consolidation of parliamentary power. Controversy over gender segregation resurfaced after liberal members of parliament submitted a draft bill in February 2008 to allow coeducation. Kuwait's previous mandatory-segregation laws had not yet been fully implemented due to the high cost of building separate facilities for men and women. Islamist MPs nevertheless insisted that gender segregation was required by Islamic law. Over this issue, the cabinet resigned and the parliament elected in June 2006 was dissolved in March 2008. In the general elections of May 2008, no women made it to the legislature as voters returned many Islamist and tribal politicians from the previous house. It appears that the confrontational relationship between the cabinet and the parliament in Kuwait will continue.

Political developments in Bahrain were less eventful after the controversial parliamentary elections of 2007, though human-rights issues stayed in the political forefront. A Bahraini court charged political activist Hussain Mansoor in January 2008 with the assault and attempted murder of a security officer during a protest. A month later, 55 local, regional and international human-rights organisations issued a call to King Hamad to release demonstrators and human-rights activists and to refrain from torturing detainees. The regime seems reluctant to suppress an energetic civil society with sufficient muscularity to stop further gradual change, despite discord within the ruling family over the pace of reform. Qatar's first legislative elections were scheduled for early 2007, but then postponed until June 2008. The constitution allows for a legislative body with 30 members elected by universal suffrage and 15 appointed by the emir. In April 2008, municipal elections took place in which for the first time a woman won a seat, after her two competitors dropped out of the race.

While Kuwait, Bahrain and Qatar do not yet qualify as genuine democracies, incremental political liberalisation has occurred. The main drivers of change are domestic, though external factors and actors can both facilitate and obstruct liberalisation. On the regional level, both positive and negative 'demonstration' or 'contagion' effects could emanate from developments in Palestine, Lebanon and Iraq. In terms of foreign policy, though worries about possible fallout from developments in Iraq and US military or other punitive action against Iran remained, all of the small Gulf states maintained their respective strategic alignments with the United States. Thus, at the strategic level, discreet American urging towards reform is likely to persist. The experience in Kuwait, however, where an illiberal parliament has paradoxically stalled the more liberal approach of the ruling family, is likely to slow momentum in other GCC states towards fuller parliamentary processes at the national level.

Prospects

While the new succession law of 2007 to some extent institutionalised the succession practice in Saudi Arabia, it is widely accepted that it will be relevant in practice only when no more sons of King Abdul Aziz Al Saud (1876–1953) are available to rule. Until then, consultation among the brothers will determine succession. In this light, reform-minded Saudis have expressed worry about whether the reforms cautiously initiated by the 84-year old Abdullah will be carried through by his successor, who would likely be one of three of his half-brothers – called *al-Thaluth* ('the trio') – from the Sudeiri branch the family: Crown Prince Sultan (the heir apparent), Prince Salman (governor of Riyadh), and Prince Nayef (the interior minister). The Sudeiris are considered a tightly knit conservative group. Recent unofficial reports have raised questions about the health of Sultan, who was flown to Geneva for 'regular medical tests' in late April 2008. The fact that Abdullah has not selected a second deputy is telling of Sudeiri power: he appears unable to appoint a non-Sudeiri and unwilling to appoint Nayef, who is much less progressively inclined. If Sultan were to die before Abdullah, the Sudeiri power base might diminish, leaving room for other sons of Abdul Aziz, such as Prince Mishal or intelligence chief Prince Muqrin, both of whom are considered close to Abdullah.

Who succeeds Abdullah will probably affect the pace and nature of Saudi domestic reform significantly, but incrementally delegitimating Salafi jihadism in the kingdom will remain a long-term priority, and Saudi Arabia's foreign-policy imperatives are unlikely to change substantially. For one thing, the country enjoys substantial strategic consensus within the GCC. More important, the oil-and-security fundamentals of the Saudi–US relationship are intact, as confirmed by the $20bn arms deal. The deal itself seems intended to reassure the Saudi elite of continued American support against the backdrop of growing Iranian regional influence in Lebanon (through Hizbullah) and the Palestinian territories (through Hamas), the prospect of Iran's going nuclear, and eventual American withdrawal from Iraq. This reassurance, in turn, would aim to discourage Riyadh from seeking its own nuclear-weapons capability and induce it instead to rely on extended American conventional and nuclear deterrence. More broadly, on major strategic issues, the two countries' interests are as convergent as ever. Both are concerned not just about Iran, but also the spillover of Iraqi unrest, terrorism perpetrated by al-Qaeda and its followers, and the destabilising effects of the Israeli–Palestinian conflict. At the same time, the bilateral relationship is not popular in either country, which leads to a degree of tactical distancing on both sides. Moreover, although Saudi regional diplomacy will be cued to an extent by US policy, as a regional actor and a Muslim power, the Saudi government is still compelled to apprehend the region in customary balance-of-power terms, quietly inflected by sectarian (Sunni versus Shia) concerns.

While Riyadh is likely to discourage precipitous US withdrawal from Iraq in order to moderate the return of Saudi jihadis and temper Iranian inroads in the Gulf, it will probably become more active in shaping Sunni–Shia reconciliation in Iraqi affairs in the knowledge that a US departure is inevitably drawing closer. Greater Saudi activism on the Israeli–Arab and Lebanese fronts, though broadly conducive to containing Iran, is likely to come more slowly due to the discouraging state of play of the respective peace processes. In any case, Riyadh and Washington are likely to continue to differ tactically over the handling of Hamas. Riyadh would prefer to co-opt the organisation through reconciliation with Fatah while Washington will probably – even with a new administration – continue to prefer to isolate it completely. Since rolling back Iran will remain an American imperative, it is in Riyadh's strategic interest to continue to avoid any direct confrontation with Tehran – so as not to become a military target – while subtly supporting US efforts. If the US administration were to lose patience and launch a military strike on Iran, Riyadh would find its strategic balancing act far more difficult to execute.

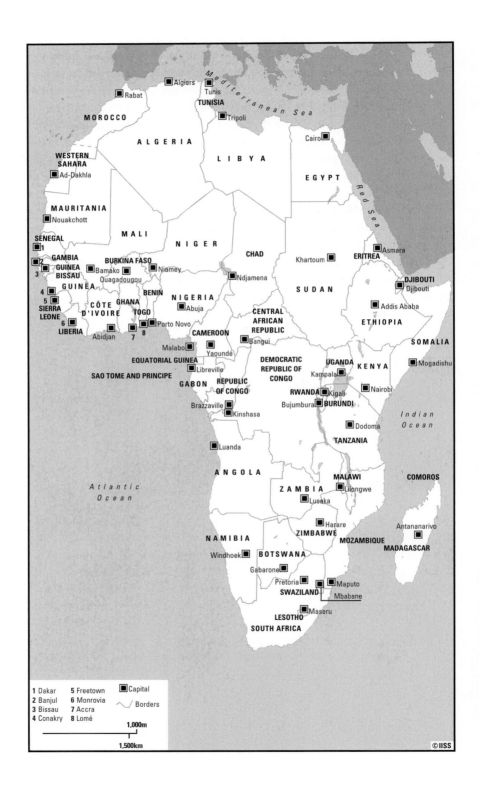

Mediterranean Sea

Algiers
Tunis
TUNISIA
Rabat
MOROCCO
Tripoli
Cairo
ALGERIA
LIBYA
EGYPT
Red Sea
WESTERN SAHARA
Ad-Dakhla
MAURITANIA
Nouakchott
MALI
NIGER
CHAD
Khartoum
Asmara
ERITREA
SENEGAL
1
GAMBIA
2
GUINEA BISSAU
3
Bamako
BURKINA FASO
Ouagadougou
Niamey
Ndjamena
SUDAN
DJIBOUTI
Djibouti
GUINEA
4
5
SIERRA LEONE
6
CÔTE D'IVOIRE
GHANA
BENIN
TOGO
NIGERIA
Abuja
CENTRAL AFRICAN REPUBLIC
Addis Ababa
ETHIOPIA
LIBERIA
Abidjan
7
8
Porto Novo
CAMEROON
Malabo
Yaoundé
Bangui
SOMALIA
EQUATORIAL GUINEA
Libreville
SAO TOME AND PRINCIPE
GABON
REPUBLIC OF CONGO
DEMOCRATIC REPUBLIC OF CONGO
UGANDA
Kampala
KENYA
Mogadishu
Brazzaville
Kinshasa
RWANDA
Kigali
Bujumbura
BURUNDI
Nairobi
Indian Ocean
Dodoma
Luanda
TANZANIA
Atlantic Ocean
ANGOLA
MALAWI
Lilongwe
COMOROS
ZAMBIA
Lusaka
Harare
Antananarivo
NAMIBIA
ZIMBABWE
BOTSWANA
MOZAMBIQUE
MADAGASCAR
Windhoek
Gabarone
Pretoria
Maputo
SWAZILAND
Mbabane
Maseru
LESOTHO
SOUTH AFRICA

1 Dakar   5 Freetown   ■ Capital
2 Banjul   6 Monrovia
3 Bissau   7 Accra   / Borders
4 Conakry   8 Lomé
1,000m
1,500km

©IISS

7 Africa

The quest for a more stable and secure environment in Africa took as many steps backward as forward in the past year. The political scene was dominated by the desperate attempts of the regime of Robert Mugabe in Zimbabwe to prolong its stay in power, the explosion of inter-ethnic violence after elections in Kenya, and continuing conflicts and humanitarian emergencies in Somalia, Sudan and Chad, despite the deployment of new international peacekeeping operations. The victimisation of civilians in these crises prompted calls for more forceful outside intervention, but there were few signs of greater willingness to undertake such action.

Coinciding with these developments, the political outlook in South Africa, the pre-eminent regional power, was unsettled by a successful and divisive challenge for leadership of the governing African National Congress by the controversial Jacob Zuma. This internal revolt and the disputed elections in Kenya and Zimbabwe all demonstrated an increased readiness at the grassroots level of African politics to repudiate leaders who fail to respond to public pressures.

Relatively strong economic performances masked growing inequalities. While the developing world as a whole appeared likely to meet the UN target of halving the proportion of people in extreme poverty by 2015, Africa did not. This was despite expectations of a fifth successive year of high growth in 2008, with a forecast rate of around 6%. Increased involvement by China, India and Russia in the exploitation of African resources has shaken complacency among the continent's traditional Western partners. Africa has taken on increased relevance to the extent that its affairs impinge on energy security, immigration policies and international terrorism. Among the signs of renewed interest were the first EU–Africa summit for more than seven years, held in Lisbon in December 2007, a second African tour by US President George W. Bush in February 2008, and the establishment of a unified US military command for Africa, AFRICOM, scheduled to become fully operational in October 2008. However, it became clear that the doubling of aid promised by the Group of Eight (G8) industrialised countries over the second half of the decade was not materialising, resulting in an erosion of trust among African governments.

While Africa has recently shown more consistent economic vigour than at any time since decolonisation, and has in many countries improved standards of government and made more room for democracy, the result has not so far been to make the continent more predictable or less volatile.

Challenges of Peace Enforcement

At the beginning of 2008 there were four times as many UN troops, police and military observers in Africa as there had been in all UN peacekeeping operations around the world ten years previously. Africa took up 65% of UN-deployed forces, including three of the four biggest missions. The build-up in 2008 of a new joint operation in Sudan's Darfur region pushed the global total of UN peacekeepers to a record of over 90,000 and further increased the proportion dedicated to Africa. Almost all these operations dealt with internal conflicts rather than the classic task of overseeing international ceasefires. The exception was the mission on the Ethiopia–Eritrea border, where the UNMEE operation was under reconsideration in early 2008 after Eritrea cut off supplies and forced the withdrawal of most peacekeepers from the buffer zone.

Growing demands on military resources for complex peace tasks have led to an ad hoc division of responsibilities among organisations, with regionally organised interim operations complemented by short-term European Union missions, the third of which has begun in Chad. The African Union (AU) has progressively increased its participation, with operations in Darfur (now shared with the UN) and Somalia. These were exceptionally tough missions, severely testing the AU's capacities. They were set up with the idea that they should be subsumed by the UN after an initial period, as had happened earlier in Burundi. But this has been a difficult process. In Darfur, AU soldiers were sent initially because Sudan would not accept any others. Expanding and strengthening the force has been painfully slow, and has not set an encouraging precedent for 'hybrid' peace operations.

Increased assertiveness in AU security policy was demonstrated in March 2008 by the dispatch of more than 1,000 troops to back the Comoros government in an amphibious invasion of Anjouan Island, overturning its secessionist leader. Meanwhile, an African standby force that would be able to deploy in 30 days, based on brigades in each of five African regions, was scheduled to become operational by 2010. But progress in the different regions has been uneven, the most advanced being West Africa through the Economic Community of West African States (ECOWAS). The AU faced big challenges in management, logistics and harmonisation, and there have been severe constraints on its ability to carry out anything more than short-term missions. With African countries already supplying 40% of the troops on UN peacekeeping duties around the continent, the AU had limited numbers of competent personnel available for its own operations, and depended on donor finance as well as airlift and other support, with training and assistance coming from a hotchpotch of multilateral and bilateral programmes. In April 2008, the UN Security Council agreed to carry out a review to seek ways of improving support and funding.

Complex mission in Darfur

Deployment of a joint UN–AU force in the Darfur region of western Sudan finally got under way in late 2007, after long and intensive international lobbying and public pressure for action to stop further atrocities. The 'hybrid' nature of the UNAMID mission was dictated by the need for Khartoum's consent to the deployment. It was set to be the largest active peacekeeping operation and one of the most complicated and expensive ever undertaken. When fully deployed it was expected to cost more than $2 billion annually, approximately twice the budget of the UN operation in the Democratic Republic of the Congo (DRC). The force was in addition to 10,000 UNMIS peacekeepers supporting a 2005 peace deal in southern Sudan.

However, with Darfur's rebel conflict in its sixth year, the mission's prospects were dogged by the Khartoum regime's delaying tactics, stalled movement towards a new peace agreement for the region, and an increasingly confused pattern of fighting. The UN–AU force was meant to reach full strength in early 2008. But by March, barely 9,000 of the planned 26,000 troops and police were in place, mainly African soldiers plus some Chinese and Bangladeshi contingents. One cause of delay was Sudanese resistance to having non-African troops in Darfur. Sweden and Norway had to withdraw plans for a 400-strong engineering unit. Other difficulties arose over land for bases and approval of night flights, among other issues, while the force had its own problems securing commitments of troops and equipment, especially helicopters.

This was the UN's second attempt to mount a large operation in Darfur, the Security Council having authorised a force of about 23,000 almost a year earlier. The Council approved the new force in July 2007, in a resolution tabled by Britain and France and passed unanimously, with a mandate including protection of civilians and humanitarian workers. The threat of further UN sanctions against

Khartoum was dropped in order to overcome objections from China which, while it helped to press Sudan to agree to the UN peacekeepers, continued to oppose tough measures. With respect to the UN embargo on arms to the region, UNAMID was restricted to a monitoring role.

UNAMID took over from the AU's 7,000-strong AMIS force, incorporating the latter's troops along with support elements already provided by the UN. Built up from an observer mission first sent in 2004 to monitor a ceasefire neither side observed, AMIS lacked the means to contain violence and suffered from an inadequate mandate, lack of clarity about its task, under-equipment and irregular donor funding. It was also the target of intermittent attacks: in September 2007 ten of its peacekeepers were killed when rebels stormed a base in north Darfur. Within days of UNAMID taking up its mission, a supply convoy was fired on by the Sudanese army, which subsequently apologised.

One of the new mission's first tasks was to improve security in camps that accommodated about 2 million displaced people, a third of Darfur's population. The situation continued to worsen during the past year. Violence, categorised as genocide by the United States four years ago, had since become more generalised, with a proliferation of armed groups, widespread banditry and infighting between and among Arab tribal factions. According to UN estimates, the conflict may have caused 300,000 deaths so far, although Sudan disputed such high figures. A fresh wave of air and ground attacks by Sudanese forces and militias on towns in west Darfur in February, aimed at pushing back the Justice and Equality Movement (JEM) rebel group, drove more refugees across the Chad border, adding to the 240,000 already there. In May JEM fighters staged a bold and unprecedented attack, penetrating east from Darfur as far as Omdurman, just outside the seat of government in Khartoum.

Peace talks mediated by the UN and AU were launched in Sirte, Libya, in October 2007 but fizzled out when the principal rebel groups refused to join. This was despite attempts made in the Tanzanian town of Arusha and the southern Sudanese capital Juba to forge a unified rebel negotiating stance. The Sudan Liberation Movement, one part of which signed a peace deal in 2006, fragmented further along tribal lines, and the JEM later divided as well, creating a dozen or more factions in total. The outlook for a settlement was clouded by Sudan's difficult relations with Chad, which served as a rear base for Darfur rebels.

Meanwhile, clouds were gathering over the future of the Comprehensive Peace Agreement (CPA) signed in 2005 between Sudan's north and south. While international attention was concentrated on Darfur, the carefully worked out north–south deal came under serious strain. The two issues were closely tied, since any political settlement on greater autonomy and power-sharing in Darfur had to fit in with the overarching CPA arrangements. North–south discord came to a head in October 2007 when the southern partner, the Sudan People's

Liberation Movement (SPLM), withdrew from the national unity government in Khartoum. Although it had returned to the government by year's end, the relationship remained precarious. The parties were positioning themselves ahead of nationwide elections due by July 2009, in which the regime survival of the dominant National Congress Party (NCP) will be at stake. Among steps prescribed by the CPA, a census, necessary for the elections and for the south's planned referendum on independence in 2011, went ahead in April 2008, nine months behind schedule. A draft election law was also agreed. But critical elements lagged behind, including troop redeployment and border demarcation, which could be crucial for access to oil if the south, which has most of the reserves, were to secede. The SPLM sought greater transparency on oil contracts and production, revenues from which are split between north and south. Tension rose sharply in the oil-producing Abyei district adjacent to southern Sudan. Skirmishes starting in December 2007 between southern forces and Arab tribal fighters were followed in May 2008 by direct clashes with Sudanese government troops.

The NCP, which is likely to have difficulty in winning southern support for a unified Sudan, may seek to keep delaying the issue. A breakdown in the CPA arrangements could in turn threaten the new-found peace in neighbouring northern Uganda, where expectations continued in early 2008 of a formal deal with the elusive leader of the Lord's Resistance Army, Joseph Kony. At the same time, while fighting continues in Darfur, it risks spreading to other areas of Sudan. A more complex or volatile situation would be hard to imagine.

Europe's intervention in Chad

An EU military operation in Chad and the Central African Republic (CAR) began in early 2008. Designed as an interim military mission to complement the UN–AU deployment in Darfur, the operation appeared particularly challenging. With 3,700 troops, the EU took on the task of protecting a displaced population of more than 460,000, mostly refugees from Darfur and the CAR, in dozens of sites across the inhospitable terrain of eastern Chad. During planning for the mission, the region suffered heavy fighting, as Sudan and Chad continued to fuel each other's rebellions.

The idea of an EU force surfaced in June 2007 after an unsuccessful attempt by French Foreign Minister Bernard Kouchner to establish a 'humanitarian corridor' through Chad to Darfur. Chad's President Idriss Déby had until then shown no willingness to host an international force, which might have cramped his government's own operations, but France brought him round to the idea. The force, called EUFOR Chad/CAR, was authorised by the UN Security Council in September as a one-year bridging operation to protect refugees and other civilians, facilitate aid delivery and provide security for UN staff.

This was the EU's third military operation in Africa. The others, both in the DRC, were smaller and more short term with narrow remits, first to secure the flashpoint town of Bunia in 2003, pending the arrival of a larger UN peacekeeping force, and then to bolster security in Kinshasa during elections in 2006. It was unclear how the Chad/CAR mission could work without having its neutrality called into question. Concerns were raised among some EU members that the operation, the biggest undertaken autonomously by the EU outside Europe, might be seen as an extension of French policy in two fragile former colonies which had seen six French military interventions since independence. The danger of ambiguity in this regard was underlined in late 2007 when Chad's principal Sudanese-backed rebel group said it was 'in a state of belligerence against the French army or any other foreign forces'.

Set up alongside a smaller UN mission, MINURCAT, as part of a 'multi-dimensional' operation including police training, the EU force was to concentrate on three main refugee areas in Chad, together with the northeastern border zone of the CAR, to stop that area being used for the transit of fighters between Sudan and Chad. France would contribute more than half the troops, incorporating a detachment already sent to the CAR. But French troops already stationed in Chad, numbering about 1,250, would remain separate.

The risks that awaited the EU operation became clear in November 2007 when, after a month's ceasefire, intense battles took place in eastern Chad, causing hundreds of casualties. Deployment had then to be temporarily suspended in February when a rebel alliance staged a major assault on the capital N'Djamena, the second in two years. Advancing in a column of about 300 vehicles with machine guns and artillery, the rebels travelled 800km and succeeded in entering the capital. Held at bay at the presidential palace, they were finally repelled after three days of fighting involving government tanks and helicopters. At least 160 people were killed in the assault, including Chad's army chief of staff. Thousand of residents fled on foot to nearby Cameroon.

French commanders were put on the spot. They had tried in recent years to play a discreet role, providing logistics and reconnaissance for Chad's forces without becoming directly involved in combat operations. But French forces this time played an important part, tracking the rebel advance with *Mirage* F1s and securing N'Djamena's airport, permitting the evacuation of foreign nationals. French troops came under attack by rocket-propelled grenades near the airport, and returned fire. Officials in Paris later admitted to transporting ammunition for government forces, some of it from Libya. France also came to Déby's aid by drafting a UN Security Council statement condemning the attack and urging other countries to support his government. Déby was prompted to pardon six French charity workers convicted of attempting to kidnap Chadian children (the workers had been repatriated and jailed in France under a bilateral agreement).

EUFOR, which had an advance team in Chad at the time of the rebel attack, resumed deployment in time to declare initial operating capability in March. The mission fit in with France's aims of strengthening the EU's security role and 'Europeanising' its military presence in Africa, which includes bases in Djibouti, Gabon and Senegal. The idea of reducing France's exposure had been aired during the presidency of Jacques Chirac. President Nicolas Sarkozy repeated Chirac's position that France had no wish to 'play the role of gendarme in Africa'. In a speech to the South African parliament in late February, he said France had no vocation to keep armed forces in Africa indefinitely. It was now, he added, 'unthinkable ... for us to be drawn into domestic conflicts'. This was just after he had visited Chad, where French forces had come close to crossing that line. The French Defence White Paper published in June 2008 confirmed that one of the two West African bases would be closed, and clauses in Franco-African defence agreements detailing France's possible role in internal security would be abrogated.

The task facing peacekeepers on both sides of the Chad–Sudan border was made more difficult by acute friction and distrust between the two governments. In March, following mediation by Senegal, Déby signed a fresh non-aggression pact with Sudan's President Omar al-Bashir, agreeing to stop armed groups using the territory of one country to attack the other. It was their sixth pact in five years and, like the others, soon collapsed. When Darfur rebels surged to the metropolitan area of Khartoum in May, mirroring the Chadian rebel attack on N'Djamena three months earlier, Sudan broke off relations. Chad closed its frontier in response. Hopes that the new international deployments might be accompanied by an easing of cross-border tensions appeared baseless.

Somalia: from bad to worse

Fighting in Somalia showed no sign of remission in 2007 and early 2008. It became increasingly apparent that the US-favoured Ethiopian military intervention, while enabling the Transitional Federal Government (TFG) to assert greater authority, had not brought a solution. Instead it had created a new dynamic in Somalia's 17 years of stateless turmoil, with a growing insurgency by jihadist and other militant groups against the TFG and Ethiopian forces. It was equally clear that any apparent threat to international security had not been lessened by the ousting of the short-lived Islamic Courts regime, which exercised control in much of central and southern Somalia in the second half of 2006, and that the internal situation was worse than before.

A sustained Islamist insurgent campaign was marked by bouts of fighting in the capital Mogadishu and an unrelenting succession of bombings, kidnappings and assassinations. Somali civil servants, journalists, African peacekeepers and humanitarian workers were among the targets. Retaliatory operations caused heavy casualties. Some 2m Somalis, more than a fifth of the population, were reckoned to be in need of assistance, but relief work was badly disrupted. Hardship was aggravated by an exceptionally harsh dry season in the first months of 2008, driving some residents who had fled the capital to return.

Ethiopian troops, who had been expected to leave quickly after their decisive intervention in December 2006, were still engaged in Somalia well over a year later. An under-strength AU force, AMISOM, authorised by the UN as an interim mission, also had its stay extended much longer than planned. Deployment stalled after the arrival of the first Ugandan contingents. Short of funding and equipment, AMISOM looked unlikely to achieve much more than half its planned strength of 8,000.

International officials dealing with Somalia mostly stayed outside the country, with diminishing access to reliable information. While the insurgency attracted foreign fighters and outside support, the extent of this external involvement may have been exaggerated. Certainly, the presence and sometimes ruthless conduct of Ethiopian troops solidified resistance. After some of the worst fighting of recent years in April 2007, further heavy clashes took place in November, less widespread but by all accounts more vicious. In the following months, insurgents strengthened their control in the south, around Kismayo. Relative security in the semi-autonomous Puntland region of the north showed signs of crumbling, while a border dispute flared up again with Somaliland, the self-governing but internationally unrecognised state in the northwest. In March and April 2008, more fierce battles broke out in Mogadishu, with shell and mortar fire causing dozens of civilian deaths.

Pressure was building up at the UN for more decisive action. With little sign of willingness to countenance a full-scale peace-enforcement exercise, Secretary-General Ban Ki Moon put forward the idea that a 'coalition of the willing' might field a short-term force to cover an Ethiopian withdrawal. In March he presented a list of phased contingency plans involving up to 28,500 peacekeeping troops and police. But this was impractical in view of the absence of any commitments to peace, and in light of the demands of other large peacekeeping operations and previous experience in Somalia 15 years ago, when an even larger US-led task force and a major UN deployment both failed.

Discussion centred instead on ways of strengthening AMISOM, increasing the UN's civilian presence and protecting shipping from Somalia-based pirates through UN-authorised patrols. After three attacks on vessels contracted by the UN's World Food Programme, France started to provide naval escorts for food-aid shipments in late 2007, a task subsequently taken up by Denmark and the Netherlands. The piracy issue gained prominence in April with the seizure of a French luxury charter yacht. After payment of ransom to free the 30 crew members, French commandos captured six of the men believed to have taken part in the attack in an elaborately planned raid.

UN-sponsored talks began in Djibouti in May aimed at promoting reconciliation between the TFG and the opposition Alliance for the Re-liberation of Somalia, a coalition formed in the Eritrean capital Asmara between the Islamic Courts, ex-parliamentarians and Somali diaspora leaders. International diplomats pinned their hopes on the open stance taken by the TFG's new prime minister, Nur Adde, a former humanitarian administrator appointed in November 2007. But prospects for substantive negotiations were fragile. A key issue will be how to deal with the jihadist insurgent group al-Shabaab, the Islamic Courts' former youth wing, which has distanced itself from the Asmara-based opposition. The group increased its impact in early 2008 with a series of hit-and-run operations on small towns. In late February the United States placed it on its list of designated foreign terrorist organisations, citing alleged links to al-Qaeda. US forces meanwhile continued with periodic air-strikes, begun in early 2007, aimed at a small number of 'high value terrorist targets'. After a sea-launched missile strike in Puntland in June 2007, and another in the far south in March 2008, an attack in central Somalia in May killed the al-Shabaab military commander Aden Hashi Ayro.

With wide international agreement on the need to end Ethiopia's military involvement, the challenge was how to arrange a gradual withdrawal without jeopardising the TFG's survival. Uncertainties in the coming months included the approach to be taken by the next US administration, and the possible succession to the TFG's ailing hard-line president, Abdullahi Yusuf Ahmed. It was also becoming increasingly clear that elections planned for late 2009 would be impracticable.

Congo's elusive peace

Pockets of conflict in the DRC continued into 2008, six years after the country's last civil war was formally brought to an end, despite the efforts of a large and costly UN peacekeeping mission. Concentrated in the combustible eastern provinces of North and South Kivu, on the borders of Uganda, Rwanda and Burundi, the fighting showed up failures in the implementation of peace arrangements, especially with respect to disarmament and the integration of forces into a unified national army.

The fighting involved forces aligned with the region's Rwandan-origin ethnic Tutsi community under the renegade Congolese general Laurent Nkunda; Rwandan Hutu rebel forces made up largely of ex-army soldiers and extremist militias who crossed the border after Rwanda's 1994 genocide; Congolese government forces; and local Mayi-Mayi militias. This cauldron of internal conflict with external components has been kept on the boil by competition for resources and the ability of armed groups to finance themselves through illegal exploitation of timber and minerals.

The DRC represents an important precedent for the UN in the handling of peace enforcement in complex intra-state conflicts. As requirements build up for peacekeepers to be deployed elsewhere, it will also be a test of the UN's capacity to follow through with support after completion of a post-war political transition, which officially ended in the DRC with elections in 2006. The MONUC mission, totalling 18,000 troops and police, will be exceeded in size only by the new Darfur operation. Its presence, as well as enabling the 2006 elections to take place, undoubtedly reduced the extent of renewed fighting and helped facilitate aid. But the mission has been overstretched and has not fulfilled its mandate to protect civilians under imminent threat of violence. Its reputation has been damaged by allegations of smuggling and sexual misconduct. In providing support for government forces in the east, it could risk being sucked into a domestic conflict.

An agreement between the government and Nkunda in early 2007 to merge his 4,000 or so troops into the national army, Forces Armées de la République Démocratique du Congo (FARDC), proved to be defective, since Nkunda's units remained under his commanders' control. Heavy fighting began again when newly formed mixed brigades launched offensives against the largely Rwandan Hutu fighters of the Democratic Forces for the Liberation of Rwanda (FDLR), numbering about 6,000. There were subsequent confrontations involving troops loyal to Nkunda, which continued despite UN attempts to impose a ceasefire in September. Violence during the year was reckoned to have caused the fresh displacement of 375,000 people in North Kivu alone.

The danger of wider regional conflict was reduced, however, by improvement in relations between the DRC and Rwanda. Under international pressure for a peaceful solution, the DRC suspended operations against Nkunda's troops in October, and a deadline for them to disarm was relaxed. At a UN-brokered agreement in Nairobi in November the DRC, accused of collaborating with the FDLR, committed itself to disarming the force and repatriating members to Rwanda, while Rwanda, under suspicion of backing Nkunda, pledged to stop rebel groups in the DRC from receiving cross-border support.

After further clashes the FARDC, with logistical assistance from MONUC, launched a drive against a strategic Nkunda base, but only temporarily succeeded in dislodging his forces. Declaration of a ceasefire by Nkunda opened the way to talks in January 2008 in the border city of Goma, sponsored by the United States, EU and AU. These produced a deal committing the DRC government and 22 Congolese factions from the two provinces, including Nkunda's, to a full ceasefire, disarmament of non-state militias, demobilisation of fighters or their absorption into the FARDC alongside soldiers of different ethnic groups, and adherence to international humanitarian and human-rights law. The FDLR was not party to the talks. The deal included limited amnesty for rebel groups but left open the question of possible war-crimes charges. It also provided for the supervised return of Congolese refugees from Tanzania and other neighbouring countries. Although the agreement was hailed as a breakthrough, there were further clashes, discouraging the return of displaced populations. The situation looked likely to remain precarious.

West Africa and Nigerian oil unrest

West Africa was more at peace in the past year that at any time since the end of the 1980s. The epidemic of bloody civil conflicts in coastal states subsided, even if the potential for further outbreaks remained.

Recent UN peacekeeping missions succeeded in creating more secure environments in which to consolidate democratic institutions. But the combination of large numbers of former combatants, broken-down infrastructure and services and a shortage of formal sector jobs still posed considerable risks. Escalating food costs created an additional focus of discontent in a number of countries in the region in 2008.

Côte d'Ivoire has been spared serious fighting since late 2004. The presence of French, West African and UN peacekeepers was crucial in holding the country back from catastrophe. A peace deal brokered by neighbouring Burkina Faso in March 2007 led to the dismantling of the buffer zone between the country's rebel-controlled northern half and the south. An airport rocket attack in June 2007 against former rebel leader and current prime minister Guillaume Soro failed to derail the process. A presidential election, originally due at the end of President Laurent Gbagbo's mandate in October 2005, was scheduled for June this year, but then postponed again to November. Gbagbo insisted that disarmament be completed first, but the process was slow.

In Liberia, the UN presence was provisionally set to be reduced from more than 14,000 to below 10,000 in 2010, ahead of elections the following year. President Ellen Johnson-Sirleaf was credited with making progress on better governance, but much remained to be done to secure sustainable peace throughout the country.

In Sierra Leone, opposition candidate Ernest Bai Koroma won a run-off vote for the presidency in September 2007, in the first elections conducted without support from peacekeepers since the country's civil war ended in 2002. In a decisive turnaround, his All People's Congress party also took control of parliament. Observers said they found irregularities in the vote, but not enough to affect the outcome. Tension meanwhile revived in neighbouring Guinea after a political deal last year, amidst frustration over economic conditions and the slow pace of reform.

Despite a change of approach under Nigeria's President Umaru Yar'Adua, who took office in May 2007, one of the most intractable of West Africa's problems remained oil-related violence affecting that country. After particularly shoddy elections, Yar'Adua faced the task of establishing his government's authority and legitimacy, not least in the Niger Delta region, Africa's largest oil-production zone and source of almost all Nigeria's export earnings. Although there were some signs of slackening in the rhythm of attacks, unrest in the delta contributed to record oil prices in early 2008, in a market highly sensitive to any disruption in supply. Indeed, the loss of Nigerian crude reaching the market-place was not compensated for by the amount of increase in Saudi oil production in June 2008.

The spectre of an election re-run was lifted when a special tribunal rejected the opposition case in February 2008, although a lengthy appeal process was expected. Yar'Adua took steps to make government more accountable with the announcement of a new body to monitor state-sector transactions. Charges against a series of prominent figures, including at least eight former state governors and two former health ministers, helped ease concern that the government might be relaxing its anti-corruption drive. Yar'Adua also moved to overhaul oil and gas policies, rescinding pre-election contracts for the privatisation of refineries and ordering a revamp of the monolithic Nigerian National Oil Corporation.

Defusing tensions in the Niger Delta was clearly a priority. With Vice-President Goodluck Jonathan (who, like most of the militants, was a member of the Ijaw ethnic group), Yar'Adua made progress in building dialogue with local organisations. Two high-profile Ijaw leaders were released from jail, and a structure of peace and conflict resolution committees was set up. Yar'Adua's con-ciliatory approach contrasted with the brusque style of his predecessor Olusegun Obasanjo. But there are no easy solutions to violence in the region, which arises from a combination of criminality, corrupt politics and genuine grievances over access to revenues and environmental degradation. Oil operations have been subject to bombings, sabotage, hostage-taking and large-scale theft of crude oil. Production has been curtailed by about a fifth over the past two years.

The situation has been complicated by a proliferation of armed groups and 'cults', used by local politicians as election-time private armies. In July and August 2007 fierce fighting in Port Harcourt between rival gangs armed with automatic weapons and rocket-propelled grenades caused dozens of deaths, prompting the authorities to deploy a heavy security presence. The Movement for the Emancipation of the Niger Delta, which gained prominence in 2006, sus-pended attacks after Yar'Adua's election. But it resumed its campaign after one of its leaders, Henry Okah, was arrested with an associate in Angola. The two were handed over to Nigeria in February to face treason and terrorism charges. While hostage incidents involving foreigners have become less frequent, partly reflecting the fact that many expatriates have left the region, repeated attacks have been made on installations of Royal Dutch Shell and other international oil companies, as well as government buildings. Pipelines, oil terminals and ships continued to be targeted, and there were threats of attacks beyond the delta. In December the government said losses due to militant attacks had reached 500,000 barrels a day, with another 400,000 due too 'technical disruptions', for a total of 30% of potential production. At the same time, Nigerian military authorities were accused of heavy-handed action by its Joint Task Force in the region. With no short-term solutions available, the best prospect would appear to be for the violence to be contained at a lower level while more serious efforts are devoted to the region's development needs.

Radicalisation in the Maghreb

Beginning in 2006, North Africa in general, and Algeria in particular, suffered a resurgence of Islamist suicide terrorism. There appeared to be no serious threat to the regimes in the region, which exercise rigid control over state security, and broad-based popular uprisings such as the one that gripped Algeria in the 1990s are highly unlikely. But Algerians' alienation from formal politics and high unemployment may provide the country's numerically diminished but increasingly aggressive Islamists with opportunities for expansion into neighbouring Tunisia, Morocco and Libya. Such a development would be of considerable strategic concern for several reasons.

First, political and economic stasis in Algeria, Morocco and Tunisia – the Maghreb proper – present a fertile political opportunity to al-Qaeda to generate a new wave of radicalisation. Secondly, pre-existing terrorist infrastructure and a recent history of extreme Islamist political violence provide ready operational and cultural toeholds for a terrorist revival, particularly in Algeria. Thirdly, North Africa's location on Europe's southern flank could portend an accelerated emigration of experienced terrorists to Europe, which in turn could facilitate direct terrorist attacks there and the re-establishment of Europe as a recruiting, planning and staging platform for attacks on the United States. Those North Africans seeking to flee terrorism and instability could also opt for illegal migration to Europe, adding to demographic and economic pressures there. Finally, an enlarging trend of political violence in the Maghreb would sap confidence in a region trying to attract investors, boost regional trade and provide its population with prospects of stability and prosperity.

Algeria: setting the tone

In April 2004, Algerian President Abdelaziz Bouteflika was re-elected with 85% of the popular vote. Algeria's vicious civil war between Islamists and secularists, which had claimed up to 200,000 lives starting in 1992, when ruthless army-supported rulers aborted legislative elections that a radical Islamic party was about to win, appeared to have simmered down to a manageable level, as the government induced the disarming of tens of thousands of rebels with repeated amnesties. With oil prices approaching the $50 a barrel level in mid 2004 and rising to over $100 a barrel by 2008, Algeria's macroeconomic profile improved. By the same token, oil and gas revenues allowed the Algerian government to bankroll muscular police and army forces that ensure regime security. Yet the country's microeconomic condition remained stagnant, and left ordinary Algerians struggling for basic necessities.

Most Algerians believed that Bouteflika's election merely consolidated the power of a secretive military elite that has dominated Algerian government since the country's independence from France in 1962. The Algerian press, enterprising and forward-leaning by Arab standards, considered Bouteflika a virtual autocrat. While daily violence in Algeria declined and terrorist attacks diminished following the killing and capture of leading figures of the Salafist Group for Preaching and Combat (GSPC) – a several-hundred-strong offshoot, formed in 1998, of the Armed Islamic Group that spearheaded the civil war in the 1990s – the Algerian government's human-rights record remained dismal. Arbitrary arrests, prolonged incommunicado detentions, excessive use of force, extra-judicial killings, torture and official impunity all appeared to be standard operating procedure for the regime, as did the suppression of free speech, assembly and political activity. In 2005, al-Jazeera's Algiers bureau was closed after airing reports that prisoners deemed 'threats to national security' had disappeared.

Although Islamists have been the only group in Algeria and elsewhere in the Maghreb cohesive enough to mobilise – albeit often violently – to challenge the authoritarian political order, signs of broader-based resistance have begun to emerge. In February 2008, in response to Bouteflika's initiative to amend Article 74 of the Algerian constitution (which provides that a president may only renew his term once) to allow him to serve a third term, a group of former members of parliament, political activists, academics, professionals and journalists published online and in print a petition opposing the proposal. The published statement indicated that they considered it an undemocratic attempt to establish a 'presidency-for-life' and return to a one-party political system, and offered a bleak future of widespread arrests, torture, deteriorating purchasing power, illegal immigration and suicide under such a regime. The signatories called on all citizens to join the cause, saying that 'every Algerian who opposes unilateral rule should join their efforts in order to protect democratic freedoms'. The government, they said, should instead address day-to-day problems facing citizens, such as declining purchasing power and stagnating economic growth.

At the same time, Islamists in Algeria were stimulated by outside developments. Before the US-led invasion of Iraq, North African Islamist terrorist groups distanced themselves from al-Qaeda because it remained unclear that fighting the United States would dislodge secular regimes in the region. The invasion of Iraq, however, convinced younger leaders that Osama bin Laden's portrayal of a longstanding Western conspiracy to humiliate and subjugate Muslims was valid. In Algeria, the nearly flattened GSPC again had a cause célèbre to spur recruitment, which was also aided by sustained violence and lack of political progress in the Israeli–Palestinian conflict. Some enlistees were promised transport to Iraq to fight Americans, while others were told that the Algerian regime was a puppet of the power responsible for the Abu Ghraib prison abuses in Iraq. In September 2006, on the fifth anniversary of the 11 September attacks, the al-Qaeda leadership designated the Algeria-based GSPC its representative in North Africa. The GSPC had considerable institutional knowledge and international experience and ambitions, having been linked to planned attacks in France on the Paris Metro, Orly Airport and the headquarters of the Direction de la Surveillance du Territoire (France's domestic intelligence agency), and in Italy on Milan's police headquarters and the Basilica of San Petronio (which depicts Muhammad burning in hell) in Bologna. It also claimed responsibility for the April 2002 bombing of a synagogue on the Tunisian island of Djerba.

In January 2007, the GCSP rebranded itself 'al-Qaeda in the Islamic Maghreb' (AQIM). The following month, the group claimed credit for seven bombs that exploded in the Kabylia region of eastern Algeria, killing six people. In April 2007, AQIM killed 30 people in bomb attacks on government buildings in Algiers. Attacks subsequently occurred on buses carrying foreign oil workers, American diplomats and Algerian soldiers. In September 2007, a suicide-bomb attack was made on Bouteflika's motorcade in Batna. The president was not injured, but 20 others died. Two days later, a car bomb killed more than 30 people at a coast-guard barracks in the town of Dellys. Then, on 24 December 2007, suspected AQIM operatives shot dead four French tourists, two of them children, in southern Mauritania. In February 2008, the group attacked the Israeli Embassy in Nouakchott, Mauritania's capital, wounding three people. Security concerns prompted the cancellation of the Dakar Rally for automobiles and motorcycles, which traditionally crosses the Sahara through Mauritania, for the first time in its 30-year history.

AQIM's plan to target American and British embassies across the region was thwarted in January 2007 in a series of bloody enforcement operations in Tunisia, in which a dozen terrorists and two Tunisian policemen were killed and another 15 terrorists captured. But hope, or perception, that the group was a flash in the pan appeared dubious, given that in 2007 North Africa was the largest regional source of foreign jihadists (some 40%) in Iraq, and major attacks in Algeria remained frequent. Furthermore, intelligence officials from North Africa, Europe and the United States agreed that AQIM was establishing links with other terrorist groups in Morocco, Nigeria, Mauritania and Tunisia, sending jihadists into Iraq, and dispatching them to their home countries. AQIM is believed to comprise 600–800 fighters across North Africa and Europe. In April 2008 Ayman al-Zawahiri, al-Qaeda's second-in-command, characterised the group's purpose in targeting civilians in Algeria as efforts to secure the lives and property of Algerian citizens and liberate Algerians from 'America, France and the children of France'. This statement, which appeared on a jihadist website, echoed AQIM's anti-French rhetoric and seemed to harmonise the GSPC's anti-colonial objectives and al-Qaeda's broader anti-Western and anti-Israeli ones.

The establishment of AQIM thus appeared to consolidate a trend of al-Qaeda-linked radicalisation in the Maghreb initiated by the formation of the Moroccan Islamic Combatant Group (GICM), which was involved in the Casablanca suicide bombings in May 2003 and the Madrid bombings of March 2004. A police raid on Islamist militants in Morocco in summer 2006 uncovered documents contemplating an operational union among the GSPC, the GICM and several Tunisian groups. Both AQIM and the GICM pose significant security threats not only to North Africa but also to Europe – the GICM to Spain, where Muslims are mainly of Moroccan origin, AQIM to France, where Muslims are predominantly of Algerian lineage, and to a lesser extent Italy, to which a large number of Algerians have emigrated in the past decade.

Illiberal politics elsewhere
The widening disassociation between political leaders in the Maghreb and their putative constituents has loomed as a threat to political stability in the region for the last several years. Such concerns were reinforced in 2007 by the suicide bombings in Algeria and record low turnouts of 35% and 37% in Algerian and Moroccan parliamentary elections, respectively. There are major political and economic differences among North African countries. Libya's 30-year-old no-party system of popular rule is unique, Morocco's royal dynasty has ruled for four centuries, and army-backed leaders have been the norm in Algeria for 45 years. Algeria and Libya have oil and gas but are otherwise economically weak. Morocco and Tunisia lack energy resources, but have cultivated diversified private sectors to which foreign investors have warmed. These differences make the similarities all the more striking: high unemployment, low economic productivity, curbs on political participation, poor education, bureaucratic inefficiency and negligible levels of regional and international trade prevail throughout the region. Earlier in the decade, prospects in the Maghreb appeared far better. Modernising social reforms in Morocco and the removal of Western sanctions on Libya were salutary, and hinted that the region was heading for stability.

Momentum towards reform, however, has proved unsustainable. Illiberal authoritarian governments, as weak as they are in terms of economic fundamentals, still enjoy considerable political autonomy. While North African economies under-perform and fail to take advantage of human and material resources, the overall fiscal health of Algeria, Morocco and Tunisia is good enough to nourish robust security apparatuses. The Maghreb ranked noticeably above average in the proportion of GDP spent on security, approaching 5% in 2000 against a world average of 3.8%. Rentier income derived from oil and gas in Algeria and Libya continued to enable the regimes to maintain their coercive apparatuses. While Morocco and Tunisia lack natural resources in large enough quantities to meet the state's financial demands, foreign aid, tourism revenues and remittances from expatriates serve the same function in allowing the state to ensure regime security through generous security-sector expenditures.

Furthermore, the Algerian and Libyan governments have suppressed dissent by distributing oil and gas revenues among the broader population. Governments without such economic inducements at their disposal use other means. In Morocco, although the monarchy enjoys wide popular support and King Mohammed VI is ostensibly a modern political reformer, a tradition of corruption and of apparently rigged elections has bred voter apathy. Prime Minister Driss Jettou is seen as obeisant to the king and royal-appointed technocrats who wield the real political power. Tunisia has North Africa's best-educated population and largest middle class, but human-rights groups assert that the government runs a de facto police state. Tunisian President Zine al-Abidine Ben Ali had the Tunisian constitution amended so he could run for a fourth term in October 2004 following his 99% victories in 1989, 1994 and 1999. Tunisia's security apparatus, once small by Arab standards, has ballooned under Ben Ali. Libyan President Muammar Gadhafi, who has ruled the country since wresting power in a 1969 coup, is slowly loosening its statist economy but has indicated that political reform will not occur on his watch. Maghrebi governments all reject a legitimate role in government for Islamist groups – a stance that arguably provokes Islamists into violence as the only way of gaining a voice in the political process. However, Islamist groups are, for the most part, the only purposefully mobilised bodies in the region, which means that quick democratisation would pose the substantial risk of their elevation to power.

Perverse international interest

Intense concern about the Maghreb as an incubator of terrorists preceded the inception of AQIM, dating back to the 11 September attacks if not before. Counter-terrorism and access to hydrocarbons became the two key strategic interests justifying close foreign involvement with existing army-backed regimes in Algeria, Morocco and Tunisia. The United States' Pan Sahel Initiative, succeeded by the even more substantial Trans-Sahara Counterterrorism Initiative in 2005, was originally conceived by State Department planners in 2002 as a way of bolstering Sahelian armed forces against the terrorist threat. In its implementation, however, it became a broader vehicle for cracking down on al-Qaeda's penetration of the Sahel and North Africa via groups like the GSPC.

Washington's counter-terrorism interest in southern Algeria fits awkwardly with Bouteflika's domestic political imperative of maintaining a robust authoritarian state. Thus, the United States has courted the once-isolated Algiers as an ally in the 'war on terror'. For example, almost $600,000 in funding for US-based training of Algerian military officers under the International Military Education and Training (IMET) programme was provided in 2003, compared to only $30,000 in 2002. In the first four years after 11 September, Algeria received more than ten times the total amount of military assistance from the United States that it received in the previous 12 years. In 2002–06, US military assistance (including IMET and foreign military financing) to Algeria totalled about $2m, compared to roughly $500,000 in 1997–2001. US military sales (foreign military sales plus direct commercial sales) during the same periods were $600m and zero, respectively. While such American policies aimed to produce greater global security, they also reinforced the authoritarian state and rendered it even less inclined to respond to popular demands for more equitable and democratic governance, and antagonised Islamists.

Even more extensive American support was extended to Morocco and Tunisia, which were slated to receive $3.95m and $3.56m, respectively, in US military assistance in FY2008. Furthermore, in June 2004 the United States granted Morocco the status of 'major non-NATO ally' and signed a free-trade agreement with Rabat. Other negative effects of increased US and other international military, political and economic support for the three Maghrebi countries included crackdowns on press freedoms, heightened human-rights violations on the pretext of anti-terrorist security, and a general deterioration of political and civil rights. The recent experience of Egypt and Saudi Arabia – and indeed that of Algeria in the 1990s – demonstrates that such corroded political environments yield the most zealous terrorist recruits.

Containment and slow reform

The strong security apparatuses of the regimes in the Maghreb can probably contain terrorism, but cannot eliminate its deeper causes; indeed, they constitute one such cause themselves. Thus, political reform remains key to any thoroughgoing counter-terrorism effort. No fundamental political transition to democracy from authoritarianism is likely to occur in any of the three Maghrebi countries in the medium term. Nevertheless, the recent protests in Algeria over the attempt to amend the constitution suggest that a fairly energetic civil society may be emerging slowly, and over the longer term may challenge illiberal regimes to give way to the evolution of more equitable systems. In the meantime, active diplomacy on the part of the United States and Europe to encourage incremental political reform that might dampen the impulse towards radicalisation without unduly sacrificing security would be in order. Washington, for its part, could gently encourage – perhaps by way of conditions attached to security assistance – the establishment of independent political parties, the institutionalisation of truly representative legislative bodies, and the application of the rule of law. European capitals could do the same in their bilateral political and economic relationships with North African governments.

In the absence of such efforts there is no reason to believe that the Maghreb's robust authoritarianism – and hence its hospitableness to Islamist impulses – will recede. At the same time, the people of the Maghreb – secular, moderate or Islamist – tend to be sensitive to bilateral European involvement in their countries and region as a vestige of colonial oppression, and to American insinuations into their national and regional affairs as harbingers of neo-colonial control. Filtering political and economic influence through multilateral forums in which North African capitals have an equal place at the table would make such influence less inflammatory. In that light, it may be fortuitous that worries about the democratic deficit in North Africa partly prompted Sarkozy's rather vague proposal, first mooted in a February 2007 campaign speech, for a Mediterranean Union to coordinate government activities related to migration, terrorism and economic development. This idea, however, was modified in the face of opposition from other countries, and is likely to be built on the existing Barcelona Process, also known as the Euro-Mediterranean Partnership, which includes all EU members as well as states bordering the Mediterranean. A focus on economic and business-orientated initiatives makes this body attractive to the authoritarian Arab regimes, though Israel's prospective participation in Sarkozy's concept of a Mediterranean Union. However, human-rights organisations are concerned that opt-out provisions will marginalise democracy and rule-of-law requirements. Although economic reform is integral to tamping down Islamist radicalisation and terrorism in southern Europe and North Africa, so too is political reform. Unless the two are combined, economic advantages may continue primarily to benefit groups close to the political elite, as opposed to populations at large, which would therefore remain rich recruiting grounds for jihadist groups.

AFRICOM and US Regional Diplomacy

The past year saw the development of Africa Command (AFRICOM), the US military's new regional combatant command, first instituted in February 2007. Previously, responsibility for the continent had been split between European

Command (EUCOM), Central Command (CENTCOM, responsible the Middle East/Persian Gulf region) and Pacific Command (PACOM), each of which regarded Africa as only marginally important. Creation of the new command stemmed from a confluence of American interests: balancing China's strategic interest in the continent, containing Islamic radicalism and protecting non-Middle East oil supplies.

AFRICOM has a very small footprint in terms of military operations, and a substantial State Department staff, including a civilian deputy commander. From a military standpoint, its emphasis will be on prevention and preparation through building African military capacity, rather than reaction by the US military to regional crises. On the diplomatic front, Washington's aim is to make AFRICOM part of an integrated inter-agency effort to bring benefits to Africa, including humanitarian assistance, development and improved defence infrastructure, and to encourage enlightened and enterprising African leadership. This would be done especially through the use of 'non-kinetic' military resources such as command, control and communication assets, engineering capabilities and public-health expertise.

AFRICOM's creation followed a series of US military activities around Africa. US Marines spearheaded what became a successful UN peacekeeping and state-building effort in Liberia in 2003. EUCOM had established forward-operating locations along Africa's west coast. Through NATO, the US Air Force provided logistical support for relief efforts in Darfur. After 11 September 2001, American train-and-equip programmes in most African countries gathered momentum. And the US special-operations forces of the 2,000-strong Combined Joint Task Force–Horn of Africa (CJTF–HOA) based in Djibouti collected intelligence, bolstered regional governments' internal security capabilities and civic programmes, and occasionally took direct action against terrorists.

These activities were on a small scale. However, some American actions that indicated heightened military involvement seemed less benign – and potentially ominous – to Africans. Most important among these was the operation undertaken in January 2007 by US-trained Ethiopian troops, assisted by a few small US special-operations advisory units from CJTF–HOA, to help Somalia's secular government in exile to oust the Islamic Courts movement, which had taken de facto control of southern Somalia six months earlier. Subsequently, several US attacks on suspected terrorist targets in Somalia with AC-130 gunships claimed civilian casualties. This use of CJTF–HOA, which is likely to fall under AFRICOM's command, was an early example of a reconfiguring of US ground forces to devote more resources to small, agile special-operations units suitable for discreetly combating terrorists and dramatically expanding the remit of Special Operations Command. But while tactically effective in supporting Ethiopian troops, it appeared to intensify the determination of Somali

Islamists to regain control of the country. CJTF–HOA has made some Africans, both officials and the wider population, nervous about the nature and extent of prospective US military activities on the continent. This apprehension was not helped by the manner of Washington's announcement of plans for AFRICOM at the end of 2006, when the Defense Department suggested it would be establishing military bases as it set up the new command, then backed off and characterised AFRICOM as a mere bureaucratic reform. The State Department, meanwhile, suggested that AFRICOM could signal a bold new policy focus on Africa.

The United States' new attention to Africa sprang from several motivations. It has a strategic interest in protecting access to rich reserves of sub-Saharan oil and gas, mainly in the vicinity of the Gulf of Guinea, as part of its effort to reduce dependence on unstable Middle East suppliers. Sub-Saharan Africa accounts for about 15% of US oil imports. By 2010, oil production from Angola, Equatorial Guinea, Chad and South Africa could double to over 10m barrels per day, depending on the pace of Western investments, and Africa's share of US oil imports could rise to 20%. Furthermore, sub-Saharan Africa has entered the early stages of a geopolitical contest for hydrocarbons and other economic and political benefits between the United States and China. China's primary interests in Africa are strategic rather than ideological – namely, to establish resource security, trade and investment opportunities, and diplomatic legitimacy. China's fast-growing economy is increasingly thirsty for foreign oil, gets 28% of its imported oil from Africa, and has forged strong ties with regimes including those in Sudan and Zimbabwe.

Islamic radicalism has also been on the rise in countries such as Nigeria and Somalia. Because weak states are highly susceptible to becoming terrorist havens, preventing jihadist infiltration of weak or failed states is a broad US strategic imperative. There are more weak and failed states – a partial list would include Somalia, Sudan and Zimbabwe – in sub-Saharan Africa than in any other region in the world. The United States and its partners have provided considerable help in training and financial support to cooperative governments in East Africa and the Horn (under the East Africa Counterterrorism Initiative) and predominantly Muslim Chad, Mali, Mauritania and Niger in north-central Africa (under the Trans-Sahara Counterterrorism Initiative). AFRICOM is intended to function as a coordinating mechanism for these efforts.

The United States, in common with other industrialised nations, has also felt a duty to help alleviate chronic problems such as poverty and disease (HIV/AIDS in particular) throughout the continent. At the press conference announcing AFRICOM's creation, a Pentagon spokesman indicated that many of its missions would be non-coercive, such as humanitarian assistance and disaster relief, and that the command would generally be geared for prevention and stability.

Although AFRICOM's physical presence on the continent is intended to be small and its military assets relatively light – its budget for FY2009 is modest, in the $300m range – the mixed signals given by its official portrayals stoked rising fears of US 'militarisation' of its relationship with Africa and its 'recolonisation' of the continent. Only Liberia offered to host AFRICOM's headquarters. The South African Development Community (SADC) voted expressly not to do so. In December 2007, Nigeria officially rejected Washington's request to host a regional AFRICOM headquarters and encouraged other African nations to follow its lead. Ghana, traditionally the most pro-American country in West Africa, promptly followed Nigeria's lead. Kenya and perhaps Senegal were left as the default choices. Until an African headquarters site is agreed on, AFRICOM will operate out of the headquarters of EUCOM in Stuttgart, Germany. As of spring 2008, the resistance of African governments to AFRICOM appeared to be receding substantially. But the unease among African populations and governments is unlikely to disappear.

Given African concern about ground-based troops, inherently less intrusive maritime initiatives such as the Africa Partnership Station (APS) take on new importance. The APS is part of the US Navy's Global Fleet Station (GFS) programme, whereby American ships establish a relatively light and mobile presence in various parts of the world and provide several types of assistance to local people and institutions. In South America, the GFS enterprise has focused fairly narrowly on humanitarian assistance. The APS concept is broader, and builds on a recently refined strategic concept of maritime safety and security. The operational objective is to improve African naval capabilities in four main areas: maritime domain awareness; military professionalism; technical infrastructure; and operational response. The strategic objective is to render African nations at once self-sufficient in securing the maritime domain and favourably aligned with the United States by virtue of relationships established and cultivated through the execution of the APS itself, which will also come under AFRICOM's authority.

The APS's lead element is the USS *Fort McHenry*, a 186m amphibious landing ship. Other navy ships involved include the high-speed vessel *Swift*, a 98m catamaran originally tagged for mine warfare and for developing littoral combat concepts, and the USS *Annapolis*, a nuclear attack submarine. The APS's first tour began in November 2007 in Senegal and ended there in April 2008. The other countries visited were Cameroon, Gabon, Ghana, Liberia, and São Tomé and Príncipe. In each country, the US Navy (and, for some courses, the US Coast Guard) conducted compressed training programmes in areas ranging from tactical tasks such as sentry duty and search-and-seizure to aspects of security-sector reform like maritime law. Some training took place on board the *Fort McHenry*, and some occurred on shore at nearby naval bases and other military facilities of the host nation. In all, the navy offered courses in 13 subjects to roughly 1,800 students drawn from the navies and coast guards of the six countries visited. Although there were some shortfalls in implementation, the APS got a generally enthusiastic reception from African military officers, civilian officials and ordinary citizens. The navy plans to improve and enhance the programme.

In spite of its emphasis on 'non-kinetic' activities and conflict prevention, some US ground-based military efforts in Africa may be unavoidable. Given the ignominy of its inaction in Rwanda during the 1994 genocide and its slender contribution to the international response to Darfur, the United States is unlikely to invariably stay its hand with respect to direct and urgent military needs, such as preserving access to hydrocarbons or quelling large-scale ethnic violence in failing states. It is also possible that, with AFRICOM in place, the United States will take a bigger role in peace enforcement or peacekeeping operations. There remains an urgent need for troops and related capacity in countries such as the DRC, Somalia and Sudan, where African contingents have been either insufficient or lacked the clout to execute a robust mandate. But to maintain positive relationships with African partners, the United States would have to undertake military ground operations through the UN rather than unilaterally, and ideally in consultation with the AU. AFRICOM has a strong diplomatic component and is establishing liaisons with organisations such as the AU and ECOWAS; it provides a suitable bureaucratic and diplomatic mechanism for conducting diplomatic and operational relationships with these bodies. By increasing funding for foreign military financing, international military education and training, and peacekeeping operations through AFRICOM, the United States could at once advance its objective of building African military capacity, improve interoperability that would be critical for combined peacekeeping deployments, and validate its intention to help Africans to help themselves. With these adjustments in policy and public diplomacy, AFRICOM should become more palatable than it has initially been to African governments – including Nigeria, the ranking regional power in the Gulf of Guinea – and ultimately win their approval, or at least acquiescence.

Kenya's Political Crisis

The turmoil in the aftermath of Kenya's elections in December 2007 was the worst the country experienced since independence from Britain in 1963. The violence, which claimed more than 1,200 lives, widened existing ethnic divisions, inflicted lasting damage on social cohesion, and may not yet have burnt itself out.

This was a political crisis that found expression in the exploitation of long-standing tribal grievances. In a remorseless battle for control of a government system flawed by patronage and graft, the elections were at best grossly misman-aged, and at worst stolen. The aftermath revealed dire deficiencies in internal intelligence and policing. The violence and chaos were all the more striking because of Kenya's standing as East Africa's economic hub and best-functioning state, with relatively strong institutions and a record of stability. It has also been an important ally for the United States in its counter-terrorism strategy. The post-election upheaval therefore had a broader effect on Africa's international reputation, undermining confidence in the ability of countries such as Kenya to lead by example.

The December elections were the fourth since Kenya's return to multi-party politics and, up to the final stages of vote-counting, the most openly com-petitive. President Mwai Kibaki's triumphant victory five years earlier, which overturned almost four decades of rule by the Kenya African National Union (KANU), had brought a climate of greater freedom and economic hope. Until mid 2007 he seemed to be well placed for a second win, in spite of the sluggish-ness of promised reforms, evidence of continued systemic corruption, and his own remoteness. Having captured 62% of the vote in 2002, he presided over steady economic recovery, with annual growth rising to about 7%, and retained all the levers of centralised power. In 2005, voters inflicted a stinging referendum defeat, rejecting a watered-down proposal for a new constitution. However, in a shifting political landscape of fickle alliances, the opposition appeared too disu-nited to repeat this victory in general elections.

Opposition challenge

Opinion polls changed sharply after Raila Odinga's selection as the presidential candidate of the Orange Democratic Movement (ODM), the party that formed around the 'No' campaign in the constitutional referendum. Odinga had run for president ten years earlier. Like his prominent politician father, he could count on solid backing from the large Luo ethnic community, based near Lake Victoria in southwest Kenya. In 2002 he lent vital support to Kibaki's presidential bid on the understanding that he would get a new prime minister's post, but the deal never materialised and the two fell out.

Two rivals for the opposition candidacy went their own ways. Stephen Kalonzo Musyoka, a former foreign minister, stood separately for an ODM splin-ter party, while Uhuru Kenyatta, the defeated KANU candidate in 2002, threw in his party's lot with Kibaki. Also backing Kibaki was former president Daniel arap Moi, but he proved unable to deliver mass support in his home Rift Valley province, the epicentre of the subsequent inter-ethnic violence.

The association between the two main sides from the previous election proved to be much less than the sum of its parts. In a particularly inept move, Kibaki abandoned his former election vehicle, the National Rainbow Coalition, and recast his alliance under a new Party of National Unity (PNU). This had less resonance with many Kenyans and increased suspicions about a closing of ranks among political leaders from the Kikuyu, the largest of Kenya's 40-plus ethnic communities, to which both Kibaki and Kenyatta belong. Since Kenya's independence, the Kikuyu of central Kenya, about 22% of the national population, have had a disproportionate role in both business and public life. One of the failings of Kibaki's first term was the perceived favour meted out to Kikuyu appointees. Tribal tensions, which erupted in serious violence near the time of previous elections in 1992 and 1997, had been left to fester.

While the PNU based its platform on continuing economic growth, the ODM pitched its campaign to the poor who had participated the least in the gains, pledging more equitable distribution of resources, constitutional change and devolution. Late opinion polls warned of a close contest, with the ODM's lead still tight enough to allow the chance of a Kibaki victory.

Following generally peaceful voting in presidential, parliamentary and local council elections on 27 December, initial figures announced by the media showed Odinga pulling clearly ahead. In a country where politics has remained tied to tribal identity, the government was taken aback by the extent to which Odinga had been able to mobilise allegiance not just from his own community but also from the two other main ethnic groups of western Kenya, and to win substantial support in the capital, Nairobi. The ODM declared victory, but the gap closed as more results came through. A slowdown in the announcement of official results was a clear sign that something was amiss, triggering the first protests. Having set the stage for confrontation with prior warnings about ballot-rigging, the ODM called on Kibaki to concede or allow a recount. The suspense ended when, three days after the vote, Samuel Kivuitu, the experienced and hitherto respected Electoral Commission chairman, announced that Kibaki had won with 46% to Odinga's 44%. Kibaki lost no time in having himself sworn in. But by then order had already broken down in several flashpoints.

What the results actually were will never be known. It seems likely that there was manipulation at polling stations by both sides, inflating the number of ballots in heartland constituencies, but that totals were also doctored at the Electoral Commission's tallying headquarters in Nairobi's Kenyatta International Conference Centre. The credibility of the commission, most of whose members had been unilaterally appointed by Kibaki, was shattered. Three days later, Kivuitu said he had been put under pressure to announce the results by allies of both Kibaki and Musyoka, who was subsequently made vice-president. He added the astonishing admission that he did not know whether Kibaki had won.

Discrepancies between ballot totals for the presidential contest and the parliamentary elections, in which the ODM came out on top, suggested that manipulation in the former could have amounted to several hundred thousand votes, while Kibaki's official margin of victory was 230,000. In the Kikuyu-dominated Central province, he scored 97%, on the country's highest turnout. To avoid a run-off under Kenya's election rules, he needed to attain 25% in at least five of the country's eight provinces. He managed to secure this tally in seven.

The government was routed in the parliamentary elections. No fewer than 22 ministers, two-thirds of the cabinet, including Vice-President and Home Affairs Minister Moody Awori, along with the foreign, defence and information ministers, lost their national assembly seats. In a resounding rejection of politicians considered by voters to be mainly interested in their own benefit, 70% of those elected were new. With six of the 210 elected seats still vacant pending by-elections, including those of two new ODM legislators who were shot dead in late January, the ODM and allied parties had a narrow majority.

Cycle of violence

Worsening violence during January forced hundreds of thousands from their homes, with parts of the country subject to widespread arson, ransacking of shops and the forced closure of many businesses. Several different elements contributed to the breakdown. In a first phase, it involved spontaneous urban rioting in reaction to the mishandled election process, by opposition supporters who believed they were being cheated of victory. As protests degenerated, there was also looting and vandalism of homes and other premises. Heavy-handed and often indiscriminate police action added a further element, with at least 123 deaths attributed to police. Finally, there were waves of organised attacks and reprisals against members of different ethnic groups. The swiftness and effectiveness with which these attacks were mounted indicated a high degree of planning at local level, although they may not have been centrally orchestrated.

Inter-ethnic attacks demonstrated the survival of militia structures established during the Moi regime. There were widespread stories of bounties being offered. Weapons were bought ahead of time by organisers on both sides. During the campaign, stocks of machetes, called *pangas*, were found in cars used by an assistant minister and a pro-government member of parliament, both from western Kenya.

The initial outbreak of protests over thwarted election hopes recalled Zambia's 2006 election, when an early opposition lead was similarly reversed by late results. But in Zambia's case the presidential challenger Michael Sata quickly and firmly called on supporters to remain calm and refrain from violence. In Kenya, appeals for non-violence were half-hearted. The ODM had stoked expectations of tangible economic benefits, and many tenants, encouraged to expect lower rents, had already stopped paying their landlords, often

Kikuyus. The violence took place mainly in Kenya's three western provinces, as well as in Nairobi slums. Despite clashes between protesters and police in the port city of Mombasa, the coastal region, where most of Kenya's Muslims live, was largely calm, but it remained a potential focus of unrest.

The first wave of violence was directed principally against Kikuyus, along with other tribal communities associated with them or seen as Kibaki supporters. It was particularly fierce in the Rift Valley, where there has long been simmering resentment against Kikuyu settlers, particularly since the early independence years when they were enabled to buy formerly white-owned farmland. A further reason for grievance among people from the region's Kalenjin tribes was a recent cutback in state-sector jobs that were handed out under Moi, himself a Kalenjin. The worst incident was the setting alight of a church in Eldoret being used as a refuge by mainly Kikuyu women and children, causing more than 30 deaths. The second wave, later in January, mainly involved reprisals by organised Kikuyu gangs, especially the outlawed Mungiki sect.

Sustained international television coverage invited disturbing if misleading comparisons with the Rwandan genocide of 1994. Paul Kagame, Rwanda's president, suggested the military should step in to halt ethnic bloodshed, and Odinga raised the prospect of UN or AU troops. Police said in February they had opened 5,600 case files over the incidents. During the subsequent lull, as talks went on towards a political settlement, security forces used helicopters to root out a Kalenjin militia group, the Saboat Land Defence Force, on the Ugandan border.

According to UN estimates, 42,000 homes were looted or destroyed and some 300,000 people displaced. The violence and the resulting bitterness increased polarisation between ethnic groups in Nairobi and elsewhere, and drew new lines of division. In the absence of an agreement, the confrontation threatened to split the country along a north–south line situated to the west of the capital, much in the way Côte d'Ivoire had broken into two halves with the outbreak of civil conflict in 2002, an ominous precedent for the collapse of a previously successful African state following unsatisfactory elections.

The upheaval put at risk Kenya's status as an anchor of stability in the region. The country hosts a large international presence, serving as regional headquarters for aid agencies and humanitarian organisations and as a platform for emergency relief. Having avoided becoming embroiled in other countries' conflicts, Kenya has built a significant role in recent years as a regional peace broker, notably in Sudan and Somalia. As eastern Africa's most diversified and, apart from oil-exporting Sudan, largest economy, it is the centrepiece of moves towards regional integration. Kenya is also the main transit route for goods to Uganda, Rwanda, Burundi and the east of the DRC. The post-electoral violence made an immediate impact by choking transport of fuel and other supplies along the highway from Mombasa to the Ugandan border. Businesses in Kenya were hit by damage to premises, looting, increased transport costs and the loss of experienced workers such as tea-pickers displaced from homes and jobs. As the economy began slowly to recover, the government forecast a fall in growth for 2008. Some effects appeared likely to take years to overcome.

International response

Few in the diplomatic community foresaw such a crisis, and those who did were surprised by its ferocity. Reaction was rapid, however, and an exceptional degree of unity emerged in the response of African and international partners. This common front contrasted sharply with the divergent international positions taken on other African crises, notably in Rwanda and Darfur. The US State Department, apparently anxious to ensure there would be no political vacuum, initially congratulated Kibaki and called for official results to be respected, but quickly pulled back from that position. Along with the EU, it made clear there would be no 'business as usual'. The United States, Canada and Switzerland led moves to impose visa sanctions against selected politicians. However, donors were reluctant to use their aid, which in any case contributes only 6% of Kenya's budget, as a means of pressing the government into a deal.

Very few African countries acknowledged the official outcome, although Kibaki was able to attend an AU summit in Ethiopia in late January. Significantly, election monitors from the East African Community and the Pan-African Parliament joined EU, Commonwealth and independent monitoring teams in finding that vote tallying was not credible. This could mark a watershed for Africa, where elections criticised by external organisations have frequently been approved as fair by African representatives. The judgement is particularly notable given Kenya's prominence in the region. Under Kibaki, it was one of the first countries to put itself forward for Africa's 'peer review mechanism', designed to show Western partners the continent's seriousness about governance. Events in Kenya proved this review exercise to be of little use.

During a tortuous series of mediation efforts, Nairobi saw the arrival of a procession of international dignitaries, provoking some ill-disguised irritation among Kenyan authorities about outside interference. The outgoing AU chairman, Ghana's President John Kufuor, brokered a tentative deal between government and opposition, but Kibaki refused to sign. Kofi Annan, former UN secretary-general, arrived in mid January at the AU's behest to head a panel of 'eminent African persons'. He managed to bring the chief protagonists into a first face-to-face meeting four weeks after the election. Kibaki, once widely thought of as a weak president at the mercy of hardliners, showed himself as obdurate as any, seemingly ready to brazen it out and try to stay in government at all costs, banking on public fear and weariness of conflict.

However, Annan got the PNU to drop its argument that only a Kenyan court could challenge the election result, and the ODM to ditch its demand that Kibaki step down. Agreement was reached on an independent inquiry and proposals for a truth, justice and reconciliation commission. The main argument remaining was about the form a new government would take, with the ODM pushing for a more parliamentary-based system with executive powers vested in a revived post of prime minister, abolished when Kenya became a republic in 1964. A compromise broadly resembling the French 'cohabitation' model was finally agreed by the two contenders at the end of February, with some additional persuasion from the new AU chairman, Tanzania's President Jakaya Kikwete. As prime minister, Odinga would have authority to co-ordinate and supervise government functions, with two deputy prime ministers. All three would be removable only by an assembly vote, while posts in a 'grand coalition' government would be shared equitably between both sides. Annan's patient negotiating appeared to have resulted in a breakthrough. But it then took more than six weeks of agonising argument, punctuated by a further outbreak of rioting, for the two sides to agree on ministerial positions in a bloated 40-member cabinet.

Mending the damage

Events in Kenya provided a warning to African governments of the potential price to be paid for mishandled elections. On the other hand, they gave encouragement to contenders tempted to rely on the leverage of organised violence to guarantee a share of power.

While Kenyan voters were able to deliver an unmistakable message of displeasure by dismissing most of their parliamentarians, government remained in the hands of the same narrow political elite. Indeed, Kenya emerged from the contest in a remarkably similar position to that of five years ago – an uneasy coalition bogged down by argument over a premiership post and a new constitution. As an interim arrangement, the 'grand coalition' was seen as a means of addressing outstanding long-term issues, including constitutional reform, but not as a solution in itself. Annan's idea was that a deal would lead to fresh elections in about two years, an immediate re-run being ruled out as too risky. If that happened, Kibaki would be expected to stand aside. However, considering past performance, the reform process is likely to take longer. Kibaki may therefore seek to stay the full five years of his second term, the maximum allowed. The ODM could try to force an earlier election by a no-confidence vote in the national assembly, but would then lay itself open to a fresh parliamentary contest.

A successful period of coalition administration could clear the path for Odinga's presidential ambitions in 2012 or before. But whether the arrangement can deliver effective government is questionable. Past agreements have failed to hold, and little trust exists between the two camps. The deal could easily unravel without tackling the underlying causes of tribal friction, especially land issues. Tensions have been slow to subside, and there is every indication that militias will be better prepared and better armed. Many Kenyans fear the showdown has merely been postponed. It will take more than a patched-up political compromise to allay those fears.

Change in Southern Africa

The past year has been one of political drama in southern Africa. First came the failure of South Africa's Thabo Mbeki to retain control over his party and guide the choice of who should succeed him in 2009 as president of the continent's most developed and sophisticated nation. The internal rebellion that put his alienated former ally Jacob Zuma in line for the succession while facing corruption charges produced an atmosphere of tension, unease and uncertainty. Then came the extraordinary outcome of elections in Zimbabwe, where, amidst accelerating economic collapse, the ruling party machine was unable to engineer a majority for the first time in 28 years. Weeks of delays, confusion and political thuggery that followed the initial voting revived frustration in the West about the weak stance taken by neighbouring countries, especially South Africa, which outsiders saw as having the most power to sway Robert Mugabe's embattled regime.

The Zimbabwe crisis exposed the failings of the SADC as a regional organisation. In spite of initiatives to promote better governance and common electoral guidelines, it has proved to be a relatively ineffectual body, especially compared with West Africa's ECOWAS. It has little to hold it together beyond the solidarity linked to past liberation struggles, which is the ostensible reason for regional governments' reluctance to confront the implications of misrule in Zimbabwe. Seven of its 15 members, including most of the main economies, have had the same former liberation movements or independence parties continuously in power since the end of colonialism or white-led rule. These party hierarchies – even in a rigorously democratic country such as South Africa – tend to be inscrutable, opaque, remote and hypersensitive to criticism. The region's nations vary widely in the strength of their institutions and the quality of elections. In Angola, rapidly increasing its income as Africa's second largest oil producer, the ruling elite's openness to political competition was set to be tested in legislative elections scheduled for September 2008, after repeated postponements. The last elections were in 1992, when the presidential contest was aborted after the first round and the country went back to civil war. A presidential ballot is expected in 2009.

Zimbabwe: the end of an era?

The renewal of Robert Mugabe's presidency of Zimbabwe, after the opposition's withdrawal from a run-off contest in June 2008, was a hollow victory. It protracted a political crisis deepened by increasingly brutal repression in the three months following the first round of voting. The mood in the run-up to the March elections was one of general pessimism. There was little expectation that the contest would be clean or fair, or offer any hope of alleviating dire economic conditions. After the vote, the outlook abruptly changed, with a sudden sense of possibility that the Mugabe regime might after all have to concede defeat. This was followed by a tantalising wait of more than a month as the result of the presidential vote was withheld. The suspense, which continued as the government prepared for a delayed run-off contest, was accompanied by a fresh surge of brutality against opposition supporters. But it was already becoming clear that the endgame had begun for the regime, even though it was far from apparent how it would be played out.

By early 2008 Zimbabwe's economy was in free fall. Official inflation soared past the 100,000% mark in January. The black market rate for Zimbabwe dollars, which at the start of 2007 was about 3,000 to the US dollar, climbed to 100m, and by late June to over 20bn. Basics such as maize meal, cooking oil, sugar and fuel were hard to obtain. Since 2000, when the government launched its campaign of farm invasions, the economy had shrunk by about two-fifths, driving large numbers to emigrate and leaving about half the remaining workforce unemployed.

Southern African governments insisted that Mugabe be allowed to attend an EU–Africa summit in Lisbon in December 2007, despite an EU travel ban. This prompted Britain's Gordon Brown to boycott the event, and a defiant Mugabe to declare he had 'defeated the British'. The following week a congress of Mugabe's Zimbabwe African National Union–Popular Front (ZANU–PF) party unanimously endorsed him to stand for a sixth consecutive term.

SADC mediation efforts led by Mbeki between ZANU–PF and the opposition Movement for Democratic Change (MDC) brought changes to controversial legislation on media and public order, as well as to electoral procedures. But Mugabe called the elections before a new constitution, already agreed in draft, could be enacted. The government invited observers from Africa and close partners such as China, but not from the United States or the EU. Shortly before the election, a bill was signed into law empowering the state to take control of foreign or white-owned companies. The government backed its electoral campaign by handouts of food and farm equipment, pay rises for security forces and teachers, and an order for retailers to roll back recent price increases. State-run television and radio gave the opposition little air time. The heads of the defence forces, police and prison service made statements suggesting they would not serve under Mugabe's rivals. The US ambassador warned in an open letter that there were 'ominous signs' about the fairness of the elections.

The surprise element was the late entry of Simba Makoni, a former finance minister who at the time was still in the ZANU–PF politburo, as an independent presidential contender. This was the first time the party had been openly challenged from within. His candidacy was seen, especially among SADC countries, as offering a third way. Proposing a cross-party government, Makoni counted on sympathies within the military. But he failed to create a significant split in ZANU–PF, or to overcome suspicions about his recent links with the regime sufficiently to dig deep into opposition support.

The elections, in which parliamentary contests were brought forward by two years to coincide with presidential and local government votes, were better conducted than in the past. Despite opposition complaints, most of the violence did not take place until after the voting. The mainly urban-based MDC was able to stage rallies in parts of the countryside previously considered no-go areas. A new requirement that each polling station should display returns for each of the different elections proved to be a crucially important change. There was nonetheless confusion about the results. The MDC claimed that its candidate, Morgan Tsvangirai, the former union leader who had stood unsuccessfully six years earlier, had achieved an outright 50.3% win in the presidential vote, enough to avoid a run-off. But its figures were contradictory. There was no official announcement of the result.

Equally significant, however, was the result in the House of Assembly, where the MDC and a smaller splinter party won a combined majority, which they later consolidated by reuniting. It was the first time Mugabe's party had lost control since coming to power in 1980. In the senate, which has a limited role, elected seats were evenly split. For a while it appeared that Mbeki, vilified by critics for not standing up to Mugabe, had been vindicated. In the frenzy of meetings and rumours that followed, there were indications that Mugabe might have been prepared to step down but was dissuaded by his closest military commanders.

Two weeks after the election, with no outcome forthcoming, a special SADC summit convened in Lusaka, capital of neighbouring Zambia. Mbeki tried to persuade the 84-year-old Mugabe to attend, but failed. The summit produced only the mildest statement urging results to be verified and published 'expeditiously'. But signs of a toughening in the regional stance came as a result of union and public pressure in South Africa. A court in Durban ruled that containers of ammunition aboard a Chinese ship were not authorised for transport overland to Zimbabwe. Mozambique then denied the ship entry to its waters, and Levy Mwanawasa, Zambian president and SADC chairman, called on other countries to refuse to handle the cargo. Britain meanwhile led calls for a global arms embargo on Zimbabwe.

As results were further delayed by laborious recounts in 23 constituencies, MDC supporters came under attack by pro-Mugabe 'war veterans' and youth militias in rural areas, and armed police stormed the party's headquarters in Harare, detaining scores of people. Tsvangirai, described by Washington as being 'a clear victor', vacillated over whether he would participate in a presidential run-off. The parliamentary recounts, much to the surprise of many observers who assumed they would be fixed, confirmed the MDC's win, even though half the seats were still subject to court challenges. Faced with this loss and the likelihood that any openly run presidential second round would bring defeat for Mugabe, the government continued to play for time.

Almost five weeks after the vote, the electoral commission announced that Tsvangirai had won 47.9%, against 43.2% for Mugabe. Overriding the three-week period allowed for in the electoral law, the government eventually set a run-off ballot for 27 June, three months after the initial vote. In a renewed campaign of intimidation, many opposition supporters were beaten, tortured or forced from their homes, and the MDC said dozens were killed. Tsvangirai, who was repeatedly detained during the run-off campaign, announced five days before the vote that he would no longer participate in 'this violent, illegitimate sham of an election process', took temporary refuge in the Netherlands Embassy, and called for intervention by the UN, AU and SADC to prevent worse bloodshed. Even before the inevitable re-election announcement, Bush moved to toughen sanctions against the regime. With prospects diminishing for regional recognition of the legitimacy of Mugabe's mandate, pressure intensified on ZANU-PF to agree to transitional arrangements through the formation of a national unity government and a negotiated exit for Mugabe.

A key issue in any settlement would be the question of Mugabe's immunity from prosecution after leaving office. An international prosecution seemed unlikely. Zimbabwe has not ratified the 2002 treaty that established the International Criminal Court, and the court would anyway not have jurisdiction over earlier crimes such as massacres in Matabeleland in the 1980s.

A new government would need strong international support for urgent reforms. These would include depoliticising Zimbabwe's security forces and intelligence service, and bringing order to its chaotic and destructive land redistribution programme. Britain, the United States and the EU would be expected to provide large injections of assistance for economic recovery. But it will take time for Zimbabwe to overcome the damage done in recent years. It has lost many of its qualified people as well as medium-sized businesses, and much of its productive farmland has gone to waste. Tough policies will be required to tame hyperinflation. Managing public expectations in a post-Mugabe Zimbabwe will be a big challenge.

South Africa's uncertain leadership

The African National Congress (ANC), the party that has governed South Africa since it became a multi-racial democracy in 1994, entered unmapped territory when it chose former Deputy President Jacob Zuma over President Mbeki as its leader in December 2007. The momentum that built up behind the populist Zuma resulted in what amounted to a bloodless palace revolution. Failure to promote a compromise candidate to take over from Mbeki, who has to stand down as South African president in 2009, plunged the ANC into its first leadership election contest for 50 years. At the party's congress in Polokwane, attended by about 4,000 delegates, Zuma and his allies took all the top party posts.

It was a remarkable comeback for Zuma after being sacked from the government, tried for and acquitted of rape, charged with corruption and faced with a fresh trial that could disbar him from succeeding Mbeki as president. Zuma's challenge provided a channel for discontent among the ANC rank and file over centrist government policies that were criticised for not spreading the benefits of economic growth.

The frustration and anger felt in poor urban areas over unemployment, public services and living standards were subsequently blamed for a wave of mob attacks in May 2008 against migrants from other African countries and ethnic groups from northern South Africa. The violence, which started in townships around Johannesburg and spread to other regions, left more than 60 dead and led to intensified criticism of government inaction.

Zuma's campaign carried strong backing from the Congress of South African Trade Unions (COSATU) and the South African Communist Party (SACP), which are ANC partners, and from ANC women's and youth leagues. With a background as a recruit of the movement's clandestine armed wing, a prisoner on Robben Island, later head of ANC intelligence and, after the end of apartheid, the party's regional leader in KwaZulu–Natal, the self-taught and polygamous Zuma has a down-to-earth style totally different from that of the aloof and cerebral Mbeki. This was not the first time South Africa had had different people in the party leadership and the presidency, but it was the first in such conditions of estrangement.

In theory Zuma could attempt to force Mbeki out early, but that appeared unlikely, and Zuma would not gain immunity by becoming president. After the collapse of a first bribery prosecution in 2006, Zuma faced a fresh trial on 16 charges of fraud, corruption, money laundering and racketeering. The charges related to one part of a large defence procurement deal agreed almost ten years ago, ranging from submarines to fighter aircraft. Aspects of the deal prompted investigations in Germany, the UK and Sweden, and there were calls for Mbeki's role to be probed. Zuma was forced from his government post in 2005 when his financial adviser Schabir Shaik was jailed for fraud and corruption. Shaik had an interest in a company controlled by Thomson-CSF of France, now Thales, which won a combat suite contract for four German-built MEKO A-200 corvettes. The judge in Shaik's trial found that Shaik's company had acquired its stake through Zuma's intervention and that Shaik or one of his companies had paid Zuma for his influence. Prosecutors alleged that Zuma received payments amounting to the equivalent of about $525,000 and failed to declare them. Claiming to be the target of a political vendetta, Zuma indicated he would stand down from his party post only if convicted.

This left various possible scenarios. One would be rapid acquittal, which would clear the path for Zuma to become president. A rapid conviction might be less decisive, since his eligibility would not be settled as long as there remained the possibility of the conviction being overturned on appeal. The president is elected by the national assembly, and has first to be a member. Under the constitution, a sentence of more than 12 months would disqualify Zuma, unless he were pardoned. But the trial, initially set to start in August, was in any event expected to be delayed. The ANC could face the unpalatable prospect of going into the election with its leader still locked in a court battle. A further possible scenario would be for the case to be stopped before going to court, but that would be the most damaging for the standing of the rule of law in South Africa, one of the pillars of the country's successful transition from the apartheid era.

The ANC does not lack plausible substitutes. Zuma's second in command Kgalema Motlanthe is one of the few senior figures to have survived from the previous party team, and there are at least half a dozen other potential candidates. The party faces a difficult period. Before the Polokwane congress it seemed to be headed for an eventual split. COSATU and the SACP had resolved to ballot members on a breakaway if Zuma's leadership bid failed. A reconfiguration of South African politics now looks likely to take longer. But the ANC's overwhelming majority, with almost three-quarters of parliamentary seats, could be eroded by disaffection. Any loss of ANC turnout would bolster the position of minority parties, even though the opposition Democratic Alliance, led since 2007 by Cape Town mayor and former anti-apartheid journalist Helen Zille, has struggled to gain black support.

Zuma's legal troubles and propensity for offhand remarks raised questions about his judgement and tainted his image abroad. Although he made efforts to reassure business and to respond to concerns about violent crime, his ascendancy caused apprehension among whites and middle-class blacks at a time when confidence in government was already shaken by an electricity-supply crisis. Recent ANC criticism of the media and judiciary raised particular concern. Zuma is also clearly less comfortable with international issues than Mbeki. While he took a firmer position than the government on post-election delays and violence in Zimbabwe, he was reluctat to condemn Mugabe directly, and on a trip to London rejected the suggestion that South Africa should do more to exert pressure.

Western governments have looked to post-apartheid South Africa to use its political status and economic clout to help resolve Africa's crises. Pursuing a strongly multilateralist policy, Mbeki articulated the idea of an African renaissance, and was a driving force behind the AU. But the New Partnership for Africa's Development, of which he was a main sponsor, became lost in its own rhetoric. The countries where South Africa put the greatest diplomatic and military effort into peace-building, the DRC and Burundi, continued to be beset by residual conflicts. In Zimbabwe, where Mbeki was once anointed by Bush as 'the point man', his policy of 'quiet diplomacy' was lambasted by international and domestic critics as feeble.

Under a Zuma presidency South Africa would probably become more introverted, less inclined to play a leadership role. Combined with other events in Africa in the past year, especially the turmoil in Kenya, the prospect will cause further qualms about the direction the continent is taking.

8 South Asia and Afghanistan

This was a year of frustration for the Indian government as it faced rising inflation and a slowdown in the pace of economic growth, and struggled to put into effect the agreement on civil nuclear cooperation that it had reached in 2007 with US President George W. Bush. Although Indian Prime Minister Manmohan Singh finally made progress towards clinching the nuclear deal in July 2008, after leftist parties had blocked it for over ten months, its implementation remained uncertain. Amidst increases in fuel and food prices, a volatile stock market and rising inflation, the electoral contest between the Congress-led United Progressive Alliance government and the opposition Bharatiya Janata Party (BJP) sharpened considerably. BJP victories in provincial elections in Himachal Pradesh and Gujarat underlined the serious challenge that the Congress Party would face in parliamentary elections scheduled to be held by May 2009.

The year saw tumultuous developments in Pakistan, including the assassination of former prime minister Benazir Bhutto shortly after her return from exile. Parliamentary and provincial elections on 18 February 2008 were a key step towards democratic rule and offered an opportunity to counter violent Islamist extremism through a civilian–military effort. However, by mid 2008 the country had a weakened president, a deeply divided coalition government, a defiant judiciary and an army adversely affected by a six-year front-line campaign against militant groups. Moreover, the West and Afghanistan remained unhappy about infiltration of Pakistan-based Taliban fighters into Afghanistan, and about Islamabad's policy of negotiating with pro-Taliban militant leaders in border areas. Continuing domestic political instability could set back the army's attempts to reduce its role in civilian affairs.

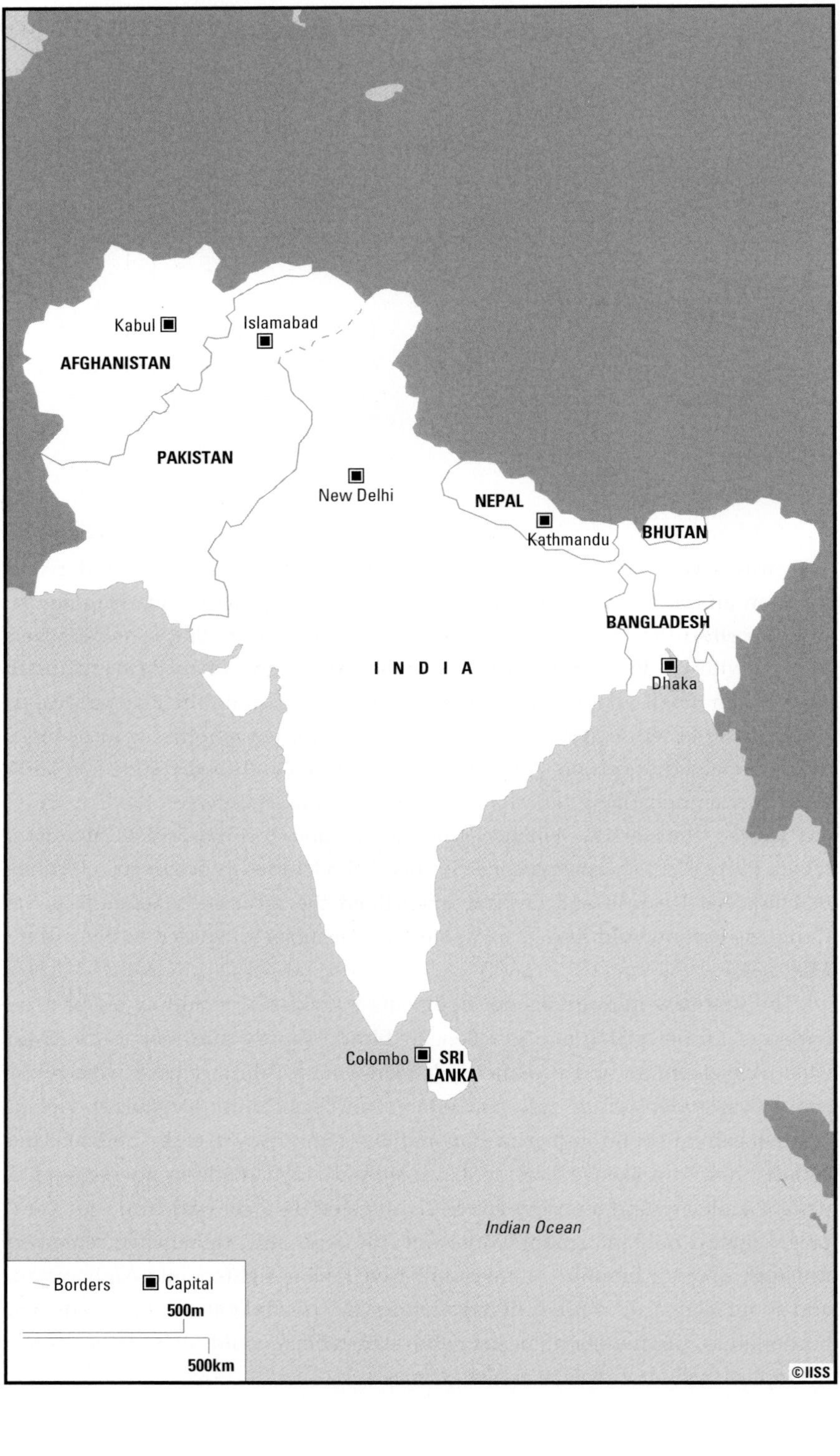

AFGHANISTAN

Kabul

Islamabad

PAKISTAN

New Delhi

NEPAL

Kathmandu

BHUTAN

INDIA

BANGLADESH

Dhaka

Colombo SRI LANKA

Indian Ocean

Borders   Capital

500m

500km

©IISS

In Afghanistan, the Taliban-led insurgency retained its momentum, and spread into new areas. The increasing violence aroused heightened concern among the international community, but prospects for a solution were undermined by a lack of coordination and weak capacity for governance in Kabul.

Following the defeat and withdrawal of the Liberation Tigers of Tamil Eelam (LTTE) from eastern Sri Lanka and President Mahinda Rajapakse's declaration of the 'Dawn of the East', the political and military leadership became more confident of defeating the LTTE militarily. However, the LTTE remained committed to the defence of its Jaffna heartland. In Bangladesh, democracy remained suspended. The caretaker government's chief adviser, Fakhruddin Ahmed, declared in May 2008 that the suspended parliamentary elections would be held in December. Much will hang on whether the elections are held on time and are free and fair.

In Nepal, elections to a Constituent Assembly held on 10 April 2008 were the culmination of the 2006 peace deal between the erstwhile Maoist rebels (Communist Party of Nepal (Maoist)) and the ruling Seven Party Alliance. The victory of the Maoists, who won the largest number of seats but fell short of a majority, reflected the people's desire for an end to the conflict and instability of the past decade, as well as disillusionment with the squabbles of the traditional political parties. The assembly voted to abolish the monarchy, and in June King Gyanendra quietly left the royal palace.

India: Growth Slows

India's economic growth slowed in the past year, and rising prices were creating a sense of short-term crisis by mid 2008. The growth rate could well remain the second-fastest in the Asia-Pacific after China's, but is projected to decline to 8.0–8.5% in 2008–09 from 8.7% in 2007–08 and rates above 9% in the preceding two years. The slowdown was caused largely by global conditions, with record fuel prices, increasing food costs and fears of a global economic slowdown brought about by the credit crisis in the United States. On 4 June 2008 the government increased petrol and diesel prices by 10%, although they remained heavily subsidised. Later that month, Indian inflation hit a 13-year high of nearly 12%. As Singh told delegates to the 1st IISS–Citi India Global Forum in New Delhi in April, India was more integrated into the global economy than ever before, and globalisation represented both a challenge and an opportunity.

Inflation and other economic factors played a part in setbacks suffered by the Congress-led United Progressive Alliance (UPA) coalition government. The ruling alliance and its leftist allies won a major victory against the Bharatiya

Janata Party (BJP) with the election of Pratibha Patil as president, with 66% of the vote, in July 2007, and again with the election of Mohammed Hamid Ansari as vice-president a month later. However, the Congress Party suffered major reverses with BJP victories in provincial elections in Himachal Pradesh and Gujarat in December 2007 and Karnataka in May 2008.

In Himachal Pradesh the BJP overthrew the ruling Congress government. In Gujarat the incumbent BJP government returned to power, providing a boost to controversial Chief Minister Narendra Modi, widely held responsible for communal violence that had broken out in 2002. Winning 117 of 182 seats, the BJP's victory in the polarised province was due largely to Modi's public stature and the ineffectiveness of the Congress opposition. In Karnataka the BJP won 110 of 224 seats, three short of a majority, in a contest with the Congress and the Janata Dal (Secular) to lead the new provincial government. This was the BJP's first victory in southern India, and took place despite a substantial farm-loan waiver scheme introduced by Finance Minister Palaniappan Chidambaram. In addition, the government had introduced in 2005 legislation guaranteeing 100 days a year of employment to any rural household whose members were willing to do manual work. The results indicated that difficult times lay ahead for the Congress in the six provincial elections scheduled to take place in November–December 2008 in Chhattisgarh, Madhya Pradesh, Rajasthan, Jammu and Kashmir, Mizoram and Delhi.

A BJP buoyed by further provincial electoral gains, and geared up for the elections both organisationally and ideologically, would represent a serious electoral challenge to the Congress, suffering from unpopularity over high inflation and poor infrastructure. The BJP's and Congress's alliances with regional and smaller political parties will also be a key factor in the parliamentary elections scheduled to be held by May 2009. In an attempt to enhance its prospects, the government sought to push forward its controversial April 2006 reservation of 27% of places in central institutions of higher education for so-called Other Backward Castes, which would increase total reservation for weaker sections of the community to 49.5%. Public opposition had led to legal challenges in the Supreme Court, but on 10 April 2008 the court upheld a phased 27% reservation.

Internal security

Several terrorist attacks occurred at places of worship and in areas with mixed Hindu–Muslim populations. The government was increasingly concerned that these were aimed at triggering communal riots. On 25 August 2007 there were twin bomb blasts in Hyderabad, a city with a prominent Muslim minority, killing 43 people and injuring 53. An explosion at the shrine in Ajmer, Rajasthan, on 12 October killed two people and injured 17. Serial blasts in Varanasi, Faizabad and Lucknow (all in Uttar Pradesh) on 23 November 2007 caused 13 deaths. But the worst attack took place in the city of Jaipur in northern India on 13 May, when seven bombs exploded within minutes, killing 61 people and injuring 100.

Although the Indian authorities blamed the Bangladesh arm of the Harkat-ul-Jihad-al-Islami (HUJI), a South Asian militant group, for the bombs in Jaipur, Hyderabad and Uttar Pradesh, there were reports, denied by both Bangladesh and Pakistan, that the attacks were linked to Pakistan's Inter-Services Intelligence (ISI). These claims came as the Indian government became concerned that Indian Muslims were increasingly being recruited for terror attacks as a result of growing radicalisation of a minority of the Muslim community. In an attempt to counter extremism, influential Islamic scholars from the powerful Dar-ul-Uloom seminary in Deoband in Uttar Pradesh came together to denounce terrorism, and issued a fatwa against it in May 2008.

The Maoist Naxalites continued to attack political leaders. Their most prominent target was former Andhra Pradesh Chief Minister Nedurumalli Janardhan Reddy and his wife, a minister in the provincial government, both of whom escaped unhurt when a landmine exploded near their convoy in Nellore on 7 September 2007, killing three people. On 27 October 2007, the son of former Jharkhand Chief Minister Babulal Marandi was killed, along with 16 others. On 29 June 2008 nearly 40 security personnel were killed when the Maoists sank their boat in a reservoir close to the Andhra Pradesh border. The Maoists proclaimed the formation of a parallel 'revolutionary government' in a remote tribal-dominated area of Chhattisgarh in central India, although Indian officials denied they had lost effective control. In the northeast, Assam continued to experience bombings in the absence of a peace process.

The India–US nuclear deal

The key foreign-policy priority for India's fragile coalition government was final agreement on and implementation of the India–US civil nuclear deal. Following passage of the United States–India Peaceful Atomic Energy Cooperation Act (the Hyde Act) by the US Congress in December 2006, Indian and American officials negotiated hard on the final agreement, known as the '123 Agreement' after Section 123 of the US Atomic Energy Act, which governs international nuclear cooperation. Unveiled on 3 August 2007, the 40-year nuclear agreement would assure fuel supplies for India's civilian nuclear reactors in return for placing them under permanent International Atomic Energy Agency (IAEA) safeguards. India would also be given the right to reprocess spent fuel resulting from nuclear materials of US origin, following New Delhi's offer, among other things, to establish a new national facility for reprocessing foreign nuclear material under IAEA safeguards. India's right to test nuclear weapons if it chose to do so was not explicitly prohibited, but the US was allowed to terminate the agreement in the event of a test.

The agreement was criticised by the non-proliferation lobby in the United States and both the left and the right wings in India. Opposition from the US non-proliferation lobby focused on the sidelining of the Nuclear Non-Proliferation Treaty (NPT) and the concessions being made to India, including the absence of direct references to Indian nuclear tests or explicit abrogation of the agreement if India carried out a nuclear test. India has maintained its refusal to sign the NPT. Although the vast majority of nuclear scientists in India expressed satisfaction with the agreement, the opposition BJP criticised it as compromising India's 'strategic autonomy' by affecting India's strategic-weapons programme.

Most important, however, was the strident criticism from the leftist and communist parties supporting the government. They opposed the deal on the basis that it was more about developing a strategic relationship with the United States, which was anathema to them, than about civilian nuclear energy which, in any case, was projected to meet only 7–10% of total energy demand by 2020. On 13 August 2007 Prime Minister Singh tried to placate the opposition by stating in parliament that 'there is no question that we will ever compromise, in any manner, our independent foreign policy. We shall retain our strategic autonomy.' But this did not put an end to leftist opposition.

Increasingly frustrated at not being able to move forward on the next step towards completing the deal – an India-specific safeguards agreement with the IAEA – Singh stated that the agreement was final and dared the leftists to withdraw their support for the government. They reacted by threatening to withdraw support if the nuclear agreement were 'operationalised' – understood to mean formalisation of the safeguards agreement with the IAEA.

With the ball in the government's court, confusion reigned. Some analysts believed the leftists' threat was a bluff that the government should call, as the leftists themselves were not prepared for early polls. However, the government saw this course as risky. The Congress Party itself was divided on the issue. While Singh was keen to move forward on the nuclear deal, party chief Sonia Gandhi and its key negotiator with the leftists, Foreign Minister Pranab Mukherjee, were reportedly not convinced that this could be done without a collapse of the government. Other major constituents of the coalition were also keen to avoid an early poll. The government ruled out concluding the nuclear deal as a minority government. Thus, in an important change of tack, Singh on 12 October said his government was not driven by a single issue and that failure to implement the nuclear deal was 'not the end of life'. Two days later, Singh reportedly told Bush that there were 'certain difficulties' in implementing the nuclear deal. This was reiterated by Mukherjee on 8 March 2008 when he stated that the government would not be sacrificed for the sake of the nuclear deal. In November the leftists agreed to allow the government to engage in discussions with the IAEA on a safeguards agreement, and by the end of the March 2008 the two sides had reached an agreed text.

The nuclear deal then stalled, with the leftist parties adamantly refusing to allow the government to move forward and the government not willing to sacrifice its future. In July, however, Singh moved forward on the deal, despite leftist threats to withdraw support from the goverment. He won a crucial vote of confidence in parliament. The additional steps required for implementation were approval by the IAEA Board of Governors of an agreed text of the safeguards agreement; the unanimous grant to India by the full 45-member Nuclear Suppliers Group of an exception to the group's guidelines on the transfer of nuclear technology and material; and passage of the final implementation legislation by the US Congress. Unless the first two steps could be completed by August 2008, the US Congress would not be able to approve the nuclear deal, which would have to await the election of new governments in both countries. This would likely affect the momentum of bilateral relations: Indian officials have been left exhausted by their struggle to implement the deal, and US officials feel let down that their efforts to rewrite the rules of international nuclear commerce specifically for India have not been recognised in India.

India–China relations

India's relationship with China appeared to be at a difficult stage, despite Singh's visit to China in mid January 2008, the first by an Indian premier for five years, and the unparalleled growth of bilateral annual trade to $40bn. There was growing concern in India over China's activities in Myanmar, where it was developing ports and pipelines; in Pakistan, where Gwadar port on the Makran coast in Baluchistan was Chinese-built; and in China's own Tibetan region, where military-related infrastructure has been substantially upgraded. Indian officials perceived these activities as an attempt by China to encircle India strategically and to gain a permanent presence in the Indian Ocean for the first time. China meanwhile expressed concern over the activities in the Indian Ocean of other regional powers, as well as over the prospective defence and strategic relationship between New Delhi and Washington, which Beijing saw as an effort to contain it. In September 2007, the Indian navy participated with the United States, Australia, Japan and Singapore in the largest multilateral naval exercise in the Bay of Bengal to date. While the Indian navy now regularly exercises and trains with Southeast Asian navies, the Chinese navy is continuing to build relations with that of Pakistan. The tendency for each country to be excluded from the international engagements of the other has raised the prospect of Sino-Indian naval rivalry in the Indian Ocean. In May 2008, Chairman of the Indian Chiefs of Staff Committee and Chief of Naval Staff Admiral Sureesh Mehta expressed concern over the growing number of Chinese nuclear submarines.

Meanwhile, however, India and China attempted to build a bilateral defence relationship. Following low-scale naval exercises, the first significant joint army counter-terrorism exercise took place in Kunming in December 2007. But prospects for far-reaching bilateral military exercises remained limited. The Indian navy plans to strengthen its fleet in the east, including basing an aircraft carrier in the Bay of Bengal within the next five years. The Indian air force reportedly re-opened an air base at Daulat Beg Oldi in Ladakh and planned to deploy two squadrons of Su-30MKI fighters at Tezpur air base in eastern India, close to the Chinese border. The Indian army reportedly moved 6,000 troops to the border in December 2007, although this was presented as a routine deployment.

In October 2007, China accused India of violating the border agreement in Sikkim by building facilities on its side of the Line of Actual Control (LAC), though India denied this. This came as a surprise to New Delhi, as it had assumed China had accepted Sikkim as part of India. In December 2007, Indian Defence Minister A.K. Antony visited Sikkim, and this was followed by a visit by Singh to Arunachal Pradesh, parts of which are claimed by China. Negotiations over the border dispute between special representatives of the two countries moved slowly. In May 2008, the Indian media gave considerable publicity to alleged Chinese incursions across the LAC into Indian territory, as well as to Chinese claims to Finger Point at the northern tip of Sikkim. Troubles in Tibet led to greater concern in China over the Dalai Lama's presence and activities in India ahead of the Beijing Olympic Games. However, India made special efforts to ensure that the Olympic torch relay was not disrupted as it passed through Delhi, deploying over 15,000 security personnel to cover a two-kilometre distance.

India and the neighbourhood

Amidst uncertainty over the India–US civil nuclear deal and growing concern over a prospective acute shortage of energy resources, India attempted to resuscitate a dormant $7.5bn project to build a gas pipeline from Iran via Pakistan. Although Iranian President Mahmoud Ahmadinejad's short visit to New Delhi on 29 April provided political impetus, problems remained over the proposed route and fees.

India's peace process with Pakistan, which had stalled due to Pakistan's domestic political turmoil, was restarted with Mukherjee's visit to Islamabad on 20 May 2008. This signalled the start of the fifth round of the composite dialogue, including discussions on the Kashmir dispute. However, a joint working group on terrorism made little headway. After a reported exchange of gunfire in May 2008 along the international border and the Line of Control for the first time since the 2003 ceasefire, the focus could again shift to Kashmir, with elections due in the Indian state of Jammu and Kashmir by the end of 2008. Meanwhile, India–Pakistan rivalry over Afghanistan sharpened; India provided over $750m in rehabilitation and reconstruction funding and Indian personnel were involved in the construction of the Zaranj–Delaram highway linking Iran to Afghanistan. But Indian construction workers and security personnel were increasingly targeted by Taliban forces.

Pakistan: Political Drama

A period of extraordinary turbulence in Pakistani politics began with the decision in March 2007 of President Pervez Musharraf to suspend Chief Justice Iftikhar Mohammed Chaudhry, as he was thought unlikely to allow Musharraf to contest presidential elections while serving as army chief. This triggered country-wide protests and strikes, and in July the Supreme Court struck a blow against Musharraf by ordering that Chaudhry be reinstated. This increased the pressure on the president, who remained the army chief and faced both presidential and parliamentary elections.

Musharraf's moves to retain his position in the face of mounting criticism began with discussions with Benazir Bhutto, former premier and leader of the Pakistan People's Party (PPP), who had gone into exile in 1999 because she and her husband faced corruption charges under the government of her arch-rival Nawaz Sharif. Each had been prime minister twice during the 1990s, and each had twice been removed from office. This period ended when Musharraf ousted Sharif in a military coup. In return for Bhutto's support for his re-election to a second five-year presidential term, Musharraf promulgated the controversial National Reconciliation Ordinance 2007 (NRO) on 5 October, which terminated all legal cases against Bhutto, but not against Sharif, leader of the Pakistan Muslim League (Nawaz) (PML(N)), who was also in exile. The following day Musharraf won the presidential elections with 57% of the electoral-college vote amidst boycotts or abstentions by opposition parties, although the Supreme Court had yet to rule on whether he was eligible for re-election while still serving as army chief.

Bhutto returned to Karachi on 18 October after eight years in self-imposed exile to a tumultuous public welcome. As she travelled through the crowds into the city, her motorcade was hit by two suicide-bomb blasts which killed 140 people and injured over 400. She was unhurt. Sharif also returned to Lahore on 25 November 2007 after eight years in exile. Musharraf had swiftly deported him after an earlier attempt on 10 September, despite a Supreme Court order permitting him to return.

Fearing that the Supreme Court would refuse to validate his election as president, Musharraf proceeded to take drastic steps. On 3 November he suspended the constitution and imposed a state of emergency, citing the worrying increase in violent attacks by jihadist groups and the need to rein in the judiciary. Chaudhry was placed under house arrest, 2,000 people were arrested, and the media were censored. Soon afterwards, Chaudhry and nearly 60 other Supreme and High Court judges were removed from office, and on 22 November a reconstituted loyalist judiciary formally upheld Musharraf's election as president. However, he had accepted that both domestically and internationally, his position would no longer be tenable if he retained his army uniform. On 28 November, Musharraf gave up his position as army chief, symbolically ending nine years of military rule in Pakistan, and was formally sworn in as president the next day. The new army chief, General Ashfaq Kayani, a former chief of the ISI, began slowly to reduce the army's role in civilian affairs, which had increased enormously under Musharraf. Now assured of remaining in office, Musharraf lifted the state of emergency to enable parliamentary and provincial elections, which were scheduled for 8 January 2008.

In spite of her earlier narrow escape, Bhutto continued to hold election rallies. On 27 December, she was killed along with 16 others at a rally in the military cantonment of Rawalpindi. There was a dispute as to whether the cause of her death was the explosion set off by a suicide bomber close to her vehicle, or a gunshot wound. The government blamed the pro-Taliban Tehrik-e-Taliban Pakistan (TTP) leader, Baitullah Mehsud, a tribal leader in South Waziristan allegedly linked to al-Qaeda. The TTP had previously threatened to kill Bhutto, as she was seen as close to the West.

Following Bhutto's murder, the elections were postponed to 18 February. The polls were widely accepted as free and fair, in spite of some reported irregularities. There was far less violence than anticipated and a high voter turnout at 45%. The results delivered yet another setback to Musharraf, as well as dealing a blow to Pakistan's religious parties. Bhutto's PPP secured 120 out of a total of 342 seats in the national assembly, while Sharif's PML(N) performed better than expected, winning 90. The Pakistan Muslim League (Quaid-i-Azam) (PML(Q)), which supported Musharraf, won only 54 seats. Meanwhile, the religious parties were routed: in the 2002 elections, grouped as the Muttahida Majlis-e-Amal (MMA) coalition, they had won 11% of the vote; in 2008, they won only 2.2% of the vote and only six national-assembly seats. The religious parties' loss was to the advantage of the more traditional and secular Pushtun Awami National Party (ANP), which won 13 seats.

Prolonged discussions among the parties after the elections finally brought together a ruling coalition of former rivals, the PPP and the PML(N), along with the ANP and the Jamiat Ulema-e-Islam Fazl (JUI-F). The coalition had a two-thirds majority in the national assembly, but not in the Senate. Yusuf Raza Gillani, a PPP national-assembly member and former speaker of the national assembly, was elected prime minister on 24 March, but it was clear that PPP leader Asif Ali Zardari, Bhutto's husband, wielded greater influence, although he himself did not stand in the election.

The issue that triggered the tensions a year beforehand continued to dog Pakistani politics. Gillani had promised that judges dismissed by Musharraf would be reinstated. But the coalition partners wrangled for months about how this should be done. The resulting tensions led to the resignation of all nine ministers from the PML(N) on 13 May. While Sharif wanted the judges restored through a prime-ministerial executive order, which could have the effect of ruling unconstitutional Musharraf's declaration of a state of emergency, and thus his election as president. Zardari appeared to favour a constitutional approach which would enable most of the judges to return but retain Musharraf as president. In spite of the ministers' withdrawal, the PML(N) continued to support the government from the outside, ensuring its survival.

Following all these events, Musharraf's authority was considerably weakened. Neither his survival as president nor that of the government could be assured. The country's lawyers remained defiant. There were deep ideological and political differences between the PPP and the PML(N). Leaders of both parties may aspire to become prime minister. Musharraf's future, too, was uncertain: although both parties pledged to abolish Article 58-2(b) of the constitution, which gives the president discretionary powers to dissolve the national assembly, there was no consensus on impeaching Musharraf. However, although there was considerable domestic pressure on Musharraf to resign, the widening rift between the PPP and the PML(N) could help Musharraf to stay in office. This political instability did not augur well for an already weakened economy, which saw rising food and fuel prices, inflation at a 30-year high of nearly 20%, electricity shortages, and growth slowing to 5.8% from an average of 7% over the previous five years.

Extremism and terrorism

The inevitable effect of these political disturbances was to weaken Pakistan's efforts to counter Islamist extremism and terrorism. A surge in suicide attacks was triggered by the storming by security forces of the Lal Masjid (Red Mosque) in the heart of Islamabad on 10 July 2007. The mosque had been under the control of Islamist militants supporting the Taliban, and had come under siege from security forces after a gun battle broke out a week beforehand. More than 100 people died in the storming of the mosque. On 14 July a suicide car bomber killed 24 paramilitary soldiers and injured 29 in North Waziristan. The next day, in two attacks, 16 people, mostly paramilitary, were killed in Matta in Swat and 29 people, mostly new police recruits, were killed in Dera Ismail Khan. On 19 July three suicide attacks killed over 50 people. In Islamabad, a suicide bomber killed 16 people and injured 47 outside a court on 17 July, and a suicide bomb attack at Aabpara market on 27 July killed 15 people, mostly policemen. A bomb attack on the Danish Embassy on 2 June 2008 killed eight people and injured more than 25. In Rawalpindi, suicide bombers killed 25 people on 4 September and 15 on 24 November. On 21 December, 56 people were killed and more than a hundred injured in a mosque in northwest Pakistan in the second assassination attempt in recent months on former Interior Minister Aftab Khan Sherpao. On 29 February 2008 in Mingora, a suicide bomber targeted a police officer's funeral parade, killing 50 people and wounding a further 50. On 2 March at least 39 people were killed in a suicide attack in Darra Adam Khel.

The 112,000 Pakistani troops in the Federally Administered Tribal Areas (FATA) and the adjoining areas of the North West Frontier Province (NWFP), including five divisions of the regular army, made little headway in curbing pro-Taliban and al-Qaeda militants, who grew in both political influence and capabilities. The abduction of 270 security personnel in South Waziristan on 30 August 2007 by an estimated 200 militants controlled by Baitullah Mehsud considerably lowered troop morale in the province and led to increased desertion. The authorities reportedly released over a hundred arrested tribesmen to secure the release of most of the abducted security personnel. Since November 2007, Swat, Darra Adam Khel in the Kohat frontier region, the Mehsud territory of South Waziristan, and Upper Khurram and Khyber Agency have been the main areas for security operations. Pakistan's ambassador to Afghanistan was kidnapped on the Peshawar–Kabul road on 11 February 2008 and held captive for 96 days before being released, reportedly in exchange for senior Taliban commanders. On 17 February, the the NWFP government and the pro-Taliban Utmanzai tribal leaders signed the North Waziristan Agreement, which stipulated the immediate cessation of militant activities and expulsion of foreigners in return for the redeployment of troops and the restoration of tribal concessions.

Soon after his appointment as prime minister, Gillani announced a three-pronged policy towards FATA, comprising political dialogue, development and force. The new ANP-led provincial coalition in NWFP, led by Chief Minister Amir Haider Hoti, was also keen to end the violence. The first peace deal by the new provincial government was signed on 21 May 2008 with militants loyal to Maulana Fazlullah, a leader of the Tehrik-e-Nifaz-e-Shariat-e-Mohammadi. The 16-point agreement stipulated an end to suicide attacks and bombings and closure of all militant training centres in return for the gradual withdrawal of the army and implementation of sharia law in Malakand Agency. This was followed on 28 May by a deal with TTP commander Umar Khalid in the Mohmand Agency bordering Afghanistan. The Swat agreement was reported to have collapsed in early June 2008 due to continuing attacks against security forces, although this was denied by Pakistani officials.

Regardless of the outcome the traditional Pakistani government policy of resolving disputes through political negotiations with militant leaders was likely to continue. This policy had been criticised by the Afghan government, which accused Pakistan of harbouring terrorists. Following the 13 June 2008 attack on Kandahar prison that released a large number of militants, Karzai stated that Afghan forces had the right to cross into Pakistan as long as Taliban and other groups launched operations from there. Washington also continued to express reservations about negotiating with extremists, fearing it would reinforce the status of the tribal areas as a sanctuary for groups planning cross-border attacks on NATO forces in Afghanistan or against Western states. Islamabad claimed it was doing what it could and that pre-conditions for the ceasefire with militant groups included the closure of training camps and the handover of foreign fighters. But criticism by Afghan and US officials of direct complicity in assistance to militants continued. The United States also continued to conduct clandestine air and missile attacks against Taliban and al-Qaeda targets in the tribal areas, causing public furore in Pakistan.

Baluchistan

The insurgency in the Pakistani province of Baluchistan continued unabated, with Baluchi nationalist groups using bombs, landmines, rockets and small arms against security forces and civilians in the provincial capital Quetta and other cities, along with attacks against gas pipelines and infrastructure, and railway lines. The security forces responded with ground and aerial attacks. Allegations that the Taliban was active in the province were officially denied by provincial authorities.

On 19 July 2007, 30 people were killed and 50 injured in an attack against a convoy of Chinese engineers in Hub. In a notable success for the security forces, Mir Balaach Marri, leader of the most active militant group, the Baluchistan Liberation Army (BLA), was reportedly killed in a clash in Afghanistan on 21 November 2007 along with two other Baluchi leaders, triggering retaliatory attacks on security forces. On 13 December, seven people were killed and approximately 20 others wounded in two suicide bombings in Quetta. In January 2008, the security forces attacked militant camps in Kohlu and Sibi districts.

The February elections were boycotted by a Baluchi nationalist alliance of eight political parties, and the new provincial government was formed by a coalition of the PPP, PML(Q) and JUI-F. The governor of Baluchistan, Nawab Zulfiqar Ali Magsi, said the new government's priority was to cease military operations and restore peace and normality through a process of reconciliation. The Baluchistan Assembly unanimously adopted a resolution calling for an immediate end to military operations in the province and the release of BNP (Mengal faction) chief Akhtar Mengal and all detained political activists. On

2 May, Gillani stated that military operations in Baluchistan had stopped. But the BLA appeared to have rejected negotiations with the government amidst continuing clashes in the province.

Afghanistan: Worsening Problems

Those involved in the building of a new Afghanistan found few reasons for optimism in the year to mid 2008. The number of conflict-related deaths exceeded 6,500 in 2007, including insurgents, the highest level since the US-led attack on the country in 2001. In July 2008 a NATO report said that 900 civilians had been killed due to the insurgency since the beginning of the year. The UN reported a 70% rise in civilian casualties compared to the same period in 2007, although the number attributed to actions by government or international forces had fallen. The Taliban-led insurgency continued unabated and spread into new areas. Counter-insurgency efforts were forced to adapt to new Taliban tactics, and seemed to make little headway, on balance, in spite of some successes. It was not clear that the presidential elections scheduled for 2009 would pave the way to a more stable future. For this reason foreign governments were cautious about pledging new aid to the country – even though they remained deeply concerned about it again becoming a haven for terrorism as well as for illicit drugs, with the opium trade continuing to account for a large share of the economy. In the absence of more positive developments and a more unified international approach, it seemed likely that some of the 40-plus countries with troops deployed in Afghanistan as part of NATO's International Security Assistance Force (ISAF) would begin to review their commitments. Tensions among NATO members about the nature of the mission undermined its effectiveness, and the capacity of the Afghan National Army to take over more operations remained limited, in spite of improvements. The flow of Taliban fighters from lawless areas of Pakistan into Afghanistan remained a very serious problem. Meanwhile, development and aid efforts lacked coordination and government capacity remained weak.

Taliban insurgency: resilient and agile

Despite the variety of factions within the Taliban-led insurgency, it remained resilient to attempts to defeat it, and made rapid changes of tactics. The wide range of its activities illustrated the flexible nature of the insurgency and its ability to regroup. Insurgents moved into previously peaceful provinces, stepped up suicide bombings and the use of improvised explosive devices (IEDs), and launched attacks on high-profile targets, including President Hamid Karzai.

After a series of defeats in open combat with better-equipped international forces in their heartland of the southern provinces of Helmand, Kandahar and Uruzgan, insurgents established bases in areas where government and ISAF forces were less strong, such as the southwestern provinces of Nimroz and Farah. (At the same time, poppy cultivation spread to Nimroz.) The Taliban also became more active in the north, particularly in the provinces of Badghis, Faryab, Faizabad and Badakhshan. Insurgent operations focused on perceived areas of weakness such as the Afghan National Police (ANP), who were poorly prepared to protect themselves. Casualties in the ANP were higher than in any other elements of the security forces, with 925 policemen killed by insurgents in 2007.

Insurgent groups resorted increasingly to suicide attacks, of which 143 occurred in 2007. Many bombers came from Pakistan, from where reports indicated that the drive to recruit new suicide bombers was continuing, with the Pakistani Taliban, or Tehrik-e-Taliban (TTP), being particularly active in this respect.

In another sign of changed tactics, the number of insurgent attacks using IEDs against international and Afghan forces increased. There were more than 700 IED attacks in 2007. Targets included the latest armoured vehicles deployed by NATO forces. According to some published reports, there was evidence of Iranian-supplied explosively formed projectiles (EFPs) in Afghanistan, just as there had been in Iraq. Four EFPs were reported to have been found near the Iranian border and several arms caches have been found in the south and east. The debate over the degree and nature of Iranian involvement in the insurgency continued. Despite the discovery of Iranian weapons, claims in the media by senior Afghan border commanders that insurgents were being trained in Iranian camps remain unsubstantiated.

The Taliban also carried out attacks on high-profile targets in Kabul and Kandahar, with the aim of bringing instability to these key population centres. On 14 January 2008, the Taliban attacked the Serena Hotel in Kabul while a foreign-ministry delegation from Norway was holding a meeting in the building. Six people, including a Norwegian journalist, died in the attack, which was carried out by four militants using a combination of small arms and suicide bombs. In another attack in Kabul on 24 April 2008, in which three people died, six Taliban militants equipped with small arms and suicide vests attempted to assassinate Karzai as he led a parade to commemorate the victory of the mujahadeen over Soviet forces. The attacks showed that security in Kabul was tenuous. There were also reports of increasing Taliban activity within Kabul University. However, the Afghan Taliban denied responsibility for the worst attack in Kabul since 2001, which occurred on 7 July when 41 people were killed in a suicide attack on the Indian Embassy.

In Kandahar more than 80 people died in a suicide bomb attack at a dog fight on 17 February 2008. The likely target was a police commander. On 13 June a

Taliban force of some 200 attacked Kandahar prison and freed over 300 prisoners. Shortly after the breakout, a force of approximately 500 insurgents took over several villages in the Arghandab district of Kandahar province. Canadian and Afghan forces conducted a joint operation to retake the area and the Taliban withdrew. The difficult terrain in Arghandab is known historically for favouring insurgent tactics: Soviet forces were unable to dominate the district during their ten-year occupation of Afghanistan.

In the east and south the insurgency continued to gain impetus from insecurity in Pakistan, which allowed fighters to undergo training and launch attacks from the relative safety of the Federally Administered Tribal Areas (FATA), in particular Waziristan. The TTP, under the leadership of Baitullah Mehsud, became one of the most potent insurgent groups in both Pakistan and Afghanistan. Mehsud's extreme practices, including beheadings, led to a divide between him and Afghan Taliban leader Mullah Omar, who was believed to be in the Pakistani city of Quetta. Mehsud supported Omar's objectives of removing foreign forces from Afghanistan and bringing down the government, but was also aligned with al-Qaeda's broader objectives of global jihad. The TTP was also linked to a spate of suicide attacks in Pakistan, including the assassination of former Prime Minister Benazir Bhutto.

The Pakistani military's approach of dealing with militant leaders, which led to a number of truces with tribal groups, was criticised by the Afghan government, which accused Pakistan of harbouring terrorists. While Islamabad claimed that pre-conditions for a ceasefire with the TTP included the closure of training camps and the handover of foreign fighters, Afghan and US officials complained that direct complicity with militants continued and noted that Mehsud was able to meet journalists and communicate through a radio station.

The readiness of the TTP to act on both sides of the Durand Line (the border between the two countries, not accepted by Afghanistan) as well as the intelligence available to it were illustrated by the kidnap of the Pakistani Ambassador to Kabul, Tariq Azizuddin, by TTP fighters inside Afghanistan on the road between Kabul and Peshawar. He was later released.

A wide variety of militant groups remained active on both sides of the Durand Line. Some were intent on controlling territory and illicit trade, others were sectarian with religious motivation, and some fell into both categories. All were acting at a local level for reasons of self-interest, often in competition with each other, as well as cooperating as parts of the insurgency, either in Pakistan or Afghanistan. A factor common to almost all of them was that spiritual leadership was provided by Mullah Omar. An exception to this loose loyalty was Gulbuddin Hekmatyar, the leader of Hizb-e-Islami, which was operating in the Afghan provinces of Kunar and Kapisa. Although well armed and equipped, it appeared less active than other groups, perhaps because of Hekmatyar's desire to play a political role in a future government. By contrast, the Haqqani group, led by Sirajuddin Haqqani and based in North Waziristan, became more active, and was blamed for the attack on the Serena Hotel.

Funding the insurgency: drugs and crime

One reason for the resilience of the insurgency was the difficulty of eradicating its sources of funding: the trade in illicit drugs as well as black markets in other goods. Methods of financing from these sources were obscure and hard to obstruct. Powerful vested interests were involved, with government corruption pervasive and the trade affected by local disputes over territory and trafficking.

In its 2008 *World Drug Report* the UN Office on Drugs and Crime (UNODC) said that, although there was a net decrease in the number of provinces affected from 28 in 2006 to 21 in 2007 and poppy-free provinces rose from 6 to 13, cultivation in 2007 had increased by 17% compared to 2006. The number of hectares under cultivation rose from 165,000 to 193,000. This rise was concentrated in Helmand, with new areas emerging in Nimroz and Farar and cultivation returning to Nangahar.

The debate about how to deal with poppy cultivation continued. Careful poppy eradication as part of the National Drug Strategy continued. However, eradication by aerial spraying, although still retained as an option, was widely regarded as counterproductive because it would cause further loss of support for the government amongst farmers. There was also a fear that spray aircraft could be attacked by insurgents. Instead, there was greater concentration by the government on finding alternative, licit livelihoods. However, with an estimated 30% of the country's total GDP coming from the illicit drug trade, which provides 92% of the world's heroin, no short-term solution was in sight. Implementation of a national control strategy continued to be hindered by government corruption, the ability of the drug trade to mutate or move, and disagreement amongst foreign allies of the government on how to deal with cultivation, production and trafficking.

The UNODC also reported that Afghanistan had become the world's largest supplier of cannabis, with some being grown in areas where poppy had been eradicated. Significant trade in hashish was indicated by the seizure of 236.8 tonnes worth $400m by the Afghan National Police Special Task Force in June 2008. In addition, the import into Afghanistan of precursor chemicals used in the production of heroin, especially acetic anhydride, was reportedly growing. The Afghani Counter-Narcotics Police had some success in interdicting precursors; on 22 May 2008 three tonnes of acetic anhydride were seized in Kabul.

As well as narcotics, the wider black market in luxury goods and other commodities may also have been sustaining the insurgency. This was facilitated by the growth in mass transportation of goods to and from Afghanistan from the north, east and west, using containers which travel principally from Pakistan's growing container port of Gwadar in Baluchistan. The volume of goods being moved through Gwadar is estimated at about 8m tonnes annually and is forecast to grow sharply. Few checks are made on containers either in transit or at destination. Weak border control undermines efforts to bring stability to Afghanistan, with the country's terrain making it difficult to control the diversity of routes. Goods smuggled through Afghanistan can be sold at a profit in Pakistan in a manner similar to the tax differential between Northern and Southern Ireland formerly used by the Irish Republican Army to help fund its campaign.

Counter-insurgency: more troops but little progress

As the insurgency spread, efforts to battle it were hampered by the failure of foreign governments and militaries to provide necessary force levels and key equipment such as helicopters. The deficiency in troop numbers and air-mobility impeded the military effort to deny territory to the Taliban, who continued to move with increasing impunity.

With combat operations taking place in a growing number of Afghan provinces, the United States put pressure on NATO allies to increase troop numbers. Before a meeting of NATO defence ministers in Vilnius in February 2008, US Secretary of Defense Robert Gates publicly criticised European member states for not sharing enough of the burden. Canada had threatened to withdraw its troops from Kandahar by February 2009 if there was not a greater involvement by other countries, but in April said it would continue its deployment beyond 2009. The American pressure won only small increases in commitments. France committed a battalion to eastern Afghanistan, which allowed US troops to redeploy to the south. Georgia, Poland, the Czech Republic and Azerbaijan pledged to deploy extra troops; in June the UK announced it would also deploy an extra 200 engineer and logistic troops, bringing its total to 8,000; and on 24 June Germany increased the number of troops it was prepared to deploy by 1,000 to 4,500.

A commitment was made at the NATO summit in Bucharest on 2–4 April 2008 to adopt what was termed a 'comprehensive approach' in the counter-insurgency operation. This would combine all aspects of governance, reconstruction, development and security into one strategy. With the same objective, UN Secretary-General Ban Ki Moon appointed the Norwegian diplomat Kai Eide as his special representative, after Karzai refused to accept Paddy Ashdown, the former British politician who had been high representative in Bosnia, in the role.

Despite the declared intention to adopt a comprehensive approach, countries contributing troops to ISAF, each of which had responsibility for a specific area of the country, were likely to continue to adopt their own approaches to security and development in those areas. The United States, for example, which commands Regional Command–East, spent more than $20m on road building and other construction projects in Khowst province alone. US commanders also had authority to spend money on so-called 'quick improvement' projects at local level. Other nations were unable to disburse this type or amount of funding in their areas. There were also differences in the way countries channelled their finances into development projects. In addition, governments continued to place restrictions on the activities their forces could undertake, limiting the flexibility of the NATO commander and the capabilities at his disposal. Pressure to lift these caveats continued to bear only limited fruit – for example, Italy allowed its troops to be deployed for limited periods into combat zones.

US General David McKiernan replaced General Dan McNeill as ISAF commander in May 2008. As of mid 2008, ISAF numbered approximately 52,700 troops from 40 countries, including 23,500 from the United States, which had a further 12,000 troops deployed in the country as part of its counter-terrorism efforts under *Operation Enduring Freedom*. ISAF had 26 Provincial Reconstruction Teams (PRTs), which enabled development projects to be undertaken by providing security as well as specialist expertise, across Afghanistan in addition to troops committed to combat. The deployment of extra troops allowed NATO better to hold territory once taken, though still only to a limited extent. A crucial reinforcement was the deployment of 24th US Marine Expeditionary Unit to southern Helmand, which boosted the capacity of the largely British contingent in a key area. As the fighting intensified in summer 2008, the UK suffered an increase in casualties, mostly caused by IED attacks. In one week in June, nine soldiers were killed, bringing total British losses from hostile action since October 2001 to 80.

The operational capability of the Afghan National Army (ANA) steadily improved, although a manpower level of approximately 57,000 remained below the desired total strength of 80,000, due to be reached by 2010. One enhancement was the inauguration of the ANA Air Corps. Additional international troops, including an extra 3,500 US Marines, were allocated to training and mentoring the ANA. ISAF had increased the number of its Operational Mentoring and Liaison Teams (OMLTs) to 36, with a further 12 pledged by donor countries. European Union police-training teams with 400 personnel were assigned to building capacity in the weak Afghan National Police.

While the international community sought to strengthen its efforts, intense counter-insurgency operations were under way in the southern provinces of Helmand, Kandahar and Uruzgan, where Taliban influence was historically greatest. The number of operations involving combat increased in provinces such as Nimroz and Farah in the southwest and Badghis, Faryab, Faizabad and Badakhshan in the north. There was a growing emphasis on using ANA units in combat operations. In October and November 2007 ISAF forces in Regional

Command–North launched their first major joint combat operations with the ANA. *Operation Harekate Yolo 1* took place in Badakhshan against insurgents and included 400 ANA troops with 160 German paratroopers. In *Operation Harekate Yolo 2* ISAF forces from Norway and Germany, with 900 ANA troops, attacked insurgents in Ghowrmach district in northwest Afghanistan, after which the ANA took over responsibility for Ghowrmach.

Operations against the Taliban resulted in some successes. Mawlawi Abdul Manan, top Taliban commander in the eastern provinces of Khost, Paktia and Paktika, was killed as he was crossing into Afghanistan from Pakistan. In Helmand province 4,500 ISAF and ANA troops in December 2007 retook the town of Musa Qala, which the Taliban had captured in February after it reneged on a deal made in 2006 with British forces. In this battle, the first in which Afghan army units were the principal fighting force, it was clear that lessons had been learned from previous engagements. Overwhelming numbers of American, British and Afghan troops forced the insurgents to withdraw, with collateral damage kept to a minimum, and the recapture was followed by deployment of a stabilisation team which immediately started to implement development projects in order to show local people the government's commitment to improving conditions. ISAF's hope was that fast development would turn the population away from the Taliban and thus deny it territory.

Following this operation a key insurgent commander, Mullah Abdul Salaam, who had been persuaded to change sides under a British initiative, was appointed governor of Musa Qala. His appointment was initially agreed by Karzai, but the president later claimed to have been misled by the British. In a separate incident, a British official working for the UN and an Irish official who had been working for the EU as part of the Afghan government's efforts to woo Taliban fighters away from the insurgency were arrested and expelled from the country, after which Karzai turned down Ashdown for the UN 'supremo' post.

Interdicting the flow of insurgents from Pakistan into Afghanistan, essential to curbing the Taliban insurgency, would depend heavily on good intelligence, and joint centres were established for sharing information across the Durand Line between Pakistani and Afghan and international forces. Relations between Karzai and Pakistan, however, continued to be poor. The attack on Kandahar prison prompted Karzai to assert that Afghan forces had the right to cross the Durand Line in pursuit of militants, further heightening tension. The presence of large numbers of Afghan refugees in camps in Pakistan along the Durand Line was a contentious issue. The camps, many of which have become virtual townships, have been a ready source of recruits for militant groups.

Attempts to turn Taliban fighters away from insurgency met limited success. In the long run, this seemed an essential part of any solution to Afghanistan's chronic problems. So too did some form of dialogue with the Taliban. The National Peace Commission, headed by former mujahadeen commander Sibghatullah Mojaddedi, was charged with the task of reconciliation but its mandate was unclear and the process was slow, allowing for the reconciliation only of individuals rather than groups. Dialogue with the Taliban was viewed with caution in Washington. In April 2008, Karzai, conscious of the upcoming presidential election and the possible need for some kind of compliance with insurgent leaders, said that US and UK arrests of Taliban members were undermining his authority. This contributed to a growing sense that dialogue of some kind with recognised Taliban leaders was an increasing possibility.

Politics, governance and development

Karzai's authority declined over the past year, damaged by continuing corruption in many parts of his government and a general inability to bring sustainable development to areas most in need. His lack of authority was highlighted by an apparent inability to root out known drug barons and by the behaviour of close associates such as his military adviser, General Rashid Dostum. The president had few opportunities to improve his standing before his re-election bid in September 2009.

At an international donors' conference in Paris on 12 June 2008, Karzai announced a five-year development strategy with three main strands:

- to achieve nationwide stabilisation, strengthen law enforcement, and improve personal security for Afghans;
- to strengthen democratic practice and institutions, human rights, the rule of law, delivery of public services and government accountability; and
- to reduce poverty, ensure sustainable development through a private-sector-led market economy, improve human-development indicators, and make significant progress towards the Millennium Development Goals.

Karzai asked donors for $50bn, but the total pledged, at $21bn, demonstrated the limited confidence of the international community in the government's ability to manage donor finance. In 2007 it was estimated that government ministries only spent between 30 and 40% of aid for its intended purposes because of corruption, mismanagement and lack of expertise. A report by the non-governmental civil-society organisation Integrity Watch Afghanistan said that, of $25bn given in aid since 2001, only some $15bn had been spent, and that for every $100 spent, sometimes only $20 reached Afghan recipients; 15–30% of aid was spent on security for aid agencies, and 85% of products, services and human resources used by agencies were imported, providing few jobs for Afghan workers. Karzai argued, however, that donor nations' practice of spending directly, rather than through the state budget, undermined the government's authority and ability to manage development programmes.

One positive indicator was a rise in foreign direct investment to take advantage of the government's privatisation policy. Three foreign companies invested in the telecommunications sector and, in March 2008, Karzai announced that 80% of the state-owned company Afghan Telecom was to be privatised. China Metallurgical Group signed a $3bn deal to develop the Aynak copper mine in Logar province. Some hopes were raised for future economic prospects with new talks on 23 June on the Turkmenistan–Afghanistan–Pakistan–India (TAPI) pipeline project, worth $3.5bn. Overall, however, the prospects for improved governance were hamstrung by lack of security and of institutional capacity. One critical gap was in linking central government to provincial and local structures. In an attempt to overcome this problem an Independent Directorate of Local Governance was created, reporting directly to the president, with the aim of improving the performance of Provincial Development Committees and bypassing the Ministry of Interior, which was regarded as the most corrupt ministry. A programme was also launched to equip local defence organisations to cope with criminals and insurgents at a local level. In addition, a National Solidarity Programme succeeded in channelling resources directly to elected Community Development Councils representing over 25,000 villages, or over 70% of the country's communities, but funding was irregular.

A further positive sign was the number of children attending schools, with 6m children in education, of whom 30% were girls, although most were in northern or western areas where there was greater stability. Access to health care was available for 85% of the population, compared with less than 10% in 2002, and there was growth in independent media with more than 60 radio stations, 15 television channels and a wealth of printed media.

These areas of successful development were offset by poor economic performance. Although there was real 13% percent growth in the economy (excluding the opium economy) in 2007, inflation was running at about 20% and unemployment in a predominantly young population was around 40%. The price of flour rose by 69% in 2007 and continued to rise in 2008. A drought in summer 2007 was particularly severe in Badghis and Ghor provinces. The Commerce Ministry estimated that Afghanistan only produced 1.2m of the 6m tonnes of grain it needed to feed the population, and in many areas the government was unable to provide support to the areas worst affected. The drought also led to areas such as Nangahar province, where licit crops had been successfully cultivated, to revert to poppy cultivation, which requires a minimal supply of water.

Against this background of insecurity and a weak economy, Karzai's prospects in the presidential elections due to take place in October 2009 seemed weak. However, most of his likely opponents will be running for the first time and are untested. One name being discussed as a possible candidate was Zalmay Khalilzad, the US Ambassador to the UN, who was born in Afghanistan and was previously US Ambassador in Afghanistan and Iraq.

The Wolesi Jirga (the lower house of parliament) remained divided along ethnic and religious lines, with several warlords as members. The exception was the multi-ethnic United National Front (UNF) (Jabhe-ye-Motahed-e-Milli), the nearest thing to a coherent political opposition party. However, its declared aim to change from a presidential form of democracy to a parliamentary system brought it into direct confrontation with Karzai. The UNF, which includes former Northern Alliance figures, resented their apparent marginalisation by the current administration. In the elections, Karzai will be dependent on the selective non-transferable voting (SNTV) system, a Western construct which some criticise for not taking enough account of the traditional Afghan democratic customs through the village *shura*. SNTV was used to retard the emergence of new parties, fragment existing opposition blocs and weaken the influence of regional warlords. At the same time, it was an attempt to create a loyal Pashtun bloc upon which Karzai could depend for legislative support. Although the first two goals were achieved, Karzai's Pashtun base was also fragmented. As a result the Wolesi Jirga became a forum for clientelism and shifting alliances, where progressive and liberal parties or candidates struggled to get their message across.

Possible outcomes

By mid 2008, Afghanistan faced a clash between two competing desires among the population. The first was a desire of the government and its largely northern support base to modernise along Western lines. The second, seen in the underdeveloped south, which was also the Taliban heartland, hankered after a traditional way of life. This clash allowed the Taliban to maintain its support. How to reconcile a democratic system with Afghan tradition and practice was an increasing challenge that could eventually lead to some form of accommodation with the Taliban. Amidst the insurgency, corruption and weak governance, Karzai's options were limited. The appointment of Eide as UN supremo offered some hope that more coherence could be brought to the nation-building effort, as did the continued support of the international community in providing military and financial resources. Looming over the nation's problems, however, was the continuing poor relationship between Pakistan and Kabul. There could be little hope while the support base for the Afghan insurgency continued to exist with relative impunity on Pakistani territory. But until relations improve between the two countries this situation is set to continue.

Sri Lanka, Bangladesh and Nepal: Conflict and Change

Sri Lanka

That the recent renewed escalation of the long ethnic conflict in Sri Lanka was likely to continue indefinitely seemed to be confirmed when the government in January 2008 formally withdrew from the 2002 ceasefire. It argued the ceasefire was already dead in practice, and that rather than constraining the Tamil Tigers it had given them time to rearm. The government's decision led to the withdrawal of the Norwegian-led Sri Lankan Monitoring Mission.

Having defeated the Liberation Tigers of Tamil Eelam (LTTE) in the east in 2007, the government's military strategy appeared to be to weaken it further with the aim of negotiating a political settlement on favourable terms. To consolidate its military victory in the eastern province, the government held nine local-council elections in the Batticaloa district in March 2008, with 60% voter turnout and over a hundred members elected to local bodies. This was followed in May by the first provincial-council elections in the eastern province for 20 years. With voter turnout of 65%, President Mahinda Rajapakse's United People's Freedom Alliance (UPFA) won a majority of seats with the support of the Tamil Makkal Viduthalai Pulikal (TMVP), a breakaway group of the LTTE. The government saw these elections as key to achieving peace and democracy in the east. Sivanesathurai Chandrakanthan, the controversial TMVP leader, was sworn in as chief minister of the Eastern Provincial Council on 16 May, despite commanding only six TMVP members among the UPFA's 20 councillors, as a reward for the TMVP's support. Both elections were disrupted by violence from the LTTE and reports of intimidation and collusion with the police on the part of the TMVP.

Following the government's success in the east, LTTE leaders in the north became priority targets. In November 2007, Suppayya Paramu Thamilchelvan, leader of the LTTE political wing, was killed in an air raid, followed in January 2008 by military intelligence leader Shanmuganathan Ravishankar and his son. The government also claimed that LTTE supremo Vellupillai Prabhakaran was wounded in the January attack. In retaliation, the LTTE killed Tamil member of parliament Thiyagarajah Maheswaran; Minister for Construction Dassanayake Mudiyanselage Dassanayake; the chief secretary of the eastern province, Herath Abeyweera; and Minister of Highways and Road Development Jeyaraj Fernandopulle, among others. The end of the ceasefire on 16 January 2008 was marked by a bomb explosion on a bus near Colombo in which approximately 25 people were killed. The LTTE also continued bomb attacks, killing eight people and injuring over 90 in Colombo on 16 May 2008, killing nine and injuring 84 on the Colombo–Panadura train on 26 May, and killing 21 and injuring over 50 on a bus in Moratuwa on 6 June. During offensive operations by the armed forces

Map 8.1 **Sri Lanka: escalating conflict**

The Sri Lankan government's official withdrawal from its six-year-old ceasefire agreement with the Liberation Tigers of Tamil Eelam (LTTE) in January 2008 followed a two-year period of escalating conflict in which it became clear that the peace process was in serious jeopardy. Even though the Sri Lankan army has gained significant ground from the LTTE in recent months and has stated its intention to bring an end to the Tamil insurgency by the end of 2008, the LTTE's determination to resist army offensives is undiminished.

Selected violent incidents, January–June 2008

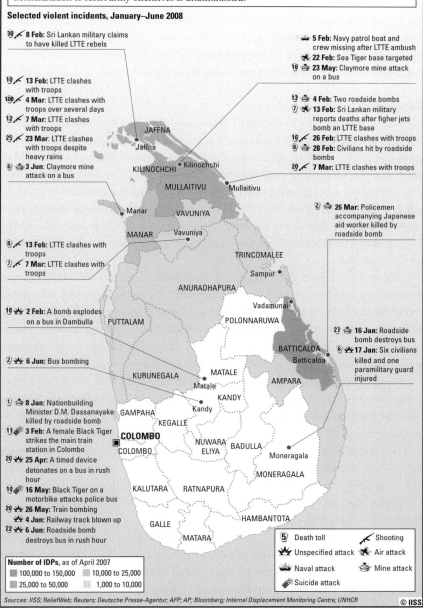

30 ✘ **8 Feb:** Sri Lankan military claims to have killed LTTE rebels

10 ✘ **13 Feb:** LTTE clashes with troops
100 ✘ **4 Mar:** LTTE clashes with troops over several days
12 ✘ **7 Mar:** LTTE clashes with troops
29 ✘ **23 Mar:** LTTE clashes with troops despite heavy rains
6 🏊 **3 Jun:** Claymore mine attack on a bus

8 ✘ **13 Feb:** LTTE clashes with troops
7 ✘ **7 Mar:** LTTE clashes with troops

18 🌊 **2 Feb:** A bomb explodes on a bus in Dambulla

2 🌊 **6 Jun:** Bus bombing

1 🏊 **8 Jan:** Nationbuilding Minister D.M. Dassanayake killed by roadside bomb
11 💥 **3 Feb:** A female Black Tiger strikes the main train station in Colombo
26 🌊 **25 Apr:** A timed device detonates on a bus in rush hour
10 💥 **16 May:** Black Tiger on a motorbike attacks police bus
26 🌊 **26 May:** Train bombing
🌊 **4 Jun:** Railway track blown up
23 🌊 **6 Jun:** Roadside bomb destroys bus in rush hour

🚤 **5 Feb:** Navy patrol boat and crew missing after LTTE ambush
✦ **22 Feb:** Sea Tiger base targeted
16 🏊 **23 May:** Claymore mine attack on a bus

13 🏊 **4 Feb:** Two roadside bombs
7 ✦ **13 Feb:** Sri Lankan military reports deaths after figher jets bomb an LTTE base
16 ✘ **26 Feb:** LTTE clashes with troops
8 🏊 **28 Feb:** Civilians hit by roadside bombs
20 ✘ **7 Mar:** LTTE clashes with troops

2 🏊 **26 Mar:** Policemen accompanying Japanese aid worker killed by roadside bomb

27 🏊 **16 Jan:** Roadside bomb destroys bus
6 🌊 **17 Jan:** Six civilians killed and one paramilitary guard injured

JAFFNA
• Jaffna
KILINOCHCHI • Kilinochchi
MULLAITIVU • Mullaitivu
• Manar
MANAR VAVUNIYA • Vavuniya
TRINCOMALEE
• Sampur
ANURADHAPURA
• Vadamunai
PUTTALAM POLONNARUWA
BATTICALOA
• Batticaloa
KURUNEGALA MATALE
• Matale AMPARA
KANDY
GAMPAHA • Kandy
KEGALLE
■ **COLOMBO**
COLOMBO NUWARA BADULLA
ELIYA • Moneragala
MONERAGALA
KALUTARA RATNAPURA
GALLE HAMBANTOTA
MATARA

Number of IDPs, as of April 2007
▮ 100,000 to 150,000   ▮ 10,000 to 25,000
▮ 25,000 to 50,000   ▯ 1,000 to 10,000

⑤ Death toll   ✘ Shooting
🌊 Unspecified attack   ✦ Air attack
🚤 Naval attack   🏊 Mine attack
💥 Suicide attack

Sources: IISS; ReliefWeb; Reuters; Deutsche Presse-Agentur; AFP; AP; Bloomberg; Internal Displacement Monitoring Centre; UNHCR

© IISS

in the north, LTTE, military and civilian casualties continued to mount. There were fears that the flow of Tamil refugees across the Palk Strait into the southern Indian province of Tamil Nadu could affect Indian security.

The All Parties Representative Council (APRC), comprising most of the major parties in Sri Lanka, endeavoured to reach cross-party consensus on the conflict. Its primary proposal was to devolve power through implementation of the 13th Amendment to the constitution, passed in 1987; previous governments had lacked the will to meaningfully devolve power in this way. For Rajapakse this recommendation was an interim measure, and he appointed a cabinet sub-committee to explore ways and means for its implementation.

Bangladesh

Following the army-backed state of emergency declared by President Iajuddin Ahmed on 11 January 2007, democracy remained suspended in Bangladesh. The caretaker government's chief adviser, Fakhruddin Ahmed, announced on 12 May 2008 that the suspended parliamentary elections would be held in December. The rationale for postponing elections had been to remove corruption, produce a new voter identification list with photographs and issue national identification cards to citizens. The previous voter list had been ruled null and void by the High Court. The Election Commission expected completion of voter registration by October 2008.

The delay allowed the caretaker government to press corruption charges against prominent politicians and to circumvent the political process. It targeted the leaders of the two major political parties, former premiers Khaleda Zia of the Bangladesh Nationalist Party (BNP) and Sheikh Hasina of the Awami League (AL). After attempts to exile both leaders in early 2007 failed, the government prosecuted them on corruption and extortion charges brought by the Anti-Corruption Commission. Hasina was jailed in July 2007 and Zia in September 2007. The caretaker government also arrested Moulana Matiur Rahman Nizami, head of Jamaat-e-Islami, the country's largest Islamic party and a minister in Zia's former BNP government. In May 2008 the government created a Truth and Accountability Commission allowing Bangladeshi nationals to voluntarily declare and deposit illegally obtained wealth, and avoid prosecution. Those who did would nevertheless be ineligible to participate in public office for five years.

Under the emergency rule, rallies, demonstrations and processions were banned, though a ban on indoor political meetings was partially lifted in May 2008. In June 2008 the government announced several local elections for 4 August, for which emergency rules were to be conditionally relaxed to permit meetings and election rallies 21 days before the election date. In August 2007, the army had responded violently to student protests sparked by a physical assault on Dhaka University students by troops at a sporting event; one person was killed and hundreds injured. Severe restrictions on the media continued to prohibit criticism of the government. As political parties could not demonstrate publicly against the government, the BNP (which recently healed a split in its ranks) and the AL refused to talk to the government. On 31 May 2008, Education Adviser Hossain Zillur Rahman announced that the government was working on a way to release Hasina and Zia to enable parliamentary elections to take place and prevent a boycott by the two major political parties. The following month Hasina was allowed to travel abroad for medical treatment. Over 20,000 people were detained by security forces for links to criminal and militant organisations in order to prevent violence in the forthcoming polls.

There were no major terrorist attacks in Bangladesh over the year to July 2008, due largely to the success of its intelligence agencies and security forces. The latter recovered bombs and seized firearms belonging to various militant groups. Some 250 militants were also arrested, with 17 sentenced to death. The banned terrorist group Jama'at-ul Mujahideen Bangladesh (JMB), however, was reportedly regrouping across the country, strengthening networks and organising training and indoctrination programmes. Partially as a response, Bangladesh adopted a controversial anti-terror law calling for seven years' imprisonment for campaigning for a banned organisation and six months' imprisonment for joining a banned organisation.

The United States labelled the Harkat-ul-Jihad-al-Islami Bangladesh (HuJI-B) as a 'specially designated global terrorist organisation', and India claimed that the group was responsible for several terror attacks. The Bangladesh government denied the allegations. In April 2008 the rail link between Kolkata in India and Dhaka in Bangladesh was re-established, giving India easier access to its northeast. However, India began to fence large stretches of its border with Bangladesh in an attempt to prevent illegal immigration, evoking strong protests from Dhaka.

Nepal

The Constituent Assembly elections in Nepal on 10 April 2008 were the culmination of the 2006 peace deal between the erstwhile Maoist rebels (Communist Party of Nepal (Maoist)) and the ruling Seven Party Alliance (SPA). The elections, which had been postponed twice over the previous year, were supported by a large UN mission and observers from the international community and were surprisingly peaceful, with 60% turnout. The Maoists won the largest number of seats (220) but fell short of a majority in the 601-member Constituent Assembly. This unexpected victory reflected the people's desire for change and an end to the conflict and political instability of the past decade, along with disillusionment with the traditional political parties. The royalist political parties boycotted the elections, and the Nepali Congress Party and Communist Party Nepal – United

Marxist Leninist (CPN-UML) fared much worse than expected, winning 110 and 103 seats respectively.

The assembly, which is to re-write the country's constitution and act as an interim parliament until general elections are held in two years' time, convened for the first time on 28 May 2008. Its first act, by a vote of 560 to 4, was to abolish the 239-year-old Hindu monarchy and declare the country a republic. Former King Gyanendra, who had already been stripped of most of his powers and had lost control of the army, now formally lost any remaining status. On 26 June, interim Prime Minister Girija Prasad Koirala announced he would step down to make way for the new government. While abolition of the monarchy had been a major issue for the Maoists, other major concerns remained, many affecting the welfare of their core constituency, the rural poor. The new government, under the lead of the Maoists, was expected to focus on land reform, greater economic control, slowing privatisation, integration of military cadres, and dealing with continuing ethnic unrest in the south. However, as major decisions required a two-thirds majority in the Constituent Assembly, this depended on being able to form a coalition. Much will therefore depend on the ability of the Maoists and the traditional parties to work together.

A new factor over the past 18 months has been increased ethnic violence, along with armed clashes, continuing civil unrest and kidnappings in the southern Terai plains bordering India. The region's Madhesi community, reportedly comprising over 40% of Nepal's population, demanded greater political representation and autonomy. Its largest political group, the Madhesi People's Rights Forum (MPRF), demanded an autonomous and unified Terai region within a federal system. On 30 August 2007 the MPRF and the interim government agreed on a federal structure with an autonomous state for the Terai, to be finalised by the Constituent Assembly. To pressure the government to implement the reform, the coalition United Democratic Madhesi Front (UDMF) began a general strike on 13 February 2008, which caused considerable hardship and crippled food and fuel supplies to the Terai and Kathmandu. It was called off 15 days later, after an eight-point agreement between the UDMF and the interim government on 28 February confirmed that the Madhesis and other federal states would be recognized as autonomous regions. Nonetheless, armed groups in the Terai remained dissatisfied. On 1 March 2008, the interim government signed an agreement with another ethnic umbrella organisation, the Federal Republic National Front (FRNF), ending another series of strikes in the south and east.

The question of the integration of the Maoist's People's Liberation Army (PLA) into the new republican army remained, although the UN lowered its estimate of the number of PLA cadres from over 30,000 to approximately 18,000. There was also concern over continued political violence by the Maoists and their Young Communist League (YCL).

The United Nations Mission in Nepal (UNMIN) arrived in January 2007 with a 12-month mandate, later extended by six months to July 2008, and reportedly by a further six months to January 2009. Prachanda, the Maoist leader who was likely to head the new government, indicated that he favoured only a limited further extension of the mandate. India also opposed growing international involvement in its immediate neighbourhood. For New Delhi, a Maoist-led government in Nepal raised perplexing questions, including alleged links with India's Maoist Naxalites and insurgent groups in the northeast, and the future of the India–Nepal relationship. Prachanda had said that a bilateral friendship treaty would be scrapped. For China, Nepal's largest neighbour, the key issue was likely to remain the stability and security of its long and sensitive Tibetan border.

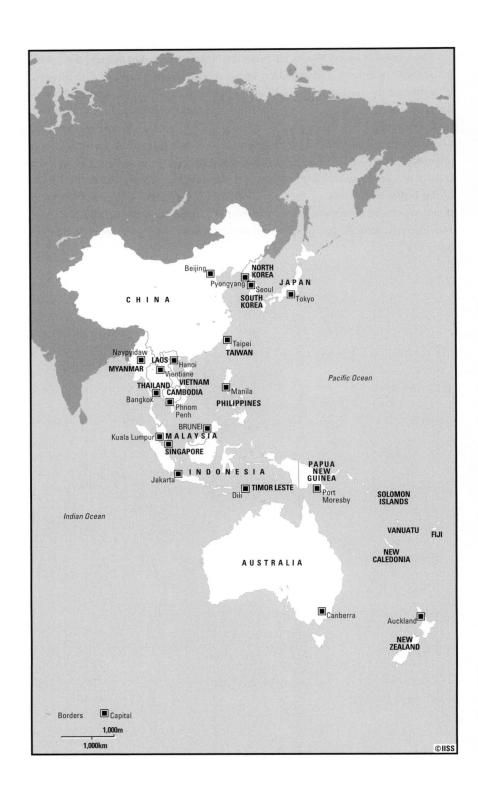

CHINA

Beijing

NORTH
KOREA

Pyongyang

Seoul
SOUTH
KOREA

JAPAN

Tokyo

Taipei
TAIWAN

Naypyidaw

LAOS

Hanoi

MYANMAR

Vientiane

THAILAND   VIETNAM

CAMBODIA

Bangkok

Phnom
Penh

Manila

PHILIPPINES

BRUNEI

Kuala Lumpur   MALAYSIA

SINGAPORE

Jakarta   INDONESIA

PAPUA
NEW
GUINEA

Dili   TIMOR LESTE

Port
Moresby

SOLOMON
ISLANDS

Pacific Ocean

VANUATU   FIJI

NEW
CALEDONIA

Indian Ocean

AUSTRALIA

Canberra

Auckland

NEW
ZEALAND

Borders   Capital

1,000m

1,000km

©IISS

The principal focus in the Asia-Pacific region was on China as it continued to consolidate its position as an economic power. Beijing's overriding concern was that the 2008 Olympic Games – to be held after *Strategic Survey* went to press – should provide a trouble-free showcase for its extraordinary development over the past 30 years. It therefore reacted in determined fashion when protests against Chinese rule broke out in Tibet, followed by demonstrations in foreign cities as the Olympic torch was paraded through them. There were changes of leadership in South Korea, where the conservative Lee Myung Bak was elected president but quickly ran into political troubles; in Japan, where Shinzo Abe lasted only a year as prime minister and was replaced by the older and more pragmatic Yasuo Fukuda; in Australia, where Kevin Rudd's Labor Party swept to victory in elections to defeat the prime minister of 12 years, John Howard; in Thailand, where democracy was restored 15 months after a military coup; and in Taiwan, where the election of Ma Ying-jeou as president heralded an immediate warming of relations with Beijing. There was some progress towards easing the confrontation over North Korea's nuclear programme, as a result of bilateral negotiations between Washington and Pyongyang.

The region suffered two natural disasters causing huge loss of life. The enormous and impressive rescue efforts made by the Chinese authorities, including the People's Liberation Army, could not prevent 70,000 deaths following an earthquake in Sichuan province. By contrast, coastal areas of Myanmar were devastated by a cyclone and the military regime prevented a flow of foreign aid while up to 130,000 people died. The regime had earlier suppressed pro-democracy protests by monks.

China's Year – For Better or Worse?

As *Strategic Survey* went to press, the 2008 Beijing Summer Olympic Games had yet to be formally opened and not a single discipline had been contested. But as a political and diplomatic phenomenon the Olympics had been in full swing for many turbulent months. The spectacle was going neither as China's ruling Communist Party had intended nor as ordinary Chinese – some perplexed, others plainly furious – had expected. Beijing had pursued the goal of hosting the 2008 games with tremendous tenacity and great powers of recovery following the acrimonious failure of its bid for the 2000 Olympics, which had been awarded to Sydney. It had thrown the full weight of the state into a renewed campaign and, once the prize had been clinched, poured its energy and resources into preparations that quickly assumed a vast and costly scale. No country seeks to host the Olympics for reasons limited entirely to sporting zeal or a sense of affinity with the athletic traditions of ancient Greece: national pride and prestige, and the thrill of the spot-lit centre-stage, are typically prominent impulses. Yet in the case of China the Olympics early on acquired unusually totemic significance. Beijing regarded them as the proper international occasion on which the Chinese could celebrate – and the outside world could be made to recognise – China's immense accomplishments over 30 years of economic reform: the stunning enrichment of vast swathes of a population whose energy and entrepreneurial flair had been unleashed; the breathtaking transformation of now soaring cityscapes; and, above all, China's arrival as a country of real consequence – a pivot of trade and diplomacy whose best days appeared still to lie ahead. In a festival of patriotic fervour, the ruling Communist Party reasoned and hoped, the Chinese might congratulate and thank the leaders whose guidance had delivered these things without the chaotic, distracting encumbrances of Western-style democracy – an alien system of government of which China had no past tradition and no future need. Indeed, the moral of the story would be that political continuity is the precondition to increased wealth at home and greater respect abroad for China.

To many outside observers, however, the games would not mark China's 'arrival' at some fixed point from which it would continue forward on a roughly familiar trajectory. Rather, they would provide only a blurred or highly pixelated snapshot of a China on a fast-moving transition to an unknown and perhaps unknowable destination. And if the games were indeed to be a showcase, then it would be of China 'warts and all'. Next to China's dynamic economic growth would be set gaping income inequalities within and between regions, the absence of meaningful welfare structures and an appalling degradation of the environment in the pursuit of rapid growth. Against the undoubted increase in economic and social freedoms since the Orwellian days of the Cultural Revolution would be set the continuing repressiveness of a Communist Party that crushes even murmurs of political dissent and, far from being overwhelmed by the private information flows made possible by mobile phones, e-mail and the Internet, has contrived to enlist these as instruments of surveillance and control. The party's self-confessed tendency towards corruption would, at the very least, qualify its claim to unique prowess in governing. And next to China's apparent craving for international recognition and approval would stand an all-too-easily ignitable nationalism that bristled at foreign criticisms and inclined to exotic theories of an international conspiracy against China.

Indeed, the uneasiness of China's relations with the outside world and the breadth of the political gulf that still separated it from large parts of international society were encapsulated in the awkward – sometimes violent, sometimes farcical – procession of the Olympic torch around the world in the months leading up to the Games. Given Beijing's familiarity with the controversy that its repressive actions in Tibet and its entanglements with the unsavoury regimes of Sudan and Myanmar – among others – have inspired abroad over many years, it never expected the procession to be received to universal acclaim. Calls from non-governmental organisations, activists and Hollywood celebrities for a boycott of what they branded the 'Genocide Olympics' – in reference to the campaign of violence prosecuted in Darfur by Beijing's ally, Khartoum – had already prompted a tactical but nevertheless public recalibration of China's relations with Sudan (and to a lesser degree with Myanmar). Intended as a triumphal march, the torch procession would no doubt meet with a political reply from those activists and campaigners who argued that the Beijing Games would, like the 1936 Olympics hosted by Nazi Germany, provide an undeserved platform for a cynical and disreputable regime. Overseas Chinese communities were therefore mobilised by Beijing to line the streets of capitals and cheer the torch on its way. The precaution was taken of permanently surrounding the Olympic flame, treated now as a symbol of Chinese dignity, with a somewhat robotic retinue of tracksuit-wearing elite members of the paramilitary People's Armed Police. Their presence, and their occasionally rough manner in handling the protesters of London, Paris and other cities, soon was seen by demonstrators as in itself a provocation. So was their elaborate route, which took them through the Tibetan capital of Lhasa in a symbolic affirmation of Chinese suzerainty there.

The outburst of ethnic violence in Tibet and in other ethnic-Tibetan communities in western China in March and April 2008, which met with a sharp response from the Chinese security forces, magnified and inflamed all these controversies. In the most scathing and withering terms, Beijing accused the exiled Dalai Lama of orchestrating a campaign of bloodshed in which around 20 Han Chinese were officially reported to have been killed. Criticism of China's crackdown from Western governments – some of which threatened to boycott the opening ceremonies of the Olympics – and by non-governmental organisations grew amidst a gale of nationalist outrage in China. Heated discussion in Chinese Internet chat rooms referred to a spiteful international effort to subvert Tibet and sabotage the Olympics. Some Western observers of Tibet, in turn, speculated that Beijing had in fact allowed disturbances – stimulated by ethnic and economic as much as political and religious grievances – to escalate there, providing a pretext for the imposition of martial law well in advance of the arrival in Lhasa of the Olympic torch in the company of the world's media and of 'troublemaker' activists who no doubt would wish to stage incidents to embarrass China and protest its policies in the 'Autonomous Region'.

Measures were at any rate soon taken in Beijing and elsewhere to prevent matters getting out of hand. Chinese officials consented to meet with representatives of the Dalai Lama, who had all the while called for violent Tibetan protests to end. The governments of those countries through which the Olympic flame had still to pass now took special care to avoid further embarrassment. The controversy was in due course smothered – but not settled – by the catastrophic consequences of the earthquake that struck Sichuan province in western China in May, killing around 70,000 people and shattering the lives of many more. It forcibly redirected China's attention and produced expressions of international sympathy and offers of practical help. The media moved on. The competence, decisiveness and openness with which the Chinese government responded to this emergency, moreover, had a certain rehabilitating effect on its international reputation when set against the admittedly rather low benchmark of Myanmar's cynical and incompetent response to the enormous death and destruction caused by a cyclone at about the same time. But left hanging in the air were the questions of what atmosphere – good-natured and sporting; or bitterly political – would attend the Olympics in Beijing, and whether the games would on this basis be judged a success or a failure. A tightening security clampdown in Beijing, leading to common references inside and outside China to the 'Killjoy Olympics', did not augur well. The final answer seemed likely to carry implications for the way in which China and others conceived of its place in the world and of the meaning of its much-heralded rise.

Reactions to China's rise

Different attitudes towards this subject can be found in China. A hubristic view regards China as undergoing a resurgence that will restore the country to the position of economic, political and cultural pre-eminence it has customarily enjoyed – or thought of itself as enjoying – for a majority of its long and continuous history. This is a history that the Chinese were encouraged to reject and even physically eradicate in the decades following the 1949 Revolution. They are now being urged to celebrate it in substitution of the vanishing relevance of communist ideology to their daily lives. China's coming pre-eminence is seen in this narrative as expressing a return to a natural state of affairs that has only temporarily been interrupted by internecine struggles within China, by the errors of certain Chinese rulers or systems of rule, and the opportunistic predations of outside powers who gained a fleeting technological and military ascendancy over China. Like most forms of hubris, it is fed by a sense of past humiliation and weakness that must be overcome – and perhaps overcompensated for. The disasters and slights visited on China by European colonial powers and Japan in the nineteenth and early twentieth centuries are to be corrected by the reunification of the motherland, including Taiwan, and a vigorous defence of Chinese sovereignty, dignity and interests on all fronts.

Yet this hubris differs from the solipsism of imperial China, with its often lofty indifference to the civilisational, scientific and economic accomplishments of other states. There is now a recognition that China's domestic fortunes are to an unusual and unprecedented extent dependent on the outside world for markets, resources, technology and capital, all of which form potential chokeholds on the re-emergence of a still vulnerable China. Allied to this sense of vulnerability is the impression that existing major powers, and chiefly the United States, are pursuing a policy of encirclement and containment that requires China to break out of its claustrophobic confinement and establish strategic relationships and partnerships almost wherever these can be found. China must in consequence learn how to exercise its economic influence to extract political loyalty from those willing to offer it and have the military means to command respect from those who are not. The possibility of conflict may not be avoidable.

This view represents a powerful undercurrent of Chinese thinking. But it is not how China officially describes its self-image or its diplomatic objectives. Official pronouncements instead focus on a sense of historical and geopolitical exceptionalism. China will break the destructive pattern of behaviour that other rising powers in modern history have been imprisoned by – reckless self-assertion and revisionism, open competition or conflict with established powers, leading at best to exhaustion or at worst to war and ruin. China will not emulate Revolutionary and Napoleonic France, Wilhelmine or Nazi Germany, the Japan of the early twentieth century, nor, implicitly, the contemporary strategic petulance of revanchist Iran and Russia. Its principal objective is economic development at home and the political stability this affords. It wishes to put relations with neighbours on a sound footing, freezing disputes, including territorial disputes, that cannot yet be mutually resolved. China seeks integration with global economic structures and engages multilateral organisations that have wider, political remits. It wishes to play a constructive role in the United Nations and its Security Council. It will join common efforts to tackle international security problems and other challenges of global governance, yet it cannot allow others to decide when and how it should do so or what specific national interests China should be prepared to sacrifice for a broader good. China demands no more respect, and avails itself of no less patriotic pride, than other large powers would claim for themselves. It feels entitled to modernise its antique military to take account of the country's continental proportions and the uncertain and fluid geopolitical environment it inhabits. China argues that the military alliances of other states, especially the United States, should, however, be dissolved as relics of an outdated 'Cold War mentality'. In East Asia, their place should be taken by a process of regional community-building in which China will play its full role, and which will form part of a tight web of interweaving economic and diplomatic ties that will constrain competition and compel cooperation.

These narratives find their echoes and resonances in the outside world, and where one stands is, as so often, governed by where one sits. In the United States, which in strategic terms is heavily invested in Asia and, as the foremost power in the world, is uniquely sensitive to the emergence of peer competitors who might wish to supplant it, it is not hard to uncover analysis of China of a determinist hue. This is an influential but hardly dominant strain of thought. It holds that a struggle for mastery is the tragic but inevitable outcome of constant historical forces that cannot be escaped even by conscious effort. Chinese behaviour and American responses are seen through the prism of this inevitability. Strategic distractions in the Balkans or the Middle East, or in the form of international terrorism, may come and go, but a reckoning with China is the principal strategic challenge with which the United States will be confronted and for which it must prepare.

By contrast, the narrative of Chinese exceptionalism finds a ready and enthusiastic audience in many parts of the European Union, with its strategic detachment from Asia, its disavowal of traditional geopolitics, its relaxed attitude towards questions of sovereignty, its limited military means and ambitions, and its multilateralist, supposedly 'postmodern' psychology. The message is also well received by China's smaller neighbours, who certainly wish it to be true.

Neither the determinist nor the exceptionalist argument is convincing, however. The content of Chinese diplomacy points to something more complicated, subtle and elusive. In many important senses China conforms to the 'normal', realist behaviour of other rising powers of the past. It is forming exclusive political relationships and economic interests around the world, becoming more confident in exercising power and in resisting foreign pressure, immersing itself in regional and global diplomacy, and acquiring significant military capabilities. At the same time, however, much of its behaviour is not typical of a rising, revisionist power. It remains agile and flexible in its diplomacy, willing to deal, prioritise and compromise – and even to show deference towards much smaller neighbours. It is embracing the world economically and sees economic globalisation, rather than autarky, as an essential ingredient of the recipe for China's future growth. It speaks the language of reassurance and pragmatism.

At issue is which of these parallel patterns of behaviour will ultimately emerge as dominant. Is China's soothing diplomacy merely a device to perpetuate the circumstances required to enlist the acquiescence and resources of other states in reaching that goal – a mere tactic to be cast aside once superpower status has been achieved? Or will the successful practice of these policies of engagement and cooperation ultimately suppress whatever traditional geopolitical instincts and impulses China may be subject to?

For those who would wish to influence the answer, a number of strategies have been suggested. In the United States, the 'responsible stakeholder' model developed by then-Deputy Secretary of State Robert Zoellick disavows the containment of China as futile and counterproductive but sets certain standards of behaviour as the terms and conditions for China's integration with the international system and its induction among the great powers. It also requires the United States and its allies to prepare for the possibility that China may find these terms too exorbitant and seek to barge its way in on its own terms. Another approach suggests that the United States should resign itself to its inevitable relative decline and ensure the endurance of Western liberal values in international affairs by strengthening the global institutions that give expression to them.

Yet grand strategies such as these are more often articulated than implemented. It is difficult to develop the consensus and coherence they require, not least because China's international behaviour is ambiguous and the outside world has little understanding of precisely how, and by whom, grand strategic decisions are made. For a country of China's size, complexity and importance, this is remarkable. Indeed, it is an astounding achievement. The Chinese political system at the highest levels is determinedly non-transparent. The ruling Communist Party leadership wishes to project an image of invincible solidarity. Public divisions are regarded as politically fatal. Factional squabbling and political dealing occurs, but only behind closed doors. For outsiders, there is large scope for speculation but little that can be asserted confidently as fact. The official Chinese media provides guidance on how decisions and leadership appointments are to be perceived and interpreted, but this gives no insight into the processes that produce a certain outcome. Often such guidance deliberately distorts.

Leadership politics

The opacity of the Chinese political system was fully on display, as it were, at the 17th Congress of the Chinese Communist Party in Beijing on 15–21 October 2007. The gathering pointed to domestic-policy continuity under the rubric of striving for a 'harmonious society' in which economic inequalities are addressed, environmental degradation is tackled, corruption is reduced and the efficiency and competence of central and local government is improved. Yet the Congress was more notable for the leadership decisions that were taken, or rather simply announced to the world. As expected, President Hu Jintao was confirmed for a second term as secretary-general of the party and chairman of its central military commission, or high command. However, fresh appointments to the Politburo Standing Committee, the highest decision-making body, strongly suggested that a succession process is now being prepared in advance of the expiry of Hu's second and final term around 2012. Xi Jinping, 54, a former governor and party secretary of Zhejiang province and briefly party secretary of Shanghai, who hails from a prestigious party family, was fast-tracked directly onto the standing committee, having not previously served on the wider Politburo (which in turn is composed of selected members of a Central Committee). Confirming his status as heir apparent, Xi was in December 2007 appointed president of the Central Party School and, at the National People's Congress in March 2008, made vice-president of China. He also was made executive secretary of the Party Secretariat, and appointed head of that group of the leadership which is overseeing the preparations for the Olympics. The main features of this process of collecting jobs and portfolios seemed to mimic that undergone by Hu Jintao ahead of his own succession to former leader Jiang Zemin in 2002–03. It was widely speculated that Xi recommended himself to the leadership because of his lack of a strong attachment to any one of the party's factions as much as by virtue of his competence. The apparent intra-party haggling also, however, ensured that Li Keqiang, considered an ally of Hu Jintao, was – like Xi – parachuted directly onto the standing committee. It was rumoured he would be groomed to eventually assume the post of prime minister from the incumbent Wen Jiabao, and also that Li might be kept in the wings to assume Xi's mantle should Xi somehow falter or fall out of favour in the next five years.

The implications of the Congress for Hu Jintao's authority were seen as mixed. The presumed rules of succession, and the imperatives of factional politics, may prevent him from naming his own replacement, but the nine-man Politburo Standing committee now features an additional ally in the form of Li Keqiang. It has also been depopulated of members of the formerly dominant 'Shanghai faction' associated with Jiang Zemin, which in the early years of Hu's first term had been construed by observers as a constraint on Hu's freedom of action and initiative: Hu's principal rival, Zeng Qinhong, retired at the Party Congress; Chen Liangyu, the former party chief of Shanghai, had already been dismissed on corruption charges in July 2007; and a third faction member, Huang Ju, had passed away in June 2007.

In the months following the 17th Party Congress, the leadership found itself not only wrestling with preparations for the Olympics but also tested by a number of unexpected challenges. In January and February 2008 the worst snow and ice storms for 50 years struck central and western China, paralysing transport systems during the annual Spring Festival and causing extensive damage to property. As with the Sichuan earthquake that followed in May, the government was given credit for its responsiveness and swift mobilisation of resources, including the People's Liberation Army and other agencies, to assist in relief efforts. The leadership deftly presented a compassionate face, epitomised by the ubiquitous presence of Wen, megaphone in hand, issuing statements of reassurance and sympathy at disaster sites and at railway stations crammed with angry, stranded passengers. The party appeared to be placing greater emphasis on demonstrating responsiveness, competence and populist appeal as part of a strategy of fending off any calls for greater transparency and accountability.

A transformation in Taiwan

Beijing's political and diplomatic attention in the second half of 2007 and the first half of 2008, however, was gripped by the momentous developments underway in Taiwan. Legislative elections held in January 2008, followed promptly by presidential elections in March, produced a resounding rejection of rule by the pro-independence Democratic Progressive Party (DPP), which had been led in government since March 2000 by Chen Shui-bian as president. His tenure had been fraught. Although his policies never brought Taiwan to the precipice of a formal declaration of independence from China, which Beijing threatened would meet with a military reply, Chen, throughout his two terms, constantly asserted an identity for Taiwan separate from China. He sought to re-brand what formally still counted as the Republic of China as simply 'Taiwan'. He conducted a campaign to widen the 'international space' the island occupied, unsuccessfully seeking admission to multilateral bodies for whom national sovereignty is a criterion for entry. And he stepped up the bitter chequebook-diplomacy contest with China for recognition among various African, Caribbean and Pacific island states. Chen was cheered on by his political base as the true champion of Taiwan's interests. But his detractors regarded him as a reckless opportunist, whose initiatives seemed intended to provoke a heavy-handed response from Beijing – and so confirm his description of China as bullying and overbearing. In the early years of his term, Beijing seemed perplexed and cumbersome in responding to Chen's antics, relying on threats of military action if the red line of formal independence were crossed, passing an 'anti-secession' law that in fact mandated such action legally, and meanwhile beseeching the United States to hurl a diplomatic strait-jacket around Chen, who was testing not only Beijing's nerves but also Washington's patience. Often Chen seemed indifferent to the wishes and interests of Washington, which, with all its Middle Eastern preoccupations, had no need of aggravated relations with Beijing or tensions in the Taiwan Strait.

Gradually, however, China regained its composure. It noted a certain estrangement between Washington and Taipei, and had the strong sense that, despite Chen's intentions and efforts, Taiwan was becoming more isolated, more controversial in international opinion, and politically more introspective. It saw, too, that Chen was presiding over a prolonged economic malaise that many in Taiwan's business community linked to an increasingly unaffordable confrontation with China. Corruption scandals swirled about Chen and members of his family. Impeachment was threatened. The government lurched from one crisis or incident to another. In a politically vicious atmosphere, cooperation among the island's political parties seemed far beyond reach, even on matters of defence policy (such as the purchase of a package of arms – including submarines, surveillance aircraft and upgraded *Patriot* missile batteries – offered by the United States in 2001, which was not approved by the legislature until the dying days of the Chen administration). Beijing gathered the confidence to change tack. It refused to rise to Chen's bait, choosing to comment only rarely on Taiwanese politics. While leaving its military posture towards the island unaltered, Beijing offered trade concessions that seemed reasonable and constructive. And, drawing some comfort from Chen's inability to seek a third term as president, it received leading members of the opposition party, the Kuomintang (KMT), in Beijing. China signalled that better relations would develop across the strait with a KMT government in place, but it also took care not to handicap the KMT by treating it as China's agent and instrument in Taiwan. At the 17th Party Congress in October 2007, Hu spoke of the need for a 'peace treaty' – albeit one predicated on Taipei's acceptance of Chinese sovereignty. For its part, the KMT positioned itself astutely with the Taiwanese electorate, arguing that it could better defend the island's interests, security and economic prospects by engaging China and improving relations with the island's only patron, the United States. It also chose as its presidential candidate the former mayor of Taipei, Ma Ying-jeou, a politician of wide appeal and with a reputation for pragmatism and probity (he was acquitted in late 2007 of charges of financial misconduct, allowing his presidential campaign to move forward with no lasting harm). The DPP sought to refresh its appeal by selecting as its candidate Frank Hsieh, the respected and able former mayor of Kaohsiung. But the political tide had turned. In the January elections to the Legislative Yuan, the KMT won 71% of the seats, trouncing and demoralising the DPP. The KMT sustained its momentum into the presidential contest, which Ma won with 58% of the votes cast, against Hsieh's 42%, on an impressively high turnout of 75%. A referendum put forward by the DPP to coincide with the election, seeking support for the notion that the island should apply to join the United Nations as 'Taiwan', failed amidst public antipathy.

A period of greater stability in relations between China and Taiwan was thus ushered in. What possibilities for an enduring accommodation or reconciliation between the two sides this might open up still seemed hard to predict. Taipei and Beijing were at pains to damp down excessive expectations of rapid progress and convergence. Given the many differences between them, and the political constraints they both operate under, this was prudent. They did, nonetheless, seek to develop a pattern of regular and systematic contact. Notable meetings after the presidential election included a brief encounter on 12 April between Hu and the Taiwanese vice-president-elect, Vincent Siew, at an annual economic conference on China's Hainan island. The honorary chairman of the KMT, Lien Chan, visited Hu in Beijing on 29 April. Following Ma's inauguration in late May, KMT Chairman Wo Poh-hsiung also called on Hu in Beijing. The sides quickly announced plans to resume a long-suspended dialogue, conducted through semi-official organisations – China's Association for Relations Across the Taiwan Straits (ARATS) and Taiwan's Straits Exchange Foundation (SEF); ARATS Chairman Chen Yunlin duly appeared in Taiwan on 11–14 June for a round of talks. Beijing and Taipei agreed to conduct such exchanges and others under a formula known as the '1992 consensus' – a reference to the period in which it was first employed. This device allows both sides to publicly subscribe to a 'one China principle' while holding entirely different views about how that concept is to be defined and what it signifies in practice. For China, the principle upholds its claim to sovereignty over Taiwan; for Taiwan, the principle indicates that there may well be only 'one China', but the island is not necessarily part of it. The formula is a knowing fudge, intended to create cover for dialogue that otherwise would be obstructed by the impractical requirement that the two sides resolve the most fundamental difference between them before they in fact sit down to talk. One of the early significant accomplishments of these contacts was the establishment at the start of July of direct charter flights between China and Taiwan (although agreement on direct cargo flights – of vital importance to the many Taiwanese businesses that have invested heavily in China – could not be reached at that time).

Ma emerged from the election empowered with a strong mandate for improving relations with Beijing, but conscious that in the wide centre ground of Taiwanese politics – the constituency to which he owes his election – there is no appetite for steps towards reunification with China. There is also a great sense of protectiveness towards Taiwan's dynamic democracy and the island's prerogatives as a de facto independent entity. Ma's pledge has been that under his tenure there will be 'no [de jure] independence; no reunification and no use of force'. Beijing cannot and will not disavow the goal of eventual reunification, but its immediate and medium-term interests are served by the maintenance of the status quo to which Ma points.

As their dialogue moves forward, both sides will face dilemmas. China is certainly relieved to have come through a seven-year period of flux and fragility in cross-strait relations. It spent much of this time engaged in the exhausting business of vilifying the Chen Shui-bian administration and being vilified in return. Now it faces in Taipei a new government whose arrival it privately hoped for and which it has publicly welcomed. Yet handling the dialogue is likely to prove complicated from the perspective both of content and appearances. Beijing will have to accord a more friendly Taipei greater respect. Suggestions and requests made by Taipei in the course of their dialogue – however unwelcome some of them may be – will need to be seen to be treated seriously. Moreover, the fact that a democratic process in Taiwan has produced a dialogue partner whom Beijing considers acceptable and responsible carries intriguing implications for the Communist Party's usual depiction of Taiwan's democracy as inherently flawed. This raised the question: if democracy can produce favourable outcomes in what China sees as one of its provinces, why would the introduction of democracy across China not bring similarly positive results?

For Taiwan, the challenge will be how to engage China in pursuit of better relations without at the same time allowing itself to be sucked so deeply into the Chinese orbit that the precious 'international space' still available to the island does not shrink irretrievably. The government's critics in the DPP were quick to charge that Ma had committed the tactical error of suspending competition with China for diplomatic recognition in order to sustain a correct atmosphere for the talks – thereby weakening his hand. Crucial will be an effective management of Taiwan's relations with the United States – a guarantor and a vital source of diplomatic leverage. Washington welcomed the altered tone in cross-strait relations and approved of the contacts between Taipei and Beijing. Yet some initial concerns were voiced privately about a lack of full consultation by Taiwan. And there was a sense that, exhilarated by the novelty of the talks, Taipei was at risk of moving without sufficient circumspection and patience into China's embrace.

Whatever specific tactical challenges the unfolding process of engagement with Taipei might hold in future, Beijing could by the middle of 2008 take considerable satisfaction from the new circumstances of the Taiwan Strait – no longer quite such a flashpoint of imminent danger, but rather holding out the promise of stability and predictability, and, if wisely handled by the Chinese side, involving the gradual marginalisation of the United States as a factor in the dispute. The transformation of the scene was important for Chinese domestic political reasons, too. The Communist Party at last had progress to report after long years in which Taiwan seemed to be slipping further and further out of China's grasp. Only so much of this could convincingly be blamed on Chen Shui-bian alone. Beijing had at times appeared helpless: it was keenly aware of the risk that its competence as the guardian of China's integrity and sovereignty might be impugned. There were also obvious implications for China's diplomacy in the Asia-Pacific, a region inhabited by a number of great or rising powers who see

China's approach to Taiwan – whether militaristic and coercive, or diplomatic and cooperative – as a barometer of China's strategic attitudes and a predictor of its broader intentions.

China in a multipolar Asia

China has viewed the evolution of a multipolar Asia with some discomfort. It resents America's heavy strategic engagement with the region and the web of military alliances Washington has cast in Asia. Its relations with India and Japan, both of which it has faced in war, have in the last 60 years mostly been unsteady and marked by mutual suspicion or open contempt. The fact that Tokyo and Washington remain tightly intertwined, and that New Delhi and Washington have put their Cold War antagonisms behind them and begun to develop a significant strategic relationship of their own, is hardly welcomed. Nor are recent signs of a mutual attraction between India and Japan. China's 'strategic partnership' with Russia, a notional but rather distant power in Asia, provides only some diplomatic relief: in the Asian geopolitical context, the significance of Beijing's relationship with Moscow derives from Russia's status as a supplier of arms, a source of energy and, through the Shanghai Co-operation Organisation, a partner in expanding China's presence in Central Asia and West Asia.

In the course of 2007 and the first half of 2008 China worked hard to interrupt some of these coagulating alignments, seeking to blunt bilateral antagonisms, establish new patterns of engagement and generally operate in a spirit of apparent goodwill. Treated with most urgency was the task of improving relations with neighbouring Japan – or rather pulling them out of the deep trough in which they had been festering for the last ten years. China and Japan have never benefited from the kind of active and determined reconciliation that France and Germany embarked on after the Second World War. They are captives of a sense of rivalry, fed by controversies about the honesty with which their historians chronicle their past encounters and by a number of unresolved territorial disputes. China fears Japan's gradual 'normalisation' as a military power and does not believe Japan has a legitimate leadership role to perform in East Asia or on the United Nations Security Council; Japan fears an increasingly assertive and militarily capable Chinese giant that is actively seeking to marginalise Tokyo in regional and global affairs. And yet the two countries are at the same time supremely important to each other as trading partners. The absence in recent years of a strategic dialogue with Japan therefore arguably represented the greatest weakness in China's foreign and security policy, and vice versa.

China was quick in 2006 to capitalise on the departure as prime minister of Junichiro Koizumi, whose repeated visits to the Yasukuni shrine – containing the remains of 12 Class A war criminals – had as far as China was concerned ruled out any bilateral summitry as a matter of principle. Koizumi's successor,

Shinzo Abe, made the strategic decision to avoid giving this offence, opening up the possibility of a visit to Beijing in October 2006 that was reciprocated by Wen's visit to Tokyo in April 2007. Abe's resignation in September of that year brought to the premiership Yasuo Fukuda. The improvement in the relationship was, however, sustained. The new prime minister recommended himself to Beijing because of his parentage and presumed diplomatic instincts. His late father, Takeo Fukuda, had as prime minister himself overseen the promulgation of the China–Japan Peace and Friendship Treaty, which in 2008 usefully has its 30th anniversary. The ground was carefully prepared for the first state visit to Japan in ten years by a Chinese president. The last such summit, featuring finger-pointing and lecturing by then President Jiang, had generally been judged a disaster in both China and Japan. Hu's visit in May 2008 was an entirely different affair. No major disagreements between the two countries were overcome, but the two leaders spoke in the spirit of identifying and developing common strategic interests concerning regional security and global challenges such as climate change. In order to give this aspiration meaning, the two sides committed themselves to annual summits.

The earthquake that struck Sichuan province soon after Hu's visit to Tokyo provided the occasion for Japan to offer, and China to accept, aid assistance. But it was a measure of continuing anti-Japan sentiment in China that an offer to fly assistance in on aircraft belonging to the Japan Self-Defense Forces could not be accepted, despite initial intimations that it might be. In the circumstances, Tokyo saw little alternative but to accept China's position with as much good grace and 'understanding' as it could muster. Significant practical accomplishments were nonetheless recorded after the summit. On 18 June, China and Japan announced that they had agreed to jointly explore undersea natural-gas and oil deposits in a part of the East China Sea to which they both lay sovereign claim. Under the terms of the agreement, which pragmatically sets the issue of sovereignty to one side, Japan will be able to invest in and profit from Chinese exploration projects at the Chunxiao fields, called Shirakaba by Japan. It was suggested that a similar approach will also be taken towards the disputed Longjin/Asunaro fields in due course. If these projects move forward successfully, and if similar pragmatism can be brought to bear in other parts of the relationship, there is a reasonable hope that relations will progress further. But official diplomacy will always have to stay within hailing distance of still antipathetic public opinion in both countries.

In parallel to this diplomacy China kept up its contacts with India. From Beijing's perspective this was warranted by India's increasing – if fairly recent – sense of itself as a rising Asian giant of global reach, with strengthening ties to the United States, the Persian Gulf and Southeast Asia, substantial investments in its defence capabilities, and growing need of energy and natural resources imported from abroad. In January 2008, Manmohan Singh made his first visit as India's prime minister to China. Burgeoning economic ties were celebrated and a target set to lift two-way trade to $60 billion by 2010 (from a mere $250 million in 1991). The official statement concluding the summit rehearsed India's ambition to occupy a permanent seat on the UN Security Council, a prospect China publicly treats with aloof 'understanding' but in practical terms resists as implying a dilution of its own status. Border disputes between the two countries – China's claim to Arunachal Pradesh and its presence in parts of the Jammu and Kashmir region India claims; demarcation disagreements regarding Indian-held Sikkim – moved no closer to final resolution in 2007 and early 2008. The subject was raised during the June 2008 visit to Beijing of Indian Foreign Minister Pranab Mukherjee. Emphasis here, however, was placed on the general stability of the borders, and both sides publicly at least emphasised that any outstanding issues should not be allowed to prejudice the development of a more substantial relationship. Each side continued vigilantly to monitor the military deployments of the other in the vicinity of the disputed areas, but they were also open to friendly contact. In December 2007, the armies of China and India held their first joint exercises. They were conducted in China's southwestern province of Yunnan, which abuts Myanmar and Tibet – both points of significant strategic interest to New Delhi as well as Beijing. Although of a modest scale, and intended as a confidence-building measure, the exercises indicated an increasing willingness to add a military dimension to the relationship (the navies of the two countries had already held joint search-and-rescue exercises).

As each country gathers greater strategic heft and expands its horizons, at issue will be whether a more overt strain of competition will emerge between them. As of mid 2008, however, neither New Delhi nor Beijing wished or needed to force disputes. Both had enough domestic preoccupations to wrestle with. Under these circumstances it seemed likely that they would for the time being continue to develop a broad if perhaps also still shallow and intermittent relationship. To a degree, this would, like China's engagement of Japan and its energetic cultivation of the ten members of the Association of Southeast Asian Nations (ASEAN), function as a sub-plot to Beijing's principal strategic relationship – that with the United States.

All change in Washington?

The 12 months to July 2008 were marked neither by dramatic breakthroughs nor striking reversals in US–China relations. Routine exchanges dealing with a wide range of economic and diplomatic matters continued at their now customary intensive pace. There were no state visits, but Presidents Bush and Hu met at the Asia-Pacific Economic Cooperation (APEC) summit in Sydney in September 2007, and then again at the meeting of the G8 in Japan in July 2008. The encounters appeared cordial enough. The improvement in Beijing's relations with both Taipei and Tokyo helped to ease irritants in the US–China relationship. The Six-Party Talks process that addresses North Korea's nuclear activities provided a venue in which Beijing and Washington continued to cooperate closely and publicly. They could, moreover, finally claim some success, as Pyongyang – gradually and partially – accounted for its past activities and submitted to the deactivation of key nuclear installations – as well as the visually striking implosion of the cooling tower at its Yongbyon facility in July 2008. But bilateral relations were not without their problems. The decision of the US Congress to award the Dalai Lama its highest civilian honour, the Gold Medal, introduced a distinct coolness. The fact that the award ceremony was not only attended by Bush but also coincided with the Communist Party's 17th Congress in October 2007 was received in China as an embarrassing and humiliating slight. These tensions revived amidst the March and April 2008 disturbances in Tibet. But, although Washington criticised China's crackdown there in strong terms, Bush ultimately resisted pressure to boycott the opening ceremony of the Olympics in the interest of keeping the broader relationship with China on an even keel.

Military-to-military contacts, meanwhile, moved forward – and back. US Secretary of Defense Robert Gates travelled to China in early November 2007, and by the end of the year the two countries had finalised the establishment of a long-planned 'hotline' between their defence establishments. In between these developments, however, tensions broke out over China's unexplained decision to deny the US aircraft carrier *Kitty Hawk* access to Hong Kong harbour, where crew members were, according to well-laid plans, to be reunited with their families for the American Thanksgiving holiday in late November. Despite lodging protests, the carrier was faced with no alternative but to set course for Japan, only to be informed once underway that Beijing had again reversed its position and that berthing in Hong Kong could now in fact go ahead. The *Kitty Hawk* declined the offer and steamed on. Beijing provided no public explanation for its actions, leading to speculation outside China about the coherence of decision-making in Beijing and the possibility of divisions between the civilian and military leaderships. Similar inferences had been drawn following China's decision in January 2007 to test an anti-satellite weapon without prior notice or subsequent explanation of its intent. The case of the *Kitty Hawk* was raised by Admiral Timothy Keating, Commander of the US Pacific Command, during his visit to China in January 2008. Later that month, Beijing agreed to allow the flagship of the US Seventh Fleet, the *Blue Ridge*, to enter Hong Kong harbour without incident. In its *Annual Report to Congress on the Military Power of the People's Republic of China*, published in March 2008, the Pentagon highlighted among other things the continuing build-up of short-range missiles opposite Taiwan, estimated at 900–1,000; the modernisation of the long-range missile force, including submarine-launched missiles; an increase in cyber attacks originating from China and directed against Western government facilities; increased efforts to develop China's submarine fleet, including nuclear-powered attack submarines; upgrades to the fighter and bomber fleet; the addition of modern battle tanks to the ground forces; and various initiatives to enhance China's defence-industrial base. To this extent the report described familiar American concerns and patterns of behaviour and planning that contradict the overall tone of Chinese foreign policy.

As the first half of 2008 slipped by, and the lame-duck status of the Bush administration became more patent, fewer bilateral initiatives were launched and China inevitably began to look more closely and with greater interest at the approaching US presidential election. From Beijing's perspective, the attitudes of the two leading presumptive candidates for the presidency – Senator John McCain of the Republican Party and Senator Barack Obama of the Democratic Party – towards China seemed at best somewhat enigmatic. Beijing was hard pressed to choose between them.

McCain at first sight appeared to imply continuity with the latterly pragmatic China policies of the Bush administration. He had the support of seasoned China hands familiar to Beijing, including former Secretary of State Henry Kissinger and former National Security Adviser Brent Scowcroft, and presumably drew on their steadying advice. And to the extent that McCain's advertised foreign-policy priorities concerned the Middle East, it seemed unlikely that he would launch rash policy initiatives towards China, or Asia more generally. On the other hand, however, China noted the importance McCain attached to further developing America's military alliances in Asia. It saw, too, that McCain's foreign-policy advisory team included prominent champions of a greater global diplomatic and military role for a 'normalised' Japan. The increasing ideological content of McCain's foreign-policy speeches, and his related call for the foundation of a League of Democracies that would by implication be ranged against a group of autocracies, was unsettling to Beijing. And with the expectation that McCain might well focus his attentions on the Middle East came the realisation that he would make far greater demands of China and Russia in confronting Iran over its nuclear programme in the United Nations Security Council and through their bilateral channels. McCain's age suggested he would be limited to a single term in office, a factor which presumably would not predispose him towards patience and restraint in meeting perceived security challenges to the United States. A McCain presidency could prove testing and turbulent, Beijing feared.

Yet Obama's views about China were regarded by Beijing as mysterious or simply unformed. The protectionist accent placed on his economic policies gave some cause for concern, but China hoped that much of this could be discounted as routine populist campaign-trail rhetoric. The questions and challenges posed by an Obama administration in any case seemed broader and more subtle. If international opinion polls were to be believed, Obama's election would be welcomed abroad as marking the cleanest break with a deeply unpopular Bush administration. The inauguration of an African-American president, whatever the specifics of his policies, would be regarded as a remarkable testimony to the vitality and progressiveness of American democracy. In this sense – and notwithstanding the risks of excessive expectations – it appeared likely to have the most rehabilitating impact on America's reputation and appeal, providing a genuine opportunity to recover leadership in those parts of the world, including Asia, that have seen a waning of US influence in recent years, but which still look to Washington for much of their protection and prosperity. How such developments would affect China's relative international standing and its key relationships remained to be guessed at. But it was conceivable, to choose one example, that a more completely healed transatlantic rift might weaken the European Union's interest in seeking out China as a 'strategic partner' in a multipolar world.

Options open

The increasing importance of China to questions of international security and global governance is by now obvious. At issue for much of 2007 and 2008, however, was the direction in which China's attitudes were evolving. The evidence was contradictory, or at least ambiguous. China was more receptive to the need to tackle environmental problems and climate change, but it continued to argue that the burden of action lay not with it but with the West. It sought to play an effective role in response to the global credit crunch, but was accused of pursuing distorting monetary policies that significantly undervalued its currency in a mercantilist manner. China played an important role – though one increasingly subsidiary to that of the United States – in cajoling North Korea towards the cessation of its nuclear activities, but seemed far more circumspect and reticent in its approach to Iran's nuclear programme. China had done much to help pave the way in 2006 for the introduction of a United Nations–African Union force in Darfur, and proved willing over the last year to criticise the Burmese junta for its use of violence against protestors. Yet in July 2008 China, with Russia, vetoed UN Security Council sanctions targeting the flagrantly oppressive and isolated regime of Robert Mugabe in Zimbabwe. China sought to work towards a new Framework Agreement with the European Union, premised on a supposed commonality of strategic interests, while at the same time tightening its links to a Russia that, to many Europeans, is worryingly overbearing and coercive in its energy diplomacy. China, in sum, appeared to be keeping its options open.

Japan's Dampened Extroversion

Japan's external security environment proved relatively stable in 2007–08, especially compared with the turbulence created in 2006–07 by North Korea's missile and nuclear tests. Although North Korea's threats and the rise of China continued to dominate Japanese external security concerns, the major developments governing Japan's short-term strategic outlook occurred on the domestic front. Prime Minister Shinzo Abe assumed the premiership in September 2006, following the extraordinarily successful tenure of Junichiro Koizumi. Many younger Liberal Democratic Party (LDP) politicians and American policymakers had high hopes for Abe – a relatively youthful 53-year-old – but he lasted just one year in office. He was replaced by the 71-year-old and more pragmatically inclined Yasuo Fukuda in September 2007.

This instability in domestic politics caused Japan to retreat from Abe's active global diplomacy, and to retrench on many of its more ambitious security-policy objectives. In particular, the government's difficulties in maintaining strong support for the US-led 'war on terror' through the extension of the Maritime Self-Defense Force (MSDF)'s refuelling mission in the Indian Ocean diminished prospects for a more globally focused US–Japan alliance. Meanwhile, Fukuda concentrated on repairing ties with East Asia, and preparing for Japan's hosting of the G8 summit at Toyako, Hokkaido in July 2008. Nevertheless, Japan still faced the same external pressures which drove changes in its security policy over the last decade, and there were also indications of a resurgence of the same domestic political forces that brought Koizumi and Abe to power.

Domestic paralysis

Koizumi's mastery of domestic politics centred on his personal charisma, and his ability persuasively to portray his brand of neo-liberal conservatism as delivering long-overdue political and economic reforms. In turn, his domestic popularity enabled him to gamble on risky foreign-policy ventures, including committing the Japan Self-Defense Forces (JSDF) to supporting the mainly American counter-terrorism efforts in the Indian Ocean in 2001 and Iraq intervention in 2003, as well as summit meetings with North Korea in 2002 and 2004. He succeeded in framing the September 2005 elections for the House of Representatives, the lower house of the Diet, with the single issue of his administration's plans for privatisation of the Japan Post Office, making it essentially a referendum on domestic reforms. In the event, Koizumi's LDP trounced the opposition Democratic Party of Japan (DPJ). But his stepping down from the premiership a year later left Abe with a difficult act to follow. Abe inherited the largest faction in the governing LDP and a two-thirds 'supermajority' in the lower house, which under Article 59 of the constitution allowed the LDP to force through legislation, but he was also compelled to manage a bigger and more diffuse LDP and to meet strong public expectations for continuing reform.

Abe proved lacking in personal charisma, political know-how and finesse. Without extensive ministerial experience, he tended to rely on ideologically kindred but equally callow younger cabinet confidants, and employed strong-arm tactics to push through legislation. Abe was unable to control the LDP and to sustain its image as a reform party. He allowed a number of high-profile rebel members who had been expelled for opposing postal privatisation to rejoin in December 2006, and failed to decisively discipline members of his cabinet for a series of gaffes and suspected corruption. Abe was also seen as preoccupied with constitutional revision and foreign policy to the neglect of fundamental domestic issues. His government was hit particularly hard by revelations in May 2007 that it had lost up to 50m pension records, leaving many pensioners unpaid. In the same month, the suicide of Minister of Agriculture Toshikatsu Matsuoka over his involvement in political funding scandals cast doubt on Abe's political judgement, as he had refused previous calls for Matsuoka's resignation. Abe's support in the opinion polls dipped below 30% by June 2007 and never recovered.

Political heavyweight Ichiro Ozawa – a near 30-year veteran of the LDP and acknowledged master of electoral strategy – assumed the DPJ leadership in April 2007, determined to practice adversarial politics and dislodge the LDP from power. The LDP suffered a humiliating defeat in elections to the upper house, the House of Councillors, in July 2007, losing its overall majority to the DPJ. Abe's position became close to untenable in a divided Diet. Although the LDP controlled the lower house, which selects the prime minister, the DPJ's majority in the upper house gave it an effective block on most legislation. Abe staked his already declining political credibility on passing an extension to the Anti-Terrorism Special Measures Law, due to expire on 1 November, stating on 9 September following a meeting with US President George W. Bush at the Asia-Pacific Economic Cooperation summit that he would otherwise resign. Beginning in 2001, the law had provided the authority for the MSDF's deployment to the Indian Ocean to provide refuelling support for the US-led counter-terrorism coalition. Ozawa, however, had made it clear that the DPJ would oppose any extension. He argued that the law was tantamount to supporting the use of force by the United States and its coalition partners, for which there was no clear legitimating UN resolution, and thus an unconstitutional act of collective self-defence. Ozawa further contended, in an article in the influential monthly journal *Sekai*, that a properly mandated UN mission would allow the deployment of Japan's Ground Self-Defense Forces to Afghanistan as part of the International Security Assistance Force, and even to engage in the use of force. Such a mission, he said, would be a more meaningful contribution to combating international terrorism than the MSDF's 'floating gasoline stand' in the Indian Ocean. The DPJ hardened its opposition, and on 12 September Abe offered his resignation as LDP president, and thus as prime minister. He was then promptly hospitalised for stress-related abdominal pains. Fukuda – a compromise candidate selected in lieu of Foreign Minister Taro Aso, whose strong right-wing views on national security were considered too divisive – was duly elected as LDP leader by 330 votes to 197, and then elected as prime minister in the Diet on 26 September.

Fukuda was never viewed as an especially inspirational choice, but was at least regarded by the LDP, media and much of the public as a safe pair of hands, having been the longest-serving chief cabinet secretary in the post-war period. Fukuda placed more experienced LDP figures in key ministerial posts. Though drawn from the same faction as Abe and Koizumi, Fukuda was viewed as a greater pragmatist than either, and better able to integrate the LDP and possibly forge a workable political accommodation with the DPJ. But despite an early public-approval rating of close to 70%, Fukuda faced as much opposition from the DPJ as Abe had done.

Fukuda's options for breaking the deadlock in the Diet were limited. His administration was able to use its two-thirds-plus supermajority in the lower house to push through the Replenishment Support Special Measures Law (a limited one-year extension of the anti-terrorism law) in November 2007 and the 2008/09 general budget in February 2008. But his declining credibility within his own party meant that this constitutional resort had to be used sparingly to ensure the necessary votes. Fukuda's main tactic was to attempt to co-opt the DPJ. He held two secret meetings with Ozawa on 31 October and 2 November in an attempt to forge a 'grand coalition' whereby the DPJ would help pass the extension in exchange for LDP support for a new permanent National Security Law which could facilitate the despatch of the JSDF on UN-mandated international peace cooperation missions in line with Ozawa's long-held aspirations. The DPJ top leadership, however, feared losing its political identity and strongly opposed any such deal. Fukuda was subsequently unable to entice the DPJ into closer cooperation. By the end of April 2008, support for his cabinet had dipped below 30%, and the DPJ appeared determined to trigger a general election and force Fukuda from office.

US–Japan relations

Abe assumed the premiership intent on strengthening the US–Japan bilateral relationship as the centrepiece of his strategy of expanding Japanese security cooperation with other US allies and democratic partners. He found it hard, however, to make significant headway. The first Abe–Bush summit in April 2007 was a relatively low-key affair, overshadowed by the pending US congressional resolution censuring Japan over its treatment of Korean 'comfort women' during the colonial period. But Abe and Bush apparently felt relatively strong personal rapport, and Abe dedicated the remainder of 2007 to making good on Japanese promises to implement the agenda of alliance restructuring set in motion by Koizumi. Abe's administration succeeded in passing the Law to Promote the Realignment of US Forces in Japan on 23 May 2007. In line with the May 2006 US–Japan Defence Policy Review Initiative, this law established the necessary finance and local-government subsidies to begin the relocation of US bases within Japan and to Guam. But after this initial success, Abe found it increasingly hard to keep US–Japan relations on track.

The first signs of tension in the relationship emerged over North Korea, with the United States intimating since spring 2007 that it was determined to move ahead with the Six-Party Talks and that it would be prepared if necessary to remove the North from the list of state sponsors of terrorism to guarantee the denuclearisation process. Japan's hard-line stance on North Korea and insistence on resolution of the issue of the abduction of Japanese citizens before providing any political support for the talks threatened to create a rift with Washington. Signs of further potential bilateral tensions came with Tokyo's unsuccessful attempts to persuade the United States to permit Japan to replace its ageing F-4J interceptors with state-of-the-art F-22A fighters. The 'comfort women' issue exacerbated bilateral tensions, but US–Japan relations were disrupted most strongly by Japan's initial inability to renew the anti-terrorism law in November 2007. The United States viewed the MSDF refuelling operation in the Indian Ocean as a useful logistical contribution, but more importantly as a political symbol of Japan's commitment to coalition solidarity. In response to fears that the DPJ would block renewal of the anti-terrorism law, Washington even attempted to intervene in Japanese domestic politics. US Ambassador Thomas Schieffer met Ozawa on 8 August and asked for the DPJ's support for the extension. Ozawa rebuffed US appeals, and Abe's failure to make good on his pledge to Bush to renew the law ultimately forced him from office. Fukuda's inability to persuade Ozawa to cooperate meant that the law expired on 1 November, and the refuelling flotilla was forced to return to Japan. In the meantime, the DPJ also threatened to introduce measures that would oblige the Air Self-Defense Force (ASDF) to withdraw from logistical missions in Kuwait and Iraq. Tensions eased when the extension passed the lower house in January 2008 enabling the MSDF to return to refuelling activities in the Indian Ocean in February.

Familiar alliance-management problems relating to the US bases in Japan then resurfaced. Japan, much to US frustration, moved slowly on the Defense Policy Review Initiative realignments, with no sign of substantive progress on the central issue of the relocation within Okinawa Prefecture of the US Marine Corps Air Station from Futenma to Nago. The prefectural government requested relocation of the new V-shaped runway at Nago on safety and environmental grounds, and the central government indicated it might be amenable to the change. The United States insisted, however, that the location agreed under the review initiative should stand. Other aspects of the review were less fraught; Iwankuni City agreed in March 2008 to accept the relocation of the US carrier wing from Atsugi.

Public perceptions of the US bases in Japan remained a broad political liability for the Japanese government. In mid February 2008, in the most recent of a long line of alleged criminal transgressions on the part of US military personnel, US Marines were accused of raping a 14-year-old Japanese schoolgirl. A similar incident in Okinawa in 1995 sparked mass protests against the US presence, shook alliance confidence, and triggered the first moves by Washington and Tokyo to reduce the US presence on Okinawa. Bilateral ties were again strained in March and April 2008 over the murder of a Japanese taxi driver by a US Navy serviceman in Yokosuka City. The Japanese media criticised the existing US–Japan Status of Forces Agreement as inadequate, given that the US military was under no formal obligation to inform the Japanese police that the US sailor in question had been absent without leave for some days before he committed the murder. Washington and Tokyo were especially keen to head off public criticism because the city was due to host a US nuclear-powered aircraft carrier for the first time in August 2008. Ambassador Schieffer publicly apologised to Yokosuka's mayor, and in April the United States pledged that in future it would inform Japan about personnel absent without leave and allow their arrest by Japanese police.

Japan–China relations

Japan–China relations, at their nadir during Koizumi's tenure, improved under Abe and Fukuda as the search for a meaningful 'mutually beneficial strategic relationship' continued. While Abe had few opportunities to follow up on Chinese Premier Wen Jiabao's successful 'ice-thawing' visit to Japan in April 2007, Beijing regarded Fukuda as a 'friend'. He had worked closely with his father on the conclusion of the 1978 Sino-Japanese Treaty of Peace and Friendship and stated at the outset of his LDP leadership campaign that, unlike Koizumi, he would not visit the controversial Yasukuni shrine in Tokyo, which commemorates Japanese war dead but is perceived by Beijing as glorifying Japanese imperialism and war crimes, many of which were perpetrated against Chinese.

Fukuda met Wen as premier for the first time on 20 November on the sidelines of the ASEAN Summit in Singapore, then travelled to China for a summit on 27–30 December. Fukuda described the visit as bringing 'springtime' to bilateral ties and sought to inject more substance into the strategic partnership. Fukuda emphasised the need for enhanced bilateral cooperation on environmental protection and announced plans for the exchange of up to 10,000 environmental researchers. Fukuda further sought Chinese assistance on Japanese plans for combating climate change, which were to be unveiled at the July G8 summit, and cooperation on halting North Korea's nuclear-weapons programmes, reform of the UN Security Council, and Africa policy (in light of the Fourth Tokyo International Conference on African Development (TICAD-IV) scheduled for May 2008). Fukuda and Chinese President Hu Jintao reiterated their intention to seek joint development of disputed gas fields in the East China Sea. With an eye on the impending March 2008 presidential election in Taiwan, Fukuda restated Japan's position, held since 1972, that it opposed an attempt by either side uni-laterally to alter Taiwan's status, and said Japan could not support a move by Taiwan to hold a referendum on UN membership. Hu visited Japan in May 2008, the first Chinese president for a decade to do so.

Despite the ostensible success of Fukuda's visit, Japan–China relations were still beset by persistent problems, especially in the security sphere. Tensions did see some improvement with the first-ever visit to Japan of a Chinese guided-missile destroyer, the *Shenzhen*, in November 2007, although the visit was marred slightly by alleged US pressure on Japan to prevent the Chinese visitors from inspecting technologically advanced Japanese *Aegis* destroyers. In March Japan and China worked on the establishment of a military hotline to avoid destabilis-ing military incidents. At the same time, Japan kept up its criticism of China's military build-up. The Ministry of Defense's 2007 White Paper expressed con-cerns at the continuing 20-year expansion of Chinese military spending. These were repeated by Foreign Minister Masahiko Komura in February 2008 and Chief Cabinet Secretary Nobutaka Machimura the following month, when the Ministry of Defense also noted its anxiety about China's growing cruise-missile force. The ministry's National Institute of Defence Studies, in its 2008 annual *East Asian Strategic Survey*, acknowledged China's attempts to project a peaceful image through defence diplomacy, but also the relentless build-up of its military, especially space capabilities.

In late 2007 and early 2008, economic and political issues also upset Japan–China relations. In December 2007, Japan protested when, after bilateral economic talks, China omitted Tokyo's call for the revaluation of the yuan from the joint communiqué. Relations were further damaged when a number of Japanese fell ill after eating Chinese-manufactured *gyoza* (dumplings) that contained traces of pesticides banned in Japan. Sales of Chinese food in Japan plunged, and there was protracted and inconclusive wrangling between Tokyo and Beijing over the source of the contamination.

Failure to resolve the East China Sea dispute was also unsettling. Hopes for a resolution were raised in February 2008 following Foreign Ministry talks, with apparent agreement that joint development should take place along the median between respective exclusive economic zones, which Japan interpreted as implicit Chinese recognition of its territorial claim. But actual agreement has proved elusive. Japan, for its part, remained relatively quiet on the Tibet issue, simply urging the Chinese government to open Tibet as soon as possible to foreign media and to engage in dialogue with the Tibetan people, and refraining from calling for the boycott of the Olympics opening ceremony. Nevertheless, Japanese leaders noted Beijing's willingness to suppress domestic dissent and the implications for possible use of force in its external relations.

Japan and the Korean Peninsula

Unlike the previous year, North Korea did not engage in overtly provocative behaviour in the region in 2007–08, and Japan was somewhat reassured that ongoing Six-Party Talks could eventually nullify the North Korean nuclear threat. Nevertheless, Japan maintained a generally hard-line stance over the talks and its willingness to engage bilaterally with the North. During his last months in office, Abe pressed Pyongyang to resolve the abductee issue, and extended Japan's unilateral economic sanctions on the North despite US attempts to advance the Six-Party Talks. Following the International Atomic Energy Agency's confirmation in August 2007 that North Korea had completed the first steps of the denuclearisation agreement, Japan felt increasing international pressure from its partners in the Six-Party Talks to engage Pyongyang, and on 5–6 September Tokyo reopened bilateral normalisation talks, ultimately unsuccessful, with the North.

In his election campaign Fukuda said he would emphasise dialogue in contrast to Abe's brand of pressure, and in October Komura appeared to offer a compromise when he said Japan might be satisfied on the abduction issue if just a 'number of abductees' were permitted to return. North Korea did not respond to Japan's overtures, drawing confidence from the progress of the Six-Party Talks and perceived Japanese fears of international isolation. In spring 2008 Japan renewed its economic sanctions.

Japanese relations with South Korea, which had been fraught under Koizumi, were more promising. Abe took the initial step in repairing ties with a summit meeting with President Roh Moo Hyun in Seoul in October 2006. But Roh declined to visit Tokyo in turn, and Japan had to wait for a new president to take power. When Lee Myung Bak – known as a pragmatist and disinclined to raise the issue of the colonial past with Japan – was elected in 2008, Fukuda visited South Korea for his inauguration on 24–25 February. The leaders agreed to put history behind them, resume bilateral 'shuttle diplomacy' in the form of annual summit visits, restart negotiations on a bilateral free-trade agreement, and enhance their coordination on North Korea policy, with Lee hinting at a generally tougher line on the North, closer to Japan's position. In turn, Fukuda invited Lee to the G8 summit, and Lee paid an advance visit to Japan on 21–22

April, confirming greater coordination on North Korea. Japan and South Korea also planned to sign their first agreement on defence exchanges, including professional military education and bilateral maritime cooperation. But questions remained about how far the relationship could progress. Tokyo and Seoul remained at loggerheads over the disputed Takeshima Islands, and there was considerable opposition among agricultural and industrial lobbies in the South towards the free-trade agreement with Japan.

Japan's wider diplomacy

Beyond the strategic relationships with the United States, China and the Koreas, Abe wanted to transform Japan into a truly global diplomatic and security player. In April and May 2007, he visited Saudi Arabia, the United Arab Emirates, Kuwait, Qatar and Egypt, seeking to assure energy supplies from the Middle East and counter rising Chinese influence in the region. On 21–23 September, as part of a larger strategy to consolidate a democratic partnership among the United States, India and Australia to balance China, Abe visited India, where both sides concluded a Joint Statement on the Roadmap for New Dimensions to the Strategic and Global Partnership, intended to enhance cooperation on economic development, climate change, and Security Council reform. India was disappointed that Japan declined to endorse the US–India civilian nuclear cooperation deal because of its potential impact on nuclear proliferation, while Japan was frustrated that India paid only lip service to its plans for countering climate change.

Fukuda was less active in regional and global diplomacy due to domestic political challenges. The highlight of Japan–ASEAN relations was the signing of a Comprehensive Economic Partnership Agreement to promote a free-trade area. Fukuda also showed less enthusiasm for the concerted democratic partnership favoured by Abe, only minimally engaging Australia and India. Conversely, new Australian Prime Minister Kevin Rudd did not include Japan on his international tour in April. However, Fukuda invited Rudd to the G8 summit, in hopes that Australia's recent change of heart over emissions targets would help Japan broker a deal on global climate change.

Closer to home, Fukuda devoted considerable attention to the re-emergence of Japan's old geopolitical rival, Russia. Moscow heavily criticised American – and by implication Japanese – plans for missile defence in October 2007, and Japan protested incursions by Russian Tupolev-5 bombers into its airspace in February 2008. Japan and Russia held their first regular strategic dialogue the following April and established a full agenda including the sovereignty of the Northern Territories and energy and climate-change policies. Fukuda made his first visit as prime minister to Russia on 25–26 April, holding summit talks with outgoing President Vladimir Putin and president-elect Dmitry Medvedev, seeking improved ties to counterbalance China and securing useful agreements on energy cooperation.

A less-ambitious security policy

Japan's developing security policy was knocked off track by Abe's departure and the domestic gridlock over the anti-terrorism law. When he assumed the premiership Fukuda had a far more cautious outlook on Japan's international security role.Although a known advocate of revisions to Article 9 of the constitution that would allow Japan greater freedom to deploy forward and use force, Fukuda made it clear that his administration had little energy to devote to the issue. He scrapped Abe's Prime Ministerial Advisory Committee on Reconstructing the Legal Basis for Security Policy, which had been investigating the conditions for Japan to exercise collective self-defence in support of the United States, and in December discarded Abe's plans for a US-style Japan National Security Council, designed to strengthen Japanese decision-making on security policy.

Fukuda's conservatism was reinforced by erratic and unsettled leadership, and a series of scandals in the newly created Ministry of Defense. There were four different ministers in 2007. The first, Fumio Kyuma, was forced to resign in July over a gaffe in which he described the US atomic bombings of Japan as 'unavoidable'. The second, Yuriko Koike, resigned in August after internal arguments with Administrative Vice-Minister Takemasa Moriya over the succession to his post. Koike was replaced by Masahiko Komura, who became foreign minister when Fukuda became prime minister and reshuffled the cabinet. Shigeru Ishiba took up the post in September 2007.

The first scandal to hit the ministry was a report by the Japanese non-governmental organisation Peace Depot in early October, based on unclassified US data, suggesting that the MSDF had supplied fuel to the US aircraft carrier *Kitty Hawk* in 2003 immediately before it took part in the Iraq War, contravening the purpose of the anti-terrorism law, which was specifically designed to support *Operation Enduring Freedom* in Afghanistan. The ministry later refuted the allegations with additional information from the United States, but faced further embarrassment when it became clear it had understated the quantity of fuel oil provided to coalition forces by the MSDF in 2003 by a factor of four. The MSDF had provided accurate information to civilian defence bureaucrats and the military's general staff, and the bureaucratic failure to promulgate correct information was seen as a major failure of civilian-control procedures.

Worse was yet to come. Moriya was alleged by prosecutors to have received up to a total of around ¥12m (about $115,000) in golf hospitality and cash bribes from Miyazaki Motonobu, a former employee of the Yamada Corporation and president of the Nihon Mirise Corporation trading companies, to steer the Ministry of Defense towards signing discretionary contracts with Nihon Mirise for the supply of General Electric engines for the ASDF's C-X transport aircraft and for the MSDF's 19DD-class destroyer. Then, in mid February, the *Aegis* destroyer *Atago*, returning to port, hit and sunk a civilian fishing vessel. The fishing vessel's crew perished, and it emerged that the *Atago*'s crew had not followed proper safety procedures and that the ministry had been slow to respond and had failed to follow prescribed investigative procedures. Fukuda's tepid response to this litany of scandals was to institute a Council for the Reform of the Ministry of Defense, charged with investigating information security, civilian control, and procurement practices.

Japan did move forward quietly with various military plans, most notably ballistic-missile defence. The ASDF completed its deployment of *Patriot* Advanced Capability-3 (PAC-3) missiles at bases around Tokyo, and conducted drills for deployment in central Tokyo in September 2007 and January 2008. The *Aegis* destroyer *Kongo* conducted Japan's first ballistic-missile interceptor test close to Hawaii in December. In August 2007, the MSDF also launched its first *Hyuga*-class helicopter destroyer, at 13,500 tonnes the largest Japanese warship in the post-war period and, with its capability of mounting 11 helicopters, in essence a light helicopter carrier. The ASDF also took delivery of its first of four KC-767 tanker aircraft in February 2008.

Fukuda's prospects, home and away

Fukuda's strategy was to hold out until the July 2008 G8 summit in the hope that he might garner international kudos that would translate into domestic confidence. He might then possibly call an election in late summer 2008. Japan's domestic political fluidity will probably constrain it from taking a more active role in the US–Japan alliance and regionally. Certain endeavours, however, could still bear fruit. Japan's security establishment has begun to search for less domestically controversial ways to expand Japanese international security cooperation. As of spring 2008, Fukuda was considering submitting a new permanent National Security Law to the Diet in the autumn. This statute would provide a regularised legal framework for the despatch of the JSDF on overseas operations other than UN peacekeeping. It would allow for faster JSDF deployment with clearer constitutional mandates, based on UN resolutions or requests from international organisations, with missions limited to non-combat areas and with prior Diet authorisation. The law had supporters in both the LDP and the DPJ. Passage of such a law would make another protracted Diet battle to renew the anti-terrorism law less likely and could open the way for the deployment of the GSDF to Afghanistan on non-combat missions. While this would not be the revolutionary change in Japan's defence posture that Koizumi and Abe appeared to advocate, it would be a step towards a more extroverted security policy.

The Korean Peninsula: Nuclear Progress

Coaxing North Korea to abandon its nuclear programmes has often seemed like trying to roll a rock up a steep mountain. As of mid 2008, it could at least be said that the rock had not rolled back downhill.

Some of the upward momentum was due to Washington's willingness to engage Pyongyang bilaterally. Starting in the immediate aftermath of North Korea's test of a nuclear device on 9 October 2006, US Assistant Secretary of State Christopher Hill met repeatedly with his North Korean counterpart, Vice Foreign Minister Kim Gye Gwan, both in sessions of the Six-Party Talks and separately. While Pyongyang's newfound willingness to negotiate may have been due partly to sanctions imposed by the UN Security Council, political steps taken by Washington to re-engage with the North seemed more telling. Although progress was slow, it was halted neither by changes of government in Seoul and Tokyo, nor by the impending change of administration in Washington. Whether or not North Korea would yet live up to its commitment in the Six-Party Joint Statement of 19 September 2005 to abandon 'all nuclear weapons and existing nuclear programmes', momentum on both disabling and disclosure was sustained.

In South Korea, the conservative Lee Myung Bak was elected in December 2007 to succeed Roh Moo Hyun as president. For Washington, this was a relief: although Roh had acceded to most American requests, including the dispatch of 3,000 troops to Iraq over the protests of many in his own party, his pursuit of South Korea's 'Sunshine Policy' with the North had strained relations with Washington. In contrast, Lee was expected to make engagement with the North conditional on denuclearisation.

Ties between South Korea and Japan had also frayed, but when Prime Minister Yasuo Fukuda of Japan showed his determination to mend fences with South Korea, Lee reciprocated by breaking with his predecessor's emphasis on Korea's unhappy past with Japan and telling a leading Japanese journalist he would leave history to the historians. Two weeks later Fukuda became the first foreign leader to meet with Lee when he attended the 25 February 2008 inauguration. Lee said afterwards: 'I fully support the prime minister's diplomacy, which places priority on Asia'.

Perhaps the year's most remarkable development was the visit of the New York Philharmonic orchestra to Pyongyang on 26 February 2008. Its performance, broadcast live throughout North Korea, must have come as a shock to ordinary North Koreans accustomed to daily denunciations of the United States. The audience listened impassively to the playing of the 'Star-Spangled Banner' and, in a few cases, tearfully as the strains of the Korean melody 'Arirang' filled the hall, then applauded vigorously for more than ten minutes at the end.

America's bilateral engagement

In spite of past progress in the Six-Party Talks, bilateral contacts between Washington and Pyongyang seemed to offer the best prospect of moving North Korea towards nuclear disarmament. Bilateral talks to date have yielded agreements on stopping the North's plutonium programme and disabling it so as to make it more difficult and time-consuming to restart. North Korea also made a declaration of its fissile material and the facilities and equipment it had to make more – which it pledged to dismantle.

In the 2005 Joint Statement, North Korea had committed itself to abandoning nuclear weapons and programmes. In return, Washington pledged to respect its sovereignty and 'to take steps to normalize' relations, and the United States, Japan, South Korea, Russia and China promised energy assistance and cooperation in trade and investment. Pyongyang asserted its 'right to peaceful uses of nuclear energy' and the others agreed to discuss 'at an appropriate time' provision of a light-water reactor, promised under the 1994 Agreed Framework but never delivered. The accord committed the parties to 'explore ways and means for promoting security cooperation in Northeast Asia'. The 'directly related parties' agreed to 'negotiate a permanent peace regime on the Korean Peninsula at an appropriate separate forum'. The accord bound the parties to synchronise implementation 'commitment for commitment, action for action'. Sequencing those actions would be the subject of subsequent agreements.

In talks in Berlin in January 2007, Hill and Kim Gye Gwan worked out what would become the 13 February 2007 six-party agreement on 'initial actions' for the implementation of the September 2005 Joint Statement. In the February agreement, the North pledged to 'shut down and seal' its plutonium facilities at Yongbyon and allow inspectors to monitor them. It also agreed to 'discuss with other parties [i.e., the United States] a list of all its nuclear programmes … that would be abandoned pursuant to the Joint Statement'. In return, the United States promised to 'begin the process' of delisting the North as a state sponsor of terrorism and to 'advance the process' of ending sanctions under the Trading with the Enemy Act. South Korea agreed to begin delivery of 50,000 tonnes of heavy fuel oil (HFO) within 60 days.

An Israeli air-strike in Syria on 6 September 2007 threatened to upset negotiations with North Korea, although this aspect of the raid was not publicly known at the time. At first, both the target and the reason for the strike were cloaked in secrecy. But Washington later said, citing intelligence, that the site attacked and destroyed by the Israelis had been a nuclear reactor that was under construction with North Korean help. Details would not be made public until April 2008, when American intelligence officials briefed Congress and the press. They disclosed that Syrian–North Korean contacts had begun in 1997. Ground-clearing for the Syrian reactor began in 2001 and North Korea was detected buying equipment in 2002. How closely North Korea's actions were linked to US actions remained unclear, but the nuclear contacts with Syria seemed to have commenced at a time when Pyongyang was complaining about the Clinton administration's failure to fulfil its obligations under the 1994 Agreed Framework. Construction of the reactor began as Pyongyang's relations with the George W. Bush administration were plummeting. In spring 2007, Israel shared intelligence with Washington, including visual evidence gathered on the ground. It notified US officials of its intention to attack the site in order to 're-establish the credibility of our deterrent power', as one Israeli official put it later. After Israeli aircraft demolished the site, there was silence on all sides for more than a week until Israeli opposition-party leader Benjamin Netanyahu confirmed the attack. Syria and North Korea condemned it.

Knowing of the Syria–North Korean link, Bush nevertheless authorised Hill to meet Kim Gye Gwan on 1–2 September 2007 in Geneva. They reached agreement on the basics of what soon became the third key six-party accord. The White House gave formal notice to Congress of preparations to ship 50,000 tonnes of HFO to North Korea and issued a presidential determination allowing exceptions to sanctions for the funding of educational and cultural exchanges. On 3 October agreement was reached at the Six-Party Talks on 'second phase actions' that went well beyond the suspension of plutonium operations at Yongbyon. North Korea was obliged to provide 'a complete and correct declaration of all its nuclear programmes' by 31 December 2007, listing the fissile material it had made and the means it had to make more. It agreed to 'disable' its nuclear facilities at Yongbyon. Importantly in view of the Syria connection, it 'reaffirmed its commitment not to transfer nuclear materials, technology or know-how'. Why the word 'reaffirmed' was used was not clear, since this was the first known North Korean pledge to its dialogue partners not to engage in nuclear proliferation.

The United States, in turn, promised to fulfil its commitments on terminating the Trading with the Enemy Act and delisting the North as a state sponsor of terrorism in parallel with North Korea's actions. In an arrangement first broached to the North by South Korea's six-party representative Chun Young Woo, energy and other assistance 'up to the equivalent of one million tons' of HFO (minus the 100,000 tonnes already delivered) would be phased in as the North complied. Seoul, China and Washington each pledged to ship 50,000 tonnes of HFO.

Separate bilateral talks conducted by US diplomats with the North also began to bear fruit. Pyongyang provided evidence that the 3,000 or so aluminium tubes it had acquired in the past from Russia were well suited for making centrifuges to enrich uranium. But, as Hill put it on 31 January 2008, 'we've seen that the tubes are not being used for the centrifuge programme' – most likely because the North was not able to acquire other vital components. The implication was that North Korea's uranium-enrichment programme posed much less of a threat because it had only a limited number of centrifuges – far fewer than the number needed for full-scale production. Testing of a sample aluminium tube showed traces of enriched uranium, however, suggesting that the tube may have been in a location where the North had been using uranium hexafluoride to test centrifuges or where contaminated Pakistani-origin centrifuges were stored.

Moves towards disarmament

Roh and Chairman Kim Jong Il of North Korea met on 2–4 October 2007 in Pyongyang. Seoul had been seeking to host a second summit ever since then President Kim Dae Jung travelled to Pyongyang in 2000, but when Kim indicated he would not be willing to travel to South Korea, Roh decided that the holding of a summit was more important than the venue. While conservatives in Seoul and Washington disparaged the summit as grandstanding by a lame-duck president, Kim Jong Il's clear indication of his engagement priorities in the joint declaration provided potential inducements for greater cooperation by Pyongyang in nuclear disarmament. Three points in their agreement seemed relevant to the six-party negotiations. First, deeper economic engagement was indicated by further development of the Kaesong Industrial Complex and construction of shipbuilding complexes at Anbyun and Nampo in North Korea. Secondly, a shared commitment to 'terminate the existing armistice regime and to build a permanent peace regime' opened the way to a series of confidence-building agreements. Thirdly, the prospect of a joint fishing area off the west coast offered a potentially creative way to link economic cooperation to security. Crabbing boats from both sides have strayed across the Northern Limit Line in that area, occasionally provoking exchanges of hostile fire between North and South Korean naval patrols. Future incidents could be averted by naval confidence-building measures.

However, many hurdles remained in the way of the steps towards nuclear disarmament that the international community desired. By early 2008, eight of the 11 disabling measures, including those at the North Korean reprocessing facility and the fuel-fabrication plant, had been completed without much difficulty. But the two most critical steps had not: removal of all the fuel rods from the Yongbyon reactor and disposal of the replacement fuel rods.

Defuelling was initially delayed to prepare the cooling pond where the spent fuel rods would be stored. Then North Korea delayed it further after accusing the other parties of not living up their obligations. Russia, which was supposed to provide North Korea with 50,000 tonnes of HFO by December, did not deliver the full shipment until late January. China and South Korea, which were supposed to supply the equivalent of 50,000 tonnes of HFO in the form of steel and other material to refurbish North Korea's conventional power plants, were also tardy with their deliveries. And the United States had not advanced the process of ending the Trading with the Enemy Act sanctions or delisting the North as a state sponsor of terrorism.

In response, Pyongyang slowed the defuelling to 32 rods per day, down from 80, at a point when fewer than 20% of the 8,000 rods had been removed. At that rate, the defueling would not be completed until the end of 2008. Since disposal of the replacement fuel rods had made no headway at all, the North was in a position to reload and restart the reactor.

Completion of the declaration of North Korean nuclear activities, which was supposed to be accomplished by the end of 2007, also encountered difficulties. The North did provide an estimate of the plutonium it had, but there were serious doubts about its accuracy. And it offered no transparency on other matters. On 5 December, Hill had raised the Syria issue in Pyongyang, showing Kim Gye Gwan evidence of North Korea's complicity in the construction of Syria's reactor. In a meeting with Foreign Minister Pak Ui Chun, he handed over a letter from Bush to Kim Jong Il urging disclosure of the North's proliferation efforts. Although some observers saw the letter as a goodwill gesture in that Bush was according Kim status as a counterpart, the new demand almost certainly contributed to North Korea delaying its declaration of all its nuclear programmes by the promised date of 31 December.

At a meeting with Hill on 19 February in Beijing, Kim Gye Gwan turned down a proposal to deliver the formal declaration of the plutonium programme and to keep this separate from a side-letter listing equipment and components it had acquired for uranium enrichment, which would be delivered to the United States. Later that month, former Secretary of Defense William Perry, who accompanied the New York Philharmonic to Pyongyang, carried a message from Secretary of State Condoleezza Rice offering to keep the side-letter confidential. Rice, meanwhile, in Tokyo and Beijing, had a message of her own on the declaration: 'I really have less concern about what form it takes or how many pieces of paper there may have to be or how many times it may have to go back and forth. I am just concerned that by the time we get to the end of this phase, we have some clarity so we know what we're looking for at the third phase.'

But the North Koreans, who had been burned when Kim Jong Il's 2002 confession of kidnappings of Japanese citizens served to raise a new hurdle to normalisation of relations with Tokyo, were wary that if the list of enrichment equipment or nuclear-proliferation activities became public, it would be held up as an example of their perfidy. They balked at itemising the approximately 20 centrifuges and components acquired from Pakistan starting in the late 1990s – equipment Pyongyang would be obliged to abandon in the next phase of Six-Party Talks. Hill opted instead to draw up his own accounting of what US intelligence believed the North had acquired. On 1 March he gave it to the Chinese to pass to the North Koreans, but at a meeting with Hill in Geneva on

13–14 March, Kim Gye Gwan refused to check off the items on the US list. Kim also denied any North Korean involvement in Syria's nuclear efforts.

The North was more forthcoming about its plutonium programme. It refused to say where it was assembling its nuclear devices but did disclose the amount of plutonium it had separated in each of its reprocessing campaigns. It reportedly said it had separated 37kg in all, including the amount expended in its nuclear test. The total, while plausible, was at the lower end of the range of US estimates – 'enough plutonium for at least a half dozen nuclear weapons', according to the annual threat assessment given to Congress last year. The North agreed to provide the reactor's operating logs which, if complete, could help verify the amount of plutonium, but it wanted to delay verification until the next phase of Six-Party Talks. In May it relented and turned over some 18,000 pages of records to Washington. It also blew up the reactor's cooling tower, a symbolic climax to the disabling process, although none of the disabling steps were irreversible.

In Singapore on 7–8 April, the two sides tentatively agreed on a compromise on uranium enrichment and Syria. In return for an end to application of the Trading with the Enemy Act and delisting as a state sponsor of terrorism, the North would 'acknowledge the US conclusions' – the list of enrichment equipment and components and the information Hill had showed Kim about Syria – 'and take serious note of US concerns'. That would allow the declaring and disabling of the plutonium programme to be completed. North Korea also gave the United States a list of enrichment equipment to be dismantled, albeit one that it might reopen in the next phase of negotiations. The agreement kept the Syria issue on the bilateral agenda, but without a final resolution.

The outcome was, arguably, a better way to achieve US near-term security objectives than waiting to obtain a possibly incomplete North Korean list that would then have had to be verified. That might have only further delayed disabling and left Pyongyang with its nuclear leverage intact. Yet the agreement outraged those in Washington who viewed the declaration as a way to extract a North Korean confession of its past misdeeds and saw this deal as another instance of cheat-and-retreat tactics by Pyongyang. It prompted anxious questioning among erstwhile supporters of deal-making and was attacked by critics who had opposed negotiating with North Korea since 1994. It also sparked anger in Japan.

The US commitment to delist North Korea as a state sponsor of terrorism despite lack of progress in resolving the abductions issue hardly came as a surprise to Japan. But the issue was a delicate one. Some Diet members saw the willingness to delist as a sign of US insensitivity to Japanese feelings. Prime Minister Yasuo Fukuda understood that, as he told the Diet on 14 October 2007, 'the abduction issue has to be solved through serious talks between Japan and North Korea'.

Elections and discord in South Korea

Dealings with Pyongyang would prove no easier for the new government in Seoul, elected in December 2007. The presidential election campaign took place against a backdrop of slowing economic growth and rising income inequality. Many of Roh's most ardent supporters on the centre-left had grown disenchanted with his economic policies and his dispatch of troops to Iraq and were even more doubtful about his would-be successor, television-newscaster-turned-politician Chung Dong Young.

Lee Myung Bak, a construction magnate who had launched his political career as mayor of Seoul, emerged as the nominee of the conservative Grand National Party in a hotly contested race against Park Geun Hye, leader of the party and daughter of late president Park Chun Hee. Lee ran on a platform of reinvigorating the Korean economy and attempted to take the North Korea issue out of the campaign by pledging to sustain economic engagement. But he added a new condition reflecting the conservative critique of Roh's 'sunshine policy', that assistance would be based on North Korean reciprocity. Even that condition did not satisfy his right wing and prompted Lee Hoi Chang, who had been the party's nominee in the last two presidential elections, to throw his hat into the ring as its champion. Lee Myung Bak won with 49% of the vote; Chung had 26% and Lee Hoi Chang 15%. Turnout was an all-time low at just under 63%, 8 percentage points below that of the 2002 election, because of disaffection on the centre-left.

Lee's post-election honeymoon was surprisingly short lived. Four scandal-tainted high-level appointees had to bow out before they could assume their new posts. Legislative elections in April confirmed the narrowness of Lee's mandate as the Grand National Party won just 153 seats in the 299-member National Assembly. The centre-left opposition fared even worse, taking 81 seats, half its previous total. Lee Hoi Chang's newly formed party won 18. Unhappy with the party's allocation of the 56 seats to be awarded by proportional representation, Park Geun Hye broke with Lee and ran her own slate, which won 14 seats along with the loyalty of an unknown number of party legislators. Lee's rivals now held the balance of power in the National Assembly.

The new president's post-inaugural debut received an inhospitable welcome from North Korea as well, which withheld comment on his election for three months. Lee had made no effort to contact the North during the interregnum. In his inaugural address on 25 February, distancing himself from his predecessors' more forthcoming approach, Lee characterised his attitude toward the North as 'pragmatic, not ideological'. He also made it clear that improving US–South Korean relations took priority over engaging with the North, as did strengthening ties with Japan, China and Russia.

Lee's approach was reflected on a number of fronts. He reiterated a campaign pledge to boost per capita income in North Korea to '$3,000 within ten years' – but only *after* the North 'abandons its nuclear programme and chooses the path to openness', rather than *as* it does so – and expressed his willingness to meet Kim Jong Il 'whenever necessary'. He pledged to sustain humanitarian assistance as needed, if the North requested it, but wanted increased transparency in distributing the aid. Whether he would attach other conditions regarding the fate of South Korea's prisoners of war or human rights was not clear. He set four conditions to additional economic investments in the North, including projects agreed at the October 2007 summit meeting: progress on denuclearisation, economic feasibility, the South's ability to bear the fiscal burden, and public support. In a clear break with the previous government, the South Korean delegate to the United Nations Human Rights Council in Geneva, instead of abstaining as South Korea had done previously, voted with the majority for a resolution on 27 March renewing the mandate of the UN special rapporteur on human rights in North Korea.

Sensing that Lee was backing away from Roh's summit commitments, North Korea was quick to demonstrate what was at stake in its own style. On 28 March it test-fired two ship-to-ship missiles off the west coast in the vicinity of an area designated to be a joint fishing zone in the summit agreement. Seizing on a response by the chairman of the South Korean chiefs of staff to a question in his National Assembly confirmation hearing that South Korea, if attacked, could launch a 'preemptive attack' on the North's nuclear sites, Pyongyang barred South Korean officials from the joint enterprise zone just across the De-Militarised Zone in Kaesong and Mount Kumgang if the remark was not retracted. On 1 April Pyongyang's party organ *Rodong Sinmun* lashed out at Lee, personally accusing him of 'sycophancy' towards the United States and 'confrontation' with North Korea by threatening 'to overturn all that has been achieved between the north and south' over the past decade.

In short, Lee's policy towards North Korea seemed still to be a work in progress as he searched for a tougher approach than those of his predecessors, but one that would not spark a new crisis on the peninsula. While the rocky patch in relations was not of concern to a South Korean public more attentive to its own economic well-being, it was not clear that this lack of interest would persist. If the United States were to make further progress with the North on the nuclear issue and to step up its own assistance to Pyongyang, as it may do in the remaining months of 2008, Lee would be under pressure not to be left behind.

As for his top foreign-policy priority, strengthening ties with the United States, Lee's visit to Washington in April 2008 for two days of meetings featured the first-ever stay at Camp David by a South Korean leader. The two countries reached important agreements to keep US troop levels at 28,500, to allow some South Korean citizens to travel to the United States without visas, and to ease South Korean restrictions on US beef imports, a key impediment in Congress to the still unratified Korea–US Free Trade Agreement. The beef deal, however, drew immediate opposition in Seoul and as protests swelled to the tens of thousands, Lee's popularity plummeted and the cabinet tendered their resignations. Lee and Bush may have established a good working relationship, but Bush will only remain in office until January 2009, so the South Korean leader will have to start over when the new US president takes over.

Lee's determination to reinvigorate the economy may also be sorely tested in the coming year. South Korea's top trading partner, China, is experiencing a slowdown in exports to the United States, which will adversely affect South Korean growth as well. The Free Trade Agreement with the United States, concluded in the last year of the Roh administration, as much for the strategic purpose of strengthening the alliance as for economic reasons, still faces an uncertain future in the legislatures of both countries.

North Korea: driving factors

North Korea's economy continues to face severe difficulties. Economic reforms, initiated in 2002, seemed to be expanding the role of markets, improving independent economic decision-making of enterprises, and opening the economy to foreign investment. Nevertheless, the Seoul-based Bank of Korea estimated that economic growth turned negative in 2006 for the first time in seven years. The downturn was partly due to worsening economic relations, which exacerbated energy shortages, in the wake of the intensifying nuclear crisis. Perhaps as a result, 2008 began with a new high-level focus on 'building economic power', with an emphasis on the role of 'service persons'. Forty percent of the national budget was earmarked for economic development, including a 60% increase in expenditures on science and technology. A number of personnel changes in leading institutions, including the appointment of a new prime minister, also seemed to underscore the renewed emphasis on economic growth. Even so, North Korea's haphazard efforts at reform seemed unlikely to stimulate enough growth to replace ageing capital stock or invest in new technology that would enhance productivity or output. Escaping this 'poverty trap' will be difficult without a fundamental improvement in political relations with the United States, South Korea and Japan that would allow North Korea to reallocate scarce skilled manpower and other resources from military to civilian use and attract substantial aid and investment from the outside.

Following its poor economic performance, the spectre of massive food shortages again haunted the country. As a result of crop failures, surging world prices for food and donor fatigue, the shortfall may reach one million tonnes, the worst since 2001, making Pyongyang unable to feed 20% of its population. Aggravating this problem, China's aid, slashed to meet its own internal needs, remained far below the levels of the last decade. South Korean deliveries, about 500,000 tonnes of rice and 300,000 tonnes of fertiliser per year, have slowed as well. It remained possible that the shortages would result in the same scale of mass starvation that occurred in the late 1990s, although this could be prevented if donors step forward. The United States has committed to send 500,000 tonnes of food aid to the beleaguered North in a move it denied was linked to nuclear talks.

Looming over the North's challenging problems is the continuing political uncertainty over who will succeed Kim Jong Il. While concerns about his health are not immediately apparent, he is now in his mid 60s. His own ascent to power was well under way when his father reached the same age. There were unsubstantiated press reports in 2007 that his middle son Kim Jong Chul had assumed a party post that his father had occupied in his climb to the top. If he wants any of his three sons to inherit his rule, Kim Jong Il needs a long period of tranquillity on his borders to make it possible.

While it was unclear whether domestic factors, such as economic problems and the risk of food shortages, were driving the North to seek a diplomatic solution to the nuclear issue, the assurance of regime security seemed likely to be an overriding priority. North Korea's relations with China have been for some time in transition from military alliance to cooperative partnership, and for two decades it has sought a strategic partnership with its long-time enemies, the United States, South Korea and Japan, so as to enhance its security and reduce reliance on China. In negotiations with the United States over denuclearisation, North Korean officials use the term 'political compensation', indicating that they want concrete evidence of movement toward reconciliation – an end to hostile relations. It remains to be seen whether, through these moves, it can feel sufficiently secure to give up its nuclear programmes and weapons.

Completion of the declaration and disablement phases of the Six-Party Talks would open the way to even more difficult negotiations on the permanent dismantlement of North Korea's nuclear facilities and the verifiable elimination of its nuclear weapons and plutonium – a dauntingly long series of steps. It would include the storage and eventual shipping out of spent fuel now being removed from the reactor, the dismantlement and decontamination of the North's nuclear facilities, declaration of the weapons and the associated weapons-assembly and -testing facilities, verification of denuclearisation, disassembly of nuclear weapons and the removal of fissile material from the country. These measures would require an unprecedented degree of cooperation. Implementation could take up to a decade and cost billions of dollars.

Carrying out these tasks would require building trust among all six parties and easing North Korea's sense of isolation and insecurity. Part of that effort would consist of incentives such as energy assistance, possibly including the construction of light-water nuclear reactors, the key inducement provided to Pyongyang in the failed 1994 Agreed Framework. Beyond tangible assistance, Pyongyang would want further steps that promote better political and economic relations with the United States, including high-level bilateral contacts, the establishment of diplomatic relations, and further lifting of economic and financial sanctions. Underlying Pyongyang's drive for better relations may be a calculation that Washington can serve as a counterbalance to Beijing. However, there will be persistent concern in Washington not only about the uncertainty of North Korea's giving up all of its plutonium, but also about security challenges posed by Pyongyang's ballistic-missile programme, chemical-weapons stocks and forward-deployed conventional forces, as well as about human rights. Meanwhile, Kim Jong Il would be careful not to embrace the outside world so that his grip on the North Korean people loosens.

Southeast Asia: A Region in Flux

Political volatility characterised parts of Southeast Asia, with large-scale demonstrations in late 2007 and a major natural disaster in May 2008 severely challenging Myanmar's repressive military regime, a major electoral setback threatening the continued tenure of Malaysia's long-established government, an apparent assassination attempt against Timor Leste's president, and unrest over fuel-price rises injecting a new element of instability in several countries by mid 2008. The conflict in southern Thailand intensified during 2007, and the inconclusiveness of peace talks in the southern Philippines jeopardised Manila's ceasefire with Muslim insurgents. Nevertheless, the threat from Jemaah Islamiah (JI, the Indonesian-based, pan-Southeast Asian terrorist network) seemed to recede. Despite the signing of the regional grouping's ambitious charter, lack of consensus and bilateral tensions among its members have continued to weaken the Association of Southeast Asian Nations (ASEAN), which failed to take a leading role in response to either Myanmar's continuing political crisis or, initially, the humanitarian emergency there. Meanwhile, regional security institutions remained embryonic and ASEAN members hedged against China's rising power and assertiveness in the region by continuing to develop their security relations with the United States.

Myanmar: Southeast Asia's pariah state
During August and September 2007, an upsurge of peaceful popular protest led by Buddhist monks gripped global attention and stimulated hopes for pro-democratic regime change in Myanmar. However, the willingness of the military State Peace and Development Council (SPDC) regime led by its chairman, Senior-General Tan Shwe, to use violence to suppress the opposition, combined with the likely ineffectiveness of Western sanctions in the face of continued Chinese and

other Asian support for the regime, did not bode well for political change in the short to medium term.

The immediate trigger for the protests, which began on 19 August, when 400 people led by pro-democracy activists marched in Yangon, Myanmar's largest city, was the government's unexpected decision to drastically reduce fuel subsidies at a time when annual inflation had already reached 40%. This element of a reform package supported by the International Monetary Fund and World Bank, aimed at reducing the government's extremely high budget deficit, had the effect of doubling petrol and diesel prices, and – even more dramatically – increased the price of compressed gas used to power buses by a factor of five. Public-transport fares increased overnight and there was a knock-on effect on the price of staples such as rice and cooking oil. Despite the arrest of demonstrators, there were further protests in other towns, such as Sittwe. In early September, troops injured three monks and arrested others who had joined protestors in Pakokku near Mandalay. In retaliation, monks there briefly took 13 senior officials and military officers hostage for several hours and burnt their vehicles.

With the expiry on 17 September of a deadline the Pakokku monks had set for a government apology, protests erupted in Yangon and elsewhere. Eventually, tens of thousands of monks took part in these peaceful demonstrations. The monks also effectively 'excommunicated' military officers and their families by refusing to accept alms from them. Though the regime's failure to apologise for the Pakokku incident was the catalyst, the protests were also aimed at the SPDC's political repression and failure to prevent the extreme economic hardship which characterised the lives of most Burmese. The previously unknown Alliance of All-Burma Buddhist Monks emerged as the coordinating body behind the protests, and on 21 September claimed that the SPDC was 'the enemy of the people'. Its declared aim was to remove the regime from power. Despite the military's efforts since the early 1990s to control religious bodies, the silence of senior abbots in the face of these mass demonstrations indicated their acquiescence in the monks' revolt.

Given that 80–90% of Myanmar's population is Buddhist and that the monks have played key roles at turning points in the country's modern history, including anti-colonial protests in the 1930s and the popular uprising against dictator Ne Win's regime in 1988, the SPDC had every reason to worry that these latest protests might escalate to threaten its hold on power. On 22 September, Aung San Suu Kyi, leader of the National League for Democracy (NLD) which had decisively won elections in 1990, who had spent 12 of the previous 18 years under house arrest, appeared outside her house to acknowledge more than 500 monks and sympathisers who had converged there. Mobile phones and digital cameras captured this event, inspiring NLD members and ordinary Burmese to respond positively to the monks' calls for them to join the protests.

Doubtless fearing a repeat of 1988, when millions of pro-democracy demonstrators took to the streets and an ensuing army crackdown claimed more than 3,000 lives, the SPDC predictably acted to defend the political status quo against forces that threatened not just its own position but also – in its view – national unity. Unlike in 1988, this time Myanmar's security forces acted in a relatively discriminate manner. The crackdown was nevertheless effective. On 24 September, General Thura Myint Maung, minister of religious affairs, appeared on television to threaten 'action' against the monks, and army vehicles were soon deployed across Yangon to announce a curfew. Arrests of pro-democracy activists followed quickly, and on 26 September the army and police took control of Yangon's iconic Shwedagon pagoda. Riot police attacked demonstrators with smoke bombs and canes, and troops fired live rounds over their heads. Troops raided monasteries across Yangon, beating and detaining monks. On 27 September, the army shot dead a number of demonstrators. While the regime admitted to ten fatalities (including a Japanese journalist shot at point-blank range), the actual figure may have been as high as 200. The authorities apparently arrested around 3,000 monks and other demonstrators and activists at this stage, by which time the security forces' crackdown had effectively ended the revolt.

Particularly because of the ubiquity of mobile telephones and the Internet, the drama in Myanmar received graphic coverage in the media worldwide, which carried images of monks who had been shot dead and of troops killing Japanese journalist Kenji Nagai. There was widespread international condemnation of the SPDC regime's suppression of the protests and its rejection of the demonstrators' demands. Western states' reactions to events in Myanmar were strident. The United States, which has attempted to promote democracy in what it still calls 'Burma' through the imposition of economic sanctions (notably in 2003 against the import of garments produced in Myanmar) and by funding opposition groups, announced new sanctions – including an expanded visa ban – targeted at the 'leaders of the regime and their financial backers'. The First Lady, Laura Bush, took a personal interest, calling in an op-ed piece published in early October for Myanmar's generals to join the 'peaceful transition to democracy or get out of the way'. For its part, the European Union broadened sanctions that already included visa bans and asset freezes on senior military officers, officials and their families, and took additional measures targeting Myanmar's timber, metals and gemstone sectors. Its position hardened by the killing of the journalist Kenji Nagai, Japan – which still gives Myanmar development aid ($25m in 2006) – announced that it would cancel plans to build a 'human resources centre' in Yangon.

While these additional sanctions may impact on Myanmar's economy and make life less comfortable for the SPDC elite, the regime's crucial economic links with China meant that the new punitive measures were unlikely to bring it to its knees. More than 700 Chinese businesses operate in Myanmar, dominating urban property markets, as well as the forestry, gem-mining, mineral exploitation and construction sectors. China is the regime's main source of military equipment. Though reports that China is constructing 'military bases' in Myanmar are almost certainly erroneous, there is no doubt that Beijing has important strategic interests there, particularly in terms of energy supply: as well as seeking to exploit Burmese natural-gas reserves, in mid September Beijing approved a pipeline project to facilitate transhipment of Middle East oil supplies through Myanmar, thus avoiding the Malacca Strait. Beijing was probably keen, ahead of the 2008 Olympic Games, to avoid international opprobrium for supporting the SPDC, and may have attempted to curb the brutality of the junta's repression. However, there was no indication that China was willing to sacrifice its economic and strategic stake in Myanmar.

India's relations with Myanmar have also grown apace since the mid 1990s, when New Delhi, to balance China's burgeoning role, protect the security of India's northeastern provinces against ethnic minority insurgents, and develop economic ties, reversed its earlier policy of attempting to isolate the junta. Significantly, in the midst of the September upheaval India's petroleum minister, Murli Deora, visited Myanmar's capital Naypyidaw to discuss energy cooperation. This all-round bilateral relationship with India benefited the SPDC as it attempted to brazen out international criticism.

The United Nations attempted to assert itself in relation to the crisis in Myanmar but did not influence the SPDC significantly. Secretary-General Ban Ki Moon despatched a special envoy, Ibrahim Gambari, who engaged in shuttle diplomacy between the SPDC and Aung San Suu Kyi in early October. Tan Shwe told Gambari that he would meet Aung San Suu Kyi if she ceased promoting 'confrontation, utter devastation, economic sanctions on Myanmar, other sanctions'. On 11 October 2007, the UN Security Council issued a unanimous statement deploring the SPDC's 'use of violence against peaceful demonstrators' and calling on the regime and other parties to 'work together toward a de-escalation of the situation and a peaceful solution'. This represented a diluted version of an original draft by Western powers, which had called directly for democracy in Myanmar. China and Russia rejected this, arguing that the crisis was an internal matter that did not threaten regional or international security. Gambari visited Myanmar again in November, but failed to persuade the SPDC to join a trilateral meeting with himself and Aung San Suu Kyi.

Nevertheless, in February 2008 the junta announced plans for a referendum on a new constitution in May 2008, with democratic multi-party elections following in 2010. However, Myanmar's opposition movement expected that the military would use every resource at its disposal to ensure that its role as political arbiter endured. Indeed, key points of the constitution that the SPDC revealed in early April were that a quarter of parliamentary seats would be reserved for the military, which would also retain exclusive control of the home-affairs ministry. Moreover, anyone who had married a foreigner would be excluded from the presidency, a caveat apparently aimed at Aung San Suu Kyi (though her British husband had died in 1999).

On 2 May 2008, Cyclone Nargis hit Myanmar's Irrawaddy Delta, resulting in the country's worst-ever recorded natural disaster and humanitarian crisis. It quickly became apparent that casualties were massive, with up to 130,000 dead or missing and as many as three million made homeless. The SPDC declared the Yangon, Ayeyerwary and Bago divisions, along with the states of Mon and Kayin, to be disaster areas. There was a large-scale and rapid international response to the emergency, with regional and Western states pledging hundreds of millions of dollars in assistance and announcing their readiness to send in large quantities of relief supplies supported by teams of aid workers. However, the regime brought renewed international opprobrium upon itself by its refusal to allow foreign relief teams into the affected areas, despite the severe dangers that survivors faced from hunger, thirst, lack of shelter and – imminently – disease. Though international relief aid from the UN, India, Malaysia, Thailand and even the United States began to arrive by air and sea from 7 May onwards, reports indicated that Myanmar's armed forces were sequestering relief supplies, some of which were soon on sale in Yangon markets.

Amidst growing international criticism over its failure to facilitate disaster relief for its own population, the SPDC announced that it intended to proceed with the constitutional referendum scheduled for 10 May, though it postponed voting in the Irrawaddy Delta and Yangon for two weeks because of the cyclone's impact there. The regime announced that the result of the 10 May vote, announced five days later – 92.4% in favour, with a 99% turnout – indicated overwhelming support for the new constitution. Subsequently, the SPDC claimed that in voting in the cyclone-affected area on 24 May, 93% turned out with 92.9% in favour. However, reports accused the SPDC of large-scale electoral fraud and intimidation, and the implausible results seemed to vindicate critics who had expected the junta to rig the referendum. But though there was apparently popular dissatisfaction in Myanmar over the SPDC's response to the cyclone disaster, there seemed little near-term prospect of renewed demonstrations against the regime.

Meanwhile, there was growing international clamour for the SPDC to accept foreign assistance for the cyclone-affected region. Australian Prime Minister Kevin Rudd promised to use diplomatic pressure to 'bash the doors down' to allow aid to reach those afflicted by the cyclone, branding the regime's obstruction as 'obscene'. France's state secretary (junior minister) for foreign affairs and human rights, Rama Yade, claimed that Britain and Germany backed French

Foreign Minister Bernard Kouchner's call for 'armed humanitarian intervention' under the 'responsibility to protect' principle that the UN General Assembly adopted in 2005. On 17 May, US congressmen asked President George W. Bush to consider 'peaceful international humanitarian intervention' in Myanmar. The fact that the United States had already deployed sizeable forces to Thailand for the annual *Cobra Gold* exercise and that British and French warships were in the vicinity gave the SPDC grounds for nervousness, but armed intervention was never likely. On 19 May, more than two weeks after the cyclone, an emergency ASEAN foreign ministers' meeting won the SPDC's agreement to allow the association to take the lead in implementing an international aid effort. While this helped to defuse the growing tension between the SPDC and concerned governments, the SPDC reiterated that it would not allow 'uncontrolled' entry of foreign aid workers, and it was unclear how effective the 'mechanism' proposed by ASEAN for bringing aid into Myanmar would prove in practice. Though ASEAN subsequently set up a task force including UN and SPDC representatives to coordinate the relief effort and provide accountability, and the SPDC allowed some international aid workers into hard-hit areas, reservations on the part of potential donor states were clear at an international 'pledging' conference in Yangon on 25 May, co-chaired by UN Secretary-General Ban Ki Moon and Singaporean Foreign Minister George Yeo. While the SPDC had requested $10.7bn for rehabilitation and reconstruction (including construction of a massive protective embankment to protect the delta's population from future storm surges), representatives of more than 50 countries promised a mere additional $50m. The United States and other potential donors said they could promise additional assistance only if they could first thoroughly assess needs on the ground. However, despite signs of disagreement within Myanmar's junta over how to proceed, by mid June it granted visas to hundreds of UN staff and foreign aid workers, who were at last heading for the worst-affected areas to assess the needs of survivors.

Malaysia's new politics

Malaysians broadly welcomed the accession in 2003 of Abdullah Badawi as prime minister in succession to Mahathir Mohamad. Indeed, along with the restoration of fast economic growth after the doldrums resulting from the regional financial crisis of 1997–8, a 'feel-good factor' associated with the new prime minister – who was widely seen as an incorruptible and moderate leader combining religious piety with tolerance – helped the Barisan Nasional (BN) coalition to a resounding victory in the March 2004 elections, the opposition taking the lowest number of seats since the 1970s. The BN also regained control of Terengganu state, which it had lost to the opposition Parti Islam se-Malaysia (PAS, Malaysian Islamic Party) in 1999. There was widespread optimism that Abdullah Badawi's administration would deal effectively with the corruption and crime that increasingly plagued Malaysia.

Compared with the Mahathir era, regional and international interlocutors found Malaysia much easier to deal with under Abdullah Badawi, who largely muted the government's previous nationalist and anti-Western rhetoric. Singapore, in particular, benefited. Under the new prime minister, Malaysia welcomed involvement from Singapore's government as well as companies in the Iskandar Development Region in southern Johor state, identified in the Ninth Malaysia Plan announced in 2006 as an important catalyst for future economic growth. However, by contrast, Malaysians themselves increasingly registered disappointment with Abdullah Badawi's administration, which demonstrated little if any progress towards reducing corruption and crime. While there had always been considerable opposition among the non-Malay communities and poor rural Malays to the BN's rule, there was now also growing discontent across a wider stratum of Malays who had previously supported the UMNO (United Malays National Organisation), the BN's largest and dominant component. There was particular unhappiness over the way that Abdullah Badawi's government apparently tolerated the further entrenchment of privilege among a small elite of affluent Malays connected to ruling circles, and discomfort with the prominent political role of Abdullah's son-in-law, Khairy Jamaluddin (deputy chief of UMNO's youth wing). While racial issues remained central to Malaysian politics, there was a growing popular view that inequality within the Malay community was also important.

During November 2007, two major anti-government demonstrations unnerved Abdullah's administration. On 10 November, as many as 40,000 people joined a rally in the commercial capital Kuala Lumpur supported by opposition parties and organised by BERSIH, the Coalition for Clean and Fair Elections, with the aim of submitting to the Yang di-Pertuan Agong (king) a petition listing specific demands relating to electoral reform. The authorities' reaction to this rally was heavy-handed, as was the case later in the month when police broke up a demonstration by tens of thousands of ethnic Indian Malaysians led by HINDRAF (the Hindu Rights Action Force), a coalition of 30 non-governmental organisations, galvanised by concern over the demolition of Hindu temples and the perceived imposition of sharia-based law. The police arrested HINDRAF leaders after the rally, and detained five under the Internal Security Act. The demonstration highlighted the inability of the Malaysian Indian Congress (MIC) to protect the interests of ethnic Indians (who represent roughly 8% of Malaysia's population) despite its membership of the BN, a multi-racial coalition including UMNO and the Malaysian Chinese Association, representing ethnic Malay and Chinese interests respectively. Together, the two demonstrations provided a livelier-than-usual backdrop to the announcement in mid February 2008 that the next general election would be held on 8 March. This was a year earlier than strictly necessary, but the government evidently wished to seek a renewed popular mandate before former Deputy Prime Minister Anwar Ibrahim (who had been detained under the Internal Security Act and subsequently imprisoned after conviction on corruption and sexual charges, widely believed to have been trumped up) was allowed to return to politics in April 2008. Another reason for calling the election relatively early may have been the expectation that the looming US recession would impact negatively on Malaysia's own economy.

The opposition parties set their sights primarily on removing the BN's symbolically important two-thirds majority (which allowed the government to change the constitution at will, if it wished) in the federal parliament and retaking control of Terengganu. But the March 2008 election results caused widespread surprise because of the extent of BN losses to the three opposition parties, the Democratic Action Party (DAP), Parti Keadilan Rakyat (PKR, People's Justice Party) and PAS, which had reached an agreement in advance of the 2008 elections to avoid contesting the same seats and presented themselves as the Barisan Rakyat (People's Front), with Anwar Ibrahim playing the role of leader despite his temporary disqualification from standing for election. Alongside widespread disillusionment with the BN, and the blossoming of on-line newspapers and blogs that provided a vibrant and critical alternative to the stodgy, progovernment newspapers and TV channels, the strategy brought a stunning success to the opposition. It was clear that the wish to punish the BN was now more important than inter-communal distrust within the opposition, with significant numbers of Malays voting for the 'Chinese' DAP, and Chinese similarly voting for the 'Malay' PAS.

In the federal parliament, the three main opposition parties took 47% of the vote, compared with 50% for the BN; only in 1969 had the opposition taken a greater proportion. No fewer than 82 seats (37% of the total of 222) fell to the opposition, by far the largest number since independence. Among those who lost their seats were several BN ministers, including Samy Vellu (leader of the discredited MIC). At the state level, the BN was shocked to lose control of four states in the heavily populated and economically important west of the peninsula: Kedah, Penang, Perak and Selangor. Though the opposition failed to win Terengganu, PAS strengthened its hold on Kelantan.

The election results remodelled Malaysia's political landscape and raised the prospect of considerable turmoil to come. Though he attempted to reassert his authority after the election, Abdullah Badawi's leadership of UMNO and the government seemed unlikely to endure beyond the short term. Soon after the polls, there were calls from within UMNO (supported by former Prime Minister Mahathir, who had led the party and the country from 1981 to 2003) for Bedawi to step aside, and it seemed possible there would be a fierce contest to succeed him in the next party elections. These were originally scheduled for August 2008, but were delayed until December because of the party's post-election disarray. One possibility appeared to be that the prime minister would resign and support his anointed successor, Deputy Prime Minister and Defence Minister Najib Tun Razak, who was in any case scheduled to take over as party and national leader in late 2009 or early 2010. If Badawi attempted to remain in post, though, he might face a challenge from the veteran UMNO politician and former finance minister, Tengku Razaleigh Hamzah, or the current international trade and industry minister, Muhyiddin Yassin, both of whom indicated their possible readiness to enter a leadership contest. In late May, Mahathir dramatically resigned his UMNO membership in protest against Badawi's refusal to step aside. Mahathir's move may have further undermined UMNO's credibility to the opposition's benefit, without having the desired effect of accelerating leadership change.

A failure to respond quickly and effectively to the message from the electorate could prove disastrous for UMNO and the BN. The opposition needs only 30 extra seats to replace the BN and immediately after the election there was already widespread talk of potential defections to the opposition, particularly from the BN's historically fickle components in Sabah and Sarawak, some of which still wished to renegotiate the relationship between the federation and their states, while securing more important positions in the federal cabinet.

Anwar Ibrahim, the leader of the Pakatan Rakyat (People's Alliance), as the opposition grouping had renamed itself in April, promised BN politicians in the two Borneo states greater political and financial autonomy (including an increase in their oil royalties to 20% from the 5% they currently receive). In May, Anwar insisted that the opposition coalition would be in a position to take power before mid September as a result of BN defections.

When announcing the formation of the Pakatan Rakyat, Anwar identified common principles uniting the three opposition parties, including 'justice, good governance, human rights, accountability and transparency'. However, in the wake of the opposition victories at state level, there were disagreements over the allocation of chief ministers' posts, and it was unclear how successfully the opposition parties could reconcile their policy positions if they took power at the federal level. Part of the answer might lie in Malaysia becoming a looser federation, with state governments allowed greater powers.

The scale of opposition success and the threat that the Pakatan Rakyat posed to the BN government's tenure carried with it a risk to Malaysia's political stability. UMNO leaders attempted to exploit fears that the opposition, if it took power, would oversee an erosion of the special privileges of the country's *bumiputra* (indigenous) population, most of whom were Malays. Soon after taking over, the new DAP-led state government in Penang spoke of dismantling pro-*bumiputra* policies. Some Malaysians feared a repeat of the events of May 1969, when opposition electoral gains appeared to threaten Malay interests, provoking violence (mainly perpetrated by Malays) which killed several hundred people, mainly Chinese-Malaysians. The government then imposed a state of emergency and effectively suspended democracy for almost two years. However, almost 40 years later the trans-ethnic character of support for the Pakatan Rakyat, and the fact that two of its three parties are Malay-led, suggested that while political instability was inevitable, communal disturbances and violence might be avoided.

The huge increase in the price of oil threatened to further undermine the government's position in mid 2008. In early June, the government announced that it would withdraw fuel subsidies, which would otherwise cost it $17bn over the year, considerably more than the country's development budget. Though the government emphasised that it would help low-income Malaysians with measures such as cash handouts and a fuel-quota system, there was widespread anger over the fuel-price increases (41% for petrol and 63% for diesel), which took effect almost immediately. The opposition capitalised on the issue, calling for mass demonstrations. Anwar promised that if the Pakatan Rakyat took power it would reduce fuel prices 'the very next day'.

The enlivening of Malaysia's democracy is likely to have important regional ramifications, notably by further strengthening political pluralism within ASEAN. There may be particular implications for neighbouring Singapore. Though the two countries' political circumstances are quite different, they remain closely linked in social terms and the Malaysian electorate's impulse to vote for the opposition could prove contagious, particularly if the Malaysian case demonstrates that vibrant politics do not spell economic disaster. And if Malaysia ultimately thrives under a more meritocratic, less ethnically driven system, the way would be open for closer collaboration in many spheres with Singapore. In the immediate future, however, while Malaysia's new politics continue to take shape, Singapore will be wary of the potential for Malaysian political turbulence to affect bilateral relations negatively, as it has on previous occasions.

Thailand's political travails

In Thailand, where a military coup in September 2006 had usurped the caretaker administration led by Prime Minister Thaksin Shinawatra following inconclusive polls earlier in the year, democracy was restored with the election in December 2007 of a new government supported by the deposed former leader. However, the country's political stability was far from assured. Following the coup, the military had set up a Constitutional Tribunal charged with investigating allegations that Thaksin's Thai Rak Thai ('Thais Love Thais', TRT) and other parties, notably the opposition Democrats, had been guilty of gross malpractice in the April 2006 general election. The TRT was accused of 'hiring' small political parties to contest the election so that its candidates could legitimately win seats. Thailand's revered and highly influential King Bhumibol Adulyadej warned Constitutional Tribunal judges, a week before they were due to announce their verdict, that they should issue a firm decision on the charges faced by the TRT and other parties, explain their rationale clearly, and recognise that their verdicts were unlikely to satisfy all constituencies. Against this background, on 30 May 2007 the tribunal ordered the TRT's dissolution and banned Thaksin, together with 110 senior TRT officials, from political participation for five years. But the judgment also absolved the opposition Democrat Party of all charges and was widely interpreted as a highly politicised ruling aimed at breaking the TRT's power and re-establishing a system of government based on coalitions of relatively weak parties, and in which the military and monarchy would have important arbitrating roles.

While the TRT had undoubtedly behaved improperly during the 2006 election campaign, and there had been drawbacks to its previously overwhelming parliamentary preponderance, with its extensive social programmes it nevertheless remained Thailand's most popular political party. Its supporters numbered millions, concentrated particularly in the north and northeast and among Bangkok's poor. Despite its forced dissolution and the temporary disqualification of its leaders, it was evident that in modified form it would endure as a major political force. Though the 30 May ruling temporarily removed the TRT's leading lights from politics, around 250 former TRT members of parliament remained eligible for re-election. It was widely – and correctly – anticipated that the party would re-form under a different name but with broadly the same populist agenda.

After publication in April 2007 of the draft of Thailand's proposed new constitution, which reduced the size of the parliamentary lower house and attempted to boost the standing of smaller parties in an effort to prevent a single party from dominating the legislature to the extent that the TRT had, movement towards restoring democratic government was surprisingly smooth during the second half of 2007. Following the removal in mid July of the ban on political activity, on 19 August a popular referendum on the new constitution saw a 58% turnout and a decisive 57% vote in its favour. With the hurdle of approving the constitution surmounted, in late August the Electoral Commission announced that the general election would be held on 23 December. During the four-month interval before the election, TRT members regrouped as the People's Power Party (PPP), under the leadership of a veteran right-wing, populist politician, 72-year-old Samak Sundaravej, whom many saw as a proxy for Thaksin.

All parties made populist promises to Thailand's rural voters during the election campaign. The main rival to the PPP, the Democrat Party led by Abhisit Vejjajiva, claimed that it would lower living costs while pursuing fiscal prudence, maintain village-level micro-credit schemes as part of a rural 'self-sufficiency economy', and reinforce the national education system. The Democrats aspired to lead the next government in coalition with minor parties, and a PPP victory was never assumed to be inevitable. However, the Democrats were unable to make significant inroads beyond their established support bases in the south and Bangkok into the TRT's heartland constituencies in the north and northeast. There, the PPP – as the TRT's successor – was now the natural party of choice.

Despite the junta's efforts to interfere with the PPP's campaign (notably through a leaked 'classified order' accusing the party of lese-majesty), the party emerged with the largest number of House of Representatives seats. However, while the PPP gained 226 seats against the Democrats' 166, it did not hold an outright majority and could not automatically form the new administration. It was not until January 2008 that the PPP was able to agree a coalition with five smaller parties, leaving the Democrats as the opposition. Prime Minister Samak's government, which took office in early February 2008, includes controversial political figures such as Sanan Kajornprasart (deputy prime minister) and Chalerm Yoobamrung (interior minister), but many of its members are politically inexperienced associates of Thaksin.

While Samak may possess sufficient political drive to pursue his own course as prime minister, there were good reasons for thinking that Thaksin would exert considerable behind-the-scenes influence on the PPP government. Indeed, Thaksin's wife, Khunying Pojaman Shinawatra, who had left Thailand in August, returned in early January 2008. Like Thaksin, she faced corruption charges; though arrested on arrival in Bangkok, she was quickly released on bail and reportedly played a significant part in deciding the cabinet's composition. Thaksin himself returned in late February 2008. In March, he pleaded not guilty in the Supreme Court to one of two corruption charges he was facing. Though the former prime minister faced further court appearances and denied that he planned a political comeback, with massive resources at his disposal it seemed possible that he might seek to overturn his and his former TRT colleagues' political disqualification, setting the stage for a major political showdown with establishment political forces led informally by Privy Councillor Prem Tinsulanond. Combined with the monarchy's unclear succession mechanism (King Bhumibol celebrated his eightieth birthday in December 2007 amidst rumours concerning his fragile health), this suggested that continuing political instability was likely. Indeed, in late March Samak warned that groups of army officers were plotting to overthrow his government, prompting Army Commander-in-Chief General Anupong Paochinda to deny the existence of coup plots. During May, political controversy intensified as the PPP promoted constitutional changes that would prevent the party and two coalition partners from being dissolved, like the TRT, for alleged electoral fraud. Amending the constitution could also lead to the lifting of the ban on political activities imposed on Thaksin and other former TRT members. At the same time, allegations of lese-majesty against one of Samak's ministers, Jakrapob Penkair (who resigned in late May), appeared to be aimed at creating the conditions favourable to another coup, though senior army officers indicated that they would not interfere in the deepening political conflict. The anti-Thaksin pressure group, the People's Alliance for Democracy (PAD), led large-scale and persistent demonstrations against the government, as it did before the 2006 military intervention. In mid June, additional protests over the rapidly rising price of fuel and other essential goods exacerbated the sense of national crisis.

The conflict involving Thai Muslim insurgents (believed to be largely from the Barisan Revolusi Nasional – Coordinate) in the three southernmost provinces of Narathiwat, Pattani and Yala continued during 2007, which saw more violent incidents than the previous year. More heavily urbanised Yala remained the worst affected of the three provinces. Insurgent attacks in the three provinces, where more than 70% of the population is Muslim – involving bombings of public places such as markets; shootings aimed at Thai troops and police, schoolteachers and civilians; and arson targeted at schools and other government buildings – were almost daily occurrences. The conflict's death toll since 2004 had reached 3,000 by May 2008, with around 5,000 injured. Though the security forces and Buddhist civilians were often targets, most of the victims were Muslim civilians.

On 20 December, days before the general election, the junta's National Legislative Assembly enacted an Internal Security Act, giving the Internal Security Operations Command extensive powers to impose curfews and house arrest, and to curtail freedom of movement. This law, which one Muslim community leader described as 'terrifying' because of the scope it seemed to provide the authorities to violate human rights, was expected to come into force in June or July 2008. Political developments in Bangkok did nothing to change the Thai state's hard-line approach to the southern conflict, and there was no indication that the new civilian government would seriously consider a political solution. The Samak government's interior minister initially indicated that the government might be willing to grant a degree of autonomy to a 'special administrative region' in the south, but he withdrew his suggestion after the new prime minister called it 'dangerous'. Despite earlier informal attempts by Malaysia and international non-governmental organisations to broker contact between Bangkok and the insurgents, there was no sign that negotiations were imminent. When Samak visited the Malaysian capital, Putrajaya, in January 2008, Prime Minister Badawi reiterated his government's willingness to assist social and economic development in Thailand's south, but the Malaysian priority in the bilateral meeting was to obtain assurances regarding the supply of Thai-produced rice amidst acute concerns over shortages and rising prices.

Continuing instability and insecurity in the Philippines

Political opponents – particularly in the opposition-controlled Senate – continued to mount legal challenges to Philippine President Gloria Macapagal Arroyo, claiming that she was corrupt and guilty of electoral fraud. In August 2007, a new scandal erupted over allegations that the president, her husband and others were improperly involved in the awarding of a contract to a Chinese company to construct the proposed National Broadband Network (NBN). There was an inept, small-scale military rebellion in November 2007, when navy lieutenant Antonio Trillanes (who had been elected to the Senate from prison in the May 2007 elections) and other personnel on trial for their part in the 2003 'Oakwood Mutiny' broke out of court and seized control of Manila's Peninsula Hotel, calling for Arroyo's overthrow because of her alleged corruption and abuses of power. However, loyal forces quickly subdued the rebellion without casualties. Public-opinion pollsters claimed that ordinary Filipinos saw Arroyo as the most corrupt president in the nation's history, and that almost half of the population was dissatisfied with her leadership. But despite this level of opposition, it seemed highly likely that Arroyo would survive until her six-year term ended in 2010. Though her former political ally, Speaker of the House of Representatives José de Venecia, turned against her over the NBN affair, necessitating his ouster, the president continued to command majority support in the lower house as well as the backing of the armed forces' leadership. However, the government-backed initiative for 'charter change' – major constitutional revisions including adoption of a parliamentary system of government – seemed unlikely to succeed during Arroyo's presidency.

Meanwhile, Arroyo – herself an economist – was overseeing an economic boom. With exports, particularly in the electronics sector, surging and remittances from millions of overseas Filipino workers boosting domestic demand, the Philippines registered 7.3% GDP growth in 2007, making it Southeast Asia's fastest-growing economy. The Philippines' impressive economic performance brought comparisons with India's contemporary surge; another similarity, however, was continuing widespread poverty alongside rapid growth. In the Philippines, more than half the population subsisted on less than $2 a day. Large-scale social inequity explained the continuing appeal of the Communist Party of the Philippines and its military wing, the New People's Army (NPA), whose Maoist guerrillas maintained their campaign of assassination, extortion and raids on military and police posts throughout the country. The detention in the Netherlands of José Maria Sison, founder of the Communist Party of the Philippines, for two weeks in August and September may have temporarily demoralised elements of the NPA, but at the end of 2007 the rebels ignored the government's declaration of a three-week 'offensive ceasefire' and intensified operations, with a 100-strong guerrilla force attacking a police station on

Samar on 24 December. Nevertheless, in January 2008 Philippine National Police chief Avelino Razon claimed that military action, including the destruction of 13 NPA bases, had reduced the insurgent army's overall strength to 5,700 personnel (by way of comparison, it had 25,000 guerrillas at its peak in the 1980s). Razon further claimed that by 2010 the NPA would be a mere 'peace and order' issue rather than a 'security problem'.

The complex problem of Muslim rebellion in the Philippines' south represented a far more acute security challenge for Manila. During *Oplan Ultimatum*, a major military operation on the island of Jolo in the Sulu archipelago to the southwest of Mindanao between August 2006 and March 2007, the Armed Forces of the Philippines (AFP) notched significant tactical successes against the Abu Sayyaf Group (ASG), a relatively small but highly aggressive, criminally inclined insurgent-cum-terrorist band responsible for a series of kidnappings-for-ransom and bombings since 2000. The AFP estimated that the operation, backed by US troops whose main role was to provide battlefield intelligence, had reduced the ASG's strength by 20% to around 430 men with 280 weapons among them and led to the deaths of the group's two top leaders. A specific aim of *Oplan Ultimatum* had been to capture or kill two Indonesians, Umar Patek and Dulmatin, who were known to have been among a dozen non-Filipino Southeast Asian jihadis who had allied themselves with ASG. These foreigners were formerly members of Indonesian-based extremist groups such as Jemaah Islamiah, KOMPAK and Darul Islam; Umar Patek and Dulmatin were allegedly bomb-makers who had been part of the team behind the 1992 Bali bombings. In mid February 2008, the AFP announced (as it had on previous occasions) that it had killed Dulmatin (for whom the US government had offered a $10m bounty) in a battle several weeks earlier and that troops had recovered his body. However, at the end of March the military admitted that DNA tests on the remains were 'inconclusive'.

Subsequent developments undermined gains made during *Oplan Ultimatum*. Despite efforts by the Ad Hoc Coordinating Group and the Peace Monitoring Group, established at the start of *Oplan Ultimatum*, to separate the ASG from local units of the Moro National Liberation Front (MNLF), whose Jolo members had retained their arms despite the Front's 1996 final peace agreement with the Philippine government, an AFP attack in April 2007 on an ASG concentration close to an MNLF camp led to fighting with the larger group. The MNLF mounted reprisals against AFP elements on the island, but the army and marines soon captured the three main MNLF camps. The conflict intensified to the extent that by the end of May 2007 it had displaced 67,000 villagers on Jolo. According to the AFP, at least seven MNLF commanders transferred their allegiance to the ASG, and the number of 'enemy combatants' on the island rose to more than 600. *Oplan Ultimatum II*, launched in July 2007, involved notably greater emphasis on civic-action projects, but the AFP emphasised that combat operations on

Jolo would continue. In early August, intense clashes re-erupted following an ambush on an AFP convoy; 26 troops and more than 30 rebels died. Though the Philippine military blamed the ASG, the MNLF claimed responsibility for the fighting. Rivalry between local clans further complicated the situation on Jolo: in February 2008, an army attack on a village during a search for ASG personnel and foreign jihadis, leading to seven civilian and two AFP deaths, may have resulted from deliberate misinformation related to such a feud.

Elsewhere in the country's south, the danger of large-scale conflict reigniting between the government and the Moro Islamic Liberation Front (MILF) seemed to increase. Following a ceasefire agreement in 1997, Manila and the MILF pursued negotiations aimed at a final settlement, but these stalled in late 2006 over the issue of Muslim 'ancestral domain' in the south, which would determine the extent of territories to be included in any new autonomous region. In October 2007, a joint statement announced that the peace process was on course again, with formal talks expected before the year's end. However, in mid December the MILF announced that it would not sign a memorandum of agreement because the government's draft agreement stated that the inclusion of new territories in the proposed autonomous 'Bangsamoro Judicial Entity' would be subject to 'constitutional processes'. From the MILF's viewpoint, the constitution was anathema, as it takes a unitary state for granted; in its view, only extra-constitutional measures can resolve the southern conflict. Though the talks remained stalled, in March 2008 the MILF's leader, Al-Haj Murad Ebrahim, emphasised his commitment to the peace process. However, the Philippine government increasingly emphasised military and developmental – rather than political – responses to the issue of Moro assertiveness.

The breakdown in negotiations had important ramifications on the ground, making armed clashes between government forces and MILF guerrillas more likely. Following a series of warnings over its frustration with repeated delays to negotiations, in April 2008 Malaysia, which had facilitated the peace talks since 2001 and had led the International Monitoring Team (IMT) since 2004, announced that it would withdraw its monitors. Most of the 41 Malaysian troops flew home in early May, and the remainder – along with ten Bruneian and eight Libyan personnel and a Japanese development official – were expected to withdraw by the end of August. The IMT had played a crucially important role in helping bilateral government–MILF committees and Local Monitoring Teams to prevent clashes between the AFP and MILF: such incidents declined from 559 in 2003 to a mere seven in 2007. Another negative development was the effective suspension of the Ad Hoc Joint Action Group (AHJAG), established by the AFP and MILF in 2005 as a mechanism to 'isolate and interdict' criminals and 'lost commands' (most obviously the ASG) who might be hiding in MILF areas, again reducing the chances of fighting between government and MILF forces. During 2005, the

AHJAG facilitated intelligence-sharing between the AFP and MILF which played a significant part in forcing ASG and foreign jihadi elements back into Sulu from mainland Mindanao, helping US-backed AFP troops to win significant victories there. However, the AHJAG's mandate expired in June 2007 and, though it was renewed the following November, with the peace talks in abeyance the group has remained inactive. The dangers of the less-regulated environment in the south became apparent in the 'Al-Barka incident' in July 2007, when insurgents on Basilan killed 14 marines (ten of whom they beheaded) out of a larger group who were searching for an Italian priest kidnapped a month earlier. The AFP troops strayed into MILF territory, provoking a major fire-fight: it was exactly the type of clash that the AHJAG might have prevented. Subsequent incidents highlighted the truce's fragility. In May 2008, both the AFP and the MILF claimed the other side had violated the ceasefire after another major clash on Basilan.

Meanwhile, the ASG and its foreign associates continued to pose a tangible security threat. In November 2007, a bombing at the Philippine Congress attributed to the ASG killed Congressman Wahab Akbar, a former Basilan governor and one-time senior member of the MNLF. In May, an AFP divisional commander in the south warned that freelance bomb-making terrorists were now operating outside the control of the ASG, and were offering their services to other criminal and insurgent groups, and speculated that the MILF might use such bomb attacks to press the government to resume talks. At month's end, Manila blamed a lethal bombing at an air base near Zamboanga on the ASG, Jemaah Islamiah and the MILF. There appeared to be a significant danger that conflating the ASG and foreign terrorist threat with concerns over the MILF and MNLF might ignite a wider conflict in the south.

Timor Leste: still a fragile state

In largely peaceful parliamentary elections at the end of June 2007, the left-wing Fretilin party led by former Prime Minister Mari Alkatiri won the largest number of seats, but lacked sufficient representation to form a government on its own. After weeks of wrangling, in early August 2007 President José Ramos-Horta appointed his predecessor, Xanana Gusmão, as prime minister of a coalition government comprising Gusmão's National Congress for Timorese Reconstruction (CNRT) and several smaller parties. In the days following the new government's formation, Fretilin supporters rampaged in towns where the party's support was strongest, burning buildings in Viqueque, Baucau and on a smaller scale in Dili. However, although Fretilin members initially boycotted parliament, in late August they took their seats.

Major Alfredo Reinado, the Timor Leste Defence Force's former naval and subsequently military police commander, remained on the run during 2007 following his leading role in provoking the country's 2006 crisis (which necessitated a new international military intervention led by Australia), his arrest in July 2006 and his escape from prison with 50 others the following month. In April 2007, then Acting Prime Minister Ramos-Horta called off the search for Reinado in the hope of relaxing tensions before the elections. In August, Ramos-Horta (by then president) met Reinado and they agreed to initiate talks aimed at reconciliation. However, over the following months negotiations intended to facilitate Reinado's return to the defence force with the proviso that he first stand trial were fruitless. In a dramatic turn of events, on 11 February 2008 Reinado and several accomplices attempted to kidnap or assassinate the president. The president's bodyguards killed Reinado; Ramos-Horta was seriously injured but survived following medical evacuation to Australia. A simultaneous attack on Prime Minister Gusmão failed. In May, Indonesia extradited four renegade soldiers who had been involved in the attacks and subsequently fled across the border to Indonesian West Timor.

At the time of the February 2008 attacks on Timor Leste's leaders, an International Security Force comprising 750 Australian and 180 New Zealand troops under Australian national command, together with a UN police force (UNPOL) of around 1,500 officers provided by Australia, Portugal and 23 other states were responsible for the country's security while the local security forces were being restructured in the wake of the events of late 2006. The commander of Timor Leste's defence force, Brigadier-General Taur Matan Rauk, blamed the international police for not preventing the attacks, though it became clear that Ramos-Horta had ordered that national personnel should provide his personal security. Two hundred additional Australian troops deployed to Timor Leste following the February attacks, but were withdrawn again by April. Though the country's political stability remained in question, the continuing and substantial international security presence effectively forestalled major public disorder.

Indonesia: consolidating stability

Indonesia, which many international observers viewed as a fragile or even potentially disintegrating state at the start of the decade, continued to manifest considerable stability under the leadership of President Susilo Bambang Yudhoyono's coalition government elected in 2004. In Aceh, a comprehensive peace agreement in 2005, which ended a long-running insurgency in return for substantial political and economic autonomy, effectively ended the central government's acute security concerns in the province by ending the armed conflict there. There was concern in Jakarta, particularly among senior military officers, in July 2007 over the re-establishment of GAM (the Aceh Freedom Movement, which had provided political direction to the insurgency) as a political party. The movement seemed likely to constitute Aceh's most important political force. However, while GAM evidently still harboured long-term separatist ambitions, the successful implementation of Aceh's special status as agreed in 2005 offered the possibility that genuine autonomy might satisfy Aceh's people.

Another notable security-related achievement for Yudhoyono's administration was the success of its counter-terrorism efforts, leading to the arrest of more than 200 members of Jemaah Islamiah (JI) between 2005 and mid 2008. The Australian and US governments provided substantial financial and operational support for these efforts. In raids in Java in June 2007, the Indonesian police counter-terrorist unit, Detachment-88, captured key JI leaders, including Zarkasih and Abu Dujana. Their trials began in December 2007, and in April they were each sentenced to 15 years in prison. Though important JI figures including Malaysian bomb-maker Noordin Top, Mas Selamat Kastari (who, embarrassingly for Singapore's government, escaped from detention in the city-state in February 2008), Umar Patek, and others in the southern Philippines remained at large, the apprehension of important suspects almost certainly circumscribed the operational capacity of JI, which had mounted no major attacks since the Bali bombings in 2005.

Nevertheless, in mid 2008 Yudhoyono's government faced significant political problems. Though the acute threat from terrorism was apparently in retreat, Islamic radicalism presented a broader and apparently growing challenge to Indonesia's secular (and, since the overthrow of Suharto's dictatorship in 1998, essentially liberal) political order. In 2008, controversy over the Ahmadiyah religious group, which many conservative Muslims view as heretical because of its insistence that its founder was the successor to the Prophet Muhammad, sparked conflict between religious hardliners and defenders of the secular order. Ahmadiyah has several hundred thousand Indonesian followers, who since 2005 had suffered intimidation in Java, Lombok, south Sulawesi and other parts of the country. In April, the country's leading religious body pronounced that Ahmadiyah's teachings deviated from Islamic principles. In early June, the Islamic Defenders Front (FPI) attacked a small demonstration by members of Ahmadiyah, Muslim liberals and Christians in Jakarta celebrating Indonesia's tradition of pluralism. Police subsequently arrested almost 60 FPI members involved in the attack, but others eluded capture. Only too aware that it relied on the support of conservative Islamic parties (whose backing Yudhoyono would need to hold on to his post in the 2009 legislative and presidential elections), days later the government announced restrictions on Ahmadiyah (essentially preventing the group from proselytising), though these stopped short of the outright ban that the FPI and other conservative groups had demanded. This enraged both sides, and police were deployed across Indonesia to protect Ahmadiyah members and mosques.

By May 2008, rising fuel prices were also undermining the standing of Yudhoyono and his government. Like its Malaysian counterpart, Yudhoyono's administration felt obliged to reduce subsidies in order to protect the national budget, with the result that prices were expected to rise by up to 30% in a matter of weeks. As was the case elsewhere, it was anticipated that fuel-price increases would in turn also push the price of food supplies, which had already become more expensive for other reasons, still higher. Though the government announced plans for cash handouts to 19m poor families, public anger mounted. The government was acutely aware that it was protests over fuel-price increases a decade earlier that had forced President Suharto to resign, and that popular discontent had led Yudhoyono's predecessor, Megawati Sukarnoputri, to reverse increased prices. Following the announcement of price increases on 24 May, students and other protestors demonstrated and clashed with police. Nervous for the country's stability, Yudhoyono temporarily banned his ministers from leaving Indonesia. Days later, Jakarta announced that it planned to withdraw from OPEC, to which it had belonged since 1962 as a major oil producer. Having become a net oil importer two years previously, membership of a cartel dedicated to seeking higher oil prices no longer made sense. Simultaneously, however, the government offered 25 new oil and gas areas for auction (with more to follow later in 2008) in an effort to stem declining national output.

Challenges for ASEAN

Political developments in Southeast Asia, particularly in Myanmar, posed important challenges for ASEAN, just as its members were attempting to intensify their politico-security cooperation. For the association, to which Myanmar had belonged since 1997, the SPDC's crackdown on dissent in late 2007 represented a flagrant breach of the principles that the grouping – or at least its longer-standing core membership – claimed to see as key to the ASEAN Community which it aims to establish by 2015. In November 2007, a summit meeting of the association in Singapore adopted the ASEAN Charter, which established the grouping as a legal entity for the first time, strengthened its secretariat, and committed members' heads of government to biannual summits. It also called for, among other things, the promotion of human rights and good governance, as well as the strengthening of democratic institutions. Taking action to implement these principles in Myanmar's case proved difficult. The association's membership is eclectic, and there was little consensus on how to deal with the challenge that developments in Myanmar posed to its credibility as an effective regional institution. Members with democratic political systems – Indonesia and the Philippines – favoured a tough stance towards the SPDC. Malaysia and Singapore had significant economic interests in Myanmar which they wished to protect, and were concerned over the probable destabilising effects on regional security of rapid democratisation, yet were also keen for ASEAN to develop as an effective institution and registered mounting frustration with the SPDC.

Despite the Thai junta's links with its SPDC counterpart and dependence on Myanmar's natural gas, it was also vexed by the SPDC's failure to control the flow of narcotics, refugees and migrants across the border and by the obstacle it posed to ASEAN's development. However, relatively new ASEAN members Cambodia, Laos and Vietnam shared Myanmar's authoritarianism and had no interest in promoting change there.

With Singapore in the chair, following the SPDC's crackdown in September 2007 ASEAN issued its strongest-ever condemnation of a member, calling on Myanmar's junta immediately to cease its repression, which had 'appalled' fellow ASEAN states. But despite anguished calls for firm action from intellectuals in the region who wanted the association to live up to its ideals in its 40th anniversary year and on the eve of the crucial November summit, ASEAN's Secretary-General Ong Keng Yong rejected any notion of suspending Myanmar's membership. Ong argued that while there could be 'no business as usual', it was important for ASEAN to use its link with the SPDC to impress on Myanmar's generals the depth of international disapproval. ASEAN would press for Aung San Suu Kyi's release from house-arrest to facilitate negotiations over Myanmar's political future, he said. Given the diversity of outlooks within ASEAN it would have been difficult for the grouping to adopt a more strident posture while retaining its cohesion. Nevertheless, ASEAN's apparently ineffectual stance brought criticism within and beyond Southeast Asia, as was the case also in the wake of the cyclone calamity despite the association's eventual efforts to mediate between the SPDC and external would-be providers of humanitarian and reconstruction assistance.

One aspect of ASEAN's efforts to move towards more highly institutionalised cooperation in the form of an ASEAN Community by 2015 involves creation of an ASEAN Political Security Community (APSC). The 2007 summit tasked members' ministers and officials to draft an APSC blueprint for adoption at the next summit in late 2008. In the meantime, the precise objectives of the APSC remained vague, though it seemed likely that the annual ASEAN Defence Ministers' Meeting (ADMM), first held in 2006 with the objective of forging 'practical cooperation to address the transnational security issues facing the region', would form an important element of the community, if not its centrepiece. For the foreseeable future, however, a range of bilateral intra-ASEAN disputes – quite apart from the SPDC's hugely undermining impact on the associations's ambitions – seemed likely to preclude the level of trust necessary for a true community in the political and security sphere. One bilateral problem which came to the fore was the territorial dispute between Malaysia and Singapore over the islet of Pedra Branca (or Pulau Batu Puteh), where the city-state had operated a lighthouse since colonial times and which had been in dispute since Malaysia claimed sovereignty in 1979. A ruling of the International Court of Justice in May 2008 found in favour of Singapore, though Malaysia was given sovereignty over the Middle Rocks, two smaller, uninhabited islets. However, under pressure from its own legislators as well as the opposition, the Malaysian government indicated that it would seek further evidence to overturn the ruling, might undertake construction work to join and enlarge the Middle Rocks, and would seek to take over a Singapore-operated lighthouse on another small island. Underlying the issue was the strategic interest of each side in increasing its capacity to control Singapore's eastern maritime approaches.

Major powers' roles in flux

Conscious that the regional roles of the major powers were in long-term flux, Southeast Asian states continued to hedge their security postures. With China emerging as a power of global significance, there were inevitably varying degrees of apprehension among Southeast Asian governments over the implications for the regional balance of power and the nature of the regional order. Beijing continued to use economic assistance to strengthen its bilateral ties with smaller Southeast Asian states, notably Cambodia, Laos and Timor Leste, while the crises in Myanmar reinforced the SPDC's all-round dependence on Beijing. However, despite Beijing's more sophisticated diplomacy and efforts at reassurance (such as subscribing to ASEAN's Treaty of Amity and Cooperation and the Declaration on the Conduct of Parties in the South China Sea), in some ASEAN members concerns grew over China's increasingly assertive regional posture. Following incidents in June and July 2007 in which Chinese naval vessels harrassed Vietnamese fishermen in the Spratly Islands, Vietnam's government allowed students to demonstrate outside Beijing's Embassy in Hanoi in November 2007 in protest at new Chinese legislation creating a symbolic administrative region in the disputed group. On the sidelines of the ASEAN Summit during the same month, Vietnamese Prime Minister Nguyen Tan Dung protested to Chinese Premier Wen Jiabao over a major Chinese naval exercise in the Paracel Islands. Vietnam simultaneously heightened efforts to improve its naval and air-defence capabilities. In the Philippines, concern grew that in a secret 'executive agreement' with Beijing in 2004, President Arroyo had made substantial concessions regarding her country's claims in the Spratly Islands in order to allow a joint seismic survey, which Vietnam later joined, to proceed. Some critics claimed that the deal provided more evidence of China gaining undue influence in the Philippines through its economic power, which was also allegedly apparent in the controversy over the National Broadband Network.

Important aspects of the ASEAN states' response to China's looming regional role have been to strengthen their own cooperation and to enmesh Beijing in a web of regional institutions. However, with the prospects for intra-ASEAN politico-security cooperation uncertain, and with wider multilateral regional institutions pretending to some sort of overarching security role in East Asia or the Asia-Pacific region likely to remain inchoate for many years, there remained widespread acceptance in Southeast Asia of the usefulness of the United States' continuing regional security role. There was some talk in the region of the United States' 'neglect' of Southeast Asia due to the major distractions of the wars in Iraq and Afghanistan, but US economic, diplomatic and strategic engagement remained extensive and since 2006 there had been signs in Washington of a clearer policy focus on the region. As well as annual two-way trade between the United States and the ASEAN states of $140bn in 2007, and growing US support for ASEAN as an institution (demonstrated by the appointment of a US ambassador to ASEAN), the involvement of the US armed forces in the region (ranging from supporting AFP operations in the southern Philippines to the staging of the major annual *Cobra Gold* exercise in Thailand and the Western Pacific Naval Symposium's Multilateral Sea Exercises) was still substantial and evolving. It was clear that the United States still provided much of the load-bearing structure of the regional security architecture.

Australia: Changing Doctrines

After nearly 12 years in office, Prime Minister John Howard and his conservative Liberal–National coalition were decisively defeated in Australia's elections on 24 November 2007, with Howard losing his own seat in parliament. Kevin Rudd, leader of the Australian Labor Party, became prime minister.

The turnaround came after Howard lost the sureness of his earlier touch with the electorate. After winning control of the parliament's upper house, the Senate, for the first time in mid 2005, Howard enacted an industrial-relations law that was perceived as worsening job conditions for ordinary workers. He also announced plans to hand over to his deputy if re-elected. Rudd meanwhile portrayed the government as complacent and promised to invest revenue from exports of raw materials to China into education, health, broadband services and other infrastructure. A withdrawal of combat forces from Iraq was also part of Labor's platform, but this was counterbalanced by strong commitments to the American alliance and to deployments in Afghanistan. A former diplomat fluent in Chinese, Rudd also offered himself as best qualified to help Australia confront the opportunities and challenges presented by Asia. Rudd's conservative personality (a workaholic, a practising Christian, and a family man) made for an easy transition from the staid Howard, who had made a virtue out of suburban ordinariness.

Rudd did not signal major changes in Australia's strategic posture and defence forces. A cautious politician, Howard steadily but substantially shifted the strategic doctrine he inherited from the 1983–96 period of Labor rule under Bob Hawke and Paul Keating. The earlier approach had been principally formulated in post-Vietnam War defence White Papers from 1976 under the conservative government of Malcolm Fraser and then under Labor Defence Minister Kim Beazley, and developed by then Deputy Defence Secretary Paul Dibb into what became known as the Defence of Australia doctrine. It represented a withdrawal from the previous policy of 'forward defence' under which Australia had contributed forces to the fight against distant global threats such as fascism or communism. The Defence of Australia doctrine was set against the background of superpower deadlock, the 'Nixon Doctrine' (which required self-reliance on the part of America's allies), stability in neighbouring Indonesia under Suharto, and small Pacific island states apparently launched successfully into independence. It put the prime focus on defence of the Australian landmass and dominance of the 'sea–air gap' between it and other territorial springboards for attack. Capabilities would be acquired for this purpose, and if these happened to be suited to more distant operations, then that was an extra option for the government.

The Defence of Australia doctrine put more emphasis on the Royal Australian Navy and the Royal Australian Air Force. The latter acquired the fourth-generation FA-18 strike fighter, while the navy purchased *Perry*-class patrol frigates, the smaller German-designed *Anzac*-class frigates and the locally built *Collins*-class submarines, though it no longer had an aircraft carrier. The army was cut back to four infantry battalions by 1991, though it managed to save its heavy armour from the mothballing recommended by Dibb.

By the end of the 1990s, a long period of relative inactivity for the armed forces was ending. An initially hesitant Australian intervention in East Timor in 1999 was followed by participation with special forces in the overthrow of the Taliban regime in Afghanistan in late 2001. Australia then contributed special forces and naval and air assets to the 2003 Iraq War, and intervened in the collapsing state of the Solomon Islands in 2003. It sent a 550-strong battlegroup into southern Iraq in 2005, and has had a deepening role in southern Afghanistan since September 2005 involving a reconstruction unit, special forces, air transport and artillery support.

A strategy of loud political endorsement of American war aims in Iraq, and of the 'war on terror' generally, gave Howard standing as one of Washington's inner circle along with former British Prime Minister Tony Blair – despite the fact that the Iraq and Afghanistan deployments were carefully tailored to minimise both casualties (with less than ten Australian fatalities in both theatres by May 2008) and domestic political costs.

By his last year in office, Howard was enunciating a shift in defence doctrine. 'We have abandoned the narrow, misguided and ultimately self-defeating nostrum that our force structure should be determined only or even mostly for the defence of Australia narrowly defined: our coastline and its approaches', he said in a speech to Canberra's Australian Strategic Policy Institute in July 2007. 'Australia's security will continue to be shaped by global trends, as it always has been. Australians have always understood intuitively that our security can be deeply affected by distant events ... The [Australian Defence Force] needs to be able to defend our mainland and its approaches in the unlikely event these ever come under direct military threat. But it must also be capable of conducting substantial operations in our immediate region – whether alone or as the leader of a coalition – and of making meaningful military contributions as a member of coalitions further abroad.'

In the election campaign, Rudd promised to withdraw the primary Australian combat force from Iraq by mid 2008, and to rely more on multilateral institutions than on US unilateralism. This played only a minor part in Labor's election win, though Rudd was accused of pursuing a 'little Australia' policy. Alexander Downer, then foreign minister, said this was based on 'cowardice and introspection' and that replacing Australia's 'network of strong bilateral relationships with mushy multilateralism would damage our achievements in areas such as Pacific policy, counter-terrorism, crime fighting, non-proliferation and trade'.

The new government
Rudd won power by successfully implanting a narrative that had Howard basking in the surpluses created by China-bound exports while ignoring domestic skills shortages and bottlenecks in infrastructure. His foreign minister, Stephen Smith, and defence minister, Joel Fitzgibbon, then set about demolishing the credentials of their predecessors, whose foreign policy was painted as unduly slavish to Washington, with defence management lacking fiscal discipline and strategic focus. On foreign policy, government pronouncements favoured a fuzziness also fashionable elsewhere in the world. Smith talked of a world shifting from an order where 'here's a nation state with its defence and security assets against another nation state' to one where security challenges were global and Australia would need to work with other nations and agencies on issues such as climate change, pandemics, transnational crime, migration, energy security and food security.

However, beyond these efforts to assert Labor's authorship of policy, changes have been less than radical. In New York, Rudd proclaimed a new 'creative middle-power diplomacy' in which the United Nations would play a more central role. But in Washington, he emphasised that Australia would continue with military training and civil support in Iraq. At the March 2008 NATO summit in Bucharest, he pledged Australia's long-term commitment to the ISAF force in

Afghanistan and called for decisive action to eliminate the country's opium production. Meeting Pakistan's President Pervez Musharraf at a business forum in
China, he demanded tougher action against Taliban bases.

In its first annual budget, the Rudd government adopted Howard's pledge
of a 3% real annual increase in the defence budget until 2016 and extended it by
another two years to 2018. For the fiscal year beginning July 2008, it allocated
A$22.7bn to defence, up 7.1% on the previous year.

A full exposition of the government's strategic thinking is expected in a
defence White Paper, the first since 2000, commissioned by Fitzgibbon for publication by early 2009. Early indications suggest the White Paper will not make
great changes. In April, Fitzgibbon said it was unlikely to please those harking
back to the Defence of Australia doctrine, or advocates of a more lightly equipped
army for use in a mix of anti-terrorism and stabilisation operations. 'There will
be no return to a Fortress Australia situation', Fitzgibbon said. 'But we want to
get the balance right. We need to be able to defend the continent and its people,
we need to be able to play a lead role in dealing with contingencies in our own
neighbourhood and, of course, we do need to maintain the capability to make
contributions to international efforts further afield.'

Work on the White Paper has triggered considerable debate about the
posture now appropriate for Australia. The people who helped to develop the
Defence of Australia position now accept that the world has changed. However,
they dispute Smith's contention that state-based rivalry is diminishing in
importance. Dibb described a new multipolar world order in which the United
States, China, Russia, Japan, India and Europe jostle in uneasy balance, without
the shared morality or political principles which underpinned the pre-1914
century of general peace in a multipolar Europe. Challenges from nation-states
with powerful armed forces are far from inconceivable in Australia's region,
Dibb argued: 'Some of the world's major concentrations of military power and
potential hot spots are in Asia: for example on the Korean peninsula, across the
Taiwan Straits and between India and Pakistan. Strong economic growth in our
region is leading to the build-up of modern military forces in China and India,
as well as in South Korea and Japan and some South-East Asian countries.'
He forecast that by 2025 China will have the strongest military in Asia, and
that India will also seek defence capabilities commensurate with its widening interests. Meanwhile, America's lead over other powers is likely to shrink,
Dibb said. Hugh White, author of the 2000 White Paper, wrote in an April 2008
paper for Sydney's Lowy Institute: 'If Australia scales back its strategic objectives significantly it will quickly find itself slipping from being a middle power
to a small power, without the military capacity to shape its own future. Which
are we to be? At the start of the Asian century, this is a critical question for
Australia.'

Matching forces to strategy

Unusually among Western economies, Australia seems likely to maintain 3% economic growth despite the global credit crunch, thanks to its links with Asia's emerging economies. Maintaining the real growth targets for defence spending is not seen as a problem. Rather, the difficulty has come from what some viewed as weakened budgetary control resulting from the flood of resources thrown at security in the wake of the 2001 terrorist attacks in the United States.

The Howard years produced a steady flow of major defence-equipment announcements. The biggest was an investment commitment to the US-led consortium developing the F-35 Joint Strike Fighter, of which the air force is expected to order 100 from 2014 at a total projected cost of A$16bn. Canberra also ordered 24 F/A-18 *Super Hornets* as a fill-in capability, at a cost of A$6.5bn. Plans for future reliance on the F-35 are viewed by some in the defence community as a gamble, although such bets have paid off for Australia in the past – for example, with the swing-wing F-111 aircraft in the 1960s, with *Collins*-class conventional submarines, and the *Jindalee* radar which tracks air and sea movements. However, the new government finally scrapped a project to install modern avionics, anti-submarine torpedo and anti-ship missile capabilities into the Kaman *Seasprite* helicopter, and terminated a A$1bn upgrade of six *Perry*-class frigates with only four ships refitted. Other major projects have been beset by delays. The acquisition of six airborne command-and-control aircraft, based on the Boeing 737, is running two years behind schedule, and several other contracts are suffering longer hold-ups. Delivery of 22 Eurocopter *Tiger* armed reconnaissance helicopters for the Australian Army is two years behind, and delays have also hit armoured-vehicle and torpedo projects.

Some procurement decisions have raised questions about whether equipment will fit into Australia's strategic requirements. These include an order for 50 reconditioned *Abrams* heavy tanks, replacing *Leopard* medium tanks which have never left Australian soil since they were acquired in the early 1980s, and an A$11bn order placed in June 2007 for three *Aegis*-equipped air-warfare destroyers of the F-100 design of Spain's Navantia yard, plus two 27,000-tonne amphibious landing ships, also of a Navantia design. To many analysts, these promised a package of capabilities that seemed designed only to deliver battalion-sized contingents and armoured support to distant hot-war engagements. It was argued that a mix of smaller ships would provide a more flexible capability suited to small-scale Pacific operations.

However, Fitzgibbon is seen as unlikely to take an axe to these programmes. Separate reviews ahead of the White Paper confirmed the *Super Hornet* and F-35 decisions. The destroyer and amphibious ship orders were crafted to maximise employment through the use of local industry. The destroyers will be completed in the Australian Submarine Corporation shipyards in Adelaide, helping to compensate for the recent closure of Mitsubishi's car factory in the city. About 70% of the ships' modules will be built in other yards around Australia. The amphibious ships are centred on Melbourne, where the Tenix yard will fit out hulls built in Spain. Assisting Fitzgibbon as parliamentary secretary for defence procurement is newly elected MP Greg Combet, previously head of the Australian Council of Trade Unions. The ambitious procurement programme nevertheless raises questions about longer-term affordability. Fitzgibbon indicated there was a A$6bn shortfall in funding over the next ten years, and ordered $1bn annual savings. The civilian strength of the Defence Department, which had grown by more than a quarter to over 20,000 since 11 September 2001, is under particular scrutiny, although the increase was partly due to civilians taking roles vacated by deployed uniformed personnel going on active deployment, and to the addition of intelligence specialists. In the event, the Defence Department achieved A$477m in projected savings for 2008/09 by cutting fuel, travel and maintenance costs, and delaying upgrades of buildings and barracks. Delays in equipment deliveries allowed a further A$1.25bn of spending to be postponed.

A further challenge for the Australian Defence Force lies in recruiting personnel when unemployment is at its lowest rate for over 30 years. In 2006, Howard announced an addition of two new infantry battalions for the Australian Army by 2012, bringing infantry strength up to eight battalions, including one parachute-commando battalion. The extra numbers are widely seen as necessary, given the strain on a small army engaged in several widely dispersed operations almost continuously for seven years. A revamped recruitment campaign, partly using new platforms such as YouTube, coupled with innovative entry schemes, has achieved a 25% lift in two years. However, the navy and air force have faced difficulties in maintaining high-end specialists, including submarine crews and combat-aircraft pilots.

The regional setting

The past year has seen an easing of some regional tensions. The departure of Howard, closely associated with the interventions of US President George W. Bush, has freshened the atmosphere in relations with Southeast Asia. Rudd, with his previous diplomatic experience in Asia, has also brought a new deftness to relations in the region.

Whereas Howard had promoted the trilateral alignment of the United States, Japan and Australia – and at one point seemed willing to accept former Japanese Prime Minister Shinzo Abe's notion of a quadrilateral security alignment of Asia-Pacific democracies including India – Rudd has tended to downplay the role of Japan in the strategic posture of America and its Asian allies. His first major overseas trip included China, but not Japan, though he was later to spend an equal amount of time in Tokyo and to stress that the trilateral security dialogue would continue with Japan and the United States. In Beijing, Rudd used the platform of an address in Chinese at Peking University to suggest Australia was a *zhengyou*, or 'true friend', who could give critical advice when it was obviously needed, and – ahead of the later furore over the Olympic torch parade – mentioned that there were issues of human-rights concern in Tibet. In speeches relating to China, Rudd has continued to argue for strategic engagement and has echoed the objective of China being a 'responsible stakeholder' in the global and Asia-Pacific order, first set out by then US Deputy Secretary of State Robert Zoellick in September 2005.

As well as supplanting Japan as Australia's biggest trading partner, China is emerging as one of the biggest foreign investors in Australian projects and corporations, as part of its effort to secure raw-material supplies. Moves by Chinese corporations to take equity in Australian mining companies – including the biggest, BHP Billiton and Rio Tinto – caused worries in Canberra that the Chinese had expectations of thwarting market mechanisms and obtaining supplies at cheap prices, rather than cementing long-term supply arrangements. The uproar over the Olympic torch parade, which provoked demonstrations in Canberra as in other cities around the world, also showed a strident side to Chinese nationalism. Balancing close economic ties with China against strategic worries continues to be a strong theme in Australia's emerging strategic policies. Divergence from the United States is a distinct possibility on questions such as the defence of Taiwan.

Australia's relations with Indonesia have steadily improved. There has been close and successful cooperation between police and security agencies on counter-terrorism and people-smuggling. The signing of a new security treaty in 2006 revived military-to-military training and other links severed since the 1999 East Timor crisis. However, the friendship remains vulnerable to the arrival in Australia of asylum-seekers from the province of West Papua. Meanwhile, human-rights activists in Australia still seek accountability for Indonesian violations in East Timor between 1975 and 1999. In November 2007, a Sydney Coroner's Court forwarded evidence against two former Indonesian special-forces soldiers, including retired Lieutenant-General Yunus Yosfiah, to federal prosecutors over the killing of five television newsmen in October 1975.

In Timor Leste itself, a new crisis flared with attacks in Dili on 11 February 2008 that wounded President José Ramos-Horta and threatened Prime Minister Xanana Gusmão. Australia rushed an additional 200 troops to the country. However, the shoot-out seemed to have precipitated an end to the rebellion by Timor Leste Defence Force elements that began in February 2006. The rebel leader, Major Alfredo Reinado, was killed in a shoot-out at the president's home. In April, Lieutenant Gastão Salsinha, leader of nearly 600 deserters from the two-battalion defence force, surrendered to Ramos-Horta in Dili. Australian forces were then reduced to the previous level of 750 personnel, augmented by a New Zealand company.

New Zealand and the Pacific islands

New Zealand appeared to be heading towards a change of government in elections due by the end of 2008, with opinion polls showing Prime Minister Helen Clark of the Labour Party trailing her conservative opponent, Jim Key of the National Party, amidst some of the highest interest rates in the developed world and worries about high tax rates. As in Australia, the battleground has been on domestic issues: tax cuts, education, health and broadband availability. Despite a generous tax cut in her last pre-election budget in May this year, Clark raised the defence force's operating budget by 9%, allowing pay rises of 10–12% to help recruitment and retention in the 9,185-strong regular services. An ongoing capital upgrade sees seven new small patrol vessels joining the navy by the end of 2008, and new Agusta 109 and NH-90 helicopters delivered to the air force in 2010–11. New Zealand has deployed about 650 personnel to operations overseas, including Afghanistan, Timor Leste and Sudan.

In the Solomon Islands, a parliamentary confidence vote in December 2007 brought down Prime Minister Manasseh Sogavare, who had been fighting the legal and fiscal discipline being promoted by the 15-country Regional Assistance Mission to the Solomon Islands (RAMSI), to which Australia and New Zealand are the principal contributors. The new leader, Derek Sikua, immediately improved relations with RAMSI and with the governments of Australia and New Zealand.

Rudd's arrival as Australian premier quickly warmed relations with Papua New Guinea (PNG), whose cabinet ministers had been shunned by the Howard government over indirect support for Sogavare's attempts to undermine RAMSI, and over their reluctance to agree to aggressive intervention by Australian personnel to shore up the PNG police force. In a visit to Port Moresby in March, Rudd declared a new start to cooperation and greater Australian interest in the country, partly involving the inclusion of PNG forest protection into Australia's emerging carbon-trading regime. The Australian-led reform of the PNG Defence Force, intended to help retire over-age soldiers and reduce numbers from 3,500 to a more wieldy 1,800-strong force, has continued.

Fiji remained the major political problem in the southwest Pacific, following the military takeover under Commodore Frank Bainimarama in December 2006. In September 2007, Bainimarama committed to holding free elections by March 2009, but later made clear he intended to sweep away Fiji's existing system of racially based electorates, risking a backlash from his fellow ethnic Fijians. Until Fiji returns to democracy, Australia and New Zealand seem likely to maintain sanctions that exclude Fiji's competent 3,500-strong regular military force (and its 6,000 reservists) from joining regional stabilisation operations, as they did earlier in Timor Leste and the Solomons.

The nearby island nation of Tonga meanwhile moved closer to democracy as the proportion of popularly elected members of its parliament was increased (to reach a majority by 2010). This followed riots in 2006 that required security assistance from New Zealand and Australia.

10 Prospectives

The economic uncertainties created throughout 2008 by the global financial crisis and the debate about its depth and nature will be easily matched in 2009 by a range of geopolitical uncertainties caused by shifts in the personalities and powers affecting global politics. Certainly the next US president will face a complex set of issues. The restoration of US standing in the world might be eased by the assumption to office of a new figure, but in time the very difficult decisions to be taken on Iran, Iraq, Pakistan and Afghanistan as well as on the general approach to managing the international system will invite controversy as much as it could inspire revived cooperation. The outcome of elections in Israel, Iran and India, among others, will establish new partners or rivals for American diplomacy. The international outlook of the 'post-Olympics' China will shape regional perspectives on how to engage the United States and Europe. Russia's approach to international crises under President Dmitry Medvedev guided by Prime Minister Vladimir Putin's residual influence will not just affect relations with Washington, but also the tendency of Europeans to act in concert or at cross purposes with the United States. As important as any of these trends will be whether the international community will be able to shrink the size of the world's ungoverned areas that, at present, especially on the Afghan–Pakistan border, are the generators of international threats and instability.

Debates on climate change, energy security, nuclear proliferation, terrorism, the management of the international financial and economic system and other transnational issues will continue to dominate summit agendas and international gatherings. But affecting these debates, and in many cases driving them, will be stated and implicit attitudes to the relationship between values and geopolitics held by the main players.

A trend set in 2007–08 and likely to be reinforced in the years ahead will be the very diverging emphasis that Western states and their public opinions place on the moral element in foreign policy as opposed to the, if anything, stiffening resistance to the perceived 'interference in internal affairs' that this approach elicits in large parts of the rest of the world. The serial mishaps of the Olympic torch relay disturbed by protests, and reactions to it, over the Tibet issue, vividly illustrated this general point last year. Other examples included: the frustrations that Southern African states could be, from a Western perspective, so possessed by anti-colonial solidarity as to be tolerant of President Robert Mugabe's dictatorial excesses in his own country; the unwillingness of China and Russia to support the Western position at the UN Security Council on the same issue; the angry reaction by the Arab League to the suggestion of the International Criminal Court (ICC) that President Omar al-Bashir of Sudan should be prosecuted for genocide and crimes against humanity; and the initially different, but eventually almost reconciled points of view held by some Asian states and Western donors on Myanmar's resistance to external help in the wake of Cyclone Nargis.

During the year, the emphasis the United States had previously placed on democracy promotion was further played down, though interestingly UK Foreign Secretary David Miliband made the idea a centrepiece of one of his more important speeches. It was the Republican, not the Democratic, candidate in the US presidential campaigns who thought this question more central, as John McCain spoke of establishing some sort of alliance of democracies. In the Middle East, which the George W. Bush administration had earlier sought to drench in the showers of democratic aspiration, disenchantment with the concept grew not just because of the failures in Iraq, or the complications created by Hamas victories in Palestine, but also because elsewhere in the region legislative gridlock created by democracy was stifling advance. In Kuwait, the ruling al-Sabah family again found that its relatively more liberal approaches on economic, political and social issues were stymied by a parliament more interested in scoring political points against particular ministers than in advancing a legislative agenda that would modernise the state. Other GCC countries looked on with a mixture of horror and dismay at how Kuwait's fuller experimentation with democratic processes was in effect hampering Kuwaiti development. Their own progress, leaders concluded, lay not in borrowing Western concepts of democracy but in adapting Asian models of guided development: more Singapore, less US would be the future watchword. While democracy of a kind was restored in Pakistan, established good governance was still a blurry mirage on the horizon. Building good governance in Afghanistan would depend less on the establishment of democratic structures than in weaving a more complex political fabric that would entail making a series of effective power-sharing deals regionally and at the centre over an extended period of time. In any case, the idea that the export of democracy was the central element of an effective grand strategy for global stability began to look much worn in 2007–08. Good governance would be a strategically satisfying goal if achieved.

In some places, like Pakistan's Federally Administered Tribal Areas, or much of Somalia, almost any governance would do. States that are too weak clearly pose a systemic threat to international affairs at a time when dangerous transnational trends dominate. One of the issues that will have seriously to be addressed over the next few years is the manner in which to deal with the violence and instability caused by the appearance of more, or at least larger, ungoverned areas. It is one thing to intervene in the internal affairs of a sovereign country; it is quite another to intervene usefully in areas that have lost sovereign control. The point is not that the first is illegitimate and the second potentially lawful, but that the first is relatively easy and the second well-nigh impossible. In these circumstances, the international effort to prevent state or 'area' failure is important. The more powers involved in this the better and the task should certainly not be seen as some sort of Western 'special subject'.

For much of the year, Americans and Europeans were alarmed by the evolution of hyper state power in Russia. For many Russians, the West seemed set on advancing its interests in Europe, through NATO enlargement, or Kosovo recognition, or missile defence in Eastern Europe, in a strategically autistic manner, almost perversely insensitive to known Russian interests, concerns and certainly emotions. For many in the West, Russian leaders had made their bad temper almost an instrument of diplomacy, rejecting often out of hand policies in other areas (such as tough sanctions on Iran) more out of pique than as a result of strategic calculus. Relations were not helped by the fact that Europe looked at Russia mainly through an energy-security prism and Russian foreign policy similarly seemed to have energy concerns at the centre of many of its preoccupations.

For a more balanced relationship to exist in 2009 it will be important for the West not to see relations with Russia as guided by the need simply to have Moscow accept the goals of Western diplomacy, and for the Russians to establish some goals of their own that they could pursue with some cooperation from the West. The indicators, however, are that Russia will seek geostrategic comfort more in forums such as the Shanghai Co-operation Organisation than elsewhere, and the West will still brood over how it lost Russia to its more 'Eastern' instincts. Reversing these trends would be good: it is hard to see who will take the lead.

Certainly the 'state capitalism' practised by Russia is by no means unique, finding counterparts in China, in a number of the Gulf countries, and in different doses, in parts of Latin America. A reality of the current international system is indeed how much of foreign policy appears guided by state commercial interests and specifically the natural-resource and energy needs of the state. China's policies in Africa have long been seen in this light, but as smaller Gulf countries in 2008 contemplated leasing large swathes of land in Pakistan or Sudan in order to attenuate the risks of food insecurity the extent of this phenomenon became more apparent. So long as state power is used in this overtly mercantile way there will be concerns about how geopolitical and financial aims mix. The concern over sovereign-wealth funds seemed to subside during the year not just as more of them accepted voluntary codes of conduct but as evidence mounted that ascribing foreign-policy goals to the investments of such funds became hard. Moreover, their money was needed to shore up key financial institutions. But the question persists as to whether the practice of state capitalism, especially by big powers, could be conducive to the establishment of a more stable international community. If this is true for Russia, it is all the more true of China, whose proclaimed value-free foreign policy regularly bumps up against a number of real-life problems with which it is engaged as a member of the UN Security Council.

Debates about the relationship between the growth of Chinese power and a parallel growth in China's sense of 'stakeholder responsibility' will continue. Chinese leaders worked hard in 2008, taking advantage of the outcome of Taiwan's elections, to introduce a sense of ease in cross-strait relations. Presented with a Japanese leader who was less prone to nationalist impulses, China also moved to improve relations with Tokyo. Some Southeast Asian countries were still nervous that China's energy needs would lead it to be more assertive in reviving territorial interests in disputed areas, despite Beijing's public promises to cooperate on joint exploration of energy opportunities. No one (outside Taiwan) truly fears the direct or overtly threatening application of Chinese power regionally, but the sheer weight of China in the area is leading more to fear an eventual 'Finlandisation' of parts of Asia, by which Asians anticipate Chinese requirements and bend to accommodate them in order to avoid direct confrontation with Beijing. In this environment, having a US presence in the region is not so much a question of balancing or containing China, but much more related to a desire to maintain great-power pluralism in Asia, so as to maximise the freedom of action of the smaller players to pursue their interests freer of the real (or imagined) pressures imposed by any single power. If ASEAN has an unexpressed geopolitical goal, it is the maintenance of a multipolar Asia. While China accepts US status as a 'resident power' (US Secretary of Defense Robert Gates's phrase at the 2008 IISS Shangri-La Dialogue) it would prefer to see America's bilateral alliance system wither on the vine. How comfortable China is with a multipolar Asia is still to be seen. How strong those poles are will much depend on how extroverted India feels it is able to be. In 2008 the government was much absorbed by its inability, until the last minute, to begin implementation of the US–India civilian nuclear deal. After elections, it will be of some importance to the future of the Asian system that India feels able to play its full role in it.

In sum, many of the big powers last year were struggling to advance their diplomatic and strategic agendas as these collided with the entrenched positions of others. Agreements to disagree seemed sometimes the best that could be hoped for. Some tactical shifts in negotiating strategies led to some advances: a less publicly polemical approach to North Korea led to some diplomatic agreement there, though US opponents of the more flexible American approach argued that the regime was in effect being appeased. Interestingly, there was one example of a small power breaking through with some diplomatic flair to address an issue others had not solved. Qatar in May 2008 was able to do what others, including the Europeans, the Arab League and big Middle East powers had been unable to do, namely achieve sufficient national agreement to allow for the election of a president of Lebanon. While Qatar's diplomacy was much celebrated, even by the Bush administration, some regretted that it came at the price of giving Hizbullah the weight within the political system it was seeking. Yet that agreement recognised the realities of the internal balance of power, something which arguably other diplomatic efforts were vainly fighting too hard against. Working too much with the grain of international trends strikes some as defeatist. Occasionally, it is the technique that avoids worse outcomes. While Israeli–Palestinian talks were so stagnant, artificial plugging of the holes in other regional trouble-spots was perhaps helpful. These are the sorts of stopgap measures that are often needed when the bigger diplomatic powers are distracted or otherwise engaged.

A new US president in 2009 will not be enough immediately to shift some of the stilled waters of international diplomacy. Economic and financial realities may lead the new president to concentrate substantially on affairs at home. The unfinished business in Iraq, Afghanistan/Pakistan, problems in the Middle East and prospectively so particularly with Iran, will command attention. The rest of the world will be interested to see how the new president thinks strategically and whether indeed a more well-rounded strategy is developed for the United States that goes beyond the 'global war on terror' to capture the richer variety of international challenges. America's friends in Europe, the Middle East, Asia and elsewhere should not (again) miss the opportunity positively to shape that strategic thinking. In Europe, increasing emphasis has been placed on the importance of public diplomacy in a globalised world – including talking direct to the public in target countries – the rituals of effective summitry, and the modernisation of institutions to deal with current demands. But public diplomacy, summitry and institutions are instruments, partial at that, for the implementation of strategy. They are means, not strategic ends in themselves, and good only insofar as the strategic thinking behind them is sound. The French Defence White Paper issued in June 2008 was a good example of strategic thinking. A Europe-wide approach that was serious could hold the promise of engaging the Americans around a set of strategic principles that could command wider acceptance. Asia and the Middle East are more strategically diverse places than Europe, but if the leading powers there constructively assert their strategic perspectives, the chances of a more informed and therefore perhaps more effective US external policy in these crucial areas increases. The structure of global power will for a while still remain fluid and essentially 'non-polar', with different states, businesses, non-state actors and others constantly influencing international events in a variety of ways. Yet, however much America's individual share of global power has been in relative decline, it remains the case that it is the 'swing' geopolitical player, the one that by its actions or inactions can have the most impact on the comity of nations and the stability of the international system as a whole. Just as America is unable to shape a global agenda alone and must find international partners, so others need to take some strategic responsibility for developing initiatives that can usefully involve the United States in effective wider coalitions. The quality of those initiatives will be the test of whether others can legitimately claim a share of global strategic leadership in a more egalitarian international order.

Index